THE BIRDWATCHERS YEARBOOK AND DIARY 2009

Designed and published by
Hilary Cromack

Edited by
David Cromack

BUCKINGHAM PRESS LTD

In association with

SWAROVSKI
OPTIK

Published in 2008 by
Buckingham Press Ltd
55 Thorpe Park Road, Peterborough
Cambridgeshire PE3 6LJ
United Kingdom

(Tel/Fax) 01733 561 739
e-mail: admin@buckinghampress.com
www.birdsillustrated.com

© Buckingham Press Ltd 2008

ISBN 978-0-955033-97-1
ISSN 0144-364 X

Cover image: Lapwings by Andrew Beckett
Address: 37 Buckingham Road, Lytham St Annes, Lancs, FY8 4EU. 01253 730 167 mobile: 07946 820 156; e-mail: andysart@freeuk.com

Black and white illustrations: By Steve Cale.
Address: Bramble Cottage, Westwood Lane, Gt Rysburgh, Fakenham, Norfolk, NR21 7AP. 01328 829 589; e-mail: steveshrike@aol.com

Printed and bound in Great Britain by
Cambridge University Press, Cambridge, UK.

CONTENTS

CONTENTS

PREFACE

WELCOME TO THE 29th edition of *The Birdwatcher's Yearbook*, which has been described by many of its fans as the most comprehensive source of information on the birding scene in Britain. I'd just like to thank all the club secretaries, reserve wardens and myriad other contributors who take the time and trouble to update the information each year — without your willing assistance, this unique publishing venture simply would not be possible.

Regular buyers of *The Yearbook* will notice that we've made big efforts this year to track down many more potential speakers for the Lecturers' Directory to make the feature even more useful to indoor meeting secretaries up and down the country.

I've been addressing bird clubs, RSPB member groups and photographic societies for a number of years, so I'm acutely aware that the recent staggering rises in fuel costs make it imperative for groups to find guest speakers closer to home to keep down costs.

Of course it is still important that guest lecturers are of the highest quality to ensure that the indoor meetings remain a key part of a club's programme — those in the hall won't thank the organiser for finding a cheap local option if they are bored stiff! Happily, you will see that our Directory is packed with fascinating topics by top photographers, artists and writers, so clubs should still be able to put together a varied, high quality programme.

The survey of English-language magazines has also been expanded in the 2009 edition and a number of new sites have been added to the Reserves section. We write to all the management bodies for updated information on their sites each year and you will note that many are now including details of their most significant non-bird species.

Conscious that *The Yearbook* is a journal of record, I've again asked Richard Facey to summarise some of the most important ornithological happenings of the past 12 months and Gordon Hamlett highlights the 50 or so most vital birding websites. To complete our major features, the BTO's Jacquie Clark celebrates 100 years of bird ringing in Britain, an activity which continues to expand our knowledge of birds' lives.

The Birdwatchers' Yearbook should be a one-stop solution to all your information needs, but if there are extra features you'd like to see added, please do not hesitate to make contact.

David Cromack
EDITOR

A MESSAGE FROM THE SPONSORS OF THIS BOOK

THE ENTHUSIASM and knowledge shown by British birdwatchers for their hobby is second-to-none. The memberships of the RSPB and The Wildlife Trusts dwarf those of similar organisations in the rest of the world and the network of county bird clubs continues to meet needs at the local level.

This commitment to the hobby means that British birdwatchers demand the very highest standards – both in the field of optics and publishing. Swarovski Optik takes pride in continually evolving the design and function of its telescopes and binoculars and it was quick to recognise that *The Birdwatcher's Yearbook* has been equally innovative throughout its 29-year history.

We were delighted to sponsor the redesigned 2002 edition as we recognised that *The Yearbook* was uniquely successful in delivering trustworthy, up-to-date information to its many readers, whether they be journalists, people working within the birding industry or simply ordinary birdwatchers. Seven years later, nothing has dented our confidence.

Regular buyers need no introduction to the virtues of this publication, but if you are a first-time reader, we feel confident it will meet nearly all your needs – from information about visiting new nature reserves, to locating the meeting place of your nearest bird club or to recording your sightings of birds, butterflies and dragonflies. Put it to the test today – and for the rest of 2009. Happy birding.

Peter Antoniou
Managing Director, Swarovski Optik UK

SWAROVSKI
OPTIK

FEATURES

Alan Williams

Habitat recreation programmes have led to an
explosion in the UK's Bittern population.

KEY ORNITHOLOGICAL NEWS OF 2008

Richard Facey evaluates masses of bird-related material generated by conservation organisations and behavioural scientists to provide a digest of the most significant bird news.

Boom time for the heron family

MEMBERS of the heron family made headlines in Britain during 2008 thanks to some encouraging breeding records. The most encouraging was an outstanding performance by Bittern *(Botaurus stellaris)*, with 2008 being the best season in more than 100 years.

In total 75 males were recorded booming in the reedbeds of England – up 47% compared to 2007 and an incredible 581% increase on the numbers heard a decade ago, when just 11 birds were heard performing their characteristic call. Thanks to habitat creation projects, the species' range has continued to expand, with booming Bitterns now being heard in ten counties, compared to four in 1997.

While Bittern numbers continue to boom, a relative has bred for the first time in the UK. Not one, but two pairs of Cattle Egrets *(Bubulcus ibis)* decided that Somerset was clearly the place for them to raise their families, and they successfully reared at least one youngster between them. The four birds were probably part of the large influx that occurred in in the South West during the preceding winter.

Once rare, the Little Egret *(Egretta garzetta)* is now firmly established within the UK, and perhaps the Cattle Egret will follow its example and become the next major coloniser of the British Isles.

Heading north, we saw Scotland's first recorded breeding of Spoonbills *(Platalea leucorodia)*, only the second record for the UK. The pair of aptly named birds chose Kirkcudbright Bay in Dumfries and Galloway to make their home and raise a family of three in 2008. It is a decade since the species last bred in the UK and 330 years since the next previous record!

Climate change impacts on threatened birds

CLIMATE CHANGE was cited as one of the biggest threats to biodiversity in several publications during 2008. The 2008 IUCN Red List of Threatened Species of birds paints an alarming picture of how changes in our climate are adding to and accelerating the potential demise of numerous species, with the number of species currently considered at risk rising to 1,226.

Species such as the Floreana Mocking Bird *(Nesomimus trifasciatus)* of the Galapagos Islands, with a population of less that 60 individuals, are becoming increasingly vulnerable to extreme weather events. Others, such as Australia's Mallee Emuwren *(Stipiturus mallee),* are being affected by continued drought. With its last significant population being found in less than 100 square kilometres of highly fragmented habitat, a single bush fire could put paid to the Mallee Emuwren.

However, help in predicting the effects of climate change, at least for European species, will be boosted by the publication of *A Climatic Atlas of European Breeding Birds* in 2008. Again it is sober reading, predicting that on average the range of Europe's birds will have moved 550km north-east by the time 2100 comes. Ranges are predicted to reduce by 20% and only overlap with current distributions by 40%. The result could be declines in three-quarters of the continent's breeding bird species. For those found only or mainly in Europe, the door to extinction could well and truly be opened.

Part of the Atlas' purpose is to galvanise practical action. The publication, which is available from www.hbw.com, also shows ways of a strengthening existing protection, connecting habitats, and planning to accommodate potential shifts in species ranges.

Sources:
A Climatic Atlas of European Breeding Birds by Brian Huntley, Rhys E. Green, Yvonne C. Collingham, Stephen G. Willis (Lynx Edicions).

Counting the wider costs of vulture disaster

A SEVERE DECLINE of any species often leads to unforeseen impacts on the natural world and possibly, human society too. A case in point is the situation brewing on the Indian subcontinent following the massive losses of Gyps vulture species as a result of dicolofenac poisoning.

In a study published in the journal *Ecology Economics*, it was reported that the decline in the three Gyps vulture species have been felt in numerous ways. As dominant scavengers, their demise has resulted in a huge number of carcasses being left without a natural means of disposal. To prevent health problems and environmental pollution, the cost of carcass disposal has fallen upon often poor local communities and authorities.

The tanning and fertiliser industries have also suffered as both rely on the availability of carcasses.

Normally a skinner would remove the hide of a dead animal, the vultures would remove the flesh, and the remaining bones would be gathered

The collapse in vulture numbers has created many public health problems in India.

9

for sale to the fertiliser trade. But now that dead animals are removed from the streets for health reasons, both trades, which often supply a much needed source of income in poorer areas, are suffering.

Populations of other scavenging species have increased to fill the void left by these birds. Feral dogs have increased by 7.3 million – a worrying development as they are a major vector for many diseases in India. It has been suggested that the increase in dogs has led to 50,000 additional deaths in the human population from rabies. And the total cost of the increase in rabies is estimated to be to the tune of $34 billion over the 14-year period of 1992 to 2006.

As well as rabies, the dogs also carry canine distemper and brucellosis, which are easily transmitted to other species, including the native and endangered dhole, a fellow member of the canine family.

Despite conservation efforts the populations of Indian's Gyps vultures continue to decline. Scientists repeated the surveys that initially detected losses in 2007, and the results were not good. India's populations of the Long-billed Vulture (*Gyps indicus*) and Slender-billed Vulture (*G. tenuirostris*) declined by 16% annually between 2000 and 2007.

More alarmingly, however was the trend for the Oriental White-back Vulture's (*G. bengalensis*) population, which over the same period has declined by nearly 44% per annum. Since 1992 this latter species' population has declined by 99%, and now stands at one thousandth of its 1992 level – around 11,000 compared to tens of millions nearly two decades ago. The populations of *G. indicus* and *G. tenuirostris* on the Indian Subcontinent stand at 45,000 and 1,000 respectively.

The cause of the decline was identified in 2004 to be the anti-inflammatory drug diclofenac, used to treat cattle. In 2006, the Indian Government banned the veterinary manufacture of the drug, but the ban has not been a complete success. The drug has remained widely available, and veterinary practitioners have circumvented the ban by supplying dicolfenac sold for human use.

However, in further step to reduce the impact of this drug, the Drug Controller General of India, has officially warned drug companies not to sell the veterinary form of the substance, and that labelling for its human counterpart should clearly state it is not intended for livestock.

Newly-discovered species in two continents
LIFTING SPIRITS when there is so much doom and gloom, is the announcement of species new to science being discovered in South America, Vietnam, Papua New Guinea and Indonesia – all places with extensive areas of under-studied habitat.

A team of scientists surveying birds in the Nonggang Natural Reserve of Guangxi on the Vietnam-China border, spotted what appeared to be an unknown species of babbler on several occasions during 2005. In January 2006, the team set out to catch specimens and two were duly caught - a male and female, as luck would have it.

These two specimens allowed a comparison with known species of babbler, which confirmed that they were indeed from a new species. The new babbler was named for the reserve in which is it was found, being christened the Nonggang Babbler (*Stachyris nonggangensis*). It inhabits the karst seasonal rainforest but has seldom been seen in the trees, preferring the limestone areas. Currently the Nanggong Babbler is only known from the one site, which indicates the species has specialised habitat requirements. Happily, the region is heavily protected, so the Nanggong Babbler's habitat is at least safe for the time being.

Brazil has always been a hotspot of diversity, and a species of Antwren is the newest of a steady stream of new species coming out of the country.

The Soncorá Antwren (*Formicivorva grantsaui*), discovered in the Chapada Diamantina region, has even more discerning habitat

The Soncorá Antwren was identified as a new species after a researcher heard sounds he could not recognise.

requirements than the Nonggang Babbler, only being found in the *campo rupestre* vegetation of the Serra do Soncorá, between 850 and 1,100m. The discovering scientist used, among other characters, the new antwren's distinctive voice and habitat preference to distinguish it from other known species.

South America also revealed a new species in the form of the Yungas Tyrannulet (*Phylloyias weedeni*). The existence of a previous un-described Tyrannulet in the Bolivian and Peruvian Andes was originally suggested in 1991, based on recordings of vocalisations that didn't fit those of known taxa. However, it would be 13 years until this would be confirmed.

Despite being found at five locations, it is believed that the species numbers no more than 10,000 mature individuals – making it an uncommon sight in its humid and semi-humid forest home, where is prefers to spend its time in the upper canopy.

It is back east for the next discovery to be announced. The Wattled Smokey Honeyeater (*Melipotes carolae*) was discovered in the Foja Mountains of Western New Guinea, during a 25-day long rapid assessment of the region's biodiversity by Conservation International

The Recurve-billed Bushbird has been rediscovered in Colombia, leading conservationists to call for greater habitat protection in the areas where it is found.

and the Indonesian Institute of Sciences. The species appears to be a common inhabitant of the region, preferring the montane forest and forest fringe.

As its common name suggests, the new species possess two fleshy wattles that hang down either side of its face – making it unique among the known members of its genus. The wattles and facial skin are a striking orange.

Indonesia is also home to another new species with a very different characteristic than the rest of its relatives. Members of the genus Zosterops are more commonly called white-eyes but the Tongian White-eye (*Zosterops somadikartai*) lacks the characteristic white eye-ring.

The species was found in the coastal regions of the Tongian Islands, Sulawesi, and was another species that scientists had to wait more than a decade before they could formally name it.

Though not a new species to science, the Recurve-billed Bushbird (*Clytoctantes alixii*) has made a recent appearance, giving hope for its survival within Colombia and Venezuala. The species, whose distinctive bill is an effective tool for cracking open bamboo to glean caterpillars and other insects, had not been seen for more than four decades.

Sources:
Nanggong Babbler - Fang and Aiwu. *The Auk*, volume 125, pages 420–424
Soncorá Antwren - Gonzaga, Carvalhaes and Buzzetti. *Zootaxa*, volume 1473, pages 25–44
Wattled Smokey Honeyeater - Beehler, Prawiradilaga, de Fretes, and Kemp. *The Auk*, volume 124, pages 1000–1009
Tongian White-eye - Indrawan, Rasmussen, and Sunarto. *The Wilson Journal of Ornithology* DOI: 10.1676/06-051.1
Recurve-billed Bushbird – *BirdLife International*

Short distance migrants are more flexible
RESEARCH FROM THE US has shown that, when it comes to migrating species, those that migrate a short distance are more likely to adapt their breeding rhythms to the weather conditions on their breeding grounds, compared to those species that decide to make a longer haul between their summer and winter homes.

The US research, conducted by Scientists from Boston University and the Manomet Center for Conservation Sciences, shows that this is because the climate of the summer and winter ranges are often linked if they are geographically close.

Short-distance migrants, such as the Swamp Sparrow (*Melospiza georgiana*), can better gauge the conditions at their destination, by the prevailing temperatures of their wintering grounds. However, long-distance migrants such as the Great-Crested Flycatcher (*Myiarchus crinitus*), which winters in South America, have no way of telling what conditions lie in wait for them in their breeding grounds. The result is that short distance migrants are in a better position to time their arrival on breeding grounds with the best conditions.

Some resident species may also be able to keep up with climatic changes. Scientists from Oxford University have studied the Great Tits (*Parus major*) of Wytham Wood for nearly five decades or so, generating 10,000 breeding records in this time.

When laying dates were analysed, the scientists (not all the same from 60 years ago!) found that the tits were keeping pace with changing conditions – laying on average two weeks earlier than they did 50 years ago. Earlier laying means the birds are keeping pace with the peak emergence of the winter moth caterpillar, which is happening earlier as a result of higher average temperatures.

Sources:
Great Tits - Charmantier, McCleery, Cole, Perrins, Kruuk, Sheldon. *Science*, volume 320, pages 800 – 803.
North American migrants - Miller-Rushing, Lloyd-Evans, Primack, *Satzinger Global Change Biology*, Volume 14, pages 1959 - 1972

Giving rare birds a helping hand

THE FUTURE of a species depends not only on overall numbers, but its distribution, and conservationists are always striving to increase the range of endangered and declining birds.

Sometimes, with the help of a little habitat creation or management, nature can be left to its own devices. In certain circumstances, however, nature needs a little boost in the form of reintroduction programmes.

The Regent Honeyeater (*Xanthonyza phrygia*) is one such species that has received a helping hand, with the introduction of 27 individuals into Australia's Chiltern-Mt Pilot National Park in north-eastern Victoria. Wild birds were soon seen with the introduced birds, the first examples reported in the park in 18 months.

More good news also came from the Antipodes at the end of 2007 with the first hatching of Stitchbirds, or Hihi, (*Notiomystus*

All the Regent Honeyeaters released into Australia's Chiltern National park carry radio transmitters so scientists can keep track of their movements.

13

cincta) in over a century on New Zealand's Auckland mainland.

The happy event took place at Cascade Kauri Park, Auckland, where 60 individuals had been introduced earlier in the year. Until the arrival of black rats, the species had been widespread over North Island, but now the last natural population stands at fewer than 2,000 individuals.

However one species' absence from its home eclipses both that of the Regent Honeyeater and Hihi. It has been nearly two centuries since the Rimitara Lorikeet (*Vini kuhlii*) occurred naturally on the island of Atiu in the Cook Islands. But this changed at the end of 2007, when 27 birds were released.

The rainbow-hued Rimitara Lorikeet has been returned to its ancestral home in the Cook Islands.

This release has been 15 years in the planning, and is down to the hard work of a few individuals. Those attending the 2006 British Bird Fair, which contributed £215,000 to the project, also aided the Rimitara Lorikeet's return to Atiu.

The species became extinct on Atui and other islands in the archipelago because of hunting and predation by introduced predators, such as rats. But on Rimitara, its future was secured thanks to the Queen of Rimitara, who placed a taboo on the taking of the species, and the island thankfully remained free of rats.

In 2007, an international team went to Rimitara, where it is symbol of joy and well being, and trapped several individuals. Atui should be able to support its new lorikeet population, as it is free of rats and has similar vegetation to Rimitara.

Sources:
BirdLife International

CELEBRATING A CENTURY
OF BIRD RINGING

2009 marks 100 years of ringing in Britain and Ireland, and Jacquie Clark (Head of Ringing at BTO) looks back over the milestones achieved in that time and speculates about the next century.

PEOPLE started ringing birds to find out where they go and ringers today are just as fascinated by migration as the original pioneers of a century ago. Though we have learnt so much in the last 100 years, there is still more that we don't know.

Some of the early results from ringing were very exciting at the time, though they may seem obvious to us today. The first BTO-ringed Swallow to be found in South Africa was an adult female ringed at the nest in Staffordshire on May 6, 1911 by JRB Masefield (brother of the poet, John) and reported in Utrecht, Natal on 23 December 1913. There are now more than 400 reports of BTO-ringed Swallows in South Africa, but we continue to learn about the distribution of this and other species and, most importantly, any changes.

Monitoring alterations in the movements of birds is becoming increasingly important as climate change leads to changes in behaviour and distribution. The *Migration Atlas*, published in 2002, drew on many years of ringing to answer some questions, but there are still many more – for instance, where **do** our Spotted Flycatchers go in winter? Knowing where our breeding birds go in winter could help us to understand why many populations, particularly of migrants, are declining.

Members of the Lincolnshire Naturalists Union hear about bird ringing at the Gibraltar Point bird observatory in 1949.

How long do they live?

Reports of ringed birds also continue to tell us how long they live. Since hard-wearing alloy rings were introduced in the 1960s, the record ages for many species have increased. The current record-holder is a Manx Shearwater ringed on Bardsey Island in 1951 when it was already an adult. More than 50 years later it is still going strong and is now on its fourth ring. The record for Bar-tailed Godwit was also increased in 2008, with a bird originally caught on the Wash in 1974 being recaptured more than 34 years later – in this case still wearing its original ring.

These exceptional birds are fascinating, but the real 'bread and butter' of the Ringing Scheme now is looking at how long the average birds survive and how this changes from year-to-year.

CELEBRATING A CENTURY OF BIRD RINGING

Ringing provides information on numbers of birds in the population, how many survive from one year to the next and how many young birds join the population.

Analysing results from ringing, nest recording and counting we can find out whether the survival rate of adult or of young birds has declined, or productivity has fallen. With this information we can start to understand declines in numbers and target action to reverse those declines, so ringing remains as relevant today as it did back before the First World War.

Pioneering spirits

Ringing in Britain & Ireland began in 1909, when two schemes were started independently. In Scotland, Arthur Landsborough Thomson announced the Aberdeen University Bird Migration Inquiry in April and Harry Forbes Witherby announced the *British Birds* Marking Scheme in June.

The first birds were ringed in Aberdeen on May 8, 1909 by Mr Lewis Ramsay, who was heavily involved with the scheme – his great nephew, Andrew Ramsay, is a ringer today! The Aberdeen Inquiry was intended to be a short-term project and came to an end during The Great War.

The *British Birds* Marking Scheme continued and was taken over by the recently-formed BTO in 1937 and was housed at the British Museum (Natural History). Despite two moves of 'home' since, the Natural History Museums' well-known and easily understood address is still used on rings today. An experiment using BTO TRING ENGLAND on alternate rings found that that about 40% of recoveries (reports of ringed birds) would be lost using this address. It also generated a complaint from a finder who wanted to know who Mr BT Otring was and why he was ringing birds!

Inititally, rings were supplied in what sounded more like clothes sizes, coming in small, medium and large. They had to be overlapped to fit a wide range of birds. The early rings were made of aluminium, with alloy rings, which wear less, being gradually introduced. Rings were

developed further by the late Bob Spencer (the Scheme's first full-time Ringing Officer, who is still remembered by older ringers), working with a bird ringer, Cecil Lambourne, who ran a company making cuff-links, belts and braces and had expertise in metal work.

For many years, Lambournes supplied rings not just to the BTO, but to many other ringing schemes around the world. Now Porzana produce more than 20 sizes of rings for us, with internal diameters from

In the days before high quality binoculars and telescopes were generally available, ringing allowed keen birdwatchers the chance to study individual birds in the hand. Bird observatories attracted a stream of eager volunteers and this shows a gathering of them with Peter Scott at a conference weekend in 1950.

CELEBRATING A CENTURY OF BIRD RINGING

2mm to 26mm, using three different metals, so that there is a suitable ring size and type of ring for each species from Goldcrest to Golden Eagle.

Growth and change

Relatively few birds were ringed in the early years, and the vast majority of these were nestlings. In a world with no mist nets, ringers had to work even harder to catch and ring birds - either relying on finding nests with pulli ready to ring or using traps. However, the large Heligoland traps were only to be found at bird observatories, which were very much a focus for ringing at that time.

The ringing total in 1931 was 29,554 with 76% of those being pulli – now we ring around 800,000 birds a year, but in an almost complete reversal, only about 20% are pulli. Ringing totals increased fairly steadily in the 1920s and 30s, though the grand total only reached half a million in 1936 – now it is more than 35 million.

Peter Wilkinson

The Scheme continued to operate during the Second World War, albeit at a reduced level. The ringing secretary, Miss Elsie Leach, who had been running the Scheme since the 1930s, tried to maintain contact with ringing schemes in Germany by sending details of reports of ringed birds to our Embassy in Dublin, to be passed onto the German Embassy. She was apparently investigated three times for 'communicating with the enemy' and was cleared on each occasion – but you can imagine how suspicious lists of numbers with geographical coordinates must have looked.

During the latter part of the 20th Century, Chris Mead of the BTO was 'Mr Ringing' and his ability to relay science to the general public in an accessible way via newspapers, magazines, TV and radio was legendary.

The 1950s were a time of increase and change for the Scheme. The grand total ringed reached one million birds at the beginning of the decade and annual totals reached 100,000 in 1955. Bob Spencer was appointed in 1954 and set about modernising the growing Scheme.

Mist nets arrived in 1956 and the ringing totals really started to increase, peaking at more than 800,000 in the 1980s, approximately what is ringed each year today. Ringing permits were also introduced in 1956. In the early days, you simply had to write to the Scheme and request a supply of rings and you were a ringer. In those days there were nine rules which were printed on the back of ringing 'schedules' (forms giving details of birds ringed).

By 1960 things had changed a bit, but you only had to ring 100 birds to get an 'A' (independent) ringing permit. Bob Spencer introduced the first *Ringers' Manual* in 1965, telling ringers that they would have to pay ten shillings (50p) for it and carefully explaining that it really was worth it! We now have a comprehensive *Ringers' Manual* which includes rules, catching techniques, data collection and submission and licensing and training. The emphasis today in training is on skills, not numbers, but 'A' permit applicants will have ringed more than 1,500 birds of a wide range of species.

CELEBRATING A CENTURY OF BIRD RINGING

The biggest change in the last two decades has been computerisation of ringing data. Many were sceptical when the idea of asking ringers to submit computerised data was mooted, but ringers rose to the challenge and using programs developed by volunteer ringers, they now send in 95% of their data electronically.

In addition, if a member of the public finds a ringed bird, they can now report it online. Computerisation means the

Waders, gulls and other species that flock together can be caught by ringers using cannon nets. Here volunteers move in quickly to extract birds (mainly Ruddy Turnstones) trapped on Reeds Beach, Delaware.

data are secure and, most importantly, are available for analysis. We can now carry out more sophisticated survival analyses as well as having an enormous data bank of measurements of birds which is increasingly being utilised.

Finding out even more

Ringers are fascinated by the birds that they are privileged to catch and ring – and are keen to learn more. This has led to the production of guides to catching, ageing and sexing birds, and a series of ringing projects over the years.

In the 1960s the Sand Martin Enquiry was launched by Bob Spencer, with the late Chris Mead (who worked for the Ringing Scheme throughout his life) using his boundless enthusiasm to encourage ringers to join in. Later, when faced with the mammoth task of analyzing more than 11,000 recoveries of Sand Martins without a computer, Chris wondered if he should have been quite so enthusiastic.

Today we have long-term projects giving us detailed information on the survival and productivity of a wide range of birds. For the Constant Effort Sites Scheme ringers go to the same site, at the same time and put up the same nets on 12 occasions between April and August. This constant effort gives us a very good measure of the changing numbers, survival rates and productivity of birds. The poor breeding season in 2007 was clearly illustrated by the low numbers of juvenile birds ringed on these Constant Effort sites.

Ringers also target particular species to learn more about their ecology – again vital

CES annual statistics (based on a typical site with two ringers, making all 12 visits a year, each visit lasting six hours and having 6 x 18m nets at 130 sites).

Statistic	Annual per site	All sites (n=130)
Total length of nets erected	6 x 18m x 12 = 1.3 km	x 130 = 169 km
Total distance walked	18 rounds x 1.3 km x 12 = 46.8 km	x 130 = 6,084 km
Total cups of tea drunk	6 x 2 x 12 = 144	x 130 = 18,720

CELEBRATING A CENTURY OF BIRD RINGING

information for conservation. We are currently analyzing the results of a five-year project to look at how our Swallows use roosts in autumn as they fatten before heading for South Africa. Preliminary results show that our birds only put on a small amount of weight before leaving the country. When they reach Spain and are faced with crossing the Sahara, they put on far more weight.

Where now?

Is there really more to learn from conventional ringing? The answer is a resounding 'yes'. As well as continuing to learn more about the movements of birds, we are now able to use all the computerised ringing data we now have to study and understand the lives of birds.

Full computerisation of all our current data is now approaching – and ringers and other volunteers are busy computerising years and years of back data. This will allow rapid processing of data and regular analyses of survival and condition, showing any changes from year to year and giving us an early warning of problems for particular species or populations. For example, recent analyses have

British ringers regularly travel overseas to support local enthusiasts and to extend their knowledge of species not seen in the UK. However, this Scops Owl in the hand was rescued from a North Sea oil platform in 2004. When weighed by Hugh Insley, he found it to be under weight.

shown us that for both Starling and Song Thrush there has been a decrease in juvenile survival, which appears to have driven the declines in numbers of these species.

We are also using the measurements and weights of birds collected by ringers to understand how and why birds' weights change during the day, through the year and between years. We will also be able to link condition (using weight and size of birds) to their survival, to help us understand why some individuals or species survive better than others and therefore to understand population change and differences in populations, both within Britain and Ireland and between countries.

Project ringing will continue to be important, focusing ringers efforts on particular issues, though the 'background' of general ringing will continue to provide vital monitoring. For example, who could have predicted that House Sparrow would have been of interest? One of the great strengths of the Scheme is that we have information from large numbers of birds in a wide range of habitats, which is only achievable by general ringing.

New technologies, developed hand-in-hand with ringing, are likely to increase in importance. Stable isotopes from a small sample of a feather can tell us about where that feather was moulted, a drop of blood can give a DNA profile so that we understand who is related to whom, adding colour marks allows us to follow the movements and behaviour of individuals and adding a radio transmitter or a satellite transmittter can give detailed information on where a bird is and what it does.

As radio transmitters become smaller, one day we will be able to find out where our Spotted

Flycatchers go – hopefully before it is too late for this rapidly declining species. None of these techniques could be used without the skill of trained ringers who are able to catch and individually mark birds.

I'm sure there will be other advances, perhaps metal rings will become obsolete as we move to different marking methods. However, I'm sure that we will still need the dedicated band of bird ringers (perhaps called bird markers in future), who understand how birds use their environment and are prepared to spend hours using their skills to catch and mark them.

FASCINATING FACTS UNCOVERED BY BIRD RINGERS

- The first birds in what became the BTO Ringing Scheme were Lapwings, ringed on Saturday May 8, 1909 at Sands of Forvie in Aberdeenshire, Scotland.

- The first record of a bird ringed in Britain & Ireland and found abroad was a Common Tern. It was ringed as a chick on July 30, 1909 in Ravenglass, Cumbria, and found exhausted in A Coruña, northwestern Spain on September 21 the same year.

- Though some British and Irish breeding Merlins do remain for the winter, ringing records have shown that numbers are boosted by birds of the Icelandic race.

- Ringing recoveries revealed that Sanderlings in Britain during autumn come from Canada/Greenland, not just Siberia.

- Ringing has revealed changing patterns of migration in the Blackcap – when birds started overwintering in Britain it was initially thought that these were simply British birds that had not migrated, but ringing revealed they are from central Europe.

- Our longest-lived birds are seabirds. The oldest bird in the BTO Ringing Scheme (so far) is a Manx Shearwater ringed at Bardsey Bird Observatory on May 17, 1957. It has been recaught on Bardsey on several occasions, the most recent being May 8, 2008. Longevity records for other seabird species include a Razorbill ringed on July 2,1962 and retrapped on June 25, 2004 and a Fulmar ringed on July 18, 1951 retrapped on June 3, 1992.

- For BTO-ringed birds, terns are the distance record-holders. The longest distance on the database is for an Arctic Tern that travelled 18,056 km from its ringing site in Anglesey to New South Wales, Australia. For Common Tern, the record is 17,641 km for a bird ringed in Co Down and reported in Australia.

Becoming a ringer

If you are interested in becoming a ringer, you will find information on our website (www.bto.org/ringing/index.htm) where you can also look for ringing trainers in your area (www.bto.org/goto/train2ring.htm). If you have any further questions, please contact us (details above).

Reporting a ringed bird
If you find a ringed bird, please report it to the BTO.

You can use the web reporting form – go to www.ring.ac.

Or contact us at:
Ringing, BTO, The Nunnery, Thetford, Norfolk IP24 2PU

Phone: 01842 750 050

E-mail: recoveries@bto.org

ENGLISH LANGUAGE BIRD MAGAZINES

To help meet the needs of active UK birdwatchers keen to learn more about birds and birding opportunities overseas, we have compiled this Directory of English language magazines. Readers are encouraged to nominate other suitable titles for future editions.

GREAT BRITAIN

BirdingASIA

The bulletin of the Oriental Bird Club, *BirdingASIA* is published twice a year for the group's membership in Britain and overseas. It provides a forum for articles on the avifauna of the Oriental zoogeographic area (from Indonesia in the south to Russia's Kamchatka region and west to Pakistan). Regular features include bird identification, taxonomy, birding hotspots, species under threat, pioneers of Oriental ornithology, news, book reviews and letters.
Editor: OBC Publications Committee.
Contact: Oriental Bird Club, PO Box 324 Bedford MK42 0WG.
E-mail: mail@orientalbirdclub.org
www.orientalbirdclub.org

Birding World

A full-colour monthly magazine that caters for keener birders interested in rarer birds in Britain and Europe, migration, identification, status, the fast-changing taxonomic scene and overseas birding. Each monthly issue details the most significant bird sightings in Britain, Europe and the remainder of the Western Palearctic.
Other regular features include ground-breaking identification articles and accounts of overseas birding trips.
Editor: Steve Gantlett.
Contact details: Birding World, Sea Lawn, Coast Road, Cley-next-the-Sea, Holt, Norfolk NR25 7RZ. Tel: 01263 740 913. E-mail: Steve@birdingworld.co.uk
www.birdingworld.co.uk

Birds

The quarterly members-only magazine issued by the Royal Society for the Protection of Birds is a full-colour super-A4 magazine that promotes the organisation's work in conservation and education. In addition to an extensive general news section, the magazine carries features on RSPB reserves, international initiatives with partner organisations, members' letters and book reviews. *Birds* is available on CD for visually-impaired members.
Editor: Rob Hume.
Contact: Birds magazine, The Lodge, Sandy, Bedfordshire SG19 2DL.
E-mail: rob.hume@rspb.org.uk
Tel: 01767 680 551. www.rspb.org.uk

Birds Illustrated

A subscription-only quarterly A4 publication, *Birds Illustrated* is very different to the monthly UK bird magazines as it emphasises the aesthetic appreciation of wild birds anywhere in the world. In-depth articles cover a broad range of ornithological topics, with regular features on leading bird artists and photographers. A column about secondhand natural history books is a unique feature of every issue.

The magazine sponsors a number of art awards at exhibitions staged by the Society of Wildlife Artists, the British Decoy and Bird Carving Association, British Birdwatching Fair and the National Exhibition of Wildlife Art.
Editor: David Cromack.
Contact: Buckingham Press Ltd, 55 Thorpe Park Road, Peterborough PE3 6LJ. 01733 561 739. E-mail: editor@ buckinghampress.com www.birdsillustrated.com

Bird Table

A quarterly full colour A4 magazine sent free to all participants in the British Trust for Ornithology's Garden BirdWatch survey, *Bird Table* presents a seasonal round-up of the most significant garden bird sightings, plus features on individual species, bird behaviour, wildlife gardening, bird migration, plus notes from Garden BirdWatch participants.
Edited by: Mike Toms, with contributions from a range of garden bird experts.
Contact: Subscribe to the magazine by joining BTO Garden BirdWatch survey (£15 per annum). Write to GBW, FREEPOST IH2784, Thetford, Norfolk, IP24 2BR. Tel: 01842 750 050 or join online at www.bto.org/gbw

Birdwatch

A monthly full-colour A4 magazine, *Birdwatch* is available on subscription and from newsagents and specialist outlets such as bird reserves. Contains a range of features on identification, birding tips, UK and foreign birding areas and taxonomic issues. Also contains news, events, readers' letters, product reviews and summaries of British, Irish and Western Palearctic bird sightings. The magazine organises the Swarovski-sponsored Birdwatch Artist of the Year competition in association with the Society of Wildlife Artists.
Managing Editor: Dominic Mitchell.
Contact: Warners Midland Plc, The Chocolate Factory, 5 Clarendon Road, London N22 6XJ. Tel: 020 8881 0550. Fax: 020 8881 0990. Email: editorial@birdwatch.co.uk www.birdwatch.co.uk

Bird Watching

Britain's best-selling monthly bird magazine since its launch in 1986, *Bird Watching* is available from all leading newsagents and on subscription. This A4 full-colour title, is part of the Bauer Media stable and caters for all active birdwatchers. Every issue contains articles on identification, plus news, readers' letters, the *Go Birding* pull-out guide to bird walks and reserves, individual product reviews, plus surveys of leading optical products. The magazine is a co-organiser of the International Wildbird Photographer competition.
Editor: Sheena Harvey.
Contact: Bird Watching, Media House, Lynchwood, Peterborough PE2 6EA. Tel: 01733 468 201.
E-mail: birdwatching@bauermedia.co.uk www.birdwatching.co.uk

ENGLISH LANGUAGE BIRD MAGAZINES

British Birds

This well respected subscription-only full colour journal of record celebrated its centenary of publication in 2007. Throughout its long history it has always aimed to publish material on behaviour, conservation, distribution, ecology, identification, status and taxonomy for birders throughout the Western Palearctic. Organises the BB Bird Photograph of the Year competition. Publishes the annual report of the British Birds Rarities Committee.

Editor: Roger Riddington.
Contact: Editor, *British Birds*, Spindrift, Eastshore, Virkie, Shetland ZE3 9JS.
Tel: 01950 460 080.
E-mail: editor@britishbirds.co.uk
www.britishbirds.co.uk

BTO News

A completely redesigned and up-dated bi-monthly full-colour A4 magazine sent to all members of the British Trust for Ornithology. Features include articles about the full range of BTO research projects, articles of general interest based on BTO research, plus the status of various species, book reviews and an events guide.

Editor: Su Gough.
Contact: BTO, The Nunnery, Thetford, Norfolk IP24 2PU. Tel; 01842 750 050.
E-mail: btonews@bto.org
www.bto.org

Cotinga

The journal of the Neotropical Bird Club, *Cotinga* will be published annually from 2009, in September, to provide a forum for scientific and birding articles concerning South and Central America and the Caribbean.

There are regular features on birding sites, site and area records, behaviour, breeding observations, range extensions, rediscoveries, conservation of Neotropical birds, sightings from the NBC region, a taxonomic round-up and book reviews.

Editor: Guy Kirwan
Contact: Neotropical Bird Club, c/o The Lodge, Sandy, Bedfordshire, SG19 2DL, UK.
E-mail secretary@neotropicalbirdclub.org.
www.neotropicalbirdclub.org.

Forktail

The journal of Asian ornithology, *Forktail* is published annually by the Oriental Bird Club. It contains original papers in the English language (occasionally also English translations of papers in Oriental languages) treating any aspect of the ornithology (e.g. distribution, biology, conservation, identification) of the same region covered by Its sister publication *BirdingASIA*. All submissions are reviewed by referees and the *Forktail* editorial committee.

Senior Editor: Suhel Quader.
Contact: Oriental Bird Club, PO Box 324 Bedford MK42 0WG.
E-mail: mail@orientalbirdclub.org
www.orientalbirdclub.org

Neotropical Birding

The birding magazine of the Neotropical Bird Club. From 2009 *Neotropical Birding* will be published twice a year for members in the UK and around the world. It is the place to find information on birding in South and Central America and the Caribbean.

There are regular features on bird identification, country guides, information on lodges and information on rare and interesting species and where and how to find them.

Editor: James Lowen
Contact: Neotropical Bird Club, c/o The Lodge, Sandy, Bedfordshire, SG19 2DL, UK.
E-mail secretary@neotropicalbirdclub.org.
www.neotropicalbirdclub.org.

ENGLISH LANGUAGE BIRD MAGAZINES

Peregrine

Members of the Hawk & Owl Trust receive copies of this full-colour A4 magazine twice a year. It reports on various research projects being carried out by the Trust, plus extensive news coverage from its reserves and local groups, plus events listings. One page is devoted to the Kestrel Club junior members.
Editor: Barbara Hall
Contact: Hawk & Owl Trust, PO Box 100, Taunton TA4 2WX.
E-mail: enquiries@hawkandowl.org
www.hawkandowl.org

Sandgrouse

This journal, produced twice a year, is sent to all members of the Ornithological Society of the Middle East, Caucasus and Central Asia (OSME) in Britain and overseas. It publishes papers and notes on the ornithology of the Middle East, Caucasus and Central/Middle Asia and includes news and recent sightings. The OSME region extends from Egypt, the Yemen and Turkey to Afghanistan and Kazakhstan.
Editor: Dr Peter Cowan.
E-mail sandgrouse@osme.org
Contact: www.osme.org for membership and further details.

Scottish Bird News

The quarterly magazine for members of the Scottish Ornithologists' Club (SOC) is a full-colour A4 publication that disseminates expert information on Scotland's bird life. Content includes articles, news, club notices and book reviews.
Editors: Jimmy Maxwell & Ian Francis

Contact: SOC, Scottish Birdwatchers' Resource Centre, Waterston House, Aberlady EH32 0PY.
Tel: 01875 871 330.
E-mail: mail@the-soc.org.uk
www.the-soc.org.uk

Scottish Birds

The official journal of the Scottish Ornithologists' Club (SOC) celebrated its 50th anniversary in 2008. This A5 annual (June) publication publishes original material on Scottish ornithology with a particular emphasis on distribution and status. Papers and notes are considered by referees and, where appropriate, the editorial panel. The journal also publishes obituaries.
Editor: Stan da Prato
Contact: SOC, Scottish Birdwatchers' Resource Centre, Waterston House, Aberlady EH32 0PY. Tel: 01875 871 330.
E-mail: mail@the-soc.org.uk
www.the-soc.org.uk

World Birdwatch

The long-established quarterly subscription-only magazine from BirdLife International promotes global bird conservation activities. An extensive round-up of world bird-related news regularly includes exciting reports of new bird species discoveries and rediscoveries, and is supported by features on the work of the BirdLife International Partnership.
Editor: Martin Fowlie.
Contact: BirdLife International, Wellbrook Court, Girton Road, Cambridge CB3 0NA.
E-mail: birdlife@birdlife.org
www.birdlife.org

ENGLISH LANGUAGE BIRD MAGAZINES

FINLAND

Alula

Started in 1995, *Alula* is an independent journal for people interested in birds and bird identification. Regular topics include ID papers by field experts, articles about birding sites, tests of optical equipment, literature reviews, competitions and current birding issues.

In order to widen its sales appeal, this high-quality quarterly A4 magazine is now available in an English-language edition as well as Finnish.

Editor: Rami Lindroos.
Contact: Alula Oy, P.O. Box 24, FI-20540 Turku, Finland.
E-mail: alula@alula.fi
www.alula.fi

HOLLAND

Ardea

The scientific, peer-reviewed journal of the Netherlands Ornithologists' Union, published twice yearly since 1912. Contributions in English, with a focus on ecology, life history and evolution of birds throughout the world. Members of the NOU also receive *Limosa* (4x per year), with contributions in Dutch on birds in The Netherlands (English summaries).
Contact: Jouke Prop, Allersmaweg 56, 9891 TD Ezinge, The Netherlands.
E-mail: ardea.nou@planet.nl
www.ardeajornal.nl

Dutch Birding

Many of the articles in this long-established bi-monthly A5 journal catering for serious birders and twitchers are published in English, and the Dutch pieces generally have an English summary.
Regular topics include ID papers by field

experts, extensive coverage of scarcer birds in Holland and the Western Palearctic generally, literature reviews, competitions and current birding issues. Good range of quality rarity photographs.
Editor: Arnoud van den Berg.
Contact: E-mail: editors@dutchbirding.nl
www.dutchbirding.nl

INDIAN SUB-CONTINENT

Indian Birds

Despite its name, this bi-monthly A4 journal publishes articles on bird behaviour, ecology and conservation, birding sites, plus notes about birds throughout Afghanistan, Bangladesh, Bhutan, India, the Maldives, Myanmar, Nepal, Pakistan and Sri Lanka.
First published in 2005, *Indian Birds* provides details of Indian bird conservation groups and web-based e-mail groups in each issue, as part of its mission to encourage awareness of birdwatching among the general public in the region.
Editor: Aasheesh Pittie.
Contact: Indian Birds, c/o The New Ornis Foundation, PO Box 2, Banjar Hills, Hyderabad 500034, India.
E-mail: editor@indianbirds.in

IRELAND

Irish Birds

The annual scientific journal of BirdWatch Ireland, the BirdLife International Partner for the Republic of Ireland, publishes peer-reviewed papers and notes on all aspects of birds and ornithology in Ireland, as well as annual reports of rarities, scarce migrants and rare breeders, and the annual Irish Ringing Report.

Papers, notes, photographs and drawings are welcome from amateurs and professionals alike, and should be submitted to the editor before July 31 each year.

Editor: Dr. Stephen Newton
Contact: Irish Birds, BirdWatch Ireland, P.O. Box 12, Greystones, Co. Wicklow, Ireland
Tel: +353-1-2819878.
E-mail: info@birdwatchireland.ie
www.birdwatchireland.ie

Wings

The quarterly members-only magazine of BirdWatch Ireland, the BirdLife International Partner for the Republic of Ireland, is a full-colour A4 magazine that highlights the organisation's conservation work and provides information on birds, birdwatching and wildlife in Ireland.

The magazine includes a general news section, a members' letters section, details of BirdWatch Ireland reserves and surveys, regional birdwatching guides, photographic features, local, national and international conservation reports, competitions and information on BirdWatch Ireland branch events across the country.

Editor: Cóilín MacLochlainn
Contact: Wings Magazine, BirdWatch Ireland, P.O. Box 12, Greystones, Co. Wicklow, Ireland
Tel: +353-1-2819878.
E-mail: info@birdwatchireland.ie
www.birdwatchireland.ie

NEW ZEALAND

Forest & Bird

Forest & Bird is the magazine of the Royal Forest & Bird Protection Society of New Zealand, the country's BirdLife International partner. Published quarterly, it includes articles about New Zealand's birdlife, as well

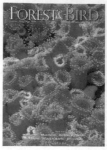

as other wildlife and conservation issues. Regular topics include efforts to protect endangered birds such as the Kiwi, Kakapo and albatrosses; places to go to see birds in New Zealand, news, research, reviews and letters.

Editor: Helen Bain
Contact: Forest & Bird, PO Box 631, Wellington, New Zealand.
E-mail: h.bain@forestandbird.org.nz
www.forestandbird.org.nz

SOUTH AFRICA

Africa Birds & Birding

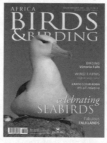

This award-winning glossy A4 bi-monthly colour magazine, first published in 1994, enjoys support from BirdLife South Africa and several other non-governmental groups but remains totally independent. The publisher (Africa Geographic Pty Ltd) strives to foster an awareness of the continent's birdlife and encourages birdwatching as a pastime and for its ecotourism potential.

High quality photographic features on birds and habitats, mainly in southern Africa, are Included along with articles on sites, book and product reviews, news and letters.

Editor: Eve Gracie
Contact: P O Box 44223, Claremont 7735, Cape Town, South Africa.
E-mail: eve@africageographic.com
www.africageographic.com

UNITED STATES

Birder's World

A bi-monthly magazine for birdwatchers who actively look for wild birds in the field. It concentrates on where to find, how to attract,

and how to identify wild birds, and on how to understand what they do. It carries features on individual bird species, hotspots across the globe, local birding hotspots in North America, conservation issues, bird behaviour, book and product reviews. Also features a question-and-answer column, and readers' letters and photography.

Editor: Charles J. Hagner.
Contact: Kalmbach Publishing Co., Birder's World editorial dept, PO Box 1612, Waukesha, WI 53187-1612, USA.
E-mail: mail@birdersworld.com
www.birdersworld.com

Birding

Issued exclusively to members six times a year by the American Birding Association, a not-for-profit organisation that aims to help field birders develop their knowledge, skills and enjoyment of wild birds.
The organisation (membership open to all birdwatchers) also encourages the conservation of birds and their habitats. In practice this means the magazine carries full-colour features, in-depth ID articles, book and product reviews, photo quizzes, fieldcraft, taxonomy and conservation articles.

Birding now features substantial online content, available free of charge at www.americanbirding.org/pubs/birding/archives/
Editor: Ted Floyd.
Contact: American Birding Association, PO Box 7974, Boulder, CO 80306 - 7974, USA.
www.americanbirding.org

Bird Watcher's Digest

This pocket-sized full-colour bi-monthly magazine is unashamedly populist in its approach and features a high proportion of articles about backyard birding and readers' birding tales, as well as helpful advice on ID and fieldcraft.
Top birding areas in North America and abroad are spotlighted and Book Notes covers the latest publications. Regular columnists include Kenn Kaufman and Julie Zickefoose. Subscribers get free access to additional material on the magazine's website, which also features a birding blog (Bill of the Birds) and a series of podcasts, called *This Birding Life*.
Editor: William H Thompson III.
Contact: Bird Watcher's Digest, PO Box 110, Marietta, Ohio 45750, USA.
E-mail: editor@birdwatchersdigest.com
www.birdwatchersdigest.com

WildBird

The bi-monthly magazine covers North American birds and birding in readers' back yards and in the Western Hemisphere. *WildBird* urges readers to share their appreciation for birds and to consider beginners' education and habitat conservation as means of ensuring avian species' survival.
The magazine features species profiles, travel articles, backyard birding tips, book reviews, and columns about conservation and birding with children. It also offers reader interaction and prizes via the Birder of the Year programme in each issue and the annual photo contest.
Editor: Amy K. Hooper
Contact: BowTie Inc., 3 Burroughs, Irvine CA 92618-2804, USA.
E-mail: wildbird@bowtieinc.com
www.wildbirdmagazine.com

THE TOP 50 MOST USEFUL WEBSITES FOR BIRDWATCHERS

Gordon Hamlett trawls the internet to highlight a broad range of bird-related sites worth visiting on a regular basis.

THE WEB is a highly transitory beast. I have hundreds of websites bookmarked for future reference which are no longer in existence. Some foundered due to lack of interest, while the cost of time and money in maintaining other sites led to them being abandoned. However, things are settling down and there is an increased stability today. Several main sites are even making money – or at least covering their costs - through selling advertising.

Money and the net are strange bedfellows. With nearly all internet content free, there has been minimal interest in sites where you have to pay to access extra content. Birders have a reputation for having long pockets and short arms and it seems that they would rather spend the extra money on a pager, a tank of petrol or an extra large pasty instead.

With this settling down of websites though has come a definite loss of the sheer joie de vivre of a few years ago when everything was new and exciting and there was a little bit of anarchy involved too. Now, everything is becoming a little bit too corporate and, dare one say it, boring.

Take for example BirdLife International (www.birdlife.org), though I could have chosen scores of other organisations. Here is one of the most important conservation bodies we have, doing fantastic work all round the world. The website contains massive amounts of information. So far, so good. But there is absolutely nothing here to set my blood boiling about the latest environmental outrage and fire off letters to politicians round the world.

Such a laid-back approach means a casual browser is just going to fall asleep instead of being exercised about major problems or the organisation's striking successes. Don't just tell me about them, SHOUT about them. Make me sit up and take notice.

So, where has all the passion gone? There was hope that blogging was going to be the answer. These online diaries allow you to vent your spleen on whatever takes your fancy. Certainly, in some fields such as politics, they are becoming hugely influential. But birding blogs just haven't taken off.

In the course of researching this article, I looked at dozens of blogs and very depressing it was, too. Don't get me wrong. Some of the blogs are very amusing or have excellent photos, or both. But they aren't reaching an audience at all. All too frequently you see something like 'Number of people who have read this article – 3. Number of comments on this article – nil.' Who wants to keep writing something that no-one's going to read?

ANNUAL WEBSITE SURVEY

A good website should draw you in and make you keep coming back. It's nice if looks pretty but not a problem if it isn't. Write with passion. Writers who love their subject should tell us what makes them excited and let us get caught up in their enthusiasm too.

One website that has done that for me this year is that of the Portland Bill Observatory. I checked it out before going on holiday, just to see what's around but I now find myself having a look every day. Congratulations to Martin Cade and the rest of the team. Of the 50 most essential websites in my survey, yours is my website of the year.

WEBSITE OF THE YEAR
www.portlandbirdobs.org.uk
Portland Bill is one of my favourite places to watch birds and the observatory's website does the area full justice. Updated daily, there are plenty of details and photos about migration that day, switching to moths if the birding is slow. All previous reports are archived. There is a spreadsheet of ringing totals and information on wildlife in the area. It's not a flashy site but it does what it sets out to extremely well and a lot of other websites could learn a lot.

MOST USEFUL BIRDING WEBSITES
Topics arranged alphabetically as follows:

Bird families	Migration	Seabirds
Bird ringing	Optics	Social networking
Bird sounds	Photography	Stamps
Blogs	Prehistoric birds	Taxonomy
Books and magazines	Quizzes	Trip reports
Conservation	Rarities	Videos
General ornithology	Research	Wildlife art
Latest sightings	Scottish islands	Wildlife news
Links		

BIRD FAMILIES

www.owlpages.com
Here you can find everything you wanted to know about owls as well as a lot that you didn't know you wanted, too. Not quite reaching the obsession stage, there are sections on sounds, behaviour, biology, mythology, photos, artwork and much, much more. Did I mention it was about owls?

www.geocities.com/RainForest/ Canopy/6181/gulls.htm
If the owl people are mildly eccentric, then the real anoraks of the birding world are the gull fanatics who enjoy nothing more than an abnormal moult pattern or an obscure hybrid and for whom a second-summer Caspian Gull is twice as interesting as a first-summer Caspian Gull (only joking). Here you get a series of beginners' articles, plus plenty of descriptions though only a few pictures. Fear not – there are plenty of links to other fanatical gull sites.

BIRD RINGING

www.euring.org
If you think that bird ringing simply involves the small metal ring placed on a bird's leg, then think again. Many projects, especially involving larger birds, now use large coloured rings as well, designed so that a birder can read the number through a scope. If you do find a colour-ringed gull, goose or wader, then this is the place to report your sighting and you will find out other places where your bird has been

seen. Everything else you want to know about ringing is here, too.

BIRD SOUNDS

www.rspb.org.uk/wildlife/birdguide/name/a/index.asp

I have criticised the RSPB's website many times in the past and in truth, it is still something of a lumbering giant. The one section I refer to regularly though is the species list, not least because the entries come complete with sound recordings – ideal for checking up on unfamiliar birds before you go out, or trying to nail down a mystery call when you return home.

BLOGS

http://10000birds.com

This is easily the slickest on-line diary around at the moment. Profusely illustrated, the site is largely North American in content though one contributor is British. There are plenty of stories such as an impressive set of photos of Red-necked Stints in Hong Long at the time of writing. Conservation projects include raising money for the Sharpe's Longclaw in Kenya. There are links to plenty of other birding blogs too.

BOOKS AND MAGAZINES

www.birdjournals.com

This is the place to try if you are looking for the odd missing volume in your collection of magazines or bird reports. The site itself is pretty crude but the prices are cheap and you have a good chance of filling those gaps. Content is mostly British.

www.eurobirding.com/birdingmagazines/articlesearch.php

When you want to refer back to a particular article but can't remember where you've seen it, turn to this site for help. It has more than 7,000 indexed articles from 12 leading European magazines. You can search by author, species, topic and country and your search should return a list of likely references. The site uses a series of pop-up windows, so you might have to temporarily change your computer settings if you normally block these to prevent spam.

www.newnaturalists.com

Collins New Naturalists are the most collected series of wildlife books, with some of the scarcer titles fetching well into four figures when they come up for sale in the secondhand market. This site has all the latest news, articles such as an interview with cover artist Robert Gillmor and, best of all, a forum for like-minded fans. While the correspondents have lots of expertise, at the time of writing the hot topic was how to stop people getting hold of a limited edition copy of *Grouse* and selling it on e-bay next day for a huge profit.

CONSERVATION

www.birdlife.org/datazone/species/index.html

How threatened is a particular bird? Here you can find conservation summaries for every species in the world, ranging from the not-at-all endangered Common Starling to the critically endangered Pohnpei Starling, just 50 of which survive on one tiny Micronesian island. The more threatened the bird is, the more information you get.

www.jncc.gov.uk/page-4

Hand in hand with conserving individual species goes the need to protect their habitats too. That is the remit of the Joint Nature Conservation Committee and this site is a portal to all the sites in Britain that have some form of special protection – Ramsar, Special Areas of Conservation, Special Protection Areas and Sites of Special Scientific Interest.

GENERAL ORNITHOLOGY

www.birds.cornell.edu

Though it is a North American site, the emphasis here is on teaching people about ornithology and there are plenty of articles, pictures, film clips and sounds to explore, culminating in 18,000 pages of information on North America's breeding birds

LATEST SIGHTINGS

www.birdguides.com

You don't have to be a twitcher to want to know what's about. At the time of writing, there is an obvious influx of Crossbills.

BirdGuides has details of all the latest sightings. You can pay to have full details of all birds reported or get free access to basic details of all that day's reports plus full details of the latest sighting called in.

www.bubo.org/listing
Having seen your rare bird, if you want to keep your lists online, then this site allows you to do just that. Lists can be set up for different geographical areas e.g. World, Western Palearctic, UK and Norfolk, or for specific periods such as year lists. You get to see just how you compare against like-minded people so there is a definite competitive element here. Not surprisingly, not many women feature; they've obviously got much better things to do with their time!

LINKS

www.fatbirder.com
Why spend hours researching something when someone else has done all the work for you? Fatbirder has thousands of links, all fully described, to other birding websites round the world. The main categories are World and British birding, bird news, travel, library, bird families, ornithology, sights and sounds, equipment and supplies and miscellaneous. Whether you are interested in birding in Botswana or have a passion for parrots, I would always start my research here.

www.bsc-eoc.org/links
http://birdingonthe.net
http://www.camacdonald.com/birding/birding.htm
One fieldguide or one encyclopaedia is never enough. They all have their strengths and weaknesses. These three sites also have huge numbers of links to other birding websites, but, being American-based, come from a slightly different angle. Between them, they should hoover up anything that Fatbirder has missed.

MIGRATION

www.bto.org/birdtrack
One of the great advantages of the internet is that the flow of information is two-way. BirdTrack, run by the British Trust for Ornithology, asks you to enter your sightings.

From the results, they plot where birds are at any given time and you can follow spring and autumn migration through a series of animated maps. This is a fantastic resource that will only get better with time.

www.rspb.org.uk/wildlife/tracking/mulleagles
www.roydennis.org
One of the recent developments in the study of bird migration and movement has been the ability to follow larger birds by fitting them with radio or satellite transmitting systems. The first site here allows you to follow the movements of the two White-tailed Eagle chicks hatched at Loch Frisa on Mull in 2008. The Highland Foundation is currently tracking a young Golden Eagle and a family of Ospreys and there is some historical data on Honey Buzzards and Marsh Harriers.
There are many similar projects online at the moment but I haven't found any umbrella site detailing them all yet. Type 'satellite tracking bird' into Google for dozens of sites involving cranes, waders, wildfowl, seabirds...

OPTICS

www.optics4birding.com/introduction.aspx
www.betterviewdesired.com/The-Ideal-Birding-Binocular.php
Optics4birding discusses the rationale behind binocular design, explaining various technical terms and looking at the merits of porro prisms versus roof prisms. Better View Desired takes a theoretical look at producing the perfect binoculars. Both sites have plenty of reviews to help you draw up a shortlist of models to be tested though, as both sites are American, not everything on their pages will be available in Britain or Europe.

PHOTOGRAPHS

www.birdpix.nl/portal.php
There are currently some 85,000 photos on this site. It is primarily a Dutch website, though there is an English version for the photos but not for the forums. The search button instantly brought up 120 Peregrine photos. There were four for White-billed Diver shots too, though one problem is that you are at the whim of the indexing and nomenclature – an American

would type in Yellow-billed Loon and get no hits at all. You can get round this by using the bird's scientific name. You can submit your own pictures and even create your own online album.

www.peregrinesbirdblog.blogspot.com

With the advent of digital photography, there has been an exponential increase in the number of bird/wildlife photography sites. Though this site is, a priori, a Northern Ireland birding blog (online diary), and a very interesting one, it has the best collection of links to other photography sites I have come across. If you want to explore further blogs, there is a good selection here too.

www.surfbirds.com

Surfbirds is a fully fledged birding on-line magazine, complete with discussion group, trip reports etc, albeit in a fairly higgledy-piggledy layout. It is however one of the best places to see the latest rarity photographs, some of which even appear online within a couple of hours of the bird being found. Look for the Photo Galleries section where you can also see rarity pictures from the rest of Europe and North America.

PREHISTORIC BIRDS

http://en.wikipedia.org/wiki/Origin_of_birds
http://en.wikipedia.org/wiki/Category: Prehistoric_birds

Wikipedia, the encyclopaedia that can be edited by its users comes in for some pretty bad press, with accusations of malicious editing and downright inaccuracies. To its credit, most of the articles have been more up-to-date and more accurate than Encyclopaedia Britannica. Here are two articles well worth exploring if you want find out about prehistoric and fossil birds. All the words in blue in the articles – and there are lots – take you to new articles so you will be browsing here for a long time.

QUIZZES

www.computerbirding.com/what/cbirding_e.html

Here's something to try when the boss isn't looking. There are six levels of difficulty featuring 2,700 pictures of 519 species. The early rounds are all multiple choice but at expert level, you have to type the answer in. Guaranteed to waste time as you try to beat your previous best score.

RARITY RECORDS

www.bbrc.org.uk
www.rbbp.org.uk

These sites cover the British Birds Rarities Committee and the Rare Breeding Birds Panel. Old reports can be downloaded from both sites, going back to 1973 in the case of breeding birds. There are details of what species are currently being assessed, forms for submitting records and the latest news – Cattle Egrets breeding for the first time in summer 2008 was the latest story.

RESEARCH

www.bsc-eoc.org/avibase

Avibase is a terrific place to start if you are researching a particular species. Once you enter the name of the species you require, you get a list of the name in about 70 languages. A series of clickable links brings up pictures, articles, maps, conservation details, published papers etc, all culled from sites elsewhere. From the website, you can also access checklists for just about anywhere on earth, trip reports, other birding links etc.

SCOTTISH ISLANDS

www.nature-shetland.co.uk
www.wildlifehebrides.com

Here's a dilemma. Because of their geographical location, the Western Isles and Northern Isles have some of the best birding in Britain, both in their breeding birds and their ability to attract rare migrants. But they are not easy places to get to. So how do you go about attracting eco-tourists to boost the local economy as well as providing a great experience for visiting birders?

These two websites take radically different approaches, yet both succeed admirably. Nature Shetland is very much sightings-led, totally up-to-date and with lots of photos. Wildlife Hebrides concentrates on locations, with 43 main sites detailed. What is interesting is that both sites see birds as just part of the package, giving equal prominence to flowers, mammals and invertebrates. Shetland even has astronomical maps.

If you run, or are planning to run a similar website, then take a look; the passion shines through. You want to visit these places. At a time when websites are getting flashier, and adding extra bells and whistles, it is a point worth remembering. Style only takes you so far; it is substance that counts in the end.

SEABIRDS

www.seawatch-sw.org

Concentrating on monitoring Balearic Shearwaters off Britain's south-west coast, this site also has details of recent seawatching totals, as well as information on cetaceans, basking sharks and sunfish. There are useful identification tips and you are encouraged to submit your own sightings.

www.oceanwanderers.com
www.seawatching.net

If you are serious about your seawatching, then these sites are a good place to start, with hundreds of stunning photos, news, reviews, conservation, mailing lists, cetaceans etc. It is not just seabirds that are discussed either, but anything seen passing at sea, such as waders and displaced landbirds. The downsides are that Ocean Wanderers does not appear to have been updated for a couple of years and navigation around the Seawatching site leaves something to be desired. There are plenty of links to other seabird sites.

SOCIAL NETWORKING

www.birdforum.net

If you want advice on which digital camera to choose, need help on a tricky identification problem or simply want to tell everyone else about the brilliant day's birding you have just had, then Bird Forum is for you. With more than 70,000 members worldwide, you can talk about anything bird related. And it's moderated, so while others might have strong, differing views to your own, you can guarantee that there won't be any abuse.

www.fatbirder.com/links/signpost_and_ discussion/mailing_lists.html
http://dir.groups.yahoo.com/dir/ Recreation___Sports/Outdoors/Birding

These two sites between them detail many hundreds of other discussion groups for you to browse and join. Not all of them are well used, though you can monitor the amount of traffic each group gets on the Yahoo site. Nor is there any relation between the quality of the birding and the number of messages posted – Norfolk groups get hardly any postings whereas just down the road, Peterbirder, which covers birds in the Peterborough area, is particularly active.

www.birdingpal.org

'A stranger is just a birder you haven't met yet' is the philosophy of Birdingpals. If you are visiting a new part of the world, the site aims to put you in touch with local birders who can show you round. The quid pro quo is that someone might e-mail you out of the blue, looking for help when he visits your particular patch. There are also lists of professional tour guides for each area.

STAMPS

www.bird-stamps.org
www.birdtheme.org

Collecting birds on stamps is by far the most popular philatelic theme. There are currently 26,000 stamps featuring more than 3,400 species and these two sites detail every one of them. You can select by either species or country and the first site even produces a distribution map for each species when you click on an individual image. Misidentifications and other errors are fully discussed.

TAXONOMY

www.worldbirdnames.org

If you want a bang up-to-date list of all the birds of the world, featuring all the latest taxonomic changes, then here it is. There are summaries of new species and suggested splits. As well as browsing the website, you can also download a couple of Excel spreadsheets. Their ultimate aim is to achieve a standardised set of English names, a topic guaranteed to upset just about everybody – I guarantee you'll violently disagree with at least one of the suggested names.

TRIP REPORTS

www.travellingbirder.com/tripreports/default.php
If you are planning a birding holiday, it makes a lot of sense to find out the best places to visit and what sort of birds you are likely to see. The easiest way to do this is to read other birders' trip reports and Travelling Birder aims to index as many as they can find. At the time of writing, more than 6,400 are listed covering the whole world. If you don't feel like reading all of those, you can filter by country and time of year to narrow your selection.

VIDEOS

http://ibc.hbw.com/ibc/
Sometimes, a picture of a bird in a fieldguide just isn't enough; you want to watch a film clip instead. Here you have nearly 27,000 videos of more than 5,300 species, about 55% of the world's total. At the time of writing, the site is due for an imminent major makeover promising much greater functionality. Given that this is an impressive site to start with, this is really exciting news.

www.birdforum.tv
As well as various video clips, you can also watch longer birding films here including various travelogues from Malcolm Rymer. All content is free and there is plenty of wildlife apart from birds on offer too. The footage is on several channels though and I kept forgetting to stop one film as I started another resulting in a somewhat confusing double commentary until I twigged what I was doing wrong. Variety of spellings makes searching for clips trickier than it might be.

WILDLIFE ART

www.birdingart.com
For anyone who loves bird art, site is an excellent place to start, each featuring a range of pictures from a selection of artists. Check the sites regularly as new exhibitions come and go. And it might be worth keeping your credit card in a different room...

www.langford-press.co.uk
Langford Press publishes of some of the best art books around at the moment, ideal if you can't afford the original pieces of art. There is a nice mix of individual artists – I can recommend the titles by James McCallum and Robert Gillmor but there are also themed titles with a variety of artists interpreting the same landscape. Look out for the *Great Fen* and *Aig an Oir – At the Edge* which is based on Scotland's Atlantic oakwoods.

www.natureartists.com
This is an American art site, so most of the artists featured will be unfamiliar to UK viewers. New pages open up for each artist and you get biographical details and a look at the artist's studio as well as seeing plenty of examples of their work. At the time of writing, there were more than 1,600 bird pictures featured with thousands more on different wildlife subjects. One word of caution; if you are planning to buy a piece of art from this site, then you should check with the Revenue and Customs website about any import duties and VAT to be paid.

www.newa-uk.com
The National Exhibition of Wildlife Art site features works from more than 180 different artists that have been featured in the annual show on the Wirral. Featured artists include the likes of Alan Harris, Thelma Sykes and John Threlfall. The next exhibition opens in July but you can still admire work from previous shows and there is an impressive set of links to individual artist's websites.

WILDLIFE NEWS

www.habitat.org.uk
Updated daily, Habitat trawls the British press – national and local – for the latest wildlife and environmental stories. You get a brief introduction to the story plus a link to the full article. There is a discussion group too but it doesn't get a lot of traffic. Simply and elegantly put together, this site is well worth checking every day.

DIARY 2009

Singing Robin by Steve Knell

EVENTS DIARY 2009

JANUARY

19-30: RSPB Big Schools Birdwatch
A new initiative to get children interested in wild birds - see RSPB website for local area information.

24: Sussex Ornithological Society annual conference
Clare Hall, Haywards Heath, Sussex, by prior booking only.
Contact: adrianrspb@btinternet.com

24-25: RSPB Big Garden Birdwatch
Nationwide survey.
Contact: RSPB on 01767 680 551.
www.rspb.org.uk

FEBRUARY

14-21: National Nest Box Week
Contact: jeff.baker@bto.org

21: North East Ringers Conference
Norton College, Malton, North Yorks.
Contact: ringingconferences@bto.org

MARCH

8: African Bird Club AGM
Venue to be announced.
Contact: info@africanbirdclub.org

21: BTO/SOC Scottish Birdwatchers Conference
Barony College, Parkgate, Dumfries.
Contact: e-mail: mail@the-soc.org.uk

27-30: Seabird Group 10th International Conference
Provinciaal Hof, Bruges, Belgium.
Contact: Conference secretariat at:
e-mail: seabirdconf2009@vliz.be

31- April 2: BOU Annual Conference: Lowland farmland birds
University of Leicester. Follows successful conferences on same theme in 1999 and 2004 with up-to-date research and conservation initiatives.
Contact: 01733 844 820.
E-mail: conferences@bou.org.uk

APRIL

3-5: BTO Bird Survey Techniques Residential Course
Dale Fort Field Studies Centre, Gower, S Wales (Led by Su Gough)
Contact: e-mail: su.gough@bto.org

17-19: BTO Bird Survey Techniques Residential Course
Slapton Ley Field Studies Centre, South Devon (Led by Su Gough)
Contact: e-mail: su.gough@bto.org

17-19: RSPB Members Weekend
York University.
Contact: e-mail: Anna.saunders@rspb.org.uk

MAY

1-3: BTO Bird Survey Techniques Residential Course
 Malham Tarn Field Studies Centre, N. Yorkshire (Led by Su Gough)
Contact: e-mail: su.gough@bto.org

5-7: BTO Bird Identification Residential Course
Dale Fort Field Studies Centre, Gower, S Wales (Led by Steve Piotrowski)
Contact: e-mail: u.gough@bto.org

16-17: Lee Valley Spring Wildlife Weekend
Waterworks Nature Reserve, Lammas Road, Leyton, London E10 7NU (10am - 4.30pm).
Contact: Vicki Sage on 01992 709 913.
E-mail: events@leevalleypark.org.uk

24: Neotropical Bird Club Spring Meeting and AGM
Illustrated talks, book sales and refreshments at Cley Village Hall, Norfolk.
Contact: Trevor Warren
e-mail: trevorwarren@trevorwarren.demon.co.uk

30-31: Birdwatcher's Spring Fair & Wildlife Digital Photo Show
Middleton Hall, near Tamworth, West Midlands
Contact: Alan Richards, 01527 852 357; e-mail: alan.richards@birdwatchers-springfair.co.uk
www.birdwatchers-springfair.co.uk

JULY

17 - Aug 2: NEWA (National Exhibition of Wildlife Art)
Gordale Nursery, Burton, The Wirral. Preview evening on July 1
Contact: e-mail: NEWA@mtuffrey.freeserve.co.uk or visit: www.newa-uk.com

18: Ornithological Society of the Middle East (OSME) AGM
The Nunnery, BTO Thetford.
Contact: Secretary W J Bartley on 01636 703 512.

EVENTS DIARY 2009

AUGUST

21-22-23: British Birdwatching Fair
Egleton Nature Reserve, Rutland Water, Rutland.
Contact: Tel: 01572 771 079 or
e-mail: info@birdfair.org.uk
www.birdfair.org.uk

21-26: 7th Conference of the European Ornithologists Union
University of Zurich, Switzerland
Contact: e-mail: info@eou2009.ch

23 - 24: Dutch Birdfair (Vogelfestival)
De Oostvaardersplassen near Lelystad.
Contact: Anna Kemp on +31 30 69 377 64 or
anna.kemp@vogelbescherming.nl

27 - 30: Marwell International Wildlife Art Society annual exhibition
Marwell Zoological Park, Hampshire.
Contact: chairman Pip McGarry at
e-mail: pip@pipmcgarry.com
www.miwas.co.uk

SEPTEMBER

5-6: 19th Scottish Nature Photography Fair
Battleby, Perth.
Contact: e-mail: Lorne.Gill@snh.gov.uk
www.snh.org.uk

5-13: Wildlife Art Exhibition
10am-5pm each day at The Friars, Aylesford, Kent.
Preview night - Sept 4.
Contact: Paul Cumberland on 01795 532 370.

12-13: Bird And Countryside Show
A festival for all people interested in birds and
conservation at The Friars, Aylesford, Kent. Sat:
10am-6pm. Sun: 10am-5pm. Admission £5 adults.
Contact: Paul Cumberland on 01795 532 370.

TBC: German Birdfair (Fokus Natur)
Radolfzell, Lake Constance.
Contact: Mrs. Marion Hammerl.
E-mail: info@bodensee-stiftung.org.
www.bodensee-stiftung.org

23 - Oct 4: Society of Wildlife Artists' annual exhibition
The Mall Galleries, Pall Mall, London SW1. Preview
Day September 22.
Contact: patriciahouchell@mallgalleries.com

29- Oct 4: Raptor Research Council Annual Conference
Pitlochry, Perthshire, Scotland.
Contact: Ruth Tingay of Scottish Raptor Group,
e-mail: dimlylit100@hotmail.com

OCTOBER

3: RSPB AGM & Members Day
Queen Elizabeth II conference centre,
Westminster, London.
Contact: e-mail: Anna.saunders@rspb.org.uk

16-18: Hawk & Owl Trust Member's Day and AGM
Skippings Barn, Chiltern Open Air Museum. Call
0870 990 3889 for details.
Contact: e-mail: enquiries@hawkandowl.org

16-18: BTO Bird Survey Techniques Residential Course
Kindrogan Field Studies Centre, Perthshire (Led by
Graeme Garner).
Contact: e-mail: su.gough@bto.org

28-30: BTO Bird Survey Techniques Residential Course
Flatford Mill Field Studies Centre, Suffolk (Led by
Su Gough).
Contact: e-mail: su.gough@bto.org

24: RSPB Feed The Birds Day
A programme of events across the UK - check local
press and RSPB website for details in your area.

NOVEMBER

9-15: Australian Birdfair
Leeton, New South Wales (NW of Canberra).
Contact: E-mail: coordinator@
australianbirdfair.org.au

8: Oriental Bird Club AGM
Venue to be confirmed.
Contact: e-mail: mail@orientalbirdclub.org

28-29: North-west Bird Fair
WWT Martin Mere, Lancashire.
Contact: e-mail: victoria.guinan@wwt.org.uk

29- Dec 4: Australasian Ornithological Conference
Keynote speaker - Jeremy Greenwood (ex-BTO).
Armidale Ex-Services Memorial Club.
Contact: e-mail: aley@northnet.com.au
(www.birdsaustralia.co.au)

DECEMBER

4-6: BTO Annual Conference: Celebrating 100 Years of Bird Ringing
Hayes Conference Centre, Swanwick, Derbyshire.
Contact: e-mail: jeff.baker@bto.org

DIARY – JANUARY 2009

1	Thu	New Year's Day
2	Fri	Holiday (Scotland)
3	Sat	
4	Sun	
5	Mon	
6	Tue	
7	Wed	
8	Thu	
9	Fri	
10	Sat	
11	Sun	
12	Mon	
13	Tue	
14	Wed	
15	Thu	
16	Fri	
17	Sat	
18	Sun	
19	Mon	
20	Tue	
21	Wed	
22	Thu	
23	Fri	
24	Sat	
25	Sun	
26	Mon	
27	Tue	
28	Wed	
29	Thu	
30	Fri	
31	Sat	

DIARY – FEBRUARY 2009

1	Sun	
2	Mon	
3	Tue	
4	Wed	
5	Thu	
6	Fri	
7	Sat	
8	Sun	
9	Mon	
10	Tue	
11	Wed	
12	Thu	
13	Fri	
14	Sat	
15	Sun	
16	Mon	
17	Tue	
18	Wed	
19	Thu	
20	Fri	
21	Sat	
22	Sun	
23	Mon	
24	Tue	
25	Wed	
26	Thu	
27	Fri	
28	Sat	

DIARY – MARCH 2009

1	Sun	
2	Mon	
3	Tue	
4	Wed	
5	Thu	
6	Fri	
7	Sat	
8	Sun	
9	Mon	
10	Tue	
11	Wed	
12	Thu	
13	Fri	
14	Sat	
15	Sun	
16	Mon	
17	Tue	
18	Wed	
19	Thu	
20	Fri	
21	Sat	
22	Sun	Mothering Sunday
23	Mon	
24	Tue	
25	Wed	
26	Thu	
27	Fri	
28	Sat	
29	Sun	British Summertime begins
30	Mon	
31	Tue	

DIARY – APRIL 2009

1	Wed	
2	Thu	
3	Fri	
4	Sat	
5	Sun	
6	Mon	
7	Tue	
8	Wed	
9	Thu	
10	Fri	Good Friday
11	Sat	
12	Sun	Easter Day
13	Mon	Easter Monday
14	Tue	
15	Wed	
16	Thu	
17	Fri	
18	Sat	
19	Sun	
20	Mon	
21	Tue	
22	Wed	
23	Thu	
24	Fri	
25	Sat	
26	Sun	
27	Mon	
28	Tue	
29	Wed	
30	Thu	

DIARY – MAY 2009

1	Fri	
2	Sat	
3	Sun	
4	Mon	May Day
5	Tue	
6	Wed	
7	Thu	
8	Fri	
9	Sat	
10	Sun	
11	Mon	
12	Tue	
13	Wed	
14	Thu	
15	Fri	
16	Sat	
17	Sun	
18	Mon	
19	Tue	
20	Wed	
21	Thu	
22	Fri	
23	Sat	
24	Sun	
25	Mon	Spring Bank Holiday
26	Tue	
27	Wed	
28	Thu	
29	Fri	
30	Sat	
31	Sun	

DIARY – JUNE 2009

1	Mon	
2	Tue	
3	Wed	
4	Thu	
5	Fri	
6	Sat	
7	Sun	
8	Mon	
9	Tue	
10	Wed	
11	Thu	
12	Fri	
13	Sat	
14	Sun	
15	Mon	
16	Tue	
17	Wed	
18	Thu	
19	Fri	
20	Sat	
21	Sun	
22	Mon	
23	Tue	
24	Wed	
25	Thu	
26	Fri	
27	Sat	
28	Sun	
29	Mon	
30	Tue	

DIARY – JULY 2009

1	Wed	
2	Thu	
3	Fri	
4	Sat	
5	Sun	
6	Mon	
7	Tue	
8	Wed	
9	Thu	
10	Fri	
11	Sat	
12	Sun	
13	Mon	
14	Tue	
15	Wed	
16	Thu	
17	Fri	
18	Sat	
19	Sun	
20	Mon	
21	Tue	
22	Wed	
23	Thu	
24	Fri	
25	Sat	
26	Sun	
27	Mon	
28	Tue	
29	Wed	
30	Thu	
31	Fri	

DIARY – AUGUST 2009

1	Sat	
2	Sun	
3	Mon	
4	Tue	
5	Wed	
6	Thu	
7	Fri	
8	Sat	
9	Sun	
10	Mon	
11	Tue	
12	Wed	
13	Thu	
14	Fri	
15	Sat	
16	Sun	
17	Mon	
18	Tue	
19	Wed	
20	Thu	
21	Fri	
22	Sat	
23	Sun	
24	Mon	
25	Tue	
26	Wed	
27	Thu	
28	Fri	
29	Sat	
30	Sun	
31	Mon	Summer Bank Holiday

DIARY – SEPTEMBER 2009

1	Tue	
2	Wed	
3	Thu	
4	Fri	
5	Sat	
6	Sun	
7	Mon	
8	Tue	
9	Wed	
10	Thu	
11	Fri	
12	Sat	
13	Sun	
14	Mon	
15	Tue	
16	Wed	
17	Thu	
18	Fri	
19	Sat	
20	Sun	
21	Mon	
22	Tue	
23	Wed	
24	Thu	
25	Fri	
26	Sat	
27	Sun	
28	Mon	
29	Tue	
30	Wed	

DIARY – OCTOBER 2009

1	Thu	
2	Fri	
3	Sat	
4	Sun	
5	Mon	
6	Tue	
7	Wed	
8	Thu	
9	Fri	
10	Sat	
11	Sun	
12	Mon	
13	Tue	
14	Wed	
15	Thu	
16	Fri	
17	Sat	
18	Sun	
19	Mon	
20	Tue	
21	Wed	
22	Thu	
23	Fri	
24	Sat	
25	Sun	British Summertime ends
26	Mon	
27	Tue	
28	Wed	
29	Thu	
30	Fri	
31	Sat	

DIARY – NOVEMBER 2009

1	Sun	
2	Mon	
3	Tue	
4	Wed	
5	Thu	
6	Fri	
7	Sat	
8	Sun	Remembrance Sunday
9	Mon	
10	Tue	
11	Wed	
12	Thu	
13	Fri	
14	Sat	
15	Sun	
16	Mon	
17	Tue	
18	Wed	
19	Thu	
20	Fri	
21	Sat	
22	Sun	
23	Mon	
24	Tue	
25	Wed	
26	Thu	
27	Fri	
28	Sat	
29	Sun	
30	Mon	

DIARY – DECEMBER 2009

1	Tue	
2	Wed	
3	Thu	
4	Fri	
5	Sat	
6	Sun	
7	Mon	
8	Tue	
9	Wed	
10	Thu	
11	Fri	
12	Sat	
13	Sun	
14	Mon	
15	Tue	
16	Wed	
17	Thu	
18	Fri	
19	Sat	
20	Sun	
21	Mon	
22	Tue	
23	Wed	
24	Thu	
25	Fri	Christmas Day
26	Sat	
27	Sun	
28	Mon	Bank holiday
29	Tue	
30	Wed	
31	Thu	

YEAR PLANNER 2010

January
February
March
April
May
June
July
August
September
October
November
December

LOG CHARTS

Tree Sparrow by Steve Knell

A CHECKLIST OF BIRDS

Based on the British List formulated by the British Ornithologists' Union

NEWCOMERS to birdwatching are sometimes baffled when they examine their first fieldguide as it is not immediately clear why the birds are arranged the way they are. The simple answer is that the order is meant to reflect the evolution of the included species. If one were to draw an evolutionary tree of birds, those families that branch off earliest (i.e are the most ancient) should be listed first.

Previously the British Ornithologists' Union British List was based on Voous Order (BOU 1977), the work of an eminent Dutch taxonomist and many of the popular fieldguides for British and European birds follow this established order.

However, more than 26 phylogenetic studies, many using DNA analysis, have been published in recent years that together form a large body of evidence showing that the order of birds in the British List did not properly reflect their evolution.

A change in order was required to reflect these new findings, so that now swans, geese and ducks have replaced divers and grebes at the head of the list.

The British Ornithologists' Union's Records Committee (BOURC) is responsible for maintaining the British List and it relies on its Taxonomic Sub-Committee (BOURC-TSC) to advise on taxonomic issues relating to the species that form the British List. The recommended changes have been accepted by the British Ornithologists' Union who have advised all book, magazine and bird report editors and publishers to begin using the new order as soon as possible and this is the third edition of The Birdwatcher's Yearbook to do so.

SPECIES, CATEGORIES, CODES – YOUR GUIDE TO GET THE BEST USE FROM THE CHECKLIST

Species list

The charts include all species from categories A, B and C on the British List, based on the latest BOU listing. Selected species included in categories D and E are listed separately at the end of the log chart.

Vagrants which are not on the British List, but which may have occurred in other parts of the British Isles, are not included. Readers who wish to record such species may use the extra rows provided on the last page. In this connection it should be noted that separate lists exist for Northern Ireland (kept by the Northern Ireland Birdwatchers' Association) and the Isle of Man (kept by the Manx Ornithological Society), and that Irish records are assessed by the Irish Rare Birds Committee.

The commoner species in the log charts are indicated by the * symbol to help make record-keeping easier.

Taxonomic changes introduced in 2002 mean there is a new order of species (as outlined above). The species names are those most widely used in the current fieldguides and each is followed by its scientific name, printed in italics.

Species categories

The following categories are those assigned by the British Ornithologists' Union.

A Species which have been recorded in an apparently natural state at least once since January 1, 1950.

B Species which would otherwise be in Category A but have not been recorded since December 31, 1949.

C Species that, though originally introduced by man, either deliberately or accidentally, have established breeding populations derived from introduced stock that maintain themselves without necessary recourse to further introduction.

D Species that would otherwise appear in

Categories A or B except that there is reasonable doubt that they have ever occurred in a natural state. (Species in this category are included in the log charts, though they do not qualify for inclusion in the British List, which comprises species in Categories A, B and C only. One of the objects of Category D is to note records of species which are not yet full additions, so that they are not overlooked if acceptable records subsequently occur. Bird report editors are encouraged to include records of species in Category D as appendices to their systematic lists).

E Species that have been recorded as introductions, transportees or escapees from captivity, and whose populations (if any) are thought not to be self-sustaining. They do not form part of the British List.

EU Species not on the British List, or in Category D, but which either breed or occur regularly elsewhere in Europe.

Life list

Ticks made in the 'Life List' column suffice for keeping a running personal total of species. However, added benefit can be obtained by replacing ticks with a note of the year of first occurrence. To take an example: one's first-ever Marsh Sandpiper, seen on April 14, 2008, would be logged with '08' in the Life List and '14' in the April column (as well as a tick in the 2008 column). As Life List entries are carried forward annually, in years to come it would be a simple matter to relocate this record.

First and last dates of migrants

Arrivals of migrants can be recorded by inserting dates instead of ticks in the relevant month columns. For example, a Common Sandpiper on March 11 would be recorded by inserting '11' against Common Sandpiper in the March column. The same applies to departures, though dates of last sightings can only be entered at the end of the year after checking one's field notebook.

Unheaded columns

The three unheaded columns on the right of the December column of each chart are for special (personal) use. This may be, for example, to cater for a second holiday, a particular county or a 'local patch'. Another use could be to indicate species on, for example, the Northern Ireland List or the Isle of Man List.

BTO species codes

British Trust for Ornithology two-letter species codes are shown in brackets in the fourth column

from the right. They exist for many species, races and hybrids recorded in recent surveys. Readers should refer to the BTO if more codes are needed.

In addition to those given in the charts, the following are available for some well-marked races or forms - Whistling Swan (WZ), European White-fronted Goose (EW), Greenland White-fronted Goose (NW), dark-bellied Brent Goose (DB), pale-bellied Brent Goose (PB), Black Brant (BB), domestic goose (ZL), Green-winged Teal (TA), domestic duck (ZF), Yellow-legged Gull (YG), Kumlien's Gull (KG), Feral Pigeon (FP), White Wagtail (WB), Black-bellied Dipper (DJ), Hooded Crow (HC), intermediate crow (HB).

Rarities

Rarities are indicated by a capital letter 'R' in the column headed BBRC (British Birds Rarities Committee).

EURING species numbers

EURING databanks collects copies of recovery records from ringing schemes throughout Europe and the official species numbers are given in the last column. As they are taken from the full Holarctic bird list there are many apparent gaps. It is important that these are not filled arbitrarily by observers wishing to record species not listed in the charts, as this would compromise the integrity of the scheme.

Similarly, the addition of a further digit to indicate sub-species is to be avoided, since EURING has already assigned numbers for this purpose. The numbering follows the Voous order of species so some species are now out of sequence following the re-ordering of the British List. For full details, visit: www.euring.org/edb/methods

Rare breeding birds

Species monitored by the Rare Breeding Birds Panel (see National Directory) comprise all those on Schedule 1 of the Wildlife and Countryside Act 1981 (see Quick Reference) together with all escaped or introduced species breeding in small numbers. The following annotations in the charts (third column from the right) reflect the RBBP's categories:

A Rare species. All breeding details requested.

B Less scarce species. Totals requested from counties with more than 10 pairs or localities; elsewhere all details requested.

C Less scarce species (specifically Barn Owl, Kingfisher, Crossbill). County summaries only requested.

D Escaped or introduced species. County summaries only requested.

SWANS, GEESE, DUCKS

BOU	Species	Scientific name	Life list	2009 list	24 hr	Garden	Holiday	Jan	Feb	Mar	Apr	May	Jun	Jul	Aug	Sep	Oct	Nov	Dec		BTO	RBBP	BBRC	EU No
* AC	Mute Swan	*Cygnus olor*																			MS			0152
* A	Bewick's Swan	*C. columbianus*																			BS	A		0153
* A	Whooper Swan	*C. cygnus*																			WS	D		0154
* A	Bean Goose	*Anser fabalis*																			BE			0157
* A	Pink-footed Goose	*A. brachyrhynchus*																			PG	D		0158
* A	White-fronted Goose	*A. albifrons*																			WG	D		0159
* A	Lesser White-fronted Goose	*A. erythropus*																			LC	D	R	0160
* AC	Greylag Goose	*A. anser*																			GJ			0161
* A	Snow Goose	*A. aerulescens*																			SJ	D		0163
* C	Canada Goose	*Branta canadensis*																			CG			0166
* A	Barnacle Goose	*B. eucopsis*																			BY	D		0167
* A	Brent Goose	*B. bernicla*																			BG			0168
* A	Red-breasted Goose	*B. ruficollis*																			EB	D	R	0169
* C	Egyptian Goose	*Alopochen aegyptiaca*																			EG	D		0170
* B	Ruddy Shelduck	*Tadorna ferruginea*																			UD	D		0171
* A	Shelduck	*T. tadorna*																			SU			0173
* C	Mandarin Duck	*Aix galericulata*																			MN			0178
* A	Wigeon	*Anas penelope*																			WN	A		0179
* A	American Wigeon	*A. americana*																			AW			0180
* AC	Gadwall	*A. strepera*																			GA	B		0182
* A	Teal	*A. crecca*																			T			0184
* A	Green-winged Teal	*A. carolinensis*																				A		1842
* AC	Mallard	*A. platyrhynchos*																			MA			0186
* A	Black Duck	*A. rubripes*																			BD	A	R	0187
	Sub total																							

DUCKS CONTINUED

BOU	Common name	Scientific name	Life list	2009 list	24 hr	Garden	Holiday	Jan	Feb	Mar	Apr	May	Jun	Jul	Aug	Sep	Oct	Nov	Dec				BTO	RBBP	BBRC	EU No
* A	Pintail	A. acuta																					PT	A		0189
* A	Garganey	A. querquedula																					GY	A		0191
A	Blue-winged Teal	A. discors																					TB	D	R	0192
* A	Shoveler	A. clypeata																					SV	A		0194
* A	Red-crested Pochard	Netta rufina																					RQ	D		0196
A	Canvasback	A. valisineria																							R	0197
* A	Pochard	A. ferina																					PO	B		0198
A	Redhead	A. americana																					AZ		R	0199
A	Ring-necked Duck	A. collaris																					NG	A		0200
A	Ferruginous Duck	A. nyroca																					FD			0202
* A	Tufted Duck	A. fuligula																					TU			0203
* A	Scaup	A. marila																					SP	A		0204
* A	Lesser Scaup	A. affinis																					AY		R	0205
* A	Eider	Somateria mollissima																					E			0206
* A	King Eider	S. spectabilis																					KE	A	R	0207
A	Steller's Eider	Polysticta stelleri																					ES		R	0209
A	Harlequin Duck	Histrionicus histrionicus																					HQ		R	0211
* A	Long-tailed Duck	Clangula hyemalis																					LN	A		0212
* A	Common Scoter	Melanitta nigra																					CX	A		0213
A	Black Scoter	M. americana																							R	2132
* A	Surf Scoter	M. perspicillata																					FS			0214
A	Velvet Scoter	M. fusca																					VS	A		0215
A	Bufflehead	Bucephala albeola																					VH		R	0216
A	Barrow's Goldeneye	B. islandica																							R	0217
	Sub total																									

DUCKS, GAMEBIRDS, DIVERS, GREBES

BOU	Species	Scientific name	Life list	2009 list	24 hr	Garden	Holiday	Jan	Feb	Mar	Apr	May	Jun	Jul	Aug	Sep	Oct	Nov	Dec	BTO	RBBP	BBRC	EU No
*A	Goldeneye	B. clangula																		GN	D		0218
*A	Smew	Mergellus albellus																		SY	A		0220
*A	Red-breasted Merganser	Mergus serrator																		RM			0221
*A	Goosander	M. merganser																		GD			0223
*C	Ruddy Duck	Oxyura jamaicensis																		BY			0225
*A	Red Grouse	Lagopus lagopus																		RG			0329
*A	Ptarmigan	Lagopus muta																		PM			0330
*A	Black Grouse	Tetrao tetrix																		BK			0332
*BC	Capercaillie	T. urogallus																		CP	A		0335
*C	Red-legged Partridge	Alectoris rufa																		RL			0358
*AC	Grey Partridge	Perdix perdix																		P			0367
*A	Quail	Coturnix coturnix																		Q	B		0370
*C	(Commom) Pheasant	Phasianus colchicus																		PH			0394
*C	Golden Pheasant	Chrysolophus pictus																		GF	D		0396
*C	Lady Amherst's Pheasant	C. amherstiae																		LM	D		0397
*A	Red-throated Diver	Gavia stellata																		RH	B		0002
*A	Black-throated Diver	G. arctica																		BV	A		0003
*A	Great Northern Diver	G. immer																		ND	A		0004
A	White-billed Diver	G. adamsii																		IW	A	R	0005
A	Pied-billed Grebe	Podilymbus podiceps																		PJ	A	R	0006
*A	Little Grebe	Tachybaptus ruficollis																		LG			0007
*A	Great Crested Grebe	Podiceps cristatus																		GG			0009
*A	Red-necked Grebe	P. grisegena																		RX	A		0010
*A	Slavonian Grebe	P. auritus																		SZ	A		0011
	Sub total																						

ALBATROSS, FULMAR, PETRELS, SHEARWATERS, CORMORANTS, FRIGATE BIRDS

BOU	Species		Life list	2009 list	24 hr	Garden	Holiday	Jan	Feb	Mar	Apr	May	Jun	Jul	Aug	Sep	Oct	Nov	Dec	BTO	RBBP	BBRC	EU No
*A	Black-necked Grebe	P. nigricollis																		BN	A		0012
A	Black-browed Albatross	Thalassarche melanophris																		AA	A	R	0014
*A	Fulmar	Fulmarus glacialis																		F			0020
A	Fea's Petrel	Pterodroma feae																				R	0026
A	Capped Petrel	Pt. hasitata																				R	0029
A	Cory's Shearwater	Calonectris diomedea																		CQ			0036
*A	Great Shearwater	Puffinus gravis																		GQ			0040
*A	Sooty Shearwater	P. griseus																		OT			0043
A	Manx Shearwater	P. puffinus																		MX			0046
A	Balearic Shearwater	P. mauretanicus																					0046
A	Macaronesian Shearwater	P. baroli																			A	R	0048
*A	Wilson's Petrel	Oceanites oceanicus																					0050
B	White-faced Petrel	Pelagodroma marina																				R	0051
*A	Storm Petrel	Hydrobates pelagicus																		TM			0052
*A	Leach's Petrel	Oceanodroma leucorhoa																		TL	A		0055
A	Swinhoe's Petrel	O. monorhis																					0056
B	Madeiran Petrel	O. castro																				R	0058
A	Red-billed Tropicbird	Phaethon aethereus																				R	0064
*A	(Northern) Gannet	Morus bassanus																		GX			0071
*A	Cormorant	Phalacrocorax carbo																		CA			0072
A	Double-crested Cormorant	P. auritus																				R	0078
*A	Shag	P. aristotelis																		SA			0080
A	Magnificent Frigatebird	Fregata magnificens																				R	0093
A	Ascension Frigatebird	F. aquila																				R	
	Sub total																						

69

BITTERNS, HERONS, STORKS, SPOONBILL, RAPTORS

BOU	Common	Scientific	Life list	2009 list	24 hr	Garden	Holiday	Jan	Feb	Mar	Apr	May	Jun	Jul	Aug	Sep	Oct	Nov	Dec		BTO	RBBP	BBRC	EU No
* A	Bittern	Botaurus stellaris																			BI	A		0095
A	American Bittern	B. lentiginosus																			AM		R	0096
A	Little Bittern	Ixobrychus minutus																			LL	A	R	0098
A	Night-heron	Nycticorax nycticorax																			NT	D		0104
A	Green Heron	Butorides virescens																			HR		R	0107
A	Squacco Heron	Ardeola ralloides																			QH		R	0108
A	Cattle Egret	Bubulcus ibis																			EC		R	0111
A	Snowy Egret	Egretta thula																					R	0115
* A	Little Egret	E. garzetta																			ET	A		0119
A	Great White Egret	Ardea alba																			HW			0121
A	Grey Heron	A. cinerea																			H			0122
A	Great Blue Heron	A. herodias																					R	
A	Purple Heron	A. purpurea																			UR	A		0124
A	Black Stork	Ciconia nigra																			OS		R	0131
A	White Stork	C. ciconia																			OR	A		0134
A	Glossy Ibis	Plegadis falcinellus																			IB		R	0136
* A	Spoonbill	Platalea leucorodia																			NB	A		0144
* A	Honey-buzzard	Pernis apivorus																			HZ	A		0231
A	Black Kite	Milvus migrans																			KB	A		0238
* AC	Red Kite	M. milvus																			KT	A		0239
* A	White-tailed Eagle	Haliaeetus albicilla																			WE	A		0243
B	Egyptian Vulture	Neophron percnopterus																					R	0247
A	Short-toed Eagle	Circaetus gallicus																					R	0256
* A	Marsh Harrier	Circus aeruginosus																			MR	A		0260
	Sub total																							

RAPTORS, RAILS AND CRAKES

BOU		Species	Scientific	Life list	2009 list	24 hr	Garden	Holiday	Jan	Feb	Mar	Apr	May	Jun	Jul	Aug	Sep	Oct	Nov	Dec	BTO	RBBP	BBRC	EU No
*	A	Hen Harrier	C. cyaneus																		HH	B		0261
	A	Pallid Harrier	C. macrourus																			A	R	0262
*	A	Montagu's Harrier	C. pygargus																		MO	A		0263
*	AC	Goshawk	Accipiter gentilis																		GI	B		0267
*	A	Sparrowhawk	A. nisus																		SH			0269
*	A	Buzzard	Buteo buteo																		BZ			0287
*	A	Rough-legged Buzzard	B. lagopus																		RF	A		0290
	B	Greater Spotted Eagle	Aquila clanga																				R	0293
*	A	Golden Eagle	A. chrysaetos																		EA	B		0296
*	A	Osprey	Pandion haliaetus																		OP	A		0301
	A	Lesser Kestrel	Falco naumanni																					0303
*	A	Kestrel	F. tinnunculus																		K			0304
	A	American Kestrel	F. sparverius																				R	0305
*	A	Red-footed Falcon	F. vespertinus																		FV			0307
*	A	Merlin	F. columbarius																		ML	B		0309
*	A	Hobby	F. subbuteo																		HY	B		0310
	A	Eleonora's Falcon	F. eleonorae																				R	0311
*	A	Gyr Falcon	F. rusticolus																		YF	A	R	0318
*	A	Peregrine	F. peregrinus																		PE	B		0320
*	A	Water Rail	Rallus aquaticus																		WA	A		0407
*	A	Spotted Crake	Porzana porzana																		AK	A		0408
	A	Sora	P. carolina																				R	0409
*	A	Little Crake	P. parva																		JC		R	0410
	A	Baillon's Crake	P. pusilla																		VC	A	R	0411
		Sub total																						

GALLINULES AND WADERS

BOU	Species	Scientific	Life list	2009 list	24 hr	Garden	Holiday	Jan	Feb	Mar	Apr	May	Jun	Jul	Aug	Sep	Oct	Nov	Dec	BTO	RBBP	BBRC	EU No
* A	Corncrake	*Crex crex*																		CE	A		0421
* A	Moorhen	*Gallinula chloropus*																		MH			0424
A	Allen's Gallinule	*Porphyrio alleni*																				R	0425
A	Purple Gallinule	*P. martinica*																				R	0426
* A	Coot	*Fulica atra*																		CO			0429
A	American Coot	*F. americana*																				R	0430
* A	Crane	*Grus grus*																		AN	A		0433
A	Sandhill Crane	*G. canadensis*																				R	0436
A	Little Bustard	*Tetrax tetrax*																				R	0442
A	Macqueen's Bustard	*Chlamydotis macqueenii*																				R	0444
A	Great Bustard	*Otis tarda*																		US	A	R	0446
* A	Oystercatcher	*Haematopus ostralegus*																		OC			0450
* A	Black-winged Stilt	*Himantopus himantopus*																		IT	A	R	0455
* A	Avocet	*Recurvirostra avosetta*																		AV	A		0456
* A	Stone-curlew	*Burhinus oedicnemus*																		TN	A		0459
A	Cream-coloured Courser	*Cursorius cursor*																				R	0464
A	Collared Pratincole	*Glareola pratincola*																				R	0465
A	Oriental Pratincole	*G. maldivarum*																		GM		R	0466
A	Black-winged Pratincole	*G. nordmanni*																		KW		R	0467
* A	Little Ringed Plover	*Charadrius dubius*																		LP	B		0469
* A	Ringed Plover	*C. hiaticula*																		RP			0470
A	Semipalmated Plover	*C. semipalmatus*																		TV		R	0471
A	Killdeer	*C. vociferus*																		KL		R	0474
A	Kentish Plover	*C. alexandrinus*																		KP	A		0477
	Sub total																						

WADERS CONTINUED

BOU	Name	Scientific name	Life list	2009 list	24 hr	Garden	Holiday	Jan	Feb	Mar	Apr	May	Jun	Jul	Aug	Sep	Oct	Nov	Dec	BTO	RBBP	BBRC	EU No
A	Lesser Sand Plover	C. mongolus																				R	0478
A	Greater Sand Plover	C. leschenaultii																				R	0479
A	Caspian Plover	C. asiaticus																				R	0480
*A	Dotterel	C. morinellus																		DO	B		0482
A	American Golden Plover	Pluvialis dominica																		ID			0484
A	Pacific Golden Plover	P. fulva																		IF		R	0484
*A	Golden Plover	P. apricaria																		GP			0485
*A	Grey Plover	P. squatarola																		GV			0486
A	Sociable Plover	Vanellus gregarius																		IP		R	0491
A	White-tailed Plover	V. leucurus																				R	0492
*A	Lapwing	V. vanellus																		L			0493
A	Great Knot	Calidris tenuirostris																		KO		R	0495
*A	Knot	C. canutus																		KN			0496
*A	Sanderling	C. alba																		SS	A		0497
A	Semipalmated Sandpiper	C. pusilla																		PZ		R	0498
A	Western Sandpiper	C. mauri																		ER		R	0499
A	Red-necked Stint	C. ruficollis																				R	0500
*A	Little Stint	C. minuta																		LX			0501
*A	Temminck's Stint	C. temminckii																		TK	A		0502
A	Long-toed Stint	C. subminuta																				R	0503
A	Least Sandpiper	C. minutilla																		EP			0504
A	White-rumped Sandpiper	C. fuscicollis																		WU			0505
A	Baird's Sandpiper	C. bairdii																		BP		R	0506
A	Pectoral Sandpiper	C. melanotos																		PP	A		0507
	Sub total																						

73

WADERS CONTINUED

BOU	Species	Scientific name	Life list	2009 list	24 hr	Garden	Holiday	Jan	Feb	Mar	Apr	May	Jun	Jul	Aug	Sep	Oct	Nov	Dec	BTO	RBBP	BBRC	EU No
A	Sharp-tailed Sandpiper	C. acuminata																		VV		R	0508
*A	Curlew Sandpiper	C. ferruginea																		CV			0509
A	Stilt Sandpiper	C. himantopus																				R	
*A	Purple Sandpiper	C. maritima																		PS	A		0510
*A	Dunlin	C. alpina																		DN			0512
A	Broad-billed Sandpiper	Limicola falcinellus																		OA	A	R	0514
A	Buff-breasted Sandpiper	Tryngites subruficollis																		BQ	A		0516
*A	Ruff	Philomachus pugnax																		RU	A		0517
*A	Jack Snipe	Lymnocryptes minimus																		JS	A		0518
*A	Snipe	Gallinago gallinago																		SN	A		0519
A	Wilson's Snipe	G. Gallinago delicata																				R	
A	Great Snipe	G. media																		DS		R	0520
A	Short-billed Dowitcher	Limnodromus griseus																				R	0526
A	Long-billed Dowitcher	Limnodromus scolopaceus																		LD		R	0527
*A	Woodcock	Scolopax rusticola																		WK			0529
*A	Black-tailed Godwit	Limosa limosa																		BW	A		0532
A	Hudsonian Godwit	L. haemastica																		HU		R	0533
*A	Bar-tailed Godwit	L. lapponica																		BA	A		0534
A	Little Whimbrel	Numenius minutus																				R	0536
B	Eskimo Curlew	N. borealis																				R	0537
*A	Whimbrel	N. phaeopus																		WM	B		0538
A	Slender-billed Curlew	N. tenuirostris																				R	0540
*A	Curlew	N. arquata																		CU			0541
A	Upland Sandpiper	Bartramia longicauda																		UP		R	0544

Sub total

WADERS CONTINUED, SKUAS, GULLS

BOU	Name	Scientific	Life list	2009 list	24 hr	Garden	Holiday	Jan	Feb	Mar	Apr	May	Jun	Jul	Aug	Sep	Oct	Nov	Dec	BTO	RBBP	BBRC	EU No
A	Terek Sandpiper	Xenus cinereus																		TR		R	0555
* A	Common Sandpiper	Actitis hypoleucos																		CS			0556
A	Spotted Sandpiper	A. macularius																		PQ	A	R	0557
* A	Green Sandpiper	Tringa ochropus																		GE	A		0553
A	Solitary Sandpiper	T. solitaria																		I		R	0552
A	Grey-tailed Tattler	T. brevipes																		YT		R	0558
* A	Spotted Redshank	T. erythropus																		DR			0545
A	Greater Yellowlegs	T. melanoleuca																		LZ		R	0550
* A	Greenshank	T. nebularia																		GK	A		0548
A	Lesser Yellowlegs	T. flavipes																		LY		R	0551
* A	Marsh Sandpiper	T. stagnatilis																		MD		R	0547
* A	Wood Sandpiper	T. glareola																		OD	A		0554
* A	Redshank	T. totanus																		RK			0546
* A	Turnstone	Arenaria interpres																		TT	A		0561
* A	Wilson's Phalarope	Phalaropus tricolor																		WF		R	0563
* A	Red-necked Phalarope	P. lobatus																		NK	A		0564
* A	Grey Phalarope	Phalaropus fulicarius																		PL			0565
* A	Pomarine Skua	Stercorarius pomarinus																		PK			0566
* A	Arctic Skua	S. parasiticus																		AC			0567
* A	Long-tailed Skua	S. longicaudus																		OG			0568
* A	Great Skua	S. skua																		NX			0569
A	Ivory Gull	Pagophila eburnea																		IV		R	0604
* A	Sabine's Gull	Larus sabini																		AB			0579
* A	Kittiwake	Rissa tridactyla																		KI			0602
	Sub total																						

75

GULLS AND TERNS

BOU	Common name	Scientific name	Life list	2009 list	24 hr	Garden	Holiday	Jan	Feb	Mar	Apr	May	Jun	Jul	Aug	Sep	Oct	Nov	Dec		BTO	RBBP	BBRC	EU No
A	Slender-billed Gull	Chroicocephalus genei																			EI	A	R	0585
A	Bonaparte's Gull	C. philadelphia																			ON		R	0581
*A	Black-headed Gull	C. ridibundus																			BH			0582
*A	Little Gull	Hydrocoloeus minutus																			LU	A		0578
A	Ross's Gull	Rhodostethia rosea																			QG		R	0601
*A	Laughing Gull	Larus atricilla																			LF		R	0576
A	Franklin's Gull	L. pipixcan																			FG		R	0577
*A	Mediterranean Gull	L. melanocephalus																			MU	A		0575
A	Audouin's Gull	L. audouinii																					R	0589
B	Great Black-headed Gull	L. ichthyaetus																					R	0573
*A	Common Gull	L. canus																			CM			0590
*A	Ring-billed Gull	L. delawarensis																			IN			0588
*A	Lesser Black-backed Gull	L. fuscus																			LB			0591
*A	Herring Gull	L. argentatus																			HG			0592
*A	Yellow-legged Gull	L. michahellis																				A		5927
A	Caspian Gull	L. cachinnans																						
A	American Herring Gull	L. smithsonianus																					R	
*A	Iceland Gull	L. glaucoides																			IG			0598
*A	Glaucous Gull	L. hyperboreus																			GZ	A		0599
*A	Great Black-backed Gull	L. marinus																			GB			0600
A	Aleutian Tern	Onychoprion aleutica																					R	0617
A	Sooty Tern	O. fuscata																					R	0623
A	Bridled Tern	O. anaethetus																					R	0622
*A	Little Tern	Sternula albifrons																			AF	B		0624
	Sub total																							

TERNS CONTINUED, AUKS, DOVES

BOU		Scientific name	Life list	2009 list	24 hr	Garden	Holiday	Jan	Feb	Mar	Apr	May	Jun	Jul	Aug	Sep	Oct	Nov	Dec	BTO	RBBP	BBRC	EU No
A	Gull-billed Tern	Gelochelidon nilotica																		TG		R	0605
A	Caspian Tern	Hydroprogne caspia																		CJ			0606
*A	Whiskered Tern	Chlidonias hybrida																		WD		R	0626
*A	Black Tern	C. niger																		BJ	A		0627
*A	White-winged Black Tern	C. leucopterus																		WJ			0628
*A	Sandwich Tern	Sterna sandvicensis																		TE			0611
A	Royal Tern	S. maxima																		QT		R	0607
A	Lesser Crested Tern	S. bengalensis																		TF	A	R	0609
A	Forster's Tern	S. forsteri																		FO		R	0618
*A	Common Tern	S. hirundo																		CN			0615
*A	Roseate Tern	S. dougallii																		RS	A		0614
*A	Arctic Tern	S. paradisaea																		AE			0616
*A	Guillemot	Uria aalge																		GU			0634
A	Brünnich's Guillemot	U. lomvia																		TZ		R	0635
*A	Razorbill	Alca torda																		RA			0636
B	Great Auk 1	Pinguinus impennis																					
*A	Black Guillemot	Cepphus grylle																		TY			0638
A	Long-billed Murrelet	Brachyramphus perdix																				R	
A	Ancient Murrelet	Synthliboramphus antiquus																				R	0645
*A	Little Auk	Alle alle																		LK			0647
*A	Puffin	Fratercula arctica																		PU			0654
A	Pallas's Sandgrouse	Syrrhaptes paradoxus																				R	0663
*AC	Rock Dove / Feral Pigeon	Columba livia																		DV			0665
*A	Stock Dove	C. oenas																		SD			0668
	Sub total																						

DOVES CONTINUED, CUCKOOS, OWLS, NIGHTJARS, SWIFTS,

BOU	Name	Scientific	Life list	2009 list	24 hr	Garden	Holiday	Jan	Feb	Mar	Apr	May	Jun	Jul	Aug	Sep	Oct	Nov	Dec		BTO	RBBP	BBRC	EU No
*A	Woodpigeon	C. palumbus																			WP			0670
*A	Collared Dove	Streptopelia decaocto																			CD			0684
*A	Turtle Dove	S. turtur																			TD			0687
A	Rufous Turtle Dove	S. orientalis																					R	0689
A	Mourning Dove	Zenaida macroura																					R	0695
*C	Ring-necked Parakeet	Psittacula krameri																			RI			0712
A	Great Spotted Cuckoo	Clamator glandarius																			UK		R	0716
*A	Cuckoo	Cuculus canorus																			CK			0724
A	Black-billed Cuckoo	Coccyzus erythrophthalmus																					R	0727
A	Yellow-billed Cuckoo	C. americanus																					R	0728
*A	Barn Owl	Tyto alba																			BO			0735
A	Scops Owl	Otus scops																					R	0739
*A	Snowy Owl	Bubo scandiacus																			SO	A	R	0749
A	Hawk Owl	Surnia ulula																					R	0750
*C	Little Owl	Athene noctua																			LO			0757
*A	Tawny Owl	Strix aluco																			TO			0761
*A	Long-eared Owl	Asio otus																			LE			0767
*A	Short-eared Owl	Asio flammeus																			SE			0768
A	Tengmalm's Owl	Aegolius funereus																					R	0770
*A	Nightjar	Caprimulgus europaeus																			NJ			0778
B	Red-necked Nightjar	C. ruficollis																					R	0779
A	Egyptian Nightjar	C. aegyptius																					R	0781
A	Common Nighthawk	Chordeiles minor																					R	0786
A	Chimney Swift	Chaetura pelagica																					R	0790
	Sub total																							

SWIFTS CONTINUED, KINGFISHERS, BEE-EATERS, WOODPECKERS, LARKS

BOU	Species	Scientific name	Life list	2009 list	24 hr	Garden	Holiday	Jan	Feb	Mar	Apr	May	Jun	Jul	Aug	Sep	Oct	Nov	Dec	BTO	RBBP	BBRC	EU No
A	Needle-tailed Swift	Hirundapus caudacutus																		NI		R	0792
*A	Swift	Apus apus																		SI			0795
A	Pallid Swift	A. pallidus																				R	0796
A	Pacific Swift	A. pacificus																				R	0797
A	Alpine Swift	A. melba																		AI			0798
A	Little Swift	A. affinis																				R	0800
*A	Kingfisher	Alcedo atthis																		KF			0831
A	Belted Kingfisher	Megaceryle alcyon																				R	0834
A	Blue-cheeked Bee-eater	Merops persicus																				R	0839
*A	Bee-eater	M. apiaster																		MZ	A		0840
A	Roller	Coracias garrulus																				R	0841
*A	Hoopoe	Upupa epops																		HP	A		0846
*A	Wryneck	Jynx torquilla																		WY	A		0848
*A	Green Woodpecker	Picus viridis																		G			0856
A	Yellow-bellied Sapsucker	Sphyrapicus varius																				R	0872
*A	Great Spotted Woodpecker	Dendrocopos major																		GS			0876
*A	Lesser Spotted Woodpecker	D. minor																		LS			0887
A	Eastern Phoebe	Sayornis phoebe																				R	0909
A	Calandra Lark	Melanocorypha calandra																				R	0961
A	Bimaculated Lark	M. bimaculata																				R	0962
A	White-winged Lark	M. leucoptera																				R	0965
A	Black Lark	M. yeltoniensis																				R	0966
A	Short-toed Lark	Calandrella brachydactyla																		VL			0968
A	Lesser Short-toed Lark	C. rufescens																				R	0970
	Sub total																						

LARKS, MARTINS, SWALLOWS, PIPITS, WAGTAILS

BOU			Life list	2009 list	24 hr	Garden	Holiday	Jan	Feb	Mar	Apr	May	Jun	Jul	Aug	Sep	Oct	Nov	Dec		BTO	RBBP	BBRC	EU No
A	Crested Lark	Galerida cristata																					R	0972
*A	Wood Lark	Lullula arborea																			WL	B		0974
*A	Sky lark	Alauda arvensis																			S			0976
*A	Shore Lark	Eremophila alpestris																			SX	A		0978
*A	Sand Martin	Riparia riparia																			SM			0981
A	Tree Swallow	Tachycineta bicolor																					R	0983
A	Purple Martin	Progne subis																					R	0989
A	Crag Martin	Ptyonoprogne rupestris																					R	0991
*A	Swallow	Hirundo rustica																			SL			0992
*A	House Martin	Delichon urbicum																			HM			1001
A	Red-rumped Swallow	Cecropis daurica																			VR			0995
A	Cliff Swallow	Petrochelidon pyrrhonota																					R	0998
A	Richard's Pipit	Anthus richardi																			PR			1002
A	Blyth's Pipit	A. godlewskii																					R	1004
A	Tawny Pipit	A. campestris																			TI			1005
A	Olive-backed Pipit	A. hodgsoni																			OV			1008
*A	Tree Pipit	A. trivialis																			TP			1009
A	Pechora Pipit	A. gustavi																					R	1010
*A	Meadow Pipit	A. pratensis																			MP			1011
A	Red-throated Pipit	A. cervinus																			VP			1012
*A	Rock Pipit	A. petrosus																			RC			1014
*A	Water Pipit	A. spinoletta																			WI			1014
A	Buff-bellied Pipit	A. rubescens																					R	1014
*A	Yellow Wagtail	Motacilla flava																			YW			1017
	Sub total																							

WAGTAILS, WAXWINGS, DIPPER, WREN, CHATS

BOU	Common name	Scientific name	Life list	2009 list	24 hr	Garden	Holiday	Jan	Feb	Mar	Apr	May	Jun	Jul	Aug	Sep	Oct	Nov	Dec	BTO	RBBP	BBRC	EU No
A	Citrine Wagtail	M. citreola																			A	R	1018
* A	Grey Wagtail	M. cinerea																		GL			1019
* A	Pied Wagtail	M. alba																		PW	A		1020
A	Cedar Waxwing	Bombycilla cedrorum																				R	1046
* A	Waxwing	B. garrulus																		WX	A		1048
* A	Dipper	Cinclus cinclus																		DI			1050
* A	Wren	Troglodytes troglodytes																		WR			1066
A	Northern Mockingbird	Mimus polyglottos																				R	1067
A	Brown Thrasher	Toxostoma rufum																				R	1069
A	Grey Catbird	Dumetella carolinensis																				R	1080
* A	Dunnock	Prunella modularis																		D			1084
A	Alpine Accentor	P. collaris																				R	1094
A	Rufous Bush Chat	Cercotrichas galactotes																				R	1095
* A	Robin	Erithacus rubecula																		R			1099
A	Rufous-tailed Robin	Luscinia sibilans																				R	1102
A	Thrush Nightingale	L. luscinia																		FN	A		1103
* A	Nightingale	L. megarhynchos																		N			1104
A	Siberian Rubythroat	L. calliope																				R	1105
A	Bluethroat	L. svecica																		BU	A		1106
A	Siberian Blue Robin	L. cyane																				R	1112
A	Red-flanked Bluetail	Tarsiger cyanurus																				R	1113
A	White-throated Robin	Irania gutturalis																				R	1117
* A	Black Redstart	Phoenicurus ochruros																		BX	A		1121
* A	Redstart	P. phoenicurus																		RT			1122
	Sub total																						

81

CHATS CONTINUED, WHEATEARS, THRUSHES

BOU	Name	Scientific	BTO	RBBP	BBRC	EU No
A	Moussier's Redstart	P. moussieri			R	1127
*A	Whinchat	Saxicola rubetra	WC			1137
*A	Stonechat	S. torquatus	SC			1139
A	Isabelline Wheatear	Oenanthe isabellina			R	1144
*A	Wheatear	O. oenanthe	W			1146
A	Pied Wheatear	O. pleschanka	PI		R	1147
A	Black-eared Wheatear	O. hispanica			R	1148
A	Desert Wheatear	O. deserti			R	1149
A	White-crowned Black Wheatear O. leucopyga				R	1157
A	Rock Thrush	Monticola saxatilis	OH		R	1162
A	Blue Rock Thrush	M. solitarius			R	1166
A	White's Thrush	Zoothera dauma			R	1170
A	Siberian Thrush	Z. sibirica			R	1171
A	Varied Thrush	Ixoreus naevius	VT		R	1172
A	Wood Thrush	Hylocichla mustelina			R	1175
A	Hermit Thrush	Catharus guttatus			R	1176
A	Swainson's Thrush	C. ustulatus			R	1177
A	Grey-cheeked Thrush	C. minimus			R	1178
A	Veery	C. fuscescens			R	1179
*A	Ring Ouzel	Turdus torquatus	RZ			1186
*A	Blackbird	T. merula	B			1187
A	Eyebrowed Thrush	T. obscurus			R	1195
A	Dusky Thrush	T. naumanni			R	1196
A	Dark-throated Thrush	T. ruficollis	XC		R	1197
	Sub total					

Column headers (full): BOU · Life list · 2009 list · 24 hr · Garden · Holiday · Jan · Feb · Mar · Apr · May · Jun · Jul · Aug · Sep · Oct · Nov · Dec · BTO · RBBP · BBRC · EU No

THRUSHES CONTINUED, WARBLERS

BOU	Name	Scientific	Life list	2009 list	24 hr	Garden	Holiday	Jan	Feb	Mar	Apr	May	Jun	Jul	Aug	Sep	Oct	Nov	Dec	BTO	RBBP	BBRC	EU No
* A	Fieldfare	T. pilaris																		FF	A		1198
* A	Song Thrush	T. philomelos																		ST			1200
* A	Redwing	T. iliacus																		RE	A		1201
* A	Mistle Thrush	T. viscivorus																		M			1202
A	American Robin	T. migratorius																		AR		R	1203
* A	Cetti's Warbler	Cettia cetti																		CW	A		1220
A	Fan-tailed Warbler	Cisticola juncidis																				R	1226
A	Pallas's Grasshopper Warbler	Locustella certhiola																					1233
A	Lanceolated Warbler	L. lanceolata																				R	1235
* A	Grasshopper Warbler	L. naevia																		GH			1236
A	River Warbler	L. fluviatilis																		VW	A	R	1237
A	Savi's Warbler	L. luscinioides																		VI	A	R	1238
A	Aquatic Warbler	Acrocephalus paludicola																		AQ			1242
* A	Sedge Warbler	A. schoenobaenus																		SW			1243
A	Paddyfield Warbler	A. agricola																		PY		R	1247
A	Blyth's Reed Warbler	A. dumetorum																			A	R	1248
* A	Marsh Warbler	A. palustris																		MW	A		1250
* A	Reed Warbler	A. scirpaceus																		RW			1251
A	Great Reed Warbler	A. arundinaceus																		QW	A	R	1253
A	Thick-billed Warbler	A. aedon																				R	1254
A	Eastern Olivaceous Warbler	Hippolais pallida																				R	1255
A	Booted Warbler	H. caligata																			A	R	1256
A	Sykes's Warbler	H. rama																				R	
A	Olive-tree Warbler	H. olivetorum																				R	
	Sub total																						

WARBLERS CONTINUED

BOU	Name	Scientific name	Life list	2009 list	24 hr	Garden	Holiday	Jan	Feb	Mar	Apr	May	Jun	Jul	Aug	Sep	Oct	Nov	Dec		BTO	RBBP	BBRC	EU No
* A	Icterine Warbler	H. icterina																			IC	A		1259
* A	Melodious Warbler	H. polyglotta																			ME			1260
* A	Blackcap	Sylvia atricapilla																			BC			1277
* A	Garden Warbler	S. borin																			GW			1276
A	Barred Warbler	S. nisoria																			RR			1273
* A	Lesser Whitethroat	S. curruca																			LW			1274
A	Orphean Warbler	S. hortensis																					R	1272
A	Asian Desert Warbler	S. nana																				A	R	1270
* A	Whitethroat	S. communis																			WH			1275
A	Spectacled Warbler	S. conspicillata																					R	1264
* A	Dartford Warbler	S. undata																			DW	B		1262
A	Marmora's Warbler	S. sarda																			MM	A	R	1261
A	Rüppell's Warbler	S. rueppelli																					R	1269
A	Subalpine Warbler	S. cantillans																				A		1265
A	Sardinian Warbler	S. melanocephala																				A	R	1267
A	Greenish Warbler	Phylloscopus trochiloides																			NP		R	1293
A	Arctic Warbler	P. borealis																			AP		R	1295
A	Pallas's Warbler	P. proregulus																			PA			1298
* A	Yellow-browed Warbler	P. inornatus																			YB			1300
A	Hume's Warbler	P. humei																					R	1300
A	Radde's Warbler	P. schwarzi																						1301
A	Dusky Warbler	P. fuscatus																			UY			1303
A	Western Bonelli's Warbler	P. bonelli																			IW		R	1307
A	Eastern Bonelli's Warbler	P. orientalis																					R	1307
	Sub total																							

FLYCATCHERS, TITS, NUTHATCHES,

BOU	Species	Scientific name	BTO	RBBP	BBRC	EU No
* A	Wood Warbler	P. sibilatrix	WO			1308
* A	Chiffchaff	P. collybita	CC			1311
A	Iberian Chiffchaff	P. ibericus			R	1311
* A	Willow Warbler	P. trochilus	WW			1312
* A	Goldcrest	Regulus regulus	GC			1314
* A	Firecrest	R. ignicapilla	FC	A		1315
* A	Spotted Flycatcher	Muscicapa striata				1335
* A	Red-breasted Flycatcher	Ficedula parva	FY			1343
A	Taiga Flycatcher	F. albicilla			R	1343
A	Collared Flycatcher	F. albicollis			R	1348
* A	Pied Flycatcher	F. hypoleuca	PF			1349
* A	Bearded Tit	Panurus biarmicus	BR	B		1364
* A	Long-tailed Tit	Aegithalos caudatus	LT			1437
* A	Blue Tit	Cyanistes caeruleus	BT			1462
* A	Great Tit	Parus major	GT			1464
* A	Crested Tit	Lophophanes cristatus	CI	B		1454
* A	Coal Tit	Periparus ater	CT			1461
* A	Willow Tit	Poecile montana	WT			1442
* A	Marsh Tit	P. palustris	MT			1440
A	Red-breasted Nuthatch	Sitta canadensis			R	1472
* A	Nuthatch	S. europaea	NH			1479
A	Wallcreeper	Tichodroma muraria			R	1482
* A	Treecreeper	Certhia familiaris	TC			1486
A	Short-toed Treecreeper	C. brachydactyla	TH	A	R	1487
	Sub total					

Other column headings (blank for all rows): Life list, 2009 list, 24 hr, Garden, Holiday, Jan, Feb, Mar, Apr, May, Jun, Jul, Aug, Sep, Oct, Nov, Dec

85

SHRIKES, CROWS, SPARROWS

BOU	Species	Scientific name	Life list	2009 list	24 hr	Garden	Holiday	Jan	Feb	Mar	Apr	May	Jun	Jul	Aug	Sep	Oct	Nov	Dec		BTO	RBBP	BBRC	EU No
A	Penduline Tit	Remiz pendulinus																			DT	A	R	1490
*A	Golden Oriole	Oriolus oriolus																			OL	A		1508
A	Brown Shrike	Lanius cristatus																					R	1513
A	Isabelline Shrike	L. isabellinus																			IL		R	1514
*A	Red-backed Shrike	L. collurio																			ED	A		1515
A	Long-tailed Shrike	L. schach																					R	1517
*A	Lesser Grey Shrike	L. minor																					R	1519
*A	Great Grey Shrike	L. excubitor																			SR	A		1520
A	Southern Grey Shrike	L. meridionalis																					R	1520
A	Woodchat Shrike	L. senator																			OO			1523
A	Masked Shrike	L. nubicus																					R	1524
*A	Jay	Garrulus glandarius																			J			1539
*A	Magpie	Pica pica																			MG			1549
A	Nutcracker	Nucifraga caryocatactes																			NC		R	1557
*A	Chough	Pyrrhocorax pyrrhocorax																			CF	B		1559
*A	Jackdaw	Corvus monedula																			JD			1560
*A	Rook	C. frugilegus																			RO			1563
*A	Carrion Crow	C. corone																			C			1567
*A	Hooded Crow	C. cornix																						1567
*A	Raven	C. corax																			RN			1572
*A	Starling	Sturnus vulgaris																			SG			1582
A	Rose-coloured Starling	S. roseus																			OE			1594
*A	House Sparrow	Passer domesticus																			HS			1591
A	Spanish Sparrow	P. hispaniolensis																					R	1592
	Sub total																							

BOU	VIREOS, FINCHES		Life list	2009 list	24 hr	Garden	Holiday	Jan	Feb	Mar	Apr	May	Jun	Jul	Aug	Sep	Oct	Nov	Dec				BTO	RBBP	BBRC	EU No
* A	Tree Sparrow	P. montanus																					TS			1598
A	Rock Sparrow	Petronia petronia																							R	1604
A	Yellow-throated Vireo	Vireo flavifrons																							R	1628
A	Philadelphia Vireo	V. philadelphicus																							R	1631
A	Red-eyed Vireo	V. olivaceus																					EV		R	1633
* A	Chaffinch	Fringilla coelebs																					CH			1636
* A	Brambling	F. montifringilla																					BL	A		1638
* A	Serin	Serinus serinus																					NS	A		1640
* A	Greenfinch	Carduelis chloris																					GR			1649
* A	Goldfinch	C. carduelis																					GO			1653
* A	Siskin	C. spinus																					SK			1654
* A	Linnet	C. cannabina																					LI			1660
* A	Twite	C. flavirostris																					TW			1662
* A	Lesser Redpoll	C. cabaret																					LR			1663
A	Mealy Redpoll	C. flammea																						A		1663
A	Arctic Redpoll	C. hornemanni																					AL			1664
* A	Two-barred Crossbill	Loxia leucoptera																					PD		R	1665
* A	Common Crossbill	L. curvirostra																					CR			1666
* A	Scottish Crossbill	L. scotica																					CY	A		1667
* A	Parrot Crossbill	L. pytyopsittacus																					PC	A	R	1668
A	Trumpeter Finch	Bucanetes githagineus																							R	1676
* A	Common Rosefinch	Carpodacus erythrinus																					SQ	A		1679
A	Pine Grosbeak	Pinicola enucleator																							R	1699
* A	Bullfinch	Pyrrhula pyrrhula																					BF			1710
	Sub total																									

NEW WORLD WARBLERS, SPARROWS

BOU		Scientific name	BTO	RBBP	BBRC	EU No
* A	Hawfinch	Coccothraustes coccothraustes	HF	A		1717
A	Evening Grosbeak	Hesperiphona vespertina			R	1718
A	Black-and-white Warbler	Mniotilta varia			R	1720
A	Golden-winged Warbler	Vermivora chrysoptera			R	1722
A	Tennessee Warbler	V. peregrina			R	1724
A	Northern Parula	Parula americana			R	1732
A	Yellow Warbler	Dendroica petechia			R	1733
A	Chestnut-sided Warbler	D. pensylvanica			R	1734
A	Blackburnian Warbler	D. fusca			R	1747
A	Cape May Warbler	D. tigrina			R	1749
A	Magnolia Warbler	D. magnolia			R	1750
A	Yellow-rumped Warbler	D. coronata			R	1751
A	Blackpoll Warbler	D. striata			R	1753
A	Bay-breasted Warbler	D. castanea			R	1754
A	American Redstart	Setophaga ruticilla	AD		R	1755
A	Ovenbird	Seiurus aurocapilla			R	1756
A	Northern Waterthrush	S. noveboracensis			R	1757
A	Common Yellowthroat	Geothlypis trichas			R	1762
A	Hooded Warbler	Wilsonia citrina			R	1771
A	Wilson's Warbler	W. pusilla			R	1772
A	Summer Tanager	Piranga rubra			R	1786
A	Scarlet Tanager	P. olivacea			R	1788
A	Eastern Towhee	Pipilo erythrophthalmus			R	1798
A	Lark Sparrow	Chondestes grammacus			R	1824
	Sub total					

Additional columns (all blank for these rows): Life list, 2009 list, 24 hr, Garden, Holiday, Jan, Feb, Mar, Apr, May, Jun, Jul, Aug, Sep, Oct, Nov, Dec.

SPARROWS CONTINUED, BUNTINGS

BOU	Species	Scientific name	Life list	2009 list	24 hr	Garden	Holiday	Jan	Feb	Mar	Apr	May	Jun	Jul	Aug	Sep	Oct	Nov	Dec		BTO	RBBP	BBRC	EU No
A	Savannah Sparrow	Passerculus sandwichensis																					R	1826
A	Song Sparrow	Melospiza melodia																					R	1835
A	White-crowned Sparrow	Zonotrichia leucophrys																					R	1839
A	White-throated Sparrow	Z. albicollis																					R	1840
A	Dark-eyed Junco	Junco hyemalis																			JU		R	1842
A	Lapland Bunting	Calcarius lapponicus																			LA	A		1847
*A	Snow Bunting	Plectrophenax nivalis																			SB	A		1850
A	Black-faced Bunting	Emberiza spodocephala																					R	1853
A	Pine Bunting	E. leucocephalos																			EL			1856
*A	Yellowhammer	E. citrinella																			Y			1857
*A	Cirl Bunting	E. cirlus																			CL	A		1958
A	Rock Bunting	E. cia																					R	1860
A	Ortolan Bunting	E. hortulana																			OB			1866
A	Cretzschmar's Bunting	E. caesia																					R	1868
A	Yellow-browed Bunting	E. chrysophrys																					R	1871
A	Rustic Bunting	E. rustica																						1873
A	Chestnut-eared Bunting	E. fucata																					R	1869
A	Little Bunting	E. pusilla																			LJ			1874
A	Yellow-breasted Bunting	E. aureola																				A	R	1876
*A	Reed Bunting	E. schoeniclus																			RB			1877
A	Pallas's Reed Bunting	E. pallasi																					R	1878
A	Black-headed Bunting	E. melanocephala																					R	1881
*A	Corn Bunting	E. calandra																			CB			1882
A	Rose-breasted Grosbeak	Pheucticus ludovicianus																					R	1887
	Sub total																							

89

BUNTIINGS CONITNUED

BOU		Species	Scientific name	Life list	2009 list	24 hr	Garden	Holiday	Jan	Feb	Mar	Apr	May	Jun	Jul	Aug	Sep	Oct	Nov	Dec				BTO	RBBP	BBRC	EU No
A		Indigo Bunting	Passerina cyanea																							R	1892
A		Bobolink	Dolichonyx oryzivorus																							R	1897
A		Brown-headed Cowbird	Molothrus ater																							R	1899
A		Baltimore Oriole	Icterus galbula																							R	1918
		Sub total																									

CATEGORY D & E SPECIES PLUS EUROPEAN

BOU	SPECIES		Life list	2009 list	24 hr	Garden	Holiday	Jan	Feb	Mar	Apr	May	Jun	Jul	Aug	Sep	Oct	Nov	Dec			BTO	RBBP	BBRC	EU No
D	Ross's Goose	Anas Vosii																				FT		R	0181
D	Falcated Duck	A. falcata																				IK		R	0183
D	Baikal Teal	A. formosa																						R	0195
D	Marbled Duck	Marmaronetta angustirostris																				WQ			0226
EU	White-headed Duck	O. Leucocephala																							
EU	Hooded Merganser	Lophodytes cucullatus																							0357
EU	Rock Partridge	Alectoris graeca																							0359
EU	Barbary Partridge	A. barbara																							0082
EU	Pygmy Cormorant	P. pygmeus																							0088
D	Great White Pelican	Pelecanus onocrotalus																				YP		R	0089
EU	Dalmatian Pelican	P. crispus																							0147
D	Greater Flamingo	Phoenicopterus roseus																				FL		R	0235
EU	Black-winged Kite	Elanus caeruleus																							0244
D	Bald Eagle	H. leucocephalus																						R	0246
EU	Lammergeier	Gypaetus barbatus																							0255
D	Black (Monk) Vulture	Aegypius monachus																						R	0273
EU	Levant Sparrowhawk	A. brevipes																							0288
EU	Long-legged Buzzard	B. rufinus																							0292
EU	Lesser Spotted Eagle	Aquila pomarina																							0295
EU	Imperial Eagle	A. heliaca																							0298
EU	Booted Eagle	Hieraaetus pennatus																							0299
EU	Bonelli's Eagle	H. fasciatus																							0314
EU	Lanner Falcon	Falco biarmicus																				FB			0316
D	Saker Falcon	F. cherrug																				JF		R	
	Sub total																								

91

BOU	CATEGORY D & E SPECIES PLUS EUROPEAN SPECIES		Life list	2009 list	24 hr	Garden	Holiday	Jan	Feb	Mar	Apr	May	Jun	Jul	Aug	Sep	Oct	Nov	Dec			BTO	RBBP	BBRC	EU No
EU	Andalusian Hemipode	Turnix sylvatica																							0400
EU	Purple (Swamp-hen) Gallinule	Porphyrio porphyrio																							0427
EL	Crested Coot	F. cristata																							0431
FA	Greater Sand Plover	C. leschenaultii																				DP		R	0479
EU	Spur-winged Plover	Hoplopterus spinosus																				UW			0487
EU	Black-bellied Sandgrouse	Pterocles orientalis																							0661
EU	Pin-tailed Sandgrouse	P. alchata																							0662
EU	(Eurasian) Eagle Owl	Bubo bubo																				EO	bD		0744
EU	Pygmy Owl	Glaucidium passerinum																							0751
EU	Ural Owl	S. uralensis																							0765
EU	Great Grey Owl	S. nebulosa																							0766
EL	White-rumped Swift	A. melba																							0799
EU	Grey-headed Woodpecker	Picus canus																							0855
EU	Black Woodpecker	Dryocopus martius																							0863
EU	Syrian Woodpecker	D. syriacus																							0878
EU	Middle Spotted Woodpecker	D. medius																							0883
EU	White-backed Woodpecker	D. leucotos																							0884
EU	Three-toed Woodpecker	Picoides tridactylus																							0898
EU	Dupont's Lark	Chersophilus duponti																							0959
EU	Thekla Lark	G. theklae																							0973
EU	Black Wheatear	O. Leucura																						R	1158
IA	Eyebrowed Thrush	T. obscurus																						R	1195
EU	Olive-tree Warbler	H. olivetorum																							1258
EU	Cyprus Warbler	S. melanothorax																							1268
	Sub total																								

CATEGORY D & E SPECIES PLUS EUROPEAN

BOU	SPECIES		Life list	2009 list	24 hr	Garden	Holiday	Jan	Feb	Mar	Apr	May	Jun	Jul	Aug	Sep	Oct	Nov	Dec				BTO	RBBP	BBRC	EU No
D	Asian Brown Flycatcher	Muscicapa dauurica																								1335
D	Mugimaki Flycatcher	F. mugimaki																								R	1344
EU	Semi-collared Flycatcher	F. semitorquata																								1347
EU	Sombre Tit	P. lugubris																								1441
EU	Siberian Tit	P. cinctus																								1448
EU	Krüper's Nuthatch	Sitta krueperi																								1469
EU	Corsican Nuthatch	S. whiteheadi																								1470
EU	Rock Nuthatch	S. neumayer																								1481
EU	Masked Shrike	L. nubicus																								1524
EU	Siberian Jay	Perisoreus infaustus																								1543
EU	Azure-winged Magpie	Cyanopica cyana																								1547
EU	Alpine Chough	Pyrrhocorax graculus																								1558
D	Daurian Starling	Sturnus sturninus																								R	1579
EU	Spotless Starling	S. unicolor																								1583
D	(White-winged) Snow Finch	Montifringilla nivalis																								R	1611
D	Palm Warbler	D. palmarum																								R	1752
D	Yellow-headed Blackbird	Xanthocephalus xanthocephalus																								1911
EU	Cinereous Bunting	E. cineracea																								1865
D	Chestnut Bunting	E. rutila																								R	1875
D	Red-headed Bunting	E. bruniceps																								1880
D	Blue Grosbeak	Guiraca caerulea																								R	1891
	Sub total																								

BRITISH DRAGONFLY LIST

SPECIES	2009 list	Life list
DAMSELFLIES		
Calopterygidae (Demoiselles)		
Banded Demoiselle		
Beautiful Demoiselle		
Lestidae (Emerald damselflies)		
Scarce Emerald Damselfly		
Emerald Damselfly		
Southern Emerald Damselfly		
Coenagrionidae (Blue, blue-tailed & red damselflies)		
Small Red Damselfly		
Norfolk Damselfly		
Northern Damselfly		
Irish Damselfly		
Southern Damselfly		
Azure Damselfly		
Variable Damselfly		
Dainty Damselfly		
Common Blue Damselfly		
Red-eyed Damselfly		
Small Red-eyed Damselfly		
Blue-tailed Damselfly		
Scarce Blue-tailed Damselfly		
Large Red Damselfly		
Platycnemididae (White-legged damselflies)		
White-legged Damselfly		
DRAGONFLIES		
Gomphidae (Club-tailed Dragonflies)		
Common Club-tail		
Aeshnidae (Hawkers and Emperors)		
Southern Migrant Hawker		
Southern Hawker		
Brown Hawker		

SPECIES	2009 list	Life list
Norfolk Hawker		
Azure Hawker		
Common Hawker		
Migrant Hawker		
Emperor		
Lesser Emperor		
Green Darner		
Hairy Dragonfly		
Vagrant Emperor		
Cordulegastridae (Golden-ringed Dragonflies)		
Golden-ringed Dragonfly		
Corduliidae (Emerald dragonflies)		
Downy Emerald		
Brilliant Emerald		
Northern Emerald		
Libellulidae (Chasers, Skimmers and Darters)		
Broad-bodied Chaser		
Scarce Chaser		
Four-spotted Chaser		
Black-tailed Skimmer		
Keeled Skimmer		
Scarlet Dragonfly		
Black Darter		
Yellow-winged Darter		
Red-veined Darter		
Ruddy Darter		
Common Darter		
Highland Darter		
Vagrant Darter		
Banded Darter		
White-faced Darter		
TOTAL		

BRITISH BUTTERFLY LIST

SPECIES	2009 list	Life list
Hesperiidae - Skippers		
Chequered Skipper		
Dingy Skipper		
Grizzled Skipper		
Lulworth Skipper		
Essex Skipper		
Small Skipper		
Silver-spotted Skipper		
Large Skipper		
Papilionidae		
Swallowtail		
Pieridae - The Whites		
Wood White		
Clouded Yellow		
Brimstone		
Large White		
Small White		
Green-veined White		
Orange Tip		
Lycaenidae - Hairstreaks, Coppers and Blues		
Green Hairstreak		
Brown Hairstreak		
Purple Hairstreak		
White-letter Hairstreak		
Black Hairstreak		
Small Copper		
Small Blue		
Silver-studded Blue		
Northern Brown Argus		
Brown Argus		
Common Blue		
Chalkhill Blue		
Adonis Blue		

SPECIES	2009 list	Life list
Holly Blue		
Large Blue		
Duke of Burgundy		
Nymphalidae - The Nymphalids		
White Admiral		
Purple Emperor		
Painted Lady		
Small Tortoiseshell		
Red Admiral		
Peacock		
Comma		
Nymphalidae -- The Fritillaries		
Small Pearl-bordered Fritillary		
Pearl-bordered Fritillary		
High Brown Fritillary		
Dark Green Fritillary		
Silver-washed Fritillary		
Marsh Fritillary		
Glanville Fritillary		
Heath Fritillary		
Nymphalidae - The Browns		
Speckled Wood		
Wall		
Mountain Ringlet		
Scotch Argus		
Marbled White		
Grayling		
Gate Keeper		
Meadow Brown		
Ringlet		
Small Heath		
Large Heath		
TOTAL		

DIRECTORY OF ARTISTS, PHOTOGRAPHERS AND LECTURERS

Nick Williams, who took this picture, of a Nuthatch, is listed in the Lecturer's Directory.

ART/PHOTOGRAPHY/LECTURERS

DIRECTORY OF
WILDLIFE ART GALLERIES

BIRDS BIRDS BIRDS

Paul and Sue Cumberland opened Birds Birds Birds in June 2001. Now it is becoming one of the nation's leading bird art galleries. A steady increase in sales has encouraged professional wildlife artists to join the roster. Prints are now being produced and published in-house, using the giclee system.
Address: 4, Limes Place, Preston St, Faversham, Kent ME13 8PQ; 01795 532 370;
email: birdsbirdsbirds@birdsbirdsbirds.co.uk
www.birdsbirdsbirds.co.uk

BIRDSCAPES

Offers top quality bird art all year round, plus landscapes and other wildlife originals, sculptures, prints, wildlife art books and cards. More than 30 regular artists, including SWLA members, are represented, with new exhibitions each month. Located next to the Cley Spy optical dealership and offering the opportunity of exploring the Farmland Bird Project on the Bayfield Estate.
Opening times: Mon-Sat, (10am-5pm), Sunday, (10am-4pm). The gallery may be closed for part of the day before a new exhibition.
Address: The BIRDscapes Gallery, Manor Farm Barns, Glandford, Holt, Norfolk. NR25 7JP. 01263 741 742. (Follow the brown signs to Cley Spy from Blakeney Church).

NATURE IN ART

The world's first museum dedicated exclusively to art inspired by nature. The collection spans 1,500 years, covers 60 countries and includes work by Tunnicliffe, Harrison, Thorburn, Scott and other bird artists. See work being created by artists in residence (see website for dates), plus a vibrant exhibitions programme. Sculpture garden, coffee shop, gift shop and children's activity areas.
Opening times: 10am-5pm (Tuesday to Sunday and bank holidays).
Address: Wallsworth Hall, Twigworth, Gloucester GL2 9PA (two miles N of city on A38). 01452 731 422. e-mail: enquiries@nature-in-art.org.uk
www.nature-in-art.org.uk

THE WILDLIFE ART GALLERY

Opened in 1988 as a specialist in 20th Century and contemporary wildlife art. It exhibits work by many of the leading European wildlife artists, both painters and sculptors, and has published several wildlife books.
Opening times: Mon-Sat (10am-4.30pm) and Sun (2pm-4.30pm).
Address: 97 High Street, Lavenham, Suffolk CO10 9PZ; 01787 248 562; (Fax) 01787 247 356.
E-mail: wildlifeartgallery@btinternet.com
www.wildlifeartgallery.com

DIRECTORY OF
WILDLIFE ARTISTS

ALLEN, Richard

Watercolour paintings, sketches and illustrations of birds, wildlife, flowers and landscapes, mainly based on extensive field sketching. Book work includes: Sunbirds (Helm) and Guide to Birds of SE Asia (New Holland). Also stamp designs for The Solomons, Ascension Island and Kiribati and in RSPB Birds magazine.
Exhibitions for 2009: NEWA; BBWF; Birdcapes Gallery, Glandford, Norfolk; Birds, Birds, Birds Gallery, Faversham, Kent, Wildlife Art Gallery, Lavenham, Suffolk.

Artwork for sale: Watercolour paintings, limited edition prints, original cover paintings from Birding World and header illustrations from British Birds. See website for details.
Address: 34 Parkwood Avenue, Wivenhoe, Essex, CO7 9AN; 01206 826 753.
e-mail: richard@richardallen31.wanadoo.co.uk
www.richardallenillustrator.com

APLIN, Roy

Born in Swanage, Isle of Purbeck, now part of the Jurassic coastline. Lives in Wareham with easy access to Arne RSPB nature reserve - Dartford Warbler habitat. Self-taught artist, carpenter/joiner by trade, also involved in aviculture since the age of 9.

Exhibitions for 2009: Purbeck art weeks - end of May to 1st Week June; British Birdwatching Fair; Dorset Coppice Group country events.

Artwork for sale: Original watercolours plus goache paintings, limited edition prints, pencil sketches, cards.

Address: 11 Brixeys Lane, Wareham, Dorset BH20 4HL; 01929 553 742.

e-mail: roy.aplin@ukonline.co.uk

www.royaplin.com

BECKETT, Andrew

Worked as a freelance illustrator for 16 years represented by the agency Illustration Ltd. Exhibited as a wildlife artist at Birds in Art and NEWA (National Exhibition of Wildlife Art). Part time lecturer of Scientific & Natural History Illustration at Blackpool & the Fylde College.

Formats: Original artwork, prints (mounted or framed).

Artwork for sale: Puffin study I (Pastel), Winter plumage (watercolour), Eider portrait (oil).

Address details: 7 Buckingham Road, Lytham St Annes, Lancs, FY8 4EU. 01253 730 167 mobile: 07946 820 156;

e-mail: andysart@freeuk.com

CALE, Steve

Steve is a keen naturalist and specialises in painting in acrylics. His paintings have gone as far afield as Hong Kong and New Zealand. Undertakes work for The Mareeba Wetland Foundation in Australia and for Pensthorpe waterfowl park. Steve produced the cover image for *Best Birdwatchng Sites in Norfolk* and *Best Birdwatching Sites in North Wales*, and is happy to consider commission requests.

Address: Bramble Cottage, Westwood Lane, Gt Rysburgh, Fakenham, Norfolk, NR21 7AP. 01328 829 589; e-mail: steveshrike@aol.com

COOK, Robert A

Rob has two main passions: drawing and observing nature, and feels extremely lucky to be able to combine these two areas in his working life. After graduating in scientific illustration, he worked as a freelance illustrator, before entering education as a lecturer in natual history illustration. He is now devoting all his time to furthering his work through drawing and paintings.

Formats: Oils, watercolour, pencil and charcoal.

Artwork for sale: Contact the artist.

Address: 16 Beverley Avenue, Poulton-le-Fylde, Lancashire, FY6 8BN; 01253 884 849.

e-mail: robcookart@hotmail.com

www.robcookart.com

GARNER, Jackie FRSA

Original paintings based on field sketches. Current projects: illustrations for Snowy Owls monograph, illustrations for research projects on Egyptian wildlife. *Birds Illustrated* contributor. See website for details.

Exhibitions for 2009: Solo exhibition in London (July, dates TBC); British Birdwatching Fair; NEWA; SWLA; Nature in Art residency; Slimbridge WWT Bird Fair. See website for details.

Artwork for sale: Originals, limited edition prints, cards. Commissions accepted.

Address: c/o Nature In Art, Wallsworth Hall, Twigworth, Glos, GL2 9PA; 01452 730 159, 07800 804 847. e-mail: artist@jackiegarner.co.uk

www.jackiegarner.co.uk

GREENHALF, Robert

Fulltime painter and printmaker. Member of SWLA. Work features in many books including *Modern Wildlife Painting* (Pica Press 1998), *Artists for Nature Foundation* books on Poland and Extremadura and *Towards the Sea* (Pica Press 1999) - first solo book.

Formats: Watercolours, oils and woodcuts.

Exhibitions for 2009: Aldeburgh Contemporary Arts - dates TBC.

Artwork for sale: Watercolours, oils and woodcuts, sold mainly through galleries but some commissions undertaken.

Address: Romney House, Saltbarn Lane, Playden, Rye, East Sussex, TN31 7PH; 01797 222 381. Search internet on 'Robert Greenhalf' for links to galleries showing examples of work.

HOOPER, Lisa

Artist/printmaker living and working in Dumfries and Galloway. Regular contributor to National Wildlife Exhibitions. Winner of Birds Birds Birds Gallery prize (2007) for the most innovative piece of wildlife art (NEWA) and *Birds Illustrated* award (2008).

Formats: Mixed print media (etchings, woodcuts etc).

Exhibitions for 2009: Programme available on website or phone for leaflet.

Artwork for sale: Work on display at address below, on website and at local outlets.

Address: Hoopoe Prints, Seymour House, 25 High Street, Port William, Newton Stewart, Dumfries,DG8 9SL; 01988 700 392.

www.hoopeprints.co.uk

DIRECTORY OF WILDLIFE ARTISTS

LEAHY, Ernest
Original watercolours and drawings of Western Palearctic birds, wildlife and country scenes. Illustrations for many publications including Poysers.
Formats: Wide range of framed and unframed originals available. Commissions accepted and enquiries welcome.
Exhibitions for 2009: Birdfair 2009, Rutland Water. E-mail for further details.
Artwork for sale: E-mail for current list. Quotes for commissions provided with a scheme.
Address: 32 Ben Austins, Redbourn, Herts, AL3 7DR; 01582 793 144
e-mail: ernest.leahy@ntlworld.com
www.wildlifewatercolours.co.uk

LINGHAM, Steven
Fulltime wildlife and landscape artist, private collectors worldwide. First prize winner for the "Best Bird Painting" & Runner-up for the "Best British Wildlife Painting" in the MIWAS 2008 exhibition.
Exhibitions for 2009: Please see website for details.
Artwork for sale: Originals, limited edition prints and greeting cards. All commissions undertaken.
Address: 169 High Street, Hook, Goole, East Yorks DN14 5PL; 01405 767313 or 07779 694576
e-mail: info@stevenlingham.com
www.stevenlingham.com or www.natureartists.com

MILLER, David
Born in Oldham, David now lives and works in the heart of west Wales in a wooded valley with the dramatic Pembrokeshire coastline on his doorstep. He paints mostly British wildlife, prefering to return to subjects he knows well, travelling widely to gather reference and inspiration for his work.
Artwork for sale: Original oils and prints of British wildlife, fish and birds.
Address: Nyth-Gwdi-Hw, New Mill, St Clears, Carmarthenshire, SA33 4HY; 01994 453 545.
e-mail: david@davidmillerart.co.uk
www.davidmillerart.co.uk

SCOTT, Dafila
Trained as a zoologist then studied art under Robin Child at the Lydgate Art Research Centre UK. Has exhibited widely in the UK. Recent work includes both figurative and abstract paintings of wildlife, people and landscape.
Formats: Oil, acrylics and pastels.
Exhibitions for 2009: SWLA (Mall Galleries, Sept 2009).
Artwork for sale: Oil, acrylics and pastels.
Address: White Roses, The Hythe, Reach, Cambridgeshire CB5 0JQ.
e-mail: dafilascott@yahoo.co.uk
www.dafilascott.co.uk

THRELFALL, John
Member of the Society of Wildlife Artists. Swarovski/Birdwatch Bird Artist of the Year 2007. Award winner at the NEWA 2001, 2004, 2006. Birdscapes Gallery award 2007.
Formats: Paintings in acrylic or pastel.
Exhibitions for 2009: Pennel Gallery, Peebles March; The Rockcliffe Gallery, Dalbeatie, Kirkcudbrightshire, May; Birdscapes Gallery, Glandford, Norfolk, November.
Artwork for sale: Contact artist.
Address: Saltflats Cottage, Rockcliffe, Dalbeattie, Kirkcudbrightshire DG5 4QQ; 01556 630 262.
www.johnthrelfall.co.uk

WARREN, Michael
Original watercolour paintings of birds, all based on field observations. Books, calendars, cards and commissions.
Exhibitions for 2009: Mixed SWLA show, Blake Gallery, York, May; Bird Fair, Rutland, August; SWLA annual exhibition, September. Please see website for other information.
Artwork for sale: Original watercolour paintings of birds, all based on field observations. Books, calendars, cards and commissions welcomed.
Address: The Laurels, The Green, Winthorpe, Nottinghamshire, NG24 2NR; 01636 673 554; (Fax)01636 611 569.
e-mail: mike.warren@tiscali.co.uk
www.mikewarren.co.uk

WATLING-FERGUSON, Jan
Fine art watercolour artist, renowned for superb detail of wildlife. Exhibits annually at NEWA, commissions undertaken.
Formats: Fine art in watercolour or gouache.
Exhibitions for 2009: NEWA, July 2009, plus others unknown at present.
Artwork for sale: Check website for galleries holding work, plus studio. Please call.
Address: The Old Smiddy, Toward, Argyll PA23 7UG; 01369 870 346.
www.janferguson.co.uk

WOOLF, Colin

Beautiful original watercolour paintings. The atmosphere of a landscape and the character of his subject are his hallmark, also the pure watercolour technique that imparts a softness to the natural subjects he paints. Owls, birds of prey and ducks are specialities. Wide range of limited editions and greetings cards, special commissions also accepted.

Formats: Original paintings, limited edition prints and greetings cards.

Exhibitions for 2009: British Birdwatching Fair and other shows - check show calendar on website or ring Colin.

Artwork for sale: New paintings are added to the website when framed. Ring Colin for more details or a private viewing.

Address: Tremallt, Penmachno, Betws y Coed, Conwy, LL24 0YL; +44 (0) 1690 760 308.

e-mail: colin@wildart.co.uk

www.wildart.co.uk

DIRECTORY OF WILDLIFE PHOTOGRAPHERS

BASTON, Bill

Photographer, lecturer.

Subjects: East Anglian rarities and common birds, Mediterranean birds and landscapes, UK wildlife and landscapes, Florida birds and landscapes, Northern Greece, Spain, western Turkey, Goa, General wildlife photography.

Products and services: Prints, slides, digital, mounted/unmounted.

Address: 86 George Street, Hadleigh, Ipswich, IP7 5BU; 01473 827 062.

e-mail: blll.baston@bt.com

www.billbaston.com

BATES, Tony

Photographer and lecturer.

Subjects: Mainly British wildlife, landscapes and astral landscapes.

Products and services: Prints (mounted or framed), original handmade photo greetings cards.

Address: 22 Fir Avenue, Bourne, Lincs, PE10 9RY; 01778 425 137.

e-mail: mtr@masher.f9.co.uk

BEJARANO, Santiago

An Ecuadorean naturalist and wildlife photographer.

Subjects: Flora and fauna of Galapagos Islands and birds of Ecuador.

Products and services: Prints and posters of the wildlife of the Glapagos Islands and birds of Ecuador. Introductory classes to wildlife photography, including digital and basic Photoshop® techniques.

Address: 25 Trinity Lane, Beverley, East Yorkshire HU17 0DY. 01482 872 716.

e-mail: info@thinkgalapagos.com

www.ghinkgalapagos.com

BELL, Graham

Ornithologist, photographer, author, cruise lecturer worldwide.

Subjects: Birds, animals, flowers, landscapes, all seven continents, from Arctic to Antarctic.

Products and services: Original slides for sale, £2 each. Lecture: 'Taking Better Photos'.

Address: Ros View, South Yearle, Wooler, Northumberland, NE71 6RB; 01668 281310.

e-mail: seabirdsdgb@hotmail.com

BRIGGS, Kevin

Freelance ecologist.

Subjects: Raptors, Oystercatcher, Ringed Plover, Goosander, Yellow Wagtail, Ring Ouzel, Lune Valley, Confessions of a Lunatic.

Address: The Bramblings, 1 Washington Drive, Warton, Carnforth, LA5 9RA; 01524 730 533.

e-mail: kbbriggs@yahoo.com

BROADBENT, David

Professional photographer.

Subjects: UK birds and wild places.

Products and services: Top quality photographic prints.

Address: Rose Cottage, Bream Road, Whitepool, St Briavels, Lydney, GL15 6TL; 07771 664 973.

www.davidbroadbent.com

e-mail: info@davidbroadbent.com

DIRECTORY OF WILDLIFE PHOTOGRAPHERS

BROOKS, Richard

Wildlife photographer, writer, lecturer.
Subjects: Owls (Barn especially), raptors, Kingfisher and a variety of European birds (Lesvos especially) and landscapes. Limited edition calendars available.
Products and services: Mounted and unmounted computer prints (6x4 - A3+ size), framed pictures, A5 greetings cards, surplus slides for sale.
Address: 24 Croxton Hamlet, Fulmodeston, Fakenham, Norfolk, NR21 0NP; 01328 878 632.
e-mail: email@richard-brooks.co.uk
www.richard-brooks.co.uk

BUCKINGHAM, John

Worldwide bird and wildlife photographer.
Subjects: Huge range of birds, botany and wildlife in UK and Europe, plus great coverage from Africa, Americas, Australia and worldwide.
Products and services: Original slides for lectures and personal use.
Address: 3 Cardinal Close, Tonbridge, Kent, TN9 2EN; (Tel/fax) 01732 354 970.
e-mail: john@buckingham7836.freeserve.co.uk

COSTER, Bill

Professional wildlife photographer, writer and photographic tour leader.
Subjects: Wildlife and landscapes from around the world.
Products and services: Images for publication, prints for sale. Stunning new digital shows (see Directory of Lecturers).
Address: 17 Elm Road, South Woodham Ferrers, Chelmsford, Essex CM3 5QB; 01245 320 066.
e-mail: billcoster@hotmail.com
www.billcoster.com

DENNING, Paul

Wildlife photographer, lecturer.
Subjects: Birds, mammals, reptiles, butterflies and plants from UK, Europe, Canaries, North and Central America.
Products and services: 35mm transparencies and digital images.
Address: 17 Maes Maelwg, Beddau, Pontypridd, CF38 2LD; (H)01443 202 607; (W)02920 673 243.
e-mail: pgdenning.naturepics@virgin.net

ELSBY, Kevin

General natural history with more than 30 years' wildlife photography experience.
Subjects: All areas especially birds, mammals, insects and plants.
Products and services: Images for sale via my website, lecturer, tour guide.
Address: Wildlife on the Web, Chapel House, Bridge Road, Colby, Norwich, NR22 8TB; 01263 732 839. e-mail: wildlife@greenbee.net
www.wildlifeontheweb.co.uk

FURNELL, Dennis

Natural history and travel writer, radio and television broadcaster, artist and photographer.
Subjects: Wildlife, landscape, plant, mammal, insect and bird photography. Large library on 35mm slides and digital images. Commissions undertaken - please telephone.
Products and services: Limited copyright on selected images. Can arrange framed and textured images by agreement. Additional images by selected photographers available - please telephone for prices.
Address: 19 Manscroft Road, Gadebridge, Hemel Hempstead, Hertfordshire, HP1 3HU; 01442 242 915. www.natureman.co.uk
e-mail: dennis.furnell@btinternet.com

GALVIN, Chris

A birding photographer with passion for birds for more than 30 years.
Subjects: Birds.
Products and services: Images for publication, muonted prints, commisions considered.
Address: 17 Henley Road, Allerton, Liverpool, Merseyside L18 2DN; 07802 428 385 or 0151 729 0123. e-mail: chris@chrisgalvinphoto.com
www.chrisgalvinphoto.com

HOBSON, Paul

Environmental science lecturer, photographer for 20+ years. Bias towards N.Europe plus conservation issues, particularly UK.
Subjects: Wildlife, UK and global, amainly UK plus N.Europe, including birds, mammals, invertebrates, amphibians and plants.
Products and services: Talks, workshops, 1:1 tuition, prints.
Address: Sheffield. 0114 232 3699.
e-mail: paul.hobson6@virgin.net
www.paulhobson.co.uk

LANGLEY, John and Tracy

Wildlife photographers, workshop tutors and lecturers.
Subjects: Birds, mammals, butterflies and other wildlife. European plus India (especially tigers).
Products and services: Digital images for publication and commercial use. Mounted images, framed images, greeting cards, bookmarks and calendars.

DIRECTORY OF WILDLIFE PHOTOGRAPHERS

Address: 16 Carrick Road, Curzon Park, Chester CH4 8AW; 01244 678 781;
e-mail: little.owl@btopenworld.com
www.ourwildlifephotography.co.uk

LANGSBURY, Gordon FRPS
Professional wildlife photographer, lecturer, author.
Subjects: Birds and mammals from UK, Europe, Scandinavia, N America, Gambia, Kenya, Tanzania, Morocco and Falklands.
Products and services: Digital and 35mm transparencies for publication, lectures and prints.
Address: Sanderlings, 80 Shepherds Close, Hurley, Maidenhead, Berkshire, SL6 5LZ; (Tel/fax)01628 824 252.
e-mail: gordonlangsbury@birdphoto.org.uk
www.birdphoto.org.uk

LENTON, Graham
PhD Ornithology/Ecology. Former lectuer at Oxford University and Oxford Brookes University. Lifetime photographer of wildlife - publications of articles and photographs of birds and wildlife.
Subjects: Worldwide birds, mammals of Africa, wildlife, worldwide travel.
Products and services: Photos available for sale or reproduction.
Address: The Old School, 25A Standlake Road, Ducklington, Witney, Oxon OX29 7UR; 01993 899 033. www.gml-art.co.uk
e-mail: grahamlenton@btopenworld.com

LINGARD, David
Wildlife photographer, retired from RAF, now UK delegate to LIPU (BirdLife Partner in Italy).
Subjects: Birds and views of places visited around the world.
Products and services: 35mm transparencies and digital images.
Address: Fernwood, Doddington Road, Whisby, Lincs LN6 9BX; 01522 689 030.
e-mail: mail@lipu-uk.org
www.lipu-uk.org

MAGENNIS, Steve
Steve Magennis Wildlife Photography, wildlife photographer, lecturer and workshop leader.
Subjects: British wildlife, bird life and landscapes.
Products and services: Commisioned photography, image library, framed and mounted prints, mounted prints (various sizes), greetings cards (cards can be personalised with personal or company details) and photo keyrings. Photographic workshops, half-day, full-day and holidays.
Address: 3 Chepstow Close, St James, Northampton, Northants, NN5 7EB; 01604 467 848; (M)07803 619 272.
www.stevemagennis.co.uk

McKAVETT, Mike
Wildlife photographer and lecturer.
Subjects: Birds and mammals from India, Kenya, The Gambia, Lesvos, N.America, Turkey and UK.
Products and services:35mm transparencies and digital images for publication and lectures.
Address: 34 Rectory Road, Churchtown, Southport, Lancs PR9 7PU; 01704 231 358;
e-mail: mike.mckavett@btinternet.com.

MOCKLER, Mike
Safari guide, tour leader, writer and photographer.
Subjects: Birds and wildlife of Britain, Europe, Central and South America, India, Japan and several African countries. Africa a speciality.
Products and services: 35mm transparencies and digital images.
Address: Gulliver's Cottage, Chapel Rise, Avon Castle, Ringwood, Hampshire, BH24 2BL; 01425 478 103. e-mail: mike@mickmockler.co.uk

MUGRIDGE, Philip ARPS
Subjects: Birds and mammals both locally and around the world.
Products and services: Prints, greeting cards and Christmas cards.
Address: Glen Cottage, Church Walk, Viney Hill, Lydney, Gloucestershire GL15 4NY; 01594 510 384. e-mail: p.mugridge@virgin.net
www.willridgeimages.co.uk

OFFORD, Keith
Photographer, writer, tour leader, conservationist.
Subjects: Raptors, UK wildlife and scenery, birds and other wildlife of USA, Africa, Spain, Australia, India.
Products and services: Conventional prints, greetings cards, framed pictures.
Address: Yew Tree Farmhouse, Craignant, Selattyn, Nr Oswestry, Shropshire, SY10 7NP; 01691 718 740. e-mail: keith-offord@virgin.net
www.keithofford.co.uk

PARKER, Susan and Allan ARPS
Professional photographers (ASPphoto - Images of Nature) lecturers and tutors.
Subjects: Birds plus other flora and fauna from the UK, Spain, Lesvos, Cyprus, Florida and Texas.
Products and services: 35mm and digital images, mounted digital images, greetings cards and digital images on CD/DVD for reproduction (high quality scans up to A3+).

Address: Ashtree House, 51 Kiveton Lane, Todwick, Sheffield, South Yorkshire, S26 1HJ; 01909 770 238.
e-mail: aspphoto@tiscali.co.uk

READ, Mike

Photographer (wildlife and landscapes), tour leader, writer.
Subjects: Birds, mammals, plants, landscapes, and some insects. UK, France, USA, Ecuador (including Galapagos) plus many more. Behaviour, action, portraits, artistic pictures available for publication. More than 100,000 images in stock.
Products and services: Prints, greetings cards, books. Extensive stock photo library.
Address: Claremont, Redwood Close, Ringwood, Hampshire, BH24 1PR; 01425 475 008.
e-mail: mike@mikeread.co.uk
www.mikeread.co.uk

SISSON, Mark

A professional nature photographer, journalist and photographic trips and workshop organiser.
Subjects: A large and constantly expanding library of wildlife images (principally European) available, either direct or through representing agencies.
Products and services: High specification digital images, complete illustrated articles, talks and personalised as group photographic workshops and tours.
Address: 4 Deer Park Drive, Newport, Shropshire, TF10 7HB. 01952 411 436.
e-mail: mark@marksissonphoto.co.uk
www.marksissonphoto.co.uk

SMART, Oliver

Photographer and lecturer.
Subjects: All wildlife subjects, mainly UK based, also Canada, Mediterranean, Madagascar and Europe.
Products and services: Bean bags, desk calendars, greeting cards, digital files, mounted prints (to A2 size), photographic workshops and digital slideshow lectures.
Address: 78 Aspen Park Road, Weston-Super-Mare, Somerset BS22 8ER; 01934 628 888; (M)07802 417 810.
e-mail: oliver@smartimages.co.uk
www.smartimages.co.uk

SWASH, Andy and Gill

Professional wildlife photographers and authors.
Subjects: Birds, habitats, landscapes and general wildlife from all continents; photographic library currently more than 3,000 bird species.

Products and services: Images for publication and duplicate slides for lectures. High resolution images on CD/DVD. Conventional and digital prints, unmounted, mounted or framed. Greetings cards.
Address: Stretton Lodge, 9 Birch Grove, West Hill, Devon, EX11 1XP; 01404 815 383, (W)07767 763 670. e-mail: w.w.i@btinternet.com
www.worldwildlifeimages.com

TIDMAN, Roger

Professional wildlife photographer since 1979. Widely travelled. Four times winner of *British Birds* photographic competition.
Subjects: Natural history in general, birds in particular.
Products and services: Photos for sale!
Address: 142 Fakenham Road, Briston, Melton Constable, Norfolk NR24 2DL; 0044 (0)1263 860 776. e-mail: roger.tidman@onetel.net

TYLER, John

Wildlife photographer.
Subjects: Plants, fungi, insects and other invertebrates.
Products and services: Images for sale.
Address: 5 Woodfield, Lacey Green, Buckinghamshire, HP27 0QQ; 07814 392 335.
e-mail: johnclarketyler@gmail.com
www.johntyler.co.uk

WARD, Chris

Lecturer, N Bucks RSPB Local Group Leader.
Subjects: Primarily birds (and some other wildlife) and landscapes from UK and worldwide (Spain, Mallorca, Cyprus, Americas, S. Africa, Goa, Australasia).
Products and services: Digital images and prints on request.
Address: 41 William Smith Close, Woolstone, Milton Keynes, MK15 0AN; 01908 669 448.
e-mail: cwphotography@hotmail.com
www.cwardphotography.co.uk

WILLIAMS, Nick

Photographer, lecturer, author.
Subjects: W.Palearctic also Cape Verde Islands and Falkland Islands.
Products and services: Duplicate slides, some originals, prints also available.
Address: Owl Cottage, Station Street, Rippingale, Lincs, PE10 0TA; (Tel/Fax)01778 440 500. e-mail: birdmanandbird@hotmail.com
http://myweb.tiscali.co.uk/nickwilliams

DIRECTORY OF LECTURERS

BASTON, Bill
Photographer, lecturer.
Subjects: East Anglian rarities and common birds, Mediterranean birds and landscapes, UK wildlife and landscapes, Florida birds and landscapes, Northern Greece, Spain, western Turkey, Goa, General wildlife photography.
Fees: Negotiable. **Limits:** Preferably within East Anglia.
Address: 86 George Street, Hadleigh, Ipswich, IP7 5BU ; 01473 827062.
e-mail: bill.baston@bt.com
www.billbaston.com

BATES, Tony
Photographer and lecturer.
Subjects: Seven dissolve projection shows (all include some music), 'A Woodland Walk', 'Seasons and Sayings', 'From a Puddle to the Sea', 'Favourite Places', 'USA, East and West', 'Folklore of Woodland and Hedgerow', The Hare and the Owls', 'A Wildlife Garden'.
Fees: £75 plus travel. **Limits:** None. **Time limitations:** To suit.
Address: 22 Fir Avenue, Bourne, Lincs, PE10 9RY; 01778 425 137.
e-mail: mtr@masher.f9.co.uk

BEJARANO, Santiago
An Ecuadorean naturalist and wildlife photographer who worked in the Galapagos for over a decade, with a great depth of knowledge and unique insight into these remarkable islands and their wildlife.
Subjects: 'Galapagos Islands', 'Birds of Galapagos', 'Ecuador land of Mega Diversity', 'Hummingbirds'.
Fees: £40. **Limits:** None.
Time limitations: None.
Address: 25 Trinity Lane, Beverley, East Yorkshire HU17 0DY. 01482 872 716.
e-mail: info@thinkgalapagos.com
www.ghinkgalapagos.com

BELL, Graham
Cruise lecturer worldwide, photographer, author, former BBRC member.
Subjects: Arctic, Antarctic, Siberia, Australia, Canada, Iceland, Seychelles, UK - identification, behaviour, seabirds, garden birds, entertaining bird sound imitations, birds in myth and fact, bird names, taking better photos, etc.
Fees: £35 plus travel. **Limits:** None.

Time limitations: None.
Address: Ros View, South Yearle, Wooler, Northumberland, NE71 6RB; 01668 281 310.
e-mail: seabirdsdgb@hotmail.com

BOND, Terry
International consultant, ex-bank director, conference speaker worldwide, photographer, group field leader, lecturer on birds for more than thirty years.
Subjects: 8 talks - including Scilly Isles, Southern Europe, North America, Scandinavia, 'Birdwatching Identification - a New Approach' (an audience participation evening).
Fees: By arrangement (usually only expenses).
Limits: Most of UK. **Time limitations:** Evenings.
Address: 3 Lapwing Crescent, Chippenham, Wiltshire, SN14 6YF; 01249 462 674.
e-mail: terryebond@btopenworld.com

BOWDEN, Paul
Birdwatcher and nature photographer (hobby) for 30+ years. Takes both video and stills of birds and other wildlife.
Subjects: Birds of UK, Europe, USA or Australia (video on Powerpoint®), butterflies and dragonflies of UK.
Fees: Travelling expenses and overnight accom. where necessary. **Limits:** None, but longer trips will require overnight stay. **Time limitations:** Generally evenings and weekends.
Address: 4 Patmore Close, Gwaelod-y-Garth, Cardiff, CF15 9SU; 029 2081 3044.
e-mail: bowden_pe@hotmail.com

BRIGGS, Kevin
Freelance ecologist.
Subjects: General wildlife in NW England; specialist topics - Raptors, Oystercatcher, Ringed Plover, Goosander, Yellow Wagtail, Ring Ouzel, Lune Valley, 'Confessions of a Lunatic'.
Fees: £60 + petrol. **Limits:** None. **Time limitations:** None.
Address: The Bramblings, 1 Washington Drive, Warton, Carnforth, LA5 9RA; 01524 730 533.
e-mail: kbbriggs@yahoo.com

BROADBENT, David
Photographer.
Subjects: UK birds and wild places. In praise of natural places.
Fees: £70 plus travel. **Limits:** 50mls without o.n

accom Anywhere otherwise. **Time limitations:** None.
Address: Rose Cottage, Bream Road, Whitepool, St Briavels, Lydney, GL15 6TL.
e-mail: info@davidbroadbent.com
www.davidbroadbent.com

BROOKS, David

Freelance naturalist.
Subjects: Various talks on wildlife, principally birds, in UK and overseas.
Fees: £50 plus petrol. **Limits:** 50 mls without o.n. accom. **Time limitations:** Any time.
Address: 2 Malthouse Court, Green Lane, Thornham, Norfolk, PE36 6NW; 01485 512 548.
e-mail: brooks472@btinternet.com

BROOKS, Richard

Wildlife photographer, writer, lecturer.
Subjects: 12 talks (including Lesvos, Evros Delta, Israel, Canaries, E.Anglia, Scotland, Wales, Oman).
Fees: £75 plus petrol. **Limits:** None if accom provided. **Time limitations:** None.
Address: 24 Croxton Hamlet, Fulmodeston, Fakenham, Norfolk, NR21 0NP; 01328 878 632.
e-mail: email@richard-brooks.co.uk
www.richard-brooks.co.uk

BUCKINGHAM, John

Lecturer, photographer, tour leader.
Subjects: 60+ titles covering birds, wildlife, botany, ecology and habitats in UK, Europe, Africa, Australia, India and the Americas.
Fees: £70 plus expenses. **Limits:** None. **Time limitations:** None.
Address: 3 Cardinal Close, Tonbridge, Kent, TN9 2EN; (Tel/fax) 01732 354 970.
e-mail: john@buckingham7836.freeserve.co.uk

CARRIER, Michael

Lifelong interest in natural history.
Subjects: 1) 'Birds in Cumbria', 2) 'The Solway and its Birds' and 3)'The Isle of May', 4)'A look at Bird Migration', 5)'A Lifetime of Birds'.
Fees: £20. **Limits:** None but rail connection helpful. **Time limitations:** Sept-March inc., afternoons or evenings.
Address: Lismore Cottage, 1 Front Street, Armathwaite, Carlisle, Cumbria, CA4 9PB; 01697 472 218. e-mail: m.carrier131@btinternet.com

CLEAVE, Andrew MBE

Wildlife photographer, author, lecturer and tour leader
Subjects: More than 30 talks (including Galapagos, Iceland, Mediterranean birds and wildlife, Lundy, Shetland, ancient woodlands,

dormice and seashore). Full list available.
Fees: £65 plus petrol. **Limits:** Approx. 60 mls without o.n accom. **Time limitations:** Afternoons and evenings, not school holidays.
Address: 31 Petersfield Close, Chineham, Basingstoke, Hampshire, RG24 8WP; 01256 320 050. e-mail: andrew@bramleyfrith.co.uk

COOK, Tony MBE

35 years employed by WWT. Travelled in Europe, Africa and N. America.
Subjects: 22 talks from Birds of The Wash, garden birds to travelogues of Kenya, E and W North America, Europe (Med to North Cape).
Fees: £35 plus 20p per ml. **Limits:** 100 mls.
Time limitations: None.
Address: 11 Carnoustie Court, Sutton Bridge, Spalding, Lincs, PE12; 01406 350 069;
e-mail: cwaltck@aol.com

COSTER, Bill

Professional wildlife photographer, writer and photographic tour leader.
Subjects: Stunning new digital shows provide a unique look at subjects around the world, including: Pacific Northwest USA, Antarctica, Shetland, Birds and Landscape of USA Deserts, Florida, Britain and more. See webite for full details (www.billcoster. com). Even if you have seen shows from the same location, these shows will be different.
Fees: £80, plus 30p per mile. **Limits:** None.
Time limitations: None.
Address: 17 Elm Road, South Woodham Ferrers, Chelmsford, Essex CM3 5QB; 01245 320 066.
e-mail: billcoster@hotmail.com
www.billcoster.com

COUZENS, Dominic

Full-time birdwatcher, tour leader (UK and overseas), writer and lecturer.
Subjects: The Secret Lives of Garden Birds', 'Birds Behaving Badly - the trials and tribulations of birds through the year', 'Bird Sounds - As You've Never Heard Them Before', 'Have Wings Will Travel' -the marvel of bird migration, 'Vive la Difference' - a look at.
Fees: £80 plus travel. **Limits:** London and south.
Time limitations: None.
Address: 3 Clifton Gardens, Ferndown, Dorset, BH22 9BE; 01202 874 330; (M)07721 918 174.
e-mail: dominic.couzens@btinternet.com
www.birdwords.co.uk

CROMACK, David

Editor of *Birds Illustrated* magazine, co-publisher of Buckingham Press Ltd, chairman of Peterborough Bird Club.

DIRECTORY OF LECTURERS

Subjects: Subjects: 1) Bird Magazines and the Art of Bird Photography (the inside story of how publications choose and use images); 2) Wild West Birding (Arizona and California); World Class Bird Images (Leading entries from International Wildbird Photographer competitions); 4) More World Class Bird Images (Outstanding entries from the 2007 IWP competition); 5) Asia's Teardrop - Birding in Sri Lanka (NEW TALK). All suitable for bird groups and photographic societies.
Leaflet available on request.
Fees: £75 plus travel expenses (30p per mile). **Limits:** 150 miles from Peterborough. **Times:** All requests considered from Januuary 2009.
Address: 55 Thorpe Park Road, Peterborough PE3 6LJ. 01733 566 815; (Fax) 01733 561 739; e-mail: editor@buckinghampress.com

DENNING, Paul
Wildlife photographer, lecturer.
Subjects: 15 talks, (birds, mammals, reptiles, butterflies etc, UK, western and eastern Europe, north and central America, Canaries).
Fees: £40 plus petrol. **Limits:** 100 mls. **Time limitations:** Evenings, weekends.
Address: 17 Maes Maelwg, Beddau, Pontypridd, CF38 2LD; (H)01443 202607; (W)02920 673243. e-mail: pgdenning.naturepics@virgin.net

DENNIS, Roy (MBE)
Ornithologist, writer and broadcaster.
Subjects: 'A Life of Ospreys', 'Raptor Reintroductions', satellite tracking. Range of other talks including special event and keynote addresses.
Fees: Negotiable. **Limits:** None.
Time limitations: None.
Address: Middle Lodge, Dunphail, Forres, Moray, IV36 2QQ ; 01309 611 771.
e-mail: roydennis@aol.com www.roydennis.org

DUGGAN, Glenn
Ex-Commander Royal Navy, tour leader, researcher.
Subjects: Ten talks including, birds of paradise and bower birds, history of bird art (caveman to present day), modern day bird art, famous Victorian bird artists (John Gould, the Birdman and John James Audubon), Trogons and Tanagers.
Fees: £70 plus expenses. **Limits:** none with o.n accom. **Time limitations:** None.
Address: 25 Hampton Grove, Fareham, Hampshire, PO15 5NL; 01329 845 976, (M)07771 605 320. e-mail: glenn.m.duggan@ntlworld.com www.birdlectures.com

ELSBY, Kevin
General naturalist with more than 40 years'

experience.
Subjects: A wide range of talks on many aspects of British and world wildlife. Tour guide.
Fees: £50 per talk plus 25p per mile. **Limits:** Anywhere considered. **Time limitations:** None.
Address: Wildlife on the Web, Chapel House, Bridge Road, Colby, Norwich NR22 8TB; 01263 732 839. e-mail: wildlife@greenbee.net www.wildlifeontheweb.co.uk

EYRE, John
Author, photographer, conservationist and chairman Hampshire Ornithological Society
Subjects: Many talks covering birding around the world (Europe, Africa, Australasia and the Americas), plus special Hampshire subjects (eg. Gilbert White's birds and 'The Changing Fortunes of Hampshire Birds').
Fees: £70 plus travel. **Limits:** Any location negotiable. **Time limitations:** None.
Address: 3 Dunmow Hill, Fleet, Hampshire, GU51 3AN; 01252 677850.
e-mail: John.Eyre@ntlworld.com

FURNELL, Dennis
Natural history writer, radio and television broadcaster, artist and wildlife sound recordist.
Subjects: British and European wildlife, France, East Africa and Costa Rica wildlife, sound recording, wildlife and disability access issues.
Fees: £100. **Limits:** 50 miles, further with o.n. accom. **Time limitations:** Afternoons or evenings according to commitments.
Address: 19 Manscroft Road, Gadebridge, Hemel Hempstead, Hertfordshire, HP1 3HU; 01442 242 915, (Fax)01442 242 032.
e-mail; dennis.furnell@btinternet.com www.natureman.co.uk

GALLOP, Brian
Speaker, photographer, tour leader.
Subjects: 35 talks covering UK, Africa, India, Galapagos, South America and Europe - All natural history subjects. Made-to-measure talks available on request. 24hr emergency service.
Fees: £50 plus 25p per ml. **Limits:** None - o.n accom. if over 100 mls. **Time limitations:** None.
Address: 13 Orchard Drive, Tonbridge, Kent, TN10 4LT; 01732 361892.
e-mail: brian_gallop@hotmail.co.uk

GALVIN, Chris
A birding photographer with passion for birds for more than 30 years.
Subjects: Northwest Year', 'Package Holiday Birding', 'Birds of Goa' and others.
Fees: £50-£80. **Limits:** 100 miles.

Address: 17 Henley Road, Allerton, Liverpool, Mersyside L18 2DN; 07802 428 385 or 0151 729 0123. e-mail: chris@chrisgalvinphoto.com www.chrisgalvinphoto.com

GARCIA, Ernest

Writer/editor Gibraltar Bird Report
Subjects: Raptor and seabird migration at Gibraltar, birding in northern, southern and western Spain (Andalucia/Extremadura) and the northern coastal regions.
Fees: £50 plus expenses. **Limits:** None. **Time limitations:** None.
Address: Woodpecker House, 2 Pine View Close, Chilworth, Surrey GU4 8RS; 01483 539 053.
e-mail: erngarcia@btinternet.com

GARNER, David

Wildlife photographer.
Subjects: 20 live talks and audio-visual shows on all aspects of wildlife in UK and some parts of Europe – list available.
Fees: £40 plus 20p per ml. **Limits:** None. **Time limitations:** Any.
Address: 73 Needingworth Road, St Ives, Cambridgeshire, PE27 5JY; (H) 01480 463 194; (W) 01480 463 194;
e-mail: david@hushwings.co.uk
www.hushwings.co.uk

GARTSHORE, Neil

23-years working in nature conservation (National Trust, South Africa, RSPB) now a freelance contractor, writer, lecturer, tour guide and natural history book seller.
Subjects: Various talks including South Africa; Sub-Antarctic Prince Edward Islands; Japan; Farne Islands; Heathlands; and Poole Harbour.
Fees: Negotiable. **Limits:** Anything considered. **Time limitations:** Flexible.
Address: Moor Edge, 2 Bere Road, Wareham, Dorset, BH20 4DD. 01929 552560;
e-mail: neil@onaga54.freeserve.co.uk

GLENN, Neil

Author of *Best Birdwatching Sites in Norfolk*; regular contributor to *Birds Illustrated* and *Bird Watching* magazines; bird tour leader for Avian Adventures.
Subjects: Wildlife of the Lower Rio Grande Valley, Texas. Birding the Arctic Circle. More to follow!
Fees: Negotiable. **Limits:** None. **Time limitations:** Any day.
Address: 13 Gladstone Avenue, Gotham, Nottingham NG11 0HN; 0115 983 0946.
e-mail: n.glenn@ntlworld.com

GUNTON, Trevor

Ex.RSPB Staff, recruitment advisor, lecturer and consultant.
Subjects: 15 different talks, featuring places such as Shetland, other UK islands, Yorkshire from dales to coast, Viking lands (four different talks on Viking history). New talks are 'A Norwegian coastal voyage' and 'Wild goose chase (Holland and Romania)', 'Starting Birdwatching', Great Gardens and Houses of East Anglia', 'Garden Birds'. Other topics include wildlife on National Trust properties and gravel pits (Paxton Pits). Write/phone for full list.
Fees: Variable (basic £60 plus expenses). **Limits:** None. **Time limitations:** Anytime, anywhere.
Address: 15 St James Road, Little Paxton, St Neots, Cambs, PE19 6QW; (tel/fax)01480 473 562.

HASSELL, David

Birdwatcher and photographer.
Subjects: Six talks (including British Seabirds, Shetland Birds, British Birds, USA Birds, including Texas, California, Florida etc.).
Fees: £45 plus petrol. **Limits:** None. **Time limitations:** None.
Address: 15 Grafton Road, Enfield, Middlesex, EN2 7EY; 020 8367 0308.
e-mail: dave@davehassell.com
www.davehassell.com

HOBSON, Paul

Environmental science lecturer and wildlife photographer.
Subjects: Birds, wildlife, wildlife photography, UK, N Europe and Global.
Fees: £60-£100 plus 30p return mileage.
Limits: 150 miles. **Time limitations:** Evenings only.
Address: Sheffield. 0114 232 3699.
e-mail: paul.hobson6@virgin.net
www.paulhobson.co.uk

LANGLEY, John and Tracy

Wildlife photographers, workshop tutors and lecturers.
Subjects: Various talks on UK wildlife, wildlife photography and Indian wildlife (with special emphasis on tigers).
Fees: Variable. **Limits:** None. **Time limitations:** None.
Address: 16 Carrick Road, Curzon Park, Chester CH4 8AW; 01244 678 781;
e-mail: little.owl@btopenworld.com
www.ourwildlifephotography.co.uk

DIRECTORY OF LECTURERS

LANGSBURY, Gordon FRPS
Professional wildlife photographer, lecturer, author.
Subjects: 20 talks - Africa, Europe, USA, Falklands and UK. Full list provided.
Fees: £90 plus travel expenses. **Limits:** None.
Time limitations: None.
Address: Sanderlings, 80 Shepherds Close, Hurley, Maidenhead, Berkshire, SL6 5LZ; (Tel/fax)01628 824 252. www.birdphoto.org.uk
e-mail: gordonlangsbury@birdphoto.org.uk

LENTON, Graham
PhD Ornithology/Ecology. Former lecuer at oxford University and Oxford Brookes University. Lifetime photographer of wildlife - publications of articles and photographs of birds and wildlife.
Subjects: Barn Owls of Malaysia and rat control; Birds of the Seychelles; Wildlife and birds of Antarctica; Birds of New Zealand.
Fees: £50. **Limits:** Preferably within 60mls. **Time limitations:** 60-90 minute talks.
Address: The Old School, 25A Standlake Road, Ducklington, Witney, Oxon OX29 7UR; 01993 899 033. e-mail: grahamlenton@btopenworld.com www.gml-art.co.uk

LINGARD, David
Photographer, retired from RAF, now UK delegate to LIPU (BirdLife Partner in Italy).
Subjects: Choice of talks on European birding and the work of LIPU.
Fees: £75 donation to LIPU, plus petrol costs.
Limits: None. **Time limitations:** None.
Address: Fernwood, Doddington Road, Whisby, Lincs LN6 9BX; 01522 689 030.
e-mail: mail@lipu-uk.org www.lipu-uk.org

LINN, Hugh ARPS
Experienced lecturer, photographer.
Subjects: 12 talks, covering UK, Europe, Africa and bird-related subjects. List available.
Fees: £40 plus petrol. **Limits:** 100 mls without o.n. accom. 150 mls otherwise.
Time limitations: Flexible.
Address: 4 Stonewalls, Rosemary Lane, Burton, Rossett, Wrexham, LL12 0LG; 01244 571 942;
e-mail: hugh.linn@btinternet.com

LOVELL, Stephen
Naturalist, RSPB lecturer, photographer.
Subjects: 18 topics including the natural history of several European destinations including Lesvos, Mallorca, Britain. Other talks available on New Zealand, Australia, St Lucia, Tanzania, Sri Lanka and Southern India.
Fees: According to distance - on request.
Limits: None. **Time limitations:** None.
Address: 6 Abingdon Close, Doddington Park, Lincoln LN6 3UH; 01522 689 456; (M)07957 618 684. e-mail: stephenlovell58@btinternet.com

MAGENNIS, Steve
Steve Magennis Wildlife Photography, wildlife photographer, lecturer and workshop leader.
Subjects: Wildlife photography, bird life and related subjects (see website for full details).
Fees: £85 plus travel @30p per mile over 40 miles.
Limits: Up to 150 miles.
Time limitations: Available all year, day or evening.
Address: 3 Chepstow Close, St James, Northampton, Northants, NN5 7EB; 01604 467 848; (M)07803 619 272.
www.stevemagennis.co.uk

MATHER, John Robert
Ornithologist, writer, tour guide, lecturer.
Subjects: Birds and other wildlife of: Kenya, Tanzania, Uganda, Ethiopia, Namibia, South Africa, Costa Rica, Romania/Bulgaria, India, Nepal, 'Algonquin to Niagara - a tour around the Great Lakes'. 'Landscapes, Flowers and Wildlife of the American West'. 'Bird on the Bench' - a fascinating account of bird biology, 'Wildlife and Scenery of Alaska, and the Canadian Rockies'.
Fees: £75 plus 30p per mile. **Limits:** 100 mls.
Time limitations: Evenings.
Address: Eagle Lodge, 44 Aspin Lane, Knaresborough, North Yorkshire, HG5 8EP; 01423 862 775.

McKAVETT, Mike
Photographer.
Subjects: Six talks — Birds and Wildlife of India, North and Western Kenya and the Gambia, Bird Migration in North America, Birds of the Eastern Mediterranean.
Fees: £50 plus expenses. **Limits:** None.
Time limitations: None.
Address: 34 Rectory Road, Churchtown, Southport, PR9 7PU; 01704 231 358;
e-mail: mike.mckavett@btinternet.com.

MOCKLER, Mike
Safari guide, tour leader, writer and photographer.
Subjects: Birds and other wildlife of: Botswana, Kenya, Tanzania, Zambia, Spain, Finland, Norway, Costa Rica, Antarctica and South Georgia, India and Brazil.
Fees: Negotiable. **Limits:** None. **Time limitations:** Evenings.
Address: Gulliver's Cottage, Chapel Rise, Avon Castle, Ringwood, Hampshire, BH24 2BL; 01425 478 103. e-mail: mike@mikemockler.co.uk

ART/PHOTOGRAPHY/LECTURERS

109

MUGRIDGE, Philip ARPS

Subjects: Various including Gloucestershire wildlife, Finland, Bulgaria, Antarctica - see website for full listing.
Fees: From £50. **Limits:** None.
Time limitations: None.
Address: Glen Cottage, Church Walk, Viney Hill, Lydney,Gloucestershire GL 15 4NY; 01594 510 384.
e-mail: p.mugridge@virgin.net
www.willridgeimages.co.uk

NOBBS, Brian

Amateur birdwatcher and photographer.
Subjects: Wildlife of the Wild West, Israel, Mediterranean, Florida, Wildlife Gardening, Reserves for Birds (RSPB), Trinidad and Tobago, The Way Birds Feed.
Fees: £40 plus 25p per ml. **Limits:** Kent, Surrey, Sussex, Essex. **Time limitations:** None.
Address: The Grebes, 36 Main Road, Sundridge, Sevenoaks, Kent, TN14 6EP; 01959 563 530.
e-mail: Brian.nobbs@tiscali.co.uk

OFFORD, Keith

Photographer, writer, tour leader, conservationist.
Subjects: 16 talks covering raptors, flight, uplands, gardens, migration, woodland wildlife, Australia, Southern USA, Tanzania, Gambia, Spain, Costa Rica, Namibia, Western Cape.
Fees: £90 plus travel. **Limits:** None. **Time limitations:** Sept - April.
Address: Yew Tree Farmhouse, Craignant, Selattyn, Nr Oswestry, Shropshire, SY10 7NP; 01691 718 740. e-mail: keith-offord@virgin.net
www.keithofford.co.uk

PARKER, Susan and Allan ARPS

Professional photographers, (ASPphoto – Images of Nature), lecturers and tutors.
Subjects: 16 plus talks on birds and natural history, natural history photography - countries include UK, USA (Texas, Florida), Spain, Greece, Cyprus.
Fees: On application. **Limits:** Any distance with o.n accom or up to 120 mls without.
Time limitations: None.
Address: Ashtree House, 51 Kiveton Lane, Todwick, Sheffield, South Yorkshire, S26 1HJ; 01909 770 238.
e-mail: aspphoto@tiscali.co.uk

READ, Mike

Photographer, tour leader, writer.
Subjects: 12 talks featuring British and foreign subjects (list available on receipt of sae or by e-mail).
Fees: £75 plus travel. **Limits:** 125 mls.
Time limitations: Talks available 1st Sept to 31st March each winter.
Address: Claremont, Redwood Close, Ringwood, Hampshire, BH24 1PR; 01425 475 008.
e-mail: mike@mikeread.co.uk
www.mikeread.co.uk

ROBINSON, Peter

Consultant ornithologist and former Scilly resident, author of *Birds of the Isles of Scilly* and bird lecturer.
Subjects: Spring Watch - The Real Story and various other subjects - see website for details.
Fees: £85 plus petrol. **Limits:** None.
Time limitations: None.
Address: 19 Pine Park Road, Honiton, Devon, EX14 2HR; 01404 549 873 (M) 07768 538 132.
e-mail: pjrobinson2@aol.com
www.birdexpertuk.com

RUMLEY-DAWSON, Ian

Wildlife photographer, course leader, cruise lecturer.
Subjects: 96 talks using twin dissolving projectors or digital PowerPoint and some with natural wildlife sounds as well. Birds, mammals, insects, plants, habitats, ethology. Arctic, Antarctic, Falklands, N and S America, N.Z, Seychelles, North Pacific islands, Albatrosses, penguins, Snowy Owls, polar bears etc. List available.
Fees: £60 plus expenses. **Limits:** None. **Time limitations:** None.
Address: Oakhurst, Whatlington Road, Battle, East Sussex, TN33 0JN; 01424 772 673;
e-mail: ian@rumleydawson.orangehome.co.uk

SCOTT, Ann and Bob

Ex-RSPB staff, tour leaders, writers, lecturers, tutors, trainers.
Subjects: 20+ talks (including nature reserves, tours, gardening, Europe, Africa, S America, after dinner talks etc).
Fees: £60 plus travel over 50 mls. **Limits:** None (by arrangement). **Time limitations:** None.
Address: 8 Woodlands, St Neots, Cambridgeshire, PE19 1UE; 01480 214 904; (fax)01480 473 009; (M)07803 608 120.
e-mail: abscott@tiscali.co.uk

SHARRATT, Vic

Professional wildlife photographer and tour leader.
Subjects: Wildlife photography.
Limits: Within Kent. **Time limitations:** 1 hour slide show/talk, anytime of day or evening.
Address: Vic Sharratt Photo Tours, 26 Streete Court, Westgate-on-Sea, Kent CT8 8BT. 01843 832 749. www.vicsharrattwildlifeimages.com

DIRECTORY OF LECTURERS

SISSON, Mark
A professional nature photographer, journalist and photographic trips and workshop organiser.
Subjects: All aspects of wildlife photography, along with specific or tailormade talks on countries such as Iceland or broader topics such as Northern European birdlife - all with a photographer's eye and style.
Fees: £75 + travel. **Limits:** Ideally 100ml radius, but willing to be persuaded to go further! **Time limitations:** Need to fit into a busy schedule so ideally plenty of notice.
Address: 4 Deer Park Drive, Newport, Shropshire TF10 7HB; 01952 411 436.
e-mail: mark@marksissonphoto.co.uk
www.marksissonphoto.co.uk

SMART, Oliver
Photographer and lecturer.
Subjects: 1)'Birds of Lesvos'; 2) 'Grizzly Bears of Alaska'; 3) 'Wildlife on Handa Island, NW Scotland'; 4) 'Cameras and Creatures, from Cumbria to Canada'.
Fees: £60 plus 20p per mile. **Limits:** None but o.n. accom. may be required.
Time limitations: None.
Address: 78 Aspen Park Road, Weston-Super-Mare, Somerset BS22 8ER; 01934 628 888; (M)07802 417 810.
e-mail: oliver@smartimages.co.uk
www.smartimages.co.uk

STEPHEN, Gerry
Subjects: More than 28 talks, mainly about wild flowers and their habitats but includes natural history of all types and cover areas of the USA, Canada, Europe and Africa. All about 60 minutes duration but can be tailored to your needs.
Limits: £30 plus travel expenses at cost. **Time limitations:** None.
Address: 10 Birch Way, Poulton-le-Fylde, Blackpool, FY6 7SF; 01253 895 195;
e-mail: melodystephen@hotmail.com

SWASH, Andy
Photographer, author, tour leader.
Subjects: Birds and general wildlife. Tales from travels in: the Andamans, Antarctica, Argentina, Australia, Brazil, Chile, China, Costa Rica, Cuba, Galápagos, Kenya, Namibia, South Africa, Sri Lanka, USA or Venezuela.
Fees: £85 plus travel. **Limits:** None. **Time limitations:** Evenings.
Address: Stretton Lodge, 9 Birch Grove, West Hill, Devon, EX11 1XP; 01404 815 383, (W)07767 763 670. e-mail: w.w.i@btinternet.com
www.worldwildlifeimages.com

TAYLOR, Mick
Co-ordinator South Peak Raptor Group, photographer, ornithologist, writer.
Subjects: Several talks including (Merlins, Peak District birds, Peak District raptors, Alaskan wildlife).
Fees: £60 plus petrol. **Limits:** Negotiable. **Time limitations:** Evenings preferred.
Address: 76 Hawksley Avenue, Chesterfield, Derbyshire, S40 4TL; 01246 277 749.

TODD, Ralph
Lecturer & photographer, course tutor and former tour leader.
Subjects: 10 talks incl. 'Galapagos Wildlife', 'On the Trail of the Crane', 'Polar Odyssey', 'Operation Osprey', 'Iceland & Pyrenees', 'Man & Birds -Travels through time', 'A summer in Northern Landscapes', 'Where Yeehaa meets Ole'.
Fees: £60 plus expenses. **Limits:** None, negotiable over 120 miles. **Time limitations:** Any - also short notice.
Address: 9 Horsham Road, Bexleyheath, Kent, DA6 7HU; (Tel/fax)01322 528 335.
e-mail: rbtodd@btinternet.com

TYLER, John
Wildlife walks and talks.
Subjects: Life in a Nutshell (The world of small things); The Island of Crabs; Volcanoes and Dragons; Changing Wildlife of the Chilterns; The Ridgeway; The Glow-worm; The World of Fungi; Making Space for Wildlife.
Fees: £70 plus 40p per mile. **Limits:** 25 mile radius from Princes Risborough, Bucks.
Time limitations: None.
Address: 5 Woodfield, Lacey Green, Buckinghamshire HP27 0QQ; 07814 392 335.
e-mail: johnclarketyler@gmail.com
www.johntyler.co.uk

WARD, Chris
Photographer, N Bucks RSPB Local Group Leader.
Subjects: 20+ talks on UK and worldwide topics (Spain, Mallorca, Cyprus, Americas, Africa, Goa, Australasia) - primarily birds, some other wildlife.
Fees: £50 plus petrol. **Limits:** 120 miles.
Time limitations: Evenings..
Address: 41 William Smith Close, Woolstone, Milton Keynes, MK15 0AN; 01908 669 448.
e-mail: cwphotography@hotmail.com
www.cwardphotography.co.uk

WILLIAMS, Nick
Photographer, lecturer, author.
Subjects: Several audio visual shows (including Spain, N.Germany, Camargue, Turkey, N.Norway,

Cape Verdi Islands, Falklands and Birds of Prey).
Fee: £90-£110 depending on group size and distance. **Limits:** None.
Time limitations: None.
Address: Owl Cottage, Station Street, Rippingale, Lincs, PE10 0TA; (Tel/Fax)01778 440 500.
e-mail: birdmanandbird@hotmail.com
http://myweb.tiscali.co.uk/nickwilliams

WREN, Graham J. ARPS
Wildlife photographer, lecturer, tour guide.

Subjects: 23 talks - birds - UK 'Breeding Birds of Southern Britain' and 'Northern Britain', including habitats, also Scandinavia. Nest-boxes (new), the environment, wildlife - Kenya. Detailed information package supplied on request.
Fees: £50-80 plus petrol. **Limits:** None. **Time limitations:** None.
Address: The Kiln House, Great Doward, Whitchurch, Ross-on-Wye, Herefordshire, HR9 6DU; 01600 890 148.
e-mail: grahamjwren@aol.com

BTO SPEAKERS

BTO speakers can be contacted by post at BTO, The Nunnery, Thetford, Norfolk IP24 2PU
Tel: 01842 750 050; Fax: 01842 750 030; www.bto.org

Fees for BTO talks are £40, plus travel expenses and distances are negotiable with the speaker. Some speakers also offer talks in a private capacity and fees for these are shown where applicable.

APPLETON, Graham (Head of Fundraising and Publicity)
E-mail: graham.appleton@bto.org
Atlas 2007–11, The Work of the BTO, Flyway to Iceland, Time to Fly – Bird Migration, Yellowhammers, Buzzards and the next Atlas.
Fee: BTO fee (£40). **Expenses:** Negotiable.
Distance: Dependant on expenses.

AUSTIN, Dr Graham (Wetland & Coastal Ecology Unit Team Leader)
E-mail: graham.austin@bto.org
Wetland Bird Survey.
Fee: BTO fee (£40). **Expenses:** Travel.
Distance: By agreement.

BAILLIE, Dr Stephen (Director of Populations Research)
E-mail: stephen.baillie@bto.org
BirdTrack, Population Monitoring.
Fee: BTO fee (£40). **Expenses:** Travel.
Distance: By agreement.

BAKER, Jeff (Head of Membership)
E-mail: jeff.baker@bto.org
Atlas 2007–11, The work of the BTO, Little brown jobs – Warblers and how to identify them.
Fee: £40. **Expenses:** Travel expenses.
Distance: Dependent on expenses.

BALMER, Dawn (Atlas Coordinator)
E-mail: dawn.balmer@bto.org
Atlas 2007–11.

Fee: BTO fee (£40). **Expenses:** Travel.
Distance: Local.

BANKS, Alex (Wetland & Coastal Ecology Unit Research Ecologist)
E-mail: alex.banks@bto.org
Wetland Bird Survey, Aerial Monitoring of Waterbirds.
Fee: BTO fee (£40). **Expenses:** Travel.
Distance: By agreement.

BARIMORE, Carl (Nest Records Officer)
E-mail: carl.barimore@bto.org
Nest Record Scheme, Barn Owl Monitoring Programme.
Fee: BTO fee (£40). **Expenses:** Travel.
Distance: By agreement.

BLACKBURN, Jez (Ringing Unit Recoveries and Licencing Team Leader)
E-mail: jez.blackburn@bto.org
Bird Moult (suitable for ringers), Sule Skerry.
Fee: BTO fee (£40) (£50 for private talks).
Expenses: Travel. **Distance:** East Anglia.

CARTER, Dr Nick (Director of Development)
E-mail: nick.carter@bto.org
Farmland birds.
Fee: £40 (donated to current BTO Appeal).
Expenses: Petrol. **Distance:** Anywhere.

CHAMBERLAIN, Dr Dan (Senior Research Ecologist)
E-mail: dan.chamberlain@bto.org

DIRECTORY OF LECTURERS

Garden BirdWatch, Breeding Bird Survey.
Fee: BTO fee (£40). **Expenses:** Travel.
Distance: By agreement.

CLARK, Jacquie (Head of Ringing Unit)
E-mail: jacquie.clark@bto.org
Waders and Severe Weather, Why Ring Birds?,
Ringing for Conservation Migration.
Fee: BTO fee (£40). **Expenses:** Petrol. **Distance:**
100 mile radlus of Thetford.

CLARK, Dr Nigel (Head of Projects Development Unit)
E-mail: nigel.clark@bto.org
Waders, Man and Estuaries, Horseshoe Crabs and
Waders, Migration through Delaware in Spring.
Fee: BTO fee (£40). **Expenses:** Petrol. **Distance:**
100 mile radius of Thetford.

COLLIER, Mark (Wetland Bird Survey Research Offi cer)
E-mail: mark.collier@bto.org
Wetland Bird Survey.
Fee: BTO fee (£40). **Expenses:** Travel.
Distance: By agreement.

CONWAY, Greg (Terrestrial Ecology Unit Research Ecologist)
E-mall: greg.conway@bto.org
Nightjars, Woodlarks and Dartford Warblers,
Wintering Warblers.
Fee: BTO fee (£40). **Expenses:** Petrol. **Distance:**
100 mile radius of Thetford.

CRICK, Dr Humphrey (Head of Demography Unit)
E-mail: humphrey.crick@bto.org
Climate Change and Birds, One Million Nests.
Fee: BTO fee (£40) (£50 for private). **Expenses:**
Mileage @ 25p per mile. **Distance:** Willing
to travel (prefer less than 100 miles from
Cambridge).

DAVIS, Dr Sarah (Census Unit Poulations Biologist)
E-mail: sarah.davis@bto.org
Food Availability and Arctic Skuas.
Fee: BTO fee (£40). **Expenses:** Travel.
Distance: By agreement.

FULLER, Dr Rob (Director of Habitats Research)
E-mail: rob.fuller@bto.org
Nightingales, Woodland Management and Birds,
Changing Times for Woodland Birds.
Fee: BTO fee (£40). **Expenses:** Travel.
Distance: Anywhere.

GILLINGS, Dr Simon (Terrestrial Ecology Unit Research Ecologist)
E-mail: simon.gillings@bto.org
Atlas 2007–11, Winter Golden Plovers and
Lapwings, Winter Farmland Birds.
Fee: BTO fee (£40). **Expenses:** Travel.
Distance: Negotiable.

GOUGH, Su (Terrestrial Ecology Unit Research Ecologist)
E-mail: su.gough@bto.org
Atlas 2007–11, Bird Biology, The Work of the BTO,
Urban Birds, Wildlife of Canada (non-BTO talk),
Wildlife of Soutwestern USA, Wildlife of European
Mountains (non-BTO talk).
Fee: BTO fee (£40) (expenses for private talks).
Expenses: Travel. **Distance:** Negotiable.

GRANTHAM, Mark (Ringing Unit Recoveries Officer)
E-mail: mark.grantham@bto.org
A range of general talks on ringing, migration and
Bird Observatories, Oiled sea-birds.
Fee: BTO fee (£40). **Expenses:** Travel.
Distance: 100 miles

GREENWOOD, Professor JJD (former BTO Director)
E-mail: jeremy.greenwood@bto.org
How to Change Government Policy by Counting
Birds, Why Ring Birds?, The Future for Birds... and
People, Purposeful birdwatching around the world.
Fee: BTO fee (£40) (£50 for private talks).
Expenses: Public transport or 35p/mile.
Distance: 100 miles from Thetford (further by
arrangement).

HENDERSON, Dr Ian (Terrestrial Ecology Unit Research Manager)
E-mail: ian.henderson@bto.org
Arable Farming and Birds.
Fee: BTO fee (£40). **Expenses:** Travel.
Distance: By agreement.

LACK, Dr Peter (Head of Information Systems Unit)
E-mail: peter.lack@bto.org
Bird Atlassing, Palearctic Migrants in Africa, On
Foot in Rwanda and Zambia, Bird Ecology in East
African Savannahs, General Natural History of
Eastern Africa. (All are given as non-BTO talks).
Fee: Negotiable. **Expenses:** Travel. **Distance:** 60
miles from Bury St Edmunds.

MARCHANT. John (Census Unit Team Leader)
E-mail: john.marchant@bto.org
Heronries, Waterways Bird Survey/Waterways

Breeding Bird Survey, Breeding Bird Trends in the UK.
Fee: BTO fee (£40). **Expenses:** Travel.
Distance: By agreement.

MACLEAN, Dr Ilya (Wetland & Coastal Ecology Unit Research Ecologist)
E-mail: ilya.mcclean@bto.org
Waterbird Trends in Protected Areas, African Wetland Conservation.
Fee: BTO fee (£40). **Expenses:** Travel.
Distance: By agreement.

MUSGROVE, Dr Andy (Wetland & Coastal Ecology Unit Research Manager)
E-mail: andy.musgrove@bto.org
The Wetland Bird Survey, Little Egrets in the UK, Recording Moths in Your Garden (non-BTO).
Fee: BTO fee (£40) (£30 for private talk).
Expenses: Travel. **Distance:** By agreement.

NEWSON, Dr Stuart (Demography Unit Population Biologist)
E-mail: stuart.newson@bto.org
Tree Nesting Cormorants.
Fee: BTO fee (£40). **Expenses:** Travel.
Distance: By agreement.

NOBLE, Dr David (Head of Census Unit)
E-mail: david.noble@bto.org
The Farmland Bird Indicator, Population Trends.
Fee: BTO fee (£40). **Expenses:** Travel.
Distance: By agreement.

RAVEN, Mike (Breeding Bird Survey Organiser)
E-mail: mike.raven@bto.org
Latest Findings from the Breeding Bird Survey.
Fee: BTO fee (£40). **Expenses:** Travel.
Distance: By agreement.

REHFISCH, Dr Mark (Head of Wetland & Coastal Ecology Unit)
E-mail: mark.rehfisch@bto.org
Wetland Work at the BTO, Water Quality and Waterbirds, Climate Change, Habitat Loss and Waterbirds, Monitoring Waterbirds, Sea Level Rise and Climate Change, Waterbird Alerts, Introduced Species including Golden Pheasants.

Fee: BTO fee (£40) (up to £40 for private talk).
Expenses: Travel. **Distance:** By agreement.

ROBINSON, Dr Rob (Demography Unit Senior Population Biologist)
E-mail: rob.robinson@bto.org
Farming and Birds, House Sparrows.
Fee: BTO fee (£40). **Expenses:** Travel.
Distance: By agreement.

SIRIWARDENA, Dr Gavin (Terrestrial Ecology Unit Research Manager)
E-mail: gavin.siriwardena@bto.org
Marsh and Willow Tits – Analysis of BTO Data; Evidence of Impacts of Nest Predation and, Competition, Quantifying Migratory Strategies, Winter Feeding of Farmland birds.
(Currently all short talks).
Fee: BTO fee (£40). **Expenses:** Travel.
Distance: 50 miles (further with accommodation).

STANCLIFFE, Paul (Promotions Officer)
E-mail: paul.stancliffe@bto.org
Atlas 2007–11, The BTO Garden BirdWatch.
Fee: £40. **Expenses:** Travel. **Distance:** By agreement.

TOMS, Mike (Garden BirdWatch Organiser)
E-mail: michael.toms@bto.org
The BTO Garden BirdWatch.
Fee: £40. **Expenses:** Petrol. **Distance:** 50 miles, further by arrangement.

VICKERY, Dr Juliet (Head of Terrestrial Ecology Unit)
E-mail: juliet.vickery@bto.org
Farmland Birds.
Fee: BTO fee (£40). **Expenses:** Travel.
Distance: 100 miles.

WERNHAM, Dr Chris (Senior Research Ecologist, BTO Scotland)
E-mail: chris.wernham@bto.org
The BTO's Migration Research (including the Migration Atlas and later developments), The work of BTO Scotland.
Fee: £40. **Expenses:** Petrol. **Distance:** Scotland and northeast England.

TRADE DIRECTORY

Grey Heron in flight by Steve Knell

BIRD GARDEN SUPPLIERS

BIRD GARDEN SUPPLIES

BAMFORDS TOP FLIGHT

Company ethos: Family-owned manufacturing company providing good quality bird foods via a network of UK stockists or mail order. RSPB Corporate Member, BTO Business Ally, Petcare Trust Member.

Key product lines: A range of wild bird mixtures containing the revolutionary new 'Pro-tec Health Aid', developed by Bamfords, to protect and promote the welfare of wild birds. Vast array of other foods and seeds for birds.

Other services: Trade suppliers of bulk and pre-packed bird and petfoods. Custom packing/own label if required.

Opening times: Mon - Fri (8am-5.30pm); Sat 8am–12 noon); (Sunday 10am–12 noon, Mill Shop only).

Address: Globe Mill, Midge Hall, Leyland, Lancashire PR26 6TN: 01772 456 300; (Fax)01772 456 302. email: sales@bamfords.co.uk www.bamfords.co.uk

BIRD VENTURES

Company ethos: A comprehensive stock of wildlife products for everyone from garden bird enthusiasts to keen birdwatchers. The business operates as an online shop and retail outlet based in Holt, Norfok. The business helps support Natural Surrounding, a wildlife centre with eight acres of gardens and education facilities for all ages, which won Environmental Small Business of the Year for north Norfolk from the district council.

Key product lines: Nest box cameras moth traps, butterfly nets, wildbird food, bird feeders, nest boxes, hedgehog homes, insect habitats, bat boxes, squirrel-proof feeders, wildflower seeds, children's nature study equipment and much more.

Other services: On-line 24 hours.

Opening times: Mon-Sat (9am-5.30pm).

Contact: Bird Ventures, 9B Chapel Yard, Albert Street, Holt, Norfolk NR25 6HG; 01263 710 203; (fax)01263 711 091.

e-mail: paullaurie100@aol.com
www.birdventures.co.uk

CJ WILDBIRD FOODS LTD

Company ethos: High quality products, no-quibble guarantee, friendly, professional service.

Key product lines: Complete range of CJ Wildlife bird feeders, bird food, nest boxes, bird tables and accessories, alongside a wide collection of other garden wildlife related products.

Other services: Mail order company, online

ordering, 24hr delivery service. Free Handbook of Garden Wildlife to all enquirers. Collect your order from us and receive 10% discount. **New for 2009:** Continuously adding new products to the range — call for a brochure or visit the website.

Opening times: Mon-Fri (9am-5pm), Saturday (9am-12pm), Website 24 hours.

Address: The Rea, Upton Magna, Shrewsbury, Shropshire SY4 4UR; 0800 731 2820; (Fax)01743 709 504. e-mail: enquiries@birdfood.co.uk www.birdfood.co.uk

ERNEST CHARLES

Company ethos: Member of Birdcare Standards Assoc. ISO 9001 registered. Offering quality bird foods/wildlife products through a friendly mail-order service. Working in association with The British Trust for Ornithology.

Key product lines: Bird foods, feeders, nest boxes and other wildlife products.

Other services: Own label work for other companies considered and trade enquiries.

New for 2009: A range of solutions to get tough on squirrels!

Opening times: Mon to Fri (8am-5pm).

Address: Stuart Christophers, Copplestone Mills, Crediton, Devon

EX17 5NF; 01363 84 842; (Fax)01363 84 147. e-mail: stuart@ernest-charles.com www.ernest-charles.com

foodforbirds.co.uk

Company ethos: Specialist mail order company supplying high quality wild bird foods via a fast and friendly next day service. Supporter of RSPB and BTO through parent company.

Key product lines: A great range of tried and tested, freshly made wild bird mixtures, together with a whole host of straight foods - peanuts, sunflowers, niger seed, fat foods etc.

Other services: Vast array of bird feeders for peanuts and seed, plus other wildlife foods, all of which can be ordered via a secure on-line website. Send for free catalogue.

BOOK PUBLISHERS

Opening times: Telesales (freephone) 8am-5.30pm (order before midday for next day delivery). Answer phone outside these hours. On-line ordering and fax, 24 hours.
Address: Foodforbirds, Leyland, PR26 6TN; (Freephone)0800 043 9022; (Fax)01772 456 302.
e-mail: sales@foodforbirds.co.uk
www.foodforbirds.co.uk

JACOBI JAYNE & CO.

Company ethos: Market-leaders for more than 20 years, offering products and expertise to individuals and professionals alike. Conservation products of highest quality and proven worth.
Key product lines: Birdfeeders, next boxes, foods and accessories. UK distributor of Schwegler nest boxes, Droll Yankees® feeders and Jacobi Jayne wildlife foods.

Other services: *Living with Birds* mail-order catalogue and online at www.livingwithbirds.com
New for 2009: Brand new Ring-Pulla™ easy-clean feeders.
Opening times: 24hrs (use websites or answering service when office is closed).
Contact: Clair Dance, Jacobi Jayne & Co, Wealden Forest Park, Canterbury, Kent CT6 7LQ; 0800 072 0130; (Fax)01227 719 235.
e-mail: enquiries@jacobijayne.com
www.jacobijayne.com

VINE HOUSE FARM BIRD FOODS

Company ethos: Growing and selling wild bird food on a family-run farm. A full range of high quality bird foods and accessories direct to the customer through our mall order service and farm shop.
Key product lines: A full range of bird food including home-grown black sunflowers and a range of specialist mixes and feeder accessories.
Other services: A number of farm walks and open days in early summer for people to view our conservation award-winning farm. We also have a range of products available for wholesale customers.
New for 2009: The Wildlife Trust now recommend our bird seed to their members and also benefit from every sale we make.
Opening times: Mon to Fri (8am-5pm), Sat (8am-4pm), Sun (10am-4pm).

Contact: Nicholas Watts, Vine House Farm, Deeping St Nicholas, Spalding PE11 3DG; 01775 630 208; (Fax)01775 630 244.
e-mail:birdseed@vinehousefarm.co.uk
www.vinehousefarm.co.uk

BOOK PUBLISHERS

BUCKINGHAM PRESS LTD

Imprints: Single imprint company - publishers of *The Birdwatcher's Yearbook* since 1980, *Who's Who in Ornithology* (1997), *Best Birdwatching Sites* series covering Norfolk, Sussex, Highlands of Scotland and North Wales, Cornwall and Scilly. Plus sets of identification cards for British birds and British butterflies. Also publishes *Birds Illustrated*, a quarterly, subscription only magazine (see survey of English language bird magazines page 22).
New for 2009: ID Insights Pocket Cards for British Dragonflies, more *Best Birdwatching Sites* books.
Address: 55 Thorpe Park Road, Peterborough, PE3 6LJ. Tel/Fax: 01733 561 739.
e-mail: admin@buckinghampress.com
www.birdsillustrated.com

CHRISTOPHER HELM PUBLISHERS

Imprints: Christopher Helm – the leading publisher of ornithology books in the world; includes many field guides, identification guides, family guides, county and country avifaunas, and a *Where to Watch Birds* series. T & AD Poyser – an acclaimed series of respected ornithology monographs. Birds of Africa – the standard series of handbooks on African birds. A & C Black – publisher of definitive natural history books.
New for 2009: *Handbook of Western Palearctic Birds: Passerines* by Hadoram Shirihai and Lars Svensson, *Shorebirds of the Northern Hemisphere* by Richard Chandler, *Reed and Bush Warblers* by Peter Kennerley and David Pearson, *Field Guide to the Birds of the Horn of Africa* by Nigel Redman,

Terry Stevenson and John Fanshawe, *Birds of Ethiopia and Eritrea* by John Ash and John Atkins, *Where to Watch Birds in Britain* 2nd edition by Simon

Harrap and Nigel Redman, *Guide to the Mammals of Europe, North Africa and the Middle East* by Francois Moutou, Patrick Haffner and J. Zima, *Handbook of the Bats of Europe and Northwest Africa* by Christian Dietz, Otto von Helversen and Dietmar Nill.
Address: 38 Soho Square, London, W1D 3HB; 020 7758 0200; (Fax)020 7758 0222.
e-mail: nredman@acblack.com
www.acblack.com/naturalhistory

HARPER COLLINS PUBLISHERS

Imprints: Collins Natural History -- the leading publisher of fieldguides to the natural world. Collins New Naturalist Series, the encyclopaedic reference for all areas of British natural history. HarperCollins, publisher of the best illustrated books.
New for 2009: *Collins Flower Guide, Collins Bird Guide*, 2nd Edition, *Last Chance to See* by Mark Carwardine & Stephen Fry, New Naturalist *Islands, Wildfowl, Badger*, Nature Publishing.
Address: 77-85 Fulham Palace Rd, Hammersmith, London, W6 8JB; 020 8307 4998; (Fax)020 8307 4037. e-mail: Myles.Archibald@harpercollins.co.uk
www.fireandwater.com
www.collins.co.uk

NEW HOLLAND PUBLISHERS (UK) LTD

Imprints; New Holland, illustrated bird books, general wildlife and personality-led natural history.
New for 2009: *Field Guide to the Birds of Borneo, Field Guide to the Birds of South East Asia* (new fully updated edition), *Birds of Australia, European Reptile and Amphibian Guide, New Holland British Wildlife Guide, Steve Backshall's Deadly 60, Steve Backshall's Adventurer's Guide to Wildlife, Wild France, Wild Spain, Photographic Guide to the Birds of Vietnam, Cambodia and Laos, Photographic Guide to the Birds of Ecuador and Galapagos, Photographic Guide to the Birds of Borneo* (new edition), *History of Ornithology, Creative Bird Photography, Garden Wildlife Photography, The Wildlife Garden Specialist, Naturalized Animals of the British Isles.*
Address: Garfield House, 86-88 Edgware Road, London W2 2EA; 020 7724 7773; (Fax)020 7258 1293. e-mail: postmaster@nhpub.co.uk
www.newhollandpublishers.com

WILDGuides LTD

Imprints; WILDGuides — natural history fieldguides. Butterflies, Dragonflies, Orchids, Arable Plants.
OCEANGuides — identification guides to marine wildlife. Antarctic, Atlantic and Pacific titles.

Destination Guides — lavishly illustrated visitor guides. Galapagos, Seychelles, South Georgia, Falklands.
European Natural History Guides -- regional heritage guides for walkers. Spain, France, Poland, Hungary.
Recently published: *Endemic Plants of Altai Mountains, Arable Bryophytes of GB, Plants of the Falklands.*
New for 2009: *Flowers of the New Forest, Britain's Bees, Britain's Reptiles & Amphibians.*
Address: PO Box 680, Maidenhead, Berkshire SL6 9ST; 01628 529 297; (Fax)01628 525 314.
e-mail: info@wildguides.co.uk
www.wildguides.co.uk

BOOK SELLERS

ATROPOS

Company ethos: Lively magazine for butterfly, moth and dragonfly enthusiasts. Mail order book service providing key titles swiftly at competitive prices.
Key subjects: Butterflies, moths, dragonflies and other insects.
Address: 36 Tinker Lane, Meltham, Holmfirth, West Yorkshire HD9 4EX. 01326 290 287.
e-mail: atropos.editor@zen.co.uk
www.atropos.info

CALLUNA BOOKS

Company ethos: We specialise in buying and selling out-of-print natural history titles, with an emphasis on quality stock at competitive prices.
Key subjects: Birds, mammals, flora, invertebrates in the UK and worldwide, including the Poyser and New Naturalist series, and general natural history, conservation and countryside titles including some reports and journals. Stock of 2000+ titles maintained.
Other services: Catalogues issued (usually 3 p.a). We exhibit at some bird fairs including Rutland Water. Wants lists welcomed – no obligation to buy.
Opening times: Mail order but viewing by appointment possible.
Address: Moor Edge, 2 Bere Road, Wareham, Dorset BH20 4DD;01929 552 560.
e-mail: enquiries@callunabooks.co.uk
www.callunabooks.co.uk

NHBS ENVIRONMENT BOOKSTORE

Company ethos: A unique natural history, conservation and environmental bookstore. The world's largest range of wildlife books and equipment.

BOOK SELLERS

Key subjects: Natural history, conservation, environmental science, zoology, habitats and

ecosystems, botany, marine biology, bat detecting, entomology, GPS, birding.
Other services: www.nhbs.com offers a searchable and browsable web catalogue with more than 100,000 titles.
New for 2009: A large range of essential wildlife equipment, from binoculars to bat detectors, from microscopes to moth traps.
Opening times: Mon-Fri (9am-5pm), for mail-order service.
Address: 2-3 Wills Road, Totnes, Devon TQ9 5XN; 01803 865 913.
e-mail: customer.services@nhbs.co.uk
www.nhbs.com

PICTURE BOOK

Company ethos: General bookshop with specialist interest in bird books and Natural History.
Key subjects: Birdwatching, natural history, local history.
Other services: Mail order, new and secondhand books.
Opening times: Tue-Fri (9.15am-4.30pm), Sat (9am-4.30pm).
Address: Picture Book, 6 Stanley Street, Leek, ST13 5HG; 01538 384 337; (Fax)01538 399 696.
e-mail: info@leekbooks.co.uk
www.birdbooksonline.co.uk

PORTLAND OBSERVATORY BOOK SHOP

Company ethos: To meet the needs of amateur and professional naturalists.
Key subjects: Ornithology, general natural history, topography, art and local history. New and secondhand.
Other services: Mail order, discount on new books, increased discount for observatory members.
Opening times: Wed, Thur, Sat and Sunday; (10am to 4pm). Other times on request.
Address: Bird Observatory, Old Lower Light, Portland Bill, Dorset DT5 2JT; 01305 820 553, (shop)01305 826 625, (home)01225 700 728.
www.portlandbirdobs.btinternet.co.uk

SECOND NATURE

Company ethos: Buying and selling out-of-print/secondhand/antiquarian books on natural history, topography and travel.

Key subjects: Birds, mammals, flowers and all other aspects of natural history.
Other services; Exhibits at bird/wildlife fairs.
New for 2009: A comprehensive website -
www.secondnaturebooks.com
Opening times: Mail order only.
Address: Knapton Book Barn, Back Lane, Knapton, York YO26 6QJ; (Tel/fax) 01904 339 493.
e-mail: SecondnatureYork@aol.com
www.secondnaturebooks.com

SUBBUTEO NATURAL HISTORY BOOKS

Company ethos: Specialist knowledge on all aspects of wildlife, travel and natural history books, friendly service.
Key subjects: Wildlife, natural history and travel books & field guides.
Other services: Source any natural history book from around

the world. Online ordering, free delivery over £50 (in-print titles and UK orders only), free catalogue.
New for 2009: Continuously adding new titles to the range, call for a brochure or visit the website.
Opening times: Bookshop - Mon-Fri (9am-5pm). Sat (9am-12pm). Website - 24hrs
Address: The Rea, Upton Magna, Shrewsbury, Shropshire SY4 4UR; 0870 010 9700; (Fax)0870 010 9699. e-mail: info@wildlifebooks.com
www.wildlifebooks.com

WILDSOUNDS

Company ethos: Committed to sound environmental practice. Donates a significant portion of profit to bird conservation (Associate sponsor of the annual British Birdwatching Fair, Birdlife International Species Champion for the Spoon-billed Sandpiper) Official bookseller to African Bird Club.
Key product lines: Mail-order, post-free books, DVDs, multi-media guides and eGuides for PDAs – mobile versions of popular fieldguides complete with bird sounds and listing software e.g. *Collins Bird eGuide* and *Sasol eBirds of Southern Africa*. Publishers and distributor of *Birding in Eastern Europe* by Gerard Gorman
New for 2009: eGuides for North America, MP3 collections: *Sounds of Zambian Wildlife*; *Birds of the Southern Cone of South America.*
Opening times: Weekdays (9.30am-5pm).
Address: Cross Street, Salthouse, Norfolk, NR25 7XH; (Tel) +44 (UK) (0)1263 741100 (Fax) +44 (0)1263 741 838; e-mail: sales@wildsounds.com
www.wildsounds.com

BOOK SELLERS AND CLOTHING SUPPLIERS

WYSEBY BOOKSHOP

Company ethos: We stock rare, out-of-print, second-hand and unusual titles which are on display in our shop or can be found on our website. Informed and friendly staff always ready to help personal shoppers or answer telephone and e mail inquiries.

Key subjects: Bird books, gardening, forestry and natural history, art, architecture, design.

Other services: A well designed website with easy to use search facility where books can be located by author, title, keyword or subject.

Opening times: Mon-Sat (9am-5pm), but we suggest you ring beforehand just in case you are travelling some distance.

Address: Kingsclere Old Bookshop, 2a, George Street, Kingsclere, Nr Newbury, Berks. RG20 5NQ. 01635 297 995; (Fax) 01635 297 677; e-mail: info@wyseby.co.uk www.wyseby.co.uk

CLOTHING

COUNTRY INNOVATION

Company ethos: Friendly advice by well-trained staff.

Key product lines: Full range of outdoor wear; Jackets; smock; fleeces; trousers; Brasher boots, poles & accessories; Tilley hats; healthy back bags; lightweight clothing; hats; gloves; rucksacks and pouches. Ladies fits available.

Other services: Mail order and website.

Opening times: Mon-Fri (9am-5pm), Sat (10am-4pm).

Address: 1 Broad Street, Congresbury, North Somerset BS49 5DG; 01934 877 333. e-mail: sales@countryinnovation.com www.countryinnovation.com

PÁRAMO DIRECTIONAL CLOTHING SYSTEMS

Company ethos: Innovators of technical mountain, birding and travel clothing using revolutionary Nikwax fabrics, functional design to provide performance and comfort for all outdoor enthusiasts and professionals, whatever their activity. Ethical manufacture.

Key product lines: Waterproof jackets and trousers, technical base layers and insulating overlayers. Of particular note: the Pájaro birdwatching jacket and Cascada waterproof trousers and the Andy Rouse Limited Edition range of Aspira smock, Cascada trousers and mountain vent pull-on.

Other services: Repair and service of Páramo garments.

Opening times For independent retailers, consult website or ring 01892 786 444 for a stockist list and catalogue pack.

Address: Unit F, Durgates Industrial Estate, Wadhurst, East Sussex, TN5 6JL, UK e-mail: info@paramo.co.uk www.paramo.co.uk

EQUIPMENT SUPLIERS AND SERVICES

ALWYCH BOOKS

Company ethos: The Bird Watcher's All-weather Flexible Pocket Book.

Key product lines: Alwych all-weather notebooks.

Address: Janette Scott, Wishaw Printing Company, 84 Stewarton Street, Wishaw, ML2 8AG; 0845 270 2828; (admin)01698 357 223.

BIRD IMAGES

Company ethos: High quality products at affordable prices.

Key product lines: Bird DVDs. Filmed and produced by Paul Doherty.

New for 2009: *Birdwatching in Norfolk.*

Opening times: Telephone first.

Address: 28 Carousel Walk, Sherburn in Elmet, North Yorkshinre LS25 6LP; 01977 684 666. e-mail: paul@birdvideodvd.com www.birdvideodvd.com

BIRDGUIDES LTD

Company ethos: Better birding through technology. A range of web and e-mail services for birders. DVD-roms, CD-roms and MP3 sound guides.

Key product lines: DVD-ROM, CD-ROM, DVD, video guides to British, European and American birds. Rare bird news services vla e-mail, website and SMS.

New for 2009: Sound guides.

Address: Birdguides Ltd, PO Box 4104, Sheffield S25 9BJ; 0114 283 1002; order line (freephone) 0800 919 391. e-mail: birdguides@birdfood.co.uk www.birdguides.com

GOLDEN VALLEY INSURANCE SERVICES

Company ethos: Knowledgeable, friendly insurance services. Free information pack on request. Freephone telephone number for all enquiries.

Key product lines: Insurance for optical/photographic/video/computer equipment for birdwatchers. Also, public liability for ornithological clubs and societies.

Opening times: Mon-Fri (9am-5pm), answering

machine at other times
Address: Sharron or Marion, Golden Valley Insurance Services, The Olde Shoppe, Ewyas Harold, Herefordshire HR2 0ES; 0800 015 4484; (Fax)01981 240 451.
e-mail: gvinsurance@aol.com
www.insuranceforcameras.co.uk

OPTREP Optical Repairs
Company ethos: To give a speedy, economical and effective repair service.
Key services: Servicing and repair of binoculars, telescopes etc. Conversant with the special needs of birdwatchers.
Opening times: Mon-Thu (9am-5pm), Fri (9am-3pm).

Address: 16 Wheatfield Road, Selsey, West Sussex PO20 0NY; 01243 601 365.
e-mail: info@opticalrepairs.com
www.opticalrepairs.com

WILDLIFE WATCHING SUPPLIES
Company ethos: To bring together a comprehensive range of materials, clothing and equipment to make it easier and more comfortable for you to blend in with the environment. Quick and friendly service.
Key product lines: Hides, camouflage, bean bags, lens and camera covers, clothing etc.
New for 2009: New on-line shop, see new products page on website.
Opening times: Mon to Fri (9am-5pm), Mail order. Visitors by appointment.
Address: Town Living Farmhouse, Puddington, Tiverton, Devon EX16 8LW; 01884 860 692(24hr); (Fax)01884 860 994.
e-mail: enquiries@wildlifewatchingsupplies.co.uk
www.wildlifewatchingsupplies.co.uk

WILDSOUNDS
Company ethos: Committed to sound environmental practice. Donates a significant portion of profit to bird conservation (Associate sponsor of the annual British Birdwatching Fair, Birdlife International Species Champion for the Spoon-billed Sandpiper) Official bookseller to African Bird Club.
Key product lines: Mail-order, post-free books, DVDs, multi-media guides and eGuides for PDAs – mobile versions of popular fieldguides complete with bird sounds and listing software e.g. *Collins Bird eGuide* and *Sasol eBirds of Southern Africa*.

Publishers and distributor of *Birding in Eastern Europe* by Gerard Gorman
New for 2009: eGuides for North America, MP3 collections: *Sounds of Zambian Wildlife; Birds of the Southern Cone of South America.*
Opening times: Weekdays (9.30am-5pm).
Address: Cross Street, Salthouse, Norfolk, NR25 7XH; (Tel) +44 (UK) (0)1263 741100 (Fax) +44 (0)1263 741 838; e-mail: sales@wlldsounds.com www.wildsounds.com

HOLIDAY COMPANIES

AIGAS QUEST LTD
Company ethos: Scotland's longest running nature holiday provider delivers outstanding wildlife watching holidays for groups and individuals. From birdwatching to pine marten, badger or beaver viewing - we've got the lot!
Types of tours: Birdwatching and wildlifewatching for all levels.
Destinations: Highlands and Islands of Scotland.
New for 2009: Skye, Orkney, Shetland, Highlands.
Opening times: Mon-Fri (8.30am-5pm).
Brochure from: Aigas Field Centre, Aigas, Beauly, Inverness-shire IV4 7AD; 01463 782 443; (Fax)01463 782 097. e-mail: info@aigas.co.uk www.aigas.co.uk

AVIAN ADVENTURES
Company ethos: Top quality, value for money tours, escorted by friendly, experienced leaders at a fairly relaxed pace. ATOL 3367.
Types of tours: Birdwatching, birds and wildlife photography and wildlife safaris, all suitable for both the first-time and the more experienced traveller.
Destinations: More than 70 tours worldwide.
Brochure from: 49 Sandy Road, Norton, Stourbridge, DY8 3AJ; 01384 372 013; (Fax)01384 441 340. e-mail: aviantours@argonet.co.uk www.avianadventures.co.uk

BIRD HOLIDAYS
Company ethos: Relaxed pace, professional leaders, small groups, exciting itineraries.
Types of tours: Birdwatching for all levels, beginners to advanced.
Destinations: Worldwide (40 tours, 6 continents).
New for 2009: SE Brazil, Okavango Delta, Hungary (bats and birds), Poland.
Brochure from: 10 Ivegate, Yeadon, Leeds, LS19 7RE; (Tel/fax)0113 3910 510.
e-mail: info@birdholidays.co.uk
www.birdholidays.co.uk

TRADE DIRECTORY

BIRDFINDERS

Company ethos: Top-value birding tours to see all specialities/endemics of a country/area, using leading UK and local guides. ATOL 5406.
Types of tours: Birdwatching holidays for all abilities.
Destinations: Nearly 60 tours in UK, Europe, Africa, Asia, Australasia, North and South America and Antarctica.
New for 2009: Arizona/California winter, Cape Verde Islands, China, India north east, Mexico - Oaxaca and Chiapas, Panama, Taiwan, Thailand south, Texas/New Mexico winter, UAE.
Brochure from: Vaughan Ashby, Westbank, Cheselbourne, Dorset DT2 7NW. 01258 839 066.
e-mail: info@birdfinders.co.uk
www.birdfinders.co.uk
Our office is open seven days a week (8am-8pm).

BIRDWATCHING BREAKS

Company ethos: Birdwatching breaks and Black Isle birding.
Types of tours: Birding tours around the world to little-known destinations along with more traditional destinations using local guides in addition to our own. These tours are aimed at all abilities and are limited to a maximum of eight clients to one leader. We also specialise in Northern Scotland, including the Highlands and Islands under the Black Isle Birding Banner. Our main interest is aimed at birds but we also take in mammals and other wildlife. Many of our tours are suitable for photography.
Destinations: Argentina, Bhutan, Bulgaria, Chile, Ethiopia, Ghana, Ireland, Japan, Scotland, Spain, Syria, Thailand, Uganda.
New for 2009: Canary Islands, Guatemala, Jamaica, Oman, Poland, Namibia, New Zealand, Texas & Washington State, Vietnam.
Brochure from: Birdwatching Breaks, Cygnus House, Gordon's Mill, Balblair, Ross-shire IV7 8LQ; 01381 610 495.
e-mail: enquiries@birdwatchingbreaks.com
www.birdwatchingbreaks.com

BRITISH-BULGARIAN FRIENDSHIP SOCIETY

Company ethos: To introduce people to the beauty of Bulgarian wildlife at exceptional value prices with expert leaders.
Types of tours: Birdwatching tours in winter, spring and autumn, also butterfly, wild flower and natural history tours. Groups size 12-14 persons.
Destinations: Specialists to Bulgaria, over 30 years experience.
New for 2009: Wallcreeper and Bears. Magical Melnik: relaxed birding from a single base.

Brochure from: Balkania Travel Ltd, Room 40, Third Floor, Morley House, 320 Regent Street, London W1B 3BE; (Tel)020 7538 8654; e-mail: ognian:balkaniatravel.com ATOL 4465. Or Dr Annie Kay 020 7237 7616 or e-mail: annie.kay@btinternet.com
www.bbfs.org.uk

CLASSIC JOURNEYS

Company ethos: Professional and friendly company, providing well organised and enjoyable birdwatching holidays.
Types of tours: General birdwatching and wildlife holidays on the Indian sub-continent and beyond.
Destinations: Nepal, India, Bhutan, Sri Lanka, Tibet, Ecuador, Galapagos, Peru, Tanzania, Spitsbergen.
New for 2009: Beyond Borneo - Orangutans & Komodo Dragons.
Opening times: Mon-Fri (9am-5pm).
Brochure from: 33 High Street, Tibshelf, Alfreton, Derbyshire DE55 5NX; 01773 873 497; (Fax)01773 590 243.
e-mail: info@classicjourneys.co.uk
www.classicjourneys.co.uk

DORSET BIRDING

Company ethos: To provide local knowledge and expertise of Dorset's birds and wildlife, catering for all levels of experience and tailor-made to your requirements.
Types of tours: A guiding service for individuals and small groups aimed at providing an experience of Dorset's birds, wildlife and landscapes. Although there is a particular emphasis on birds, all species groups are covered. Half-day, full day, weekends or longer breaks are available. Local accommodation can be arranged.
Destinations: Dorset, New Forest.
Brochure from: Neil Gartshore, Moor Edge, 2 Bere Road, Wareham, Dorset BH20 4DD;01929 552 560. www.dorsetbirdingandwildlife.co.uk
e-mail: enquiries@dorsetbirdingandwildlife.co.uk

EXPEDITION CRUISES & CRUISES FOR NATURE

Company ethos: We are specialists in cruises on expedition ships, with expertise for birdwatchers, photographers and naturalists. We also have escorted cruises, using professional guides, to amazing destinations. ATOL no 6934.
Types of cruises: Both escorted and unescorted wildlife cruises on expedition ships.
Destinations: Worldwide including Antarctica, Spitsbergen, the Galapagos Islands, Pacific and the North Pole.
New for 2009: New Zealand to Japan cruise.

HOLIDAY COMPANIES

Brochure from: 29 Straight Mile, Romsey, Hampshire SO51 9BB; 01794 523 500; (Fax)01794 523 544. e-mail: info@expeditioncruising.co.uk www.expeditioncruising.co.uk

HEATHERLEA

Company ethos: Exciting holidays to see all the birds of Scotland and selected overseas destinations. Experienced guides and comfortable award-winning hotel to give great customer service.
Types of tours: Birdwatching and other wildlife watching tours.
Destinations: Scottish Highlands, including holidays from our base in Nethybridge, plus Outer Hebrides, Orkney, Shetlands and more. Selected destinations include Pyrenees, Lesvos, Kenya and Trinidad.
New for 2009: New destinations including Holland, Sweden, Sri Lanka and our tremendous Scottish Island Adventure.
Brochure from: The Mountview Hotel, Nethybridge, Inverness-shire PH25 3EB; 01479 821 248; (Fax)01479 821 515.
e-mail: hleabirds@aol.com
www.heatherlea.co.uk

NATURETREK

Company ethos: Friendly, gentle-paced, birdwatching holidays with broad-brush approach. Sympathetic to other wildlife interests, history  and local culture. Also operate faster-paced bargain birdwatching selection. ATOL no 2692
Types of tours: Escorted birdwatching, botanical and natural history holidays worldwide.
Destinations: Worldwide - see brochure.
New for 2009: Austria's Steppes & Wildlife; Butterflies of Croatia; Chile's Blue Whales & Pumas; India - Tiger Marathon; North Spitsbergen - A Polar Bear Special; Pilots, Dolphins & Mantas - A Maldives Cruise; Scotland to Spitsbergen - The North Atlantic Islands; Snow Leopards of the Hindu Kush; Subantarctic Islands of New Zealand; Vietnam.
Brochure from: Cheriton Mill, Cheriton, Alresford, Hampshire SO24 0NG; 01962 733 051; (Fax)01962 736 426. e-mail: info@naturetrek.co.uk
www.naturetrek.co.uk

NORTH WEST BIRDS

Company ethos: Friendly, relaxed and unhurried but targetted to scarce local birds.
Types of tours: Very small groups (up to four) based on large family home in South Lakes with good home cooking. Short breaks with birding in local area. Butterflies in season.
Destinations: Local to Northwest England. Lancashire, Morecambe Bay and Lake District.
Brochure from: Mike Robinson, Barn Close, Beetham, Cumbria LA7 7AL; (Tel/fax)01539 563 191. e-mail: mike@nwbirds.co.uk
www.nwbirds.co.uk

NORTHERN FRANCE WILDLIFE TOURS

Company ethos: Friendly personal attention. Normally a maximum of five in a group. Totally flexible.
Types of tours: Mini-bus trips catering for all from beginners to experienced birders. Local birds include Bluethroat, Black Woodpecker, Melodious Warbler.
Destinations: Brittany, Normandy and Pays de la Loire.
Brochure from: Place de l'église, 53700, Averton, France; 00 33 243 00 6969. e-mail: nfwt@online.fr
www.northernfrancewildlifetours.com

ORIOLE ADVENTURES

Company ethos: Enhancing your ID skills and enjoyment of birding.
Types of tours: Norfolk-based birding tours year round, covering all the best sites and species, plus a selection of Britain's best destinations.
Destinations: Norfolk (20 tours), South Wales, Solway, Extremadura, NE England, Cornwall, Mull and Iona, Romania, Fair Isle, Isles of Scilly.
New for 2009: Ireland, Speyside, Mallorca, Israel, The Gambia, Cornwall in Winter, Norfolk Summer Wildlife.
Brochure from: Oriole Adventures, White Horse Inn, Fakenham Road, East Barsham, Fakenham, Norfolk NR21 0LH; 01328 821 795.
e-mail: ashley.saunders1@btinternet.com
www.orioleadventures.com

ORNITHOLIDAYS

Company ethos: Oldest bird tour company in the world - established 1965. Friendly and fun holidays led by full-time tour leaders. ATOL no 0743.
Types of tours: Escorted birdwatching and natural history tours.
Destinations: Worldwide including Trinidad and Tobago, Costa Rica, Bolivia, South Africa and Antarctica.

New for 2009: Slovenia, Ukraine, Thailand and Mexico.
Brochure from: 29 Straight Mile, Romsey, Hampshire SO51 9BB; 01794 519 445; (Fax)01794 523 544.
e-mail: info@ornitholidays.co.uk
www.ornitholidays.co.uk

SHETLAND WILDLIFE

Company ethos: Award-winning small group travel with the very best naturalist guides.
Types of tours: A unique blend of itineraries to bring you the very best of Shetland. Week-long or three-day holidays dedicated to birding, wildlife, photography and walking. Also overseas holidays to the very best European birding locations.
Destinations: All corners of Shetland including Fair Isle and Foula. Also overseas holidays to the very best European birding locations.
New for 2009: Foula bird migration holidays in spring and autumn.
Brochure from: Longhill, Maywick, Shetland, ZE2 9JF; 01950 422 483; (Fax)01950 422 430.
e-mail; info@shetlandwildlife.co.uk
www.shetlandwildlife.co.uk

SPEYSIDE WILDLIFE

Company ethos: Expert leaders, personal attention and a sense of fun - it's your holiday. ATOL no 4259.
Types of tours: Experts in Scotland and leaders worldwide - birdwatching, mammals and whale watching.
Destinations: Speyside and the Scottish Islands, Scandinavia, the Arctic, Europe, N and S America, Africa and India.
New for 2009: Madagascar, Bay of Biscay and Picos, New York, Canaries, Ebro Delta, Wolves of NW Spain, Romania and Iceland.
Brochure from: Garden Office, Inverdruie House, Inverdruie, Aviemore, Inverness-shire PH22 1QH; (Tel/fax)01479 812 498.
e-mail: enquiries@speysidewildlife.co.uk
www.speysidewildlife.co.uk

SUNBIRD

Company ethos: Enjoyable birdwatching tours led by full-time professional leaders. ATOL no 3003.
Types of tours: Birdwatching, Birds & Music, Birds & History, Birds & Butterflies.
Destinations: Worldwide.
New for 2009: Crimea, Cameroon, Cambodia, Nepal, Vietnam, Tibet.

Brochure from: 26B The Market Square, Potton, Sandy, Bedfordshire SG19 2NP; 01767 262 522; (Fax)01767 262 916.
e-mail: sunbird@sunbirdtours.co.uk
www.sunbirdtours.co.ukcheck new destinations

THE TRAVELLING NATURALIST

Company ethos: Friendly, easy-going, expertly-led birdwatching and wildlife tours. ATOL no.3435. AITO 1124.
Types of tours: Tours include birds and history, birds and bears, whale-watching, birds and flowers.
Destinations: Worldwide.
New for 2009: Sichuan – Pandas and Eclipse, Gabon, Alaska.
Brochure from: PO Box 3141, Dorchester, Dorset DT1 2XD; 01305 267994; (Fax) 01305 265 506.
e-mail: jamie@naturalist.co.uk
www.naturalist.co.uk

THE ULTIMATE TRAVEL COMPANY

Company ethos: Quality wildlife experiences and shared enjoyment of the natural world.
Types of tours: Relaxed, escorted wildlife and birdwatching holidays with friendly groups and Britain's most experienced leaders. Often good photographic opportunities as well.
Destinations: Various locations in Africa, South America, India and the Indian Ocean and Europe
Brochure from: The Ultimate Travel Company, 25-27 Vanston Place, London, SW6 1AZ; 020 7386 4676; (Fax)020 7381 0836.
email: enquiry@theultimatetravelcompany.co.uk

THINK GALAPAGOS LTD

Company ethos: Specialists in Ecuador and the Galapagos Islands, with a strong focus on personal service and a reputation for organising exceptional wildlife tours.

Types of tours:
Expert led trips to Ecuador and the Galapagos designed for individuals with a keen interest in wildlife and photography. Suitable for single travellers as well as couples.
Destinations: Galapagos and Ecuador.
New for 2009: A 17-day journey visiting the Galapagos, Andes and Amazon Rainforest.
Brochure from: See www.thinkgalapagos.com or contact Rachel Dex: 01482 872 761 or email info@thinkgalapagos.com

WILD INSIGHTS

Company ethos: Friendly, no-rush tours designed to savour, understand and enjoy birds and wildlife fully, rather than simply build large tick lists. Emphasis on quality. ATOL no 5429 (in association with Wildwings).

Types of tours: Relaxed UK workshops, skills-building UK courses, plus selected overseas tours.

Destinations: Various UK locations, plus selected destinations throughout USA, Africa, Northern India and Europe.

New for 2009: Estonia.

Calender brochure from: Yew Tree Farmhouse, Craignant, Selattyn, Oswestry, Salop SY10 7NP. ;(Tel/fax) 01691 718 740.

e-mail: keith.offord@virgin.net

www.wildinsights.co.uk

WILDWINGS

Company ethos: Superb value holidays led by expert guides.

Types of tours: Birdwatching holidays, whale and dolphin watching holidays, wildlife cruises, ecovolunteers.

Destinations: Europe, Arctic, Asia, The Americas, Antarctica, Africa, Trinidad and Tobago.

New for 2009: ScoTtish Islands, Azores, Israel, Kamchatka, New Zealand.

Brochure from: 577-579 Fishponds Road, FIshponds, Bristol, BS16 3AF.

e-mail: wildinfo@wildwings.co.uk

OPTICAL IMPORTERS AND MANUFACTURERS

ACE OPTICS

Company ethos: To be the best - service, price and stock.
Product lines: Importers of Avian, Optolyth, Questar and main suppliers of Leica, Swarovski, Zeiss and Kowa. All the best tripods and an array of optical related accessories.

Address: 16 Green Street, Bath, BA1 2JZ; 01225 466 364; (fax)01225 469 761. e-mail: optics@acecameras.co.uk

www.acecameras.co.uk

CARL ZEISS LTD

Company ethos: World renowned, high quality performance and innovative optical products.

Product lines: Victory FL, Conquest, Stabilised, Victory and Classic compacts and Diascope FL telescopes.

Address: PO Box 78, Woodfield Road, Welwyn Garden City, Hertfordshire AL7 1LU; 01707 871 350; (Fax)01707 871 426. www.zeiss.co.uk

e-mail: binos@zeiss.co.uk

INTRO 2020 LTD

Company ethos: Experienced importer of photo and optical products.

Product lines: Steiner Binoculars, Tamron Lenses, Crumpler Bags, Tamrac Bags, Velbon Tripods, Slik Tripods, Kenko Scopes, Summit Binoculars, Hoya and Cokin filters. Plus many other product lines.

Address: Unit 1, Priors Way, Maidenhead, Berkshire SL6 2HP; 01628 674 411; (Fax)01628 771 055. e-mail: sales@intro2020.co.uk

www.intro2020.co.uk, www.cokin.co.uk, www.metzflash.co.uk, www.sliktripod.co.uk, www.velbon.co.uk, www.tamrac.co.uk, www. steiner-binoculars.co.uk, www.sliktripod.co.uk

LEICA CAMERA LTD

Company ethos: A passion for developing innovative products that expand the natural limits of the human eye.

Product lines: Ultravid HD (High Definition) Binoculars - for the definitive full size viewing experience. Ultravid & Trinovid Compact Binoculars - small in size, big in performance. Duovid - the world's first dual magnification binocular. Televid APO 82 and 65 Spotting Scopes with angled or straight view. Also available is a new Digital Adapter 3 for digiscoping, Ideal with Leica C-Lux camera but will take other compacts. Premium range of compact digital cameras.

New for 2009: Televid APO Angled 82 & 65 Spotting Scopes plus the world's first 25:50x wide angle zoom eyepiece & a new Digital Adapter 3.

Address: Leica Camera Limited, Davy Avenue, Knowlhill, Milton Keynes MK5 8LB; 01908 256 400;(Fax)01908 671 316.

e-mail: info@leica-camera.co.uk

www.leica-camera.com

NEWPRO UK LTD

Company ethos: Some very well-established and even old brand names with new company technology and attitude.

Product lines: Minox Binoculars, telescopes and cameras, Op/tech straps and harnesses, Cullman tripods, hide clamps and monopods. LensPen optics cleaner.

TRADE DIRECTORY

125

OPITICAL IMPORTERS AND MANUFACTURERS

New for 2009: The Minox DCM - Digital Camera Module for digiscoping.
Opening times: Mon-Fri (8.30am-5pm) plus many outdoor events.
Address: Old Sawmills Road, Faringdon, Oxon SN7 7DS; 01367 242 411; (Fax)01367 241 124.
e-mail: sales@newprouk.co.uk
www.newprouk.co.uk

OPTICRON

Company ethos: To continuously develop high quality binoculars, telescopes and accessories that are useful, ergonomically sound and exceptional value for money.
Product lines: Opticron binoculars, monoculars, telescopes, telephotography/digi-scoping equipment and accessories.
New for 2009: To early to say, but they will be something!

Address: Unit 21, Titan Court, Laporte Way, Luton LU4 8EF; 01582 726 522: (Fax)01582 273 559. e-mail: sales@opticron.co.uk
www.opticron.co.uk

PYSER-SGI LTD
Company ethos:
Our primary aim is customer/dealer care and satisfaction, achieved through technological leadership, quality technical assistance and post-sales service/ support.

Product lines: Pyser-SGI quality binoculars at competitive prices, Kowa Prominar exceptional quality spotting scopes and binoculars including the new TSN-770 and TSN-880 series scopes and Prominar XD binoculars. Swift Sport Optics wide range of binoculars and spotting scopes, including the renowned original Audubon binoculars and New Reliant & Horizon ranges.

New for 2009:
Continuing enhancements to the product ranges.
Address: Fircroft Way, Edenbridge, Kent TN8 6HA; 01732 864 111; (Fax)01732 865 544.
e-mail: sales@pyser-sgi.com
www.pyser-sgi.com

SWAROVSKI UK
Company ethos: Constantly improving on what is good in terms of products and committed to conservation world-wide.
Product lines: EL 42 Swarovision binoculars and ATM/STM telescopes will be introduced during 2009 adding to a market leading range of product. Photo accessories and tripods also available.
Address: Perrywood Business Park, Salfords, Surrey RH1 5JQ; 01737 856 812: (Fax)01737 856 885.
e-mail: info@swarovskioptik.co.uk
www.swarovskioptik.com

SWAROVSKI
OPTIK

VICKERS SPORTS OPTICS
Company ethos: To supply world-leading optical products to UK and Ireland birdwatchers, exclusively distributing Bushnell®, Tasco® and Premierlight® brands to retailers.
Product lines: The extensive Bushnell range offers cutting-edge binoculars, spotting scopes, nightvision equipment and more. Binoculars and spotting scopes by Tasco offer similarly high quality at entry-level. Premierlight LED lighting instruments perform exceptionally, from the hand-held torches to the lanterns.
Other services: UK and Eire returns service.
New for 2009: Innovative new products arriving frequently.
Opening times: Mon-Thu (8.30am-5pm), Fri (8.30am-4.30pm).
Address: Unit 9, 35 Revenge Road, Lordswood, Chatham, Kent ME5 8DW; 01634 201 284.
e-mail: info@jjvickers.co.uk
www.jjvickers.co.uk

OPTICAL DEALERS

OPTICAL DEALERS

EAST MIDLANDS AND EAST ANGLIA

BIRDNET OPTICS LTD

BIRDNET OPTICS LTD
BINOCULARS, TELESCOPES & BOOKS

Company ethos: To provide the birdwatcher with the best value for money on optics, books and outdoor clothing.
Viewing facilities: Clear views to distant hills for comparison of optics at long range and wide variety of textures and edges for clarity and resolution comparison.
Optical stock: Most leading binocular and telescope ranges stocked. If we do not have it in we will endeavour to get it for you.
Non-optical stock: Books incl. New Naturalist Series and Poysers, videos, CDs, audio tapes, tripods, hide clamps, accessories and clothing.
Opening times: Mon-Sat (9:30am-5:30pm). Sundays, see website for details.
Address: 5 London Road, Buxton, Derbyshire SK17 9PA; 01298 71 844. www.birdnet.co.uk e-mail: paulflint@birdnet.co.uk

IN-FOCUS

Company ethos: The binocular and telescope specialists, offering customers informed advice at birdwatching venues throughout the country. Leading sponsor of the British Birdwatchng Fair.
Viewing facilities: Available at all shops (contact your local outlet), or at field events (10am-4pm) at bird reserves (see *Bird Watching* magazine or website www.at-infocus.co.uk for calendar)
Optical stock: Many leading makes of binoculars and telescopes, plus own-brand Delta range of binoculars and tripods.
Non-optical stock: Wide range of tripods, clamps and other accessories. Repair service available.
Opening times: Vary - please contact local shop or website before travelling.

NORFOLK

Address: Main Street, Titchwell, Nr King's Lynn, Norfolk, PE31 8BB; 01485 210 101.

RUTLAND

Address: Anglian Water Birdwatching Centre, Egleton Reserve, Rutland Water, Rutland, LE15 8BT; 01572 770 656.

LONDON CAMERA EXCHANGE

Company ethos: To supply good quality optical equipment at a competitive price, helped by knowlegeable staff.
Viewing facilities: In shop and at local shows. Contact local branch.
Optical stock: All leading makes of binoculars and scopes.
Non-optical stock: All main brands of photo, digital and video equipment.
Opening times: All leading makes of binoculars and scopes.

CHESTERFIELD

Address: 1A South Street, Chesterfield, Derbyshire, S40 1QZ; 01246 211 891; (Fax) 01246 211 563; e-mail: chesterfield@lcegroup.co.uk

COLCHESTER

Address: 12 Led Lane, Colchester, Essex CO1 1LS; 01206 573 444.

DERBY

Address: 17 Sadler Gate, Derby, Derbyshire, DE1 3NH; 01332 348 644; (Fax) 01332 369 136; e-mail: derby@lcegroup.co.uk

LINCOLN

Address: 6 Silver Street, Lincoln, LN2 1DY; 01522 514 131; (Fax) 01522 537 480; e-mail: lincoln@lcegroup.co.uk

NORWICH

Address: 12 Timber Hill, Norwich, Norfolk NR1 3LB; 01603 612 537.

NOTTINGHAM

Address: 7 Pelham Street, Nottingham, NG1 2EH; 0115 941 7486; (Fax) 0115 952 0547; e-mail: nottingham@lcegroup.co.uk

PEAK DISTRICT BINOCULARS

Company ethos: Family-run business offers good service and value with a well defined range of birdwatching optics.
Viewing facilities: Viewing facilities in beautiful rural National Park village.
Optical stock: Stockists of Opticron, Visionary, Olivon, Minox, Hawke, Bresser and a wide range of outdoor clothing and footwear.
Opening times: Mon-Sun (9am-5pm), between April and October, all weekends - please phone midweek in winter to make sure.
Address: The Old Barn, Market Place, Castleton, Hope Valley, Derbyshire SS3 8WQ; 01433 620 999; e-mail: theoldbarn1@btconnect.com www.oldbarncastleton.co.uk

TRADE DIRECTORY

OPTICAL DEALERS

WAREHOUSE EXPRESS

Company ethos: Mail-order and website.
Optical stock: All major brands including, Leica, Swarvoski, Opticron, Kowa, Zeiss, Nikon, Bushnell, Canon, etc.
Non-optical stock: All related accessories including hides, tripods and window mounts etc.
Opening times: Mon-Fri (9am-5pm).
Address: PO Box 659, Norwich, Norfolk, NW3 2WN; 01603 258 012; (Fax) 01603 258 950.
www.warehouseexpress.com

NORTHERN ENGLAND

FOCALPOINT

Company ethos: Friendly advice by well-trained staff, competitive prices, no "grey imports".
Viewing facilities: Fantastic open countryside for superb viewing from the shop, plenty of wildlife. Parking for up to 20 cars.
Optical stock: All leading brands of binoculars and telescopes from stock, plus many pre-owned binoculars and telescopes available.
Non-optical stock: Bird books, outdoor clothing, boots, tripods, plus full range of Skua products etc. available from stock.
Opening times: Mon-Sat (9:30am-5pm).
Address: Marbury House Farm, Bentleys Farm Lane, Higher Whitley, Warrington, Cheshire, WA4 4QW; 01925 730 399; (Fax) 01925 730 368; e-mail: focalpoint@dial.pipex.com
www.focalpointoptics.com

IN-FOCUS

(see entry in Eastern England).

LANCASHIRE

Address: WWT Martin Mere, Burscough, Ormskirk, Lancs, L40 0TA: 01704 897 020.

WEST YORKSHIRE

Address: Westleigh House Office Est. Wakefield Road, Denby Dale, West Yorks, HD8 8QJ: 01484 864 729.

LONDON CAMERA EXCHANGE

(see entry in Eastern England).

CHESTER

Address: 9 Bridge Street Row, CH1 1NW; 01244 326 531.

MANCHESTER

Address: 37 Parker Street, Picadilly, M1 4AJ; 0161 236 5819.

ROTHER VALLEY OPTICS

Company ethos: Selling and distributing binoculars, spotting scopes, telescopes and accessories, we aim to offer very competitive prices and an excellent customer service.
Viewing facilities: Potential buyers can test and try out binoculars and scopes on the premises.
Optical stock: Large stock levels of Nikon, Optricron, Hawke, Audubon, Leupold, Minox, Leica, Swarovski and more.
Opening times: Mon-Fri (9am-5pm); Sat (9.30pm-3pm).
Address: 36 Bridge Street, Killamarsh, Sheffield, South Yorks S21 1AH; (Tel/Fax) 0114 247 6024; e-mail: ian@rothervalleyoptics.com
www.rothervalleyoptics.com

WILKINSON CAMERAS

Company ethos: The widest range of photographic and birdwatching equipment available at competitive prices at all times.
Viewing facilities: Optical field days at selected nature reserves in northern England. See website for details of photographic courses and other events.
Optical stock: Binoculars from Bushnell, Canon, Hawke, Leica, Nikon, RSPB, Steiner, Swarovski, Vanguard and Viking. Spotting scopes from Bushnell, Hawke, Leica, Nikon, Summit, Swarovski and Vanguard. Wide range of bags, digital cameras, lenses and video equipment.
Opening times: Branches open 9am to 5:30pm Monday to Saturday. Sunday 11am to 4pm (Preston only). e-mail: sales@wilkinson.co.uk
www.wilkinson.co.uk

BLACKBURN

42 Northgate, Blackburn, Lancs BB2 1JL: 01254 581 272; (Fax) 01254 695 867.

BURNLEY

95 James Street, Burnley, Lancs BB11 1PY; 01282 424 524; (Fax) 01282 831 722.

BURY

61 The Rock, Bury, Greater Manchester BL9 0NB; 01617 643 402; (Fax) 01617 615 086.

CARLISLE

13 Grapes Lane, Carlisle, Cumbria CA3 8NQ; 01228 538 583; (Fax) 01228 514 699.

KENDAL

19A The Westmorland Centre, Kendal, Cumbria LA9 4AB; 01539 735 055; (Fax) 01539 734 929.

LANCASTER

6 James Street, Lancaster, Lancs LA1 1UP; 01524 380 510; (Fax) 01524 380 512.

OPTICAL DEALERS

PRESTON
27 Friargate, Preston, Lancs PR1 2NQ; 01772 556 250; (Fax) 01772 259 435.

SOUTHPORT
38 Eastbank Street, Southport, Merseyside, PR8 1ET. 01704 534 534; (Fax) 01704 501 546; e-mail: southport@wilkinson.co.uk

SOUTH EAST ENGLAND

IN-FOCUS
(see entry in Eastern England).

ST ALBANS
Address: Bowmans Farm, London Colney, St Albans, Herts, AL2 1BB: 01727 827 799: (Fax) 01727 827 766.

SOUTH WEST LONDON
Address: WWT The Wetland Centre, Queen Elizabeth Walk, Barnes, London, SW13 9WT: 020 8409 4433.

LONDON CAMERA EXCHANGE
(see entry in Eastern England).

FAREHAM
Address: 135 West Street, Fareham, Hampshire, PO16 0DU; 01329 236 441; (Fax) 01329 823 294; e-mail: fareham@lcegroup.co.uk

GUILDFORD
Address: 8/9 Tunsgate, Guildford, Surrey, GU1 2DH; 01483 504 040; (Fax) 01483 538 216; e-mail: guildford@lcegroup.co.uk

PORTSMOUTH
Address: 40 Kingswell Path, Cascados, Portsmouth, PO1 4RR; 023 9283 9933; (Fax) 023 9283 9955; e-mail: portsmouth@lcegroup.co.uk

READING
Address: 7 Station Road, Reading, Berkshire, RG1 1LG; 0118 959 2149; (Fax) 0118 959 2197; e-mail: reading@lcegroup.co.uk

SOUTHAMPTON
Address: 10 High Street, Southampton, Hampshire, SO14 2DH; 023 8022 1597; (Fax) 023 8023 3838; e-mail: southampton@lcegroup.co.uk

STRAND, LONDON
Address: 98 The Strand, London, WC2R 0AG; 020 7379 0200; (Fax) 020 7379 6991; e-mail: strand@lcegroup.co.uk

WINCHESTER
Address: 15 The Square, Winchester, Hampshire, SO23 9ES; 01962 866 203; (Fax)01962 840 978; e-mail: winchester@lcegroup.co.uk

SOUTH WEST ENGLAND

ACE CAMERAS
Company ethos: To be the best - service, price and stock.
Viewing facilities: Bird of prey and Leica test card to check quality at 100 metres.
Optical stock: All the top brands, including Questar and Avian.
Non-optical stock: All the best tripods and an array of optical related accessories.
Opening times: Mon-Sat (8:45am-6pm).
Address: 16 Green Street, Bath, BA1 2JZ; 01225 466 364; (Fax) 01225 469 761.
e-mail: optics@acecameras.co.uk
www.acecameras.co.uk

LONDON CAMERA EXCHANGE
(see entry in Eastern England).

BATH
Address: 13 Cheap Street, Bath, Avon, BA1 1NB; 01225 462 234; (Fax) 01225 480 334.
e-mail: bath@lcegroup,co.uk

BOURNEMOUTH
Address: 95 Old Christchurch Road, Bournemouth, Dorset, BH1 1EP; 01202 556 549; (Fax) 01202 293 288;
e-mail: bournemouth@lcegroup.co.uk

BRISTOL
Address: 53 The Horsefair, Bristol, BS1 3JP; 0117 927 6185; (Fax) 0117 925 8716;
e-mail: bristol.horsefair@lcegroup.co.uk

EXETER
Address: 174 Fore Street, Exeter, Devon, EX4 3AX; 01392 279 024/438 167; (Fax) 01392 426 988. e-mail: exeter@lcegroup.co.uk

PAIGNTON
Address: 71 Hyde Road, Paington, Devon, TQ4 5BP;01803 553 077; (Fax) 01803 664 081.
e-mail: paignton@lcegroup.co.uk

PLYMOUTH
Address: 10 Frankfort Gate, Plymouth, Devon, PL1 1QD; 01752 668 894; (Fax) 01752 604248.
e-mail: plymouth@lcegroup.co.uk

OPTICAL DEALERS

SALISBURY
Address: 6 Queen Street, Salisbury, Wiltshire, SP1 1EY; 01722 335 436; (Fax) 01722 411 670; e-mail: salisbury@lcegroup.co.uk

TAUNTON
Address: 6 North Street, Taunton, Somerset, TA1 1LH; 01823 259955; (Fax) 01823 338 001. e-mail: taunton@lcegroup.co.uk

---

WESTERN ENGLAND AND WEST MIDLANDS

FOCUS OPTICS
Company ethos: Friendly, expert service. Top quality instruments. No 'grey imports'.
Viewing facilities: Our own pool and nature reserve with feeding stations.
Optical stock: Full range of leading makes of binoculars and telescopes.
Non-optical stock: Waterproof clothing, fleeces, walking boots and shoes, bird food and feeders. Books, videos, walking poles.
Opening times: Mon-Sat (9am-5pm). Some bank holidays.
Address: Church Lane, Corley, Coventry, CV7 8BA; 01676 540 501/542 476; (Fax) 01676 540 930. e-mail: focopt1@aol.com
www.focusoptics.co.uk

IN-FOCUS
(see entry in Eastern England).

GLOUCESTERSHIRE
Address: WWT Slimbridge, Gloucestershire, GL2 7BT: 01453 890 978. 22314; (Fax) 01905 724 585; e-mail: worcester@lcegroup.co.uk

LONDON CAMERA EXCHANGE
(see entry in Eastern England).

CHELTENHAM
Address: 10-12 The Promenade, Cheltenham, Gloucestershire, GL50 1LR; 01242 519 851; (Fax) 01242 576 771; e-mail: cheltenham@lcegroup.co.uk

GLOUCESTER
Address: 12 Southgate Street, Gloucester, GL1 2DH; 01452 304 513; (Fax) 01452 387 309; e-mail: gloucester@lcegroup.co.uk

LEAMINGTON
Address: Clarendon Avenue, Leamington, Warwickshire, CV32 5PP; 01926 886 166; (Fax)01926 887 611; e-mail: leamington@lcegroup.co.uk

WORCESTER
Address: 8 Pump Street, Worcester, WR1 2QT; 01905 22314; (Fax) 01905 724 585; e-mail: worcester@lcegroup.co.uk

---

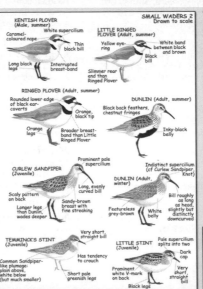

BIRD RESERVES AND OBSERVATORIES

Dundrum Bay by David Cromack

Why not widen your birdwatching horizons by visiting some new reserves in 2009? Here we detail more than 400 sites for you to explore – the information is updated each year, making it the most up-to-date guide covering the whole of Britain.

To reflect birdwatchers' growing interest in other flora and fauna, we have asked information providers for each site to highlight key mammal, insect and plant species – and elsewhere in this edition (pages 94 to 95) you can record your butterfly and dragonfly sightings.

Bedfordshire

1. BEGWARY BROOK

Beds, Cambs, Northants and Peterborough Wildlife Trust.
Location: TL 169 564. 2 miles S of St Neots. From A1 S take A428 E and continue to Wyboston Lakes complex. Pass through complex and follow nature reserve signs to car park.
Access: Open all year. Partially suitable for wheelchairs.
Facilities: None.
Public transport: Bus, St Neots to Sandy, some stop in Wyboston (Saffords Coaches - 01767 677 395).
Habitat: Former gravel pit. Marsh and open pools next to Great Ouse.
Key birds: Wildfowl and wader species. *Spring*: Sedge, Reed and Willow Warblers, Blackcap. *All year*: Reed Bunting, Kingfisher, Goldcrest.
Other notable flora and fauna: Orange-tip and speckled wood butterflies, dragonflies and grass snakes. Plants include great burnet, common fleabane and marsh woundwort.
Contact: Beds, Cambs, Northants and Peterborough Wildlife Trust, The Manor House, Broad Street, Great Cambourne, Cambridgeshire CB3 6DH. 01954 713 500; Fax 01954 710 051. www.wildlifebcnp.org e-mail:cambridgeshire@wildlifebcnp.org

2. BLOW'S DOWNS

Beds, Cambs, Northants and Peterborough Wildlife Trust.
Location: TL 033 216. On the outskirts of Dunstable. Take A5065 from W of Luton, cross M1, take first exit at roundabout, park with care on verge. Can also walk half mile from Dunstable centre to W entrance at Half Moon Lane off A5.
Access: Open all year, not suitable for wheelchairs.
Facilities: None.
Public transport: None.
Habitat: SSSI, chalk downland, scrub and grassland. This is a traditional resting place for incoming spring migrants.
Key birds: *Winter*: Lapwing, Meadow Pipit, Sky Lark, Stonechat. *Spring/autumn*: Ring Ouzel, Wheatear, Whinchat, Black Redstart, Stonechat, Willow Warbler.
Other notable flora and fauna: Chalkhill blue, brown argus and marbled white butterflies. Plants include small scabious, burnet-saxifrage, great pignut, common spotted and bee orchids.
Contact: Trust HQ. 01954 713 500; www.wildlifebcnp.org

3. FLITWICK MOOR

Beds, Cambs, Northants and Peterborough Wildlife Trust.
Location: TL 046 354. E of Flitwick. From Flitwick

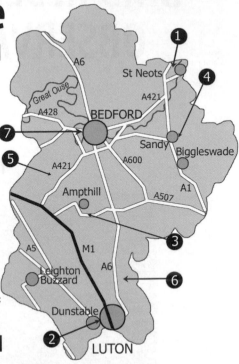

town centre (Tesco roundabout) on A5120, cross railway bridge, R at roundabout, immediately L into King's Road. After 500m, L into Moulden Road towards A507. After quarter mile R at Folly Farm, follow track to small car park. Also footpath to reserve from Moor Lane.
Access: Open all year.
Facilities: Car park. Please stick to public paths.
Public transport: Frequent buses (United Counties) from Bedford and Luton to Flitwick, or take train to Flitwick and then three-quarter mile walk.
Habitat: SSSI. Important wetland for the area, blend of fen, meadow, wet woodland and fragile peaty soil. Supports mosses ferns and flowers.
Key birds: *Winter*: Siskin, Water Rail, Great Spotted Woodpecker. *Spring*: Lesser Spotted Woodpecker, Willow Warbler, Blackcap. *Summer*: Water Rail, Grasshopper and Garden Warblers, Cuckoo. *Autumn*: Brambling.
Other notable flora and fauna: Good variety of butterflies and dragonflies, plus chimney sweeper moth and conehead bush cricket. Plants include nine species of sphagnum moss, marsh pennywort, black knapweed, water figwort plus fly agaric and yellow brain fungus in autumn.
Contact: Contact: Trust HQ. 01954 713 500; www.wildlifebcnp.org

4. LODGE (THE)

RSPB (Eastern England Office).
Location: TL 190 479. Reserve lies 1 mile/1.6km E of Sandy on the B1042 to Potton.
Access: Reserve is open daily 9am-9pm (or sunset when earlier); shop 9am-5pm weekdays, 10am-5pm weekends.
Facilities: Nature trails being extended to 5 miles, one bridleway (half mile) and gardens wheelchair/pushchair accessible. One hide (wheelchair accessible), parking 50 yards. Coach parking at weekends by arrangement.
Public transport: Buses to Sandy Market Square from Bedford, infrequent service. One mile walk or cycle from centre of Sandy or half mile from Sandy railway station, in part along trail through heathland restoration.
Habitat: This reserve is a mixture of woodland, heathland, and includes the formal gardens of the RSPB's UK headquarters. New land being restored to heathland.
Key birds: *Spring/summer*: Hobby, Spotted Flycatcher. *All year*: Woodpeckers, woodland birds.
Other notable flora and fauna: Natterjack toads, rare heathland insects. Particularly good site for fungi, and lichens. Garden pools are good for dragonflies.
Contact: RSPB, 01767 680 541. www.rspb.org.uk

5. MARSTON VALE MILLENNIUM COUNTRY PARK

Marston Vale Trust (Regd Charity No 1069229).
Location: SW of Bedford off A421 at Marston Moretaine. Only five mins from J13 of M1.
Access: Park and forest centre open seven days. Summer 10am-6pm, winter 10am-4pm. No dogs in wetlands reserve, rest of site OK for dogs and horses. Main 8km trail surfaced for wheelchair and pushchair access. All-terrain wheelchairs available for free loan. Coaches fine.
Facilities: Cafe bar, gift shop, art gallery, exhibition. Free parking.
Public transport: Bedford to Bletchley line - trains to Millbrook and Stewartby station, 20 minute walk to Forest Centre.
Habitat: Lake – 610 acres/freshwater marsh (man-made), reedbed, woodland, hawthorn scrub and grassland.
Key birds: *Winter*: Iceland and Glaucous Gulls (regular), gull roost, wildfowl, Great Crested Grebe. *Spring*: Passage waders and terns (Black Tern, Arctic Tern), Garganey. *Summer*: Nine species of breeding warblers, Hobby, Turtle Dove, Nightingale, Bearded Tit. *Autumn*: Passage waders and terns. *Rarities*: White-winged Black Tern, divers, Manx Shearwater, Bittern.
Other notable flora and fauna: Dingy and grizzled skipper butterflies, excellent for dragonflies (red-veined darter in 2007). Also otter and brown hare plus bluebells, bee and pyramidal orchids and stoneworts.
Contact: Forest Centre, 01234 767 037.
e-mail: info@marstonvale.org   www.marstonvale.org

6. PEGSDON HILL RESERVE

Beds, Cambs, Northants and Peterborough Wildlife Trust.
Location: TL 120 295. 5 miles W of Hitchin. Take B655 from Hitchin towards Barton-le-Clay. Turn R at Pegsdon then immediately L and park in lay by. Reserve entrance across B655 via footpath.
Access: Open all year. Dropping-off point for coaches only.
Facilities: None.
Public transport: Luton to Henlow buses (United Counties) stop at Pegsdon.
Habitat: Chalk grassland, scrub and woodland.
Key birds: *Winter*: Brambling, Stonechat, winter thrushes, raptors including Buzzard. *Spring*: Wheatear, Ring Ouzel, Tree Pipit, Yellowhammer. *Summer*: Turtle Dove, Grey Partridge, Lapwing, Sky Lark.
Other notable flora and fauna: Dark green fritillary, dingy and grizzled skippers, chalkhill blue, brown argus and small heath butterflies. Glow worms. Plants include pasqueflower in spring, fragrant and common spotted orchids.
Contact: Contact: Trust HQ. 01954 713 500; e-mail:cambridgeshire@wildlifebcnp.org www.wildlifebcnp.org

7. PRIORY COUNTRY PARK AND MARINA

Bedford Borough Council.
Location: TL 071 495. 1.5 miles SE from Bedford town centre. Signposted from A428 and A421. Entry point to new 'River Valley Park'
Access: Park and hides open at all times. No access to fenced/gated plantations.
Facilities: Toilets and visitor centre open daytime, disabled access to hides, nature trails, labyrinth, cycle hire, Premier Inn (meals, accomodation).
Public transport: Stagecoach (01604 676 060) – 'Blue Solo 4' every 20 mins. Mon-Sat. Alight 1st stop Riverfield Drive (200 m). Rail station – Bedford (approx 2.5 miles)
Habitat: Lakes, reedbeds, scrub and woodland, meadows – adjoining Great Ouse.
Key birds: Good numbers/variety winter wildfowl, varied mix of spring passage species, with a variety of breeding warblers and woodpeckers, augmented by feeding terns, hirundines and raptors lakeside. *Winter*: Grebes, Pochard, Shoveler, Gadwall, Merlin, Water Rail, gulls, thrushes, Chiffchaff, corvids, buntings. *Passage*: Raptors, waders, terns, pipits. *Summer*: Hobby, Turtle Dove, Swift, hirundines, *acrocephalus* and *sylvia* warblers. *All year*: Cormorant, Little Egret, Heron, Stock Dove, woodpeckers, Kingfisher, Grey Wagtail, Treecreeper, Goldfinch, Bullfinch.
Other notable flora and fauna: 23 species of dragonfly, incl small red-eyed damsel and hairy hawker. 20 species of butterfly. Large plant list. Fox, muntjac and otter.
Contact: Jon Bishop, Wardens Office, Visitor Centre, Priory CP, Barkers Lane, Bedford, MK41 9SH. 01234 211 182.

Berkshire

1. DINTON PASTURES

Wokingham District Council.
Location: SU 784 718. Country Park, E of Reading off B3030 between Hurst and Winnersh.
Access: Open all year, dawn to dusk.
Facilities: Hides, information centre, car park, café, toilets. Suitable for wheelchairs.
Public transport: Not known.
Habitat: Mature gravel pits and banks of River Loddon.
Key birds: Kingfisher, Water Rail, Little Ringed Plover, Common Tern, Nightingale. *Winter*: Wildfowl (inc. Goldeneye, Wigeon, Teal, Gadwall).
Contact: Dave Webster, Ranger, Dinton Pastures Country Park, Davis Street, Hurst, Berks. 0118 934 2 016. e-mail:countryside@wokingham.gov.uk

2. LAVELL'S LAKE

Wokingham District Council.
Location: SU 781 729. 46 acre Conservation Area one mile N of Dinton Pastures. Via Sandford Lane off B3030 between Hurst and Winnersh, E of Reading.
Access: Dawn to dusk. No permit required.
Facilities: New Tern Hide open to public.
Public transport: Information not available.
Habitat: Gravel pits, two wader scapes, although one congested with *crassula helmsii*, rough grassland, marshy area, between River Loddon, Emm Brook. To N of Lavell's Lake, gravel pits are being restored and attact birds. A lake is viewable walking N along River Lodden from Lovell's Lake over small green bridge. The lake is in a field immediately on R but is only viewable through hedge. No access is permitted.
Key birds: *All year*: Sparrowhawk. *Summer*: Garganey, Common Tern, Redshank, Lapwing, Hobby, Red Kite, Peregrine, Buzzard. *Passage* waders. *Winter*: Green Sandpiper, ducks (inc. Smew), Bittern.
Other notable flora and fauna: Grass snake, variety of dragonflies and bats.
Contact: Ranger, Dinton Pastures Country Park, Davis Street, Hurst, Berks. 0118 934 2 016. Friends of Lavell's Lake (www.foll.org.uk)

3. HUNGERFORD MARSH

Berks, Bucks and Oxon Wildlife Trust.
Location: SU 333 687. On W side of Hungerford, beside the Kennet and Avon Canal. From town centre, go along Church Street past the town hall. Turn R under the railway. Follow public footpath over swing bridge on the canal near the church. The reserve is separated from Freeman's Marsh by a line of willows and bushes.
Access: Open all year. Please keep to the footpath. Dogs on leads please.
Facilities: Car park.
Public transport: None.
Habitat: Unimproved rough grazing and reedbed.
Key birds: *Spring/summer:* Reed Warbler. *Winter:* Siskin. *All year:* Mute Swan, Mallard. Birds seen in the last ten years include Kingfisher, Yellow Wagtail, Water Rail and Grasshopper Warbler.
Contact: BBOWT, The Lodge, 1 Armstrong Road, Littlemore, Oxford OX4 4XT. 01865 775 476. www.bbowt.org.uk

4. MOOR GREEN LAKES

Blackwater Valley Countryside Partnership.
Location: SU 805 628. Main access and parking off Lower Sandhurst Road, Finchampstead. Alternatively, Rambler's car park, Mill Lane, Sandhurst (SU 820 619).
Access: Car parks open dawn-dusk. Two bird hides open to members of the Moor Green Lakes Group (contact BVCP for details). Dogs on leads. Site can be used by people in wheelchairs, though surface not particularly suitable.
Facilities: Two bird hides, footpaths around site, Blackwater Valley Long Distance Path passes through site.
Public transport: Nearest bus stop, Finchampstead (approx 1.5 miles from main entrance). Local bus companies – Stagecoach Hants and Surrey, tel 01256 464 501, First Beeline and Londonlink, tel 01344 424 938.
Habitat: Thirty-six hectares (90 acres) in total. Three lakes with gravel islands, beaches and scrapes. River Blackwater, grassland, surrounded by willow, ash, hazel and thorn hedgerows.
Key birds: *Spring/summer:* Redshank, Little Ringed Plover, Sand Martin, Willow Warbler, and of particular

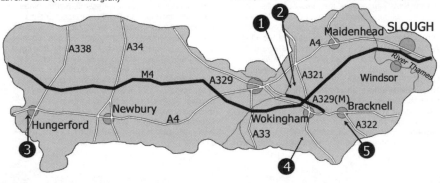

interest, a flock of Goosander. Also Whitethroat, Sedge Warbler, Common Sandpiper, Common Tern, Dunlin and Black Tern. Lapwings breed on site and several sightings of Red Kite. *Winter*: Ruddy Duck, Wigeon, Teal, Gadwall.

Other notable flora and fauna: Harvest mouse, five species of bat, good variety of dragonflies.

Contact: Blackwater VCP, Ash Lock Cottage, Government Road, Aldershot, Hants, GU11 2PS. 01252 331 353. e-mail: blackwater.valley@hants.gov.uk www.blackwater-valley.org.uk Moor Green Lakes Group (www.mglg.org.uk).

5. WILDMOOR HEATH

Berks, Bucks and Oxon Wildlife Trust.
Location: SU 842 627. Between Bracknell and Sandhurst. From Sandhurst shopping area, take the

A321 NW towards Wokingham. Turn E at the mini-roundabout on to Crowthorne Road. Continue for about one mile through one set of traffic lights. Car park is on the R at the bottom of the hill.

Access: Open all year. No access to woodland N of Rackstraw Road at Broadmoor Bottom. Please keep dogs on a lead.

Facilities: Car park.

Public transport: Train station at Sandhurst.

Habitat: Wet and dry lowland heath, bog, mixed woodland and mature Scots pine plantation.

Key birds: *Spring/summer*: Hobby, Wood Lark, Nightjar, Dartford Warbler, Stonechat.

Other notable flora and fauna: Sand lizard, reintroduced in 2002. Natterjack toad , adder, smooth snake. Good for dragonflies with 22 species recorded.

Contact: BBOWT, 01865 775 476. www.bbowt.org.uk

Buckinghamshire

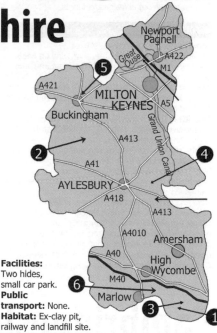

1. BURNHAM BEECHES NATIONAL NATURE RESERVE

City of London.
Location: SU 950 850. N of Slough and on W side of A355, running between J2 of the M40 and J6 of M4. Entry from A355 via Beeches Road. Also smaller parking areas in Hawthorn Lane and Pumpkin Hill to the S and Park Lane to the W.

Access: Open all year. Main Lord Mayor's Drive open from 8am-dusk.

Facilities: Car parks, toilets, café, visitor information centre. Easy access path network, suitable for wheelchairs – most start at Victory Cross. Coach parking possible, additional coach parking on request.

Public transport: Train: nearest station Slough (main line from Paddington). Buses stop in Farnham Common (between Slough and Beaconsfield), Beeline, London and Country 0870 608 2608.

Habitat: Ancient woodland, streams, pools, heathland, grassland, scrub.

Key birds: *Spring/summer*: Cuckoo, possible Turtle Dove and woodland species. *Winter*: Siskin, Crossbill, regular large flocks c100 Brambling. Possible Woodcock. *All year*: Mandarin (good population), all three woodpeckers, Sparrowhawk, Marsh Tit, possible Willow Tit, Red Kite and Buzzard.

Contact: City of London Corporation, Burnham Beeches Office, Hawthorn Lane, Farnham Common, SL2 3TE. 01753 647 358. www.cityoflondon.gov.uk e-mail: burnham.beeches@cityoflondon.gov.uk

2. CALVERT JUBILEE

Berks, Bucks and Oxon Wildlife Trust.
Location: SP 849 425. Near Steeple Claydon, NW of Aylesbury, Bucks.

Access: Access by permit (free) only. Apply to Trust who provide map and information with permit. Please keep to network of paths.

Facilities: Two hides, small car park.

Public transport: None.

Habitat: Ex-clay pit, railway and landfill site. Now with deep lake, marginal reedbed and scrub habitat.

Key birds: *Summer*: Nesting Common Tern, Kingfisher, warblers, occasional Nightingale, Lapwing. Passage migrants include Black-tailed Godwit, Greenshank. *Winter*: Bittern, Water Rail, Lesser Black-backed Gull roost. Wigeon. Rarer birds turn up regularly.

Other notable flora and fauna: Rare butterflies, including dingy and grizzled skippers.

Contact: Wildlife Trust HQ, BBOWT, 01865 775 476. www.bbowt.org.uk

3. CHURCH WOOD RSPB RESERVE

RSPB Midlands Regional Office.
Location: SU 972 872. Reserve lies three miles from J2 of M40 in Hedgerley. Park in village, walk down small track beside pond for approx 200m. Reserve entrance is on L.
Access: Open all year. Not suitable for wheelchair users.
Facilities: Two marked paths with some inclines.
Public transport: None.
Habitat: Mixed woodland.
Key birds: *Spring/summer*: Red Kite, Buzzard, Blackcap, Garden Warbler, Swallow. *Winter*: Redpoll, Siskin. *All year*: Marsh Tit, Willow Tit, Nuthatch, Great Spotted and Green Woodpeckers.
Other notable flora and fauna: Bluebells, wildflower meadow.
Contact: RSPB Midlands Regional Office, 01295 253 330. www.rspb.org.uk/wildlife/reserves

4. COLLEGE LAKE

Berks, Bucks and Oxon Wildlife Trust.
Location: SU 934 140. 2 miles N of Tring on B488, 1/4 miles N of canal bridge at Bulbourne turn L into gated entrance.
Access: Open Apr-Oct (10am-5pm); Nov-Mar (10am-4pm), closed Mondays. Wheelchair access to hides and disabled toilets.
Facilities: Large car park, coach park, many hides, interpretive buildings. Network of wheelchair-friendly paths, visitor centre, toilets.
Public transport: Tring railway station, 2 miles walk.
Habitat: Deep lake in former chalk pit, shallow pools, wet, chalk and rough grasslands, scrub.
Key birds: *Spring/summer*: Lapwing, Redshank, Little Ringed Plover, Sand Martin, Hobby, Common Tern, Sky Lark. *Winter*: Wildfowl (Wigeon, Shoveler, Teal, Gadwall), waders, inc. Snipe, Peregrine Falcon.
Other notable flora and fauna: Orchids including white helleborines, bee and fragrant. Chalk grassland flowers. Butterflies include small blue and skippers. Good numbers of dragonflies (16 species). Hares.
Contact: The Warden, College Lake, Upper Icknield

Way, Bulbourne, Tring, Herts HP23 5QG. 01442 826 774; (M)07711 821 303.

5. FOXCOTE RESERVOIR

Berks, Bucks and Oxon Wildlife Trust/Anglian Water.
Location: Reservoir is one mile NE of Buckingham, off A422 on a lane between Maids Moreton and Leckhampstead. Map and details sent with permit.
Access: Open all year. Access to hide by permit only – these are available free of charge from BBOWT.
Facilities: Hides.
Public transport: None.
Habitat: Open water.
Key birds: *Spring*: Common Tern, Hobby, Common Sandpiper, Corn Bunting. *Summer*: Spotted Flycatcher at Hydelane, warblers, Common Tern, ducks, Great Crested and Little Grebes. *Winter*: Water Rail, duck, inc. Wigeon and Goldeneye, Goosander. *All year*: Sparrowhawk, Kingfisher, Little and Tawny Owls, Grey Wagtail, Green and Great Spotted Woodpeckers, Marsh Tit, Jay.
Contact: BBOWT, 01865 775 476.

6. LITTLE MARLOW GRAVEL PITS

Lefarge Redland Aggregates.
Location: SU 876 876 (large sand pit). NE of Marlow from J4 of M40. Use permissive path from Coldmoorholm Lane to Little Marlow village. Follow path over a wooden bridge to N end of lake. Permissive path ends just past the cottages where it joins a concrete road to sewage treatment works.
Access: Open all year. Please do not enter the gravel works. Heavy lorries use concrete road from gravel workings – use footpath to N of road.
Facilities: Paths.
Public transport: None.
Habitat: Gravel pit, lake, scrub.
Key birds: *Spring*: Passage migrants, Sand Martin, Garganey, Hobby. *Summer*: Reedbed warblers, Kingfisher, wildfowl. *Autumn*: Passage migrants. *Winter*: Wildfowl, possible Smew, Goldeneye, Yellow-legged Gull in large gull roost, Lapwing, Snipe.
Contact: Buckinghamshire Bird Club organise work parties (www.bucksbirdsclub.co.uk).

Cambridgeshire

1. BRAMPTON WOOD

Beds, Cambs, Northants and Peterborough Wildlife Trust.
Location: TL 184 698. 4 miles W of Huntingdon. From A1 take A14 exit towards Huntingdon. Take first exit off A14 to Brampton (B1514). Go straight at first roundabout then R at second. Turn R at T-junction onto Grafham road, go through village, over A1,

reserve is on N side of road 1.5 miles out of Brampton. Park in small car park.
Access: Open daily. Coaches able to drop passengers off but unfortunately there is not sufficient space available for parking.
Facilities: Car park, interpretative shelter.
Public transport: Bus from Huntingdon to Brampton, then 2 mile walk.
Habitat: Ancient woodland, primarily oak, ash and

field maple with hazel coppice.

Key birds: *Autumn/winter*: Marsh Tit, woodcock, winter thrushes. *Spring/ summer*: Common woodland birds, Green Woodpecker, Spotted Flycatcher.

Other notable flora and fauna: Brown argus, white admiral and black hairstreak butterflies, pine beauty and pine hawk moths. Dormouse, glow worms, smooth and great crested newts, plus various dragonfly species. Plants include meadow grasses, cowslip, yellow rattle, devil's-bit scabious, primrose, hairy and trailing St John's wort.

Contact: Beds, Cambs, Northants and Peterborough Wildlife Trust, 01954 713 500; www.wildlifebcnp.org e-mail:cambridgeshire@wildlifebcnp.org

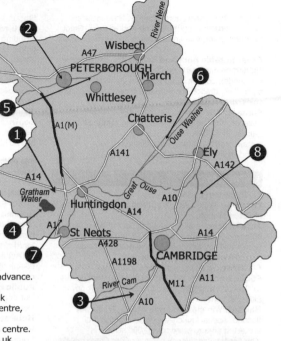

2. FERRY MEADOWS COUNTRY PARK

Nene Park Trust.

Location: TL 145 975. 500 acre site at heart of Nene Park. Three miles W of Peterborough town centre, signed off A605.

Access: Open all year. Electric scooters and wheelchair available for loan – call to book in advance. Coach parking free at all times.

Facilities: Car park (fee at weekends and bank holidays between April 1 and Oct 30). Visitor centre, toilets, café, two hides in nature reserve area.

Public transport: Stagecoach X14 from town centre. Traveline 0870 6082 608 or www.traveline.org.uk

Habitat: Lakes, meadows, scrub, broadleaved woodland and small wetland nature reserve.

Key birds: *Spring*: Terns, waders, Yellow Wagtail. *Winter*: Grebes, Siskin, Redpoll, Water Rail, occasional Hawfinch. *All year*: Good selection of woodland and water birds, Kingfisher. CES ringing site.

Contact: Visitor Services Officer, Nene Park Trust, Ham Farm House, Orton, Peterborough, PE2 5UU. 01733 234 443. www.nene-park-trust.org.uk e-mail:visitor.services@nene-park-trust.org.uk

3. FOWLMERE

RSPB (Eastern England Office).

Location: TL 407 461. 7 miles S of Cambridge. Turn off A10 Cambridge to Royston road by Shepreth and follow sign.

Access: Access at all times along marked trail.

Facilities: One and a half miles of trails. Three hides, toilets. Space for one coach, prior booking essential. Wheelchair access to one hide, toilet and some of the trails.

Public transport: Shepreth railway station 2 miles.

Habitat: Reedbeds, meres, woodland, scrub.

Key birds: *Summer*: Nine breeding warblers. *All year*: Water Rail, Kingfisher. *Winter*: Snipe, raptors.

Other notable flora and fauna: Healthy population of water shrews. 18 species of dragonfly recorded.

Contact: The Warden, RSPB, Manor Farm, High Street, Fowlmere, Royston, Herts SG8 7SH. Tel/Fax 01763 208 978.

4. GRAFHAM WATER

Beds, Cambs, Northants and Peterborough Wildlife Trust.

Location: TL 143 671. Follow signs for Grafham Water from A1 at Buckden or A14 at Ellington. Nature Reserve entrance is from Mander car park, W of Perry village.

Access: Open all year. Dogs barred in wildlife garden only, on leads elsewhere. Car parking £2 for day ticket.

Facilities: Five bird hides in nature reserve, two in the bird sanctuary area. Two hides in wildlife garden accessible to wheelchairs. Cycle track through reserve also accessible to wheelchairs. Visitor centre with restaurant, shop and toilets. Disabled parking. Use Plummer car park for lagoons and Marlow car park for the dam area (good for waders and vagrants).

Public transport: Bus, St Neots to Bedford. Get off at Great Staughton then 2 mile walk.

Habitat: Open water, settlement lagoons ranging from reedbeds, open water, wet mud and willow carr, ancient and plantation woodland, scrub, species rich grassland.

Key birds: *Resident*: Common woodland birds, wildfowl. *Winter*: Waders including Common Sandpiper and Dunlin, Great Crested Grebe, Wildfowl including large flocks of Tufted Duck and Coot, Pochard, Shoveler, Shelduck, Goldeneye, Goosander and Smew, gulls (can be up to 30,000 roosting in mid-winter). *Spring/summer*: Breeding Nightingale, Reed, Willow and Sedge Warblers, Common and Black Terns.

Autumn: Passage waders. *Rarities*: Have included Wilson's Phalarope (2007), Ring-necked Duck, Great Northern Diver, Glaucous, Iceland and Mediterranean Gulls.

Other notable flora and fauna: Bee and common spotted orchids, early purple orchid, common twyblade (in woods), cowslip. Common blue and marbled white butterflies, dragonflies including broad-bodied chaser, voles, grass snakes.

Contact: The Warden, Grafham Water Nature Reserve, c/o The Lodge, West Perry, Huntingdon, Cambs, PE28 0BX. 01480 811 075.
e-mail: matt.hamilton@wildlifebcnp.org
www.wildlifetrust.org.uk/bcnp

5. NENE WASHES

RSPB (Eastern England Office).
Location: TL 300 995. N of Whittlesey and six miles E of Peterborough.
Access: Open at all times along South Barrier Bank, accessed at Eldernell, one mile NE of Coates, off A605. Group visits by arrangement. No access to fields. No access for wheelchairs along bank.
Facilities: Small car park - one coach max.
Public transport: Bus and trains to Whittlesey, bus to Coates – alight by council houses and walk down Eldernell Lane.
Habitat: Wet grassland with ditches. Frequently flooded. Appeal launched to fund expansion of protected area to more than 2,000 acres.
Key birds: *Spring/early summer*: Corn Crake release scheme. Breeding waders, including Black-tailed Godwit, duck, including Garganey, Marsh Harrier and Hobby. *Winter*: Waterfowl including Bewick's Swan and Pintail, Barn Owl, Hen Harrier.
Contact: Charlie Kitchin, 21a East Delph, Whittlesey, Cambs PE7 1RH. 01733 205 140.

6. OUSE WASHES

RSPB (Eastern England Office).
Location: TL 471 861. Between Chatteris and March (ten miles from each) on A141, take B1093 to Manea. Reserve signposted from Manea . Reserve office and visitor centre located off Welches Dam.
Access: Access at all times from visitor centre (open every day except Christmas Day and Boxing Day). Welches Dam to public hides approached by marked paths behind boundary bank. No charge. Dogs to be kept on leads at all times. Disabled access to Welches Dam hide, 350 yards from car park.
Facilities: Car park and toilets. Space for up to two coaches. Visitor centre – unmanned but next to reserve office. Ten hides overlooking the reserve: nearest 350 yards from visitor centre (with disabled access) and furthest one mile from visitor centre. Boardwalk good for dragonflies in summer.
Public transport: No public transport to reserve entrance. Train station at Manea — three miles from reserve.
Habitat: Lowland wet grassland – seasonally flooded. Open pool systems in front of some hides, particularly

Stockdale's hide.
Key birds: *Summer*: Around 70 species breed including Black-tailed Godwit, Lapwing, Redshank, Snipe, Shoveler, Gadwall, Garganey and Spotted Crake. Also Hobby and Marsh Harrier. *Autumn*: Passage waders including Wood and Green Sandpipers, Spotted Redshank, Greenshank, Little Stint, plus terns and Marsh and Hen Harrier. *Winter*: Large numbers of Bewick's and Whooper Swans, Wigeon, Teal, Shoveler, Pintail, Pochard.
Contact: Jon Reeves, (Site Manager), Ouse Washes Reserve, Welches Dam, Manea, March, Cambs, PE15 0NF. 01354 680 212. e-mail: jon.reeves@rspb.org.uk

7. PAXTON PITS NATURE RESERVE

Huntingdonshire District Council.
Location: TL 197 629. Access from A1 at Little Paxton (sharp left off slip road), two miles N of St Neots.
Access: Free Entry. Open 24 hours. Visitor centre open 7 days a week. Dogs allowed under control. Heron trail suitable for wheelchairs during summer.
Facilities: Visitors centre provides light refreshments. Toilets available most days 9am-5pm (including disabled), two bird hides (always open), marked nature trails.
Public transport: Buses run from St Neots and Huntingdon to Little Paxton (enquiries 0845 045 5200). Nearest train station is St Neots (08457 484 950).
Habitat: Grassland, scrub, lakes.
Key birds: *Spring/summer*: Nightingale, Kingfisher, Common Tern, Sparrowhawk, Hobby, Grasshopper, Sedge and Reed Warblers, Lesser Whitethroat. *Winter*: Smew, Goldeneye, Goosander, Gadwall, Pochard.
Other notable flora and fauna: Wildflowers, butterflies and dragonflies in abundance. Meadow trail has common spotted and pyrimidal orchids. Bee ordchids are found around the car park. Otters use the reserve.
Contact: Kirsty Drew, The Rangers, The Visitor Centre, High Street, Little Paxton, St Neots, Cambs, PE19 6ET. 01480 406 795. www.paxton-pits.org.uk e-mail: paxtonpits@btconnect.com

8. WICKEN FEN

The National Trust.
Location: TL 563 705. Lies 17 miles NE of Cambridge and nine miles S of Ely. From A10 drive E along A1123.
Access: Reserve is open daily except Christmas Day. Visitor centre open daily in summer. In winter visitor centre is open (10am - 4pm) but closed on Tuesdays.
Facilities: Toilets, visitor centre, café, hides, cycle routes, boardwalk, footpaths, coach and disabled parking.
Public transport: Nearest rail link either Cambridge or Ely. Buses only on Thu and Sun.
Habitat: Open Fen – cut hay fields, sedge beds, grazing marsh – partially flooded wet grassland, reedbed, scrub, woodland.
Key birds: *Spring*: Passage waders and passerines. *Summer*: Marsh Harriers, waders and warblers. *Winter*: Wildfowl, Hen Harrier, Bittern.

Other notable flora and fauna: 7,800 species recorded: 22 species of dragonfly/damselfly, 27 species of butterfly and 1000+ species of moth. Water vole, otter.

Contact: Isobel Sedgewick, Wicken Fen, Lode Lane, Wicken, Cambs, CB7 5XP. 01353 720 274. e-mail: isobel.sedgewick@nationaltrust.org.uk
www.wicken.org.uk

Cheshire

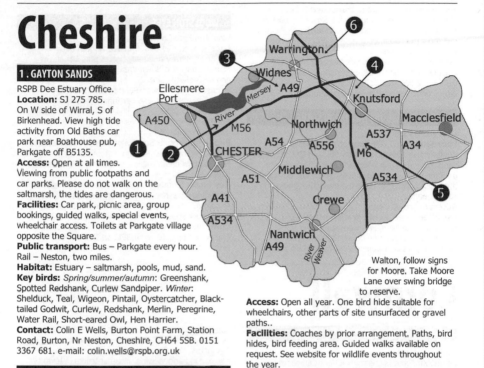

1. GAYTON SANDS

RSPB Dee Estuary Office.
Location: SJ 275 785.
On W side of Wirral, S of Birkenhead. View high tide activity from Old Baths car park near Boathouse pub, Parkgate off B5135.
Access: Open at all times. Viewing from public footpaths and car parks. Please do not walk on the saltmarsh, the tides are dangerous.
Facilities: Car park, picnic area, group bookings, guided walks, special events, wheelchair access. Toilets at Parkgate village opposite the Square.
Public transport: Bus – Parkgate every hour. Rail – Neston, two miles.
Habitat: Estuary – saltmarsh, pools, mud, sand.
Key birds: *Spring/summer/autumn*: Greenshank, Spotted Redshank, Curlew Sandpiper. *Winter*: Shelduck, Teal, Wigeon, Pintail, Oystercatcher, Black-tailed Godwit, Curlew, Redshank, Merlin, Peregrine, Water Rail, Short-eared Owl, Hen Harrier.
Contact: Colin E Wells, Burton Point Farm, Station Road, Burton, Nr Neston, Cheshire, CH64 5SB. 0151 3367 681. e-mail: colin.wells@rspb.org.uk

2. GOWY MEADOWS

Cheshire Wildlife Trust.
Location: SJ 435 740. N of M56 at Thornton-le-Moors, near Ellesmere Port.
Access: Park near church and go through public footpath gate on Thornton Green Lane. Open all year.
Facilities: None.
Public transport: The Arriva bus service stops on the Thornton Green Lane opposite the church.
Habitat: Lowland grazing marsh.
Key birds: *Spring/summer*: Wildfowl, warblers, Whinchat, Green Sandpiper, Lapwing, Jack Snipe, Snipe. *Winter*: Reed Bunting. Passage: Stonechat, Wheatear.
Contact: Cheshire Wildlife Trust, 01948 820 728; (fax) 0709 2888 469. e-mail: cheshirewt@cix.co.uk
www.cheshirewildlifetrust.co.uk

3. MOORE NATURE RESERVE

Waste Recycling Group.
Location: SJ 577 854. SW of Warrington, via A56 Warrington-to-Chester road. At traffic lights at Higher Walton, follow signs for Moore. Take Moore Lane over swing bridge to reserve.
Access: Open all year. One bird hide suitable for wheelchairs, other parts of site unsurfaced or gravel paths..
Facilities: Coaches by prior arrangement. Paths, bird hides, bird feeding area. Guided walks available on request. See website for wildlife events throughout the year.
Public transport: 62 and 66 buses from Warrington and Runcorn stop in Moore village, less than 1km from reserve. Call 0870 608 2608 for times.
Habitat: Wetland, woodland, grasslands, five pools.
Key birds: More than 130 species every year, inc. occasional rarities. *Spring/summer*: Breeding wildfowl and waders, Black-necked Grebe, warblers. *Autumn/winter*: Wide variety of wildfowl, Bittern. Also good for gulls, woodpeckers, owls and raptors. See website for list and latest sightings.
Contact: Paul Cassidy/Brian Webber, c/o Waste Recycling Centre, Arpley Landfill Site, Forest Way, Sankey Bridge, Warrington, Cheshire WA4 6YZ. 01925 444 689. e-mail: paul.cassidy@wrg.co.uk
www.wrg.co.uk/moorenaturereserve

4. ROSTHERNE MERE

Natural England (Cheshire to Lancashire team).
Location: SJ 744 843. Lies N of Knutsford and S of M56 (junction 8). Take minor road to Rostherne village.
Access: View from Rostherne churchyard and lanes;

no public access, except to A W Boyd Observatory (permits from D A Clarke, 1 Hart Avenue, Sale M33 2JY, tel: 0161 973 7122). Not suitable for coach parties but can accommodate smaller group visits by prior arrangement.
Facilities: None.   **Public transport:** None.
Habitat: Deep lake, woodland, willow bed, pasture.
Key birds: *Winter*: Good range of duck (inc Pintail), gull roost (inc. occasional Iceland and Glaucous). Passage Black Terns.
Contact: Tim Coleshaw, Site Manager, Natural England, Attingham Park, Shrewsbury, SY4 4TW. 01743 282 000; Fax 01743 709 303; e-mail tim.coleshaw@natural-england.org.uk.

5. RUDHEATH WOODS NATURE RESERVE

Cheshire Wildlife Trust.
Location: SJ 740 700. Located five miles S of Knutsford, at Allostock. From A50, turn W on to Wash Lane. Park in an unmade track which heads S after 0.25 miles. The track continues as a bridle path along the reserve, which is accessed over stiles and along various paths.
Access: Open all year.
Facilities: None. **Public transport:** None.
Habitat: Heathland, wet woodland.
Key birds: *Spring/summer*: Chiffchaff, other warblers, possible Hobby. *Autumn*: Waders, possible

Greenshank, Green Sandpiper. *Winter*: Siskin, Redpoll, Snipe. *All year*: All three woodpeckers, Willow Tit.
Contact: Cheshire Wildlife Trust, 01948 820 728; (fax) 0709 2888 469. e-mail: cheshirewt@cix.co.uk www.cheshirewildlifetrust.co.uk

6. WOOLSTON EYES

Woolston Eyes Conservation Group.
Location: SJ 654 888. E of Warrington between the River Mersey and Manchester Ship Canal. Off Manchester Road down Weir Lane or from Latchford to end of Thelwall Lane.
Access: Open all year. Permits required from Chairman, £8 each, £16 per family (see address below).
Facilities: No toilets or visitor centre. Good hides, some elevated.
Public transport: Buses along A57 nearest stop to Weir Lane, or Thelwell Lane, Latchford.
Habitat: Wetland, marsh, scrubland, wildflower meadow areas.
Key birds: Breeding Black-necked Grebe, warblers (including Grasshopper Warbler), all raptors (Merlin, Peregrine, Marsh Harrier). SSSI for wintering wildfowl, many duck species breed.
Contact: BR Ankers, Chairman, 9 Lynton Gardens, Appleton, Cheshire, WA4 5ED. 01925 267 355. www.woolstoneyes.co.uk

Cornwall

1. CROWDY RESERVOIR

South West Water.
Location: Follow signs from A39 at Camelford to Davidstow Airfield and pick up signs to the reservoir. On edge of the forestry plantation, park in pull-in spot near a cattle grid. A track leads to a hide via stiles.
Access: Open all year.
Facilities: Hide. A key and permit is required.
Public transport: None.
Habitat: Reservoir, bog, moorland, forestry.
Key birds: *Spring:* Passage migrants, inc Wheatear, Whimbrel, Ruff. *Summer:* Black-headed Gull, Reed and Sedge Warblers, returning waders. *Autumn:* Waders, raptors possible inc Peregrine, Goshawk, Merlin. *Winter:* Wild swans, wildfowl, possible Smew. Golden Plover, Woodcock, Fieldfare, Redwing.
Contact: Leisure Services Dept, South West Water, Higher Coombe Park, Lewdown, Okehampton, EX20 4QT. 01837 871 565.

2. HAYLE ESTUARY (RYAN'S FIELD)

RSPB (South West England Office).
Location: SW 550 370. In town of Hayle. From A30 take B3301 through town to Chenhalls Road.
Access: Open at all times. No permits required. No

admission charges. Not suitable for wheelchair users. Dogs on leads please. Sorry – no coaches.
Facilities: Eric Grace Memorial Hide at Ryan's Field has parking and viewing. Nearest toilets in town of Hayle. No visitor centre but information board at hide.
Public transport: Buses and trains at Hayle.
Habitat: Intertidal mudflats, saltmarsh, lagoon and islands, sandy beaches and sand dunes.
Key birds: *Winter*: Wildfowl, gulls, Kingfisher, Ring-billed Gull, Great Northern Diver. *Spring/summer*: Migrant waders, breeding Shelduck. *Autumn*: Rare waders, often from N America! Terns, gulls.
Contact: The Warden, RSPB South West Regional Office, 01458 252 805.

3. MARAZION MARSH

RSPB (South West England Office).
Location: SW 510 315. Reserve is one mile E of Penzance, 500 yards W of Marazion. Entrance off seafront road near Marazion.
Access: Open at all times. No permits required. No admission charges. Not suitable for wheelchair users. Dogs on leads please. Sorry – no coaches.
Facilities: One hide. No toilets. No visitor centre. Nearest toilets in Marazion and seafront car park.
Public transport: Bus from Penzance.

Habitat: Wet reedbed, willow carr.
Key birds: *Winter:* Wildfowl, Snipe, occasional Bittern. *Spring/summer:* Breeding Reed, Sedge and Cetti's Warblers, herons, swans. *Autumn:* Occasional Aquatic Warbler, Spotted Crake. Large roost of swallows and martins in reedbeds, migrant warblers and waders.
Contact: The Warden, RSPB South West Regional Office, 01458 252 805.

4. NARE HEAD

National Trust.
Location: Approx ten miles SE of Truro. from A390 head S on A307 to two miles S of Tregony just past the garage. Follow signs to Veryan then L signposted to Carne. Go straight over at crossroad, following Carne and Pendower. Turn L on a bend following NT signs for Nare Head. Bearing R, cross over a cattle grid to the car park. From the garage, Nare Head is about four miles.
Access: Open all year.
Facilities: Car park.
Public transport: None.
Habitat: Headland.
Key birds: *Spring/summer:* Razorbill, Guillemot, Sandwich, Common and Arctic Terns, possible Whimbrel, Fulmar. *Winter:* Black-throated and Great Northern Divers. Red-throated Diver possible, Scoter, Velvet Scoter, Slavonian, Black-necked and Red-necked Grebes.
Contact: National Trust, Lanhydrock House, Lanhydrock, Cornwall, PL30 4DE. 01208 432 691.

5. STITHIANS RESERVOIR

South West Lakes Trust.
Location: SS 715 365. From B3297 S of Redruth. At Rame turn L at Spar shop, then L and R to southern causeway.
Access: Viewing from north and south causeways.
Facilities: Three hides near causeways only for CBWPS members.
Public transport: Nearest bus service is to Zennor.
Habitat: Open water, marshland.
Key birds: Wildfowl in winter and waders at passage times (inc. rarities, eg. Pectoral and Semipalmated Sandpipers, Lesser Yellowlegs). Good site for rarities.

Contact: South West Lakes Trust, Lidn Park, Quarry Crescent, Pennygillam Industrial Estate, Launceston, Cornwall PL15 7PF. 01566 771 930. www.swlakestrust.org.uk

6. TAMAR ESTUARY

Cornwall Wildlife Trust.
Location: SX 434 631 (Northern Boundary). SX 421 604 (Southern Boundary). From Plymouth head W on A38. Access parking at Cargreen and Landulph from minor roads off A388.
Access: Open at all times. Access bird hides from China Fleet Club car park, Saltash. Follow path alongside golf course – do not walk on course itself. Combination number for hide locks available at club reception.
Facilities: Two hides on foreshore, first (0.25 miles from car park) overlooks estuary, second (0.5 miles) has excellent views across Kingsmill Lake.
Public transport: None.
Habitat: Tidal mudflat with some saltmarsh.
Key birds: *Winter:* Avocet, Snipe, Black-tailed Godwit, Redshank, Dunlin, Curlew, Whimbrel, Spotted Redshank, Green Sandpiper, Golden Plover, Kingfisher.
Contact: Cornwall Wildlife Trust, 01872 273 939.
E-mail: peter@cornwt.demon.co.uk
www.cornwallwildlifetrust.org.uk

For a comprehensive survey of bird reserves in Cornwall and The Isles of Scilly, see the latest, highly acclaimed *Best Birdwatching Sites in Cornwall and Scilly*.

See on page 349 for details.

Cumbria

1. CAMPFIELD MARSH

RSPB (North of England Office).
Location: NY 207 620. On S shore of Solway estuary, W of Bowness-on-Solway. Follow signs from B5307 from Carlisle.
Access: Open at all times, no charge. View high-tide roosts from roadside (suitable for disabled).
Facilities: Hide overlooking wetland areas, along nature trail (1.5 miles). No toilets or visitor centre.
Public transport: Nearest railway station – Carlisle (13 miles). Infrequent bus service to reserve.
Habitat: Saltmarsh/intertidal areas, open water, peat bog, wet grassland.
Key birds: *Winter*: Waders and wildfowl include Barnacle Goose, Shoveler, Scaup, Grey Plover. *Spring/ summer*: Breeding Lapwing, Redshank, Snipe, Tree Sparrow and warblers. *Autumn*: Passage waders.
Contact: North Plain Farm, Bowness-on-Solway, Wigton, Cumbria, CA7 5AG.
e-mail: dave.blackledge@rspb.org.uk
www.rspb.org.uk

2. DRUMBURGH NNR

Cumbria Wildlife Trust.
Location: NY 264 597. From Carlisle city centre, head W on B5307 to Kirkbride. After about one mile, turn R to Burgh by Sands. Follow road for 7.5 miles to Drumburgh village. Turn L by post office, continue down track and park on R past Moss Cottage.
Access: Open all year.
Facilities: None.
Public transport: None.
Habitat: Raised bog, woodland, grassland.
Key birds: *Summer*: Red Grouse, Curlew, Grasshopper Warbler.
Other notable flora and fauna: Large heath butterfly, adder.
Contact: Cumbria Wildlife Trust, Plumgarths, Crook Road, Kendal, LA8 8LX. 01539 816 300; (Fax) 01539 816 301. E-mail: mail@cumbriawildlifetrust.org.uk
www.cumbriawildlifetrust.org.uk

3. FOULNEY ISLAND

Cumbria Wildlife Trust.
Location: SD 246 640. Three miles SE of Barrow town centre on A5087 from Barrow or Ulverston. At roundabout 2.5 miles S of Barrow take minor road through Rampside to Roa Island. Turn L into reserve car park. Walk to main island along stone causeway.
Access: Open all year. Access restricted to designated paths during bird breeding season. Slitch Ridge is closed at this time. No dogs allowed during bird breeding season. The island may be cut off for several hours around high-tide – please consult tide tables.
Facilities: None.

Public transport: Bus: regular service from Barrow to Roa Island.
Habitat: Shingle, sand, grassland.
Key birds: *Summer*: Arctic and Little Terns, Oystercatcher, Ringed Plover, Eider Duck. *Winter*: Brent Goose, Redshank, Dunlin, Sanderling.
Other notable flora and fauna: Sea campion, yellow horned poppy. Six spot burnet and common blue butterfly.
Contact: Cumbria Wildlife Trust, 01539 816 300; Fax 01539 816 301.
e-mail: mail@cumbriawildlifetrust.org.uk
www.cumbriawildlifetrust.org.uk

4. HAWESWATER

RSPB and United Utilities.
Location: NY 470 108. Golden Eagle viewpoint, near Bampton, 5 miles NW of Shap, off A6. Turn L in Bampton to car park at S of reservoir.
Access: The viewpoint is always open but only manned as below. Visitors are asked not to go beyond the viewpoint. There is no wheelchair access.
Facilities: Golden Eagle viewpoint, open Friday to Sunday, Apr to end Aug (11am-4pm), telescopes available. There is no coach parking.
Public transport: None.
Habitat: Fells with rocky streams, steep oak and birch woodlands.
Key birds: *Upland breeders*: Golden Eagle, Peregrine, Raven, Ring Ouzel, Curlew, Redshank, Snipe. *Woodlands*: Pied Flycatcher, Wood Warbler, Tree Pipit, Redstart, Buzzard, Sparrowhawk.
Contact: 7 Naddlegate, Burn Banks, Haweswater, Penrith, Cumbria CA10 2RL.

5. SMARDALE GILL NATIONAL NATURE RESERVE

Cumbria Wildlife Trust.
Location: NY 727 070. Six miles SW of Brough, approx 2.5 miles W of Ravenstonedale on A685 or 0.5 miles S of Kirkby Stephen station take turning signed to Smardale. Cross over railway and turn L to junction ignoring turn to Waitby. Cross over railway and turn L at junction ignoring sign for Smardale. Cross disused railway, turn L immediately and L again to car park.
Access: 3.5 mile disused railway line is open to members and non-members but non-members should obtain a permit before visiting other parts of the reserve.
Facilities: None. Terrain not suitable for wheelchair users.
Public transport: Nearest train station at Kirkby Stephen.
Habitat: Limestone grassland, river, ancient semi-natural woodland, quarry.
Key birds: *Summer*: Redstart, Pied Flycatcher, Wood Warbler. *All year*: usual woodland birds.

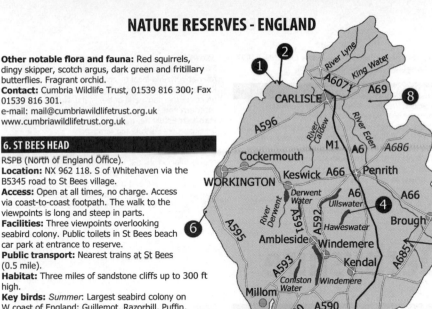

Other notable flora and fauna: Red squirrels, dingy skipper, scotch argus, dark green and fritillary butterflies. Fragrant orchid.
Contact: Cumbria Wildlife Trust, 01539 816 300; Fax 01539 816 301.
e-mail: mail@cumbriawildlifetrust.org.uk
www.cumbriawildlifetrust.org.uk

6. ST BEES HEAD

RSPB (North of England Office).
Location: NX 962 118. S of Whitehaven via the B5345 road to St Bees village.
Access: Open at all times, no charge. Access via coast-to-coast footpath. The walk to the viewpoints is long and steep in parts.
Facilities: Three viewpoints overlooking seabird colony. Public toilets in St Bees beach car park at entrance to reserve.
Public transport: Nearest trains at St Bees (0.5 mile).
Habitat: Three miles of sandstone cliffs up to 300 ft high.
Key birds: *Summer*: Largest seabird colony on W coast of England: Guillemot, Razorbill, Puffin, Kittiwake, Fulmar and England's only breeding pairs of Black Guillemot.
Contact: North Plain Farm, Bowness-on-Solway, Wigton, Cumbria, CA7 5AG. 01697 351 330.
e-mail: dave.blackledge@rspb.org.uk
www.rspb.org.uk

7. SOUTH WALNEY

Cumbria Wildlife Trust.
Location: SD 215 620. Six miles S of Barrow-in-Furness. From Barrow, cross Jubilee Bridge onto Walney Island, turn L at lights. Continue through Biggar village to South End Caravan Park. Follow road for 1 mile to reserve.
Access: Open daily (10am-5pm) plus Bank Holidays. No dogs except assistance dogs. Day permits: £2 adults, 50p children. Cumbria Wildlife Trust members free.
Facilities: Toilets, nature trails, eight hides (two are wheelchair accessible), 200m boardwalk, cottage available to rent – sleeps 10.
Public transport: Bus service as far as Biggar.
Habitat: Shingle, lagoon, sand dune, saltmarsh.
Key birds: *Spring/autumn*: Passage migrants. *Summer*: 14,000 breeding pairs of Herring, Greater and Lesser Black-backed Gulls, Shelduck, Eider. *Winter*: Teal, Wigeon, Goldeneye, Redshank, Greenshank, Curlew, Oystercatcher, Knot, Dunlin, Merlin, Short-eared Owl, Twite.
Other notable flora and fauna: 450 species of flowering plants. Natterjack toad at North Walney.
Contact: The Warden, No 1 Coastguard Cottages, South Walney Nature Reserve, Walney Island, Barrow-in-Furness, Cumbria LA14 3YQ. 01229 471 066.
e-mail: mail@cumbriawildlifetrust.org.uk
www.cumbriawildlifetrust.org.uk

8. TALKIN TARN COUNTRY PARK

Carlisle City Council
Location: NY 544 591. Twelve miles E of Carlisle. From A69 E at Brampton, head S on B6413 for two miles. Talkin Tarn is on E just after level crossing.
Access: All year. Wheelchair access around tarn, two kissing gates accessible. Tearoom has lift. Coaches welcome.
Facilities: Toilets and restaurant open all year (11am-4pm Easter-Oct, limited opening times in winter). Dogs allowed around Tarn. Rowing boat hire at weekends and school holidays. Angling by day permit (with closed season).
Public transport: Bus: infrequent. Tel: 0870 608 2608. Train: nearest station is Brampton Junction. Tel: 0845 748 4950. Footpath from Brampton Junction 1 mile.
Habitat: Natural glacial tarn, mature oak/beech woodland, orchid meadow (traditionally managed), wet mire and farmland.
Key birds: *Spring/summer*: Pied Flycatcher, Spotted Flycatcher, Redstart, Chiffchaff, Wood Warbler. *Winter*: Grebes, Smew, Long-tailed Duck, Goosander, Gadwall, Wigeon, Brambling, swans.
Other notable flora and fauna: Common blue damselfly, common darter, small copper butterfly, otter, red squirrel.
Contact: Countryside Ranger, Talking Tarn Country

143

Park, Tarn Road, Brampton, Cumbria CA8 1HN. 01697 73129. e-mail: fionash@carlisle.gov.uk

9. WALNEY BIRD OBSERVATORY

Location: Walney Island, Barrow-in-Furness, Cumbria.
Access: Although several areas are restricted, notably the golf course and airfield, the narrow width of the island means most sites are viewable from the road or footpaths. Access to South Walney Nature Reserve (10am-5pm) is along permitted trails.
Facilities: Monitoring and ringing of breeding and migrant birds occurs across the island.
Ringing facilities are available for qualified ringers – write to Walney Bird Observatory (see address

below) for availability.
Public transport: Barrow-in-Furness connects to the rail network and local bus routes serve Walney Island. Routes 1 and 1A cover the central area while 6 and 6A cover the north end of the island. No bus route to southern end.
Habitat: Estuarine, maritime, dunes, freshwater and brackish pools, scrub and farmland.
Key birds: Renowned Eider and gull colonies at south end. The winter months provide a wildfowl and wader spectacular across the island. Migrants aplenty appear during both passage periods with a proven pedigree for attracting rare and unusual species.
Contact: Walney Bird Observatory, Coastguard Cottages, Walney Island, Barrow-in-Furness, Cumbria LA14 3YQ.

Derbyshire

1. CARR VALE NATURE RESERVE

Derbyshire Wildlife Trust.
Location: SK 45 70. 1km W of Bolsover on A632 to Chesterfield. Turn L at roundabout (follow brown tourist signs) into Riverside Way. Car park at end of road. Follow footpath (waymarked) around Peter Fidler reserve.
Access: Open all year.
Facilities: Car park, coach parking on approach road, good disabled access, paths, viewing platforms.
Public transport: Various Stagecoach services from Chesterfield (Stephenson Place) all pass close to the reserve: Mon to Sat - 83 serves Villas Road, 81, 82, 82A and 83 serve the roundabout on the A632. Sun - 81A, 82A serve the roundabout on the A632.
Habitat: Lakes, wader flashes, reed bed, sewage farm, scrub, arable fields.
Key birds: *Winter:* Large numbers of wildfowl including flocks of Wigeon and Teal also wintering flocks of finches and buntings, Water Rail. Large skeins of geese fly over in early and late winter. *Spring/autumn:* In September Swallows gather in the marsh, in a gigantic roost of between 10-12,000 birds. They usually attract Hobbies. *Early summer:* Breeding birds, including Reed and Sedge Warblers, Whitethroat, Yellowhammer, Moorhen and Gadwall, plus Sky Lark.
Other notable flora and fauna: Dragonflies, mammals (hare, water vole, harvest mouse, water shrew).
Contact: Derbyshire Wildlife Trust, East Mill, Bridgefoot, Belper, Derbyshire, DE56 1XH. 01773 881 188. e-mail: enquiries@derbyshirewt.co.uk www.derbyshirewildlifetrust.org.uk

2. CARSINGTON RESERVOIR

Severn Trent Water.
Location: SK 24 51 (for visitor centre and main

facilities). Off the B5035 Ashbourne to Cromford road.
Access: Open all year except Christmas Day. The car parks are open from 7am to sunset (Apr - end Oct) and 7.30am to sunset in winter. There are various access points. Track is very steep in places and can be slippery in winter.
Facilities: Visitor centre with exhibition, restaurant, shops, play area and toilets. RSPB 'Aren't Birds Brilliant' project operates here twice a week. Four bird hides and three car parks (two chargeable, one free).
Public transport: TM Travel operates service 411 from Matlock and Ashbourne. The nearest train station is at Cromford.
Habitat: Open water, islands, mixed woodland, scrub and grasslands, small reedbed.
Key birds: *Winter:* Wildfowl and a large gull roost plus possibility of divers and rare grebes. *Spring:* Good spring passage including Yellow and White Wagtails, Whimbrel, Black and Arctic Terns. *Summer:* Warblers and breeding waders. *All year:* Tree Sparrows and Willow Tits.
Other notable flora and fauna: Species-rich hay meadows, ancient woodlands with bluebells, three species of orchid, 21 species of butterfly and water vole.
Contact: Carsington Water, The Visitor Centre, Ashbourne, Derbyshire DE6 1ST. 01629 540 696. e-mail: customer.relations@severntrent.co.uk www.moretoexperience.co.uk and www.carsingtonbirdclub.co.uk

3. DRAKELOW WILDFOWL RESERVE

E-ON, leased to Derbyshire Wildlife Trust.
Location: SK 22 72 07. Drakelow Power Station, one mile NE of Walton-on-Trent.
Access: Dawn to dusk permit holders only. Annual permit can be obtained from Derbyshire Wildlife Trust.
Facilities: Seven hides, no other facilities.

NATURE RESERVES - ENGLAND

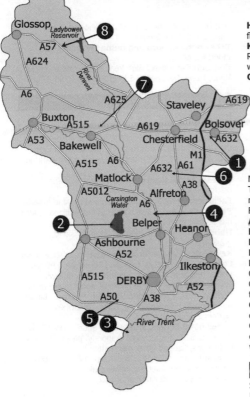

Public transport: None.
Habitat: Disused flooded gravel pits with wooded islands and reedbeds.
Key birds: *Summer:* Breeding Reed and Sedge Warblers. Water Rail, Hobby. *Winter:* Wildfowl (Goldeneye, Gadwall, Smew), Merlin, Peregrine. Recent rarities include Great White and Little Egret, Bittern and Spotted Crake, Ring-necked Duck and American Wigeon.
Other notable flora and fauna: Good for common species of dragonflies and butterflies.
Contact: Derbyshire Wildlife Trust, 01773 881 188.
e-mail: enquiries@derbyshirewt.co.uk
www.derbyshirewildlifetrust.org.uk

4. EREWASH MEADOWS

Derbyshire and Notts Wildlife Trusts
Location: SK 441 517. In three parts – Aldercar Flash, Brinsley Meadows and part of Cromford Canal. Ripley is nearest large town.
Access: Open all year – please keep to paths.
Facilities: None.
Public transport: Local bus services.

Habitat: The sites are now part of the largest floodplain grassland and wetlands in Erewash Valley.
Key birds: *Spring/summer:* Breeding Lapwing, Snipe, Reed Bunting and warblers. Raptors, waders and wildfowl seen on passage. *Winter:* Wildfowl species.
Other notable flora and fauna: Grass snake, amphibians, dragonflies, butterflies.
Contact: Derbyshire Wildlife Trust, 01773 881 188.
e-mail: enquiries@derbyshirewt.co.uk
www.derbyshirewildlifetrust.org.uk

5. HILTON GRAVEL PITS

Derbyshire Wildlife Trust.
Location: SK 24 31. From Derby, take A516 from Mickleover W past Etwall onto A50 junction at Hilton. Turn R at first island onto Willow Pit Lane. Turn L next to a large white house and park next to the gate. Follow track along S side of the pools.
Access: Open all year.
Facilities: Tracks and boardwalks, viewing screens.
Public transport: Local bus services from Derby.
Habitat: Ponds, scrub, wood, fen.
Key birds: *Spring/summer:* Great Crested Grebe, Common Tern, warblers. *Winter:* Wildfowl, Siskin, Goldcrest. *All year:* All three woodpeckers, Kingfisher, tits inc possible Willow Tit, Tawny Owl, Bullfinch.
Other notable flora and fauna: Dragonflies, orchids, black poplar.
Contact: Derbyshire Wildlife Trust, 01773 881 188.
e-mail: enquiries@derbyshirewt.co.uk
www.derbyshirewildlifetrust.org.uk

6. OGSTON RESERVOIR

Severn Trent Water Plc.
Location: From Matlock, take A615 E to B6014, just after Tansley. From Chesterfield take A61 S of Clay Cross onto B6014, towards Tansley. Cross railway, the reservoir is on L after the hill.
Access: View from roads, car parks or hides. Suitable for coaches. Heronry in nearby Ogston Carr Wood (Derbyshire Wildlife Trust) viewable from road, W of reservoir.
Facilities: Four hides (three for Ogston BC members, one public), toilets. Information pack on request.
Public transport: TM Travel 63 bus service (Chesterfield to Clay Cross) serves N end of reservoir and 64 service (Clay Cross to Matlock) not Sundays.
Habitat: Open water, pasture, mixed woodland.
Key birds: All three woodpeckers, Little and Tawny Owls, Kingfisher, Grey Wagtail, warblers. Passage raptors (inc. Osprey), terns and waders. *Winter:* Gull roost, wildfowl, tit and finch flocks.
Contact: Malcolm Hill, Treasurer, Ogston Bird Club, c/o 2 Sycamore Avenue, Glapwell, Chesterfield, S44 5LH. 01623 812 159. www.ogstonbirdclub.co.uk

7. PADLEY GORGE

The National Trust (East Midlands).
Location: From Sheffield, take A625. After eight miles, turn L on B6521 to Nether Padley. Grindleford

Station is just off B6521 (NW of Nether Padley) and one mile NE of Grindleford village.

Access: All year. Not suitable for disabled people or those unused to steep climbs. Some of the paths are rocky. No dogs allowed.

Facilities: Café and toilets at Longshaw lodge.

Public transport: Bus: from Sheffield to Bakewell stops at Grindleford/Nether Padley. Tel: 01709 566 000. Train: from Sheffield to Manchester Piccadilly stops at Grindleford Station. Tel: 0161 228 2141.

Habitat: Steep-sided valley containing largest area of sessile oak woodland in south Pennines.

Key birds: *Summer*: Pied Flycatcher, Spotted Flycatcher, Redstart, Wheatear, Whinchat, Wood Warbler, Tree Pipit.

Contact: National Trust, High Peak Estate Office, Edale End, Edale Road, Hope S33 2RF. 01433 670 368. www.nationaltrust.org.uk

8. UPPER DERWENT VALLEY

National Trust (High Peak Estate)

Location: Either side of A57 from Ladybower Reservoir viaduct.

Access: Open all year but may be inaccessible in harsh winter weather. Not suitable for disabled. No dogs allowed.

Facilities: Toilets, café and visitor centre at National Park Centre, Fourholmes.

Public transport: Bus from Sheffield to Fairholmes and from Bamford train station to Kings Tree at weekends. Call Travelline on 0870 608 2608.

Habitat: Wooded valley running through extensive upland moors.

Key birds: Breeding Goshawk, Buzzard and occasional

Hen Harrier, plus breeding Golden Plover, Dunlin, Curlew and Black Grouse.

Other notable flora and fauna: Mountain hare, moorland plants.

Contact: Derbyshire, High Peak Estate Office, Edale Road, Hope, Derbyshire, S33 2RF. 01433 760 368.

9. WILLINGTON GRAVEL PITS

Derbyshire Wildlife Trust.

Location: SK 285 274. From A50 'Toyota Island' turn onto Repton Road towards Willington and Repton. Go through village towards Repton. Just before bridge over River Trent, turn R onto un-made track. Park on track and walk along lane.

Access: Access along Meadow Lane to viewing platforms all year. No access on site.

Facilities: Viewing platforms. Limited parking in lane.

Public transport: Local trains stop at Willington, local bus service from Derby.

Habitat: Open water, reedbed, shingle island, grassland.

Key birds: *Summer*: Breeding Lapwing, other waders, Common Tern, raptors, including Peregrine, Kestrel, Hobby and Sparrowhawk, Sand Martin, wildfowl. *Winter*: Waders and large flocks of wildfowl including Wigeon, Teal, Pochard and Shoveler. *Passage*: Large numbers of Curlew in spring, up to 20 species of waders in spring/autumn.

Other notable flora and fauna: Short-leaved water starwort. Several species of dragonfly, plus occasional otter signs, fox and other mammals.

Contact: Derbyshire Wildlife Trust, 01773 881 188. e-mail: enquiries@derbyshirewt.co.uk www.derbyshirewildlifetrust.org.uk

Devon

1. AYLESBEARE COMMON RSPB RESERVE

RSPB (South West England Office).

Location: SY 058 897. Five miles E of J30 of M5 at Exeter, 0.5 miles past Halfway Inn on B3052. Turn R to Hawkerland, car park is on L. The reserve is on the opposite side of the main road.

Access: Open all year. One track suitable for wheelchairs and pushchairs.

Facilities: Car park, picnic area, group bookings, guided walks and special events. Disabled access via metalled track to private farm

Public transport: Buses (Exeter to Sidmouth, 52a, 52b). Request stop at Joneys Cross (reserve entrance).

Habitat: Heathland, wood fringes, streams and ponds.

Key birds: *Spring/summer*: Nightjar, Stonechat. *All year*: Dartford Warbler, Buzzard.

Winter: Possible Hen Harrier.

Contact: RSPB warden 01395 233 655. e-mail: aylesbeare.common@rspb.org.uk

2. BOWLING GREEN MARSH

RSPB (South West England Office).

Location: SX 972 876. On the E side of River Exe, four miles SE of Exeter, 0.5 miles SE of Topsham.

Access: Open at all times. Please park at the public car parks in Topsham, not in the lane by the reserve.

Facilities: RSPB shop at Darts Farm, 1.5km from reserve, east of Topsham across River Clyst.

Public transport: Exeter to Exmouth railway has regular (every 30 mins) service to Topsham station (half a mile from reserve). Stagecoach Devon 57 bus has frequent service (Mon-Sat every 12 mins, Sun every half-hour) from Exeter to Topsham. Travel line 0871 200 2233.

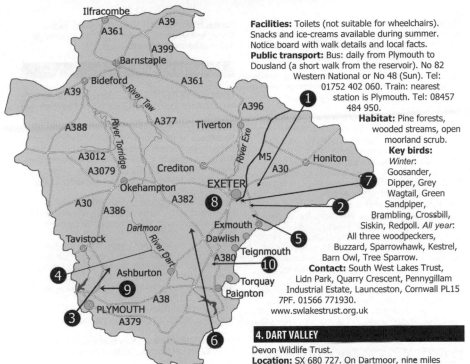

Facilities: Toilets (not suitable for wheelchairs). Snacks and ice-creams available during summer. Notice board with walk details and local facts.
Public transport: Bus: daily from Plymouth to Dousland (a short walk from the reservoir). No 82 Western National or No 48 (Sun). Tel: 01752 402 060. Train: nearest station is Plymouth. Tel: 08457 484 950.

Habitat: Pine forests, wooded streams, open moorland scrub.
Key birds: *Winter*: Goosander, Dipper, Grey Wagtail, Green Sandpiper, Brambling, Crossbill, Siskin, Redpoll. *All year*: All three woodpeckers, Buzzard, Sparrowhawk, Kestrel, Barn Owl, Tree Sparrow.
Contact: South West Lakes Trust, Lidn Park, Quarry Crescent, Pennygillam Industrial Estate, Launceston, Cornwall PL15 7PF. 01566 771930.
www.swlakestrust.org.uk

Habitat: Coastal grassland, open water/marsh, hedgerows.
Key birds: *Winter*: Wigeon, Shoveler, Teal, Black-tailed Godwit, Curlew, Golden Plover. *Spring*: Shelduck, passage waders, Whimbrel, passage Garganey and Yellow Wagtail. *Summer*: Gull/tern roosts, high tide wader roosts contain many passage birds. *Autumn*: Wildfowl, Peregrine, wader roosts.
Other notable flora and fauna: Hairy dragonfly, wasp spider.
Contact: RSPB, Darts Farm Shopping Village, Clyst St. George, Exeter EX3 0QH. 01392 879 438 or, RSPB, Unit 3, Lions Rest Estate, Station Road, Exminster, Exeter, EX6 8DZ. 01392 824 614.
www.rspb.org.uk

3. BURRATOR RESERVOIR

South West Lakes Trust.
Location: SX 551 681. Lies 10 miles NE of Plymouth, off A386 (Tavistock road). At Yelverton take B3212 towards Princeton. Turn R at Burrator Inn and follow signs to reservoir.
Access: Open all year. Numerous free parking areas around reservoir. Main route is suitable for disabled but is also used by motorists and cyclists. There are about 25 stiles around the reservoir.

4. DART VALLEY

Devon Wildlife Trust.
Location: SX 680 727. On Dartmoor, nine miles NW from Ashburton. From A38 'Peartree Cross' near Ashburton, follow signs towards Princetown. Access from National Park car parks at New Bridge (S) or Dartmeet (N).
Access: Designated 'access land' but terrain is rough with few paths. It is possible to walk the length of the river (eight miles). A level, well-made track runs for a mile from Newbridge to give easy access to some interesting areas. Not suitable for large coaches (narrow bridges). Probably too rough for wheelchairs.
Facilities: Dartmoor National Park toilets in car parks at New Bridge and Dartmeet.
Public transport: Enquiry line 01392 382 800. Summer-only bus service from Newton Abbot/Totnes to Dartmeet.
Habitat: Upland moor, wooded valley and river.
Key birds: *All year*: Raven, Buzzard. *Spring/summer*: Wood Warbler, Pied Flycatcher, Redstart in woodland, Stonechat and Whinchat on moorland, Dipper, Grey Wagtail, Goosander on river.
Contact: Devon Wildlife Trust, Cricklepit Mill, Commercial Road, Exeter, EX1 4AB. 01392 279 244.
www.devonwildlifetrust.org

5. DAWLISH WARREN NATIONAL NATURE RESERVE

Teignbridge District Council.
Location: SX 983 788. At Dawlish Warren on S side of Exe estuary mouth. Turn off A379 at sign to

Warren Golf Club, between Cockwood and Dawlish. Turn into car park adjacent to Lea Cliff Holiday Park. Pass under tunnel and turn L away from amusements. Park at far end of car park and pass through two pedestrian gates.

Access: Open public access, but avoid mudflats. Also avoid beach beyond groyne nine around high tide due to roosting birds. Parking charges apply. Restricted access for dogs (none allowed in hide).

Facilities: Visitor centre (tel 01626 863 980) open most weekends all year (10.30am-1pm and 2pm-5pm). Summer also open most weekdays as before, can be closed if warden on site.

Toilets at entrance tunnel and in resort area only. Hide open at all times – best around high tide.

Public transport: Train station at site, also regular bus service operated by Stagecoach.

Habitat: High tide roost site for wildfowl and waders of Exe estuary on mudflats and shore. Dunes, dune grassland, woodland, scrub, ponds.

Key birds: *Winter*: Waders and wildfowl – large numbers. Also good for divers and Slavonian Grebe offshore. *Summer*: Particularly good for terns. Excellent variety of birds all year, especially on migration.

Contact: Steve Ayres/Philip Chambers, Countryside Management Section, Teignbridge District Council, Forde House, Brunel Road, Newton Abbot, Devon, TQ12 4XX. Visitor centre: 01626 863 980. Teignbridge District Council: 01626 361 101 (Ext 5754).

6. EAST DARTMOOR WOODS and HEATHS NNR

Natural England (Devon team).

Location: SX 778 787. The NNR is two miles from Bovey Tracey on road to Becky Falls and Manaton. Road continues across Trendlebere Down where there are roadside car parks and adjacent paths.

Access: Yarner Wood car park open from 8.30am-7pm or dusk if earlier. Outside these hours, access on foot from Trendlebere Down. Some restrictions on dogs.

Facilities: Information/interpretation display and self-guided trails available in Yarner Wood car park also hide with feeding station (Nov-Mar).

Public transport: Nearest bus stops are in Bovey Tracey. Buses from here to Exeter and Newton Abbot (hourly).

Habitat: The reserve consists of three adjacent sites (Yarner Wood, Trendlebere Down and Bovey Valley Woodlands) totalling 365 hectares of upland oakwood and heathland.

Key birds: *All year*: Raven, Buzzard, Goshawk, Sparrowhawk, Lesser Spotted, Great Spotted and Green Woodpeckers, Grey Wagtail and Dartford Warbler (on Trendlebere Down). *Spring/summer*: Pied Flycatcher, Wood Warbler, Redstart, Tree Pipit, Linnet, Stonechat, Cuckoo, Whitethroat, Sky Lark. *Autumn/winter*: Good range of birds with feeding at hide – Siskin, Redpoll, plus Hen Harrier on Trendlebere Down.

Contact: Site Manager, Natural England, Yarner Wood, Bovey Tracey, Devon, TQ13 9LJ. 01626 832 330. www.natural-england.org.uk

7. EXMINSTER MARSHES

RSPB (South West England Office).

Location: SX 954 872. Five miles S of Exeter on W bank of River Exe. Marshes lie between Exminster and the estuary.

Access: Open at all times.

Facilities: No toilets or visitor centre. Information in RSPB car park and marked footpaths across reserve.

Public transport: Exeter to Newton Abbot/Torquay buses – stops are 400 yds from car park. Traveline 0871 200 2233. No 85 buses Mon-Sat every 15 mins, Sun 1/2 hourly.

Habitat: Coastal grazing marsh with freshwater ditches and pools, reeds, scrub-covered canal banks, winter stubbles and crops managed for farmland birds.

Key birds: *Winter*: Brent Goose, Wigeon, Water Rail, Short-eared Owl. *Spring*: Lapwing, Redshank and wildfowl breed, Cetti's Warbler on canal banks. *Summer*: Gull roosts, passage waders. *Autumn*: Peregrine, winter wildfowl, finch flocks. There are also records of Cirl Bunting and Wood Lark.

Other notable flora and fauna: 23 species of dragonfly, including hairy dragonfly and scarce chaser.

Contact: RSPB, Unit 3, Lions Rest Estate, Station Road, Exminster, Exeter, Devon, EX6 8DZ. 01392 824 614. www.rspb.org.uk

8. HALDON FOREST RAPTOR VIEWPOINT

Forestry Commission.

Location: Five miles W of Exeter. Turn off A38 at Haldon Racecourse junction, then follow signs for Dunchideock and Forest Walks. After just over 1 mile, turn L into Haldon Forest Park car park. Follow all-ability trail to the viewpoint.

Access: Open all year.

Facilities: Toilets in car park. Viewing point with benches. Path suitable for wheelchairs.

Public transport: None.

Habitat: Plantations, clearings.

Key birds: *Summer*: Hobby, Nightjar, Turtle Dove, Tree Pipit. *All year*: Peregrine, Goshawk, Sparrowhawk, Buzzard, all woodpeckers, Crossbill, Siskin.

Other notable flora and fauna: Butterfly trail.

Contact: Forestry Commission, Bullers Hill, Kennford, Exeter, Devon, EX6 7XR. 01392 832 262. www.forestry.gov.uk/england

9. PLYMBRIDGE WOOD

National Trust/Forest Enterprise.

Location: SX 524 594. At the Estover roundabout, Plymouth (near the Wrigley company factory), take the narrow, steep Plymbridge Road. Park at the bridge area at the bottom of the hill. Coming from Plympton, pick up Plymbridge Road from either Plymouth Road or Glen Road.

Access: Open all year. Cycle ride (10 miles from Plymouth to edge of Dartmoor) and 124 acres of wooded valley. No admission charge.

Facilities: Car park, woodland paths, picnic area, visitor centre.

Public transport: None.

Habitat: Mixed woodland, river, conifers.

Key birds: *Spring/summer:* Cuckoo, Wood Warbler, Redstart, Blackcap, possible Nightjar, Crossbill. *Winter:* Woodcock, Snipe, Fieldfare, Redwing, Brambling, Siskin, Redpoll, possible Crossbill. *All year:* Mandarin Duck, Sparrowhawk, Buzzard, Kestrel, Tawny Owl, all three woodpeckers, Kingfisher, Grey Wagtail, Dipper, Goldcrest, common woodland passerines, Marsh Tit, Raven.

Other notable flora and fauna: Spring flowers, plus many butterflies and dragonflies.

Contact: National Trust, Lanhydrock House, Lanhydrock, Cornwall, PL30 4DE. 01208 432 691.

10. STOVER LAKE COUNTRY PARK AND LNR

Devon County Council.

Location: Two miles N of Newton Abbot off A38 Exeter-Plymouth road. Follow the A382 L at Drumbridges roundabout, signed to Newton Abbot. After 0.25 miles follow the brown tourist sign L into the car park (fee payable).

Access: Open all year. Wheelchairs available for visitor use.

Facilities: Car park, information centre, notice board display, site leaflets, maps, feeding station, 90 metre aerial walkway.

Public transport: From Newton Abbot, Exeter or Plymouth. Info from Traveline 0870 608 2608.

Habitat: Mixed woodland, lake and lowland heath. SSSI.

Key birds: *Spring/summer:* Sand Martin, Chiffchaff, Willow Warbler, Spotted Flycatcher, Nightjar Great crested Grebe. *Winter:* Water Rail, Marsh Tit, Snipe. *All year:* woodpeckers, Jay, Siskin, Kingfisher.

Other notable flora and fauna: More than 20 species of dragonfly and damselfly including hairy dragonfly, downy emerald and red-eyed damselfly. 34 species of butterfly have been recorded including white admiral, pearl bordered and silver washed fritillary. A good site for bat watching with 10 species identified.

Contact: Rangers Office, Devon County Council, Stover Country Park, Stover, Newton Abbot, Devon, TQ12 6QG. 01626 835 236.

Dorset

1. ARNE

RSPB (South West England Office).

Location: SY 971 876. Four miles SE of Wareham, turn off A351 at Stoborough.

Access: Shipstal Point and Coombe Birdwatchers' trails open all year. Bird hides available on both trails. Accessed from car park. Coaches and escorted parties by prior arrangement. Dogs on lead in breeding season (Mar 1 – Aug 31).

Facilities: Toilets in car park. Car park charge applies to non-members. Various footpaths. Reception hut (open end-May-early Sept).

Public transport: None.

Habitat: Lowland heath, oak woodland, reedbed and saltmarsh, extensive mudflats of Poole Harbour.

Key birds: *All year:* Dartford Warbler, Little Egret, Stonechat. *Winter:* Hen Harrier, Red-breasted Merganser, Black-tailed Godwit, Avocet. *Summer:* Nightjar, warblers. *Passage:* Spotted Redshank, Whimbrel, Greenshank, Osprey.

Other notable flora and fauna: 22 species of dragonfly recorded. Green water beetle, sika deer and various reptile species.

Contact: RSPB, Syldata, Arne, Wareham, Dorset, BH20 5BJ. 01929 553 360. www.rspb.org.uk

2. BROWNSEA ISLAND

Dorset Wildlife Trust.

Location: SZ 026 883. Half hour boat rides from Poole Quay with Greenslade Pleasure Boats (01202 631 828) and Brownsea Island Ferries (01929 462 383). Ten minutes from Sandbanks Quay (next to Studland chain-ferry).

Access: Apr, May, Jun, Sept and Oct. Access by self-guided nature trail. Costs £2 adults, £1 children. Jul, Aug access by afternoon guided tour (2pm daily, duration 105 minutes). Costs £2 adults, £1 children.

Facilities: Toilets, information centre and shop, six hides, nature trail.

Public transport: Poole rail/bus station for access to Poole Quay and boats. Tel: 01202 673 555.

Habitat: Saline lagoon, reedbed, lakes, coniferous and mixed woodland.

Key birds: *Spring:* Avocet, Black-tailed Godwit, waders, gulls and wildfowl. *Summer:* Common and Sandwich Terns, Yellow-legged Gull, Little Egret, Little Grebe, Golden Pheasant. *Autumn:* Curlew Sandpiper, Little Stint.

Other notable flora and fauna: Red Squirrel, water vole, Bechstein's bat found in 2007.

Contact: Dorset Wildlife Trust, The Villa, Brownsea

149

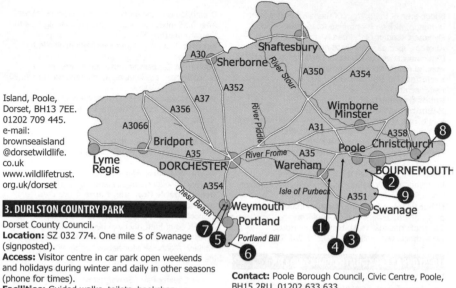

Island, Poole, Dorset, BH13 7EE. 01202 709 445. e-mail: brownseaisland @dorsetwildlife. co.uk www.wildlifetrust. org.uk/dorset

3. DURLSTON COUNTRY PARK

Dorset County Council.
Location: SZ 032 774. One mile S of Swanage (signposted).
Access: Visitor centre in car park open weekends and holidays during winter and daily in other seasons (phone for times).
Facilities: Guided walks, toilets, bookshop.
Public transport: Two buses per day except Sundays and Bank Holidays.
Habitat: Grassland, hedges, cliff, meadows.
Key birds: Cliff-nesting seabird colonies; good variety of scrub and woodland breeding species; spring and autumn migrants; seawatching esp. Apr/May and Aug/Nov.
Other notable flora and fauna: Nine species of orchid, plus more than 500 plant species. Notable butterflies: Lulworth skipper, adonis blue and chalkhill blue.
Contact: The Ranger, Durlston Country Park, Lighthouse Road, Swanage, Dorset BH19 2JL. 01929 424 443. e-mail: info@durlston.co.uk www.durlston.co.uk

4. HAM COMMON LNR

Poole Borough Council.
Location: SY 99. W of Poole. In Hamworthy, take the Blandford Road S along Lake Road, W along Lake Drive and Napier Road, leading to Rockley Park. Park in the beach car park by Hamworthy Pier or Rockley Viewpoint car park, off Napier Road, opposite the entrance to Gorse Hill Central Park.
Access: Open all year. Not suitable for coaches.
Facilities: None.
Habitat: Heathland, scrub, reedbeds, lake. Views over Wareham Channel and Poole Harbour.
Key birds: *Spring/summer*: Stonechat, Dartford Warbler. *Winter*: Brent Goose, Red-breasted Merganser, occasional divers, rarer grebes, Scaup. Waders inc Whimbrel, Greenshank and Common Sandpiper. *All year*: Little Egret.

Contact: Poole Borough Council, Civic Centre, Poole, BH15 2RU. 01202 633 633..
e-mail: information@poole.gov.uk

5. LODMOOR

RSPB (South West England Office).
Location: SY 686 807. Adjacent Lodmoor Country Park, in Weymouth, off A353 to Wareham.
Access: Open all times.
Facilities: One viewing shelter, network of paths.
Public transport: Local bus service.
Habitat: Marsh, shallow pools, reeds and scrub, remnant saltmarsh.
Key birds: *Spring/summer*: Breeding Common Tern, warblers (including Reed, Sedge, Grasshopper and Cetti's), Bearded Tit, Hobby. *Winter*: Wildfowl, waders, Bittern. *Passage*: Waders and other migrants.
Contact: Nick Tomlinson, RSPB Visitor Centre, Swannery Car Park, Weymouth, DT4 7TZ. 01305 778 313. www.rspb.org.uk

6. PORTLAND BIRD OBSERVATORY

Portland Bird Observatory (registered charity).
Location: SY 681 690. Six miles S of Weymouth beside the road to Portland Bill.
Access: Open at all times. Parking only for members of Portland Bird Observatory. Self-catering accommodation for up to 20. Take own towels, sheets, sleeping bags.
Facilities: Displays and information, toilets, natural history bookshop, equipped kitchen.
Public transport: Bus service from Weymouth (First Dorset Transit Route 1).
Habitat: Scrub and ponds.

Key birds: *Spring/autumn*: Migrants including many rarities. *Summer*: Breeding auks, Fulmar, Kittiwake.
Contact: Martin Cade, Old Lower Light, Portland Bill, Dorset, DT5 2JT. 01305 820 553.
e-mail: obs@btinternet.com
www.portlandbirdobs.btinternet.co.uk

7. RADIPOLE LAKE

RSPB (South West England Office).
Location: SY 677 796. In Weymouth alongside A354 (Weymouth Way). Enter from Swannery car park on footpaths.
Access: Visitor centre and nature trail open every day, summer (9am-5pm), winter (9am-4pm). Hide open (8.30am-4.30pm). Permit available from visitor centre required by non-RSPB members.
Facilities: Network of paths, one hide, one viewing shelter.
Public transport: Less than 400m from train station serving London and Bristol.
Habitat: Lake, reedbeds.
Key birds: *Winter*: Wildfowl. *Summer*: Breeding reedbed warblers (including Cetti's), Bearded Tit, passage waders and other migrants. Garganey regular in spring. Good for rarer gulls.
Contact: Nick Tomlinson, RSPB Visitor Centre, Swannery Car Park, Weymouth, DT4 7TZ. 01305 778 313. www.rspb.org.uk

8. STANPIT MARSH LNR

Community Services, Christchurch Borough Council. (Stanpit Marsh Advisory Panel)
Location: SZ 167 924. In Christchurch, close to confluence of Rivers Avon and Stour.
Access: Public open space SSSI. Limited disabled access across marshy terrain. Nearest coach parking

is at Two Riversmeet Leisure Centre, Stony Lane.
Facilities: Information centre.
Public transport: Wilts and Dorset bus no 123 (tel 01202 673 555) Stanpit recreation ground stop. Bournemouth Yellow Buses no 20 (tel 01202 636 000) Purewell Cross roundabout stop.
Habitat: Salt, fresh, brackish marsh, sand dune and scrub.
Key birds: *Estuarine*: Waders, winter wildfowl, migrants. *Reedbed*: Bearded Tit, Cetti's Warbler. *Scrub*: Sedge Warbler, Reed Warbler. *River/streams/bankside*: Kingfisher. Feeding and roosting site.
Contact: Peter Holloway, Christchurch Countryside Service, Steamer Point Nature Reserve, Highcliffe, Christchurch, Dorset BH23 4AU. 01425 272 479.
e-mail: countryside.service@christchurch.gov.uk

9. STUDLAND and GODLINGSTON HEATHS

National Trust.
Location: SZ 030 846. N of Swanage. From Ferry Road, N of Studland village.
Access: Open all year.
Facilities: Hides, nature trails.
Public transport: No 150 bus hourly to and from Bournemouth. 142/3 from Swanage and Wareham.
Habitat: Woodland, heath, dunes, inter-tidal mudflats, saltings, freshwater lake, reedbeds, carr.
Key birds: Water Rail, Reed and Dartford Warblers, Nightjar (summer-only), Stonechat.
Winter: Wildfowl. Studland Bay, outside the reserve, has winter Black-necked and Slavonian Grebes, Scoter, Eider.
Contact: The National Trust, Countryside Office, Middle Beach Car Park, Studland, Swanage, BH19 3AX.

Durham

1. HAMSTERLEY FOREST

Forestry Commission
Location: NZ 093 315. Eight miles W of Bishop Auckland. Main entrance is five miles from A68, S of Witton-le-Wear and signposted through Hamsterley village and Bedburn.
Access: Open all year. Toll charge. Forest closes 8pm (dusk in winter).
Facilities: Visitor centre, toilets, shop, access for disabled. Visitors should not enter fenced farmland.
Public transport: None.
Habitat: Commercial woodland, mixed and broadleaved trees.
Key birds: *Spring/summer*: Willow Warbler, Chiffchaff, Wood Warbler, Redstart, Pied Flycatcher.

Winter: Crossbill, Redwing, Fieldfare. *All year*: Jay, Dipper, Green Woodpecker.
Other notable flora and fauna: Hay meadows have wide variety of plants, including globe flower.
Contact: Forestry Commission, 01434 220 242.
e-mail: richard.gilchrist@forestry.gsi.gov.uk

2. JOE'S POND NATURE RESERVE

Durham Wildlife Trust.
Location: NZ 32 48. Between Durham and Sunderland on A690. N from Durham, leave A690 S of Houghton-le-Spring on B21284 to Fence Houses and Hetton-le-Hole. Head W towards Fence Houses and turn L at 1st roundabout, after 800 metres, into an opencast colliery site, signed Rye Hill Site.

NATURE RESERVES - ENGLAND

Access: Open all year.
Facilities: Car park, bird hide.
Public transport: None.
Habitat: Scrub, pond, grassland.
Key birds: *Spring/summer*: Ruddy Duck, hirundines, Whinchat, Lesser Whitethroat, Whitethroat, Blackcap. Possible Yellow Wagtail, Redstart, Grasshopper Warbler. *Passage*: Waders, Wheatear. *Winter*: Teal, Pochard, Water Rail, Woodcock, Short-eared Owl, Kingfisher, thrushes. Chance of Merlin, Jack Snipe.
Contact: Rainton Meadows, Chilton Moor, Houghton-le-Spring, Tyne and Wear, DH4 6PU. 01388 488 728.
e-mail: info@durhamwt.co.uk www. durhamwildlifetrust.org.uk

3 . MAZE PARK AND PORTRACK MARSH

Tees Valley Wildlife Trust.
Location: Maze Park: NZ 467 191, Portrack Marsh: NZ 465 194. Located midway between Middlesbrough and Stockton. Access from A66 at Tees Barrage. Sites are located on opposite banks to the River Tees, E of the barrage.
Access: No permits required. National cycle route passes through Maze Park. Surfaced paths at both sites. Hide suitable for disabled users at Portrack Marsh. Please keep to the permissive paths and public rights of way.
Facilities: Hide at Portrack Marsh. No toilets or visitor centre.
Public transport: Regular buses between Middlesbrough and Stockton stop at the Tees Barrage (Arriva, tel 0870 608 2608). Thornaby Station one mile. Frequent trains from Darlington and Middlesbrough.
Habitat: Freshwater marsh, scrub, post-industrial grassland, riverside.
Key birds: *Winter*: Ducks, passage waders, Redshank, Snipe and Jack Snipe, Lapwing, Grey Heron, Sky Lark, Grey Partridge, Sand Martin, occasional Kingfisher and Grasshopper Warbler.
Contact: Steve Ashton, Tees Valley Wildlife Trust, Margrove Heritage Centre, Margrove Park, Boosbeck, Saltburn TS12 3BZ. 01287 636 382; Fax 01287 636 383; e-mail:info@teeswildlife.co.uk www.wildlifetrust.org.uk/teesvalley

4. RAINTON MEADOWS

Durham Wildlife Trust / City of Sunderland / RJB Mining (UK) Ltd.
Location: NZ 326 486. Located W of A690 between Durham and Sunderland. Just S of Houghton-le-Spring turn onto B1284, signposted to Fence Houses and Hetton-le-Hole. Head W towards Fence Houses and turn L at the first roundabout after 0.5 miles into Rye Hill Site.
Access: Park at visitor centre (entrance gate locked at 4.30pm) or Mallard Way. Paths generally wheelchair-accessible but there are some muddy areas. Main circular walk.
Facilities: Visitor centre, toilets, café, log book, shop, wildlife display. Dogs on lead.
Public transport: Buses from Sunderland and Durham (222 and 220) stop at Mill Inn. Reserve is reached via B1284 passing under A690. Bus from Chester-le-Street (231) stops at Fencehouses Station. Walk E along B1284. Tel: Traveline 0870 608 2608.
Habitat: Reedbed, ponds, grassland, young tree plantation.
Key birds: *Spring/summer*: Great Crested Grebe, Ruddy Duck, Whinchat, Reed Warbler. *Winter*: Water Rail, Kingfisher, Peregrine, Merlin, Long and Short-eared Owls. *Passage*: Waders.
Contact: Durham Wildlife Trust, 0191 5843 112. www.wildlifetrust.org.uk/durham

5. STANG FOREST AND HOPE MOOR

Forestry Commission
Location: NZ 022 075. The wood is six miles S of Barnard Castle. On A66 follow signs for Reeth after the turn-off to Barnard Castle on the W-bound carriageway. Stang is then about 3.5 miles from the A66 (car park for Hope Edge Walk).
Access: Open all year. Road hazardous in frost.
Facilities: Number of parking lay-bys and forest trails. Trail best for birdwatchers heads E and then N to Hope Edge.
Public transport: None.
Habitat: Woodland, moorland.
Key birds: *Spring/summer*: Whinchat, Wheatear, Cuckoo. *All year*: Red Grouse, Crossbill.
Contact: Forestry Commission, 01434 220 242.

6. TEESMOUTH

Natural England (North East Region).
Location: Two components, centred on NZ 535 276 and NZ 530 260, three and five miles S of Hartlepool, E of A178. Access to northern component from car park at NZ 534 282, 0.5 miles E of A178. Access to southern part from A178 bridge over Greatham Creek

at NZ 510 254. Car park adjacent to A178 at NZ 508 251. Both car parks can accommodate coaches.
Access: Open at all times. In northern component, no restrictions over most of dunes and North Gare Sands (avoid golf course, dogs must be kept under close control).
In southern component, disabled access path to public hides at NZ 516 255 and NZ 516 252 (no other access).
Facilities: Nearest toilets at Seaton Carew, one mile to the N. Disabled access path and hides (see above), interpretive panels and leaflet. Teesmouth Field Centre (Tel: 01429 264 912).
Public transport: Half-hourly bus service (service 1) operates Mon-Sat between Middlesbrough and Hartlepool (hourly on Sundays), along A178,

Stagecoach Hartlepool, Tel: 01429 267 082.
Habitat: Grazing marsh, dunes, intertidal flats.
Key birds: Passage and winter wildfowl and waders. Passage terns and skuas in late summer. Scarce passerine migrants and rarities. *Winter*: Merlin, Peregrine, Snow Bunting, Twite, divers, grebes.
Other notable flora and fauna: Northern component has large marsh orchid populations in damp dune grassland. Seal Sands supports a colony of 70 common seals.
Contact: Mike Leakey, Natural England, c/o British Energy, Tees Road, Hartlepool, TS25 2BZ. 01429 853 325. email: northumbria@naturalengland.org.uk www.naturalengland.org.uk

Essex

1. ABBERTON RESERVOIR

Essex Wildlife Trust.
Location: TL 963 185. Five miles SW of Colchester on B1026. Follow signs from Layer-de-la-Haye.
Access: Open Tue-Sun and Bank Holiday Mondays (9am-5pm). Closed Christmas Day and Boxing Day.
Facilities: Visitor centre, toilets, nature trail, five hides (3 with disabled access). Ample parking, including coaches. Also good viewing where roads cross reservoir.
Public transport: Phone Trust for advice.
Habitat: 100 acres on edge of 1200a reservoir.
Key birds: *Winter*: Nationally important for Mallard, Teal, Wigeon, Shoveler, Gadwall, Pochard, Tufted Duck, Goldeneye (most important inland site in Britain). Smew and Goosander regular. Passage waders, terns, birds of prey. Tree-nesting Cormorant colony; raft-nesting Common Tern. *Summer*: Hobby, Yellow Wagtail, warblers, Nightingale, Corn Bunting; *Autumn*: Red-crested Pochard, Water Rail.
Other notable flora and fauna: Dragonflies including broad-bodied chaser, small red-eyed damselfly, butterflies including green and purple hairstreak, roesel's bush-cricket. Brown hare.
Contact: Centre Manager, Essex Wildlife Trust,, Abberton Reservoir Visitor Centre, Church Road, Layer-de-la-Haye, Colchester CO2 0EU. 01206 738 172. e-mail: abberton@essexwt.org.uk

2. ABBOTTS HALL FARM

Essex Wildlife Trust.
Location: TL 963 145. Seven miles SW from Colchester. Turn E off B1026 (Colchester–Maldon road) towards Peldon. Entrance is about 0.5 mile on R.
Access: Weekdays (9am-5pm). No dogs please. Working farm so please take care.
Facilities: Toilets, hides, guided walks, fact-sheets.

Public transport: None.
Habitat: Nearly 700 acres of saltmarsh, saline lagoons, grazing marsh, farmland on the Blackwater Estuary.
Key birds: *Winter*: Waders and wildfowl. *Summer*: Little Tern, waders, Shelduck, Grey Partridge.
Contact: Essex Wildlife Trust, 01621 862 960. e-mail: admin@essexwt.org.uk

3. BRADWELL BIRD OBSERVATORY

Essex Birdwatching Society
Location: 100 yards S of St Peter's Chapel, Bradwell-on-Sea. Mouth of Blackwater estuary, between Maldon and Foulness.
Access: Open all year.
Facilities: Accommodation for eight in hut; two rooms each with four bunks; blankets, cutlery, etc. supplied.
Public transport: None.
Habitat: Mudflats, saltmarsh.
Key birds: *Winter*: Wildfowl (inc. Brent Geese, Red-throated Diver, Red-breasted Merganser), large numbers of waders; small numbers of Twite, Snow Bunting and occasional Shore Lark on beaches, also Hen Harrier, Merlin and Peregrine. Good passage of migrants usual in spring and autumn. *Summer*: Small breeding population of terns and other estuarine species.
Contact: Graham Smith, 48 The Meads, Ingatestone, Essex, CM4 0AE. 01277 354 034.

4. CHIGBOROUGH LAKES

Essex Wildlife Trust.
Location: GR 877 086. Lies NE of Maldon, about one mile from Heybridge on the B1026 towards Tolleshunt d'Arcy, turn N into Chigborough Road. Continue past fishery entrance and Chigborough Farm buildings until you see an entrance gate to Chigborough Quarry. The

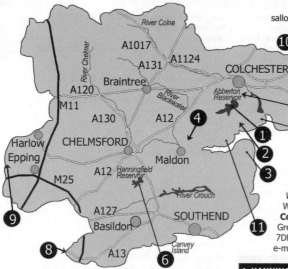

sallow/birch thickets, young scrub, reedbeds, saltmarsh, gorse heathland.

Other notable flora and fauna: 350 species of flowering plants, 13 species of breeding dragonfly, common lizard, great crested newt.

Key birds: *Autumn/winter*: Brent Goose, waders, Hen Harrier, Little Egret. *Spring*: 30 male Nightingales. Good variety of warblers in scrub, thickets, reedbeds and Turtle Dove, Green/Great Spotted Woodpeckers. *Winter*: Little Grebe, Mute Swan, Teal, Wigeon, Shoveler, Gadwall on lake.

Contact: Laurie Forsyth, Wick Farm, South Green Road, Fingringhoe, Colchester, CO5 7DN. 01206 729 678.

e-mail: admin@essexwt.org.uk

---

reserve entrance is just beyond this point on the L.

Access: Open all year. Do not obstruct the gravel pit entrance.

Facilities: Car park with height restriction barrier of 5ft 9in.

Public transport: Bus: Colchester to Maldon Leisure Centre along the B1026.

Habitat: Flooded gravel pits, small ponds, willow carr, grassland, scrub.

Key birds: *Spring/summer*: Sedge and Reed Warblers, Whitethroat, Reed Bunting, Willow Warbler, Great Crested and Little Grebes, Kingfisher, Water Rail. *Passage*: Waders, including Greenshank.

Other notable flora and fauna: Grass snakes and common lizards, good numbers of common blue, small copper and ringlet butterflies, plus dragonflies.

Contact: Essex Wildlife Trust, 01621 862 960.

e-mail: admin@essexwt.org.uk www.essexwt.org.uk

5. FINGRINGHOE WICK

Essex Wildlife Trust.

Location: TM 048 143. Colchester five miles. The Trust's flagship reserve is signposted from B1025 to Mersea Island, S of Colchester.

Access: Open six days per week (not Mon or Christmas or Boxing Day). No permits needed. Donations invited. Centre/reserve open (9am-5pm). Dogs must be on a lead.

Facilities: Visitor centre – toilets, shop, light refreshments, car park, displays. Reserve – seven bird hides, two nature trails, plus one that wheelchair users could use with assistance. Late night opening for nocturnal mammals – booking essential on 01206 729 678.

Public transport: None.

Habitat: Old gravel pit, large lake, many ponds,

6. HANNINGFIELD RESERVOIR

Essex Wildlife Trust.

Location: TQ 725 972. Three miles N of Wickford. Exit off Southend Road (Old A130) at Rettendon onto South Hanningfield Road. Follow this for two miles until reaching the T-junction with Hawkswood Road. Turn R and the entrance to the Visitor Centre and reserve is one mile on the R.

Access: Open Mon-Sun (9am-5pm) all year. Disabled parking, toilets, and adapted birdwatching hide. No dogs. No cycling.

Facilities: Visitor centre, gift shop, optics, refreshments, toilets, four bird hides, nature trails, picnic area, coach parking, education room.

Public transport: Chelmsford to Wickford bus no 14 to Downham village and walk half mile down Crowsheath Lane.

Habitat: Mixed woodland (110 acres) with grassy glades and rides, adjoining 870-acre Hanningfield Reservoir, designated an SSSI due to its high numbers of wildfowl.

Key birds: *Spring*: Good numbers and mix of woodland warblers. *Summer*: Vast numbers of Swifts, Swallows and martins feeding over the water. Hobby and Osprey. *Winter*: Good numbers and mix of waterfowl. Large gull roost.

Other notable flora and fauna: Spectacular displays of bluebells in spring. Damselflies and dragonflies around the ponds. Grass snakes and common lizards sometimes seen basking in rides.

Contact: Bill Godsafe, Hanningfield Reservoir Visitor Centre, Hawkswood Road, Downham, Billericay, CM11 1WT. 01268 711 001. www.essexwt.org.uk

7. OLD HALL MARSHES

RSPB (Eastern England Office).

Location: TL 97 51 25. Approx eight miles S of

Colchester. From A12 take B1023, via Tiptree, to Tolleshunt D'Arcy. Then take Chapel Road (back road to Tollesbury), after one mile turn L into Old Hall Lane. Continue up Old Hall Lane, over speed ramp and through iron gates to cattle grid, then follow signs to car park.
Access: By permit only in advance from Warden, write to address below. Open 9am-9pm or dusk, closed Tues. No coaches.
Facilities: Two trails – one of three miles and one of 6.5 miles. Two viewing screens overlooking saline lagoon area at E end of reserve. No visitor centre or toilets.
Habitat: Coastal grazing marsh, reedbed, open water saline lagoon, saltmarsh and mudflat.
Key birds: *Summer*: Breeding Avocet, Redshank, Lapwing, Pochard, Shoveler, Gadwall, Garganey, Barn Owl. *Winter*: Brent Goose, Wigeon, Teal, Shoveler, Goldeneye, Red-breasted Merganser, all the expected waders, Hen Harrier, Merlin, Short-eared Owl and Twite.
Passage: All expected waders (particularly Spotted Redshank, Green Sandpiper and Whimbrel), Yellow Wagtail, Whinchat and Wheatear.
Contact: Paul Charlton, Site Manager, c/o 1 Old Hall Lane, Tolleshunt D'Arcy, Maldon, Essex CM9 8TP. 01621 869 015. e-mail: paul.charlton@rspb.org.uk

8. RAINHAM MARSHES

RSPB (Eastern England Office).
Location: On N bank of River Thames, SE of Dagenham. From London take A13 to A1306 turn-off and head towards Purfleet for half a mile. At traffic lights, turn right, signposted A1090 and reserve entrance is 300 metres along this road.
Access: Open all year. Extensive programme of guided walks – check RSPB website for details. Approx 3.5 miles of boardwalks suitable for wheelchairs and pushchairs.
Facilities: Visitor centre, disabled toilets, car park on site, picnic area, shop, refreshments available. One bird hide.
Public transport: Route 44 (Ensignbus – 01708 865 656) runs daily between Grays and Lakeside via Purfleet. Arriva service (0870 120 1088) hourly Sundays and most Public Holidays.
Habitat: A former MoD shooting range, the site is the largest remaining expanse of wetland along the upper reaches of the Thames.
Key birds: *Spring*: Marsh Harrier, Hobby, Wheatear, hirundines and other migrants. *Summer*: Many waders, including Black-tailed Godwit, Whimbrel, Greenshank, Snipe, Lapwing, Avocet. Yellow-legged Gull. Merlin and Peregrine hunt among the gathering wader flocks.
Winter: Waders, wildfowl, Water Pipit, Short-eared owl, Little Egret.
Other notable flora and fauna: Bank and water voles, water shrew, fox, stoat, weasel, dragonflies.
Contact: The Warden, RSPB Eastern England Office, Stalham House, The Green, 65 Thorpe Road, Norwich,
Norfolk NR1 1UD. 01603 661 662. www.rspb.org.uk/reserves/

9. RIVER LEE COUNTRY PARK

Lee Valley Park
Location: Close to Waltham Abbey, Essex. Fishers Green entrance off B194.
Access: All hides open to public at weekends and Bank Holidays (excepting Christmas Day). Permit needed for weekday use - contact Lee Valley Park for details. Groups should also book with Info Centre.
Hides and paths suitable for wheelchairs.
Facilities: Café, toilet and shop at Hayes Hill Farm. Information centre off A121 in Waltham Abbey. Bittern Watchpoint at Lee Valley Park.
Public transport: All sites served by buses - call Essex Bus Info on 0345 000 333 or Herts Travel Line on 01992 556 765.
Habitat: Former gravel pits now flooded, with wooded islands, reedbeds and marshy corners.
Key birds: *Winter*: Bittern at Fishers Green (hide open every day). Wide variety of wildfowl inc Smew, Goosander, Shoveler and Gadwall. *Summer*: Breeding warblers, Nightingale, Little Ringed Plover, Turtle Dove. Wide variety of species on spring/autumn passage.
Contact: Lee Valley Regional Park Authority, Myddelton House, Bulls Cross, Enfield, Middlesex EN2 9HG. 01992 717 711. www.leevalleypark.org.uk E-mail: Info@leevalleypark.org.uk

10. STOUR ESTUARY

RSPB (Eastern England Office).
Location: Between Manningtree and Harwich. From Manningtree, stay on B1352 past Strangers Home pub in Bradfield, then look for brown sign to reserve.
Access: Open all year. Stour wood walk (1 mile) OK for wheelchairs in dry conditions. Walks to estuary and furthest hide not suitable, due to terrain and kissing gates. Dogs only allowed in Stour Wood.
Facilities: Two hides, one viewing screen. Two picnic tables.
Public transport: Nearest train station (One Railway) at Wrabness is 1 mile away. Hourly buses (Mon - Sat) running between Colchester and Harwich will stop at entrance to woods on request.
Habitat: Extensive woodland leading down to the River Stour estuary, saltmarsh at Deep Fleet and mudflats at Copperas Bay.
Key birds: *Spring/autumn*: Black-tailed Godwit, Dunlin, Ringed Plover. *Summer*: Nightingale and warblers. *Winter*: Brent Goose, plus nationally important numbers of wildfowl and waders.
Other notable flora and fauna: Woodland wildflowers in spring.
Contact: The Warden, RSPB Eastern England Office, Stalham House, The Green, 65 Thorpe Road, Norwich, Norfolk NR1 1UD. 01603 661 662. www.rspb.org.uk/reserves/

11. TOLLESBURY WICK MARSHES NATURE RESERVE

Essex Wildlife Trust.
Location: TL 969 104. On Blackwater Estuary eight miles E of Maldon. Follow B1023 to Tollesbury via Tiptree, leaving A12 at Kelvedon. Then follow Woodrolfe Road S towards marina. Use small public car park at Woodrolfe Green (TL 964 107), 500m before reserve entrance on sea wall.
Car park suitable for mini-buses and small coaches.
Access: Open all times along public footpath on top of sea wall. Route exposed to elements, so be prepared with adequate clothing and footwear. Motorised wheelchair access possible to Block House Bay.
Facilities: Public toilets at Woodrolfe Green car park.
Public transport: Hedingham bus services run to Tollesbury from Maldon, Colchester and Witham – call 01621 869 214 for information.

Habitat: Estuary with fringing saltmarsh and mudflats with some shingle. Extensive freshwater grazing marsh, brackish borrowdyke and small reedbeds.
Key birds: *Winter*: Large numbers of wintering wildfowl and waders, particularly Brent Geese and Wigeon, Lapwing and Golden Plover. Short-eared Owl, Hen Harrier and, increasingly, Marsh Harrier. *Summer*: Breeding Avocet, Redshank, Lapwing, Little Tern, Reed and Sedge Warblers, Reed Bunting, Barn Owl. *Passage*: Whimbrel, Spotted Redshank, Green Sandpiper.
Other notable flora and fauna: Plants include spiny resharrow, grass vetchling, slender hare's ear, yellow horned poppy. Hairy dragonfly, Roesel's and great green bush chrickets – all can be seen from the footpath on top of the sea wall.
Contact: Jonathan Smith, Tollesbury, Maldon, Essex, CM9 8RJ. 01621 868 628.
e-mail: jonathans@essexwt.org.uk

Gloucestershire

1. ASHLEWORTH HAM NATURE RESERVE

Gloucestershire Wildlife Trust.
Location: SO 830 265. Leave Gloucester N on A417; R at Hartpury and follow minor road through Ashleworth towards Hasfield.
Access: Access prohibited at all times but birds may be viewed from new hide in Meerend Thicket.
Facilities: Bird viewing hide and screen, interpretation panels.
Public transport: None.
Habitat: Low-lying grassland flood plain.
Key birds: *Winter*: Wildfowl (inc. 4,000 Wlgeon, 1,500 Teal, Pintail, Goldeneye, Bewick's Swan), passage waders, Peregrine. *Summer*: Hobby, breeding waders and warblers.
Contact: Gloucestershire Wildlife Trust, Conservation Centre, Robinswood Hill Country Park, Reservoir Road, Gloucester, GL4 6SX. 01452 383 333. e-mail: info@gloucestershirewildlifetrust.co.uk www.gloucestershirewildlifetrust.co.uk

2. COTSWOLD WATER PARK

Cotswold Water Park Society.
Location: The CWP comprises 140 lakes in the Upper Thames Valley, between Cirencester and Swindon. Many of these lakes can be accessed by the public using rights of way. Start from Cotswold Water Park Gateway visitor centre (SU 072 971). The visitor centre is immediately on L after A419.
For Millenium visitor centre at Keynes Country Park (SU 026 957) from A419, take B4696 towards Ashton

Keynes. At staggered crossroads, go straight over, heading towards Somerford Keynes. Take next R turn to Circencester. The entrance to Keynes Country Park is the second entrance on the R.
Access: Cotswold Water Park is open all year round. The visitor centres are open every day except Christmas Day.
Facilities: Paths are flat but with stiles and footbridges. Many are wheelchair accessible. Toilets, refreshments, car parking and information available from the visitor centres. Hides available at Cleveland Lakes/Waterhay (lakes 68a and 68c), Shorncote Reed Bed (lakes 84/85), Cokes Pit (Lake 34) and Whelford Pools (Lake 111).
Free copies of the CWP Leisure Guide are available from the visitor centres. These have maps showing the lake numbering. The guidebook *Wildlife in the Cotswold Water Park: Where to go and what to see* also available from centres.
Public transport: Bus: from Kemble, Cheltenham, Cirencester and Swindon. Tel: 08457 090 899. Train: nearest station is four miles away at Kemble. Tel: 08457 484 950.
Habitat: Gravel extraction has created more than 1,000ha of standing open water or 140 lakes, plus other associated wetland habitats, creating one of the largest man-made wetlands in Europe.
Key birds: *Winter*: Common wildfowl, Smew, Red-crested Pochard, Merlin, Peregrine. *Summer*: Breeding ducks, warblers, Nightingale, Hobby, Common Tern, Black-headed Gull colony, Reed Bunting, hirundines.

Contact: Cotswold Water Park Society, Cotswold House, Down Ampney Estate, Cirencester, Glos GL7 5QF. 01793 752 413. e-mail: info@waterpark.org www.waterpark.org

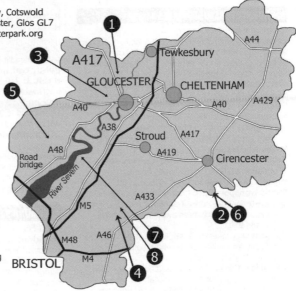

3. HIGHNAM WOODS

RSPB South West Regional Office.
Location: SO 778 190. Signed on A40 three miles W of Gloucester.
Access: Open at all times, no permit required. The nature trails can be very muddy. Some limited wheelchair access. Dogs allowed on leads.
Facilities: One nature trail (approx 1.5 miles).
Public transport: Contact Glos. County Council public transport information line. Tel: 0871 2002 233.
Habitat: Ancient woodland in the Severn Vale with areas of coppice and scrub.
Key birds: *Spring/summer*: The reserve has about 12 pairs of breeding Nightingales. Resident birds include all three woodpeckers, Buzzard and Sparrowhawk. Ravens are frequently seen. *Winter*: Feeding site near car park for woodland birds.
Other notable flora and fauna: Tintern spurge in late June-early July. White-letter hairstreak and white admiral butterflies seen annually.
Contact: Barry Embling, Site Manager, The Puffins, Parkend, Lydney, Glos, GL15 4JA. 01594 562 852. e-mail: barry.embling@rspb.org.uk www.rspb.org.uk

4. LOWER WOODS NATURE RESERVE

Gloucestershire Wildlife Trust.
Location: Reserve is about one mile E of Wickwar. Main parking is at Lower Woods Lodge, via a track off the Wickwar-Hawkesbury road. Public footpaths and bridleways cross the reserve.
Access: Open all year.
Facilities: Footpaths and bridleways. Walk leaflet available.
Public transport: None.
Habitat: Mixed woodland, mildly acidic or slightly calcareous clay, grassland, river, springs.
Key birds: *Spring/summer*: Nightingale. *All year*: Usual woodland species.
Contact: Gloucestershire Wildlife Trust, 01452 383 333. e-mail: info@gloucestershirewildlifetrust.co.uk www.gloucestershirewildlifetrust.co.uk

5. NAGSHEAD

RSPB South West Regional Office.
Location: SO 097 085. In Forest of Dean, N of Lydney. Signed immediately W of Parkend village on the road to Coleford.
Access: Open at all times, no permit required. The reserve is hilly and there are some stiles on nature trails. Some limited wheelchair access. Dogs must be kept on leads during bird nesting season and under close control at all other times.
Facilities: There are two nature trails (one mile and 2.25 miles). Information centre, with toilet facilities (including disabled), open at weekends mid-Apr to end Aug. Schools education programme available.
Public transport: Contact Glos. County Council public transport information line, 0871 2002 233.
Habitat: Much of the reserve is 200-year-old oak plantations, grazed in some areas by sheep. The rest of the reserve is a mixture of open areas and conifer/ mixed woodland.
Key birds: *Spring*: Pied Flycatcher, Wood Warbler, Redstart, warblers. *Winter*: Siskin, Crossbill in some years. *All year*: Buzzard, Raven, Hawfinch, all three woodpeckers.
Other notable flora and fauna: Golden ringed dragonfly seen annually. Silver-washed and pearl-bordered fritillary and white admiral butterflies present.
Contact: Barry Embling, Site Manager, The Puffins, Parkend, Lydney, Glos, GL15 4JA. 01594 562 852. e-mail:barry.embling@rspb.org.uk www.rspb.org.uk

6. SHORNCOTE REEDBED (LAKES 84/85)

Cotswold Water Park Society.
Location: SU 026 957. Lakes 84/85 located adjacent to Keynes Country Park and most easily accessed from here. From A419, take B4696 towards Ashton Keynes. At the staggered crossroads, go straight over, heading towards Somerford Keynes. Take the next R turn to Circencester. The entrance to Keynes Country Park is the second entrance on the R.
Access: Open at all times to walkers. Seasonal opening hours - check website for details. Per person charges apply. Paths are uneven with footbridges. No disabled access.
Facilities: Toilets, refreshments, car parking and information available from Keynes Country Park adjacent. A hide with log book is located on E shore.
Public transport: Bus: from Kemble, Cheltenham, Cirencester and Swindon. Tel: 08457 090 899. Train: nearest station is four miles away at Kemble. Tel: 08457 484 950.
Habitat: Only lakes in Cotswold Water Park restored specifically for wildlife. Lakes with reedbed, marsh, ditches, islands and loafing areas.
Key birds: *Winter*: Common wildfowl, Smew, Peregrine, Merlin, Bittern, Stonechat. *Summer*: Breeding ducks, warblers, Hobby, Reed Bunting.
Contact: Cotswold Water Park Society, 01793 752 413.

7. SLIMBRIDGE

The Wildfowl and Wetlands Trust.
Location: SO 723 048. Famous Ramsar site, S of Gloucester. Signposted from M5 (exit 13 or 14).
Access: Open daily except Christmas Day, (9am-5.30pm, 5pm in winter). Group visits a speciality. Contact Bookings Officer 01453 891 900.

Facilities: Hides, observatory, observation tower, Hanson Discovery Centre, wildlife art gallery, tropical house, facilities for disabled, worldwide collection of wildfowl species. Land-Rover safaris on selected dates. Floodlit bird feeds in winter.
Public transport: Not known.
Habitat: 350 hectares of reedbed, saltmarsh, freshwater pools, mudflats.
Key birds: Water Rail, Kingfisher, waders, raptors. *Winter*; Up to 35,000 wildfowl esp. Bewick's Swans, White-fronted Geese, Wigeon, Teal.
Other notable flora and fauna: Otter, orchids, dragonflies.
Contact: Samantha Snow, Marketing Manager, The Wildfowl and Wetlands Trust, Slimbridge, Gloucester, GL2 7BT. 01453 891 900; Fax 01453 890 927. e-mail: info.slimbridge@wwt.org.uk

8. SYMOND'S YAT

RSPB/Forestry Commission England.
Location: SO 563 160. Hill-top site on the edge of Forest of Dean, three miles N of Coleford on B4432, signposted from Forest Enterprise car park. Also signposted from A40, S of Ross-on-Wye.
Access: Open at all times. RSPB Information Officer on site daily, April to August..
Facilities: Car park, toilets with adapted facilities for disabled visitors, picnic area, drinks and light snacks. Environmental education programmes available.
Public transport: None.
Habitat: Cliff above the River Wye and woodland.
Key birds: *Summer*: Peregrine, Buzzard, Goshawk, Raven and woodland species. Telescope is set up daily for members of public to watch the Peregrines on the nest.
Contact: The Puffins, Parkend, Lydney, Gloucestershire, GL15 4JA. 01594 562 852.

Hampshire

1. BLASHFORD LAKES

Hampshire and Isle of Wight Wildlife Trust / Wessex Water / Bournemouth and West Hampshire Water / New Forest District Council.
Location: SU 153 080. From Ringwood take A338 for two miles towards Fordingbridge/Salisbury, pass Ivy Lane R and take next R to Moyles Court / Linwood at Ellingham Cross, into Ellingham Drove.
The main car park for hides is first L (entrance shared with Hanson works) after 400 yards. For Education Centre turn R opposite (entrance shared with Wessex Water and water-ski club) and straight on through gate and bear R between wooden pillars.
Parking is just inside pillars or in front of centre.

Access: A network of permissive paths through the reserve link New Forest and Avon Valley Long Distance footpaths. These paths and a number of wildlife viewing screens are always open. The six hides and centre are open daily (9am-4.30pm).
For school and other organised visits, please phone for further details. No dogs allowed on the reserve. The paths are fully wheelchair accessible and kissing gates are RADAR key operated to allow passage of disability buggies.
Facilities: Parking, footpaths, six hides, viewing screens, toilets and information including recent sightings board. Coach parking by arrangement. Picnic tables available beside the centre when not being used by booked groups.

Public transport: A bus route runs along the A338 Ringwood to Salisbury/Fordingbridge road with stops just north of Ivy Lane, Ellingham Cross and Ibsley Church.

Habitat: Flooded gravel pits, areas of wet woodland, some of it ancient, also dry grassland and lichen heath.

Key birds: *Winter*: Large number of over-wintering wildfowl, with species such as Tufted Duck, Pochard, Wigeon, Shoveler, Goosander and internationally important numbers of Gadwall. Also a large gull roost. *Spring/summer*: Breeding birds include Common Tern, Lapwing, Redshank, Oystercatcher, Kingfisher, Garden Warblers are especially common. *Autumn*: Waders on migration including Green and Common Sandpipers and Greenshank, also Hobby, Black Tern and passerines.

Other notable flora and fauna: Dragonflies (23 species recorded) including brown hawker, scarce chaser and large and small red-eyed damselfly. Roe deer are regular, badger, otter, fox. Reptiles include adder and grass snake.

Contact: Blashford Lakes Centre, Ellingham Drove, Ringwood, Hampshire BH24 3PJ. 01425 472 760. e mail: feedback@hwt.org.uk, www.hwt.org.uk

2. FARLINGTON MARSHES

Hampshire and Isle of Wight Wildlife Trust.

Location: SU 685 045. North of Langstone Harbour. Main entrance off roundabout junction A2030/A27.

Access: Open at all times, no charge or permits, but donations welcome. Dogs on leads only. Wheelchair access via RADAR gates. Short slopes up to sea wall, flat but uneven surfaces. Paths around site are mostly on level ground but main path running along sea wall can be uneven and muddy in wet weather. Groups – please book to avoid clash of dates.

Facilities: 2.5 mile trail. Information at entrance and shelter. No toilets.

Public transport: By bus: Several bus routes pass along the A2030 (Easter Road), close to the western entrance to the marsh. Contact First bus service on 023 8058 4321. By train: Hilsea station is one mile from reserve. Contact South West Trains on 0845 6000 650.

Habitat: Coastal grazing marsh with pools and reedbed within reserve. Views over intertidal mudflats/ saltmarshes of Langstone Harbour.

Key birds: *Summer*: Breeding waders and wildfowl (including Lapwing, Redshank and Shelduck) also breeding Cetti's, Sedge and Reed Warbler, Bearded Tit. *Autumn to spring*: Waders and wildfowl, good numbers of migrating Yellow Wagtail among the cattle. *Winter*: Brent Goose, Wigeon, Pintail etc and waders (Dunlin, Grey Plover etc). On migration wide range of waders including rarities. Reedbeds with Bearded Tit, Water

Rail etc, scrub areas attract small migrants (Redstart, Wryneck, warblers etc).

Contact: Mike Allen, Hampshire and Isle of Wight Wildlife Trust, Beechcroft House, Vicarage Lane, Curdridge, Hants SO32 2DP. 01489 774 439. www.hwt.org.uk - go to 'Reserves' and then 'news' for sightings, etc

3. FLEET POND LNR

Hart District Council Service / Fleet Pond Society.

Location: SY 85. Located in Fleet, W of Farnborough. From the B3013, head to Fleet Station. Park in the long-stay car park at Fleet Station. Parking also available in Chestnut Grove and Westover Road. Pond car park off B3013.

Access: Open all year.

Facilities: Some surfaced paths, boardwalks in wet areas.

Public transport: Fleet railway station lies N of site.

Habitat: SSSI. Lake, marshes, reedbeds, heathland, wet and dry woodland.

Key birds: *Spring/autumn*: Migrant waders incl. Little Ringed Plover, Dunlin, Greenshank, Little Gull, Lesser Spotted Woodpecker, occasional Kittiwake, terns, Wood Lark, Sky Lark, occasional Ring Ouzel, Firecrest, Pied Flycatcher. *Summer*: Hobby, Common Tern, Tree Pipit, occasional Red Kite and Osprey. *Winter*: Bittern, wildfowl, occasional Smew, Snipe, Jack Snipe, Siskin, Redpoll.

Other notable flora and fauna: Dragonflies and

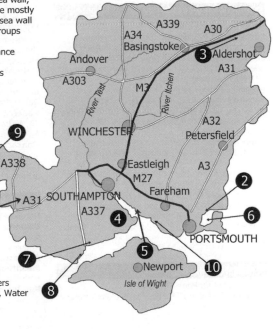

damselflies in wet areas of marshes and heathlands. Butterflies, roe deer. Plants include ling and bell heather, phragmites reeds.
Contact: Hart District Council, Civic Office,, Harlington Way, Fleet, Hampshire, GU51 4AE. 01252 622 122. e-mail: countryside@hart.gov.uk

4. HAMBLE COMMON AND COPSE

Eastleigh Borough Council (Countryside Service).
Location: SU 48 09. Hamble Common is reached via Copse Lane from the B3397 Hamble Lane, which links with A27 and M27 (junction B) at Windhover roundabout near Bursledon.
Access: Open all year.
Facilities: Car parks are linked to each other and the rest of the site by a good network of footpaths. Ground conditions good in summer, but in winter/after rain, stout waterproof footwear is advisable.
Public transport: None.
Habitat: Wet heathland, scrub, woodland, meadow, grassland overlookimg Southampton Water.
Key birds: *Winter*: Wildfowl and waders. On the Southampton Water shore, Oystercatcher, Grey Plover, Ringed Plover, Dunlin, Turnstone, Curlew and Brent Geese common. In the creek wader numbers are lower, with Redshank, Lapwing and Dunlin, occasional Greenshank, Teal, Mallard, Shelduck, Grey Heron, Kingfisher most years.
Contact: Eastleigh Borough Council, Civic Office, Leigh Road, Eastleigh, Hampshire, SO50 9YN. 023 8046 6 091. e-mail: ivcp@eastleigh.gov.uk www.eastleigh.gov.uk

5. HOOK-WITH-WARSASH LNR

Hampshire County Council.
Location: SU 490 050. Six miles W of Fareham on shore of River Hamble and Solent. Take junction 9 off M27 towards Southampton and follow signs for Warsash. Car parks by foreshore at Warsash. Reserve includes Hook Lake.
Access: Open all year.
Facilities: Public footpaths. Kissing gates at entrances. Wheelchair users can gain access at Bunay Meadows and Shore Road, Warsash. RADAR lock on toilet at Passage Lane.
Public transport: Nearest bus stop in Warsash.
Habitat: Shingle beach, saltings, marsh, reedbed, scrape.
Key birds: Winter: Brent Geese on Hamble estuary. Waders. Stonechat, Cetti's Warbler.
Other notable flora and fauna: White letter hairstreak, green hairstreak and small copper butterflies. Reptiles and various dragonfly species.
Contact: Barry Duffin, Titchfield Haven Visitor Centre, Cliff Road, Hill Head, Fareham, Hants PO14 3JT. 01329 662 145; Fax 01329 667 113.

6. LANGSTONE HARBOUR

RSPB (South East Region Office).
Location: SU 695 035. Harbour lies E of Portsmouth,

one mile S of Havant. Car parks at Broadmarsh (SE of A27/A3(M) junction) and West Hayling LNR (first R on A2030 after Esso garage).
Access: Restricted access. Good views from West Hayling LNR, Broadmarsh and Farlington Marshes LNR (qv).
Facilities: Mainline trains all stop at Havant. Local bus service to W Hayling LNR.
Public transport:
Habitat: Intertidal mud, saltmarsh, shingle islands.
Key birds: *Summer*: Breeding waders and seabirds inc. Mediterranean Gull and Little Tern. *Passage/winter*: Waterfowl, inc. Black-necked Grebes, c5,000 dark-bellied Brent Geese, Shelduck, Shoveler, Goldeneye and Red-breasted Merganser. Waders inc. Oystercatcher, Ringed and Grey Plover, Dunlin, Black and Bar-tailed Godwits and Greenshank. Peregrine, Merlin and Short-eared Owl.
Contact: Chris Cockburn (Warden), RSPB Langstone Harbour, Unit B3, Wren Centre, Emsworth, Hants PO10 7SU. 01243 378 784.
e-mail: chris.cockburn@rspb.org.uk

7. LYMINGTON REEDBEDS

Hampshire and Isle of Wight Wildlife Trust.
Location: SZ 324 965. From Lyndhurst in New Forest take A337 to Lymington. Turn L after railway bridge into Marsh Lane. Park in the lay-by next to allotments. The reserve entrance is on opposite side, to R of the house and over railway crossing. The footpath exits the reserve near the Old Ampress Works, leading to a minor road between the A337 and Boldre.
Access: Open all year. The best viewpoint over the reedbeds is from Bridge Road or from the Undershore leading from the B3054.
Facilities: None.
Public transport: Bus: at either end of the footpath through site, Marsh Lane and on the A337 (route 112). Five minutes walk from train station.
Habitat: One of largest reedbeds on S coast, fringed by alder and willow woodland.
Key birds: One of highest concentrations of Water Rail in the country; resident but most evident in winter. *Spring/summer*: Cetti's Warbler, Bearded Tit, Yellow Wagtail, Swallow, martins, Reed Warbler. *Passage*: Snipe, ducks. Otters are in the area.
Contact: Michael Boxall, Hampshire and Isle of Wight Wildlife Trust, Beechcroft House, Vicarage Lane, Curdridge, Hants SO32 2DP. 01489 774 400.
e-mail: feedback@hwt.org.uk www.hwt.org.uk

8. LYMINGTON-KEYHAVEN NNR

Hampshire County Council.
Location: SZ 315 920. S of Lymington along seawall footpath; car parks at Bath Road, Lymington and at Keyhaven Harbour.
Access: Open all year.
Facilities: None.
Habitat: Coastal marshland and lagoons.
Key birds: Nationally important for breeding and

wintering species. *Spring*: Passage waders (inc. Knot, Sanderling, Bar-tailed and Black-tailed Godwits, Whimbrel, Spotted Redshank), Pomarine and Great Skuas. Breeding Oystercatcher, Ringed Plover, Sandwich, Common and Little Terns. *Autumn*: Passage raptors, waders and passerines. *Winter*: Wildfowl inc. Brent Goose, Wigeon, Pintail, Red-breasted Merganser, waders inc. Golden Plover, Little Egret, gulls.
Contact: Hampshire County Council, Mottisfont Court, High Street, Winchester, Hants SO23 8ZF.

9. MARTIN DOWN

Natural England (Wiltshire Team).
Location: SU 05 19. Nine miles SW of Salisbury. Car park on A354.
Access: Open access, organised groups of 10+ should book in advance. Car park height barrier of 7ft 6 ins. Coaches only by prior arrangement. Hard flat track from A354 car park suitable for wheelchairs.
Facilities: Two car parks, interpretative boards.
Public transport: One bus Salisbury/Blandford. Call 01722 336 855 or visit www.wdbus.co.uk
Habitat: Chalk downland and scub.
Key birds: *Spring/summer*: Grey Partridge, Turtle Dove, warblers, Nightingale. *Winter*: Occasional Merlin, Hen Harrier.
Other notable flora and fauna: Species-rich chalk downland with a variety of orchids. The Times online rates Martin Dowin in its Britian's Best 50 Days Out list.

Contact: South Wiltshire NNR Office, Parsonage Down NNR, Cherry Lodge, Shrewton, Nr Salisbury, Wilts, SP3 4ET. 01980 620 485.
email: wiltshire@naturalengland.org.uk
www.naturalengland.org.uk

10. TITCHFIELD HAVEN

Hampshire County Council.
Location: SU 535 025. From A27 W of Fareham, head for Stubbington/Lee-on-Solent on B3334. Located in Cliff Road, car park is adjacent to Hill Head Sailing Club. Public footpath follows derelict canal along W of reserve and road skirts S edge.
Access: Admission charge to reserve. Open Wed-Sun all year, plus Bank Hols, except Christmas and Boxing Days.
Facilities: Centre has information desk, toilets, tea room and shop. Guided tours (book in advance). Hides.
Public transport: Nearest bus stop in Solent Road (quarter mile from reserve).
Habitat: Reedbeds, freshwater scrapes, wet grazing meadows.
Key birds: *Spring/summer*: Bearded Tit, waders inc. Black-tailed Godwit and Ruff, wildfowl, Common Tern, breeding Cetti's Warbler, Water Rail. *Winter*: Bittern.
Contact: Barry Duffin, Titchfield Haven Visitor Centre, Cliff Road, Hill Head, Fareham, Hants PO14 3JT. 01329 662 145; Fax 01329 667 113.

Herefordshire

1. HOLYWELL DINGLE

Hereford Nature Trust.
Location: SO 313 510, NE of Hay-on-Wye. Take A438 N then L on A4111. Park in lay-by on R, 1 mile N of Eardisley and take footpath to reserve.
Access: Open at all times. Some parts near the stream can be wet and muddy, so waterproof footwear is advised. The northern part of the reserve is very steep-sided in places, and there are precipitous drops into the stream-bed.
Facilities: Good network of marked paths and two footbridges crossing the stream.
Public transport:
Habitat: Narrow, steep-sided, wooded valley (19 acres), mainly oak and ash. Fast-flowing freshwater stream.
Key birds: Good variety of woodland birds, including breeding Nuthatch, Pied Flycatcher, Marsh Tit, Treecreeper, Great Spotted Woodpecker, Chiffchaff, Rook and Blackcap.
Other notable flora and fauna: Rich ground flora,

including early purple orchids and eight species of fern. Badger
Contact: Herefordshire Nature Trust, Lower House Farm, Ledbury Rd, Tupsley, Hereford HR1 1UT. 01432 356 872. e-mail: enquiries@herefordshirewt.co.uk
www.wildlifetrust.org.uk/hereford

2. LEA AND PAGETS WOOD

Hereford Nature Trust.
Location: SO 598 343, SE of Hereford. Take B4224 S towards Ross-on-Wye. Turn L on small road 0.25 mile S of Fownhope towards Woolhope. Footpath is on R after turning for Common Hill. Parking for two cars at top of the hill.
Access: Open at all times. Upper paths generally dry in spring and summer, but the low-lying main track can be very muddy and treacherous in places in winter. Take extra care in the vicinity of the old quarry in Church Wood. This is partly fenced off, but there are still unguarded near-vertical drops.
Facilities: Footpaths.

Habitat: Ancient broad-leaved woodland (27 acres).
Key birds: Small breeding population of Pied Flycatchers in nest-boxes, good range of woodland species, including all three woodpeckers (though Lesser Spotted Woodpeckers have not been recorded for some years) and warblers including Blackcap, Willow Warbler, Chiffchaff and the occasional Wood Warbler. Also Nuthatch, Treecreeper, Marsh Tit, Jay. Buzzard, Tawny Owl and Sparrowhawk also seen.
Other notable flora and fauna: Greater butterfly, early purple and bird's nest orchids, dormouse and yellow-necked mouse.
Contact: Herefordshire Nature Trust, 01432 356 872. e-mail: enquiries@herefordshirewt.co.uk
www.wildlifetrust.org.uk/hereford

3. LUGG MEADOW SSSI

Hereford Nature Trust.
Location: SO 539405, NE of Hereford. Take A438 from Hereford towards Ledbury. Near Lugwardine, park in lane on L adjacent to Lower House Farm,
before crossing Lungwardine bridge.
Access: Access over Upper Lugg Meadow unrestricted but do not walk in the growing hay between late April and July. In winter, the whole area may be flooded to a depth of more than 1m. for long periods, and access becomes impossible or distinctly dangerous. Take care when walking near the river as there are vertical cliffs along its banks.
Facilities: Permissive path and footpath. Not suitable for wheelchairs.
Public transport: None.
Habitat: Ancient hay meadows, flooded in winter, river, 115 acres in all.
Key birds: *Spring*: Curlew, Sky Lark. *Passage*: Greenshank, Redshank, Black-tailed Godwit, Snipe, Lapwing and Common Sandpiper *Winter*: Roosting gulls, wildfowl, swans and geese, Peregrine, Merlin.
Other notable flora and fauna: Otter, dragonflies, meadow plants and butterflies.
Contact: Herefordshire Nature Trust, 01432 356 872. e-mail: enquiries@herefordshirewt.co.uk
www.wildlifetrust.org.uk/hereford

Hertfordshire

1. AMWELL NATURE RESERVE

Herts and Middlesex Wildlife Trust.
Location: TL 375 125. Site lies between Hoddesdon and Ware, on the back road to Stanstead Abbotts near Great Amwell village. Park in Amwell Lane and walk up Footpath 17.
Access: No access to lakes, but Great Hardmead, Hollycross and Bittern Pool can be viewed from footpaths, viewpoints and Water Rail hide.
Facilities: Public hide and viewing area.
Public transport: None.
Habitat: Disused gravel pit with reedbeds and woodland.
Key birds: *Spring/summer:* Hobby and other raptors, Ringed Plover, Little Ringed Plover. *Winter:* Smew, ducks, Bittern, Little Egret. In process of becoming SSSI for wintering Gadwall and Shoveler.
Other notable flora and fauna: Otter, 17 species of dragonfly, early and southern orchids.
Contact: Herts and Middlesex Wildlife Trust, Grebe House, St Michael's Street, St Albans, Herts, AL3 4SN. 01727 858 901. e-mail: info@hmwt.org
www.wildlifetrust.org.uk/herts

2. CASSIOBURY PARK

Watford Borough Council / Herts and Middlesex Wildlife Trust.
Location: TL 093 968. Close to Watford town centre in Gade Road, off A412 Watford-to-Rickmansworth road.
Access: Open all year.

Facilities: Car park, footpaths.
Public transport: Watford Metropolitan Underground station.
Habitat: Old watercress beds within urban park, wetland, river, alder/willow wood.
Key birds: Lesser Spotted Woodpecker, Water Rail. *Spring/summer*: Kingfisher, Grey Wagtail. *Winter*: Snipe, Water Rail, occasional Bearded Tit.
Other notable flora and fauna: Invertebrates and water meadow plants.
Contact: Herts and Middlesex Wildlife Trust, 01727 858 901. e-mail: info@hmwt.org
www.wildlifetrust.org.uk/herts

3. KINGS MEADS

Herts and Middlesex Wildlife Trust /Thames Water/ Smith Kline Wellcome / East Herts District Council/ Environment Agency.
Location: Between Hertford and Ware, lying alongside A119 Ware Road. Park in Priory Street and Broadmeads (Ware) and streets in Hertford.
Access: Open all year. Wearing waterproof footwear in winter is recommended.
Facilities: None.
Public transport: Bus stops on Hertford Road (A119). Trains to Ware station (5 mins) and Hertford East Station (10 mins).
Habitat: Largest remaining area of grazed riverside flood meadow in Hertfordshire.
Key birds: *Summer:* Sky Lark, Reed Warbler, Reed Bunting, Sedge Warbler, Yellow Wagtail. *Winter/*

spring: Gadwall, Gargeney, passage migrants, Shoveler, Wigeon, Teal, Snipe, gulls, waders, Stonechat.
Other notable flora and fauna: 275 species of wildflower, 19 species of dragonfly.
Contact: Herts and Middlesex Wildlife Trust, 01727 858 901. e-mail: info@hmwt.org
www.wildlifetrust.org.uk/herts

4. LEMSFORD SPRINGS

Herts and Middlesex Wildlife Trust.
Location: TL 223 123. Lies 1.5 miles W of Welwyn Garden City town centre, off roundabout leading to Lemsford village on B197, W of A1(M).
Access: Access, via key, by arrangement with warden. Open at all times, unless work parties or group visits in progress. Keep to paths. Dogs on leads. Wheelchair access ramp to hide. Coaches welcome and room to park on road, but limit of 30 persons.
Facilities: Two hides, classroom, chemical toilet, paths and bridges. Circular walk.
Public transport: Bus service to Valley Road, WGC and Lemsford Village No 366 (Arriva, Traveline 0871 200 2233). Nearest railway station Welwyn Garden City.
Habitat: Former water-cress beds, open shallow lagoons. Stretch of the River Lea, marsh, hedgerows. Nine acres.
Key birds: *Spring/summer*: Breeding warblers, Grey Wagtail, Kestrel. *Autumn/winter*: Green Sandpiper, Water Rail, Snipe, Siskin, occasional Jack Snipe, Little Egret. *All year*: Mandarin Duck, Kingfisher, Grey Heron, Sparrowhawk.
Other notable flora and fauna: Muntjac, fox and stoat. Common butterflies and damselflies in summer.
Contact: Barry Trevis, Warden, 11 Lemsford Village, Welwyn Garden City, Herts, AL8 7TN. 01707 335 517.
e-mail: info@hmwt.org
www.wildlifetrust.org.uk/herts

5. MAPLE LODGE NATURE RESERVE

Thames Water / Maple Lodge Conservation Society
Location: TQ 036 925. South of Ricksmanworth, close to village of Maple Cross. From M25 (Jt 17) turn left at traffic lights by The Cross pub. Drive down Maple Lodge Close and park in social club car park.
Access: Restricted to members of MLCS – combination locks on entrance gates. Visits by non-members and groups can be arranged in advance. Site can be boggy – please keep to designated paths.
Facilities: Information centre,

toilets. Eight bird hides – two wheelchair-friendly. Winter feeding station.
Public transport: Not known.
Habitat: A man-made wetland habitat formed from two gravel pits and a sludge settlement area. Mixed broadleaf plantation on eastern side.
Key birds: Wildfowl throughout year, numbers building in winter. All three woodpeckers, plus variety of finches, thrushes and woodland species. Nesting species include Kingfisher, Tawny Owl, migrant warblers.
Green, Common and Wood Sandpipers on passage.
Other notable flora and fauna: 170 species of moth recorded, plus many butterflies and aquatic insects. 125 species of wildflower recorded.
Contact: For membership of MLCS or to arrange visits, contact chairman Mrs Gwyneth Bellis on 01923 230 277.

6. RYE MEADS

RSPB / Hertfordshire and Middlesex Wildlife Trust.
Location: TL 389 103. Take Hoddesdon turn off A10 and follow brown duck signs. Near Rye House railway station.
Access: Open every day 10am-5pm (or dusk if earlier), except Christmas Day and Boxing Day.
Facilities: Disabled access and toilets. Drinks machine, staffed reception, classrooms, picnic area, car park, bird feeding area. Nature trails, hides. RSPB reserve has close-circuit TV on Kingfisher and Common Terns in summer.
Public transport: Rail (Rye House) 1km distance, bus (310) stops 600 metres from entrance.

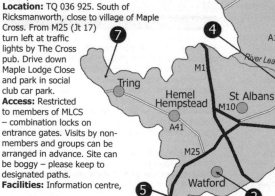

Habitat: Marsh, willow scrub, pools, scrapes, lagoons and reedbed.
Key birds: *Summer*: Breeding Tufted Duck, Gadwall, Common Tern, Kestrel, Kingfisher, nine species of warblers.
Winter: Bittern, Shoveler, Water Rail, Teal, Snipe, Jack Snipe, Redpoll and Siskin.
Other notable flora and fauna: Fen vegetation, invertebrates and reptiles.
Contact: RSPB Rye Meads Visitor Centre, Rye Road, Stanstead Abbotts, Herts, SG12 8JS. 01992 708 383; Fax 01992 708 389.

7. TRING RESERVOIRS

All four reservoirs – British Waterways/Herts and Middlesex Wildlife Trust/Friends of Tring Res. WTW lagoon – Thames Water/FOTR.
Location: Wilstone Reservoir SP 905 134. Other reservoirs SP 920 135. WTW Lagoon SP 923 134 adjacent to Marsworth Reservoir. Reservoirs 1.5 miles due N of Tring, all accessible from B489 which crosses A41 Aston Clinton by-pass. NB: exit from by-pass only southbound, entry only northbound.
Access: *Reservoirs* – open at all times. All group visits need to be cleared with British Waterways. *WTW Lagoon*: open at all times by permit from FOTR. Coaches can only drop off and pick up.
Wilstone Reservoir has restricted height access of 2.1 metres.
Facilities: Café and public house adjacent to Startops

Reservoir car park, safe parking for cycles. Also disabled trail from here. Wilstone Reservoir: Public houses about 0.5 mile away in village and cafe about 0.25 mile from car park at Farm Shop. Hides with disabled access at Startops/Marsworth Reservoir and WTW Lagoon. Also other hides.
Public transport: Buses from Aylesbury and Tring including a weekend service, tel. 0871 200 2233. Tring Station is 2.5 miles away via canal towpath.
Habitat: Four reservoirs with surrounding woodland, scrub and meadows. Two of the reservoirs with extensive reedbeds. WTW Lagoon with islands and dragonfly scrape, surrounding hedgerows and scrub.
Key birds: *Spring/summer*: Breeding water birds and heronry. Occasional Black Tern. Regular Hobby, Red Kite, Marsh Harrier and Osprey. Warblers including Cetti's. *Autumn/passage*: Waders. *Winter*: Gull roost, large wildfowl flocks, bunting roosts, Bittern.
Other notable flora and fauna: Black poplar trees, some locally rare plants in damp areas. Dragonflies include black-tailed skimmer, ruddy darter and emerald damselfly. Holly blue and small copper butterflies. Chinese water deer, Daubenton's and both pipistrelle bats.
Contact: Herts and Middsx Wildlife Trust: see Directory entry, FOTR: see Peter Hearn in Bucks BTO entry, www.fotr.org.uk,
British Waterways, 510-524 Elder House, Eldergate, Milton Keynes MK9 1BW. 01908 302 500, www.waterscape.com
e-mail:enquiries.southeast@britishwaterways.co.uk

Kent

1. BLEAN WOODS NNR

RSPB (South East Region Office).
Location: TR 126 592. From Rough Common (off A290, one and a half miles NW of Canterbury).
Access: Open 8am-9pm for cars, open at all times for visitors on foot. No parking for coaches – please drop passengers off in Rough Common village. Green Trail suitable for wheelchair users.
Facilities: Public footpaths and five waymarked trails.
Public transport: No 27 from Canterbury hourly, stops at reserve entrance (ask for Lovell Road).
No 4/4A every 20 minutes from Canterbury to Whitstable. Ask for Rough Common Road, 500m walk from site entrance. Local bus company Stagecoach 0870 243 3711.
Habitat: Mature oak woodland, plus birch, chestnut and sweet chestnut coppice. Grazed and ungrazed heathland.
Key birds: Good for Woodpeckers, warblers and Nightingale in spring, fairly quiet the rest of the year. *All year*: Woodpecker (3 species), Nuthatch, Treecreeper, tits (5 species). *Spring*: Nightingale, Blackcap, Garden Warbler, Hobby, Nightjar, Tree Pipit.

Other notable flora and fauna: Badger, dormouse. Heath fritillary, white admiral, silver-washed fritillary. Common spotted orchid, wild service tree.
Contact: Michael Walter, Site Manager, 11 Garden Close, Rough Common, Canterbury, Kent CT2 9BP. 01227 455 972.

2. BOUGH BEECH RESERVOIR

Kent Wildlife Trust.
Location: TQ 49 64 89. Bough Beech is situated 3.5 miles S of Ide Hill, signposted off B2042.
Access: Confined to holders of permits granted for recording and study purposes only on application to the warden. The whole of the reserve may be viewed from the public road just S of Winkhurst Green (TQ 49 64 94). Park on roadside (one side only).
Facilities: Toilets and visitor centre open between Apr-Oct, Wed, Sat, Sun and Bank Holiday Mon (11am-4.30pm).
Public transport: Rail service to Penshurst Station (two miles south)
Habitat: Reservoir and adjacent woodland and farmland.

NATURE RESERVES - ENGLAND

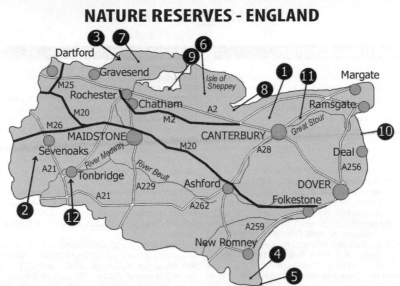

Key birds: Approx 60 species of birds breed in and around the reserve annually, with Mallard, Tufted Duck, Mandarin, Canada Goose, Coot and Great Crested Grebe notable among the waterfowl. Little Ring Plover nest most years.

Autumn especially good for numbers of waders like Green and Common Sandpipers and Greenshank. Many rarities have been recorded. Ospreys recorded most years. Winter wildfowl numbers are much higher than summer, including Goldeneye and Goosander.

Other notable flora and fauna: Great crested newt, toad, dragonflies (black-tailed skimmer, ruddy darter, emperor, southern aeshna, migrant hawker, red-eyed damselfly), common lizard, roesel's bush cricket, long-winged conehead, dormouse, water shrew, white admiral butterflies, glow-worm, bats (pipistrelle, Daubenton, noctule, brown long-eared).

Contact: Kent Wildlife Trust, Tyland Barn, Sandling, Maidstone, Kent ME14 3BD. 01622 662 012. e-mail: info@kentwildlife.org.uk www.kentwildlife.org.uk

3. CLIFFE POOLS

RSPB (South East Region Office).
Location: TQ 722 757. On S bank of River Thames, N of Rochester. Take A289 off the A2 at Strood and follow B2000 to reserve. See RSPB website for more detailed directions.
Access: Free admission at all times, but donations welcome. Group bookings welcome. Monthly guided walks available. Dogs only on public footpaths.
Facilities: Six viewing points. Public rights of way encircle reserve and bisect it.
Public transport: Nearest bus stop at Six Bells pub in Cliffe.
Habitat: A mix of saline lagoons, freshwater pools, grassland, saltmarsh and scrub.
Key birds: Massed flocks of waders in winter, plus a wide range of wildfowl. A great variety of passage

birds in spring and autumn. Breeding species include Lapwing, Redshank, Avocet, Ringed Plover, Shelduck. Also look out for Nightingale, Hobby and Turtle Dove.
Other notable flora and fauna: Essex skipper and other butterflies, various bee, grasshopper and cricket species.
Contact: Paul Hyde, RSPB North Kent Marshes, Bromhey Farm, Eastborough, Cooling, Rochester ME3 8DS. 01272 775 333.

4. DUNGENESS

RSPB (South East Region Office).
Location: TR 063 196. SE of Lydd.
Access: Open daily (9am-9pm) or sunset when earlier. Visitor centre open (10am-5pm, or 4pm Nov-Feb). Parties over 12 by prior arrangement. Closed Dec 25 and 26.
Facilities: Visitor centre, toilets (including disabled access), seven hides, viewing screen, two nature trails, wheelchair access to visitor centre and four hides. Fully equipped classroom/meeting room.
Public transport: Limited service. Bus 11 from Ashford stops at reserve entrance on request – one mile walk to visitor centre. Contact reserve for details.
Habitat: Shingle, flooded gravel pits, sallow scrub, reedbed, wet grassland.
Key birds: *Resident:* Bearded Tit. *Winter:* Bittern, Wildfowl (including Wigeon, Goldeneye, Goosander, Smew), divers and grebes. Migrant waders, landfall for passerines. *Summer:* Breeding Lapwing, Redshank, wildfowl, gulls, Cetti's Warbler.
Other notable flora and fauna: Marsh frog, migrant butterflies.
Contact: Christine Hawkins/Bob Gomes, Boulderwall Farm, Dungeness Road, Lydd, Romney Marsh, Kent, TN29 9PN. 01797 320 588/Fax 01797 321 962. e-mail: dungeness@rspb.org.uk www.rspb.org.uk

5. DUNGENESS BIRD OBSERVATORY

Dungeness Bird Observatory Trust.
Location: TR 085 173. Three miles SE of Lydd. Turn south off Dungeness Road at TR 087 185 and continue to end of road.
Access: Observatory open throughout the year. No wheelchair access.
Facilities: Accommodation available. Bring own sleeping bag/sheets and toiletries. Shared facilities including fully-equipped kitchen. Coach parking available at railway station.
Public transport: Bus service between Rye and Folkestone, numbers 11, 12, 711, 712. Alight at the Pilot Inn, Lydd-on-Sea. Tel: 01227 472 082.
Habitat: Shingle promontory with scrub and gravel pits. RSPB reserve nearby.
Key birds: Breeding birds include Wheatear and Black Redstart and seabirds on RSPB Reserve. Important migration site. Excellent seawatching when weather conditions are suitable. Power station outfall, known as 'The Patch' good for gulls and terns.
Other notable flora and fauna: Long Pits are excellent for dragonflies, including small red-eyed damselfly. Moth trapping throughout the year.
Contact: Dungeness Bird Observatory, 01797 321 309. e-mail dungeness.obs@tinyonline.co.uk www.dungenessbirdobs.org.uk

6. ELMLEY MARSHES

RSPB (South East Region Office).
Location: TQ 93 86 80. Isle of Sheppey signposted from A249, one mile beyond old Kingsferry Bridge. Reserve car park is two miles from the main road.
Access: Use old bridge road – access road is one mile from bridge. Open every day except Tue, Christmas and Boxing days. (9am-9pm or dusk if earlier). No charge to RSPB members.
Dogs are not allowed on the reserve. Less able may drive closer to the hides.
Facilities: Five hides. Disabled access to Wellmarsh hide. No visitor centre. Toilets located in car park 1.25 miles from hides.
Public transport: Swale Halt, a request stop is nearest railway station on Sittingbourne to Sheerness line. From there it is a three mile walk to reserve
Habitat: Coastal grazing marsh, ditches and pools alongside the Swale Estuary with extensive intertidal mudflats and saltmarsh
Key birds: *Spring/summer*: Breeding waders – Redshank, Lapwing, Avocet, Yellow Wagtail, passage waders, Hobby. *Autumn*: Passage waders. *Winter*: Spectacular numbers of wildfowl, especially Wigeon and White-fronted Goose. Waders. Hunting raptors – Peregrine, Merlin, Hen Harrier and Short-eared Owl.
Contact: Barry O'Dowd, Elmley RSPB Reserve, Kingshill Farm, Elmley, Sheerness, Kent ME12 3RW. 01795 665 969.

7. NORTHWARD HILL

RSPB (South East Region Office).
Location: TQ 781 757. Adjacent to High Halstow, off A228, approx four miles NE of Rochester.
Access: Open all year, free access, trails in public area of wood joining Saxon Shoreway link to grazing marsh. Dogs allowed in public area on leads. Trails often steep and not suitable for wheelchair users.
Facilities: Four trails varying in length from 0.5 to 4 miles. New trail takes visitors to viewpoint overlooking heronry. Three nature trails in the wood and one joining with long distance footpath. Toilets at village hall. New car park at Bromhey Farm (Marshland car park) is signposted from High Halstow village. Information and public toilet in this car park.
Public transport: Buses to village of High Halstow. Contact Arriva buses (01634 283 600) for timetable details.
Habitat: Ancient and scrub woodland (approximately 130 acres), grazing marsh (approximately 350 acres).
Key birds: *Spring/summer*: Wood holds UK's largest heronry (between 150 and 200 pairs most years), inc growing colony of Little Egrets (50 pairs in 2007), breeding Nightingale, Turtle Dove, scrub warblers and woodpeckers. Marshes – breeding Lapwing, Redshank, Avocet, Marsh Harrier, Shoveler, Pochard. *Winter*: Wigeon, Teal, Shoveler. Passage waders (ie Black-tailed Godwit), raptors, Tree Sparrow, Corn Bunting. Long-eared Owl roost.
Contact: Gordon Allison, RSPB North Kent Marshes, Bromhey Farm, Eastborough, Cooling, Rochester ME3 8DS. 01634 222 480.

8. OARE MARSHES LNR

Kent Wildlife Trust.
Location: TR 01 36 48 (car park). Two miles N of Faversham. From A2 follow signs to Oare and Harty Ferry.
Access: Open at all times. Access along marked paths only. Dogs under strict control to avoid disturbance to birds and livestock. Visitor centre open at weekends an dbank holidays (11am-5pm or dusk).
Facilities: Visitor centre, three hides. Roadside viewpoint of East Hide accessible to wheelchairs. Those with pneumatic tyres can reach seawall path and hide. Small car park, restricted turning space, not suitable for coaches. No toilets.
Public transport: Bus to Oare Village one mile from reserve. Arriva service (Mon-Sat), Jaycrest (Sun) - call Traveline on 0870 608 2608. Train: Faversham (two miles distance).
Habitat: Grazing marsh, mudflats/estuary.
Key birds: *All year*: Waders and wildfowl. *Winter*: Merlin, Peregrine. Divers, grebes and sea ducks on Swale. *Spring/summer*: Avocet, Garganey, Green, Wood and Curlew Sandpipers, Little Stint, Black-tailed Godwit, Little Tern, Marsh Harrier.
Contact: Kent Wildlife Trust, 01622 662 012. e-mail: info@kentwildlife.org.uk www.kentwildlife.org.uk

NATURE RESERVES - ENGLAND

9. RIVERSIDE COUNTRY PARK

Medway Council.

Location: TQ 808 683. From Rochester, take the A2 E into Gillingham and turn L onto the A289. After one mile, turn R onto the B2004 at Grange. After one mile, the visitor centre is on the L.

Access: Open all year, free access to all paths from 8.30am-4.30pm (winter) or 8.30am-dusk (summer). Shoreline and paths are wheelchair friendly.

Facilities: Visitor centre with cafe and toilets open every day from 10am-5pm summer (4pm winter) except Christmas, Boxing and New Year's Days (no parking on these days except New Year's Day). Large car park and smaller one at Rainham Dock. Car park locked at dusk. Check times on arrival. Coach parking by arrangement only.

Public transport: Bus: contact Arriva tel: 08706 082 608 (summer Sunday service only). Train: nearest stations at Rainham and Gillingham. Cycle racks at visitor centre and a Sustrans cycle route.

Habitat: Mudflats, saltmarsh, ponds, reedbeds, grassland and scrub.

Key birds: *Winter:* Good water and wildfowl watching. Regular species include Pintail, Shoveler, Wigeon, Red-breasted Merganser, Black-tailed Godwit and Avocet. *Summer:* Lesser Whitethroat, Whitethroat, Nightingale and Turtle Dove. Peregrine, Marsh Harrier, Little Egret, Cetti's Warbler and Mediterranean Gull may seen throughout the year.

Other notable flora and fauna: Adders, including many dark forms, may be found.

Contact: Riverside Country Park, Lower Rainham Road, Gillingham, Kent, ME7 2XH. 01634 337 432. e-mail: riversidecp@medway.gov.uk

10. SANDWICH BAY BIRD OBSERVATORY

Sandwich Bay Bird Observatory Trust.

Location: TR 355 575. 2.5 miles from Sandwich, five miles from Deal. Take A256 to Sandwich from Dover or Ramsgate. Follow signs to Sandwich Station and then Sandwich Bay.

Access: Open daily. Disabled access.

Facilities: Field Study Centre. Visitor centre, toilets, refreshments, hostel-type accommodation, plus self-contained flat.

Public transport: Sandwich train station two miles from Observatory.

Habitat: Coastal, dune land, farmland, marsh, two small scrapes.

Key birds: *Spring/autumn passage:* Good variety of migrants and waders, specially Corn Bunting. Annual Golden Oriole. *Winter:* Golden Plover.

Other notable flora and fauna: Sand dune plants such as lady's bedstraw and sand sedge.

Contact: The Secretary, Sandwich Bay Bird Observatory, Guildford Road, Sandwich Bay, Sandwich, Kent, CT13 9PF. 01304 617 341. e-mail: sbbot@talk21.com www.sbbo.co.uk

11. STODMARSH NNR

Natural England (Kent Team).

Location: TR 221 609. Lies alongside River Stour and A28, five miles NE of Canterbury.

Access: Open at all times. Keep to reserve paths. No dogs allowed.

Facilities: Fully accessible toilets are available at entrance car park. Five hides (one fully accessible), easy access nature trail, footpaths and information panels.

Car park, picnic area and toilets adjoining the Grove Ferry entrance with easily accessible path, viewing mound and two hides.

Public transport: There is a regular Stagecoach bus service from Canterbury to Margate/Ramsgate. Alight at Upstreet for Grove Ferry. Hourly on Sun.

Habitat: Open water, reedbeds, wet meadows, dry meadows, woodland.

Key birds: *Spring/summer:* Breeding Bearded Tit, Cetti's Warbler, Garganey, Reed, Sedge and Willow Warblers, Nightingale. Migrant Black Tern, Hobby, Osprey, Little Egret. *Winter:* Wildfowl, Hen Harrier, Bittern.

Other notable flora and fauna: Nationally rare plants and invertebrates, including shining ram's horn snail.

Contact: David Feast, Natural England, Coldharbour Farm, Wye, Ashford, Kent, TN25 5DB. 07767 321 058 (mobile).

12. TUDELEY WOODS

RSPB (South East Region Office).

Location: TQ 618 434. Beside A21, one mile S of Tonbridge. Take minor road to Capel on L immediately before Fairthorne Garage. Car park 0.25 miles on L.

Access: Open every day except Christmas Day. No dogs. No disabled facilities. No coaches. Car park open 9am-6pm or dusk if earlier.

Facilities: Leaflet, three nature trails. No coach parking.

Public transport: No buses within one mile.

Habitat: Semi-natural ancient woodland, lowland heathland (restored), pasture.

Key birds: *Spring/summer:* Willow Warbler, Garden Warbler, Blackcap, Turtle Dove, Spotted Flycatcher, Nightingale, Tree Pipit, Nightjar, Hobby, Whitethroat. *All year:* Marsh Tit, Willow Tit, Nuthatch, three woodpecker species, Yellowhammer, Treecreeper.

Other notable flora and fauna: Common spotted and early purple orchids, golden-ringed and hairy dragonfly, beautiful demoiselle, silver-washed fritillary, white admiral and purple hairstreak butterlies.

Contact: Martin Allison, Unit 10, Sham Farm Business Units, Eridge Green, Tonbridge Wells, TN3 9JA.01892 752 730. e-mail: martin.allison@rspb.org.uk www.rspb.org.uk

Lancashire

1. CUERDEN VALLEY PARK

Cuerden Valley Park Trust.
Location: SD 565 238. S of Preston on A49. Easy access from J28 and J29 of the M6, J8 and J9 on M61 and the end of M65.
Access: Open all year.
Facilities: Visitor centre, toilets.
Public transport: None.
Habitat: Mixed woodland, river, pond, lake, wildflower meadow, agricultural grassland.
Key birds: *All year:* Great Crested Grebe, Little Grebe, Kingfisher, Dipper, Great Spotted Woodpecker, Goldcrest, Little Owl and usual woodland and river birds.
Other notable flora and fauna: Dragonflies including emperor, emerald, black darter and migrant hawker. Butterflies including large and small skipper, holly blue, small copper, comma and gate keeper. Roe deer and seven species of bat. Common spotted and marsh orchid, moschatel.
Contact: Cuerden Valley Park Trust, The Barn, Berkeley Drive, Bamber, Preston PR5 6BY. 01772 324 436. e-mail: rangers@cuerdenvalleypark.org

2. HEYSHAM NATURE RESERVE & BIRD OBSERVATORY

Wildlife Trust for Lancashire, Manchester and North Merseyside / British Energy Estates.
Location: Main reserve is at SD 404 596, W of Lancaster. Take A683 to Heysham port. Turn L at traffic lights by Duke of Rothesay pub, then first R after 300m.
Access: Reserve car park usually open 9.30am-6pm (longer in summer and shorter in winter). Pedestrian access at all times. Dogs on lead. Limited disabled access.
Facilities: Hide overlooks Power Station outfalls. Map giving access details at the reserve car park. No manned visitor centre or toilet access, but someone usually in reserve office, next to the main car park, in the morning. Latest sightings board can be viewed through the window if office closed.
Public transport: Train services connect with nearby Isle of Man ferry. Plenty of buses to Lancaster from various Heysham sites within walking distance (ask for nearest stop to the harbour).
Habitat: Varied: wetland, acid grassland, alkaline grassland, foreshore.
Key birds: Passerine migrants in the correct conditions. Good passage of seabirds in spring, especially Arctic Tern. Storm Petrel and Leach's Petrel during strong onshore (SW-WW NW) winds in midsummer and autumn respectively. Good variety of breeding birds (e.g. eight species of warbler on the reserve itself). Two-three scarce land-birds each year,

most frequent being Yellow-browed Warbler.
Other notable flora and fauna: Notable area for dragonflies, red-veined darter breed at nearby Middleton Community Woodland main pond SD 418 592 (mid June - mid July). Bee orchid in several areas.
Contact: Reuben Neville, Reserve Warden, The Wildlife Trust, The Barn, Berkeley Drive, Bamber Bridge, Preston PR5 6BY. 01524 855 030; 07979 652 138. www.lancswt.org.uk
http://heyshamobservatory.blogspot.com
Annual report from Leighton Moss RSPB reserve shop.

3. LEIGHTON MOSS

RSPB (Northern England Region).
Location: SD 478 750. Four miles NW of Carnforth. Signposted from A6 N of Carnforth.
Access: Reserve open daily 9am-dusk. Visitor centre open daily 9.30am-5pm (9.30am-4.30pm Nov-Jan inclusive), except Christmas Day. No charge to RSPB members or those who arrive by public transport or bike. Dogs allowed on causeway only. Groups and coaches welcome – please book in advance.
Facilities: Visitor centre, shop, tea-room and toilets. Nature trails and five hides (four have wheelchair access), plus two hides at saltmarsh pools.
Public transport: Silverdale train station 150 metres from reserve. Tel: 08457 484 950.
Habitat: Reedbed, shallow meres and woodland. Saltmarsh pool approx 1 mile.
Key birds: *All year:* Bittern, Bearded Tit, Water Rail, Pochard and Shoveler. *Summer:* Marsh Harrier, Reed and Sedge Warblers. Avocet at saltmarsh pools.
Other notable flora and fauna: Common reed, otters, red deer.
Contact: RSPB Leighton Moss Nature Reserve, Myers Farm, Silverdale, Carnforth, Lancashire, LA5 0SW. 01524 701 601. e-mail: leighton.moss@rspb.org.uk www.rspb.org.uk

4. MARTIN MERE

The Wildfowl and Wetlands Trust.
Location: SD 428 145. Six miles N of Ormskirk via Burscough Bridge (A59), 20 miles from Liverpool and Preston.
Access: Opening times: 9.30am-5.00pm (Nov-Feb), 9.30am-5.30pm (rest of year). Special dawn and evening events. Guide dogs only allowed. Admission charge. No charge for members. Fully accessible to disabled, all hides suitable for wheelchairs. Coach park available. Special rates for coach parties.
Facilities: Visitor centre with toilets, gift shop, restaurant, education centre, play area, nature reserve and nature trails, hides, waterfowl collection and sustainable garden. Provision for disabled visitors.
Public transport: Bus service to WWT Martin Mere from Ormskirk. Train to Burscough Bridge or New Lane

Stations (both 1.5 miles from reserve). For bus times contact Traveline 0870 608 2608.

Habitat: Open water, wet grassland, moss, copses, reedbed, parkland (326 acres).

Key birds: *Winter*: Whooper and Bewick's Swans, Pink-footed Goose, various duck, Ruff, Black-tailed Godwit, Peregrine, Hen Harrier, Tree Sparrow. *Spring*: Ruff, Shelduck, Little Ringed and Ringed Plover, Lapwing, Redshank. *Summer*: Marsh Harrier, Garganey, hirundines, Tree Sparrow. Breeding Avocets, Lapwing, Redshank, Shelduck. *Autumn*: Pink-footed Goose, waders on passage.

Other notable flora and fauna: Whorled caraway, golden dock, tubular dropwort, 300 species of moth.

Contact: Senior Operations Manager, WWT Martin Mere, Fish Lane, Burscough, Lancs, L40 0TA. 01704 895 181.
e-mail: info.martinmere@wwt.org.uk
www.wwt.org.uk

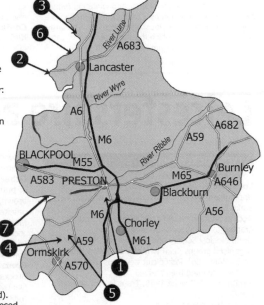

5. MERE SANDS WOOD

The Wildlife Trust for Lancashire, Manchester and North Merseyside.

Location: SD 44 71 57. 12 miles by road from Southport, 0.5 miles off A59 Preston – Liverpool road, in Rufford along B5246 (Holmeswood Road).

Access: Visitor centre open 9.30am-4.30pm - closed Fridays and Christmas Day. Car park open until 8pm in summer. Three miles of wheelchair-accessible footpaths. All hides accessible to wheelchairs.

Facilities: Visitor centre with toilets (disabled), six viewing hides, three trails, exhibition room, latest sightings board. Feeding stations. Booking essential for two motorised buggies.

Public transport: Bus: Southport-Chorley (347) stops in Rufford, 0.5 mile walk. Train: Preston-Ormskirk train stops at Rufford station, one mile walk.

Habitat: Freshwater lakes, mixed woodland, sandy grassland/heath. 105h.

Key birds: *Winter*: Regionally important for Teal and Gadwall, good range of waterfowl, Kingfisher. Feeding stations attract Tree Sparrow, Bullfinch, Reed Bunting, Water Rail. *Woodland*: Treecreeper, Nuthatch. *Summer*: Kingfisher. *Passage*: Most years, Osprey, Crossbill, Green Sandpiper, Greenshank.

Other notable flora and fauna: 18 species of dragonfly recorded annually.

Contact: Warden, Mere Sands Wood Nature Reserve, Holmeswood Road, Rufford, Ormskirk, Lancs L40 1TG. 01704 821 809. www.wildlifetrust.org/lancashire
e-mail: meresandswood@lancswt.org.uk

6. MORECAMBE BAY (HEST BANK)

RSPB (Northern England Region).

Location: SD 468 667. Two miles N of Morecambe at Hest Bank.

Access: Open at all times. Do not venture onto saltmarsh or intertidal area, because there are dangerous channels and quicksands.

Facilities: Viewpoint at car park.

Public transport: No 5 bus runs between Carnforth and Morecambe. Tel: 0870 608 2608.

Habitat: Saltmarsh, estuary.

Key birds: *Winter*: Wildfowl (Pintail, Shelduck, Wigeon) and waders – important high tide roost for Oystercatcher, Curlew, Redshank, Dunlin, Bar-tailed Godwit.

Contact: RSPB Leighton Moss and Morecambe Bay Nature Reserves, Myers Farm, Silverdale, Carnforth, Lancashire, LA5 0SW. 01524 701 601.
e-mail: leighton.moss@rspb.org.uk
www.rspb.org.uk

7. RIBBLE ESTUARY

Natural England (Cheshire to Lancashire team).

Location: SD 380 240. 7 km W of Preston. Access via minor roads from A584 and A59.

Access: Open at all times.

Facilities: No formal visiting facilities. RSPB Ribble Discovery Centre, located next to Fairhaven Lake, 5km W of Lytham St Annes, offers interpretive displays about the area, plus a shop. Open 10am-5pm. For event details call 01253 796 292.

Public transport: None.

Habitat: Ramsar site and SPA. 4,520 hectares of saltmarsh, mudflats.

Key birds: High water wader roosts (of Knot, Dunlin, Black-tailed Godwit, Oystercatcher and Grey Plover) are best viewed from Southport, Marshside, Lytham and St Annes. Pink-footed Geese and wintering swans are present in large numbers from Oct-Feb on Banks Marsh and along River Douglas respectively. The large flocks of Wigeon, for which the site is renowned, can be seen on high tides from Marshside but feed on saltmarsh areas at night. Good numbers of raptors also present in winter.

Contact: Site Manager, English Nature, Ribble Estuary NNR, Old Hollow, Marsh Road, Banks, Southport PR9 8DU. 01704 225 624.

Leicestershire and Rutland

1. EYEBROOK RESERVOIR

Corby and District Water Co.
Location: SP 853 964. Reservoir built 1940. S of Uppingham, from unclassified road W of A6003 at Stoke Dry.
Access: Access to 150 acres of private grounds granted to members of Leics and Rutland Ornithological Society and Rutland Nat Hist Soc. Organised groups need written permission (from Corby Water Co). Public can view most parts from road surrounding the reservoir.
Facilities: SSSI since 1955. Trout fishery season Apr-Oct.
Public transport: None.
Habitat: Open water, plantations and pasture.
Key birds: *Summer*: Good populations of breeding birds, sightings of Ospreys and Red Kite. Passage waders and Black Tern. *Winter*: Wildfowl (inc. Goldeneye, Goosander, Smew) and waders. Feeding station at SP 848 950 attracts Tree Sparrows and other passerines.
Contact: Corby (Northants) and District Water Co Fishing lodge 01536 770 264.
www.eyebrook.com or www.eyebrook.org.uk.
Also see Leics and Rutland OS website (www.lros.org.uk/eyebrook).

2. NARBOROUGH BOG NATURE RESERVE SSSI

Leics and Rutland Wildlife Trust. .
Location: SP 549 979. Reserve lies between River Soar and M1, 8km S of Leicester. From city, turn L off B4114 just before going under motorway, follow track to sports club. Park near club house and walk across recreation ground to reserve entrance.
Access: Open at all times, please keep to paths. Not suitable for wheelchairs. Dogs on short leads only.
Facilities: None. Small bus/coach could park in sports field car park
Public transport: Narborough train station. Buses X5, 140 to Narborough then 1km walk.
Habitat: Peat bog (the only substantial deposit in Leicestershire), wet woodland, reedbed, dense scrub and fen meadow.
Key birds: More than 130 species of birds have been recorded, including all three species of woodpeckers, six species of tits, Tawny Owl, Sparrowhawk and Kingfisher.
Other notable flora and fauna: Good varieties of butterfly including common blue, meadow brown, large and small skippers, small heath and gatekeeper. Banded demoiselles, also good for moths and beetles. Harvest mice and water voles recorded, also breeding grass snakes.
In the meadow area, look for meadow saxifrage, common meadow-rue and marsh thistle.
Contact: Leicester and Rutland Wildlife Trust, Brocks Hill Environment Centre, Washbrook Lane, Oadby, Leicestershire LE2 5JJ . 0116 272 0444. e-mail: info@lrwt.org.uk

3. RUTLAND WATER

Leics and Rutland Wildlife Trust.
Location: SK 866 6760 72. Two reserves –
1. Egleton Reserve: from Egleton village off A6003 S of Oakham. Hosts British Birdwatching Fair every August.
2. Lyndon Reserve: south shore E of Manton village off A6003, S of Oakham.
Access: 1. Open daily 9am-5pm, (4pm Nov to Jan). **2.** Open winter (Sat, Sun 10am-5pm), summer daily (9am-5pm). Day permits available for both.
Facilities: 1: Anglian Water Birdwatching Centre has toilets and disabled access to 11 hides, mobility scooter to hire, conference facilities. Annual Birdfair in August. **2:** Interpretive centre now upgraded with new toilets, including disabled, new paths, use of a mobility scooter and new interpretive material, covers climate change and the impact to UK wildlife. Marked nature trail leaflet.
Public transport: Oakham train station two miles away.
Habitat: Reservoir, lagoons, scrapes, woods, meadows, plantations, reedbeds. 2008/9 start of 3yr project to create 9 new lagoons on extensive area to N of Anglian Water Centre. First opened in winter 2008.
Key birds: *Spring/autumn*: Outstanding wader passage. Also harriers, owls, passerine flocks, terns (Black, Arctic, breeding Common, occasional Little and Sandwich). *Winter*: Wildfowl (inc Goldeneye, Smew, Goosander, rare grebes, all divers), Ruff.

Summer: Breeding Ospreys on Lyndon reserve.
Other notable flora and fauna: Up to 20 species of dragon and damselflies.
Contact: Tim Appleton, Fishponds Cottage, Stamford Road, Oakham, Rutland LE15 8AB. 01572 770 651; Fax 01572 755 931; e-mail awbc@rutlandwater.org.uk; www.rutlandwater.org. uk www.ospreys.org.uk www.birdfair.org.uk.

4. SENCE VALLEY FOREST PARK

Forestry Commission
Location: SK 404 113. Within The National Forest. Ten miles NW of Leicester and two miles SW of Coalville, between Ibstock and Ravenstone. The car park is signed from A447 N of Ibstock.
Access: Open all year. Car park open 8.30am-dusk (precise times on noticeboard). Lower car park (2.2m height barrier) gives easy access to wheelchair-friendly surfaced paths. Week's notice required for coach or minibuses visits.

Facilities: Two car parks, toilets (including disabled and baby-changing facilities), information and recent sightings boards, hide, surfaced trails.
Public transport: None.
Habitat: New forest (native broadleaf, mixed and pine), rough grassland, wildflower meadow, pools, wader scrape, river.
Key birds: *Spring/summer*: Artificial Sand Martin nesting wall, Wheatear, Whinchat, Redstart, Common and Green Sandpiper, Ringed and Little Ringed Plovers, Redshank. Dunlin and Greenshank frequent, possible Wood Sandpiper. Reed Bunting, Meadow Pipit, Sky Lark, Linnet, Yellow Wagtail. Possible Quail. Kestrel and Barn Owl seen occasionally. *Winter*: Stonechat, Redpoll, Short-eared Owl, Goosander and Wigeon possible.
Contact: Chris Mansell, Community Ranger, Lady Hill, Birches Valley, Rugely, Staffs, WS15 2UQ. 01889 586 593. www.forestry.gov.uk

Lincolnshire

1. DONNA NOOK

Lincolnshire Wildlife Trust.
Location: TF 422 998. Near North Somercotes, off A1031 coast road, S of Grimsby.
Access: Donna Nook beach is closed on weekdays as this is an active bombing range, but dunes remain open. Dogs on leads. Some disabled access.
Facilities: No toilets or visitor centre.
Public transport: None.
Habitat: Dunes, slacks and intertidal areas, seashore, mudflats, sandflats.
Key birds: *Summer:* Little Tern, Ringed Plover, Oystercatcher. *Winter:* Brent Goose, Shelduck, Twite, Lapland Bunting, Shore Lark, Linnet.
Other notable flora and fauna: The reserve has one of the largest and most accessible breeding colonies of grey seals in the UK. Other mammals include fox, badger, stoat and weasel and three species of shrew have been identified. Common lizard.
Contact: Lincolnshire Wildlife Trust, Banavallum House, Manor House Street, Horncastle, Lincs, LN9 5HF. 01507 526 667. e-mail: lincstrust@cix.co.uk www.lincstrust.co.uk

2. FRAMPTON MARSH

RSPB (Eastern England Office).
Location: TR 356 393. Four miles SE of Boston. From A16 follow signs to Frampton then Frampton Marsh.
Access: Open at all times. Free to enter. Coaches by prior arrangement.
Facilities: Footpaths, benches, car park, bicycle rack. Free information leaflets available (please contact the

office), guided walks programme.
Public transport: Nearest bus stop in Kirton (3 miles).
Habitat: Saltmarsh, wet grassland, freshwater scrapes (being created) and reedbed (being created).
Key birds: *Summer:* Breeding Redshank, passage waders (inc Greenshank, Ruff and Black-tailed Godwit) and Hobby. *Winter:* Hen Harrier, Short-eared Owl, Merlin, dark-bellied Brent Goose, Twite, Golden Plover, Lapland Bunting.
Contact: John Badley, Site Manager, Roads Farmhouse, Frampton Roads, Frampton, Boston, Lincs PE20 1AY.
01205 724 678; (Fax) 01205 723 599; (M) 07766 441 853. e-mail: john.badley@rspb.org.uk www.rspb.org.uk

3. FREISTON SHORE

RSPB (Eastern England Office).
Location: TF 398 425. Four miles E of Boston. From A52 at Haltoft End follow signs to Freiston Shore.
Access: Open at all times, free. Coaches by prior arrangement.
Facilities: Footpaths, two car parks, bird hide. Free information leaflets available on site, guided walks programme. Bicycle rack.
Public transport: None.
Habitat: Saltmarsh, saline lagoon, mudflats, wet grassland.
Key birds: *Summer:* Breeding waders including Avocets, Ringed Plovers and Oystercatchers, Corn Bunting and Tree Sparrow. *Winter:* Twite, dark-bellied Brent Goose, wildfowl, waders, birds of prey including

Short-eared Owl and Hen Harrier.
Passage: Waders, including Curlew
Sandpiper and Little Stint. *Autumn*:
Occasional seabirds including Arctic
and Great Skuas.
Contact: John Badley, 01205 724 678.
e-mail: john.badley@rspb.org.uk
www.rspb.org.uk

4. GIBRALTAR POINT NNR and BIRD OBSERVATORY

Lincolnshire Wildlife Trust.
Location: TF 556 580. Three miles S of
Skegness, signposted from town centre.
Access: Reserve open dawn-dusk all year.
Charges for car parking. Free admission
to reserve, visitor centre and toilets. Some
access restrictions to sensitive sites at S end,
open access to N. Dogs on leads at all times
– no dogs on beach during summer.
Visitor centre, toilets and surfaced paths
suitable for wheelchairs. Bird observatory and
four hides suitable for wheelchairs. Day visit
groups must be booked in advance. Access for
coaches. Contact The Wash Study Centre for
residential or day visits.
Facilities: Wash Study Centre and Bird
Observatory. Field centre is an ideal base for
birdwatching/natural history groups in spring,
summer and autumn. Visitor centre, gift shop and
cafe. Toilets open daily. Network of footpaths bisect all
major habitats. Public hides overlook freshwater and
brackish lagoons. Wash viewpoint overlooks saltmarsh
and mudflats.
Public transport: Bus service from Skegness runs
occasionally but summer service only. Otherwise taxi/
car from Skegness. Cycle route from Skegness.
Habitat: Sand dune grassland and scrub, saltmarshes
and mudflats, freshwater marsh and lagoons.
Key birds: Large scale visible migration during
spring and autumn passage. Internationally important
populations of non-breeding waders Jul-Mar (peak
Sep/Oct). Winter flocks of Brent Geese, Shelduck and
Wigeon on flats and marshes with Hen Harrier, Merlin
and Short-eared Owl often present. Regular Shore
Lark and Snow Bunting. Red-throated Divers offshore,
peak Feb. A colony of Little Tern and Ringed Plover in
summer. More than 100 species can be seen in a day
during May and Sept.
Other notable flora and fauna: Pyramidal orchids.
Large tracts of sea buckthorn. Danish scurvy grass
and shrubby sea blite are local specialities. Grey and
common seal colonies, with porpoises offshore in most
months. UK's first confirmed nursery roost of nathusius
pipistrelle. Great crested newt and a reintroduced
population of natterjack toads are key amphibian
species. At least 13 species of breeding dragonfly.
Contact: Kev Wilson, (Site Manager), Sykes Farm,
Gibraltar Point Nature Reserve, 01754 898 057.
e-mail: lincstrust@gibpoint.freeserve.co.uk
www.lincstrust.org.uk

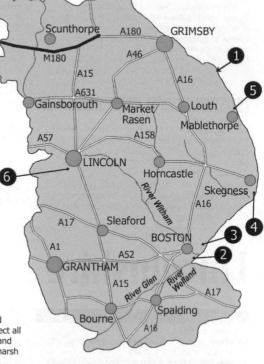

5. SALTFLEETBY-THEDDLETHORPE DUNES

Natural England (East Midlands Team).
Location: TF 46 59 24 - TF 49 08 83. Approx two
miles N of Mablethorpe. All the following car parks may
be accessed from the A1031: Crook Bank, Brickyard
Lane, Churchill Lane, Rimac, Sea View.
Access: Open all year at all times. Keep dogs under
close control. Easy access half mile trail suitable
for wheelchair users starts adjacent to Rimac car
park. Includes pond-viewing and saltmarsh-viewing
platforms.
Facilities: Toilets, including wheelchair suitability
at Rimac car park. May to end of Sept events
programme.
Public transport: Grayscroft coaches (01507 473
236) and Lincolnshire Roadcar (01522 532 424) run
services past Rimac entrance (Louth to Mablethorpe
service). Lincs Roadcar can connect with trains at
Lincoln. Applebys Coaches (01507 357 900) Grimsby
to Saltfleet bus connects with Grimsby train service.
Habitat: 13th Century dunes, freshwater marsh,
new dune ridge with large areas of sea buckthorn,
saltmarsh, shingle ridge and foreshore.
Key birds: *Summer*: Breeding birds in scrub include
Nightingale, Grasshopper Warbler, Whitethroat, Lesser
Whitethroat, Redpoll. *Winter*: Large flocks of Brent

Goose, Shelduck, Teal and Wigeon. Wintering Short-eared Owl, Hen Harrier. Migrant birds in scrub and waders on Paradise scrape.

Other notable flora and fauna: Impressive show of sea lavendar in late summer, orchids in marsh and dunes including pyramidal, marsh and bee. 14 species of dragonfly including emperor. Water vole, roe and muntjac deer, foxes and badgers common.

Contact: Reserve Manager, Natural England Workshops, Seaview, Saltfleetby St Clements, Louth, Lincs LN11 7TR. 01507 338 611. www.naturalengland.org.uk

6. WHISBY NATURE PARK

Lincolnshire Wildlife Trust.

Location: SK 914 661. SW of Lincoln off A46 southern end of Lincoln relief road. Brown tourist signs.

Access: Nature Park open dawn to dusk. Car park (charges soon to be introduced), closed out of hours. Natural World Visitor Centre open (10am-5pm). Some special exhibitions will have a charge. Disabled access. Dogs on leads. Electric buggy for hire by prior arrangement.

Facilities: Seven bird hides, coach park, toilets, visitor centre, café, education centre, waymarked routes, interpretation signs, leaflets.

Public transport: No. 46 bus Mon-Sat from Lincoln to Thorpe-on-the-Hill (infrequent), (quarter mile away).

Habitat: Flooded sand, gravel pits, scrub woodland and grassland.

Key birds: *All year*: Little and Great Crested Grebe, Sparrowhawk, Kestrel, Stock Dove, Green and Great Spotted Woodpeckers, Mistle Thrush, Willow Tit, Treecreeper, Jay, Bullfinch. *Spring/summer*: Egyptian Goose, Shelduck, Hobby, Little Ringed Plover, Common Sandpiper, Little Gull (occasional), Black-headed Gull colony, Lesser Black-backed and Yellow-legged Gulls, Common Tern colony, Arctic and Black Terns occasional, Turtle Dove, Cuckoo, Sand Martin colony, Nightingale, Grasshopper (scarce) Sedge and Reed Warblers and leaf warblers. *Autumn/winter*: Wigeon, Teal, Shoveler, Red-crested Pochard (scarce), Pochard, Goldeneye, Lapwing, Snipe, Woodcock, Green Sandpiper, Kingfisher, Grey Wagtail, winter thrushes, Goldcrest, Siskin, Lesser Redpoll.

Other notable flora and fauna: 23 species of dragonfly including emerald damselfly, migrant hawker, black-tailed skimmer and ruddy darter. 25 species of butterfly including Essex skipper, purple hairstreak and brown argus. Seven species of orchid including green-flowered helleborine.

Contact: Phil Porter, Whisby Nature Park, Moor Lane, Thorpe-on-the-Hill, Lincoln, LN6 9BW. 01522 500 676. e-mail: whisby@cix.co.uk www.lincstrust.org.uk

London, Greater

BEDFONT LAKES COUNTRY PARK

Ecology and Countryside Parks Service.

Location: TQ 080 728. OS map sheet 176 (west London). 0.5 miles from Ashford, Middx, 0.5 miles S of A30, Clockhouse Roundabout, on B3003 (Clockhouse Lane).

Access: Open (7.30am-9pm or dusk, whichever is earlier), all days except Christmas Day. Disabled friendly. Dogs on leads. Main nature reserve only open Sun (2pm-4pm). Keyholder membership available.

Facilities: Toilets, information centre, several hides, nature trail, free parking, up-to-date information.

Public transport: Train to Feltham and Ashford. Bus – H26 and 116 from Hounslow.

Habitat: Lakes, wildflower meadows, woodland, scrub.

Key birds: *Winter*: Water Rail, Bittern, Smew and other wildfowl, Meadow Pipit. *Summer*: Common Tern, Willow, Garden, Reed and Sedge Warblers, Whitethroat, Lesser Whitethroat, hirundines, Hobby, Blackcap, Chiffchaff, Sky Lark. *Passage*: Wheatear, Wood Warbler, Spotted Flycatcher, Ring Ouzel, Redstart, Yellow Wagtail.

Other notable flora and fauna: 140 plant species, wasp spider, butterflies and dragonflies

Contact: James Herd, Ranger, BLCP, Clockhouse Lane, Bedfont, Middx, TW14 8QA. 01784 423 556; Fax: 423 451. e-mail: bedfont_lakes@dip.org.uk

CHASE (THE) LNR

London Wildlife Trust.

Location: TQ 515 830. Lies in the Dagenham Corridor, an area of green belt between the London Boroughs of Barking and Dagenham and Havering. Entrances in Dagenham Rd, Dagenham and Upper Rainham Rd, Elm Park.

Access: Open at all times. No wheelchair access. Eastbrookend Country Park which borders The Chase LNR has surfaced footpaths for wheelchair use.

Facilities: Millennium visitor centre, toilets, ample car parking, Timberland Trail walk.

Public transport: Rail: Dagenham East (District Line) 15 minute walk. Bus: 174 from Romford five minute walk.

Habitat: Shallow wetlands, reedbeds, horse-grazed pasture, scrub and wetland. These harbour an impressive range of animals and plants, including the nationally rare black poplar tree. A haven for birds, with approx 200 different species recorded.

Key birds: *Summer*: Breeding Reed Warbler, Lapwing, Water Rail, Lesser Whitethroat, Little Ringed Plover, Kingfisher, Reed Bunting. *Winter*: Significant numbers of Teal, Shoveler, Redwing, Fieldfare and Snipe dominate the scene. *Spring/autumn migration*: Yellow Wagtail, Wheatear, Ruff, Wood Sandpiper, Sand Martin, Ring Ouzel, Black Redstart and Hobby regularly seen.

Other notable flora and fauna: Black poplar, spring restharrow grass, water vole.
Contact: Gareth Winn/Tom Clarke, Project Manager/ Project Officer, The Millennium Centre, The Chase, Off Dagenham Road, Rush Green, Romford, Essex, RM7 0SS.
02085 938 096. e-mail: lwtchase@cix.co.uk
www.wildlifetrust.org.uk/london/

LONDON WETLAND CENTRE

The Wildfowl and Wetlands Trust.
Location: TQ 228 770. Less than one mile from South Circular (A205) at Roehampton. In London, Zone 2/3, one mile from Hammersmith.
Access: Winter (9.30am-5pm: last admission 4pm), summer (9.30am-6pm: last admission 5pm). Charge for admission.
Facilities: Visitor centre, hides, nature trails, discovery centre and children's adventure area, restaurant (hot and cold food), cinema, shop, observatory centre, seven hides (all wheelchair accessible), three interpretative buildings.
Public transport: Train: Barnes. Tube: Hammersmith then Duckbus 283 (comes into centre). Bus from Hammersmith – 283, 33, 72, 209. Bus from Richmond 33.
Habitat: Four concrete reservoirs now redeveloped into main lake, reedbeds, wader scrape, mudflats, open water lakes, grazing marsh.
Key birds: As well as a collection of wildfowl from around the globe, the site now attracts many wild birds. *Winter*: Nationally important numbers of wintering waterfowl, including Gadwall and Shoveler. Important numbers of wetland breeding birds, including grebes, swans, a range of duck species such as Pochard, plus Lapwing, Little Ringed Plover,

Redshank, warblers, Reed Bunting and Bittern.
Contact: The Receptionist, London Wetland Centre, Queen Elizabeth Walk, Barnes, London, SW13 9WT. 020 8409 4400. e-mail: info.london@wwt.org.uk
www.wwt.org.uk

SYDENHAM HILL WOOD

London Wildlife Trust.
Location: TQ 344 725. Forest Hill, SE London, SE26, between Forest Hill and Crystal Palace, just off South Circular (A205). Entrances as Crescent Wood Road and Cox's Walk.
Access: Open at all times, no permits required. Some steep slopes – no wheelchair access.
Facilities: Nature trail, no toilets.
Public transport: Train stations: Forest Hill (from London Bridge) or Sydenham Hill (from Victoria). Bus 363,202, 356, 185, 312, 176, P4 - Transport for London 0207 5657 299.
Habitat: Ancient woodland, reclaimed Victorian gardens, meadow and small pond.
Key birds: Woodland and gardens species all year round. *All year*: All three woodpeckers, Tawny Owl, Kestrel, Sparrowhawk, Goldcrest, Nuthatch, Treecreeper, Stock Dove. *Summer*: Blackcap, Chiffchaff, Willow Warbler. *Winter*: Fieldfare, Redwing.
Other notable flora and fauna: Five species of bat, including noctule and brown long-eared. Bluebells, wood anemone and ramsons. Oak and hornbeam. Speckled wood butterfly.
Contact: Colin Higgins, London Wildlife Trust, Centre for Wildlife Gardening, 28 Marsden Road, London SE15 4EE. 0207 252 9186.
e-mail: chiggins@wildlondon.org.uk
www.wildlondon.org.uk

Manchester, Greater

1. ASTLEY MOSS

The Wildlife Trust for Lancashire, Manchester and North Merseyside.
Location: Lancs WT SJ 692 975. Lies seven miles S of Leigh. S of A580 at Astley; follow Higher Green Lane to Rindle Farm.
Access: Permit from Trust required.
Facilities: No parking on site. Leave car on Rindle Road.
Public transport: Bus service to Astley.
Habitat: Remnant peat bog, scrub, oak/birch woodland.
Key birds: *Spring/summer*: Breeding Tree Pipit. *Winter*: Raptors (inc. Merlin, Hen Harrier), finch flocks, thrush flocks; Long- and Short-eared Owls.
Other notable flora and fauna: Sphagnum

mosses, 10 species of dragonfly recorded.
Contact: The Wildlife Trust for Lancashire, Manchester and North Merseyside, Cuerden Park Wildlife Centre, The Barn, Berkeley Drive, Bamber Bridge, Preston PR5 6BY. 01772 324 129.
e-mail: lancswt@cix.co.uk www.wildlifetrust.org.uk/lancashire/

2. ETHEROW COUNTRY PARK

Stockport Metropolitan Borough Council.
Location: SJ 965 908. Well signposted from B6104 at Compstall near Romiley, Stockport.
Access: Open at all times; permit required for conservation area. Keep to paths.
Facilities: Reserve area has SSSI status. Hide, nature trail, visitor centre, scooters for disabled.

Public transport: None.
Habitat: 240 acres around River Etherow. Woodlands, marshy area.
Key birds: Sparrowhawk, Buzzard, Dipper, all three woodpeckers, Pied Flycatcher, warblers. *Winter*: Brambling, Siskin, Water Rail. Frequent sightings of Merlin and Raven over hills.
Other notable flora and fauna: 200 species of plant.
Contact: John Rowland, Etherow Country Park, Compstall, Stockport, Cheshire SK6 5JD. 01614 276 937; Fax 01614 273 643.
e-mail: parks@stockport.gov.uk

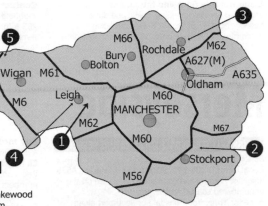

3. HOLLINGWORTH LAKE COUNTRY PARK

Hollingworth Lake – Rochdale MBC.
Location: SD 939 153 (visitor centre) off Rakewood Road. Four miles NE of Rochdale, signed from A58 Halifax Road and J21 of M62 – B6225 to Littleborough.
Access: Access open to lake and surroundings at all times.
Facilities: Cafes, hide, trails and education service, car parks, coach park by prior arrangement. Free wheelchair hire, disabled toilets and baby changing facilities, fishing. Visitor centre open 10.30am-6pm (Mon-Sun) in summer, 11am-4pm (Mon-Fri), 10.30am-5pm (Sat and Sun) in winter.
Public transport: Bus Nos 452, 450. Train to Littleborough or Smithy Bridge.
Habitat: Lake (116 acres, includes 20 acre nature reserve), woodland, streams, marsh, willow scrub.
Key birds: *All year*: Great Crested Grebe, Kingfisher, Lapwing, Little Owl, Bullfinch, Cormorant. Occasional Peregrine, Sedge Warbler, Water Rail, Snipe. *Spring/autumn*: Passage waders, wildfowl, Kittiwake. *Summer*: Reed Bunting, Dipper, Common Sandpiper, Curlew, Oystercatcher, Black Tern, 'Commic' Tern, Grey Partridge, Blackcap. *Winter*: Goosander, Goldeneye, Siskin, Redpoll, Golden Plover.
Contact: The Ranger, Hollingworth Lake Visitor Centre, Rakewood Road, Littleborough, OL15 0AQ. 01706 373 421. e-mail: hollilakecp@rochdale.gov.uk www.rochdale.gov.uk

4. PENNINGTON FLASH COUNTRY PARK

Wigan Leisure and Culture Trust
Location: SJ 640 990. One mile from Leigh town centre. Main entrance on A572 (St Helens Road).
Access: Park is signposted from A580 (East Lancs Road) and is permanently open. Four largest hides, toilets and information point open 9am-dusk (except Christmas Day). Main paths flat and suitable for disabled. Coach parking available if booked in advance.
Facilities: Toilets including disabled and information point. Total of seven bird hides. Site leaflet available

and Rangers based on site. Group visits welcome, guided tours or a site introduction can be arranged subject to staff availability.
Public transport: Only one mile from Leigh bus station. Several services stop on St Helens Road near entrance to park. Contact GMPTE 0161 228 7811.
Habitat: Lowland lake, ponds and scrapes, fringed with reeds, rough grassland, scrub and young woodland.
Key birds: Waterfowl all year, waders mainly passage spring and autumn (14-plus species). Breeding Common Tern and Little Ringed Plover. Feeding station attracts Willow Tit and Bullfinch all year.
Other notable flora and fauna: Wide variety of butterflies and dragonflies.
Contact: Peter Alker, Pennington Flash Country Park, St Helens Road, Leigh, WN7 3PA. 01942 605 253 (Also Fax number).
e-mail: pfcp@wlct.org

5. WIGAN FLASHES LNR

Lancashire Wildlife Trust/Wigan Council.
Location: SD 585 030. One mile from J25 of M6. Head N on A49, then into Poolstock Lane (B5238).
Access: Free access, open at all times. Areas suitable for wheelchairs but some motorcycle barriers (gates can be opened by reserve manager for large groups). Paths being upgraded. Access for coaches – contact reserve manager for details.
Facilities: Six hide screens.
Public transport: 610 bus (Hawkley Hall Circular). Local timetable info - call 0161 228 7811.
Habitat: Wetland with reedbed.
Key birds: Black Tern on migration. *Summer*: Nationally important for Reed Warbler and breeding Common Tern. Willow Tit, Cetti's and Grasshopper Warbler, Kingfisher. *Winter*: Wildfowl, especially

diving duck and Gadwall. Bittern (especially winter).
Other notable flora and fauna: Interesting orchids, 8 species including marsh and dune helleborine. One of the UK's largest feeding assemblage of noctule bats. 18 species of dragonfly

which has included red-veined darter.
Contact: Mark Champion, Lancashire Wildlife Trust, Highfield Grange, Wigan, Lancs WN3 6SU. 01942 233 976.
e-mail:wiganflashes@lancswt.org.uk

Merseyside

1. BIRKDALE & AINSDALE LOCAL NATURE RESERVE

Sefton Council.
Location: SD 305 145. SD 310 138. Leave the A565 just N of Formby and car parking areas are off the unnumbered coastal road.
Access: Track from Ainsdale or Southport along the shore. Wheelchair access across boardwalks at Ainsdale Sands Lake Nature Trail and the Queen's Jubilee Nature Trail, opposite Weld Road.
Facilities: Ainsdale Visitor Centre open summer and toilets (Easter-Oct).
Public transport: Ainsdale and Southport stations 20 minute walk. Hillside Station is a 30 minute walk across the Birkdale Sandhills to beach.
Habitat: Foreshore, dune scrub and pine woodland.

Key birds: *Spring/summer*: Ringed Plover, Long-eared Owl, Warblers including Grasshopper Warbler, Chiffchaff, waders. *Winter*: Blackcap, Stonechat, Redwing, Fieldfare, internationally important numbers of waders and wildfowl, white-winged gulls. *All year*: Sky Lark, Grey Partridge.
Contact: Coast and Countryside Service, Ainsdale Discovery Centre PR8 2Q8.
www.sefton.gov.uk

2. DEE ESTUARY, HESWALL

Metropolitan Borough of Wirral.
Location: SJ 255 815. Leave A540 Chester to Hoylake road at Heswall and head downhill (one mile) to the free car park at the shore end of Banks Road. Heswall is 30 minutes from South Liverpool and Chester by car.
Access: Open at all times. Best viewpoint 600 yards along shore N of Banks Road. No disabled access along shore, but good birdwatching from bottom of Banks Road. Arrive 2.5 hours before high tide. Coach parking available.
Facilities: Information board. No toilets in car park. Wirral Country Park Centre three miles N off A540 has toilets, hide, café, kiosk (all accessible to wheelchairs). Birdwatching events programme on RSPB website.
Public transport: Bus service to Banks Road car park from Heswall bus station, or bus to Irby village then walk one mile. Contact Mersey Travel (tel 0151 236 7676).
Habitat: Saltmarsh and mudflats.
Key birds: *Autumn/winter*: Large passage and winter wader roosts – Redshank, Curlew, Black-tailed Godwit, Oystercatcher, Golden Plover, Knot, Shelduck, Teal, Red-breasted Merganser, Peregrine, Merlin, Hen Harrier, Short-eared Owl. Smaller numbers of Pintail, Wigeon, Bar-tailed Godwit, Greenshank, Spotted Redshank, Grey and Ringed Plovers, Whimbrel, Curlew Sandpiper, Little Stint, occasional Scaup and Little Egret.

Contact: The Senior Ranger, Wirral Country Park Centre, Station Road, Thustaston, Wirral, Merseyside, CH61 0HN. 01516 484 371/3884.
e-mail: wirralcountrypark@wirral.gov.uk
www.wirral.gov.uk/er

3. HILBRE ISLAND LOCAL NATURE RESERVE

Wirral Country Park Centre (Metropolitan Borough of Wirral).
Location: SJ 184 880. Three tidal islands in the mouth of the Dee Estuary. Park in West Kirby which is on the A540 Chester-to-Hoylake road – 30 minutes from Liverpool, 45 minutes from Chester. Follow the brown Marine Lake signs to Dee Lane pay-and-display car park. Coach parking available at West Kirby but please apply for permit to visit island well in advance as numbers limited.
Access: Two mile walk across the sands from Dee Lane slipway. No disabled access. Do not cross either way within 3.5 hours of high water – tide times and suggested safe route on noticeboard at slipway. Prior booking and permit needed for parties of five or more – maximum of 50. Book early.
Facilities: Toilets at Marine Lake and Hilbre (primitive!). Permits, leaflets and tide times from Wirral Country Park Centre. Hilbre Bird Observatory.
Public transport: Bus and train station (from Liverpool) within 0.5 mile of Dee Lane slipway. Contact Mersey Travel, tel 0151 236 7676.
Habitat: Sandflats, rocky shore and open sea.
Key birds: *Late summer/autumn*: Seabird passage – Gannets, terns, skuas, shearwaters and after NW gales good numbers of Leach's Petrel. *Winter*: Wader roosts at high tide, Purple Sandpiper, Turnstone, sea ducks, divers, grebes. Passage migrants.
Other notable flora and fauna: Nationally scarce rock sea lavender.
Contact: The Senior Ranger, Wirral Country Park Centre, Station Road, Thustaston, Wirral, Merseyside, CH61 0HN. 01516 484 371/3884.
e-mail: wirralcountrypark@wirral.gov.uk
www.wirral.gov.uk/er

4. MARSHSIDE

RSPB (North England Office).
Location: SD 355 202. On south shore of Ribble Estuary, one mile north of Southport centre on Marine Drive.
Access: Open 8.30am-5pm all year. Toilets. No dogs please. Coach parties please book in advance. No charges but donations welcomed. Park in Sefton Council car park along Marine Drive.
Facilities: Two hides and trails accessible to wheelchairs. Two viewing screens and a viewing platform.
Public transport: Bus service to Elswick Road/Marshside Road half-hourly, bus No 44, from Lord Street. Contact Traveline (0870 608 2608).
Habitat: Coastal grazing marsh and lagoons.

Key birds: *Winter*: Pink-footed Goose, wildfowl, waders, raptors. *Spring*: Breeding waders, inc. Avocet and wildfowl, Garganey, migrants. *Autumn*: Migrants. *All year*: Black-tailed Godwit.
Other notable flora and fauna: Hares, various plants includnig marsh orchid, migrant hawker dragonfly.
Contact: The Warden, RSPB, 24 Hoghton Street, Southport, PR9 0PA. 01704 536 378.
e-mail: graham.clarkson@rspb.org.uk

5. RED ROCKS MARSH

Cheshire Wildlife Trust.
Location: SJ 206 880. 9km west of Birkenhead immediately W of Hoylake. Situated behind the Royal Liverpool Golf Course, north of West Kirby Parade, Hoylake.
Access: Open all year.
Facilities: Car park, hide.
Public transport: None.
Habitat: Sand dune, reedbed.
Key birds: *Spring/summer*: Wildfowl, warblers. *Passage*: finches, Snow Bunting, thrushes.
Other notable flora and fauna: The only breeding colony of natterjack toads on the Wirral Peninsula. More than 50 species of flowering plant recorded, including parsley piert, quaking grass, Danish scurvy grass, wild asparagus and various orchid species.
Contact: Cheshire Wildlife Trust, Bickley Hall Farm, Bickley, Malpas, Cheshire SY14 8EF. 01948 820 728; (fax) 0709 2888 469. e-mail: cheshirewt@cix.co.uk
www.cheshirewildlifetrust.co.uk

6. SEAFORTH NATURE RESERVE

The Wildlife Trust for Lancashire, Manchester and North Merseyside.
Location: SJ 315 970. Five miles from Liverpool city centre. From M57/M58 take A5036 to docks.
Access: Only organised groups which pre-book are now allowed access. Groups should contact the reserve office (see below) at least seven days in advance of their planned trip. Coaches welcome.
Facilities: Toilets when visitor centre open, three hides.
Public transport: Train to Waterloo or Seaforth stations from Liverpool. Buses to dock gates from Liverpool.
Habitat: Saltwater and freshwater lagoons, scrub grassland.
Key birds: Little Gull on passage (Apr) plus Roseate, Little and Black Terns. Breeding and passage Common Tern (Apr-Sept) plus Roseate, Little and Black Terns on passage. Passage and winter waders and gulls. Passage passerines, especially White Wagtail, pipits and Wheatear.
Contact: Steve White, Seaforth Nature Reserve, Port of Liverpool, L21 1JD. 0151 9203 769.
e-mail: swhite@lancswt.org.uk

NATURE RESERVES - ENGLAND

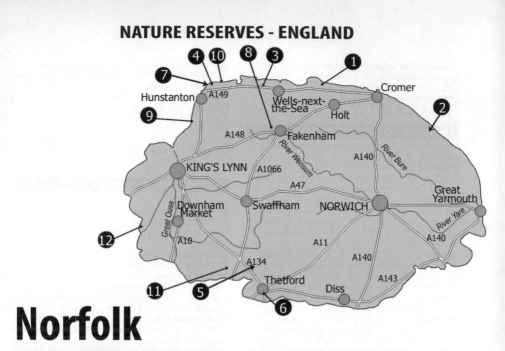

Norfolk

1. CLEY MARSHES

Norfolk Wildlife Trust.

Location: TG 054 441. NWT Cley Marshes is situated four miles N of Holt on A149 coast road, half a mile E of Cley-next-the-Sea. Visitor centre and car park on inland side of road.

Access: Open all year round, except Christmas Day. Visitor centre open Apr-Oct (10am-5pm daily), Nov-early Dec (10am-4pm Wed-Sun). Cost: adults £3.75, children under 16 free. NWT members free. Out of season, obtain permit from Watcher's Cottage, 400m along coast road towards Cley village.

Facilities: Brand new environmentally-friendly visitor centre incorporates an observation area, interactive interpretation including a remote controllable wildlife camera, a café, and sales area. Four hides (with excellent wheelchair access) provide birdwatching within metres of the pools where the birds congregate. Audio trail. Wildlife Detective Bumbags for children are free to hire. Boardwalk and information boards. Reserve leaflet.

Public transport: Coasthopper bus service stops outside, every two hours. Connections for train and bus services at Sheringham. Special discounts to visitors arriving by bus. Call Norfolk County Bus Information Line on 01603 223 800 for info.

Habitat: Reedbeds, salt and freshwater marshes, scrapes and shingle ridge with international reputation as one of the finest birdwatching sites in Britain.

Key birds: Bittern, Avocet, Marsh Harrier, Spoonbill, Bearded Tit and large numbers of wildfowl, including Wigeon, Teal, Pintail and Brent Goose. Migrating waders such as Ruff and Temminck's Stint. Many rarities.

Contact: NWT, 01603 625 540.
e-mail admin@norfolkwildlifetrust.org.uk
www.wildlifetrust.org.uk.Norfolk

2. HICKLING BROAD NNR

Norfolk Wildlife Trust.

Location: TG 428 222. Approx four miles SE of Stalham, just off A149 Yarmouth Road. From Hickling village, follow the brown badger tourist signs into Stubb Road at the Greyhound Inn. Take first turning L to follow Stubb Road for another mile. Turn R at the end for the nature reserve. The car park is ahead of you.

Access: Open all year. Visitor centre open Apr-Sep (10am-5pm daily). Cost: adults £3.25, children under 16 and NWT members free.

Facilities: Visitor centre, boardwalk trail through reedbeds to open water, birdwatching hides, wildlife gift shop, refreshments, picnic site, toilets, coach parking, car parking, disabled access to broad, boardwalk and toilets. Groups welcome. Water trail mid-May to mid-Sept (additional charge – booking essential).

Public transport: Morning bus service only Mon-Fri from Norwich (Neaves Coaches) Cromer to North Walsham (Sanders). Buses stop in Hickling village, a 25 minute walk away.

Habitat: Hickling is the largest and wildest of the Norfolk Broads with reedbeds, grazing marshes and wide open skies.

Key birds: Cranes, Marsh Harriers, Bittern, warblers. Raptor roost at Stubb Mill (Oct – Mar).

Other notable flora and fauna: Swallowtail butterfly, Norfolk hawker (rare dragonfly)

Contact: John Blackburn, Hickling Broad Visitor Centre, Stubb Road, Hickling, NR12 0BW.
e-mail johnb@norfolkwildlifetrust.co.uk
www.norfolkwildlifetrust.org.uk

3 . HOLKHAM NNR

Natural England (Norfolk and Suffolk Team).
Location: TF 890 450. From Holkham village turn N off A149 down Lady Ann's Drive (fee charged); alternatively, free parking at Burnham Overy.
Access: Access unrestricted, but keep to paths and off grazing marshes and farmland.
Facilities: Two hides. Disabled access.
Public transport: Bus Norbic Norfolk bus information line 0845 3006 116.
Habitat: Sandflats, dunes, marshes, pinewoods (4,000 hectares).
Key birds: *Passage*: Migrants. *Winter*: Wildfowl, inc. Brent, Pink-footed and White-fronted Geese. *Summer*: Breeding Little Tern.
Other notable flora and fauna: Seablite bushes, attractive to incoming migrant birds, sea aster and sea lavender.
Contact: M. Rooney, Hill Farm Offices, Main Road, Holkham, Wells-next-the-Sea, NR23 1AB. 01328 711 183; Fax 01328 711 893.

4. HOLME BIRD OBSERVATORY

Norfolk Ornithologists' Association (NOA).
Location: TF 717 450. E of Hunstanton, signposted from A149. Access from Broadwater Road, Holme. The reserve and visitors centre are beyond the White House at the end of the track.
Access: Reserve open daily to members dawn to dusk; non-members (9am-5pm) by permit from the Observatory. Please keep dogs on leads in the reserve. Parties by prior arrangement.
Facilities: Accredited Bird Observatory operating 12 months of the year for bird ringing, MV moth trapping and other scientific monitoring. Visitor centre, car park and several hides (seawatch hide reserved for NOA members), together with access to beach and coastal path.
Public transport: Coastal bus service runs from Hunstanton to Sheringham roughly every 30 mins but is seasonal and times may vary. Phone Norfolk Green Bus, 01553 776 980.
Habitat: In ten acres of diverse habitat: sand dunes, Corsican pines, scrub and reed-fringed lagoon make this a migration hotspot.
Key birds: Species list over 320. Ringed species over 150. Recent rarities have included Red Kite, Common Crane, Red-backed Shrike, Osprey, Pallas', Yellow-browed, Greenish and Barred Warblers.
Contact: Jed Andrews, Holme Bird Observatory, Broadwater Road, Holme, Hunstanton, Norfolk PE36 6LQ. 01485 525 406. e-mail: info@noa.org.uk www.noa.org.uk

5. LYNFORD ARBORETUM

Forest Enterprise.
Location: TL 822 942. On the Downham Market-Thetford road on A134. At the Mundford roundabout, follow signs to Swaffham. Take the first R to Lynford Hall. Follow road past the hall to the car park on the L. Disabled drivers can turn R.
Alternatively, from the roundabout head S towards Thetford. Take the minor road (signed L almost immediately) to Lynford Lakes. Follow the road to the L turn, signed to the lakes. There is a car park at the bottom of the track.
Access: Open all year.
Facilities: Two car parks, tracks. Suitable for wheelchairs. No dogs in arboretum.
Public transport: None.
Habitat: Plantations, arboretum, lake.
Key birds: *Spring/summer*: Possible Wood Lark, Tree Pipit, possible Nightjar, Kingfisher, waterfowl. *Winter*: Crossbill, possible Hawfinch. *All year*: usual woodland species, woodpeckers.
Other notable flora and fauna: More than 200 species of tree.
Contact: Forest Enterprise, Santon Downham. Brandon, Suffolk, IP27 0TJ. 01842 810 271.

6. NUNNERY LAKES

British Trust for Ornithology.
Location: TL 873 815. On the S edge of Thetford, adjacent to the BTO's headquarters at The Nunnery. Main access point is via Nun's Bridges car park, across pedestrian bridge at TL 874 821.
Access: Open dawn to dusk. Public access along permissive paths. Keep dogs on leads at all times. Call reception in advance to arrange wheelchair access to the lakes and hide.
Facilities: Waymarked paths, nformation panels, bird hide, boardwalk through wet woodland. Pre-booked coaches can park in grounds.
Public transport: Thetford railway station approx 1mile (0845 7484 950). Thetford bus terminal approx 1/2 mile (0870 6082 608).
Habitat: Flood meadows, scrape, flooded gravel pits, woodland.
Key birds: Wide range of species present throughout the year including Grey Heron, Egyptian Goose, Kingfisher, Willow Tit. *Spring*: Passage waders, hirundines, Swift, passerines. *Summer*: Warblers, Cuckoo, Oystercatcher, Hobby, Turtle Dove. *Winter*: Goosander, Teal, Water Rail, Snipe, Siskin, Hawfinch.
Other notable flora and fauna: Otter, brown hare, muntjac, grass snake, common lizard. Emperor dragonfly, red-eyed damselfly. Speckled wood and orange tip butterflies. Mossy stonecrop, tower mustard.
Contact: Chris Gregory, The British Trust for Ornithology, The Nunnery, Thetford, Norfolk, IP24 2PU. 01842 750 050. e-mail: chris.gregory@bto.org www.bto.org

7. REDWELL MARSH

Norfolk Ornithologists' Association (NOA).
Location: TF 702 436. In Holme, off A149, E of
Hunstanton. Access from Broadwater Road.
Access: View from public footpath from centre of
Holme village to Broadwater Road. Open at all times.
Facilities: Member's hide, offering free wheelchair
access, (access from Broadwater Road).
Public transport: As for Holme Bird Observatory.
Habitat: Wet grazing marsh with ditches, pond and
two large wader scrapes.
Key birds: Wildfowl and waders inc. Curlew/
Green/Wood and Pectoral Sandpipers, Greenshank,
Spotted Redshank, Avocet and Black-tailed Godwit.
Recent rarities have included American Wigeon, Ring
Ouzel, Black-winged Stilt, Mediterranean Gull and
Grasshopper Warbler. Also a raptor flight path.
Contact: Holme Bird Observatory, Broadwater Road,
Holme, Hunstanton, Norfolk PE36 6LQ. 01485 525
406. e-mail: info@noa.org.uk www.noa.org.uk

8. SCULTHORPE MOOR COMMUNITY NATURE RESERVE

The Hawk and Owl Trust
Location: TF 900 305. In Wensum Valley, just W
of Fakenham, on A148 to King's Lynn. Brown sign
signposted 'Nature Reserve' opposite village of
Sculthorpe. Follow Turf Moor Road to the Visitor and
Education Centre.
Access: Open Tue-Sun plus Bank Holiday Mondays
(except Christmas Day). April to September: Tues-Wed
(8am-6pm), Thur-Sun (8am-dusk). October to March:
Tues-Sun (8am-4pm). Free admission – donations
requested. Car park at Visitor and Education Centre.
No dogs except assistance dogs.
Facilities: Visitor and Education Centre open 10am-
4pm Tuesday - Sunday, with adapted toilets, hot
drinks dispenser, interpretive displays and live CCTV
coverage from around the reserve. Base for specialist
courses, school visits and other events. Boardwalks
to viewing platforms and two hides, all accessible by
wheelchair. Further hide accessed by bark path.
Public transport: Norfolk Green (tel: 01553 776 980
website: www.norfolkgreen.co.uk) bus X8 Fakenham
to King's Lynn stops at the end of Turf Moor Road.
Sustrans no.1 cycle route from Harwich to Hull runs
within 200 metres of the end of Turf Moor Road.
Habitat: Wetland reserve, with fen containing saw
sedge (a European priority habitat), reedbed, wet
woodland, pools, ditches and riverbank.
Key birds: More than 80 species recorded, including
breeding Marsh Harrier, Barn Owl and Tawny Owl,
visiting Buzzard, Goshawk, Hobby, Kestrel, Osprey,
Sparrowhawk, also Water Rail, Kingfisher, Marsh Tit
and Willow Tit.
Other notable flora and fauna: Otter, water vole
and roe deer, 19 species of dragonfly/damselfly,
butterflies including white admiral, glow-worms, fungi
including scarlet elf cup and a host of plants including

marsh fern and saw sedge.
Contact: The Hawk and Owl Trust, Sculthorpe
Moor Community Nature Reserve, Turf Moor Road,
Sculthorpe, Fakenham, Norfolk NR21 9GN, 01328 856
788, e-mail: sculthorpe@hawkandowl.org

9. SNETTISHAM

RSPB.
Location: TF 630 310. Car park two miles along
Beach Road, signposted off A149 King's Lynn to
Hunstanton, opposite Snettisham village.
Access: Open at all times. Dogs to be kept on leads.
Two hides are suitable for wheelchairs. Disabled
access is across a private road. Please phone office
number for permit and directions. Coaches welcome,
but please book in advance as a height barrier needs
to be removed.
Facilities: Four birdwatching hides, connected by
reserve footpath. No toilets on site.
Public transport: Nearest over two miles away.
Habitat: Intertidal mudflats, saltmarsh, shingle beach,
brackish lagoons, and unimproved grassland/scrub.
Best visited on a high tide.
Key birds: *Autumn/winter/spring:* Waders (particularly
Knot, Bar and Black-tailed Godwits, Dunlin, Grey
Plover), wildfowl (particularly Pink-footed and Brent
Geese, Wigeon, Gadwall, Goldeneye), Peregrine, Hen
Harrier, Merlin, owls. Migrants in season. *Summer:*
Breeding Mediterranean Gull, Ringed Plover, Redshank,
Avocet, Common Tern. Marsh Harrier regular.
Contact: Jim Scott, RSPB, Barn A, Home Farm Barns,
Common Road, Snettisham, King's Lynn, Norfolk PE31
7PD. 01485 542 689.

10. TITCHWELL MARSH

RSPB (Eastern England Office).
Location: TF 749 436. E of Hunstanton, off A149.
Access: Wheelchairs available free of charge. All
paths and trails suitable for wheelchairs. Reserve and
hides open at all times. Coach parking available but
pre-booking essential.
Facilities: Visitor centre, shop with large selection
of binoculars, telescopes and books, open every
day 9.30am to 5pm (Nov 5 - Feb 10, 9.30 to 4pm).
Tearoom open from 9.30am to 4.30pm every day (Nov
5 - Feb 10, 9.30 to 4pm). Visitor centre and tearoom
closed on Christmas Day and Boxing Day.
Public transport: Phone Traveline East Anglia on
0870 608 2608.
Habitat: Freshwater reedbed, brackish and fresh
water lagoons, extensive salt marsh, dunes, sandy
beach with associated exposed peat beds. RSPB to
adopt a policy of 'managed retreat' in the face of sea
incursion to outer part of reserve.
Key birds: Diverse range of breeding reedbed and
wetland birds with good numbers of passage waders
during late summer/autumn. *Spring/summer:* Breeding
Avocet, Bearded Tit, Bittern, Marsh Harrier, Reed
Sedge and Cetti's Warbler, Redshank, Ringed Plover
and Common Tern. *Summer/autumn:* Passage waders
including Knot, Wood and Green Sandpiper, Little

Stint, Spotted Redshank, Curlew Sandpiper and many more. *Winter*: Brent Goose, Hen/Marsh Harrier roost, Snow Bunting. Offshore Common and Velvet Scoter, Long-tailed Duck, Great Northern and Red-throated Diver.
Other notable flora and fauna: 25 species of butterfly including Essex skipper and annual clouded yellow. 21 species of dragonfly including small red-eyed damselfly. Good diversity of salt marsh plants including shrubby sea-blite and three species of sea lavender.
Contact: Centre Manager, Titchwell Marsh Reserve, King's Lynn, Norfolk, PE31 8BB. Tel/Fax 01485 210 779.

11. NWT WEETING HEATH

Norfolk Wildlife Trust.
Location: TL 756 881. Weeting Heath is signposted from the Weeting-Hockwold road, two miles W of Weeting near to Brandon in Suffolk. Nature reserve can be reached via B1112 at Hockwold or B1106 at Weeting.
Access: Open daily from Apr-Sep. Cost: adults £2.50, children free. NWT members free. Disabled access to visitor centre and hides.
Facilities: Visitor centre open daily Apr-Aug, birdwatching hides, gift shop, refreshments, toilets, coach parking, car park, groups welcome (book first).
Public transport: Train services to Brandon and bus connections (limited) from Brandon High Street.
Habitat: Breckland, grass heath.
Key birds: Stone-curlew, migrant passerines, Wood Lark.
Contact: Bev Nichols, Norfolk Wildlife Trust, Bewick house, 22 Thorpe Road, Norwich NR1 1RY. 01603 625 540. e-mail: BevN@norfolkwildlifetrust.org.uk www.wildlifetrust.org.uk/Norfolk

12. WELNEY

The Wildfowl and Wetlands Trust.
Location: TL 546 944. Ten miles N of Ely, signposted from A10 and A1101.
Access: Open daily (10am-5pm) except Christmas Day. Free admission to WWT members, otherwise £5.95 (adult), £4.50 (senior), £2.95 (child). Wheelchair accessible.
Facilities: Visitor centre (wheelchair friendly), café open 9.30am-430pm) daily. Large, heated observatory, additional 6 hides. Free parking and coach parking. Provision for disabled visitors.
Public transport: Poor. Train to Littleport (6 miles away), but from there, taxi is only option or cycling – Welney is on the National Cycle route.
Habitat: 1,000 acres of washland reserve, spring damp meadows, winter wildfowl marsh (SPA, Ramsar site, SSSI, SAC).
Key birds: Large numbers of wintering wildfowl are replaced by breeding waders, gulls, terns and warblers. *Winter*: Bewick and Whooper Swans, wintering wildfowl e.g. Wigeon. *Spring/summer*: Common Tern, Avocets, Lapwing, Black-tailed Godwits, House Martins, occasional rarities.
Other notable flora and fauna: Purple loosestrife, meadow rue, mixed grasses. Dragonflies include emperor, scarce chaser, banded damselfly, small red-eyed damselfly. Approx. 400 species of moth including goat moth, butterflies including brown argus.
Contact: Sarah Graves, Marketing and Learning Manager, WWT, Hundred Foot Bank, Welney, Nr Wisbech, PE14 9TN. 01353 860 711.

Northamptonshire

1. HOLLOWELL RESERVOIR

Anglian Water.
Location: SP 683 738. From Northampton, take the A5199 NW. After eight miles, turn L. The car park is on the L.
Access: Open all year. Permit required. Keep dogs on lead.
Facilities: None.
Public transport: Bus: No 60 from Northampton, first one arriving at 8.58am. Tel: 01604 676 060.
Habitat: Grass, mature, mixed and conifer plantations.
Key birds: *Autumn/winter*: Dunlin, Greenshank, Redshank, Green Sandpiper, Mediterranean Gull, ducks. Crossbill occurs in invasion years. Bearded Tit and Dartford Warbler occasional.
Contact: Anglian Water, Area Manager, Pitsford Fishing Lodge, Brixworth Road, Holcot, Northampton NN6 9SJ. 01604 781 350. www.anglianwaterleisure.co.uk

2. PITSFORD RESERVOIR

Beds, Cambs, Northants and Peterborough Wildlife Trust.
Location: SP 787 702. Five miles N of Northampton. On A43 take turn to Holcot and Brixworth. On A508 take turn to Brixworth and Holcot.
Access: Lodge open mid-Mar to mid-Nov from 8am-dusk. Winter opening times variable, check in advance. Permits for reserve available from Lodge on daily or annual basis. Reserve open to permit holders 365 days a year. No dogs. Disabled access from Lodge to first hide.

Facilities: Toilets available in Lodge, 15 miles of paths, eight bird hides, car parking.
Public transport: None.
Habitat: Open water (up to 120 ha), marginal vegetation and reed grasses, wet woodland, grassland and mixed woodland (40 ha).
Key birds: Typically 160-170 species per year with a total list of 248 species. *Summer*: Breeding warblers, terns, Hobby, Tree Sparrow. *Autumn*: Waders only if water levels suitable. *Winter*: Wildfowl, feeding station with Tree Sparrow and Corn Bunting.
Other notable flora and fauna: 31 butterfly species, 382 macro moths, 20 dragonfly species (including damselflies) , 371 species of flora and 101 bryophytes, 392 macro fungi.
Contact: Dave Francis, Pitsford Water Lodge, Brixworth Road, Holcot, Northampton, NN6 9SJ. 01604 780 148. e-mail: pitsford@cix.compulink.co.uk

3. SUMMER LEYS LNR

Northamptonshire County Council.
Location: SP 886 634. Three miles from Wellingborough, accessible from A45 and A509, situated on Great Doddington to Wollaston Road.
Access: Open 24 hours a day, 365 days a year, no permits required. Dogs welcome but must be kept on leads at all times. 40 space car park, small tarmaced circular route suitable for wheelchairs.
Facilities: Three hides, one feeding station. No toilets, nearest are at Irchester Country Park on A509 towards Wellingborough.
Public transport: Nearest main station is Wellingborough. No direct bus service, though buses run regularly to Great Doddington and Wollaston, both about a mile away. Tel: 01604 670 060 (24 hrs) for copies of timetables.
Habitat: Scrape, two ponds, lake, scrub, grassland, hedgerow.
Key birds: Hobby, Lapwing, Golden Plover, Ruff, Gadwall, Garganey, Pintail, Shelduck, Shoveler, Little Ringed Plover, Tree Sparrow, Redshank, Green Sandpiper, Oystercatcher, Black-headed Gull colony, terns.
Contact: Chris Haines, Countryside Service, Northamptonshire Council, PO Box 163, County Hall, Northampton, NN1 1AX. 01604 237 227. e-mail: countryside@northamptonshire.gov.uk

4. THRAPSTON GRAVEL PITS and TITCHMARSH LNR

Beds, Cambs, Northants and Peterborough Wildlife Trust/ Natural England.
Location: TL 008 804.
Access: Public footpath from

layby on A605 N of Thrapston. Car park at Aldwincle, W of A605 at Thorpe Waterville.
Facilities: Six hides.
Public transport: Bus service to Thrapston.
Habitat: Alder/birch/willow wood; old duck decoy, series of water-filled gravel pits.
Key birds: *Summer*: Breeding Grey Heron (no access to heronry), Common Tern, Little Ringed Plover; warblers. Migrants, inc. Red-necked and Slavonian Grebes, Bittern and Marsh Harrier recorded.
Contact: Northants Wildlife Trust, Ling House, Billing Lings, Northampton, NN3 8BE. 01604 405 285; Fax 01604 784 835.
e-mail:northamptonshire@wildlifebcnp.org
www.wildlifebcnp.org

5. TOP LODGE FINESHADE WOOD

Forestry Commission
Location: SP 978 983. Off the A43 between Stamford and Corby. Follow village signs to Fineshade and Top Lodge opposite the turning to Wakerley Woods.
Access: Visitor Centre (10am – 5pm), Car parking (7am – 7pm), open everyday except Christmas Day. Caravan club site open Mar – Nov – please see caravan club website for more details of yearly opening dates. Visitor Centre is fully accessible – smelter's walk is an all-ability trail and leads you to the wildlife hide
Facilities: Visitor centre, toilets, Top Lodge Café, RSPB shop. Guided walks and events throughout the year. Wildlife hide, 3 waymarked walking trails – 1 all ability, 2 are

surfaced, 1 horse trail, 1 family cycle trail, dedicated coach and horse box parking.

Public transport: None.

Habitat: Ancient woodland, coniferous woodland, beech woodland, open areas, small pond.

Key birds: A wide range of birds of mixed woodlands. *All year*: Red Kite, Great Spotted Woodpecker, Goshawk, Nuthatch, Crossbill, Marsh Tit, Willow Tit. *Summer*: Turtle Dove, warblers. *Winter*: Hawfinch.

Other notable flora and fauna: Adders, grass snakes, slow worms, common lizards. Fallow deer, badger. Orchids including greater butterfly, early purple and common spotted, other flora of ancient woodland.

Contact: Susan Taylor, Visitor and Community Services Manager, Forestry Commission Northants, Top Lodge, Fineshade, Nr. Corby, Northamptonshire NN17 3BB. 01780 444 920.
e-mail: susan.taylor@forestry.gsi.gov.uk
www.forestry.gov.uk/toplodge

Northumberland

1. ARNOLD MEMORIAL, CRASTER

Northumberland Wildlife Trust.

Location: NU255197. Lies NE of Alnwick and SW of Craster village.

Access: Public footpath from car park in disused quarry.

Facilities: Information centre (not NWT) open in summer. Interpretation boards. Toilets (incl disabled) and picnic site in quarry car park. Easy-going access along path through site. Coach parking in adjacent public car park.

Public transport: Arriva Northumberland nos. 401, 500, 501.

Habitat: Semi-natural woodland and scrub near coast.

Key birds: Good site for migrant passerines to rest and feed. Interesting visitors can inc. Bluethroat, Red-breasted Flycatcher, Barred and Icterine Warblers, Wryneck; moulting site for Lesser Redpoll. Breeding warblers in summer.

Other notable flora and fauna: Spring flora including primrose and non-native periwinkle.

Contact: Northumberland Wildlife Trust, The Garden House, St Nicholas Park, Jubilee Road, Newcastle upon Tyne NE3 3XT. 01912 846 884; e-mail: mail@northwt.org.uk
www.nwt.org.uk

2. DRURIDGE POOLS - CRESSWELL POND

Northumberland Wildlife Trust.

Location: 1. Druridge Pools NZ 272 965.
2. Cresswell Pond NZ 283 945. Half mile N of Cresswell.

Access: Day permits for both reserves. Wheelchair users can view northern part of Cresswell Pond from public footpath or roadside.

Facilities: 1. Three hides. **2.** Hide.

Public transport: None.

Habitat: 1. Deep lake and wet meadows with pools behind dunes. **2.** Shallow brackish lagoon behind dunes fringed by saltmarsh and reedbed, some mudflats.

Key birds: 1. Especially good in spring. Winter and breeding wildfowl; passage and breeding waders. **2.** Good for waders, esp. on passage.

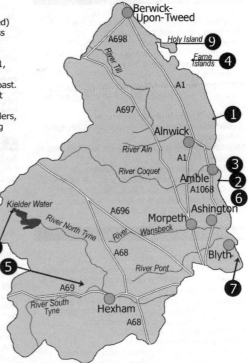

Contact: Jim Martin, Hauxley Nature Reserve, Low Hauxley, Amble, Morpeth, Northumberland. 01665 711 578.

3. EAST CHEVINGTON

Northumberland Wildlife Trust.
Location: NZ 265 985. Overlooking Druridge Bay, off A1068 between Hauxley and Cresswell.
Access: Main access from overflow car park at Druridge Bay Country Park (signed from main road).
Facilities: Four public hides, café, toilets and information at Country Park. ID boards for coastal plants.
Public transport: Arriva 420 and 423 bus services.
Habitat: Ponds and reedbeds created from former open cast coal mine. Areas of scrub and grassland.
Key birds: Large numbers of wildfowl, including Greylag and Pink-footed Geese in winter. Breeding Sky Lark, Stonechat , Reed Bunting, plus Reed, Sedge and Grasshopper Warblers. Capable of attracting rarities at any time of year.
Other notable flora and fauna: Coastal wildflowers.
Contact: Northumberland Wildlife Trust – 01912 846 884; e-mail: mail@northwt.org.uk
www.nwt.org.uk

4. FARNE ISLANDS

The National Trust.
Location: NU 230 370. Access by boat from Seahouses Harbour. Access from A1.
Access: Apr and Aug-Sept: Inner Farne and Staple 10.30am-6pm (majority of boats land at Inner Farne when conditions are calm). May-Jul: Staple Island 10.30am-1.30pm, Inner Farne: 1.30pm-5pm. Disabled access possible on Inner Farne, telephone Property Manager for details. Dogs allowed on boats – not on islands.
Facilities: Toilets on Inner Farne.
Public transport: Nearest rail stations at Alnmouth and Berwick.
Habitat: Maritime islands – between 15-28 depending on height of tide.
Key birds: 18 species of seabirds/waders, four species of tern (including Roseate), 55,000-plus pairs of Puffin, 1,200 Eider, Rock Pipit, Pied Wagtail etc.
Contact: John Walton, 8 St Aidans, Seahouses, Northumberland NE68 7SR. 01665 720 651.

5. GREENLEE LOUGH NNR

Northumberland National Park Authority
Location: NY 770 697. From Hexham or Carlisle, take A69 to Bardon Mill. Head to Housesteads Roman fort on B6318. Walk from car park on Pennine Way to Greenlee Lough.
Access: Open all year. Access via footpaths and boardwalks. Remoter locations accessed by public rights of way. Not suitable for wheelchairs.
Facilities: Bird hide, boardwalks.
Public transport: None.
Habitat: Greenlee is a shallow lake fringed by emergent vegetation, reedbeds, tall herb fen, sedges,

willow carr, peat bogs and sandbanks.
Key birds: Important with other loughs for overwintering wildfowl, Whooper Swan, Greylag Geese, Bean Geese, Goldeneye, Wigeon. *Summer*: Mute Swan, Great Crested Grebe, Reed Bunting, Sedge and Willow Warblers, Snipe, sandpipers, Lapwing, Curlew, Redshank, Oystercatcher.
Other notable flora and fauna: Marsh cinquefoil, bog bean, pond weeds, cross-leaved heath, bog asphodel, sundew. Roe deer, fox and otter also regularly use the site.
Contact: Rangers Office, National Park Centre, Once Brewed Visitor Centre, Military Road, Bardon Mill, Hexham NE47 7AN. 01434 344 430.
e-mail: tic.oncebrewed@nnpa.org.uk
www.northumberlandnationalpark.org.uk

6. HAUXLEY

Northumberland Wildlife Trust
Location: NU 285 023. South of Amble.
Access: Day permit required. Access through High Hauxley village. Site is signposted off A1068.
Facilities: Reception hide open daily from 10am-5pm (summer) or 10am-3pm (winter) and five public hides. Toilets and information.
Public transport: Arriva 420 and 423 bus services.
Habitat: Ponds created from former opencast coal mine. Areas of woodland and grassland.
Key birds: Large numbers of wildfowl use the site in winter, while waders use the site at high tide. Roseate Terns sometimes join commoner species in late summer. Waders and migrants on passage. *Winter*: Bewick's Swan, Shoveler, Lapwing and Purple Sandpiper.
Other notable flora and fauna: A variety of invertebrates, including butterflies, dragonflies and amphibians such as great crested newt.
Contact: Northumberland Wildlife Trust, 01912 846 884; e-mail: mail@northwt.org.uk www.nwt.org.uk

7. HOLYWELL POND

Northumberland Wildlife Trust.
Location: NZ 319 752. N of Holywell near Seaton Delaval on A192.
Access: Open all year. Access is limited to path to hide and adjacent routes.
Facilities: Public hide (suitable for disabled) accessed from public footpath leading from housing estate open at all times. Members hide is locked, keys are available to Trust members.
Public transport: Arriva Northumberland buses to Seaton Delaval and Holywell.
Habitat: Pond and reedbed.
Key birds: Good for winter wildfowl (inc. Goldeneye, Greylag Geese) and passage species.
Other notable flora and fauna: Northern marsh orchid and other meadow plants in grassland by ponds visible from public footpath.
Contact: Northumberland Wildlife Trust, 01912 846 884; e-mail: mail@northwt.org.uk
www.nwt.org.uk

8. KIELDER FOREST

Forestry Commission
Location: NY 632 934. Kielder Castle is situated at N end of Kielder Water, NW of Bellingham.
Access: Forest open all year. Toll charge on 12-mile forest drive and car park charge applies. Visitor centre has limited opening in winter.
Facilities: Visitor centre, exhibition, toilets, shop, access for disabled, licensed café. Local facilities include youth hostel, camp site, pub and garage.
Public transport: Bus: 814, 815, 816 from Hexham and seasonal service 714 from Newcastle.
Habitat: Commercial woodland, mixed and broadleaved trees.
Key birds: *Spring/summer*: Goshawk, Chiffchaff, Willow Warbler, Redstart, Siskin. *Winter*: Crossbill. Resident: Jay, Dipper, Great Spotted Woodpecker, Tawny Owl, Song Thrush, Goldcrest.
Other notable flora and fauna: Impressive display of northern marsh orchids at entrance to Kielder Castle.
Contact: Forestry Commission, Eals Burn, Bellingham, Hexham, Northumberland, NE48 2HP. 01434 220 242. e-mail: richard.gilchrist@forestry.gsi.gov.uk

9. LINDISFARNE NNR

Natural England (Northumbria Team).
Location: NU 090 430. Island causeway access lies two miles E of A1 at Beal, eight miles S of Berwick-on-Tweed.
Access: Open all hours. Some restricted access (refuges). Coach parking available on Holy Island.
Facilities: Toilets, visitor centre in village. Hide on island (new hide with disabled access at Fenham-le-Moor). Self-guided trail on island.
Public transport: Irregular bus service to Holy Island, mainly in summer. Main bus route follows mainland boundary of site north-south.
Habitat: Dunes, sand, mudflats and saltmarsh.
Key birds: *Passage and winter*: Wildfowl and waders, including pale-bellied Brent Goose, Long-tailed Duck and Whooper Swan. Rare migrants.
Other notable flora and fauna: Butterflies include dark green fritillary (July) and grayling (August). Guided walks advertised for 9 species of orchid including coralroot and Lindisfarne helleborine.
Contact: Phil Davey, Senior Reserve Manager, Beal Station, Berwick-on-Tweed, TD15 2PB. 01289 381 470.

Nottinghamshire

1. ATTENBOROUGH NATURE RESERVE

Nottinghamshire Wildlife Trust.
Location: SK 516 340. On A6005, seven miles SW of Nottingham alongside River Trent. Signposted from main road.
Access: Open at all times. Dogs on leads (guide dogs only in visitor centre). Paths suitable for disabled access. Coaches welcome by prior appointment. £1.50 parking donation.
Facilities: Education and visitor centre with café and shop, all accessible to wheelchair users. Nature trail (leaflet from Notts WT), one hide.
Public transport: Railway station at Attenborough – reserve is five mins walk away, visitor centre a further 10 minutes. Rainbow 5 bus service between Nottingham Broadmarsh and Derby bus station runs regularly throughout day. Alight at Chilwell Retail Park and walk 500m along Barton Lane.
Habitat: Disused, flooded gravel workings with associated marginal and wetland vegetation.
Key birds: *Spring/summer*: Breeding Common Tern (40-plus pairs), Reed Warbler, Black Tern regular (bred once). *Winter*: Wildfowl (including Bittern), Grey Heron colony, adjacent Cormorant roost.
Other notable flora and fauna: Smooth newt, dragonflies including four-spotted chaser and migrant hawker.
Contact: Attenborough Nature Centre, Barton Lane, Attenborough, Nottingham, NG9 6DY. 01159 721 777. e-mail: enquiries@attenboroughnaturecentre.co.uk www.attenboroughnaturecentre.co.uk

2. BESTHORPE NATURE RESERVE

Nottinghamshire Wildlife Trust.
Location: SK 817 640 and SK813 646 (access points). Take A1133 N of Newark. Turn into Trent Lane S of Besthorpe village, reserve entrances second turn on L and R turn at end of lane (at River Trent).
Access: Open access to two hides (one with disabled access from car park at present). No access to SSSI meadows. Limited access to areas grazed with sheep. Dogs on leads.
Facilities: No toilets (pubs etc in Besthorpe village), two hides, paths, nature trail (northern part).
Public transport: Buses (numbers 22, 67, 68, 6, S7L) run by Marshalls, Lincs, Road Car and Travel Wright along A1133 to Besthorpe village (0.75 mile away). Tel: 0115 924 0000 or 01777 710 550 for information.
Habitat: Gravel pit with islands, SSSI neutral grasslands, hedges, reedbed, etc.
Key birds: *Spring/summer*: Breeding Grey Heron, Cormorant, Little Ringed Plover, Kingfisher, Grasshopper Warbler. *Winter*: Large numbers of ducks (Pochard, Tufted Duck, Pintail, Wigeon) and Peregrine.
Contact: Nottinghamshire Wildlife Trust, 01159 588 242. e-mail: info@nottswt.co.uk www.wildlifetrust.org.uk/nottinghamshire

3. BUNNY OLD WOOD WEST

Nottinghamshire Wildlife Trust.
Location: Limited parking off the A60 at SK 579 283.
Please do not obstruct access. Further footpath access
is at SK 584 293 off Wysall Lane.
Access: Open all year. No coach parking available.
Facilities: None
Public transport: None.
Habitat: Mixed woodland.
Key birds: *All year*: Usual woodland species, all three
woodpeckers, Tawny and Little Owls. *Spring/summer*:
Usual visitors, including Blackcap. Possible Brambling
and Hawfinch.
Other notable flora and fauna: Bluebells, plus
good selection of common woodland plants. Butterflies
including white-letter hairstreak.
Contact: Nottinghamshire Wildlife Trust, 01159 588
242. e-mail: info@nottswt.co.uk
www.wildlifetrust.org.uk/nottinghamshire

4. COLWICK COUNTRY PARK

Nottingham City Council.
Location: SK 610 395. Off A612 three miles E of
Nottingham city centre.
Access: Open at all times, but no vehicle access after
dusk or before 7am. Park at Colwick Hall access road
or Mile End Road.
Facilities: Nature trails. Sightings log book in Fishing
Lodge.
Public transport: Call park office for advice
Habitat: Lakes, pools, woodlands, grasslands, new
plantations, River Trent.
Key birds: *Summer*: 64 breeding species. Warblers,
Hobby, Common Tern (15+ pairs). *Winter*: Wildfowl
and gulls. Lesser Spotted Woodpecker, Water Rail,
Kingfisher, passage migrants.
Other notable flora and fauna: Purple and white
letter hairstreak butterflies.
Contact: Head Ranger, The Fishing Lodge, Colwick,
Country Park, River Road, Colwick, NG4 2DW. 01159
870 785. www.colwick2000.freeserve.co.uk

5. LOUND GRAVEL PITS

Tarmac / Hanson / Nottinghamshire Wildlife Trust.
Location: SK 690 856. Two miles N of Retford off
A638 adjacent to Sutton and Lound villages.
Access: Open at all times. Use public rights of way
only (use OS Map Sheet No 120 - 1:50,000 Landranger
Series).
Facilities: Public viewing platform/screen off
Chainbridge Lane (overlooking Chainbridge NR
Scrape).
Public transport: Buses from Bawtry (Church
Street), Retford bus station and Worksop (Hardy
Street) on services 27/27A/83/83A/84 to Lound Village
crossroads (Chainbridge Lane).
Habitat: Working sand and gravel quarries, restored
gravel workings, woodland, reedbeds, fishing ponds,
river valley, in-filled and disused fly ash tanks,
farmland, scrub, willow plantations, open water.

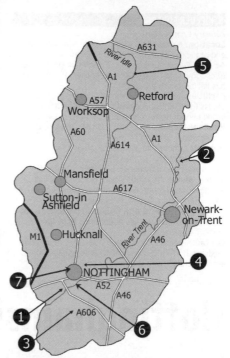

Key birds: More than 249 species recorded. *Summer*:
Gulls, terns, wildfowl and waders. Passage waders,
terns, passerines and raptors. *Winter*: Wildfowl, gulls,
raptors. Rarities have inc. Ring-billed Gull, Caspian,
White-winged Black, Gull-billed and Whiskered Terns,
Green-winged and Blue-winged Teal, Richard's
Pipit, Baird's, Pectoral and Buff-breasted Sandpiper,
Bluethroat, Nightingale, Snow Bunting, Cattle Egret
and Great White Egret.
Contact: Lound Bird Club, Gary Hobson (Secretary),
18 Barnes Avenue, Wrenthorpe, Wakefield WF1 2BH.
01924 384 419. e-mail: gary.lbc1@tiscali.co.uk
www.loundbirdclub.piczo.com

6. WILWELL FARM CUTTING NATURE RESERVE

Nottinghamshire Wildlife Trust / Rushcliffe Borough
Council.
Location: Situated on the outskirts of Nottingham
between Ruddington and Wilford.
Access: Open all year. Unsuitable for wheelchairs. No
parking for coaches.
Facilities: None.
Public transport: None.
Habitat: Abandoned railway cutting, neutral
grassland, limestone, track bed, acid fen and scrub
woodland.
Key birds: *All year*: Green Woodpecker,
Sparrowhawk, usual woodland species, Tawny Owl. 91

species have been recorded on the reserve.

Other notable flora and fauna: Cowslips, bee, green-winged and marsh orchids, plus good selection of wildflowers.

Contact: Nottinghamshire Wildlife Trust, 01159 588 242. e-mail: nottswt@cix.co.uk
www.wildlifetrust.org.uk/nottinghamshire

7. WOLLATON PARK

Wollaton Hall.

Location: Situated approx 5 miles W of Nottingham City Centre.

Access: Open all year from dawn-dusk.

Facilities: Pay/display car parks. Some restricted access (deer), leaflets.

Public transport: Trent Buses: no 22, and Nottingham City Transport: no's 31, and 28 running at about every 15 mins.

Habitat: Lake, small reedbed, woodland.

Key birds: *All year:* Main woodland species present, with good numbers of Nuthatch, Treecreeper and all three woodpeckers. *Summer:* commoner warblers, incl Reed Warbler, all four hirundine species, Spotted Flycatcher. *Winter:* Pochard, Gadwall, Wigeon, Goosander, occasional Smew and Goldeneye. Flocks of Siskin and Redpoll, often feeding by the lake, Redwing and occasional Fieldfare.

Contact: Wollaton Hall and Park, Wollaton, Nottingham, NG8 2AE. 01159 153 900.
e-mail: wollaton@ncmg.org.uk
www.wollatonhall.org.uk

Oxfordshire

1. ASTON ROWANT NNR

Natural England (Thames and Chilterns).
Location: SU 731 966. From the M40 Lewknor interchange at J6, travel NE for a short distance and turn R onto A40. After 1.5 miles at the top of the hill,

turn R and R again into a narrow, metalled lane. Drive to car park, which is signposted from the A40.

Access: Open all year. Some wheelchair access, please contact site manager for more information.

Facilities: On-site parking, easy access path to viewpoint, seats, interpretation panels.

Public transport: Regular bus services to Stokenchurch, 2km S of reserve. Red Rose Travel bus goes to Aston Rowant village (call 01296 747 926).

Habitat: Chalk grassland, chalk scrub, beech woodland.

Key birds: *Spring/summer:* Blackcap, warblers, Turtle Dove, Tree Pipit. *Winter:* Possible Short-eared Owl, Brambling, Siskin, winter thrushes. *Passage:* Whinchat, Wheatear, Ring Ouzel. *All year:* Red Kite, Buzzard, Sparrowhawk, Woodcock, Little and Tawny Owls, Green and Great Spotted Woodpeckers, Sky Lark, Meadow Pipit, Marsh Tit.

Other notable flora and fauna: Rich chalk grassland flora, including Chiltern gentian clustered bellflower, frog, bee, pyramidal and fragrant orchids. Good range of less common butterflies.

Contact: Natural England (Chiltern and North Wessex Downs Team), Aston Rowant Reserve Office, Aston Hill, Lewknor, Watlington, OX49 5SG. 01844 351 833. www.naturalengland.org.uk

2. CHIMNEY MEADOWS NATURE RESERVE

Berks, Bucks and Oxon Wildlife Trust.
Location: SP 353 014. Take A4095 from Witney to Bampton or A420 from Oxford to Buckland. The reserve is on an unclassified road between Bampton and Buckland. Head N from Tadpole Bridge, turn R after half mile. Go 1.25 miles E and turn R towards Chimney. Car park is on L at first bend – do not drive beyond it into hamlet.

Access: Open all year but limited access.

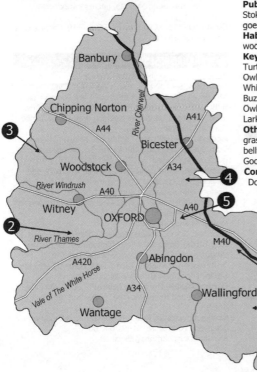

Dogs on leads to avoid disturbance to breeding and wintering waders. Leaflets available from dispenser at car park.
Facilities: Car park, two hides, leaflets.
Public transport: None.
Habitat: Six meadows next to the River Thames and 500 acres of recently-acquired farmland with meadows and wet grassland.
Key birds: *Spring/summer*: Whitethroat, Willow Warbler, Chiffchaff, Sedge Warbler. Curlew, Redshank. *Winter*: Waders, Snipe, Short-eared Owl.
Other notable flora and fauna: Nationally rare dry neutral grassland plants including meadow barley, crested dog's-tail, lady's bedstraw, bird's-foot-trefoil, meadow buttercup and tufted vetch. Good range of common butterflies.
Contact: Berkshire, Buckinghamshire and Oxfordshire Wildlife Trust, 01865 775 476. www.bbowt.org.uk

3. FOXHOLES RESERVE

Berks, Bucks and Oxon Wildlife Trust.
Location: SP 254 206. Head N out of Burford on the A424 towards Stow-on-the-Wold. Take third turning on R. Head NE on unclassified road to Bruern for 3.5km. Just before reaching Bruern, turn L along track following Cocksmoor Copse. After 750m, park in car park on R just before some farm buildings.
Access: Open all year. Please keep to the paths.
Facilities: Car park, footpaths. Can be very muddy in winter.
Public transport: None.
Habitat: River, woodland, wet meadow.
Key birds: *Spring/summer*: Nightingale, Yellow Wagtail, possible Redstart, Wood Warbler, Spotted Flycatcher. *Winter*: Redwing, Fieldfare, Woodcock. *All year*: Little Owl, all three woodpeckers, possible Hawfinch.
Contact: Berkshire, Buckinghamshire and Oxfordshire Wildlife Trust, 01865 775 476. www.bbowt.org.uk

4. OTMOOR NATURE RESERVE

RSPB (Central England Office).
Location: SP 570 126. Car park seven miles NE of Oxford city centre. From B4027, take turn to Horton-cum-Studley, then first L to Beckley. After 0.67 miles at the bottom of a short hill turn R (before the Abingdon Arms public house). After 200 yards, turn L into Otmoor Lane. Reserve car park is at the end of the lane (approx one mile).
Access: Open dawn-dusk. No permits or fees. No dogs allowed on the reserve visitor trail (except public rights of way). In wet conditions, the visitor route can be muddy and wellingtons are essential.
Facilities: Limited. Small car park with cycle racks, visitor trail (3 mile round trip) and two screened viewpoints. The reserve is not accessible by coach and is unsuitable for large groups.
Public transport: None.
Habitat: Wet grassland, reedbed and open water.
Key birds: *Summer*: Breeding birds include Cetti's

and Grasshopper Warblers, Lapwing, Redshank, Curlew, Snipe, Yellow Wagtail, Shoveler, Gadwall, Pochard, Tufted Duck, Little and Great Crested Grebes. Hobby breeds locally. *Winter*: Wigeon, Teal, Shoveler, Pintail, Gadwall, Pochard, Tufted Duck, Lapwing, Golden Plover, Hen Harrier, Peregrine, Merlin. *Autumn and spring passage*: Marsh Harrier, Short-eared Owl, Greenshank, Green Sandpiper, Common Sandpiper, Spotted Redshank and occasional Black Tern.
Contact: RSPB, c/o Folly Farm, Common Road, Bexley, OX3 9YR. 01865 351 163. www.rspb.org.uk

5. SHOTOVER COUNTRY PARK

Oxford City Council.
Location: SP 565 055. W of Oxford. From Headington take B4495 S and turn L into Old Road, continue into car park.
Access: Open all year, best early morning or late in the evening.
Facilities: Car park, toilets, nature trails, booklets.
Public transport: None.
Habitat: Woodland, farmland, heathland, grassland, scrub.
Key birds: *Spring/summer*: Willow Warbler, Blackcap, Garden Warbler, Spotted Flycatcher, Whitethroat, Lesser Whitethroat, Pied Flycatcher, Redstart, Tree Pipit. *Autumn*: Crossbill, Redpoll, Siskin, thrushes. *All year*: Sparrowhawk, Jay, tits, finches, woodpeckers, Corn Bunting.
Contact: Oxford City Council, PO Box 10, Oxford, OX1 1EN. 01865 249 811.

6. WARBURG RESERVE

Berks, Bucks and Oxon Wildlife Trust.
Location: SU 720 879. Leave Henley-on-Thames NW on A4130. Turn R at the end of the Fair Mile onto B480. L fork in Middle Assendon. After 1 mile, follow road round to R at grassy triangle, then on for 1 mile. Car park is on R.
Access: Open all year – visitor centre opens 9am-5pm. Please keep dogs on a lead. In some areas, only guide dogs allowed.
Facilities: Visitor centre, toilets, car park, two hides (one with disabled access), nature trail, leaflets. Visitors with disabilities and groups should contact the warden before visits. Car park not suitable for coaches, only mini-buses.
Public transport: None.
Habitat: Scrub, mixed woodland, grassland, ponds.
Key birds: *Spring/summer*: Whitethroat, Lesser Whitethroat. *All year*: Sparrowhawk, Red Kite, Treecreeper, Nuthatch, Tawny Owl. *Winter*: Redpoll, Siskin, sometimes Crossbill, Woodcock.
Other notable flora and fauna: Good for orchids, butterflies and mammals (roe, fallow and muntjac deer).
Contact: Warburg Reserve, Bix Bottom, Henley-on-Thames, Oxfordshire, 01491 642 001.
e-mail: bbowtwarburg@cix.co.uk

Shropshire

1. BUSHMOOR COPPICE

Shropshire Wildlife Trust
Location: SO 430 880. Head S from Church Stretton and take first R off A49 signed Bushmoor.
Access: Park in Busmoor village and follow track leading from right-angled bend. Follow green lane to gate and carry onto wood along field margin.
Facilities: None.
Public transport: No information available.
Habitat: Small mixed woodland and scrub.
Key birds: *Spring/summer*: Migrant warblers and flycatchers, plus common woodland species.
Other notable flora and fauna: Golden saxifrage, bluebells and yellow archangel. Dormouse, wood and yellow-necked mice. Copper underwing moth.
Contact: Shropshire Wildlife Trust, 193 Abbey Foregate, Shrewsbury, Shropshire SY2 6AH. 01743 284 280. e-mail: shropshirewt@cix.co.uk www. shropshirewildlifetrust.org.uk

2. CHELMARSH RESERVOIR

South Staffordshire Water/Shropshire Wildlife Trust.
Location: SO 726 880. Reservoir lies next to the reservoir, 6km south of Bridgnorth, off the B4555. From Chelmarsh village head S towards Highley. Turn L at Sutton and L at the T-junction. From the car park, walk to the other end of the reservoir to the hides.
Access: Open all year. No public car park at Dinney Farm. Park in Bull's Head car park in chelmarsh village.
Facilities: Car park.
Public transport: None.
Habitat: Reservoir, wader scrape, reedbed.
Key birds: *Winter*: Wildfowl, inc Pintail, Smew, geese, swans, Water Rail. Large gull roost on reservoir. *Spring/summer*: Little Ringed Plover, Reed and Sedge Warblers, Reed Bunting. *Passage*: Possible Osprey.
Contact: Shropshire Wildlife Trust, 01743 284 280 Fax 01743 284 281.

3. CLUNTON COPPICE

Shropshire Wildlife Trust.
Location: SO 343 806. From Craven Arms, take B4368 to Clunton village, go straight over bridge and up the hill to small car park just before reserve sign.
Access: Open at all times. Access along road and public rights of way only.
Facilities: Limited parking in small quarry entrance on R, or opposite The Crown pub.
Public transport: Not known.
Habitat: Sessile oak coppice. Good for ferns, mosses and fungi.

Key birds: Buzzard and Raven regular. *Spring/summer*: Wide range of woodland birds, inc. Redstart, Wood Warbler and Pied Flycatcher, Woodcock.
Other notable flora and fauna: Ferns, mosses and fungi including very rare *phillenus robustus*.
Contact: Shropshire Wildlife Trust, 01743 284 280.
e-mail: shropshirewt@cix.co.uk
www.shropshirewildlifetrust.org.uk

4. EARL'S HILL

Shropshire Wildlife Trust
Location: SJ 409 048. Near Minsterley, SW of Shrewsbury. Turn off A488 at Pontesford along lane by Rea Valley Tractors. Park in Forestry Commisson car park 700 yards further on.
Access: Follow green route for easier walking. Purple route leads to summit. Park in lane leading to reserve but do not block FC vehicles.
Facilities: None.
Public transport: No Information available.
Habitat: Steep-sided volcanic hill, scree slopes and crags, topped by Iron Age fort. Ancient woodland on eastern slopes.
Key birds: *Spring*: Migrants species such as Redstart, Pied Flycatcher and warblers. Dipper and Grey Wagtail on stream. Green Woodpecker common on open grassland.

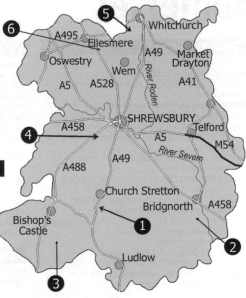

189

Other notable flora and fauna: More than 30 species of butterfly recorded, plus many wildflowers. Yellow meadow ant.
Contact: Shropshire Wildlife Trust, 01743 284 280. e-mail: shropshirewt@cix.co.uk www. shropshirewildlifetrust.org.uk

5. FENN'S WHIXALL AND BETTISFIELD MOSSES NNR

Natural England (North Mercia Team).
Location: Located four miles SW of Whitchurch, ten miles SW of Wrexham. S of the A495 between Fenn's bank, Whixall and Bettisfield. There is roadside parking at entrances, car parks at Morris's Bridge, Roundthorn Bridge, World's End and a large car park at Manor House. Disabled access by prior arrangement along the railway line.
Access: Permit required except on Mosses' trail routes.
Facilities: There are panels at all of the main entrances to the site, and leaflets are available when permits are applied for. Three interlinking Mosses trails explore the NNR and canal from Morris's and Roundthorn bridges.
Public transport: Bus passes nearby. Railway two miles away.
Habitat: Peatland meres and mosses.
Key birds: *Spring/summer*: Nightjar, Hobby, Curlew, Tree Sparrow. *All year*: Sky Lark, Linnet. *Winter*:

Short-eared Owl.
Other notable flora and fauna: Water vole, brown hare.
Contact: Natural England, Attingham Park, Shrewsbury, Shropshire SY4 4TW. 01743 282 000; Fax 01743 709 303.
e-mail: north.mercia@natural-england.org.uk

6. WOOD LANE

Shropshire Wildlife Trust.
Location: SJ 421 331. Turn off A528 at Spurnhill, 1 mile SE of Ellesmere. Car park is .75 miles down on R.
Access: Open at all times. Apply to Trust for permit to use hides. Reserve accessible to people of all abilities.
Facilities: Car parks clearly signed. Hides (access by permit).
Public transport: None.
Habitat: Gravel pit restored by Tudor Griffiths.
Key birds: *Summer*: Breeding Sand Martin, Lapwing, Little Ringed Plover and Tree Sparrow. Osprey platforms erected to tempt over-flying birds. Popular staging post for waders (inc. Redshank, Greenshank, Ruff, Dunlin, Little Stint, Green and Wood Sandpiper). *Winter*: Lapwing and Curlew.
Other notable flora and fauna: Hay meadow plants. Good variety of butterflies.
Contact: Shropshire Wildlife Trust, 01743 284 280. e-mail: shropshirewt@cix.co.uk
www.shropshirewildlifetrust.org.uk
www.woodlanereserve.co.uk

Somerset

1. BRIDGWATER BAY NNR

Natural England (Dorset and Somerset Team)
Location: ST 270 470. Nine miles N of Bridgwater. Take J23 or 24 off M5. Turn N on minor roads off A39 at Cannington.
Access: Hides open every day except Christmas Day. Permits needed for Steart Island (by boat only). Dogs on leads – grazing animals/nesting birds. Disabled access to hides by arrangement, other areas accessible.
Facilities: Car park at Steart. Footpath approx 0.5 miles to tower and hides.
Public transport: First Group buses to Stockland Bristol (2km SW of Steart).
Habitat: Estuary, intertidal mudflats, saltmarsh.
Key birds: *All year*: 190 bird species recorded. Wildfowl and waders, birds of prey. Large gatherings of Shelduck when moulting in summer. *Spring/autumn*: Passage migrants.
Contact: The Reserve Manager, Natural England (Dorset and Somerset Team), Riverside Chambers, Castle Street, Taunton, Somerset TA1 4AS. 01823 285 500. www.naturalengland.org.uk

2. CATCOTT LOWS

Somerset Wildlife Trust.
Location: ST 400 415. Approx one mile N of Catcott village (off A39 from J23 of M5).
Access: No public footpaths cross reserve – view from droves or hides.
Facilities: Two hides, one with ramp, one with steps. Car park by ramped hide at ST 400 416. No toilets.
Public transport: Daily bus service (375) between Bridgewater and Wells stops in Catcott village.
Habitat: Wet meadows with winter flooding and summer grazing.
Key birds: *Winter:* Wigeon, Teal, Pintail, Shoveler, Gadwall, Bewick's Swan, Peregrine. *Spring:* Little Egret, passage waders, breeding Lapwing, Snipe, Redshank, Yellow Wagtail.
Contact: Mark Blake
(mark.blake@somersetwildlife.org)

3. CHEW VALLEY LAKE

Avon Wildlife Trust, Bristol Water Plc.
Location: ST 570 600. Reservoir (partly a Trust

reserve) between Chew Stoke and West Harptree, crossed by A368 and B3114, nine miles S of Bristol.
Access: Permit for access to hides (five at Chew, two at Blagdon). Best roadside viewing from causeways at Herriott's Bridge (nature reserve) and Herons Green Bay.
Day, half-year and year permits from Bristol Water, Recreation Department, Woodford Lodge, Chew Stoke, Bristol BS18 8SH. Tel/Fax 01275 332 339. Parking for coaches available.
Facilities: Hides.
Public transport: Travel line, 0870 6082 608.
Habitat: Reservoir.
Key birds: *Autumn/winter*: Concentrations of wildfowl (inc. Bewick's Swan, Goldeneye, Smew), gull roost (inc. regular Mediterranean, occasional Ring-billed). Migrant waders and terns (inc. Black). Recent rarities inc. Blue-winged Teal, Spoonbill, Alpine Swift, Citrine Wagtail, Little Bunting, Ring-necked Duck, Kumlien's Gull.
Contact: Avon Wildlife Trust HQ or Bristol Water Recreation Dept, Woodford Lodge, Chew Stoke, Bristol, BS40 8XH. 01275 332 339.
e-mail: mail@avonwildlifetrust.org.uk
www.avonwildlifetrust.org.uk

4. HORNER WOOD NATURE RESERVE

National Trust
Location: SS 897 454. From Minehead, take A39 W to a minor road 0.8km E of Porlock signed to Horner. Park in village car park.
Access: Open all year. Car parking in Horner village, extensive footpath system.
Facilities: Tea-room and toilets. Walks leaflets available from Holnicote Estate office and Porlock visitor centre. Interpretation boards in car parks.
Public transport: Bus: Porlock.
Habitat: Oak woodland, moorland.
Key birds: *Spring/summer*: Wood Warbler, Pied Flycatcher, Redstart, Stonechat, Whinchat, Tree Pipit, Dartford Warbler possible. *All year*: Dipper, Grey Wagtail, woodpeckers, Buzzard, Sparrowhawk.
Other notable flora and fauna: Silver-washed fritillary in July.
Contact: National Trust, Holnicote Estate, Selworthy, Minehead, Somerset TA24 8TJ.
01643 862 452.
e-mail: holnicote@ nationaltrust.org.uk
www.nationaltrust. org.uk

5. GREYLAKE

RSPB (South West England Office).
Location: ST 399 346. Off A361 Taunton to Glastonbury road between Othery and Greinton.

Access: Open all year, dawn to dusk, free admission. No dogs, apart from guide-dogs. Wheelchair users can access a 700 metre-long boardwalk and viewing hide.
Facilities: Surfaced nature trail, interpretive signs. No toilets on site.
Public transport: No information available.
Habitat: A large wet grassland reserve bought by RSPB in 2003. Formerly arable farmland.
Key birds: *Spring/summer*: Breeding Snipe, Lapwing, Sky Lark, Yellow Wagtail, Kingfisher. Grey Heron, Little Egret. *Autumn*: Large Starling roost, Green Sandpiper, waders on passage. *Winter*: Wildfowl, waders, Peregrine.
Other notable flora and fauna: Roe deer, water vole, otter, dragonflies including four-spotted chaser.
Contact: The Warden, RSPB South West Regional Office, Keble House, Southernhay Gardens, Exeter EX1 1NT. 01458 252 805.

6. HAM WALL

RSPB (South West England Office).
Location: ST 449 397. W of Glastonbury. From A39 turn N in Ashcott and follow road onto the moor. After three miles pass Church Farm Horticultural building. Shortly after, at metal bridge, reserve is opposite side of road to Shapwick Heath NNR.
Access: Open all year. Dogs only on public footpaths and disused railway line. Wheelchair users can access viewing areas from main track. Other rougher tracks cover 3.8 miles.
Facilities: Two open-air viewing platforms, four roofed viewing screens. Part-time education officer available for school visits.
Public transport: Information not available.
Habitat: Newly-created 200-plus hectare wetland, including region's largest reedbed.
Key birds: *Spring/summer*: Cetti's Warbler, Water

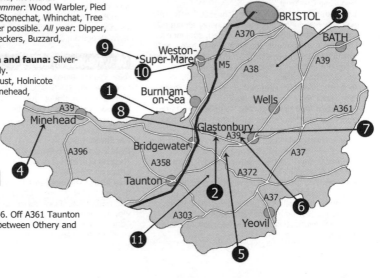

Rail. Bittern, warblers, Hobby, Barn Owl. *Autumn*: Migrant thrushes, Lesser Redpoll, Siskin, Kingfisher, Bearded Tit. *Winter*: Millions of Starlings roost, plus large flocks of ducks, Bittern, Little Egret, Peregrine, Merlin, Short-eared Owl.
Other notable flora and fauna: Otter, water vole, dragonflies, butterflies.
Contact: The Warden, RSPB South West Regional Office, 01458 252 805.

7. SHAPWICK HEATH NNR

Natural England (Dorset and Somerset Team)
Location: ST 426 415. Situated between Shapwick and Westhay, near Glastonbury. The nearest car park is 400 metres away at the Peat Moors centre, south of Westhay.
Access: Open all year. Disabled access to displays, hides. No dogs.
Facilities: Network of paths, hides, elevated boardwalk. Toilets, leaflets and refreshments available at the Peat Moors Centre.
Public transport: Train to Bridgwater, then First Bus (01278 434 574) No 375 Bridgwater–Glastonbury, to Shapwick village. Sustrans National Route 3 passes through Shapwick village.
Habitat: Traditionally managed herb-rich grassland, ferny wet woodland, fen, scrub, ditches, open water, reedswamp and reedbed.
Key birds: *All year*: Ducks and waders. *Summer*: Hobby, Cuckoo, Cetti's Warbler. *Winter*: Starling roost.
Other notable flora and fauna: Wetland plants, otter and roe deer.
Contact: The Reserve Manager, Natural England , Riverside Chambers, Castle Street, Taunton, Somerset TA1 4AS. 01823 285 500. www.naturalengland.org.uk

8. SHAPWICK MOOR RESERVE

Hawk and Owl Trust
Location: ST 417 398. On the Somerset Levels. Take A39 between Bridgwater and Glastonbury and turn N, signposted Shapwick, on to minor road, straight over crossroads and through Shapwick village, turn L at 'T' junction following signs for 'Peat Moors Centre'. The reserve is less than a mile north of village
Access: Open all year. Access only along public footpaths and permissive path (closed on Christmas Day). Dogs must be kept on leads.
Facilities: Information panels. No toilets on site (but at nearby Peat Moors Centre). There is a small parking area off the Shapwick to Westhay road.
Public transport: Train to Bridgwater, then First Bus (01278 434 574) No 375 Bridgwater–Glastonbury, to Shapwick village. Sustrans National Route 3 passes through Shapwick village.
Habitat: Wet grassland reserve being created from arable farmland as part of the Avalon Marshes project to restore the traditional, bird-rich Somerset Levels landscape. Grazing pasture with rough grass edges, fen, open ditches (known as rhynes), pollard willows and hedges.

Key birds: *Spring/summer*: Hobby, Barn Owl, Reed Bunting, and Cetti's Warbler. Waders on passage. Sky Lark. Passerines such as Bullfinch and Yellowhammer. *Autumn/winter*: Flocks of finches, Snipe, Shoveler, Gadwall, Stonechat. Peregrine and harriers may fly over. *All year*: Buzzard, Kestrel, Sparrowhawk, Kingfisher, Lapwing.
Other notable flora and fauna: Roe deer, brown hare, badger, otter and water vole.
Contact: Hawk and Owl Trust, PO Box 100, Taunton TA4 2NR, 0870 990 3889; e-mail enquiries@hawkandowl.org www.hawkandowl.org

9. STEEP HOLM ISLAND

Kenneth Allsop Memorial Trust.
Location: ST 229 607. Small island in Severn River, five miles from Weston-super-Mare harbour.
Access: Scheduled service depending on tides, via Knightstone Pier ferry. Advance booking necessary to ensure a place, contact Mrs Joy Wilson (01934 522 125). No animals allowed. Not suitable for disabled.
Facilities: Visitor centre, toilets, trails, basic refreshments and sales counter, postal service. Guidebook available, exhibition indoor area now open.
Public transport: None.
Habitat: Limestone grassland, scrub, rare flora, small sycamore wood.
Key birds: Important breeding station for Greater and Lesser Black-backed and Herring Gulls, largest colony of Cormorants in England. On migration routes.
Other notable flora and fauna: Rare plants include Steep Holm peony, henbane and many herbal/ medicinal species. Butterflies are often abundant, dragonflies in migratory season and moths, particularly lackey and brown-tail larva/caterpillars. Muntjac deer roam wild.
Contact: For direct bookings: Mrs Joy Wilson, 01934 522 125. For enquiries and general information: Mrs Joan Rendell, Stonedale, 11 Fairfield Close, Milton, Weston-super-Mare, BS22 8EA. 01934 632 307. www.steepholm.org.uk

10. WALBOROUGH LNR

Avon Wildlife Trust.
Location: ST 315 579. On S edge of Weston-super-Mare at mouth of River Axe.
Access: Access from Uphill boatyard. Special access trail suitable for less able visitors. Parking for coach available.
Facilities: None.
Public transport: Travel line, 0870 6082 608.
Habitat: Limestone grassland, scrub, saltmarsh, estuary.
Key birds: The Axe Estuary holds good numbers of migrant and wintering wildfowl (inc. Teal, Shelduck) and waders (inc. Black-tailed Godwit, Lapwing, Golden Plover, Dunlin, Redshank). Other migrants inc. Little Stint, Curlew Sandpiper, Ruff. Little Egret occurs each year, mostly in late summer.

Contact: Avon Wildlife Trust, 01179 177 270; Fax 01179 297 273. e-mail: mail@avonwildlifetrust.org.uk www.avonwildlifetrust.org.uk

11. WEST SEDGEMOOR

RSPB (South West England Office).
Location: ST 361 238. Entrance down by-road off A378 Taunton-Langport road, one mile E of Fivehead.
Access: Access at all times to woodland car park and heronry hide. Coach parking in lay-by across main road. Heronry hide and part of the woodland trail are wheelchair accessible.
Facilities: Heronry hide, two nature trails: Woodland Trail and Scarp trail (link to public footpaths), disabled parking area.

Public transport: Bus from Taunton to Fivehead. First Southern National Ltd 01823 272 033.
Habitat: Semi-natural ancient oak woodland and wet grassland. Part of the Somerset Levels and Moors.
Key birds: *Spring/summer*: Breeding Grey Heron, Little Egret, Curlew, Lapwing, Redshank, Snipe, Buzzard, Sedge Warbler, Yellow Wagtail, Sky Lark, Nightingale. Passage Whimbrel and Hobby.
Winter: Large flocks of waders and wildfowl (including Lapwing, Golden Plover, Shoveler, Pintail, Teal and Wigeon).
Contact: Site Manager, Dewlands Farm, Redhill, Curry Rivel, Langport, Somerset, TA10 0PH. 01458 252 805, Fax 01458 252 184.
e-mail: west.sedgemoor@rspb.org.uk
www.rspb.org.uk

Staffordshire

1. BELVIDE RESERVOIR

British Waterways Board / West Midland Bird Club.
Location: SJ865102. Near Brewood, 7 miles NW of Wolverhampton.
Access: Access only by permit from the West Midland Bird Club.
Facilities: Hides.
Public transport: Bus to Kiddermore Green – eight minute walk. Traveline – 0870 6082608.
Habitat: Canal feeder reservoir with marshy margins and gravel islands.
Key birds: Important breeding, moulting and wintering ground for wildfowl), including Ruddy Duck, Goldeneye and Goosander), passage terns and waders. Night roost for gulls.
Contact: Barbara Oakley, 147 Worlds End Lane, Quinton, Birmingham B32 1JX.
E-mail: permits@westmidlandbirdclub.com
www.westmidlandbirdclub.com/belvide

2. BLITHFIELD RESERVOIR

South Staffs Waterworks Co.
Location: SK 058 237. View from causeway on B5013 (Rugeley/Uttoxeter road).
Access: Access to reservoir and hides by permit from West Midland Bird Club.
Facilities: None.
Public transport: None.
Habitat: Large reservoir.
Key birds: *Winter*: Good populations of wildfowl (inc. Bewick's Swan, Goosander, Goldeneye, Ruddy Duck), large gull roost (can inc. Glaucous, Iceland). Passage terns (Common, Arctic, Black) and waders, esp. in autumn (Little Stint, Curlew Sandpiper, Spotted Redshank regular).
Contact: Barbara Oakley (see Belvide Reservoir above).

3. BRANSTON WATER PARK

East Staffordshire Borough Council.
Location: SK 217 207. Follow brown tourist sign from A38 N. No access from A38 S - instead head to the Barton-under-Needwood exit and return N. The park is 0.5 miles S of A5121 Burton-upon-Trent exit.
Access: Open all year, flat wheelchair accessible stoned path, all round the lake.
Facilities: Disabled toilets, picnic area (some wheelchair accessible tables), modern children's play area.
Public transport: Contact ESBC Tourist information 01283 508 111.
Habitat: Largest reedbed in Staffordshire, willow carr woodland, scrub, meadow area in former open cast gravel pit.
Key birds: *Spring/summer*: Reed Warbler, Cuckoo, Reed Bunting. Important roost for Swallow and Sand Martin. *Winter*: Waders, Little Ringed Plover occasionally, Pied Wagtail roost.
Other notable flora and fauna: Wide range of dragonflies and butterflies.
Contact: East Staffordshire Borough Council, Midland Grain Warehouse, Derby Street, Burton-on-Trent, Staffordshire DE14 2JJ. 01283 508 573.

4. CASTERN WOOD

Staffordshire Wildlife Trust.
Location: SK 119 537. E of Leek. Unclassified road SE of Wetton, seven miles NW of Ashbourne.
Access: Use parking area at end of minor road running due SE from Wetton.
Facilities: None.
Public transport: None.
Habitat: Limestone grassland and woodland, spoil heaps from former lead mines.
Key birds: All three woodpeckers, warblers, Pied

Flycatcher, Redstart, Sparrowhawk, Tawny Owl.
Other notable flora and fauna: More than 240 species of plants have been recorded, including cowslips and violets, several species of orchids, small scabious, ladies mantle and salad burnet, plus good numbers of woodland flowers and ferns. Five species of bats have been known to over-winter.
Contact: Staffordshire Wildlife Trust, The Wolseley Centre, Wolseley Bridge, Stafford, ST17 0WT. 01889 880 100. e-mail: staffswt@cix.co.uk www.staffs-wildlife.org.uk

5. COOMBES VALLEY

RSPB (North West England Office).
Location: SK 005 530. Four miles from Leek along A523 to Ashbourne and 0.5 miles down unclassified road – signposted.
Access: Open daily – no charge. Free parking. Coach groups welcome by prior arrangement. No dogs allowed. Most of the trails are unsuitable for disabled.
Facilities: Visitor centre, toilets, two miles of nature trail, one hide.
Public transport: Contact local bus company First PMT on 01782 207 999.
Habitat: Sessile oak woodland, unimproved pasture and meadow.
Key birds: *Spring*: Tree Pipit, woodpeckers, Pied Flycatcher, Redstart, Wood Warbler, displaying Woodcock over Chough Meadow. *Jan-Mar*: Displaying birds of prey. *Autumn*: Finches and thrushes.
Other notable flora and fauna: Bluebells, various butterflies.
Contact: Jarrod Sneyd, Six Oaks Farm, Bradnop, Leek, Staffs, ST13 7EU. 01538 384 017. www.RSPB.org.uk

6. DOXEY MARSHES

Staffordshire Wildlife Trust.
Location: SJ 903 250. In Stafford. Parking 0.25 miles off M6 J14/A513 Eccleshall Road or walk from town centre.
Access: Open at all times. Dogs on leads. Disabled access being improved. Coach and car parking off Wooton Drive.
Facilities: One hide, three viewing platforms, two are accessible to wheelchairs.
Public transport: Walk from town centre via Sainsbury's.
Habitat: Marsh, pools, reedbeds, hedgerows, reed sweet-grass swamp.
Key birds: *Spring/summer*: Breeding Snipe, Lapwing, Redshank, Little Ringed Plover, Oystercatcher, warblers, buntings, Sky Lark, Water Rail. *Winter*: Snipe, wildfowl, thrushes, Short-eared Owl. Passage waders, vagrants.
Other notable flora and fauna: Otter, noctule bat, musk beetle.
Contact: Staffordshire Wildlife Trust, 01889 880 100. e-mail: info@staffs-wildlife.org.uk www.staffs-wildlife.org.uk

7. LOYNTON MOSS

Staffordshire Wildlife Trust.
Location: SJ 789 243. Go through Woodseaves on the A519 towards Newport. Within a mile you will cross the Shropshire Union Canal, which forms the E boundary of the reserve. Approx 200m past the canal on the R is the entrance to the reserve into a small car park.
Access: Open all year. Bridle path and permissive paths throughout reserve. Some paths inaccessible during the winter months.
Facilities: None.
Public transport: None.
Habitat: Fen, woodland mire, willow/alder carr, secondary woodland, wet pasture.
Key birds: *Spring/summer*: Sky Lark, Marsh Tit, Willow Tit, Sedge Warbler, Greater and Lesser Spotted Woodpeckers, Woodcock.
Other notable flora and fauna: The areas of fen and carr are especially important for invertebrates with some very rare species of moth such as the dentated pug, small yellow wave and the round winged muslin. Plants in reedbed include marsh cinquefoil, cowbane, branched bur-reed and lesser pond sedge.
Contact: Staffordshire Wildlife Trust. 01889 880 100. e-mail: staffswt@cix.co.uk www.staffs-wildlife.org.uk

8. RADFORD MEADOWS

Staffordshire Wildlife Trust.
Location: SJ 938 216. South of Radford Bridge on A34, Stafford and alongside Staffs and Worcs Canal.

Access: View reserve from canal towpath only (access from A34 between bridge and BMW garage or via Hazelstrine Lane (over canal bridge). On-site visits restricted to special events only. No formal carpark.
Facilities: Trust intends to erect information boards along towpath.
Public transport: Site is close to National Cycle Network routes (www.sustrans.co.uk).
Habitat: 104 acres of lowland wet grassland, forming part of River Penk floodplain.
Key birds: Largest heronry in county (more than 20 pairs of Grey Heron). Breeding Sky Lark, Lapwing, Snipe and Reed Bunting. *Winter*: Wildfowl, Kingfisher, Buzzard.
Other notable flora and fauna: Several veteran black poplar trees.
Contact: Staffordshire Wildlife Trust, The Wolseley Centre, Wolseley Bridge, Stafford, ST17 0WT. 01889 880 100. e-mail: info@staffs-wildlife.org.uk www.staffs-wildlife.org.uk
Leaflet about birding the Trent Valley available on request.

Suffolk

1. CASTLE MARSHES

Suffolk Wildlife Trust.
Location: TM 471 904. Head E on the A146 from Beccles to Lowestoft. Take the first L turn after Three Horseshoes pub. Continue on the minor road which bends round to the R. Carry straight on until the road bends to the R again. The car park is on the L just after White Gables house.
Access: Public right of way. Unsuitable for wheelchairs. Stiles where path leaves the reserve. Unmanned level crossing is gated.
Facilities: None.
Public transport: Bus: nearest bus route is on the A146 Lowestoft to Beccles road. Tel: 0845 958 3358. Train: Beccles and Oulton Broad South on the Ipswich to Lowestoft line.
Habitat: Grazing marshes, riverbank.
Key birds: *Spring/summer*: Marsh Harrier, Cetti's Warbler, occasional Grasshopper Warbler. *Winter*: Hen Harrier, wildfowl, Snipe.
Contact: Suffolk Wildlife Trust, Brooke House, Ashbocking, Ipswich, IP6 9JY. 01473 890 089. e-mail: info@suffolkwildlifetrust.org www.suffolkwildlifetrust.org

2. DINGLE MARSHES, DUNWICH

Suffolk Wildlife Trust/RSPB.
Location: TM 48 07 20. Eight miles from Saxmundham. Follow brown signs from A12 to Minsmere and continue to Dunwich. Forest car park (hide) – TM 467 710. Beach car park – TM 479 707. The reserve forms part of the Suffolk Coast NNR.
Access: Open at all times. Access via public rights of way and permissive path along beach. Dogs on lead please. Coaches can park on beach car park.
Facilities: Toilets at beach car park, Dunwich. Hide in Dunwich Forest overlooking reedbed, accessed via Forest car park. Circular trail waymarked from car park.
Public transport: Via Coastlink, Dial a ride service to Dingle 01728 833 546 links to buses and trains.
Habitat: Grazing marsh, reedbed, shingle beach and saline lagoons
Key birds: *All year*: In reedbed, Bittern, Marsh Harrier, Bearded Tit. *Winter*: Hen harrier, White-fronted Goose, Wigeon, Snipe, Teal on grazing marsh. *Summer*: Lapwing, Avocet, Snipe, Black-tailed Godwit, Hobby. Good for passage waders.
Other notable flora and fauna: The site is internationally important for starlet sea anemone – the rarest sea anemone in Britain. Otter and water vole.
Contact: Alan Miller, Suffolk Wildlife Trust, Moonrakers, Back Road, Wenhaston, Halesworth Suffolk IP16 4AP. www.suffolkwildlife.co.uk e-mail: alan.miller@suffolkwildlifetrust.org

3. HAVERGATE ISLAND

RSPB (Eastern England Office).
Location: TM 425 496. Part of the Orfordness-Havergate Island NNR on the Alde/Ore estuary. Orford is 17km NE of Woodbridge, signposted off the A12.
Access: Open Apr-Aug (1st and 3rd weekends and every Thu), Sep-Mar (1st Sat every month). Book in advance through Minsmere RSPB visitor centre, tel 01728 648 281. Park in Orford at the large pay and display car park next to the quay.
Facilities: Toilets, picnic area, five birdwatching hides, viewing platform, visitor trail (approx 2km).
Public transport: Orford served by local buses (route 160). For timetable info call 0870 608 2608. Bus stop is 0.25 miles from quay. Boat trips from Orford (one mile)
Habitat: Shallow brackish water, lagoons with islands, saltmarsh, shingle beaches.
Key birds: *Summer*: Breeding gulls, terns, Avocet, Redshank and Oystercatcher. *Winter*: Wildfowl and waders.
Contact: RSPB Havergate Reserves, Unit 3, Richmond Old Dairy, Cedgrave, Woodbridge, Suffolk IP12 2BU. 01394 450 732.

4. HEN REEDBED NATIONAL NATURE RESERVE

Suffolk Wildlife Trust.
Location: TM 470 770. Three miles from Southwold. Turn off A12 at Blythburgh and follow along A1095 for two miles where brown signs guide you to the car park. Not suitable for coaches.
Access: Open at all times.
Facilities: Two hides and two viewing platforms on waymarked trails.
Public transport: Bus service between Halesworth and Southwold.
Habitat: Reedbed, grazing marsh, scrape and estuary.
Key birds: *Spring/summer*: Marsh Harrier, Bittern, Bearded Tit, Hobby, Lapwing, Snipe, Avocet, Black-tailed and Bar-tailed Godwits. *Passage*: Wood and Green Sandpipers.
Other notable flora and fauna: Norfolk hawker dragonfly.
Contact: Suffolk Wildlife Trust, Moonrakers, Back Road, Wenhaston, Halesworth, Suffolk IP16 4AP.
www.suffolkwildlife.co.uk

5. LACKFORD LAKES NATURE RESERVE

Suffolk Wildlife Trust.
Location: TL 803 708. Via track off N side of A1101 (Bury St Edmunds to Mildenhall road), between Lackford and Flempton. Five miles from Bury.
Access: Visitor centre open winter (10am-4pm), summer (10am-5pm) Wed to Sun, (closed Mon and Tues). Tea and coffee facilities, toilets. Visitor centre and four hides with wheelchair access.
Facilities: Visitor centre with viewing area upstairs. Tea and coffee facilities, toilets. Eight hides. Coaches should pre-book.

Public transport: Bus to Lackford village (Bury St Edmunds to Mildenhall service) – walk from church.
Habitat: Restored gravel pit with open water, lagoons, islands, willow scrub, reedbeds.
Key birds: *Winter*: Bittern, Water Rail, Bearded Tit. Large gull roost. Wide range of waders and wildfowl (inc. Goosander, Pochard, Tufted Duck, Shoveler). *Spring/autumn*: Migrants, inc. raptors. Breeding Shelduck, Little Ringed Plover and reedbed warblers.
Other notable flora and fauna: 17 species of dragonfly including hairy and emperor. Early marsh and southern orchid.
Contact: Lackford Lakes Visitor Centre, Lackford Lakes, Lackford, Bury St Edmunds, Suffolk IP28 6HX. 01284 728 706.
e-mail: lackford@suffolkwildlifetrust.org
www.suffolkwildlifetrust.org

6. LAKENHEATH FEN

RSPB (Eastern England Office).
Location: TL722 864. W of Thetford, straddling the Norfolk/Suffolk border. From A11, head N on B1112 to Lakenheath and then two miles further. Entrance is 200 metres after level crossing.
Access: Dawn to dusk, year round. Group bookings welcome. Visitor centre accessible to wheelchair users and a few points on the reserve.
Facilities: Visitor centre, toilets (inc disabled). Coach parking (must book). Hard and grass paths. Viewpoints. Picnic area with tables. Events programme.
Public transport: None.
Habitat: Reedbed, riverside pools, poplar woods.
Key birds: Principally a site for nesting migrants with ducks and some wild swans in winter.

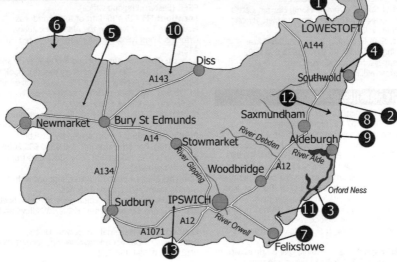

Spring: Marsh Harrier. *Summer*: Golden Oriole, Hobby, Reed and Sedge Warblers. *Autumn*: Harriers. *Winter*: Bearded Tits, Ducks.
Other notable flora and fauna: More than 15 species of dragonflies and damselflies. Range of fenland plants e.g. yellow iris, purple loosestrife. Roe deer.
Contact: Information Officer, 01842 863 400.
e-mail: lakenheath@rspb.org.uk
www.rspb.org.uk/reserves/

7. LANDGUARD BIRD OBSERVATORY

Landguard Conservation Trust
Location: TM 283 317. Road S of Felixstowe to Landguard Nature Reserve and Fort.
Access: Visiting by appointment.
Facilities: Migration watch point and ringing station.
Public transport: Call for advice.
Habitat: Close grazed turf, raised banks with holm oak, tamarisk, etc.
Key birds: Unusual species and common migrants.
Other notable flora and fauna: 18 species of dragonfly and 29 species of butterfly have been recorded on the site. Several small mammal species plus sightings of cetaceans and seals off-shore.
Contact: The Warden, Landguard Bird Observatory, View Point Road, Felixstowe, Suffolk IP11 3TW. 01394 673782. e.mail: landguardbo@yahoo.co.uk
www.lbo.co.uk

8. MINSMERE

RSPB (Eastern England Regional Office)
Location: TM 452 680. Six miles NE of Saxmundham. From A12 head for Westleton, N of Yoxford. Access from Westleton (follow the brown tourist signs).
Access: Open every day, except Christmas Day and Boxing Day (9am-9pm or dusk if earlier). Visitor centre open 9am-5pm (9am-4pm Nov-Jan). Tea-room 10am-4.30pm (10am-4pm Nov-Jan). Free to RSPB members, otherwise £5 adults, £1.50 children, £3 concession. Site partially accessible to wheelchairs.
Facilities: Toilets, visitor centre, hides, nature trails, family activity packs. Extensive events programme (see website for details). Coaches by appointment only (max two per day, not bank holidays).
Public transport: Train to Saxmundham then Coastlink (book in advance on 01728 833 526).
Habitat: Woodland, wetland (reedbed and grazing marsh), heathland, dunes and beach, farmland (arable conversion to heath), coastal lagoons, 'the scrape'.
Key birds: *Summer*: Hobby, Avocet, Spotted Redshank, Redstart, Nightingale, Nightjar, Mediterranean Gull, terns. *Winter*: Wigeon, Teal, White-fronted Goose, Bewick's Swan, Hen Harrier, Starling roost. *Autumn/spring*: Passage migrants, waders etc. *All year*: Marsh Harrier, Bearded Tit, Bittern, Cetti's and Dartford Warblers.
Other notable flora and fauna: Norfolk hawker dragonfly, red deer, otter, water vole, adder. Shingle

flora including marsh mallow.
Contact: RSPB Minsmere Nature Reserve, Westleton, Saxmundham, Suffolk, IP17 3BY. 01728 648 281.
e-mail: minsmere@rspb.org.uk
www.rspb.org.uk

9. NORTH WARREN & ALDRINGHAM WALKS

RSPB (Eastern England Office).
Location: TM 468 575. Directly N of Aldeburgh on Suffolk coast. Use signposted main car park on beach.
Access: Open at all times. Please keep dogs under close control. Beach area suitable for disabled. Three spaces at Thorpeness Beach pay-and-display car park on a first-come first-served basis only.
Facilities: Three nature trails, leaflet available from TIC Aldeburgh or Minsmere RSPB. Toilets in Aldeburgh and Thorpeness.
Public transport: Bus service to Aldeburgh. First Eastern Counties (08456 020 121).
Habitat: Grazing marsh, lowland heath, reedbed, woodland.
Key birds: *Winter*: White-fronted Goose, Tundra Bean Goose, Wigeon, Shoveler, Teal, Gadwall, Pintail, Snow Bunting. *Spring/summer*: Breeding Bittern, Marsh Harrier, Hobby, Nightjar, Wood Lark, Nightingale, Dartford Warbler.
Contact: Dave Thurlow, 1 Ness House Cottages, Sizewell, Leiston, Suffolk IP16 4UB. 01728 832 719.
e-mail: dave.thurlow@rspb.org.uk

10. REDGRAVE AND LOPHAM FENS

Suffolk Wildlife Trust.
Location: TM 05 07 97. Five miles from Diss, signposted and easily accessed from A1066 and A143 roads.
Access: Open all year, dogs strictly on short leads only. Visitor centre open all year at weekends and sometimes during the week in school holidays: call for details on 01379 688 333.
Facilities: Visitor centre with coffee shop, toilets, including disabled toilets, car park with coach space. Bike parking area, wheelchair access to visitor centre and viewing platform/short boardwalk. Other general circular trails (not wheelchair accessible).
Public transport: Buses and trains to Diss town – Simonds coaches to local villages of Redgrave and South Lopham from Diss.
Habitat: Calcareous fen, wet acid heath, scrub and woodland
Key birds: *All year*: Water Rail, Snipe, Teal, Shelduck, Gadwall, Woodcock, Sparrowhawk, Kestrel, Great Spotted, Lesser Spotted and Green Woodpeckers, Tawny, Little and Barn Owls, Reed Bunting, Bearded Tit, Willow Tit, Linnet.
Summer: Reed, Sedge and Grasshopper Warblers, Willow Warbler, Whitethroat, Hobby plus large Swallow and Starling roosts.
Winter/occasionals on passage: Marsh Harrier, Greenshank, Green Sandpiper, Shoveler, Pintail, Garganey, Jack Snipe, Bittern, Little Ringed Plover.

197

Contact: Andrew Excell, Redgrave and Lopham Fens, Low Common Road, South Lopham, Diss, Norfolk IP22 2HX. 01379 687 618.
e-mail: redgrave@suffolkwildlifetrust.org
www.suffolkwildlifetrust.org

11. TRIMLEY MARSHES

Suffolk Wildlife Trust.
Location: TM 260 352. Main Road A14 – Felixstowe two miles – Ipswich ten miles. Parking at top of Cordy's Lane, Trimley St Mary two miles from reserve.
Access: Reserve open at all times. Visitor centre open at weekends. Dogs on lead. Best time to visit – all year.
Facilities: Visitor centre, toilets (open at weekends), five hides.
Public transport: Train station at Trimley (Station Road/Cordy's Lane).
Habitat: Wetland (84 hectares).
Key birds: Summer: Avocet, Marsh Harrier, Redshank, Garganey, etc. Passage: Curlew Sandpiper, Wood Sandpiper. Winter: Wildfowl, Spoonbill, Little Egret.
Other notable flora and fauna: Good for dragonflies including emperor.
Contact: Suffolk Wildlife Trust, 01473 890 089; fax: 01473 890 165; www.wildlifetrust.org.uk/suffolk
e-mail: enquiries: info@suffolkwildlifetrust.org

12. WESTLETON HEATH NNR

Natural England (Suffolk team)
Location: Lies either side of Dunwich-Westleton minor road, E of A12.
Access: Open all year – please keep dogs on leads between March-August breeding season.
Facilities: Car park next to minor road.

Public transport: Train station in Darsham, 5 km to W, served by One Railway. First Group bus services on A12 (closest stop 5km distance).
Habitat: Lowland heath with heather-burning regime.
Key birds: Breeding Tree Pipit, Stonechat, Dartford Warbler and Nightjar on open heathland, Nightingale in woods.
Other notable flora and fauna: Silver-studded blue and white admiral butterflies, solitary bees and wasps. Adder.
Contact: Natural England (Suffolk team), 110 Northgate Street, Bury St Edmunds, IP33 1HP. 01284 762 218.
E-mail: enquiries.east@naturalengland.org.uk

13. WOLVES WOOD RESERVE

RSPB (Eastern England Office).
Location: Two miles E of Hadleigh on the A1071 to Ipswich.
Access: Open all year (9am-6pm or dusk if earlier). Wellington boots advisable between Sept-May. Unsuitable for wheelchairs. Donations welcome.
Facilities: Car park for 15 cars (no coaches), group bookings, guided walks, no dogs except guide dogs.
Public transport: Bus: Hadleigh (two miles). Train: nearest station Ipswich.
Habitat: Ancient woodland.
Key birds: *Spring/summer*: Nightingale, usual woodland species.
Other notable flora and fauna: Twelve species of dragonfly occur, including emerald damselfly.
Contact: Mark Nowers, Warden, RSPB, Unit 13, Court Farm, Stutton Road, Brantham, Manningtree, Essex CO11 1PW. 01473 328 006.
e-mail: mark.nowers@rspb.org.uk www.rspb.org.uk

Surrey

1. BRENTMOOR HEATH LOCAL NATURE RESERVE

Surrey Wildlife Trust.
Location: SU 936 612. The reserve runs along the A322 Guildford to Bagshot road, at the intersection with the A319/B311 between Chobham and Camberley. Best access is by Brentmoor Road, which runs W from West End past Donkey Town.
Access: Open all year.
Facilities: Local buses, nos 34, 590 and 591 stop under 0.5 miles away. Programme of moth nights, guided walks, fungi forays.
Public transport: None.
Habitat: Lowland heath, woodland, grassland, ponds.
Key birds: *Spring/summer*: Stonechat, Nightjar, Hobby. *All year*: Usual woodland birds.

Other notable flora and fauna: Silver-studded blue butterfly.
Contact: Surrey Wildlife Trust, School Lane, Pirbright, Woking, Surrey, GU24 0JN. 01483 795 440.
e-mail: surreywt@cix.co.uk
www.surreywildlifetrust.org.uk

2. FRENSHAM COMMON AND COUNTRY PARK

Waverley Borough Council / National Trust.
Location: SU 855 405. Common lies on either side of A287 between Farnham and Hindhead.
Access: Open at all times. Car park (locked 9pm-9am). Keep to paths.
Facilities: Information rooms, toilets and refreshment kiosk at Great Pond.

NATURE RESERVES - ENGLAND

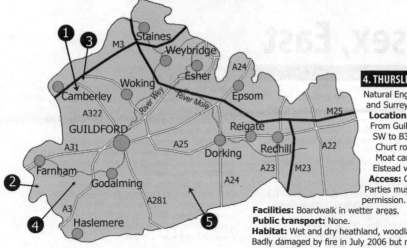

Natural England (Sussex and Surrey Team).
Location: SU 900 417. From Guildford, take A3 SW to B3001 (Elstead/Churt road). Use the Moat car park, S of Elstead village.
Access: Open access. Parties must obtain prior permission.
Facilities: Boardwalk in wetter areas.
Public transport: None.
Habitat: Wet and dry heathland, woodland, bog. Badly damaged by fire in July 2006 but recovering well.
Key birds: *Winter*: Hen Harrier and Great Grey Shrike. *Summer*: Hobby, Wood Lark, Dartford Warbler, Stonechat, Curlew, Snipe, Nightjar.
Other notable flora and fauna: Large populations of silver-studded blue, grayling and purple emperor butterflies can be seen here alongside 26 recorded dragonfly species.
Sandier sites on the reserve provide homes for many species of solitary bees and wasps. Damp areas support carnivorous plants such as sundew and bladderwort. Bog asphodel and marsh orchid may also be seen.
Contact: Simon Nobes, Natural England, The Barn, Heathhall Farm, Bowlhead Green, Godalming, Surrey, GU8 6NW. 01483 307 703.
e-mail: enquiries.southeast@naturalengland.org.uk
www.naturalengland.org.uk

5. WALLIS WOOD LOCAL NATURE RESERVE

Surrey Wildlife Trust.
Location: TQ 121 388. Wallis Wood Village is about 5 miles NW of Horsham. The reserve is 0.5 miles N of the village, on the E side of Walliswood Green Road to Forest Green.
Access: Open all year.
Facilities: None.
Public transport: None.
Habitat: Oak/hazel coppice woodland, stream, small pond.
Key birds: *All year*: Usual woodland species.
Other notable flora and fauna: Coppicing encourages a wide variety of understorey plants. Broad-leaved helleborine and violet helleborine orchids. Woodland butterflies, dormouse.
Contact: Surrey Wildlife Trust, 01483 795 440.
e-mail: surreywt@cix.co.uk
www.surreywildlifetrust.org.uk

Public transport: Call Trust for advice.
Habitat: Dry and humid heath, woodland, two large ponds, reedbeds.
Key birds: *Summer*: Dartford Warbler, Wood Lark, Hobby, Nightjar, Stonechat. *Winter*: Wildfowl (inc. occasional Smew), Bittern, Great Grey Shrike.
Other notable flora and fauna: Tiger beetle, purple hairstreak and silver-studded blue butterflies, sand lizard, smooth snake.
Contact: Rangers Office, Bacon Lane, Churt, Surrey, GU10 2QB. 01252 792 416.

3. LIGHTWATER COUNTRY PARK

Surreyheath Council
Location: SU 921 622. From J3 of M3, take the A322 and follow brown Country Park signs. From the Guildford Road in Lightwater, turn into The Avenue. Entrance to the park is at the bottom of the road.
Access: Open all year dawn-dusk.
Facilities: Car park, visitor centre open most days during summer, toilets, leaflets.
Public transport: Train: Bagshot two miles. Tel 08457 484950. Bus: No 34 from Woking, Guildford and Camberley. Tel: 08706 082608.
Habitat: Reclaimed gravel quarries. Heath, woodland, bog.
Key birds: *Summer*: Dartford Warbler, Stonechat, Wood Lark, Tree Pipit, Hobby, Nightjar, all three woodpeckers. *Autumn*: Ring Ouzel, Crossbill, Siskin, Fieldfare, Redwing, possible Woodcock.
Other notable flora and fauna: Badger, deer, fox, adder, bog myrtle.
Contact: Surreyheath Council, Surrey Heath House, Knoll Road, Camberley, Surrey GU15 3HD. 01276 707 100. www.surreycc.gov.uk

Sussex, East

1. FORE WOOD

RSPB (South East Region Office).
Location: TQ 758 123. From the A2100 (Battle/
Hastings) take lane to Crowhurst at Crowhurst Park
Caravan Park. Park at Crowhurst village hall and
walk up Forewood Lane for 500 yards. Look for the
finger post on L and follow the public footpath across
farmland to reserve entrance.
Access: Open all year. No disabled facilities. No dogs.
No coaches.
Facilities: Two nature trails.
Public transport: Station at Crowhurst, about 0.5
mile walk (Charing Cross/Hastings line). No buses
within one mile.
Habitat: Semi-natural ancient woodland.
Key birds: A wide range of woodland birds. *Spring*:
Chiffchaff, Greater Spotted Woodpecker, Nuthatch,
Treecreeper. *Summer*: Blackcap, Bullfinch, Mistle
Thrush, Green Woodpecker. *Autumn*: Goldcrest, Jay,
Marsh Tit. *Winter*: Fieldfare, Rook , Redwing.
Other notable flora and fauna: Rare ferns,
bluebells, wood anemonies, purple orchid. Butterflies
including silver-washed fritillaries and white admirals.
Contact: Gordon Allison, c/o RSPB South East Region
Office, 01272 775 333.

2. LULLINGTON HEATH

Natural England (Sussex and Surrey Team).
Location: TQ 525 026. W of Eastbourne, between
Jevington and Litlington, on northern edge of Friston
Forest.
Access: Via footpaths and bridleways. Site open for
access on foot as defined by CROW Act 2000.
Facilities: Picnic areas in nearby Friston Forest.
Interpretation panels. Nearest toilets/refreshmenst
at pubs in Jevington, Litlington or Seven
Sisters CP, 2km to S.
Public transport: Nearest bus stop is Seven Sisters
Country Park. Phone Brighton and Hove services on
01273 886 200 or visit: www.buses.co.uk/bustimes/
Habitat: Grazed chalk downland and heath, with
mixed scrub and gorse.
Key birds: *Summer*: Breeding Nightingale, Turtle
Dove, Nightjar and diverse range of grassland/scrub-
nesting species. Passage migrants include Wheatear,
Redstart, Ring Ouzel.
Winter: Raptors (inc. Hen Harrier), Woodcock.
Contact: The Site Manager, East Sussex NNRs,
Natural England, Phoenix House, 33 North Street,
Lewes, E Sussex BN7 2PH. 01273 476 595;
e-mail sussex.surrey@natural-england.org.uk
www.natural-england.org.uk

3. OLD LODGE RESERVE

Sussex Wildlife Trust.
Location: Near Crowborough. Car park off B2026.
Part of Ashdown Forest.
Access: Open all year.
Facilities: Car park, public footpaths, nature trails.
No dogs.
Public transport: None.
Habitat: Heather, pine woodland.
Key birds: *Spring/summer:* Breeding Nightjar,
Redstart, Woodcock, Tree Pipit, Redstart, Stonechat.
Other notable flora and fauna: Good for
dragonflies including black darter, golden-ringed and
small red damselfly. Small colony of silver-studded
blue butterflies.
Contact: Sussex Wildlife Trust, 01273 492 630.
e-mail: enquiries@sussexwt.org.uk
www.sussexwt.org.uk

4. PEVENSEY LEVELS

Natural England (Sussex and Surrey Team)/Sussex
Wildlife Trust.
Location: TQ 665 054. A small reserve of 12 fields,
within the 3,500 ha SSSI/Ramsar site of
Pevensey Levels. NE of Eastbourne.
S of A259, one mile along
minor road from Pevensey
E towards Norman's Bay.
Access: Please view
from road to avoid
disturbance to summer
nesting birds and
sheltering flocks in winter.
Access on foot allowed at
Rockhouse Bank (TQ 675 057)
– panoramic view of whole reserve.
Facilities: None. Nearest toilets at Star Inn
(TQ 687 062) or petrol station (TQ 652 052).

Public transport: Nearest railway stations: Pevensey Bay or Cooden Beach. Eastbourne buses to Pevensey Bay - call 01323 416 416.

Habitat: Freshwater grazing marsh with extensive ditch system, subject to flooding.

Key birds: *Summer*: Breeding Reed and Sedge Warblers, Yellow Wagtail, Snipe, Redshank, Lapwing. Raptors include Peregrine and Hobby. Passage migrants include Whimbrel, Curlew, Brent Geese. *Winter*: Flocks of wildfowl and waders, Short-eared Owl, Merlin and other raptors.

Other notable flora and fauna: Variable damselfly, many rare snails and other molluscs, the most important site in the UK for fen raft spider. Unusual wetland plants.

Contact: Site Manager, Natural England, 01273 476 595; www.natural-england.org.uk.

5. RYE HARBOUR

Rye Harbour Local Nature Reserve Management Committee.

Location: TQ 941 188. One mile from Rye off A259 signed Rye Harbour. From J10 of M20 take A2070 until it joins A259.

Access: Open at all times by footpaths. Organised groups please book.

Facilities: Car park in Rye Harbour village. Information kiosk in car park. Shop, 2 pubs, toilets and disabled facilities near car park, four hides (wheelchair access, two with induction sound loop fitted), information centre open most days (10am-4pm) by volunteers.

Public transport: Train (tel: 08457 484 950), bus (tel: 0870 608 2608), Rye tourist information (tel: 01797 226 696).

Habitat: Sea, sand, shingle, pits and grassland.

Key birds: *Spring*: Passage waders, especially roosting Whimbrel. *Summer*: Turtle Dove, terns (3 species), waders (7 species), gulls (6 species), Garganey, Shoveler, Cetti's Warbler, Bearded Tit. *Winter*: Wildfowl, Water Rail, Bittern, Smew.

Other notable flora and fauna: Good shingle flora including sea kale, sea pea, least lettuce and stinging hawksbeard. Excellent range of dragonflies including breeding red-veined darter and scarce emerald damselfly.

Contact: Barry Yates, (Manager), 2 Watch Cottages, Winchelsea, East Sussex, TN36 4LU. 01797 223 862. e-mail: yates@clara.net www.wildrye.info
See www.rxwildlife.org.uk for latest sightings in area.

Sussex, West

1. ARUNDEL

The Wildfowl and Wetlands Trust.

Location: TQ 020 081. Clearly signposted from Arundel, just N of A27.

Access: Summer (9.30am-5.30pm) winter (9.30am-4.30pm). Closed Christmas Day. Approx 1.5 miles of level footpaths, suitable for wheelchairs. No dogs except guide dogs.

Facilities: Visitor centre, restaurant, shop, hides, picnic area, seasonal nature trails. Corporate hire facilities.

Public transport: Arundel station, 15-20 minute walk. Tel: 01903 882 131.

Habitat: Lakes, wader scrapes, reedbed.

Key birds: *Summer*: Nesting Redshank, Lapwing, Oystercatcher, Common Tern, Sedge, Reed and Cetti's Warblers, Peregrine, Hobby. *Winter*: Teal, Wigeon, Reed Bunting, Water Rail, Cetti's Warbler and occasionally roosting Bewick's Swan.

Contact: James Sharpe, Mill Road, Arundel, West Sussex, BN18 9PB. 01903 883 355. e-mail: info.arundel@wwt.org.uk www.wwt.org.uk

2. PAGHAM HARBOUR

West Sussex County Council.

Location: SZ 857 966. Five miles S of Chichester on B2145 towards Selsey.

Access: Open at all times, dogs must be on leads, disabled trail with accessible hide. All groups and coach parties must book in advance.

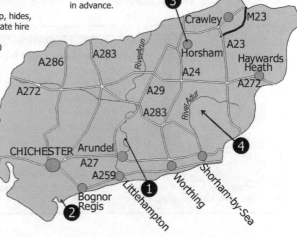

Facilities: Visitor centre open at weekends (10am-4pm), toilets (including disabled), three hides, one nature trail.

Public transport: Bus stop by visitor centre.

Habitat: Intertidal saltmarsh, shingle beaches, lagoons and farmland.

Key birds: *Spring*: Passage migrants. *Autumn*: Passage waders, other migrants. *Winter*: Brent Goose, Slavonian Grebe, wildfowl. *All year*: Little Egret, divers and grebes offshore.

Other notable flora and fauna: Wide range of grasses, butterflies and dragonflies.

Contact: Sarah Patton, Pagham Harbour LNR, Selsey Road, Sidlesham, Chichester, West Sussex, PO20 7NE. 01243 641 508.

e-mail: pagham.nr@westsussex.gov.uk

3. WARNHAM LOCAL NATURE RESERVE

Horsham District Council.

Location: TQ 167 324. One mile from Horsham town centre, just off A24 'Robin Hood' roundabout on B2237.

Access: Open everyday, all year, including bank holidays (10am-6pm or dusk if earlier). Day permits: Adults £1, children under 16 free. Annual permits also available. No dogs or cycling allowed. Good wheelchair access.

Facilities: Visitor centre and café open everyday (10am-5.30pm) except Christmas Day and Boxing Day. Also new stag beetle loggery. Ample car park – coaches by request. Toilets (including disabled), two hides, reserve leaflets, millpond nature trail, bird feeding station, boardwalks, benches and hardstanding paths.

Public transport: From Horsham Railway Station it is a mile walk along Hurst Road, with a R turn onto Warnham Road. Buses from 'CarFax' in Horsham Centre stop within 150 yards of the reserve. Travel line, 0870 608 2608.

Habitat: 17 acre millpond, reedbeds, marsh, meadow and woodland.

Key birds: *Summer*: Breeding Common Tern,

Kingfisher, woodpeckers, Mandarin Duck, Little Owl, Marsh Tit, Goldcrest, hirundines, Hobby, warblers. *Winter*: Cormorant, gulls, Little Grebe, Water Rail, Brambling, Siskin, Lesser Redpoll, thrushes and wildfowl. *Passage*: Waders, pipits, terns and Sand Martin.

Other notable flora and fauna: Extensive invertebrate interest, including 33 species of butterfly and 25 species of dragonfly. Harvest mouse, water vole and badger. More than 450 species of plant including broad-leaved helliborine and common spotted orchid.

Contact: Sam Bayley, Countryside Warden, Leisure Services, Park House Lodge, North Street , Horsham, W Sussex, RH12 1RL. 01403 256 890.

e-mail: sam.bayley@horsham.gov.uk

www.horshamdistrictcountryside.org

4. WOODS MILL

Sussex Wildlife Trust.

Location: TQ 218 138. Located NW of Bron, one mile S of Henfield on A2037.

Access: Open every day except Christmas week. All-weather surface nature trail suitable for wheelchairs. HQ of Sussex Wildlife Trust.

Facilities: Toilets (including disabled), nature trail, car parking and parking for two coaches.

Public transport: Bus route 100 stops outside. Compass Travel 01903 690 025.

Habitat: Wetland and woodland habitats.

Key birds: General woodland birds and Kingfisher all year. *Summer*: Warblers (Reed, Blackcap, Garden, Whitethroat, Lesser Whitethroat) and Nightingales.

Other notable flora and fauna: Dragon and damselflies including beautiful demoiselle, red and ruddy darter and the rare scarce chaser. Wide range of water, woodland and meadow plants. Spring flowers include bluebells, wood anemones and common spotted orchids.

Contact: Woods Mill, Henfield, West Sussex, BN5 9SD. 01273 492 630. www.sussexwt.co.uk

e-mail: enquiries@sussexwt.co.uk

Tyne & Wear

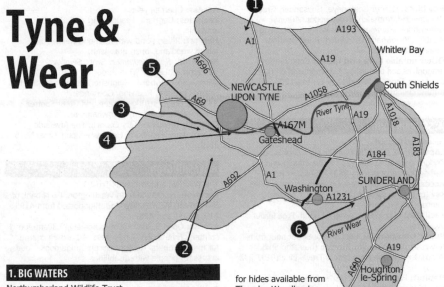

1. BIG WATERS

Northumberland Wildlife Trust.
Location: NZ 227 734. Turn N from Wide Open to Dinnington road. Brown sign to adjacent country park. Use country park car park.
Access: Hides are locked, keys avaiable to NWT members. Public viewing areas.
Facilities: Two hides, viewing areas, easy going footpath access.
Public transport: Arriva Northumberland – 45, 45a, 45b services.
Habitat: Pond with surrounding reedbed.
Key birds: Wintering wildfowl including Teal, Tufted Duck and Shoveler. Breeding species include Great Crested and Little Grebe and Coot. Tree Sparrow, Yellowhammer and Great Spotted Woodpecker use feeding station all year.
Other notable flora and fauna: Otter are frequently seen from the hide. The small pond on site is used by dragonflies, while woodland edges and fields are used by a variety of butterflies including large skipper and small copper.
Contact: Northumberland Wildlife Trust, The Garden House, St Nicholas Park, Jubilee Road, Newcastle upon Tyne NE3 3XT. 01912 846 884; www.nwt.org.uk
e-mail: mail@northwt.org.uk

2. DERWENT WALK COUNTRY PARK AND DERWENTHAUGH PARK

Gateshead Council.
Location: NZ 178 604. Along River Derwent, four miles SW of Newcastle and Gateshead. Several car parks along A694.
Access: Site open all times. Thornley visitor centre open weekends and Bank Holidays (12-5pm). Keys for hides available from Thornley Woodlands Centre. Swalwell visitor centre open daily (9am-5pm).
Facilities: Toilets at Thornley and Swalwell visitor centres. Hides at Far Pasture Ponds and Thornley feeding station.
Public transport: 45, 46, 46A, 47/47A/47B buses from Newcastle/Gateshead to Swalwell/Rowlands Gill. Bus stop Thornley Woodlands Centre. (Regular bus service from Newcastle). Information from Nexus Travel Information, 0919 203 3333, www.nexus.org.uk
Habitat: Mixed woodland, river, ponds, meadows.
Key birds: *Summer*: Red Kite, Grashopper Warbler, Lesser Whitethroat, Kingfisher, Dipper, Great Spotted and Green Woodpeckers, Blackcap, Garden Warbler, Nuthatch. *Winter*: Teal, Tufted Duck, Brambling, Marsh Tit, Bullfinch, Great Spotted Woodpecker, Nuthatch, Goosander, Kingfisher.
Contact: Thornley Woodlands Centre, Rowlands Gill, Tyne and Wear, NE39 1AU. 01207 545 212.
e-mail: countryside@gateshead.gov.uk
www.gatesheadbirders.co.uk www.gateshead.gov.uk

3. RYTON WILLOWS

Gateshead Council.
Location: NZ 155 650. Five miles W of Newcastle. Access along several tracks running N from Ryton.
Access: Open at all times.
Facilities: Nature trail and free leaflet.
Public transport: Regular service to Ryton from Newcastle/Gateshead. Information from Nexus Travelline on 0191 232 5325.
Habitat: Deciduous woodland, scrub, riverside, tidal river.

Key birds: *Winter*: Goldeneye, Goosander, Green Woodpecker, Nuthatch, Treecreeper. *Autumn*: Greenshank. *Summer*: Lesser Whitethroat, Sedge Warbler, Yellowhammer, Linnet, Reed Bunting, Common Sandpiper.
Other notable flora and fauna: Good range of dragonflies and butterflies. Common seal on river.
Contact: Thornley Woodlands Centre, 1208 545 212. e-mail: countryside@gateshead.gov.uk
www.gatesheadbirders.co.uk

4. SHIBDON POND

Gateshead Council.
Location: NZ 192 628. E of Blaydon, S of Scotswood Bridge, close to A1. Car park at Blaydon swimming baths. Open access from B6317 (Shibdon Road).
Access: Open at all times. Disabled access to hide. Key for hide available from Thornley Woodlands Centre (£2).
Facilities: Hide in SW corner of pond. Free leaflet available.
Public transport: At least six buses per hour from Newcastle/Gateshead to Blaydon (bus stop Shibdon Road). Information from Nexus Travel Line (0191 232 5325).
Habitat: Pond, marsh, scrub and damp grassland.
Key birds: *Winter*: Wildfowl, Water Rail, white-winged gulls. *Summer*: Reed Warbler, Sedge Warbler, Lesser Whitethroat, Grasshopper Warbler, Water Rail. *Autumn*: Passage waders and wildfowl, Kingfisher.
Contact: Thornley Woodlands Centre, 1209 545 212. e-mail: countryside@gateshead.gov.uk
www.gatesheadbirders.co.uk

5. TYNE RIVERSIDE COUNTRY PARK AND THE REIGH

Newcastle City Council
Location: NZ 158 658. From the Newcastle to Carlisle by-pass on the A69(T) take the A6085 into Newburn. The park is signposted along the road to Blaydon. 0.25 miles after this junction, turn due W (the Newburn Hotel is on the corner) and after 0.5 miles the parking and information area is signed just beyond the Newburn Leisure Centre.

Access: Open all year.
Facilities: Car park. Leaflets and walk details available.
Habitat: River, pond with reed and willow stands, mixed woodland, open grassland.
Key birds: *Spring/summer*: Swift, Swallow, Whitethroat, Lesser Whitethroat.
Winter: Sparrowhawk, Kingfisher, Little Grebe, finches, Siskin, Fieldfare, Redwing, Goosander.
All year: Grey Partridge, Green and Great Spotted Woodpecker, Bullfinch, Yellowhammer.
Contact: Newcastle City Council, The Riverside Country Park, Newburn, Newcastle upon Tyne, NE15 8BW.

6. WASHINGTON

The Wildfowl and Wetlands Trust.
Location: NZ 331 566. In Washington. On N bank of River Wear, W of Sunderland. Signposted from A195, A19, A1231 and A182.
Access: Open 9.30am-5pm (summer), 9.30am-4pm (winter). Free to WWT members. Admission charge for non-members. No dogs except guide dogs. Good access for people with disabilities.
Facilities: Visitor centre, toilets, parent and baby room, range of hides. Shop and café.
Public transport: Buses to Waterview Park (250 yards walk) from Washington, from Sunderland, Newcastle-upon-Tyne, Durham and South Shields. Tel: 0845 6060 260 for details.
Habitat: Wetlands, woodland and meadows.
Key birds: *Spring/summer*: Nesting colony of Grey Heron, other breeders include Common Tern, Oystercatcher, Lapwing. *Winter*: Bird-feeding station visited by Great Spotted Woodpecker, Bullfinch, Jay and Sparrowhawk. Goldeneye and other ducks.
Other notable flora and fauna: Wildflower meadows – cuckoo flowers, bee orchids and yellow rattle. Dragonfly and amphibian ponds.
Contact: Wildfowl and Wetlands Trust, Pottinson, Washington, NE38 8LE. 01914 165 454 ext 231. e-mail: dean.heward@wwt.org.uk
www.wwt.org.uk

Warwickshire

1. ALVECOTE POOLS

Warwickshire Wildlife Trust.
Location: SK 253 034. Located alongside River Anker E of Tamworth. Access via Robey's Lane (off B5000) just past Alvecote Priory car park. Also along towpath via Pooley Hall visitor centre, also number of points along towpath.
Access: Some parts of extensive path system are accessible to wheelchair-users. Parking at Alvecote Priory car park.

Facilities: Nature trail.
Public transport: Within walking distance of the Alvecote village bus stop.
Habitat: Marsh, pools (open and reedbeds) and woodland.
Key birds: *Spring/summer*: Breeding Oystercatcher, Common Tern and Little Ringed Plover. Common species include Great Crested Grebe, Tufted Duck and Snipe. Important for wintering, passage and breeding wetland birds.
Other notable flora and fauna: *Spring*: Dingy

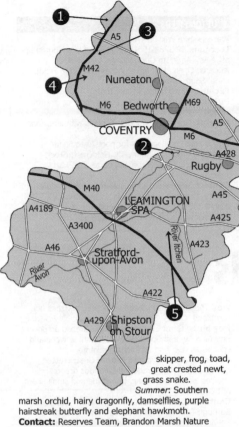

acres, designated SSSI in 1972.

Key birds: *Spring/summer*: Garden and Grasshopper Warblers, Whitethroat, Lesser Whitethroat, Hobby, Little Ringed Plover, Whinchat, Wheatear. *Autumn/winter*: Bittern (last two winters), Dunlin, Ruff, Snipe, Greenshank, Green and Common Sandpipers, Wigeon, Shoveler, Pochard, Goldeneye, Siskin, Redpoll. *All year*: Cetti's Warbler, Kingfisher, Water Rail, Gadwall, Little Grebe, Buzzard.

Other notable flora and fauna: More than 20 species of butterfly and 18 species of dragonfly recorded. Almost 500 plant species listed on www.brandonbirding.co.uk

Contact: Brandon Marsh Voluntary Conservation Team, 54 Wiclif Way, Stockingford, Nuneaton, Warwickshire, CV10 8NF. 02476 328 785.

3. KINGSBURY WATER PARK

Warwickshire County Council.

Location: SP 203 960. Signposted `Water Park' from J9 M42, A4097 NE of Birmingham.

Access: Open all year except Christmas Day.

Facilities: Four hides, two with wheelchair access. Miles of flat surfaced footpaths, free loan scheme for mobility scooters. Cafes, Information Centre with gift shop.

Public transport: Call for advice.

Habitat: Open water; numerous small pools, some with gravel islands; gravel pits; silt beds with reedmace, reed, willow and alder; rough areas and grassland.

Key birds: *Summer*: Breeding warblers (nine species), Little Ringed Plover, Great Crested and Little Grebes. Shoveler, Shelduck and a thriving Common Tern colony. Passage waders (esp. spring). *Winter*: Wildfowl, Short-eared Owl.

Contact: Paula Cheesman, Kingsbury Water Park, Bodymoor Heath Lane, Sutton Coldfield, West Midlands B76 0DY. 01827 872 660.
e-mail parks@warwickshire.gov.uk
www.warwickshire.gov.uk/countryside.

4. MARSH LANE NATURE RESERVE

Packington Estate Enterprises Limited.

Location: SP 217 804. Equidistant between Birmingham and Coventry, both approx 7-8 miles away. Off A452 between A45 and Balsall Common, S of B4102/A452 junction.
Turn R into Marsh Lane and immediately R onto Old Kenilworth Road (now a public footpath), to locked gate. Key required for access.

Access: Only guide dogs allowed. Site suitable for disabled. Access by day or year permit only. Contact reserve for membership rates: day permit adult £4, OAP £3.50, children (under 16) £3 obtained from Golf Professional Shop, Stonebridge Golf Centre, Somers Road, off Hampton Lane, Meriden, (tel 01676 522 442), four minutes' car journey from site.
Open Mon-Sun (7am-7pm). Golf Centre open to non-members for drinks and meals. £33 deposit required for key. Readily accessible for coaches.

skipper, frog, toad, great crested newt, grass snake. *Summer*: Southern marsh orchid, hairy dragonfly, damselflies, purple hairstreak butterfly and elephant hawkmoth.

Contact: Reserves Team, Brandon Marsh Nature Centre, Brandon Lane, Brandon, Coventry, CV3 3GW. 02476 302 912. e-mail: enquiries@wrwt.org.uk
www.warwickshire-wildlife-trust.org.uk

2. BRANDON MARSH

Warwickshire Wildlife Trust.

Location: SP 386 762. Three miles SE of Coventry, 200 yards SE of A45/A46 junction (Tollbar End). Turn E off A45 into Brandon Lane. Reserve entrance 1.25 miles on R.

Access: Open weekdays (9am-4.30pm), weekends (10am-4pm). Entrance charge currently £2.50 (free to Wildlife Trust members). Wheelchair access to nature trail and Wright hide. No dogs. Parking for 2 coaches.

Facilities: Visitor centre, toilets, tea-room (open daily 10am-3pm weekdays, 10am-4pm weekends), nature trail, seven hides.

Public transport: Bus service from Coventry to Tollbar End then 1.25 mile walk. Tel Travel West Midlands 02476 817 032 for bus times.

Habitat: Ten pools, together with marsh, reedbeds, willow carr, scrub and small mixed woodland in 260

Facilities: No toilets or visitor centre. Four hides and hard tracks between hides. Car park behind locked gates.

Public transport: Hampton-in-Arden railway station within walking distance on footpath loop. Bus no 194 stops at N end of Old Kenilworth Road, one mile from reserve gate.

Habitat: Two large pools with islands, three small areas of woodland, five acre field set aside for arable growth for finches and buntings as winter feed.

Key birds: 177 species. *Summer*: Breeding birds include Little Ringed Plover, Common Tern, most species of warbler including Grasshopper. Good passage of waders in Apr, May, Aug and Sept. Hobby and Buzzard breed locally.

Contact: Nicholas P Barlow, Packington Hall, Packington Park, Meriden, Nr Coventry CV7 7HF. 01676 522 020. www.packingtonestate.net

5. UFTON FIELDS

Warwickshire Wildlife Trust.

Location: SP 378 615. Located SE of Leamington Spa off A425. At South Ufton village, take B4452.

Access: Open at all times. Access via Ufton Fields Lane, South Ufton village.

Facilities: Two hides, nature trail.

Public transport: Within walking distance of Ufton village bus stop.

Habitat: Grassland, woodland, pools with limestone quarry.

Key birds: Usual species for pools/woodland/ grassland including Willow Tit, Goldcrest, Green Woodpecker, Little Grebe and up to nine warbler species.

Contact: Reserves Team, Brandon Marsh Nature Centre, Brandon Lane, Brandon, Coventry, CV3 3GW. 02476 302 912. e-mail: reserves@warkswt.cix.co.uk www.warwickshire-wildlife-trust.org.uk

West Midlands

LICKEY HILLS COUNTRY PARK

Birmingham County Council.

Location: Eleven miles SW of Birmingham City Centre.

Access: Open all year, (10am-7pm in summer; 10am-4.30pm in winter). Land-Rover tours can be arranged for less able visitors.

Facilities: Car park, visitor centre with wheelchair pathway with viewing gallery, picnic site, toilets, café, shop.

Public transport: Bus: West Midlands 62 Rednal (20 mins walk to visitor centre. Rail: Barnt Green (25 mins walk through woods to the centre).

Habitat: Hills covered with mixed deciduous woodland, conifer plantations and heathland.

Key birds: *Spring/summer*: Warblers, Tree Pipit, Redstart. *Winter*: Redwing, Fieldfare. *All year*: Common woodland species.

Contact: The Visitor Centre, Lickey Hills Country Park, Warren Lane, Rednal, Birmingham, B45 8ER. 01214 477 106.

e-mail: lickey.hills@birmingham.gov.uk

ROUGH WOOD CHASE

Walsall Metropolitan Borough Council

Location: SJ 987 012. From M6 (Jt 10) head for Willenhall and A462. Turn right into Bloxwich Road North and right again into Hunts Lane. Park by site entrance.

Access: Open all year. Circular nature trail.

Facilities: None.

Public transport: WMT bus 341 from Walsall.

Habitat: 70 acres of oakwood, significant for

West Midlands. Also meadows, ponds, marshes and scrubland.

Key birds: Great Crested and Little Grebes on pools. Breeding Jay and Sparrowhawk. Common woodland species all year and warblers in summer.

Other notable flora and fauna: Great crested and smooth newts, water vole, various dragonfly species, purple hairstreak, brimstone and small heath butterflies.

Contact: Countryside Services, Walsall Metropolitan Borough Council, Dept of Leisure and Community Services, PO box 42, The Civic Centre, Darwall Street, Walsall WS1 1TZ. 01922 650 000; Fax 01922 721 862. www.walsall.gov.uk

SANDWELL VALLEY COUNTRY PARK

Sandwell Metropolitan Borough Council.

Location: Entrances at SP 012 918 and SP 028 992. Located approx. 1 mile NE of West Bromwich town centre. Main entrance off Salters Lane or Forge Lane.

Access: Car parks open 8am to sunset. Wheelchair access to Priory Woods LNR, Forge Mill Lake LNR and other parts of the counrty park.

Facilities: 1,700 acre site. Visitor centre, toilets, café at Sandwell Park Farm (10am-4.30pm). Good footpaths around LNRs and much of the country park. Coach parking by appointment. Also 20 acre RSPB reserve with visitor centre and hides.

Public transport: West Bromwich bus station West Bromwich central metro stop. (Traveline 0871 200 2233).

Habitat: Pools, including 3 local nature reserves.

Key birds: Wintering wildfowl including regular flock of Goosander, up to 8 species of Warber breeding,

small heronry. *All year*: Grey Heron, Great Crested Grebe, Lapwing, Reed Bunting Great Spotted and Gree Woodpecker, Sparrowhawk, Kestrel. *Spring*: Little Ringed Plover, Oystercatcher, warblers, passage migrants. *Autumn*: Passage migrants. *Winter*: Goodander, Shoveler, Teal, Wigeon, Snipe.
Other notable flora and fauna: Common spotted and southern marsh orchid. Ringlet butterfly. Water vole, weasel.
Contact: Senior Countryside Ranger, Sandwell Park Farm, Salters Lane, West Bromwich, W Midlands B71 4BG. 01215 530 220 or 2147.

SANDWELL VALLEY (RSPB)

RSPB (Midlands Regional Office).
Location: SP 035 928. Great Barr, Birmingham. Follow signs S from M6 J7 via A34. Take R at 1st junction onto A4041. Take 4th L onto Hamstead Road (B4167), then R at 1st mini roundabout onto Tanhouse Avenue.
Access: 800 metres of paths accessible to assisted and powered wheelchairs with some gradients (please ring centre for further information), centre fully accessible to wheelchairs.
Facilities: Visitor Centre and car park (open Tue-Fri 9am-5pm, Sat-Sun 10am-5pm. Closes at dusk in winter), with viewing area, small shop and hot drinks, four viewing screens, one hide. Phone centre for details on coach parking.
Public transport: Bus: 16 from Corporation Street (Stand CJ), Birmingham City Centre (ask for Tanhouse Avenue). Train: Hamstead Station, then 16 bus for one mile towards West Bromwich from Hamstead (ask for Tanhouse Avenue).
Habitat: Open water, wet grassland, reedbed, dry grassland and scrub.
Key birds: *Summer*: Lapwing, Little-Ringed Plover, Reed Warbler, Whitethroat, Sedge Warbler, Willow Tit. *Passage*: Sandpipers, Yellow Wagtail, chats, Common Tern. *Winter*: Water Rail, Snipe, Jack Snipe, Goosander, Bullfinch, woodpeckers and wildfowl.
Contact: Lee Copplestone, 20 Tanhouse Avenue, Great Barr, Birmingham, B43 5AG. 0121 3577 395.

Wiltshire

FYFIELD DOWNS NATIONAL NATURE RESERVE

Natural England (Wiltshire team).
Location: On the Marlborough Downs. From the A345 at N end of Marlborough, a minor road signed Broad Hinton, bisects the downs, dipping steeply at Hackpen Hill to the A361 just before Broad Hinton. From Hackpen Hill walk S to Fyfield Down.
Access: Open all year but avoid the racing gallops. Keep dogs on leads.
Facilities: Car park.
Public transport: None.
Habitat: Downs.
Key birds: *Spring*: Ring Ouzel possible on passage, Wheatear, Cuckoo, Redstart, common warblers. *Summer*: Possible Quail. *Winter*: Occasional Hen Harrier, possible Merlin, Golden Plover, Short-eared Owl, thrushes. *All year*: Sparrowhawk, Buzzard, Kestrel, partridges, Green and Great Spotted Woodpeckers, Goldfinch, Corn Bunting.
Contact: Natural England, Prince Maurice Court, Hambleton, Devizes, Wiltshire SN10 2RT. 01380 726 344. email: wiltshire@naturalengland.org.uk

LANGFORD LAKES

Wiltshire Wildlife Trust.
Location: SU 037 370. Nr Steeple Langford, S of A36, approx eight miles W of Salisbury. In the centre of the village, turn S into Duck Street, signposted Hanging Langford. Langford Lakes is the first turning on the L just after a small bridge across the River Wylye.
Access: Opened to the public in Sept 2002. Main gates open during the day — ample parking. Advance notice required for coaches. No dogs allowed on this reserve.
Facilities: Four hides, all accessible to wheelchairs. Cycle stands provided (250m from Wiltshire Cycleway between Great Wishford and Hanging Langford).
Public transport: Nearest bus stop 500m - X4 Service between Salisbury and Warminster.
Habitat: Three former gravel pits, with newly created islands and developing reed fringes. 12 ha (29 acres) of open water; also wet woodland, scrub, chalk river.
Key birds: *Summer*: Breeding Coot, Moorhen, Mallard Tufted Duck, Pochard, Gadwall, Little Grebe, Great Crested Grebe. Also Kingfisher, Common Sandpiper, Grey Wagtail, warblers (8 species). *Winter*: wildfowl, sometimes also Wigeon, Shoveler, Teal, Water Rail, Little Egret, Bittern. *Passage*: Sand Martin, Green Sandpiper, waders, Black Tern.
Contact: Wiltshire Wildlife Trust, Langford Lakes, Duck Street, Steeple Langford, Salisbury, Wiltshire, SP3 4NH. 01722 790 770.
e-mail: admin@wiltshirewildlife.org
www.wiltshirewildlife.org

SAVERNAKE FOREST

Savernake Estate Trustees.
Location: From Marlborough the A4 Hungerford road runs along the N side of the forest. Two pillars mark the Forest Hill entrance, 1.5 miles E of the A346/A4 junction. The Grand Avenue leads straight through

the middle of the woodland to join a minor road from Stibb Green on the A346 N of Burbage to the A4 W of Froxfield.
Access: Privately owned but open all year to public.
Facilities: Car park, picnic site at NW end by A346. Fenced-off areas should not be entered unless there is a footpath.
Public transport: None.
Habitat: Ancient woodland, with one of the largest collections of veteran trees in Britain.
Key birds: *Spring/summer:* Garden Warbler, Blackcap, Willow Warbler, Chiffchaff, Wood Warbler, Redstart, occasional Nightingale, Tree Pipit, Spotted Flycatcher. *Winter:* Finch flocks possibly inc Siskin Redpoll, Brambling.
All year: Sparrowhawk, Buzzard, Woodcock, owls, all three woodpeckers, Marsh, Tit, Willow Tit, Jay and other woodland birds.
Contact: Savernake Estate Office, Savernake Forest, Marlborough SN8 3HP. 01672 512 161;
e-mail: savernakeestate@hotmail.com
www.savernakeestate.co.uk

SWILLBROOK LAKES

Wiltshire Wildlife Trust.
Location: SU 018 934. NW of Swindon, one mile S of Somerford Keynes on Cotswold Water Park spine road; turn off down Minety Lane (parking).
Access: Open at all times.
Facilities: Footpath along N and E sides of lakes.
Public transport: None.
Habitat: Gravel pits with shallow pools, rough grassland and scrub around edges.
Key birds: *Winter:* Wildfowl (inc. Gadwall, Pochard, Smew, Goosander). *Summer:* Breeding Nightingale, Garden, Reed and Sedge Warblers; one of the best sites for Hobby and Nightingale in Cotswold WP.
Other notable flora and fauna: 18 species of dragonfly, including downy emerald and lesser emperor in recent years.
Contact: Wiltshire Wildlife Trust, Elm Tree Court, Long Street, Devizes, Wiltshire, SN10 1NJ. 01380 725 670. e-mail: admin@wiltshirewildlife.org
www.wiltshirewildlife.org

Worcestershire

1. BROADWAY GRAVEL PIT

Worcestershire Wildlife Trust.
Location: SP 087 379. Approx. half mile NW of Broadway on the N side of the Broadway to Childswickham road and E of the old disused railway line.
Access: Open access at all times. Disabled access to hide only. Parts of circular path sometimes flooded but hide is usually clear.
Facilities: 1 hide. Cafes and toilets in Broadway. Very limited car parking (2-3 cars), no room for a coach. Large car park within half a mile in Broadway.
Public transport: No rail connection. Buses to Broadway from Evesham etc. Check the timetable.
Habitat: Open water, wet woodland, dry scrub.
Key birds: As this is a very small site (1.6ha), it does not hold great numbers of bird species. Wintering Chiffchaff with tit and crest flocks, finches and buntings.
Spring/summer: Whitethroat, Blackcap, Chiffchaff, Cuckoo.
Other notable flora and fauna: A good dragonfly site for commoner species. Butterflies in dryer, grassy areas. Mare's tail (unusual in Worcestershire wetland sites) found in abundance in June and August.
Contact: Worcestershire Wildlife Trust, 01905 754 919. e-mail: enquiries@worcestershirewildlifetrust.org
www.worcswildlifetrust.co.uk

2. KNAPP AND PAPERMILL

Worcestershire Wildlife Trust.
Location: SO 749 522. Take A4103 SW from

Worcester; R at Bransford roundabout then L towards Suckley and reserve is approx three miles (do not turn off for Alfrick). Park at Bridges Stone layby (SO 751 522), cross road and follow path to the Knapp House.
Access: Open daily exc Christmas Day. Large parties should contact Warden
Facilities: Nature trail, small visitor centre, wildlife garden, Kingfisher viewing screen.
Public transport: None.
Habitat: Broadleaved woodland, unimproved grassland, fast stream, old orchard in Leigh Brook Valley.
Key birds: *Summer:* Breeding Grey Wagtail, Kingfisher, Spotted Flycatcher nests in Warden's garden, all three woodpeckers. Buzzard, Sparrowhawk and Redstart also occur. Also otter.
Contact: The Warden, Knapp and Papermill Reserve, The Knapp, Alfrick, Worcester, WR6 5HR. 01886 832 065.

3. TIDDESLEY WOOD NATURE RESERVE

Worcestershire Wildlife Trust.
Location: SO 929 462. Take the A44 from Pershore to Worcester. Turn L towards Besford and Croome near town boundary just before the summit of the hill. Entrance is on L after about 0.75 miles.
Access: Open all year except Christmas Day. Cycles and horses only allowed on the bridleway. Please keep dogs fully under control. Military firing range at the SW corner of wood, so do not enter the area marked by red flags. The NE plot is private property and visitors should not enter the area. Main ride stoned, with some

potholes. Small pathways difficult if wet. Coach parking by appointment.
Facilities: Information board. May find numbered posts around the reserve which were described in an old leaflet. Circular trail around small pathways.
Public transport: First Midland Red services (see above).
Habitat: Ancient woodland, conifers.
Key birds: *Spring*: Chiffchaff, Blackcap, Cuckoo. *All year*: Crossbill, Coal Tit, Goldcrest, Sparrowhawk, Willow Tit, Marsh Tit. *Winter*: Redwing, Fieldfare.
Other notable flora and fauna: Dragonflies including club-tailed and white-legged damselflies. Good for butterflies including white admiral, peacock and gatekeeper. Invertebrates include nationally rare noble chafer beetle. Plants include uncommon violet helleborine and herb paris, greater butterfly orchid and twayblade.
Contact: Worcestershire Wildlife Trust, 01905 754 919. e-mail: enquiries@worcestershirewildlifetrust.org www.worcswildlifetrust.co.uk

4. UPTON WARREN

Worcestershire Wildlife Trust.
Location: SO 936 675. Two miles S of Bromsgrove on A38. Leave M5 at junction 5.
Access: Christopher Cadbury Wetland Reserve divided into two parts – Moors Pools and Flashes Pools. Always open except Christmas Day. Trust membership gives access, or day permit from sailing centre. Disabled access to hides at moors only. Dogs on leads.
Facilities: Seven hides, maps at entrances, paths can be very muddy. Coach parking at sailing centre by previous booking.
Public transport: Birmingham/Worcester bus passes reserve entrance.
Habitat: Fresh and saline pools with muddy islands, some woodland and scrub.
Key birds: *Winter*: Wildfowl. *Spring/autumn*: Passage waders, Common Tern, Cetti's Warbler, Oystercatcher and Little Ringed Plover, Avocet, many breeding warblers and a good track record of rarities.
Other notable flora and fauna: Saltmarsh plants, dragonflies.
Contact: A F Jacobs, 3 The Beeches, Upton Warren, Bromsgrove, Worcs B61 7EL. 01527 861 370.

5. WYRE FOREST

Natural England / Worcs Wildlife Trust.
Location: SO 750 760. Half a mile NW of Bewdley (on the A456) and four and a half miles W of Kidderminster.
Access: Observe reserve signs and keep to paths. Forestry Commission visitor centre at Callow Hill. Fred Dale Reserve is reached by footpath W of B4194 (parking at SO 776 763).

Facilities: Toilet and refreshment facilities at Wyre Forest Visitor Centre (near the Discovery Centre) at Callow Hill. Several waymarked trails in the Forest (some suitable for wheelchair users) as well as regular guided walks, also family cycle routes through the reserve. The Visitor Centre and Discovery Centre provide facilities for disabled visitors.
Public transport: The nearest train station is in Bewdley, served by the Severn Valley Railway (01299 403 816) although seasonal and sometimes infrequent service. Also Central Trains to Kidderminster (0121 634 2040) and local bus services between Bewdley and Kidderminster.
Habitat: Oak forest, conifer areas, birch heath, lowland grassland, stream.
Key birds: Breeding birds include Redstart, Pied Flycatcher, Wood Warbler, Buzzard and Raven, with Dipper, Grey Wagtail and Kingfisher found on the larger streams.
Other notable flora and fauna: Mammals found in the reserve include fallow, roe and muntjac deer, polecat, otter and mink. Yellow-necked mice, dormouse, vole and water shrew are also found. Bat species include pipistrelle and Daubenton's. The site supports an important invertebrate population that includes England's largest colony of pearl-bordered fritillary butterflies.
Contact: Tim Dixon, Natural England, Block B, Government Buildings, Whittington Road, Worcester WR5 2LQ. 01905 763 355; (Fax)01905 764 973 e-mail: herefordshire.worcestershire@naturalengland.org.uk

Yorkshire, East

1. BEMPTON CLIFFS

RSPB
Location: TA 197 738. Near Bridlington. Take Cliff Lane N from Bempton Village off B1229 to car park and visitor centre.
Access: Visitor centre open year round (phone for opening times). Public footpath along cliff top with observation points. Limited access for wheelchairs along narrow paths.
Facilities: Visitor centre, toilets, light refreshments, observation points, picnic area, limited coach parking. Four miles of chalk cliffs, highest in the county.
Public transport: Bempton railway station (limited service) 1.5 miles from reserve - irregular bus service to village 1.25 miles.
Habitat: Seabird nesting cliffs, farmland, coastal scrub.
Key birds: Breeding seabirds from March to October, peak in May to July. Largest mainland Gannet colony in England. Also Kittiwake, Puffin, Guillemot, Razorbill. Nesting Tree Sparrow and Corn Bunting. Passage skuas, shearwaters, terns and passerine migrants.
Other notable flora and fauna: Harbour porpoise offshore. Also bee and northern marsh orchid occur.
Contact: Site Manager, RSPB, Bempton Cliffs Nature Reserve, 11 Cliff Lane, Bempton, Bridlington, E Yorks, YO15 1JF. 01262 851 179.

2. BLACKTOFT SANDS

RSPB (North of England Office).
Location: SE 843 232. Eight miles E of Goole on minor road between Ousefleet and Adlingfleet.
Access: Open 9am-9pm or dusk if earlier. RSPB members free, £3 permit for non-members, £2 concessionary, £1 children, £6 family.
Facilities: Car park, toilets, visitor centre, six hides, footpaths suitable for wheelchairs.
Public transport: Goole/Scunthorpe bus (Sweynes' Coaches) stops outside reserve entrance .Bus timetable on main RSPB website (see Blacktoft Reserve details).
Habitat: Reedbed, saline lagoons, lowland wet grassland, willow scrub.
Key birds: *Summer*: Breeding Avocet, Marsh Harrier, Bittern, Bearded Tit, passage waders (exceptional list inc many rarities). *Winter*: Hen Harrier, Merlin, Peregrine, wildfowl.
Other notable flora and fauna: Good place to see water vole. Small number of dragonflies and

damselflies including black-tailed skimmer, four-spotted chaser, large red damselfly. Marsh sow thistle easily seen from footpaths in summer.
Contact: Pete Short (Warden) and Mike Pilsworth (Asst Warden), Hillcrest, Whitgift, Nr Goole, E Yorks, DN14 8HL. 01405 704 665. www.RSPB.org
e-mail: pete.short@RSPB.org.uk
mike.pilsworth@RSPB.org.uk

3. FLAMBOROUGH CLIFFS NATURE RESERVE

Yorkshire Wildlife Trust
Location: TA 240 722. The reserve is part of the Flamborough headland approx 4 miles NE of Bridlington. From Bridlington take B1255 to Flamborough and follow signs for the North Landing.
Access: Open all year. Public pay and display car park at North Landing gives access to both parts of the reserve. Paths not suitable for wheelchairs.
Facilities: Car park (pay and display), trails, refreshments available at café at North Landing (open Apr-Oct 10am-5pm), toilets.
Public transport: Flamborough is served by buses from Bridlington and Bempton. Phone 01482 222 222.
Habitat: Coastal cliffs, rough grassland and scrub, farmland.
Key birds: *Summer*: Puffin, Guillemot, Razorbill, Kittiwake, Shag, Fulmar, Sky Lark, Meadow Pipit, Linnet, Whitethroat, Yellowhammer, Tree Sparrow, occasional Corn Bunting. *Passage migrants*: Fieldfare, Redwing and occasional rarities such as Wryneck and Red-backed Shrike.
Contact: Yorkshire Wildlife Trust, 01904 659 570.
e-mail: info@ywt.org.uk www.ywt.org.uk

4. NORTH CAVE WETLANDS

Yorkshire Wildlife Trust
Location: SE 887 328. At NW of North Cave village,

approx 10 miles W of Hull. From junction 28 of M62, follow signs to North Cave on B1230. In village, turn L and follow road to next crossroads where you go L, then take next L onto Dryham Lane. Alternatively, from N, follow minor road direct from Market Weighton. After the turning for Hotham, take the next R (Dryham Lane), which is one mile further down the road.

Access: Open all year with car parking on Dryham Lane. Some footpaths are suitable for all abilities.

Facilities: Three bird-viewing hides, two accessible to wheelchair users. Nearest toilet and refreshment facilities In North Cave, one mile away,

Public transport: Buses serve North Cave from Hull and Goole: telephone 01482 222 222 for details.

Habitat: Six former gravel pits have been converted into various lagoons for wetland birds, including one reedbed. There are also grasslands, scrub and hedgerows.

Key birds: More than 150 different species have been recorded including Great Crested Grebe, Gadwall, Pochard, Sparrowhawk, Avocet, Ringed Plover, Golden Plover, Dunlin, Ruff, Redshank, Green Sandpiper, Common Sandpiper and Tree Sparrow.

Contact: Yorkshire Wildlife Trust, 01904 659 570. e-mail: info@ywt.org.uk www.ywt.org.uk

5. SPURN NATIONAL NATURE RESERVE

Yorkshire Wildlife Trust.

Location: Entrance Gate TA 417 151. 26 miles from Hull. Take A1033 from Hull to Patrington then B1445 from Patrington to Easington and unclassed roads on to Kilnsea and Spurn Head.

Access: Normally open at all times. Vehicle admission fee (at present £3). No charge for pedestrians. No dogs allowed under any circumstances, not even in cars. Coaches by permit only (must be in advance).

Facilities: Centre open weekends, Bank Holidays, school holidays. Three hides. Cafe at point open weekends Apr to Oct 10am to 5pm. Public toilets in Blue Bell car park.

Public transport: Nearest bus service is at Easington (3.5 miles away).

Habitat: Sand dunes with marram and sea buckthorn scrub. Mudflats around Humber Estuary.

Key birds: *Spring*: Many migrants on passage and often rare birds such as Red-backed Shrike, Bluethroat etc. *Autumn*: Passage migrants and rarities such as Wryneck, Pallas's Warbler. *Winter*: Waders and Brent Goose.

Other notable flora and fauna: Unique habitats and geographical position make Spurn the most important site in Yorkshire for butterflies (25 species recorded) and moths.

Contact: Spurn Reserves Officer, Spurn NNR, Blue Bell, Kilnsea, Hull HU12 0UB. e-mail: spurnywt@ukonline.co.uk

6. TOPHILL LOW NATURE RESERVE

Yorkshire Water.

Location: TA 071 482. Nine miles SE of Driffield and ten miles NE of Beverley. Signposted from village of Watton on A164.

Access: Open Wed-Sun and Bank Holiday Mon. Apr-Oct (9am-6pm). Nov-Mar (9am-4pm). Charges: £2.50 per person. £1 concessions. No dogs allowed. Provision for disabled visitors (paths, ramps, hides, toilet etc). Coaches welcome.

Facilities: Visitor Centre with toilets. 12 hides (five with access for wheelchairs). Nature trails.

Public transport: None.

Habitat: Open water (two reservoirs), marshes, wader scrapes, woodland and thorn scrub.

Key birds: *Winter:* Wildfowl, gulls, Water Rail, Kingfisher. *Spring/early summer:* Passage Wood Sandpiper and Black Tern. Breeding Pochard, Little Ringed plover, Common Tern, Kingfisher and Barn Owl. *Late Summer/autumn:* Up to 20 species of passage wader.

Other notable flora and fauna: Specialist grassland and wetland flora including orchids. Fauna includes red-eyed damselfly, marbled white and brown argus butterflies, grass snake, otter, water vole and roe deer.

Contact: Richard Hampshire, Tophill Low Nature Reserve, Watton Carrs, Driffield, YO25 9RH. 01377 270 690. e-mail: richard.hampshire@yorkshirewater.co.uk

Yorkshire, North

1. BOWESFIELD

Tees Valley Wildlife Trust.

Location: NZ 440 160. SE of Stockton on Tees. From A66 take A135 to Yarm. At first roundabout turn L along Concord Way. At next roundabout go straight onto the new Bowesfield Industrial Estate, the reserve is on the floodplain below the development.

Access: Public footpaths around the site open at all times.

Facilities: None.

Habitat: New wetland reserve on the edge of the River Tees.

Key birds: The reserve is home to a growing number of birds including Reed Bunting, Stonechat, Water Rail, Lapwing and Curlew which roost and feed in the rich, wet grassland and lakes found on the site.

Other notable flora and fauna: The reserve offers opportunities to see otter, harvest mouse and roe deer.

Contact: Tees Valley Wildlife Trust, 01287 636 382; e-mail: info@teeswildlife.org www.teeswildlife.org

NATURE RESERVES - ENGLAND

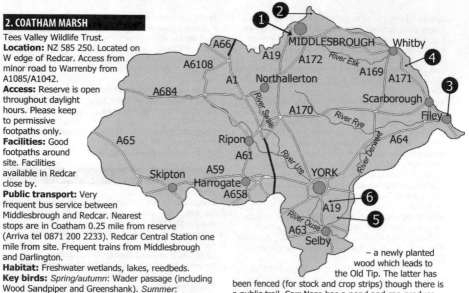

2. COATHAM MARSH

Tees Valley Wildlife Trust.
Location: NZ 585 250. Located on W edge of Redcar. Access from minor road to Warrenby from A1085/A1042.
Access: Reserve is open throughout daylight hours. Please keep to permissive footpaths only.
Facilities: Good footpaths around site. Facilities available in Redcar close by.
Public transport: Very frequent bus service between Middlesbrough and Redcar. Nearest stops are in Coatham 0.25 mile from reserve (Arriva tel 0871 200 2233). Redcar Central Station one mile from site. Frequent trains from Middlesbrough and Darlington.
Habitat: Freshwater wetlands, lakes, reedbeds.
Key birds: *Spring/autumn:* Wader passage (including Wood Sandpiper and Greenshank). *Summer:* Passerines (including Sedge Warbler, Yellow Wagtail). *Winter:* Ducks (including Smew). *Occasional rarities:* Water Rail, Great White Egret, Avocet, Bearded Tit and Bittern.
Other notable flora and fauna: The lime-rich soil allows meadow wildflowers to grow around the site including northern marsh orchid. Also good for insects including migrant hawker dragonfly.
Contact: Tees Valley Wildlife Trust, 01287 636 382; Fax 01287 636 383. e-mail: info@teeswildlife.org www.teeswildlife.org

3. FILEY BRIGG ORNITHOLOGICAL GROUP BIRD OBSERVATORY

FBOG / Yorkshire Wildlife Trust (The Dams).
Location: TA 10 68 07. Two access roads into Filey from A165 (Scarborough to Bridlington road). Filey is ten miles N of Bridlington and eight miles S of Scarborough.
Access: Opening times – no restrictions. Dogs only in Parish Wood and The Old Tip (on lead). Coaches welcome. Park in the North Cliff Country Park.
Facilities: No provisions for disabled at present. Two hides at The Dams, one on The Brigg (open most weekends from late Jul-Oct, key can be hired from Country Park café). Toilets in Country Park (Apr-Nov 1) and town centre. Nature trails at The Dams, Parish Wood/Old Tip. Cliff top walk for seabirds along Cleveland Way.
Public transport: All areas within a mile of Filey railway station. Trains into Filey tel. 08457 484 950; buses into Filey tel. 01723 503 020
Habitat: The Dams – two freshwater lakes, fringed with some tree cover and small reedbeds. Parish Wood

– a newly planted wood which leads to the Old Tip. The latter has been fenced (for stock and crop strips) though there is a public trail. Carr Naze has a pond and can produce newly arrived migrants.
Key birds: The Dams: Breeding and wintering water birds, breeding Sedge Warbler, Reed Warbler and Tree Sparrow. The Tip: important for breeding Sky Lark, Meadow Pipit, common warblers and Grey Partridge. *Winter:* Buntings, including Lapland. Seawatch Hide: Jul-Oct. All four skuas, shearwaters, terns. *Winter:* Divers and grebes. Totem Pole Field: A new project should encourage breeding species and wintering larks, buntings etc. Many sub-rare/rare migrants possible at all sites. www.fbog.co.uk
Contact: e-mail: recorder@fbog.co.uk

4. FYLINGDALES MOOR CONSERVATION AREA

Strickland Estate / Hawk and Owl Trust
Location: NZ 947 003. Off A171 S of Whitby. On eastern side of North York Moors National Park, stretching between Sneaton High Moor (Newton House Plantation) and the coast at Ravenscar. Crossed by A171 Scarborough to Whitby road.
Access: Open access. Parking available at Jugger Howe Layby (OS NZ 947 003) on A171 Scarborough to Whitby road.
Facilities: Numerous footpaths including the Lyke Wake Walk and Robin Hood's Bay Road.
Public transport: Half-hourly bus service (No. 93 and X93) between Scarborough and Whitby, nearest stop at Flask Inn (approx. 1 mile N of Jugger Howe Layby). Services run by Arriva (0191 281 1313) www.arrivabus.co.uk
Habitat: About 6,800 acres (2,750 hectares) of heather moorland (former grouse moor), with scattered trees and wooded valleys and gulleys. Managed exclusively for wildlife and archaeological

remains, the moor is an SSSI and SPA (Merlin and Golden Plover) and a special area of conservation (SAC).

Key birds: As well as more than 80 more common bird species, rare and endangered breeding birds include harriers, Merlin, Golden Plover, Red Grouse, Curlew, Wheatear, Stonechat, Whinchat, Sky Lark, Marsh Tit, Willow Tit, Linnet, Bullfinch, Reed Bunting and Yellowhammer.

The moor is also home to Kestrel, Lapwing, Snipe, Cuckoo, Meadow Pipit, Grey Wagtail and Wood Warbler.

Other notable flora and fauna: Many mammals including otter, roe deer, brown hare, stoat, weasel and badger. Also an important stronghold for water vole. Three species of heather, plus cranberry, cowberry, moonwort and, in wetter parts, bog myrtle, lesser twayblade, bog asphodel, butterwort, marsh helleborine, and sundews can be found. Also rare orchids and sedges. Notable insect species include large heath and small pearl-bordered fritillary butterflies, and emperor moth.

Contact: Professor John Edwards, The Hawk and Owl Trust. 01751 417 398. www.hawkandowl.org e-mail: john.edwards@wildflyingdales.co.uk

5. LOWER DERWENT VALLEY

Natural England (Yorkshire and Humber Region), Yorkshire Wildlife Trust and Countryside Trust.

Location: Six miles SE of York, stretching 12 miles S along the River Derwent from Newton-on-Derwent to Wressle and along the Pocklington Canal. Visitor facilities at Bank Island (SE 691 448), Wheldrake Ings YWT (SE 691 444 see separate entry), Thorganby (SE 692 418) and North Duffield Carrs (SE 697 367).

Access: Open all year. No dogs. Disabled access at North Duffield Carrs.

Facilities: Bank Island - two hides, viewing tower. Wheldrake Ings - four hides. Thorganby - viewing platform, North Duffield Carrs - two hides and wheelchair access. Car parks at all sites, height restriction of 2.1m at Bank Island and North Duffield Carrs. Bicycle stands in car parks at Bank Island and North Duffield Carrs.

Public transport: Bus from York/Selby – contact First (01904 622 992).

Habitat: Hay meadow and pasture, swamp, open water and alder/willow woodland.

Key birds: *Spring/summer:* Breeding wildfowl and waders, incl. Garganey, Snipe and Ruff. Barn Owl and warblers. *Winter/spring:* 20,000-plus waterfowl including Whooper Swan, wild geese, Teal and Wigeon. Large gull roost, incl. white-winged gulls. Also passage waders, incl. Whimbrel.

Other notable flora and fauna: A walk alongside the Pocklington Canal is particularly good for a wide range of aquatic plants and animals.

Contact: Senior Reserve Manager, Natural England, 01904 435 500. www.naturalengland.org. email: york@naturalengland.org.uk

6. WHELDRAKE INGS LOWER DERWENT VALLEY NATIONAL NATURE RESERVE

Yorkshire Wildlife Trust.

Location: From York ring-road head S onto A19 Selby road. After one mile turn L, signed Wheldrake and Thorganby. Continue through Wheldrake towards Thorganby. After a sharp R bend, turn L after 0.5 miles onto an unsigned tarmac track. Look for two stone gateposts with pointed tops. Car park is about 0.25 miles down the track. To reach the reserve, cross the bridge over river and turn R over a stile.

Access: Open all year. Please keep to the riverside path. From Apr-Sep.

Facilities: Car park, four hides.

Habitat: Water meadows, river, scrub, open water.

Key birds: *Spring/summer:* Duck species, Grey Partridge, Turtle Dove, some waders, Spotted Flycatcher, warblers. *Winter:* Occasional divers and scarce grebes. wildfowl inc. Pintail, Pochard, Goshawk, Hen Harrier, Water Rail, Short-eared Owl, thrushes, good mix of other birds.

Contact: Yorkshire Wildlife Trust, 1 St George's Place, York YO24 1GN. 01904 659 570. e-mail: info@ywt.org.uk   www.ywt.org.uk

Yorkshire, South & West

1. DENABY INGS NATURE RESERVE

Yorkshire Wildlife Trust.

Location: Reserve on A6023 from Mexborough. Look for L fork, signed Denaby Ings Nature Reserve. Proceed along Pastures Road for 0.5 miles and watch for a 2nd sign on R marking entrance to car park. From car park, walk back to the road to a set of concrete steps on R leading to a small visitor centre and a hide.

Access: Open all year.

Facilities: Car park, visitor centre, hide, nature trail.

Public transport: None.

Habitat: Water, deciduous woodland, marsh, willows.

Key birds: *Spring/summer:* Waterfowl, Little Ringed Plover, Turtle Dove, Cuckoo, Little Owl, Tawny Owl, Sand Martin, Swallow, Whinchat, possible Grasshopper Warbler, Lesser Whitethroat, Whitethroat, other warblers, Spotted Flycatcher, Red-legged and Grey Partridges, Kingfisher.

Passage: Waders, Common, Arctic and Black Terns, Redstart, Wheatear. *Winter:* Whooper Swan, wildfowl,

Jack Snipe, waders, Grey Wagtail, Short-eared Owl, Stonchat, Fieldfare, Redwing, Brambling, Siskin. *All year*: Corn Bunting, Yellowhammer, all three woodpeckers possible, Willow Tit, common woodland birds.
Contact: Yorkshire Wildlife Trust, 1 St George's Place, York YO24 1GN. 01904 659 570. www.ywt.org.uk e-mail: info@ywt.org.uk

2. DENSO MARSTON NATURE RESERVE

Denso Marston.
Location: SE 167 389. At Baildon, two miles from Shipley on Otley Road, entrance through kissing gate past end of Denso Marston factory.
Access: Open at all times.
Facilities: None.
Public transport: Bus from Bradford and Leeds 655, 652, 755.
Habitat: Two pools, woodland areas, meadow areas, site next to River Aire.
Key birds: *Summer*: Garden Warbler, Blackcap, Whitethroat. *Winter*: Lesser Redpoll, Siskin, Water Rail.
Other notable flora and fauna: Good selection of insects such as common blue and brimstone butterflies and common hawker, migrant hawker, four-spotted chaser dragonflies.
Contact: Denso Marston Ltd, Otley Road, Baildon, Shipley, West Yorkshire, BD17 7UR. 01274 582 266.

3. FAIRBURN INGS

RSPB (North West England Office).
Location: : SE 452 277. 12.5 miles from Leeds, six miles from Pontefract, 3.5 miles from Castleford

situated next to A1 at Fairburn turn-off.
Access: Reserve and hides open every day (9am-dusk). Centre with shop open weekdays and weekends (9am-5pm) and Bank Holidays. Hot and cold drinks available. Dogs on leads at all times. Boardwalk leading to Pickup Pool and feeding station and paths to centre wheelchair-friendly.
Facilities: Reserve hides: three open at all times with one locked at dusk. Toilets open when centre open or 9am-5pm. Disabled access to toilets. All nature trails follow public paths and are open at all times.
Public transport: Nearest train stations are Castleford or Pontefract. Buses approx every hour from Pontefract and Tadcaster. Infrequent from Castleford and Selby.
Habitat: Open water due to mining subsidence, wet grassland, marsh and willow scrub, reclaimed colliery spoil heaps.
Key birds: *Winter*: A herd of Whooper Swans usually roost. Normally up to five Smew including male, Wigeon, Gadwall, Goosander, Goldeney. *Spring*: Osprey, Wheatear, Little Gull and five species of tern pass through. *Summer*: Breeding birds include Reed and Sedge Warblers, Shoveler, Gadwall, Cormorant.
Contact: James Dean, Visitor Officer, Fairburn Ings Visitor Centre, Newton Lane, Fairburn, Castleford WF10 2BH. 01977 603 796.

4. HARDCASTLE CRAGS

National Trust.
Location: From Halifax, follow A646 W for five miles to Hebden Bridge and pick up National Trust signs in town centre to the A6033 Keighley Road. Follow this for 0.75 miles. Turn L at the National Trust sign to the car parks. Alternate pay-and-display car park at Clough Hole, Widdop Road, on R above Gibson Mill.
Access: Open all year. NT car park charges: £2.50 up to 3 hours, £3 all day weekdays, £4 at weekends and bank holidays. No charge for NT members and disabled badge holders.
Facilities: 2 small pay car parks, cycle racks and several way-marked trails. Gibson Mill has toilets, café, exhibitions. Not connected to any mains services, in extreme conditions the mill may be closed for health and safety reasons.
Public transport: Good public transport links. Trains to Hebden Bridge from Manchester or Leeds every 30 minutes. Call 08457 484 950. Weekday buses every 30 minutes to Keighley Road, then 1 mile walk to Midghole. Summer weekend bus 906 Widdop-Hardcastle Crags leaves Hebden Bridge rail station every 90 minutes 9.20am-6.05pm. Tel: 0113 245 7676.
Habitat: Wooded valleys, ravines, streams, hay meadows and moorland edge.
Key birds: *Spring/summer*: Cuckoo, Redstart, Lesser Whitethroat, Garden

Warbler, Blackcap, Wood Warbler, Chiffchaff, Spotted Flycatcher, Pied Flycatcher, Curlew, Lapwing, Meadow Pipit. *All year*: Sparrowhawk, Kestrel, Green and Greater Spotted Woodpeckers, Tawny Owl, Barn Owl, Little Owl, Jay, Coal Tit and other woodland species.
Contact: National Trust, Hardcastle Crags, Hollin Hall Office, Hebden Bridge, HX7 7AP. 01422 844 518.

5. MALTBY LOW COMMON

Yorkshire Wildlife Trust.
Location: SK 543 914. 1 mile SE of Maltby. From M18 J1 take A631 to Maltby. Take R fork to A634 Blyth road. After Maltby Craggs School, turn L at next signpost, then R after 100 yards. Pass Sports Ground and park near corner where road turns L into the Birks Holt housing estate. Proceed on foot over railway bridge, along track and descend to Low Common.
Access: Open all hours, all year. Keep dogs on leads and on the footpaths please.
Facilities: Footpaths, roadside parking, facilities in Maltby.
Habitat: Dry grassland and fen meadow
Key birds: Buzzard, Kestrel, Turtle Dove, Cuckoo, Barn Owl, Common Whitethroat and Garden Warbler. In the winter, flocks of foraging tits and thrushes.
Other notable flora and fauna: More than 400 invertebrate species recorded to date. Many species of butterfly and moth can be seen including brimstone, orange tip, small copper, wall heath, cinnabar and silver Y. Plants include marsh valerian, mat grass, tufted hair grass, pepper saxifrage, sneezewort, lousewort and aspen, common spotted-orchid..
Contact: Yorkshire Wildlife Trust, 1 St George's Place, York YO24 1GN. 01904 659 570.
e-mail: info@ywt.org.uk www.ywt.org.uk

6. OLD MOOR

RSPB North West Office.
Location: SE 422 011. From M1 J36, then A6195. From A1 J37, then A635 and A6195 – follow brown signs.
Access: Open Apr 1-Oct 31 (Wed-Sun 9am-5pm), Nov 1-Mar 31 (Wed/Thu/Sat/Sun 10am-4pm). Members free. Non-member adults – £2.50. Concessions – £2.
Facilities: Toilets (including disabled), large visitor centre and shop, five superb hides. All sites including hides fully accessible for disabled.
Public transport: Buses – information from South Yorkshire Passenger Transport 01709 589 200.
Habitat: Lakes and flood meadows, wader scrape and reedbeds.
Key birds: *Winter*: Large numbers of wildfowl. *Summer*: Breeding waders and wildfowl. Rare vagrants recorded annually.
Contact: RSPB Old Moor, Old Moor Lane, Wombwell, Barnsley, South Yorkshire, S73 0YF. 01226 751 593 Fax: 01226 341 078. www.rspb.org.uk

7. POTTERIC CARR

Yorkshire Wildlife Trust.
Location: SE 589 007. From M18 junction 3 take A6182 (Doncaster) and at first roundabout take third exit; entrance and car park are on R after 50m.
Access: Access by permit only. Parties must obtain prior permission. Field Centre (hot and cold drinks, snacks and meals, toilet) open 9.30am-4pm Thursdays to Sundays all year round. Bank Holiday Mondays open, also Tues 9.30am-1.30pm.
Facilities: Approx 12 km of footpaths including 8km suitable for disabled unaided. Twelve new/refurbished hides, 10 suitable for wheelchairs.
See website for more details and events programme.
Public transport: Buses from Doncaster to new B &Q store travel within easy reach of entrance.
Habitat: Reed fen, subsidence ponds, artificial pools, grassland, woodland.
Key birds: 96 species have bred. Nesting waterfowl (inc. Shoveler, Gadwall, Pochard), Water Rail, Kingfisher, all three woodpeckers, Lesser Whitethroat, Reed and Sedge Warblers, Willow Tit. *Passage/winter*: Bittern, Marsh Harrier, Black Tern, waders, wildfowl.
Other notable flora and fauna: 20 species of dragonfly recorded, 28 species of butterfly including purple hairstreak and dingy skipper. Palmate and great crested newt.
Contact: For further contact information, telephone nos. etc. Website, www.potteric-carr.org.uk. Owners: Yorkshire Wildlife Trust, 10 Toft Green, York YO1 6JT. 01302 364 152.

8. SPROTBOROUGH FLASH & THE DON GORGE

Yorkshire Wildlife Trust.
Location: From A1, follow A630 to Rotherham 4.8km W of Doncaster. After 0.8km, turn R at traffic lights to Sprotborough. After approx 1.6km road drops down slopes of the Gorse. Cross bridge over river, then another over a canal, turn Immedlately L.
Park in a small roadside parking area 45m on L beside canal. Walk along canal bank, past The Boat Inn to reserve entrance approx 90m further on.
Access: Open all year.
Facilities: Three hides, footpaths.
Public transport: River bus from Doncaster in summer months.
Habitat: River, reed, gorge, woodland.
Key birds: Summer: Turtle Dove, Cuckoo, hirundines, Lesser Whitethroat, Whitethroat, Garden Warbler, Blackcap, Chiffchaff, Willow Warbler, Spotted Flycatcher. Spring/autumn passage: Little Ringed Plover, Dunlin, Greenshank, Green Sandpiper, waders, Yellow Wagtail. Winter/all year: Wildfowl, Water Rail, Snipe, Little Owl, Tawny Owl, all three woodpeckers, thrushes, Siskin, possible Corn Bunting.
Contact: Yorkshire Wildlife Trust, 1 St George's Place, York YO24 1GN. 01904 659 570.
e-mail: info@ywt.org.uk www.ywt.org.uk

SCOTLAND
Border Counties

Borders

1. DUNS CASTLE

Scottish Wildlife Trust.
Location: NT 778 550. Located N of the centre of Duns. From Berwick-upon-Tweed head W on A6105.
Access: Access from Castle Street or at N end of reserve from B6365.
Facilities: Car park at site entrance. Some wheelchair-friendly paths. RADAR toilets in village.
Public transport: None.
Habitat: Two man-made lochs and mature woodland.

Key birds: Woodland birds, including Green and Great Spotted Woodpeckers, Goldcrest. Mute Swan and other waterfowl.
Other notable flora and fauna: Red squirrel, roe and red deer, badger and occasional otter.
Contact: SWT headquarters132 312 7765.

2. GUNKNOWE LOCH AND PARK

Scottish Borders Council.
Location: NT 523 51. 3.2km from Galashiels on the A6091. Park at Gunknowe Loch.
Access: Open all year. Surfaced paths suitable for wheelchair use.
Facilities: Car park, paths.

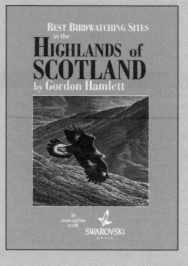
216

Public transport: Tweedbank is on the Melrose to Peebles bus route.
Habitat: River, parkland, scrub, woodland.
Key birds: *Spring/summer*: Grey Wagtail, Kingfisher, Sand Martin, Blackcap, Sedge and Grasshopper Warblers. *Passage*: Yellow Wagtail, Whinchat, Wheatear. *Winter*: Thrushes, Brambling, Wigeon, Tufted Duck, Pochard, Goldeneye. *All year*: Great Spotted and Green Woodpeckers, Redpoll, Goosander, possible Marsh Tit.
Contact: Countryside Ranger Service, Harestanes, Ancrum, Jedburgh, TD8 6UQ. 01835 830 281; Fax: 01835 830 717. www.scotborders.gov.uk

3. ST ABB'S HEAD

National Trust for Scotland.
Location: NT 914 693. Lies five miles N of Eyemouth. Follow A1107 from A1.
Access: Reserve open all year. Keep dogs under control. Viewpoint at Starney accessible for disabled visitors. Coach parking at Northfield Farm by prior arrangement.
Facilities: Visitor centre and toilets open daily Apr-Oct.
Public transport: Nearest rail station is Berwick-upon-Tweed. Bus service from Berwick, tel 018907 81533.
Habitat: Cliffs, coastal grasslands and freshwater loch.
Key birds: Apr-Aug: Seabird colonies with large numbers of Kittiwake, auks, Shag, Fulmar, migrants. Apr-May and Sept-Oct: Good autumn seawatching.
Other notable flora and fauna: Northern brown argus butterfly. Rock-rose, purple milk-vetch, sandwort.
Contact: Kevin Rideout, Rangers Cottage, Northfield, St Abbs, Borders TD14 5QF. 01890 771 443. e-mail: krideout@nts.org.uk www.nts.org.uk

4. THE HIRSEL

The Estate Office, The Hirsel.
Location: NT 827 403. Signed off the A698 on the outskirts of Coldstream.
Access: Open all year. Private estate, so please stick to the public paths. Coaches by appointment.
Facilities: Car parks, visitor centre, toilets, hide, walks, café.
Public transport: Bus: Coldstream, Kelso, Berwick-upon-Tweed, Edinburgh.
Habitat: Freshwater loch, reeds, woods.
Key birds: *Spring/summer*: Redstart, Garden Warbler, Blackcap, flycatchers, possible Water Rail, wildfowl.
Autumn: Wildfowl, Goosander, possible Green Sandpiper.
Winter: Whooper Swan, Pink-footed Goose, Wigeon, Goldeneye, Pochard, occasional Smew, Scaup, Slavonian Grebe.

Contact: The Managing Factor, Roger Dodd, Bridge Street, Kelso, TD5 7JD. 01573 224 144.

5. YETHOLM LOCH

Scottish Wildlife Trust.
Location: NT 803 275. 7.6 miles SE of Kelso. Off B6352, turning to Lochtower (unmetalled road).
Access: No access to marsh during breeding season.
Facilities: Hide. Car park along rough track.
Public transport: None.
Habitat: Marshland and loch.
Key birds: *Summer*: Breeding wildfowl (inc. Great Crested Grebe, Shoveler and Teal). *Winter*: Whooper Swan, Pink-footed Goose and wide range of ducks.
Contact: SWT Headquarters. 01313 127 765.

Dumfries & Galloway

6. CAERLAVEROCK WETLAND CENTRE

The Wildfowl & Wetlands Trust.
Location: NY 051 656. From Dumfries take B725 towards Bankend.
Access: Open daily (10am-5pm), except Christmas Day.
Facilities: 20 hides, heated observatory, four towers, Salcot Merse Observatory, sheltered picnic area. Self-catering accommodation and camping facilities. Nature trails in summer. Old Granary visitor building with fair-trade coffee shop serving light meals and snacks; natural history bookshop; binoculars & telescopes for sale. Theatre/conference room. Binoculars for hire. Parking for coaches.
Public transport: Bus 371 from Dumfries stops 30 mins walk from reserve. Stagecoach 01387 253 496.
Habitat: Saltmarsh, grassland, wetland.
Key birds: *Winter*: Wildfowl esp. Barnacle Geese (max 25,000) and Whooper Swans. *Summer*: Ospreys, Avocets, Sky Larks.
Other notable flora and fauna: Natterjack toad. Northern marsh, common spotted and twayblade orchids.
Contact: The Wildfowl & Wetlands Trust, Eastpark Farm, Caerlaverock, Dumfries DG1 4RS. 01387 770 200.

7. KEN/DEE MARSHES

RSPB (South & West Scotland Office).
Location: NX 699 684. Six miles from Castle Douglas – good views from A762 and A713 roads to New Galloway.
Access: From car park at entrance to farm Mains of Duchrae. Open during daylight hours. No dogs.
Facilities: Hides, nature trails. Three miles of trails available, nearer parking for elderly and disabled, but phone warden first. Part of Red Kite trail.

Public transport: None.
Habitat: Marshes, woodlands, open water.
Key birds: *All year*: Mallard, Grey Heron, Buzzard. *Spring/summer*: Pied Flycatcher, Redstart, Tree Pipit, Sedge Warbler. *Winter*: Greenland White-fronted and Greylag Geese, birds of prey (Hen Harrier, Peregrine, Merlin, Red Kite).
Contact: Paul Collin, Gairland, Old Edinburgh Road, Minnigaff, Newton Stewart DG8 6PL. 01671 402 861.

8. MERSEHEAD

RSPB (South & West Scotland Office).
Location: NX 925 560. From Dalbeattie, take B793 or A710 SE to Caulkerbush.
Access: Open at all times.
Facilities: Hide, nature trails, information centre and toilets.
Public transport: None.
Habitat: Wet grassland, arable farmland, saltmarsh, inter-tidal mudflats.
Key birds: *Winter*: Up to 9,500 Barnacle Geese, 4,000 Teal, 2,000 Wigeon, 1,000 Pintail, waders (inc. Dunlin, Knot, Oystercatcher). *Summer*: Breeding birds include Lapwing, Redshank, Sky Lark.
Contact: Eric Nielson, Mersehead, Southwick, Mersehead, Dumfries DG2 8AH. 01387 780 298.

9. MULL OF GALLOWAY

RSPB (South & West Scotland Office).
Location: NX 156 304. Most southerly tip of Scotland – five miles from village of Drummore, S of Stranraer.
Access: Open at all times. Access suitable for disabled. Disabled parking by centre. Centre open summer only (Apr-Oct).
Facilities: Visitor centre, toilets, nature trails, CCTV on cliffs. **Public transport:** None.
Habitat: Sea cliffs, coastal heath.
Key birds: *Spring/summer*: Guillemot, Razorbill, Kittiwake, Black Guillemot, Puffin, Fulmar, Raven, Wheatear, Rock Pipit, Twite. Migrating Manx Shearwater. *All year*: Peregrine.
Contact: Paul Collin, Gairland, Old Edinburgh Road, Minnigaff, Newton Stewart DG8 6PL. 01671 402 851.

10. WIGTOWN BAY LNR

Dumfries & Galloway Council.
Location: NX 465 545. Between Wigtown and Creetown, S of Newton Stewart. It is the largest LNR in Britain at 2,845 ha. The A75 runs along E side with A714 S to Wigtown and B7004 providing superb views of the LNR.
Access: Open at all times. The hide is disabled friendly. Main accesses: Roadside lay-bys on A75 near Creetown and parking at Martyr's Stake and Wigtown Harbour. All suitable for coaches. The visitor facility in Wigtown County Building has full disabled access, including lift and toilets.
Facilities: A hide at Wigtown Harbour with views over the River Bladnoch, saltmarsh and fresh water wetland has disabled access from harbour car park. Walks and interpretation in this area.
Visitor centre in Wigtown County Buildings has interpretation facilities and a commanding view of the bay, plus CCTV of Ospreys breeding in Galloway during summer and wetland birds in winter. Open Mon-Sat (10am-5pm, later some days). Sun (2pm-5pm).
Public transport: Travel Information Line 08457 090 510 (local rate 9am-5pm Mon-Fri). Bus No 415 for Wigtown and W side. Bus No 431 or 500 X75 for Creetown and E side.
Habitat: Estuary with extensive saltmarsh/merse and mudflats with developed fresh water wetland at Wigtown Harbour.
Key birds: *Winter*: Internationally important for Pink-footed Goose, nationally important for Curlew, Whooper Swan and Pintail, with major gull roost and other migratory coastal birds. *Summer*: Breeding waders and duck.

Other notable flora and fauna: Fish including smelt and shads. Lax flowered sea lavender, thrift, sea aster.

Contact: Elizabeth Tindal, Countryside Ranger, Dumfries and Galloway Council, County Buildings, Wigtown Bay Visitors Centre, Wigtown, Dumfries & Galloway DG8 9JH
01988 402 401, mobile 07702 212 728.
e-mail: wblnr@dumgal.gov.uk
www.dgcommunity.net/wblr

11. WOOD OF CREE

RSPB (South & West Scotland Office).
Location: NX 382 708. Four miles N of Newton Stewart on minor road from Minnigaff, parallel to A714.

Access: Open during daylight hours. Dogs on lead. Not suitable for disabled.
Facilities: Nature trails.
Public transport: None.
Habitat: Oak woodland, marshes, river.
Key birds: *Spring/summer:* Pied Flycatcher, Wood Warbler, Tree Pipit, Redstart, Buzzard, Great Spotted Woodpecker.
Other notable flora and fauna: Red squirrel, otter.
Contact: Paul Collin, Gairland, Old Edinburgh Road, Minnigaff, Newton Stewart DG8 6PL.
01671 402 861.

Central Scotland

Argyll

1. COLL RESERVE

RSPB (South & West Scotland Office).
Location: NM 168 561. Inner Hebrides island reached by ferry from Oban. On island, take the B8070 W from Arinagour for five miles. Turn R at Arileod. Continue for about one mile. Park at end of the road. Reception point at Totronald.
Access: Open all year. Please avoid walking through fields and crops.
Facilities: Car park, information bothy at Totronald, guided walks in summer. Corn Crake viewing bench.
Public transport: None.
Habitat: Sand dunes, beaches, machair grassland, moorland, farmland.
Key birds: *Spring/summer:* Corn Crake, Redshank, Lapwing, Snipe. *Winter:* Barnacle and Greenland White-fronted Geese.
Contact: RSPB Coll Nature Reserve, Totronald, Isle of Coll, Argyll, PA78 6TB, 01879 230 301.

2. LOCH GRUINART, ISLAY

RSPB (South & West Scotland Office).
Location: Sea loch on N coast of Inner Hebridean island, seven miles NW from Bridgend.
Access: Hide open all hours, visitor centre open (10am-5pm), disabled access to hide, toilets. Assistance required for wheelchair users. Coach parking at visitor centre only. No dogs.
Facilities: Toilets, visitor centre, hide, trail.
Public transport: None.
Habitat: Lowland wet grasslands, sea loch, moorland.

Key birds: Oct-Apr: Barnacle and Greenland White-fronted Goose. May-Aug: Corn Crake. Sept-Nov: Migrating wading birds.
Contact: Liz Hathaway, RSPB Scotland, Bushmills Cottage, Gruinart, Isle of Islay PA44 7PP.
01496 850 505. e-mail: loch.gruinart@rspb.org.uk
www.rspb.org.uk/scotland

3. MACHRIHANISH SEABIRD OBSERVATORY

John McGlynn, Nancie Smith and Eddie Maguire (sponsored by SNH and Leader+).
Location: NR 628 209. Southwest Kintyre, Argyll. Six miles W of Campbeltown on A83, then B843.
Access: Daily April-Oct. Wheelchair access. Dogs welcome. Parking for three cars. Digiscoping facilities include electricity and monitor.
Facilities: Seawatching hide, toilets in nearby village. Coach parking.
Public transport: Regular buses from Campbeltown (West Coast Motors, tel 01586 552 319).
Habitat: Marine, rocky shore and upland habitats.
Key birds: *Summer:* Golden Eagle, Peregrine, Storm Petrel and Twite. *Autumn:* Passage seabirds and waders. On-shore gales often produce inshore movements of Leach's Petrel and other scarce seabirds, including Balearic Shearwater, Sabine's Gull and Grey Phalarope. *Winter:* Great Northern Diver, Purple Sandpiper, Ruddy Turnstone with occasional Glaucous and Iceland Gulls.
Other notable flora and fauna: Grey and common seals, otters and wild goats.
Contact: Eddie Maguire, Warden, Seabird & Wildlife Observatory, Lossit Park, Machrihanish, SW Kintyre, Argyll PA28 6PZ. 07919 660 292.
e-mail: machrihanishbirds@btinternet.com
www.machrihanishbirds.org.uk

Ayrshire

4. AILSA CRAIG

(RSPB South & West Scotland Office).
Location: NX 020 998. Island 9 miles offshore, nearest town is Girvan – take A77 S from Ayr.
Access: Accessible only by boat - tours are available on the MFV Glorious (tel: 01465 713 219) or Kintyre Express (tel: 01294 270 160) from Girvan during the summer period, also from Campbeltown by Mull of Kintyre Seatours fast rib (Tel: 07785 542 811).
Facilities: None
Public transport: None.
Habitat: Dramatic seacliffs.
Key birds: Ailsa Craig is the third largest gannetry in the UK and supports 73,000 breeding seabirds including Guillemots, Razorbills, Puffins, Kittiwakes and up to 36,000 pairs of Gannets. Twite can also be found here.
Other notable flora and fauna: Slow worm.
Contact: RSPB South & West Scotland Office, 10 Park Quadrant, Glasgow, G3 6BS. 0141 331 0993.
e-mail: glasgow@rspb.org.uk

5. GARNOCK FLOODS

Scottish Wildlife Trust.
Location: NS 306 417. Lies S of Kilwinning and W of Irvine, sandwiched between railway line, Sandy Road and the river. From B779 N, take the one-way road to Bogside, just beyond A737 interchange. Park on roadside. Best viewed from cycle track along E boundary.
Access: Open all year.
Facilities: Parking.
Public transport: None.
Habitat: River, ponds, rush pasture.
Key birds: *Spring/summer:* Sedge and Willow Warblers, Lesser Whitethroat, Sand Martin, occasional Garganey.
Winter: Wildfowl inc Goldeneye, Mute Swan, waders including Ruff and Snipe.
Contact: SWT headquarters 0131 312 7765.

Clyde

6. BARONS HAUGH

RSPB (South & West Scotland Office).
Location: RSPB NS755552. On SW edge of Motherwell, overlooking River Clyde. Via Adele Street, then lane off North Lodge Avenue.
Access: Open all year.
Facilities: Four hides.
Public transport: None.
Habitat: Marshland, flooded areas, woodland, parkland, meadows, scrub, river.
Key birds: *Summer:* Breeding Gadwall, warblers (inc. Garden, Grasshopper); Whinchat, Common Sandpiper, Kingfisher. *Autumn:* Excellent for waders (22 species). *Winter:* Whooper Swan.
Contact: RSPB South & West Scotland Office, 10 Park Quadrant, Glasgow, G3 6BS. 01413 3 0 993.

7. FALLS OF CLYDE

Scottish Wildlife Trust.
Location: NS 88 34 14. Approx one mile S of Lanark. Directions from Glasgow – travel S on M74 until J7 then along A72, following signs for Lanark and New Lanark.
Access: Open during daylight hours all year. Disabled access limited.
Facilities: Visitor centre open 11am-5pm Mar-Dec, 12-4pm Jan-Feb. Toilets and cafeteria on site. Seasonal viewing facility for Peregrines. Numerous walkways. Ranger service offers comprehensive guided walks programme.
Public transport: Scotrail trains run to Lanark (0845 7484 950). Local bus service from Lanark to New Lanark.
Habitat: River Clyde gorge, waterfalls, mixed woodland and broadleaved riparian gorge, meadow, pond.
Key birds: More than 100 species of bird recorded on the reserve, including unrivalled views of breeding Peregrine. Others include Tawny Owl, Kingfisher, Dipper, Great Spotted Woodpecker, Spotted Flycatcher and Goosander.
Contact: Miss Lindsay Cook, The Scottish Wildlife Trust Visitor Centre, The Falls of Clyde Reserve & Visitor Centre, New Lanark, South Lanark ML11 9DB. 01555 665 262.
e-mail: fallsofclyde@swt.co.uk
www.swt.org.uk

8. LOCHWINNOCH

RSPB (South & West Scotland Office).
Location: NS 358 582. At Castle Semple Water, 18 miles SW of Glasgow, adjacent to A760.
Access: Open every day except Christmas and Boxing Day, Jan 1 and Jan 2. (10am-5pm).
Facilities: Special facilities for schools and disabled. Refreshments available. Visitor centre, hides.
Public transport: Rail station adjacent, bus services nearby.
Habitat: Shallow lochs, marsh, mixed woodland.
Key birds: *Winter:* Wildfowl (esp. Whooper Swan, Wigeon, Goosander, Goldeneye). Occasional passage migrants inc. Whimbrel, Greenshank.
Summer: Breeding Great Crested Grebe, Water Rail, Sedge and Grasshopper Warblers, Reed Bunting.
Contact: RSPB Nature Centre, Largs Road, Lochwinnoch, Renfrewshire PA12 4JF. 01505 842 663; Fax 01505 843 026;
e-mail lochwinnoch@rspb.org.uk.

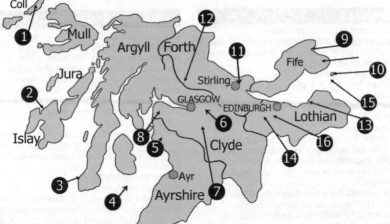

Fife

9. EDEN ESTUARY

Fife Council.
Location: NO 470 195. The reserve can be accessed from Guardbridge, St Andrews (one mile) on A91, and from Leuchars via Tentsmuir Forest off A919 (four miles).
Access: The Eden Estuary Centre is open (9am-5pm) every day except Christmas Day, New Year's Day and the day of the Leuchars airshow in September. Reserve is open all year, but a permit (from Ranger Service) is required to access the N shore. Limited coach access and coach charge if using Kinshaldy car park.
Facilities: Visitor centre at Guardbridge. Information panels at Outhead. Hide at Balgove Bay (key from Ranger Service).
Public transport: Leuchars train station. Regular buses Cupar-Dundee-St Andrews. Tel: 01334 474238.
Habitat: Saltmarsh, river, tidal flats, sand dunes.
Key birds: *Winter*: Main interest is wildfowl and waders, best place in Scotland to see Black-tailed Godwit. Other species include Grey Plover, Shelduck, Bar-tailed Godwit. Offshore Common and Velvet Scoter occur and Surf Scoter is regularly seen. Peregrine, Merlin and Short-eared Owl occur in winter.
Contact: Les Hatton, Fife Ranger Service, Craigtown Country Park, St Andrews, Fife KY16 8NX. 01334 473 047/07985 707 593 (mobile).
e-mail: refrs@craigtoun.freserve.co.uk A

10. ISLE OF MAY NNR

Scottish Natural Heritage.
Location: NT 655 995. This small island lying six miles off Fife Ness in the Firth of Forth is a National Nature Reserve.
Access: Boats run from Anstruther and North Berwick. Contact SNH for details 01334 654 038. Keep to paths. Fishing boat from Anstruther arranged for those using Observatory accommodation. Delays are possible, both arriving and leaving, because of weather.
Facilities: No dogs; no camping; no fires. Prior permission required if scientific work or filming is to be carried out.
Public transport: Regular bus service to Anstruther and North Berwick harbour.
Habitat: Sea cliffs, rocky shoreline.
Key birds: Early *Summer*: Breeding auks and terns, Kittiwake, Shag, Eider, Fulmar. Over 68,000 pairs of Puffins.
Autumn/spring: Weather-related migrations include rarities each year.
Contact: For Observatory accomodation: David Thorne, Craigurd House, Blyth Bridge, West Linton, Peeblesshire EH46 7AH. For all other enquiries: SNH, 46 Crossgate, Cupar, Fife Ky15 5HS.

Forth

11. CAMBUS POOLS

Scottish Wildlife Trust.
Location: NS 846 937. ENE of Alloa on A907. Park by river in Cambus village.
Access: Cross River Devon by bridge at NS 853 940 and walk down stream on R bank past bonded warehouses. Open all year.
Facilities: None.
Public transport: None.
Habitat: Wet grassland and pools.
Key birds: Used extensively by migrants, inc. wildfowl and waders.
Contact: SWT headquarters. 01313 127 765.

12. INVERSNAID

RSPB (South & West Scotland Office).
Location: NN 337 088. On E side of Loch Lomond.
Via B829 W from Aberfoyle, then along minor road to
car park by Inversnaid Hotel.
Access: Open all year.
Facilities: New car park and trail at Garrison Farm
(NN 348 095).
Public transport: None.
Habitat: Deciduous woodland rises to craggy ridge
and moorland.
Key birds: *Summer*: Breeding Black Grouse, Snipe,
Wheatear and Twite. Grey Wagtail, Dipper, Wood
Warbler, Redstart, Pied Flycatcher, Tree Pipit. The
loch is on a migration route, especially for wildfowl
and waders.
Other notable flora and fauna: Small pearl-
bordered fritillary on nature trail at Inversaid.
Wilson's and Tunbridge filmy ferns on boulders
through woodland.
Contact: RSPB South & West Scotland Office, 10
Park Quadrant, Glasgow, G3 6BS. 01413 310 993.

Lothian

13. ABERLADY BAY

East Lothian Council (LNR).
Location: NT 472 806. From Edinburgh take A198
E to Aberlady. Reserve is 1.5 miles E of Aberlady
village.
Access: Open at all times. Please stay on footpaths
to avoid disturbance. Disabled access from reserve
car park. No dogs please.
Facilities: Small car park and toilets. Notice board
with recent sightings at end of footbridge.
Public transport: Edinburgh to N Berwick bus
service stops at reserve (request); service no 124.
Railway 4 miles away at Longniddry.
Habitat: Tidal mudflats, saltmarsh, freshwater
marsh, dune grassland, scrub, open sea.
Key birds: *Summer*: Breeding birds include
Shelduck, Eider, Reed Bunting and up to eight
species of warbler. Passage waders inc. Green, Wood
and Curlew Sandpipers, Little Stint, Greenshank,
Whimbrel, Black-tailed Godwit. *Winter*: Divers (esp.
Red-throated), Red-necked and Slavonian Grebes
and geese (large numbers of Pink-footed roost);
sea-ducks, waders.
Contact: John Harrison, Reserve Warden,
Landscape & Countryside Management, East Lothian
Council, Council Buildings, East Lothian EH41 3HA.
01875 870 588. email: jharrison@eastlothian.gov.uk
www.aberlady.org

14. ALMONDELL & CALDERWOOD COUNTRY PARK

West Lothian Council.
Location: NT 091 697. East of Livingston. North
entrance, the closest to the visitor centre, is
signposted off A89, two miles S of Broxburn.
Access: Open all year. Parking available at N
entrance, S entrance at East Calder and Mid Calder
and Oakbank on A71 (furthest from visitor centre).
Disabled car park at visitor centre. Coach parking
available with prior notice.
Facilities: Car park, picnic area, hot and cold
drinks, toilets, pushchair access, partial access for
wheelchairs, visitor centre (open every day), gift
shop, countryside ranger service.
Public transport: None.
Habitat: Woodland, river.
Key birds: *Spring/summer*: Woodcock, Tawny Owl,
Grasshopper Warbler, Yellowhammer, Blackcap,
Garden Warbler. *Winter*: Goldcrest, Redpoll, Willow
Tit. *All year*: Dipper, Grey Wagtail, Sparrowhawk.
Contact: Head Ranger, Almondell and Calderwood
Country Park Visitor Centre, Broxburn, West Lothian,
EH52 5PE, 01506 882 254.
e-mail: almondell&calderwood@westlothian.gov.uk
www.beecraigs.com

15. BASS ROCK

Location: NT 602 873. Island in Firth of Forth, lying
E of North Berwick.
Access: Private property. Regular daily sailings from
N Berwick around Rock; local boatman has owner's
permission to land individuals or parties by prior
arrangement. For details contact 01620 892 838 or
The Scottish Seabird Centre 01620 890 202;
www.seabird.org
Facilities: None. **Habitat:** Sea cliffs.
Key birds: The spectacular cliffs hold a large Gannet
colony, (up to 9,000 pairs), plus auks, Kittiwake,
Shag and Fulmer.

16. GLADHOUSE RESERVOIR LNR

Scottish Water.
Location: NT 295 535. S of Edinburgh off the A703.
Access: Open all year although there is no access to
the reservoir itself. Most viewing can be done from
the road (telescope required).
Facilities: Small car park on north side. Not suitable
for coaches.
Habitat: Reservoir, grassland, farmland.
Key birds: *Spring/summer*: Oystercatcher, Lapwing,
Curlew. Possible Black Grouse. *Winter*: Geese,
including Pinkfeet, Twite, Brambling, Hen Harrier.
Contact: Scottish Water, PO Box 8855, Edinburgh,
EH10 6YQ, 084 6 018 855.
e-mail: customer.service@Scottishwater.co.uk
www.Scottishwater.co.uk A

Eastern Scotland

Angus & Dundee

1. LOCH OF KINNORDY

RSPB (East Scotland).
Location: NO 351 539. Car park on B951 one mile W of Kirriemuir. Perth 45 minutes drive, Dundee 30 minutes drive, Aberdeen one hour drive.
Access: Open dawn-dusk (occasionally closed on Saturdays during Sep and Oct). Disabled access to two hides via short trails. Admission free, parking £1 for non-RSPB members.
Facilities: Three birdwatching hides (two wheelchair accessible). There are no toilets (nearest in Kirriemuir).
Public transport: Nearest centre is Kirriemuir.
Habitat: Freshwater loch, fen, carr, marsh.
Key birds: *Spring*: Black-necked Grebe, Osprey, Black-headed Gull, Lapwing, Oystercatcher. *Summer*: Breeding wildfowl including Mallard, Gadwall and Mute Swan, Warblers including Blackcap, Garden, Willow and Sedge, Reed Bunting.
Autumn: Returning Whooper Swans, Pink-footed and Greylag Geese. Greenshank, Snipe, mixed tit flocks.
Winter: Wildfowl including Goosander, Goldeneye and Whooper Swan, Water Rail, Great Spotted Woodpecker, roosts of corvids and Starlings.
Other notable flora and fauna: Otters, roe deer. Good site for butterflies and dragonflies.
Contact: Hannah Morton, RSPB, 1 Atholl Crescent, Perth PH1 5NG. 01738 630 783.
e-mail: loch.kinnordy@rspb.org www.rspb.org

2. LOCH OF LINTRATHEN

Scottish Wildlife Trust.
Location: H 278 550. Seven miles W of Kirriemuir. Take B951 and choose circular route on unclassified roads round loch.
Access: Public hide planned but to date, Scottish Wildlife Trust hide (members' permit system) only. Good viewing points from several places along unclassified roads.
Facilities: Parking
Public transport: None.
Habitat: Oligatrophic/mesotrophic loch. Surrounded by mainly coniferous woodland.
Key birds: *Summer*: Osprey. *Winter*: Greylag Goose, Goosander, Whooper Swan, Wigeon, Teal.
Contact: SWT, Annat House, South Anag, Ferryden, Montrose, Angus DD10 9UT. 01674 676 555.
e-mail: swtnero@cix.co.uk

3. MONTROSE BASIN

Scottish Wildlife Trust on behalf of Angus Council.
Location: NO 690 580 – centre of basin. NO 702 565 – Wildlife SWT Centre on A92. 1.5 miles from centre of Montrose.
Access: Apr 1-Oct 31 (10.30am-5pm). Nov 1-Mar 31, (10.30am-4pm).
Facilities: Visitor centre, shop, vending machine, toilets, disabled access to centre, two hides on western half of reserve.
Public transport: Train 1.5 miles in Montrose. Buses same as above.
Habitat: Estuary, saltmarsh, reedbeds, farmland.
Key birds: Pink-footed Goose – up to 35,000 arrive each Oct. Wintering wildfowl and waders. Breeding Eider Ducks.
Contact: Scottish Wildlife Trust, Montrose Basin Wildlife Centre, Rossie Braes, Montrose DD10 9TJ. 01674 676 336. e-mail: montrosebasin@swt.org.uk www.swt.org.uk

4. SEATON CLIFFS

Scottish Wildlife Trust.
Location: NO 667 416. 30-acre cliff reserve, nearest town Arbroath 2.2 miles. Car parking at N end of promenade at Arbroath.
Access: Open all year.
Facilities: Nature trail with interpretation boards. Parking area.
Public transport: None.
Habitat: Red sandstone cliffs with nature trail.
Key birds: Seabirds including, Eider, auks, terns; Rock Dove and House Martin breed.
Contact: SWT headquarters, 0131 312 7765.

Moray & Nairn

5. CULBIN SANDS

RSPB (North Scotland Office).
Location: NH 900 580. Approx half mile from Nairn. Access to parking at East Beach car park, signed off A96.
Access: Open at all times. Path to reserve suitable for all abilities.
Facilities: Toilets at car park. Track along dunes and saltmarsh.
Public transport: Buses stop in Nairn, half mile W of site. Train station in Nairn three-quarters of mile W of reserve.

Habitat: Saltmarsh, sandflats, dunes.
Key birds: *Winter:* Flocks of Common Scoter, Long-tailed Duck, Knot, Bar-tailed Godwit, Red-breasted Merganser. Raptors including Peregrine, Merlin and Hen Harrier attracted by wader flocks. Roosting geese, Snow Bunting flocks. *Summer:* Breeding Ringed Plover, Oystercatcher.
Contact: RSPB North Scotland Office, Etive House, Beechwood Park, Inverness IV2 3BW. 01463 715 000. e-mail: nsro@rspb.org.uk
www.rspb.org.uk

6. SPEY BAY

Scottish Wildlife Trust.
Location: NJ 335 657. Eight miles NE of Elgin. From Elgin take A96 and B9015 to Kingston. Reserve is immediately E of village. Car parks at Kingston and Tugnet.
Access: Open all year.
Facilities: Car park, information board.
Public transport: None.
Habitat: Shingle, rivermouth and coastal habitats.
Key birds: *Summer:* Osprey, waders, wildfowl. *Winter:* Seaduck and divers offshore, esp. Long-tailed Duck, Common and Velvet Scoters, Red-throated Diver.
Contact: SWT Headquarters. 0131 312 7765.

7. TROUP HEAD

RSPB (East Scotland).
Location: NJ 825 672. Troup Head is between Pennan and Gardenstown on B9031, E along coast from Macduff. It is signposted off B9031. Look for small RSPB signs which direct you past the farm buildings to car park.
Access: Unrestricted, but not suitable for wheelchair users. **Facilities:** Parking for small number of cars. Not suitable for coaches. Live pictures are beamed from the reserve to the Macduff Marine Aquarium during the summer. Boat trips run from Macduff (contact Puffin Cruises 07900 920 445) and Banff or Gardenstown (contact North 580 01261 819 900).
Public transport: None.
Habitat: Sea cliffs, farmland.
Key birds: Spectacular seabird colony, including Scotland's only mainland nesting Gannets. Bonxies linger in summer. Migrants occur during spring/ autumn.
Other notable flora and fauna: Impressive common flower assemblage in spring. Ceteaceans possible offshore in summer including minke whale. Brown hare common.

Contact: RSPB Troup Head Warden , c/o Starnafin Farmhouse, Crimond, Fraserburgh AB43 8QN. 01346 532 017. E-mail: troup@rspb.org.uk

NE Scotland

8. FORVIE NNR

Scottish Natural Heritage.
Location: NK 034 289.
Access: Dogs on leads only. Reserve open at all times but ternery closed Apr 1-end of Aug annually. Stevenson Forvie Centre open every day (Apr-Sept) and, when staff are available, outside those months. Wheelchair access to the centre.
Facilities: Interpretive display and toilets in Stevenson Forvie Centre. Bird hide, waymarked trail. Space is available for coach parking at the Stevenson Forvie Centre or at Waterside Car Park.
Public transport: Bluebird No 263 to Cruden Bay. Ask for the Newburgh or Collieston Crossroads stop. Tel: 01224 591 381.
Habitat: Estuary, dunes, coastal heath.
Key birds: *Spring/summer:* Eider and terns nesting. *Winter:* Waders and wildfowl on estuary.
Contact: Annabel Drysdale (Reserve Manager), Scottish Natural Heritage, Stevenson Forvie Centre, Little Collieston Croft, Collieston, Aberdeenshire AB41 8RU. 01358 751 330. www.snh.org.uk B

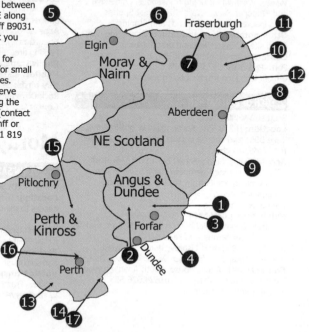

9. FOWLSHEUGH

RSPB
Location: NO 879 80. Cliff top path N from Crawton, signposted from A92, three miles S of Stonehaven.
Access: Unrestricted. Not suitable for wheelchair users.
Facilities: Car park with 12 spaces, 200 yards from reserve.
Public transport: Request bus stop (Stonehaven to Johnshaven route). Mile walk to reserve entrance.
Habitat: Sea cliffs.
Key birds: Spectacular seabird colony, mainly Kittiwakes and Guillemots, plus many Razorbills, Fulmars and Puffins. Bonxies lingering in summer.
Other notable flora and fauna: Grey and common seals, bottle-nosed dolphin regular, white-beaked dolphin and minke whale occasional in summer. Spring flowers and common butterflies and moths.
Contact: RSPB Fowlsheugh Warden , c/o Starnafin Farmhouse, Crimond, Fraserburgh AB43 8QN. 01346 532 017. e-mail: strathbeg@rspb.org.uk www.rspb.org.uk

10. HADDO COUNTRY PARK

Aberdeenshire Council.
Location: NJ 875 345. On the A90 Aberdeen-Peterhead road. After Bridge of Don, turn on to the B999. Continue to Tarves for about 20km and pick up signs for Haddo House.
Access: Open all year.
Facilities: Car parks, display boards, more than 5,000m of surfaced paths, toilets open all year (inc disabled) and bird hides with wheelchair access. Coach parking.
Public transport: Bus: Aberdeen-Tarves stop 3.2km from house. Call Stagecoach on 01224 212 266.
Habitat: Parkland, woodland, wetland, loch, ponds.
Key birds: *Spring/summer:* Sedge Warbler, Blackcap, Chiffchaff, Lapwing. *Winter:* Canada and Greylag geese, Teal, Wigeon, Goldeneye, Goosander, Brambling. *All year:* Buzzard, Sparrowhawk, Grey Partridge, Great Spotted Woodpecker, Grey Wagtail, Tawny Owl, herons, Mute Swan, Cormorant.
Other notable flora and fauna: Meadow brown, ringlet and common blue butterflies, burnet moths, blue damselfly. Plants include eyebright, yellow rattle, meadow cranesbill, meadowsweet, angelica, rock rose, valerian, tansy. Fauna includes red squirrels and pipistrelle bats.
Contact: Aberdeenshire Council Ranger Service, 29 Bridge Street, Ellon, AB41 9QX. 01358 726 417. e-mail: formartine.ranger@aberdeenshire.gov.uk

11. LOCH OF STRATHBEG

RSPB.
Location: NK 057 581. Near Crimond on the A90, nine miles S of Fraserburgh.

Access: Visitor Centre open daily 8am - 6pm. Tower Pool hide open dawn-dusk. Loch hides open 8am - 4pm. Visitor centre wheelchair accessible. Coach parking available but book in advance.
Facilities: Visitor centre, with toilets and coffee machine. Tower Pool hide accessible via 700 metre footpath. Two hides overlooking loch accessed via drive to airfield. Wildlife garden, indoor children's area - kid's backpacks available to borrow.
Public transport: Access to whole reserve difficult without vehicle. Buses from Fraserburgh and Peterhead to Crimond, one mile from centre. Details at www.travelinescotland.com.
Habitat: Dune loch with surrounding marshes, reedbeds, grasslands and dunes.
Key birds: Breeding wetland species, passage waders, internationally important numbers of wintering wildfowl. Scarcities year round. *Winter:* Pink-footed and Barnacle Geese, Whooper Swan, large numbers of duck. Snow Goose and Smew annual. Raptors including Hen Harrier. Great Northern Diver offshore. *Summer:* Common Tern, Water Rail, Corn Bunting. *Spring/autumn:* Little Egret, Spoonbill, Avocet, Marsh Harrier, Garganey, Little Gull, Pectoral Sandpiper.
Other notable flora and fauna: Otter, dark green fritillary.
Contact: RSPB Loch of Strathbeg, Starnafin, Crimond, Fraserburgh, AB43 8QN. 01346 532 017. e-mail: strathbeg@rspb.org.uk www.rspb.org.uk/reserves/guide/l/lochofstrathbeg

12. LONGHAVEN CLIFFS

Scottish Wildlife Trust.
Location: NK 116 394. 3.8 miles S of Peterhead. Take A952 S from Peterhead and then A975 to Bullers of Buchan (gorge).
Access: Access from car park at Blackhills quarry or Bullers of Buchan.
Facilities: Leaflet available. Parking.
Habitat: Rugged red granite cliffs and cliff-top vegetation.
Key birds: May-July: Nine species of breeding seabird, including Kittiwake, Shag, Guillemot, Razorbill, Puffin.
Contact: SWT Headquarters. 0131 312 7765.

Perth & Kinross

13. DOUNE PONDS

Stirling Council.
Location: NN 726 019. Take the A820 Dunblane road E from the junction with the A84 Callander-Stirling road. Turn L onto Moray Street just before Doune Church.
Access: Open all year.
Facilities: Information board, nature trail, hides.

Wheelchair access to both hides. Leaflet from local tourist information offices, local library.
Public transport: Bus: from Stirling and Callander to Doune. Traveline 0870 608 2608.
Habitat: Pools, scrape, plantations, birch woodlands.
Key birds: *All year*: Grey Heron, Buzzard, Snipe, Goldcrest, Siskin, Red Kite. *Spring/summer*: Common Sandpiper, Whitethroat, warblers.
Contact: Stirling Council Countryside Ranger Service, Viewforth, Stirling FK8 2ET. 0845 2777 000.

14. LOCH LEVEN NNR

SNH / Loch Leven Laboratory.
Location: NO 150 010. Head S from Perth and leave M90 at exit 6, to Kinross.
Access: Traditional access areas at three stretches of shoreline. New local access guidance is in place at the site. See www.snh.org.uk for details or pick up leaflet locally. New paths are in place between Kinross and Burleigh Sands.
Facilities: Hides and paths along the west shore. Café and toilets at Kinross harbour. Observation room, café, shop and toilets at Vane Farm.
Public transport: Bus from Perth or Edinburgh to Kinross. **Habitat:** Lowland loch with islands.
Key birds: *Winter*: Flocks of geese (more than 20,000 Pinkfeet), huge numbers of the full range of ducks, Whooper Swan. *Summer*: Greatest concentration of inland breeding ducks in Britain (10 species), Ospreys and grebes. *Passage*: Waders (Golden Plover flocks up to 500).
Contact: SNH, Loch Leven Laboratory, The Pier, Kinross KY13 8UF. 01577 864 439. www.snh.org.uk

15. LOCH OF THE LOWES

Scottish Wildlife Trust.
Location: NO 042 435. Sixteen miles N of Perth, two miles NE of Dunkeld – just off A923 (signposted).
Access: Visitor centre open Apr-Sept inclusive (10am-5pm). Observation hide open all year – daylight hours. No dogs allowed. Full access for wheelchairs.
Facilities: Visitor centre with toilets, hide.
Public transport: Railway station – Birnam/Dunkeld – three miles from reserve. Bus from Dunkeld – two miles from reserve.
Habitat: Freshwater loch with fringing woodland.
Key birds: Breeding Ospreys (Apr-end Aug). Nest in view, 200 metres from hide. Wildfowl and woodland birds. Greylag roost (Oct-Mar).
Contact: Peter Ferns, (Manager), Scottish Wildlife Trust, Loch of the Lowes, Visitor Centre, Dunkeld, Perthshire PH8 0HH. 01350 727 337.

16. QUARRYMILL WOODLAND PARK

Gannochy Trust.
Location: NO 121 253. From Perth on the A93, cross the River Tay. Follow it on the Isla Road to Blairgowrie. The Park is signposted on the R, opposite the Upper Springland building.
Access: Open all year.
Facilities: Visitor centre, coffee shop with disabled facilities. Dogs on leads.
Public transport: Bus: Perth to Blairgowrie stops at Quarrymill. Tel: 0870 550 5050.
Habitat: Wood, stream.
Key birds: *Spring/summer:* Blackcap, Willow and Garden Warblers, Spotted Flycatcher, Chiffchaff. *All year:* Buzzard, Great Spotted Woodpecker, Jay, Goldcrest. Possible Mandarin.
Contact: Isle Road, Perth, Perthshire, 01738 633 890.

17. VANE FARM NNR

RSPB Scotland
Location: NT 160 990. By Loch Leven. Well signposted two miles E of J5 from M90 onto B9097. Drive for approx two miles. The nature centre car park is on R.
Access: Open daily (10am-5pm) except Christmas Day, Boxing Day, Jan 1 and Jan 2. Cost £3 adults, £2 concessions, 50p children, £6 family. Free to members. No dogs except guide dogs. Disabled access to shop, coffee shop, observation room and toilets. Parking available for two coaches. Free car parking.
Facilities: Shop, coffee shop and observation room overlooking Loch Leven and the reserve with five telescopes. There is a 1.25 mile hill trail through woodland and moorland. Wetland trail with three observation hides. Toilets, including disabled. binoculars can be hired from shop.
Public transport: Trains to Cowdenbeath (seven miles). There is no public transport from here. A limited bus service (204) runs to the reserve from Kinross (4 miles) on Wednesdays and Saturdays. Contact Stagecoach Fife on 01383 511911 for further details.
Habitat: Wet grassland and flooded areas by Loch Leven. Arable farmland. Native woodland and heath moorland.
Key birds: *Spring/summer*: Breeding and passage waders (including Lapwing, Redshank, Snipe, Curlew). Farmland birds (including Sky Lark and Yellowhammer), Tree Pipit. *Autumn*: Migrating waders on exposed mud. *Winter*: Whooper Swan, Bewick's Swan, Pink-footed Goose, finch and tit flocks.
Other notable flora and fauna: 237 butterfly and moth species. 25 mammal species including pipstrelle bat and roe deer.
Contact: Uwe Stoneman, Business Manager, Vane Farm Nature Centre, Kinross, Tayside KY13 9LX. 01577 862 355.
e-mail: vanefarm@rspb.co.uk

Highlands & Islands

Highlands & Caithness

1. ABERNETHY FOREST RESERVE – LOCH GARTEN

RSPB (North Scotland Office).
Location: NH 981 184. 2.5 miles from Boat of Garten, eight miles from Aviemore. Off B970, follow 'RSPB Ospreys' road signs (between Apr - Aug only).
Access: Osprey Centre open daily 10am-6pm (Apr to end Aug). Disabled access. No dogs (guide dogs only). No charge to RSPB members. Non-members: adults £3, senior citizens £2, children 50p.
Facilities: Osprey Centre overlooking nesting Ospreys. Toilets, optics and CCTV live pictures.
Public transport: Bus service to Boat of Garten from Aviemore, 2.5 mile footpath to Osprey Centre. Steam railway to Boat of Garten from Aviemore.
Habitat: Caledonian pine wood.
Key birds: Ospreys nesting from Apr to Aug), Crested Tit, Crossbill. Possible views of lekking Capercaillies from the hide, Apr to mid-May.
Other notable flora and fauna: Red squirrel, otter, fungi.
Contact: R W Thaxton, RSPB, Forest Lodge, Nethybridge, Inverness-shire PH25 3EF. 01479 821 894.

2. FORSINARD

RSPB (North Scotland Office).
Location: NC 890 425. 30 miles SW of Thurso on A897. Turn off at Helmsdale from S (24 miles) or A836 at Melvich from N coast road (14 miles).
Access: Open at all times. Contact reserve office during breeding season (mid-Apr to end Jul) and during deerstalking season (Jul 1 to Feb 15) for advice. Families welcome. Self-guided trail open all year. No dogs. Terrain not suitable for wheelchairs.
Facilities: Visitor centre open Apr 1 to Oct 31 (9am-5.30pm), seven days per week. Static and AV displays, Hen Harrier nest CCTV. Wheelchair access to centre and toilet. Guided walks Tue and Thu afternoon, May-Aug. Hotel and B&B nearby.
Public transport: Train from Inverness and Thurso (08457 484 950) – RSPB visitor centre in former Forsinard Station building.
Habitat: Blanket bog, upland hill farm.
Key birds: The best time to visit for birds is May-July. Red-throated Diver, Golden Plover, Greenshank, Dunlin, Hen Harrier, Merlin, Short-eared Owl. Join a guided walk for the best chance of views. Few birds Sep-Feb.

Other notable flora and fauna: Red deer, azure hawker dragonfly, emperor moth.
Contact: RSPB, Forsinard Flows Reserve Office, Forsinard, Sutherland KW13 6YT. 01641 571 225.
e-mail: forsinard@rspb.org.uk
www.rspb.org.uk

3. INSH MARSHES

RSPB (North Scotland Office).
Location: NN 775 999. In Spey Valley, two miles NE of Kingussie on B970 minor road.
Access: Open at all times. No disabled access. Coach parking available along access road to car park.
Facilities: Information viewpoint, two hides, three nature trails. Not suitable for disabled. No toilets.
Public transport: Nearest rail station Kingussie (two miles).
Habitat: Marshes, woodland, river, open water.
Key birds: *Spring/summer*: Waders (Lapwing, Curlew, Redshank, Snipe), wildfowl (including Goldeneye and Wigeon), Wood Warbler, Redstart, Tree Pipit. *Winter*: Hen Harrier, Whooper Swan, other wildfowl.
Other notable flora and fauna: Black and highland darter dragonflies along Invertromie trail plus northern brown argus butterflies. Five species of orchid in Tromie Meadow. Roe deer.
Contact: Pete Moore, Ivy Cottage, Insh, Kingussie, Inverness-shire PH21 1NT. 01540 661 518.
e-mail: pete.moore@rspb.org.uk
www.visitkincraig.com

4. ISLE OF EIGG

Scottish Wildlife Trust.
Location: NM 38 48. Small island S of Skye, reached by ferry from Mallaig or Arisaig (approx 12 miles).
Access: Ferries seven days per week (weather permitting) during summer. Four days per week (weather permitting) Sept-Apr. Coach parties would need to transfer to ferries for visit to Eigg. Please contact ferry companies prior to trip.
Facilities: Pier centre – shops/Post Office, tea-room, craftshop, toilets.
Public transport: Train service from Glasgow, via Arisaig to Mallaig. Cal-Mac ferries (no sailing Wed and Sun), MV Sheerwater (no sailing Thurs). Island minibus/taxi usually available at the pier.
Habitat: Moorland (leading to sgurr pitchstone ridge), extensive woodland and scrub, marshland, and bog, haymeadows, sandy bays and rocky shorelines.

227

Key birds: *All year*: Red-throated Diver, Golden Eagle, Hen Harrier, Woodcock, Raven. *Summer*: Cuckoo, Whinchat, wheatear, various warblers, Twite.

Other notable flora and fauna: 17 species of butterfly recorded including green hairstreak, small pearl-bordered and dark green fritillaries. Nine species of damsel/dragonfly occur with golden ringed, common hawker and highland darter the most numerous.

Approx 500 species of 'higher' plants listed, including 12 species of orchid, and alpine/arctic species such as mountain aven and moss campion. Carpet of primroses, bluebells and wild garlic in spring. Otters not uncommon and minke whales, bottle-nosed and common dolphins and harbour porpoises regularly recorded offshore. Basking sharks can be quite numerous in early summer.

Contact: John Chester, Millers Cottage, Isle of Eigg, Small Isles PH42 4RL. 01687 482 477.
www.isleofeigg.org

5. BEINN EIGHE

Scottish Natural Heritage.
Location: NG 990 620. By Kinlochewe, Wester Ross, 50 miles from Inverness and 20 miles from Gairloch on A832.
Access: Reserve open at all times, no charge. Visitor centre open Easter-Oct (10am-5pm).
Facilities: Visitor centre, toilets, woodland trail and mountain trail – self-guided with leaflets from visitor centre. Trails suitable for all abilities.
Public transport: Very limited.
Habitat: Caledonian pine forest, dwarf shrub heath, mountain tops, freshwater loch shore.
Key birds: Golden Eagle, Scottish Crossbill, Ptarmigan, Red Grouse, Siskin. Summer: Black-throated Diver, Redwing, Snow Bunting.
Other notable flora and fauna: Wide range of dragonflies, including golden ringed and common hawker.
Contact: Eughain Maclean, Reserve Manager, Scottish Natural Heritage, Anancaun, Kinlochewe, Ross-shire IV22 2PD. 01445 760 254.
e-mail: david.miller@snh.gov.uk

6. HANDA

Scottish Wildlife Trust.
Location: NC 138 480. Accessible by boat from Tarbet, near Scourie – follow A894 N from Ullapool 40 miles. Continue another three miles, turn L down single track road for another three miles to Tarbet.
Access: Open April-Sept. Boats leave 9.30am-2pm (last boat back 5pm). Dogs not allowed. Visitors are asked for a contribution of £2 towards costs. Not suitable for disabled due to uneven terrain.
Facilities: Three mile circular path, shelter (no toilets on island - use those in Tarbet car park). Visitors are given introductory talk and a leaflet with

map on arrival.
Public transport: Post bus to Scourie (tel 01549 402357 Lairg Post Office). Train to Lairg (tel 0845 484950 National Train enquiries). No connecting public transport between Scourie and Tarbet.
Habitat: Sea cliffs, blanket bog.
Key birds: *Spring/summer:* Biggest Guillemot and Razorbill colony in Britain and Ireland. Also nationally important for Kittiwakes, Arctic and Great Skuas. Puffin, Shag, Fulmar and Common and Arctic Terns also present.
Contact: Mark Foxwell, Conservation Manager, Unit 4A, 3 Carsegate Road North, Inverness IV3 8PU. 01463 714 746
Charles Thomson (Boatman) 01971 502 347.
e-mail: mfoxwell@swt.org.uk www.swt.org.uk a

7. ISLE OF RUM

Scottish Natural Heritage
Location: NM 370 970. Island lying S of Skye. Passenger ferry from Mallaig, take A830 from Fort William.
Access: Contact Reserve Office for details of special access arrangements relating to breeding birds, deer stalking and deer research.
Facilities: Kinloch Castle Hostel, 01687 462 037, Lea Cottage B&B, 01687 462 036. General store and post office, Kinloch Castle tea shop and bar. Guided walks in summer.
Public transport: The Shearwater boat from Arisaig - 01687 450 224, also Caledonian MacBrayne ferry from Mallaig, 01687 450224, www.arisaig.co.uk
Habitat: Coast, moorland, woodland restoration, montane.
Key birds: *Summer*: Unique mountain top Manx Shearwater colony (one third of the world population). Seabird breeding colony including auks, Kittiwake, Fulmar, Eider, Shag. Gull colonies including Common, Herring, Lesser and Greater Black-backed. Upland breeding species including Golden Plover, Wheatear, Merlin, Kestrel. *Late autumn/spring*: Thrush passage. *Winter*: Greylag Goose, Oystercatcher, Red-breasted Merganser.
Other notable flora and fauna: Butterflies including small white, green-veined, large white, green hairstreak, small copper, common blue, red admiral, small tortoiseshell, dark green fritillary, peacock etc. Various dragonflies. Heath spotted orchid. Feral goat, red deer, otter, Rhum highland pony, palmate newt, lizard.
Contact: SNH Reserve Office, Isle of Rum, PH43 4RR. 01687 462 026; Fax 01687 462805.

8. LOCH FLEET

Scottish Wildlife Trust.
Location: NH 794 965. Site lies two miles S of Golspie on the A9 and five miles N of Dornoch. View across tidal basin from A9 or unclassified road to Skelbo.

Access: Park at Little Ferry or in lay-bys around the basin.
Facilities: Guided walks in summer. Interpretive centre.
Public transport: None.
Habitat: Tidal basin, sand dunes, shingle, woodland, marshes.
Key birds: Winter: Important feeding place for ducks and waders. The sea off the mouth of Loch Fleet is a major wintering area for Long-tailed Duck, Common and Velvet Scoters, Eider Duck. In pine wood off minor road S from Golspie to Little Ferry: Crossbill, occasional Crested Tit.
Contact: SWT headquarters 01313 127 765.

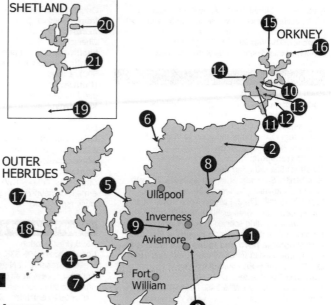

9. LOCH RUTHVEN

RSPB (North Scotland Office).
Location: NH 638 281. From Inverness, take A9 SE to junction with B851. Head SW until the minor road NE at Croachy; car park one mile.
Access: Open at all times.
Facilities: Hide, car park.
Public transport: None.
Habitat: Freshwater loch and woodland.
Key birds: Best breeding site in Britain for Slavonian Grebe. Teal, Wigeon and other wildfowl breed. Peregrine, Hen Harrier and Osprey often seen.
Contact: RSPB North Scotland Office. Etive House, Beechwood Park, Inverness IV2 3BW. 01463 715 000.
e-mail: nsro@rspb.org.uk

Orkney

10. BIRSAY MOORS

RSPB (East Scotland).
Location: Access to hide at Burgar Hill (HY 344 257), signposted from A966 at Evie. Birsay Moors viewed from layby on B9057 NW of Dounby (HY 347 245).
Access: Open access all year round.
Facilities: One hide at Burgar Hill very good for watching breeding Red-throated Divers Apr to Aug. Wheelchair access.
Public transport: Orkney Coaches. Service stops within 0.5 mile of reserve. Tel: 01856 870 555.
Habitat: Diverse example of Orkney moorland – wet and dry heath, bog, mire, scrub and some farmland.

Key birds: Spring/summer: Nesting Hen Harrier, Merlin, Great and Arctic Skuas, Short-eared Owl, Golden Plover, Curlew, Red-throated Diver. Winter: Hen Harrier roost.
Contact: The Warden, 12/14 North End Road, Stromness, Orkney KW16 3AG. 01856 850 176.
e-mail: orkney@rspb.org.uk www.rspb.co.uk

11. BRODGAR

RSPB (East Scotland).
Location: HY 296 134. Reserve surrounds the Ring of Brodgar, part of the Heart of Neolithic Orkney World Heritage Site on the B9055 off the Stromness-Finstown Road.
Access: Open all year.
Facilities: Footpath, circular route approx one mile.
Public transport: Orkney Coaches. Service within 0.5 mile of reserve. Tel: 01856 870 555. Occasional service past reserve.
Habitat: Wetland and farmland including species rich grassland, loch shores.
Key birds: Spring/summer: Breeding waterfowl on farmland and nine species of waders breed here. The farmed grassland is suitable for Corn Crake and provides water, food and shelter for finches, larks and buntings. Winter: Large numbers of Golden Plover, Curlew and Lapwing.
Other notable flora and fauna: A hotspot for

great yellow bumblebee in August. Possibility of otter, while common seals haul out nearby on Loch of Stenness.
Contact: The Warden, 01856 850 176.
e-mail: orkney@rspb.org.uk www.rspb.co.uk

12. COPINSAY

RSPB (East Scotland).
Location: HY 610 010. Access by private boat or hire boat from mainland Orkney.
Access: Open all year round.
Facilities: House on island open to visitors, but no facilities. No toilets or hides.
Public transport: None.
Habitat: Sea cliffs, farmland.
Key birds: *Summer:* Stunning seabird-cliffs with breeding Kittiwake, Guillemot, Black Guillemot, Puffin, Razorbill, Shag, Fulmar, Rock Dove, Eider, Twite, Raven and Greater Black-backed Gull, Great Skua (new breeding species in recent years). Passage migrants esp. during periods of E winds.
Other notable flora and fauna: The island is a key breeding location for Atlantic grey seals from Oct-Dec. 2,385 pups counted in 2006.
Contact: The Warden, 12/14 North End Road, Stromness, Orkney KW16 3AG. 01856 850 176.
e-mail: orkney@rspb.org.uk   www.rspb.co.uk
S Foubisher (boatman) 01856 741252 - cannot sail if wind is in the east

13. HOBBISTER

RSPB (East Scotland).
Location: HY 396 070 or HY 381 068. Near Kirkwall.
Access: Open access between A964 and the sea. Dogs on leads please.
Facilities: A council-maintained footpath to Waulkmill Bay, two car parks. New circular walk from RSPB car park along cliff top and Scapa Flow.
Public transport: Orkney Coaches. Tel: 01856 877 500.
Habitat: Orkney moorland, bog, fen, saltmarsh, coastal cliffs, scrub.
Key birds: *Summer:* Breeding Hen Harrier, Merlin, Short-eared Owl, Red Grouse, Red-throated Diver, Eider, Merganser, Black Guillemot. Wildfowl and waders at Waulkmill Bay. *Autumn/winter:* Waulkmill for sea ducks, divers, auks and grebes (Long-tailed Duck, Red-throated, Black-throated and Great Northern Divers, Slavonian Grebe).
Other notable flora and fauna: Otter occasionally seen from the Scapa trail. Grey and common seal both possible towards Scapa Flow.
Contact: The Warden, 01856 850 176.
e-mail: orkney@rspb.org.uk www.rspb.co.uk

14. MARWICK HEAD

RSPB (East Scotland).
Location: HY 229 242. On W coast of mainland

Orkney, near Dounby. Path N from Marwick Bay, or from council car park at Cumlaquoy at HY 232 252.
Access: Open all year. Rough terrain not suitable for wheelchairs.
Facilities: Cliff top path.
Public transport: Orkney Coaches (01856 877 500), 1 mile.
Habitat: Rocky bay, sandstone cliffs. Beach path good place for great yellow bumble bee in Aug.
Key birds: May-Jul best. Huge numbers of Kittiwakes and auks, inc. Puffins, also nesting Fulmar, Rock Dove, Raven, Rock Pipit.
Other notable flora and fauna: Cetaceans are a possibility from Marwick with porpoise and minke whale occasionally seen.
Contact: The Warden, 12/14 North End Road, Stromness, Orkney KW16 3AG. 01856 850 176.
e-mail: orkney@rspb.org.uk
www.rspb.co.uk

15. NORTH HILL, PAPA WESTRAY

RSPB (East Scotland).
Location: HY 496 538. Small island lying NE of Westray, reserve at N end of island's main road.
Access: Access at all times. During breeding season report to summer warden at Rose Cottage, 650 yards S of reserve entrance (Tel 01857 644240) or use trail guide.
Facilities: Nature trails, hide/info hut.
Public transport: Orkney Ferries (01856 872044), Loganair (01856 872494).
Habitat: Sea cliffs, maritime heath.
Key birds: *Summer:* Close views of colony of Puffin, Guillemot, Razorbill and Kittiwake. Black Guillemot nest under flagstones around reserve's coastline. One of UK's largest colonies of Arctic Tern, also Arctic Skua.
Other notable flora and fauna: North Hill is one of the best areas to see 'Scottish primrose' (*primula scotica*) which has two flowering periods that just overlap (May-Aug).
Contact (Apr-Aug): The Warden at Rose Cottage, Papay Westray DW17 2BU. 01857 644240.
RSPB Orkney Office 01856 850 176.

16. NORTH RONALDSAY BIRD OBSERVATORY

Location: HY 64 52. 35 miles from Kirkwall, Orkney mainland.
Access: Open all year except Christmas.
Facilities: Three star guest house and hostel accommodation, restaurant, cafe, fully licenced, croft walk.
Public transport: Daily subsidised flights from Kirkwall (Loganair 01856 872 494). Once weekly ferry from Kirkwall (Fri or Sat), Tuesday and some Sunday sailings in summer (Orkney Ferries Ltd 01856 872 044).
Habitat: Crofting island with a number of eutrophic and oligotrophic wetlands. Coastline has both sandy

bays and rocky shore. Walled gardens concentrate passerines.
Key birds: Prime migration site in *Spring/Autumn* including regular BBRC species. Wide variety of breeding seabirds, wildfowl and waders. *Winter*: Waders and wildfowl include Whooper Swan and hard weather movements occur.
Contact: Alison Duncan, North Ronaldsay Bird Observatory, Twingness, North Ronaldsay, Orkney KW17 2BE. 01857 633 200. www.nrbo.f2s.com
e-mail: alison@nrbo.prestel.co.uk

Outer Hebrides

17. BALRANALD

RSPB (North Scotland Office).
Location: NF 705 707. From Skye take ferry to Lochmaddy, North Uist. Drive W on A867 for 20 miles to reserve. Turn off main road three miles NW of Bayhead at signpost to Houghharry.
Access: Open at all times, no charge. Dogs on leads. Disabled access.
Facilities: Visitor Centre and toilets – disabled access. Marked nature trail.
Public transport: Bus service (tel 01876 560 244).
Habitat: Freshwater loch, machair, coast and croft lands.
Key birds: *Summer*: Corn Crake, Corn Bunting, Lapwing, Oystercatcher, Dunlin, Ringed Plover, Redshank, Snipe. *Winter*: Twite, Greylag Goose, Wigeon, Teal, Shoveler. *Passage*: Barnacle Goose, Pomarine Skua, Long-tailed Skua.
Contact: Jamie Boyle, 9 Grenitote, Isle of North Uist, H56 5BP. 01876 560 287.
e-mail: james.boyle3@btinternet.com

18. LOCH DRUIDIBEG NNR

SNH (Western Isles Area).
Location: NF 782 378. Reserve of 1,577 ha on South Uist.
Access: Open all year. Several tracks and one walk covering a range of habitats – most not suitable for wheelchair use. Stout footwear essential. Observe National Access Code in all areas with livestock. View of E part of reserve from public roads but parking and turning areas for coaches is limited.
Facilities: None.
Public transport: Regular bus service stops at reserve. Hebridean Coaches 01870 620 345, MacDonald Coaches 01870 620 288. Large print timetable - call 01851 709 592.
Habitat: Range of freshwater lochs and marshes, machair, coast and moorland.
Key birds: *Summer*: Breeding waders, Corn Crake, wildfowl, terns and raptors. *Spring and autumn*: Migrant waders and wildfowl. *Winter*: Waders, wildfowl and raptors.

Contact: SNH Area Officer, SNH Office, Stilligarry, South Uist, HS8 5RS. 01870 620 238; Fax 01870 620 350. website: www.nnr-scotland.org.uk

Shetland

19. FAIR ISLE BIRD OBSERVATORY

Fair Isle Bird Observatory.
Location: HZ 2172.
Access: Open from end Apr-end Oct. Free to roam.
Facilities: Public toilets at Airstrip and Stackhoull Stores (shop). Accommodation at Fair Isle Bird Observatory (phone/e-mail: for brochure/details). Guests can be involved in observatory work and get to see birds in the hand. Slide shows, guided walks through Ranger Service.
Public transport: Tue, Thurs, Sat – ferry (12 passengers) from Grutness, Shetland. Tel: Neil or Pat Thomson on 01595 760 363.
Mon, Wed, Fri, Sat – air (7 seater) from Tingwall, Shetland. Tel: Direct Flight 01595 840 246.
Habitat: Heather moor and lowland pasture/crofting land. Cliffs.
Key birds: Large breeding seabird colonies (auks, Gannet, Arctic Tern, Kittiwake, Shag, Arctic Skua and Great Skua). Many common and rare migrants Apr/May/early Jun, late Aug-Nov.
Other notable flora and fauna: Northern marsh, heath spotted and frog orchid, lesser twayblade, small adders tongue, oyster plant. Orca, minke whale, white-backed, white-sided and Risso's dolphins. Endemic field mouse.
Contact: Deryk Shaw (Warden), Hollie Shaw (Administrator), Fair Isle Bird Observatory, Fair Isle, Shetland ZE2 9JU. 01595 760 258.
e-mail: fairisle.birdobs@zetnet.co.uk
www.fairislebirdobs.co.uk

20. FETLAR

RSPB Scotland
Location: HU 603 917. Lies E of Yell. Take car ferry from Gutcher, N Yell. Booking advised. Tel: 01957 722 259.
Access: Apart from the footpath to Hjaltadance circle, Vord Hill, the Special Protection Area is closed mid May to end July. Entry during this period is only by arrangement with warden. Hide at Mires of Funzie open Apr-Nov.
Facilities: Hide at Mires of Funzie. Toilets and payphone at ferry terminal, interpretive centre at Houbie, campsite, shop.
Public transport: None.
Habitat: Serpentine heath, rough hill lane, upland mire.
Key birds: *Summer*: Breeding Red-throated Diver, Eider, Shag, Whimbrel, Golden Plover, Dunlin, skuas, Manx Shearwater, Storm Petrel. Red-necked

Phalarope on Loch of Funzie (HU 655 899) viewed from road or RSPB hide overlooking Mires of Funzie.
Other notable flora and fauna: Heath spotted orchid and autumn gentian. Otters are common, harbour and grey seals breed.
Contact: RSPB North Isles Warden, Bealance, Fetlar, Shetland ZE2 9DJ. Tel/Fax: 01957 733 246.
e-mail: malcolm.smith@rspb.org.uk

21. NOSS NNR

Scottish Natural Heritage (Shetland Office).
Location: HU 531 410. Take car ferry to Bressay from Lerwick and follow signs for Noss (5km). At end of road walk to shore (600 mtrs) where inflatable ferry (passenger only) to island will collect you (if red flag is flying, island is closed due to sea conditions). Freephone 0800 107 7818 for daily ferry information.
Access: Access (Tue, Wed, Fri, Sat, Sun) 10am-5pm, late Apr-late Aug. Access by zodiac inflatable. Sorry, no dogs allowed on ferry. Steep rough track down to ferry. Groups or anyone requiring asistance

to board ferry should contact SNH as far in advance as possible.
Facilities: Visitor centre, toilets. Bike rack/car park on Bressay side. Parking for small coaches.
Public transport: None. Post bus available, phone Royal Mail on 01595 820 200. Cycle hire in Lerwick.
Habitat: Dune and coastal grassland, moorland, heath, blanket bog, sea cliffs.
Key birds: *Spring/summer:* Breeding Fulmar, Shag, Gannet, Arctic Tern, Kittiwake, Herring and Great Black-backed Gull, Great Skua, Arctic Skua, Guillemot, Razorbill, Puffin, Black Guillemot, Eider, Lapwing, Dunlin, Snipe, Wheatear, Twite plus migrant birds at any time.
Other notable flora and fauna: Grey and common seals, otter porpoise regularly seen, killer whales annual in recent years.
Contact: Simon Smith, Scottish Natural Heritage, Stewart Building, Alexandra Wharf, Lerwick, Shetland ZE1 0LL. 01595 693 345.
e-mail: noss_nnr@snh.gov.uk

CHANNEL ISLANDS

COLIN McCATHIE RESERVE

La Société Guernesiaise.
Location: Perry's Island Guide for Guernsey (page 6 B5).
Access: Open at all times.
Facilities: Hide on road to Vale Church must be used.
Public transport: Hourly bus service 7/7A (island circular), tel: 01481 720 210.
Habitat: Brackish tidal pond, reed fringes.
Key birds: Passage waders. *Summer:* Breeding Reed Warbler, Moorhen, Coot. *Winter:* Wildfowl, Water Rail, Little Egret, Snipe, Kingfisher.
Contact: Vic Froome, La Cloture, Courtil de Bas Lane, St Sampson's, Guernsey GY2 4XJ. 01481 254 841. www.societe.org.gg

LA CLAIRE MARE

La Société Guernesiaise.
Location: *Perry's Island Guide* for Guernsey (page 12 C5).
Access: Open at all times.
Facilities: Hide down concrete track off the Rue de la Rocque Road then footpath to second hide.
Public transport: Hourly bus service 7/7A (island circular), tel: 01481 720 210.

Habitat: Reedbeds, pasture, willow thickets, scrape.
Key birds: Passage waders and passerines.
Summer: Breeding Reed Warbler, Moorhen, Coot, Kestrel. *Winter:* Wildfowl, Water Rail, Snipe, Kingfisher.
Contact: Vic Froome, La Cloture, Courtil de Bas Lane, St Sampson's, Guernsey GY2 4XJ. 01481 254 841. www.societe.org.gg

PLEINMONT

La Société Guernesiaise.
Location: Perry's Island Guide for Guernsey (Page 32 B3).
Access: Open at all times.
Facilities: Public footpath around reserve.
Public transport: Hourly bus service 7/7A (island circular) 0.5 miles from Imperial Hotel, tel 01481 720 210.
Habitat: Cliff-top headland of scrub, remnant heathland and small fields.
Key birds: Passage passerines. *Summer:* Breeding Shag, Fulmar, gulls, Dartford Warbler, Whitethroat, Stonechat and Linnet.
Contact: Vic Froome, La Cloture, Courtil Le Bas Lane, St Sampson's, Guernsey GY2 4XT. 01481 254 841. www.societe.org.gg

WALES

East Wales

1. CARNGAFALLT

RSPB Wales
Location: SN 935 653. From Rhayader take the B4518 W to Elan village. Carry on over bridge into Elan village. Continue through village to cattle grid where nature trail starts.
Access: The nature trail is open at all times.
Facilities: Nature trail.
Public transport: None.
Habitat: Ancient oak woodland, grassland and moorland. Spectacular upland scenery.
Key birds: Red Kite, Buzzard, Sparrowhawk, Peregrine, Raven, Green Woodpecker, Grey Wagtail and Marsh Tit are joined in the summer by Pied Flycatcher, Spotted Flycatcher, Wood Warbler, Redstart, Tree Pipit and Cuckoo.
Other notable flora and fauna: Golden-ringed dragonfly, silver-washed, small pearl-bordered and dark-green fritillaries and purple hairstreak butterflies.
Contact: RSPB Ynys-Hir Reserve, Eglwys-fach, Machynlleth, Powys SY20 8TA. 01654 700 222. e-mail: ynyshir@rspb.org.uk

2. DOLYDD HAFREN

Montgomeryshire Wildlife Trust.
Location: SJ 208 005. W of B4388. Go through Forden village and on about 1.5 miles. Turn R at sharp L bend at Gaer Farm and down farm track to car park at the other end.
Access: Open at all times – dogs to be kept on lead at all times.
Facilities: Two bird hides.
Public transport: None.
Habitat: Riverside flood meadow – bare shingle, permanent grassland, ox-bow lakes and new pools.
Key birds: Goosander, Redshank, Lapwing, Snipe, Oystercatcher, Little Ringed Plover, Osprey. *Winter*: Curlew.
Contact: Montgomeryshire Wildlife Trust, Collot House, 20 Severn Street, Welshpool, Powys SY21 7AD. 01938 555 654. e-mail: info@montwt.co.uk www.montwt.co.uk

3. ELAN VALLEY

Dwr Cymru / Welsh Water / Elan Valley Trust.
Location: SN 928 646 (visitor centre). Three miles SW of Rhayader, off B4518.
Access: Mostly open access.
Facilities: Visitor centre and toilets (open mid Mar-end Oct), nature trails all year and hide at SN 905 617.
Public transport: Post bus from Rhayader and Llandrindod Wells.

Habitat: 45,000 acres of moorland, woodland, river and reservoir.
Key birds: *Spring/summer*: Birds of prey, upland birds including Golden Plover and Dunlin. Woodland birds include Redstart and Pied Flycatcher.
Other notable flora and fauna: 27 species of butterfly have been recorded including purple hairstreak. More than 200 species of moth including the emperor. 17 species of dragonfly recorded including golden-ringed. More than 20 mammal species including badger, otter, polecat, mink, stoat and weasel.
Contact: Pete Jennings, Rangers Office, Elan Valley Visitor Centre, Rhayader, Powys LD6 5HP. 01597 810 880. e-mail: pete@elanvalley.org.uk www.elanvalley.org.uk

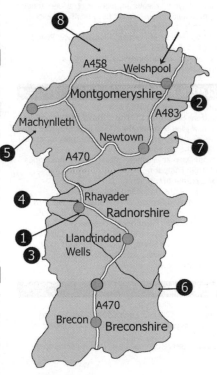

4. GILFACH

Radnorshire Wildlife Trust.
Location: SN 952 714. Two miles NW from Rhayader/ Rhaeadr-Gwy. Take minor road to St Harmon from A470 at Marteg Bridge.
Access: Open every day, all year.
Facilities: Visitor centre opening times may vary – contact Trust for details.
Public transport: None.
Habitat: Upland hill farm, river, oak woods, meadows, hill-land.
Key birds: 73 species of bird recorded on reserve. *Breeding species*: Dipper, Grey Wagtail, Common Sandpiper, Pied Flycatcher, Redstart, Wood Warbler, Tree Pipit, Raven, Whinchat, Stonechat, Linnet, Yellowhammer, Siskin, Redpoll, Marsh and Willow Tit, Stock Dove, Wheatear, Bullfinch, Buzzard, Kestrel, Barn Owl, Spotted Flycatcher, Meadow Pipit, Sky Lark. *All year*: Curlew, Merlin, Red Kite, Goshawk, Sparrowhawk, Peregrine, Goosander, Kingfisher, Reed Bunting.
Other notable flora and fauna: Several dragonfly species. Otter, polecat, badger. bats include Daubenton's, natterers and brown long-eared among the six species recorded. Butterflies incl small heath, green hairstreak, and small pearl-bordered fritillary. Plants incl dyers greenweed, moonwort, adders-tongue fern, mountain pansy, parsley fern, heath dog-violet, and eyebright. Waxcap fungi.
Contact: Gilfach, St Harmon, Rhaeadr-Gwy, Powys LD6 5LF. 01597 823 298.
e-mail: info@radnorshirewildlifetrust.org.uk
www.radnorshirewildlifetrust.org.uk

5. GLASLYN, PLYNLIMON

Montgomeryshire Wildlife Trust.
Location: SN 826 941. Nine miles SE of Machynlleth. Off minor road between the B4518 near Staylittle and the A489 at Machynlleth. Go down the track for about a mile to the car park.
Access: Open at all times – dogs on lead at all times.
Facilities: Footpath.
Public transport: None.
Habitat: Heather moorland and upland lake.
Key birds: Red Grouse, Short-eared Owl, Meadow Pipit, Sky Lark, Wheatear and Ring Ouzel, Red Kite, Merlin, Peregrine. Goldeneye – occasional.
Contact: Montgomeryshire Wildlife Trust, Collot House, 20 Severn Street, Welshpool, Powys SY21 7AD. 01938 555 654. e-mail: info@montwt.co.uk
www.montwt.co.uk

6. PWLL-Y-WRACH

Brecknock Wildlife Trust.
Location: SJ 020 193. Located WSW of Oswestry. Nearest village is Llanfyllin on A490. Take B4393 to lake.
Access: Reserve open all year. Visitor centre open Apr-Dec (10.30am-4.30pm), Dec-Apr weekends only (10.30am-4.30pm).
Facilities: Toilets, visitor centre, hides, nature trails, coffee shop, RSPB shop, craft workshops.
Public transport: Nothing closer than train and bus at Welshpool (25 miles away).
Habitat: Heather moorland, woodland, meadows, rocky streams and large reservoir.
Key birds: Dipper, Kingfisher, Pied Flycatcher, Wood Warbler, Redstart, Peregrine and Buzzard.
Contact: Brecknock Wildlife Trust, Lion House, Bethel Square, Brecon, Powys LD3 7AY. 01874 625 708.
e-mail: enquiries@bricknockwildlifetrust.org.uk
www.brecknockwildlifetrust.org.uk

7. ROUNDTON HILL NNR

Montgomeryshire Wildlife Trust.
Location: SO 293 947. SE of Montgomery. From Churchstoke on A489, take minor road to Old Churchstoke, R at phone box, then first R.
Access: Open access. Tracks rough in places. Dogs on lead at all times.
Facilities: Car park. Waymarked trails.
Public transport: None.
Habitat: Ancient hill grassland, woodland, streamside wet flushes, scree, rock outcrops. Designated SSSI.
Key birds: Peregrine, Buzzard, Raven, Wheatear, all three woodpeckers, Tawny Owl, Redstart, Linnet, Goldfinch.
Other notable flora and fauna: Horseshoe and Daubenton's bats roost. Plants include heath bedstraw, sheep's sorrel and birdsfoot trefoil.
Contact: Montgomeryshire Wildlife Trust, 01938 555 654. e-mail: info@montwt.co.uk
www.montwt.co.uk

8. VYRNWY (LAKE)

RSPB (North Wales Office).
Location: SJ 020 193. Located WSW of Oswestry. Nearest village is Llanfyllin on A490. Take B4393 to lake.
Access: Reserve open all year. Visitor centre open Apr-Dec (10.30am-4.30pm), Dec-Apr weekends only (10.30am-4.30pm).
Facilities: Toilets, visitor centre, hides, nature trails, coffee shop, RSPB shop, craft workshops.
Public transport: Train and bus Welshpool (25 miles away).
Habitat: Heather moorland, woodland, meadows, rocky streams and large reservoir.
Key birds: Dipper, Kingfisher, Pied Flycatcher, Wood Warbler, Redstart, Peregrine and Buzzard.
Other notable flora and fauna: Mammals include otter, mink, brown hare. Golden-ringed dragonflies frequent in summer.
Contact: Centre Manager, RSPB Lake Vyrnwy Reserve, Bryn Awel, Llanwddyn, Oswestry, Salop SY10 0LZ. 01691 870 278.
e-mail: lake.vyrnwy@rspb.org.uk

North Wales

1. BARDSEY BIRD OBSERVATORY

Bardsey Bird Observatory.
Location: SH 11 21. Private 444 acre island. Twenty minute boat journey from Aberdaron.
Access: Mar-Nov. No dogs. Visitor accommodation in 150-year-old farmhouse (two single, two double, one x four dorm). Day visitors by Bardsey Ferries (07971 769 895).
Facilities: Public toilets available for day visitors. Three hides, one on small bay, two seawatching. Gift shops and payphone.
Public transport: Trains from Birmingham to Pwllheli. Tel: 0345 484 950. Arriva bus from Bangor to Pwllheli. Tel: 0870 6082 608.
Habitat: Sea-birds cliffs viewable from boat only. Farm and scrubland, Spruce plantation, willow copses and gorse-covered hillside.
Key birds: *All year*: Chough, Peregrine. *Spring/ summer*: Manx Shearwater (16,000 pairs), other seabirds. Migrant warblers, chats, Redstart, thrushes. *Autumn*: Many rarities including Eye-browed Thrush, Lanceolated Warbler, American Robin, Yellowthroat, Summer Tanager.
Other notable flora and fauna: Autumn ladies tresses.
Contact: Steven Stansfield, Cristin, Ynys Enlli (Bardsey), off Aberaron, via Pwllheil, Gwynedd LL53 8DE. 07855 264 151. e-mail: warden@bbfo.org.uk www.bbfo.org.uk
To stay at the Observatory contact Alicia Normand (tel 01626 773 908) e-mail bookings@bbfo.org.uk).

2. CEMLYN

North Wales Wildlife Trust.
Location: SH 329 936 and SH 336 932. Cemlyn is signposted from Tregele on A5025 between Valley and Amlwch on Anglesey.
Access: Open all the time. Dogs on leads. No wheelchair access. During summer months walk on seaward side of ridge and follow signs.
Facilities: Car parks at either end of reserve.
Public transport: None within a mile.
Habitat: Brackish lagoon, shingle ridge, salt marsh, mixed scrub.
Key birds: Wintering wildfowl and waders, breeding terns, gulls and warblers, pipits and passing migrants. *Spring*: Wheatears, Whitethroat, Sedge Warbler, Manx Shearwater, Sandwich Tern, Whimbrel, Dunlin, Knot and Black-tailed Godwit.
Summer: Breeding Arctic, Common and Sandwich Terns, Black-headed Gull, Oystercatcher and Ringed Plover. *Autumn*: Golden Plover, Lapwing, Curlew, Manx Shearwater, Gannet, Kittiwake, Guillemot.
Winter: Little and Great Crested Grebe, Shoveler, Shelduck, Wigeon, Red-breasted Merganser, Coot, Turnstone, Purple Sandpiper.

Other notable flora and fauna: 20 species of butterfly recorded. Sea kale, yellow horned poppy, sea purselane, sea beet, glasswort. Grey seal, harbour porpoise, bottlenose dolphin.
Contact: Conservation Officer, North Wales Wildlife Trust, 01248 351 541.
e-mail: nwwt@wildlifetrustswales.org www.wildlifetrust.org.uk/northwales

3. CONNAHS QUAY POWER STATION RESERVE

Deeside Naturalists' Society / E.ON UK.
Location: SJ 275 715. From England: Take A550 from Liverpool/N Wirral or A5117 from Ellesmere Port/M56, follow road to Queensferry. 200 metres after junction of A550 and A5117, turn L at A548 and follow signs to Flint. Cross Dee Bridge and turn off dual carriageway at B5129, signed Connah's Key. Turn R under A548 then L, following signs to power station.
From Flint: Take A548 towards Connah's Quay/ Queensferry. After 2.5 miles, take B5129 (Connah's Quay exit). Turn L following signs to power station.
From Connah's Quay: Take B5129 towards Flint. Go under A548, turn L following signs to power station.
Access: Advance permit required (group bookings only). Wheelchair access. Public welcome on open days – see website for details.
Facilities: Field studies centre, five hides.
Public transport: Contact Arriva Cymru on 01745 343 492.
Habitat: Saltmarsh, mudflats, grassland scrub, open water, wetland meadow.
Key birds: *Summer*: Small roosts of non-breeding estuarine birds. *Winter*: High water roosts of waders and wildfowl including, Black-tailed Godwit, Oystercatcher, Redshank, Spotted Redshank, Curlew, Lapwing, Teal, Pintail and Wigeon.
Contact: Secretary, Deeside Naturalist's Society, 21 Woodlands Court, Hawarden, Deeside, Flintshire CH5 3NB. 01224 537 440. www.deesidenaturalists.org.uk email: deenaturalists@btinternet.com

4. CONWY

RSPB (North Wales Office).
Location: SH 799 773. On E bank of Conwy Estuary. Access from A55 at exit signed to Conwy and Deganwy.
Access: Open daily (9.30am-5pm) or dusk if earlier. Closed for Christmas Day. Ample parking for coaches. Toilets, buildings and trails accessible to pushchairs and wheelchairs.
Facilities: Visitor centre, gift shop, coffee shop, toilets including disabled. Four hides (accessible to wheelchairs) two viewing screens. Trails firm and level, though a little rough in places and wet in winter.
Public transport: Train service to Llandudno

Junction, 10 minute walk. Bus service to Tesco supermarket, Llandudno Junction 5 minutes walk. Tel: 01492 596 969.

Habitat: Lagoons, islands, reedbed, grassland, estuary.

Key birds: Wildfowl and waders in winter, warblers and wetland breeding birds in summer. *Spring*: Passage waders, hirundines and wagtails. *Summer*: Lapwings, waterbirds and warblers. *Winter*: Kingfisher, Goldeneye, Water Rail, Red-breasted Merganser, wildfow, huge Starling roost.

Other notable flora and fauna: Common butterflies through summer, expecially common blues. Great display of cowslips in March, bee orchids in summer. Otters seen earling mornings.

Contact: Conwy RSPB Nature Reserve, Llandudno Junction, Conwy, North Wales LL31 9XZ. 01492 584 091.

5. GORS MAEN LLWYD

North Wales Wildlife Trust.

Location: SH 975 580. Follow A5 to Cerrigydrudion (seven miles S of site), then take B4501 and go past the Llyn Brennig Visitor Centre. Approx two miles beyond centre, turn R (still on B4501). First car park on R approx 300 yards after the cattle grid.

Access: Open all the time. Dogs on leads. Keep to the paths. Rare breeding birds on the heather so keep to paths.

Facilities: In second car park by lake shore there are toilets and short walk to bird hide. Paths are waymarked, but can be very wet and muddy in poor weather.

Public transport: Nearest bus stop is Nantglyn (3 miles from the reserve). No.61 from Lenton Pool, Denbigh. Contact (01352) 714035 for times.

Habitat: Heathland. Heather and grass overlooking large lake.

Key birds: *Summer*: Red and Black Grouse, Hen Harrier, Merlin, Sky Lark, Curlew. *Winter*: Wildfowl on lake.

Contact: NWWT, 01248 351 541.
e-mail: nwwt@wildlifetrustswales.org
www.wildlifetrust.org.uk/northwales

6. LLYN ALAW

Welsh Water/United Utilities.

Location: SH 390 865. North Anglesey, SW of Amlwch. Signposted from J5 of A55. Main car park at SH375 856.

Access: Open all year. No dogs to hides or sanctuary area but dogs allowed (maximum two per adult) other areas. Limited wheelchair access. Coach parking in main car park (SH 373 856).

Facilities: Visitor centre, Toilets (including disabled), earth paths, boardwalks. Two hides,car parks, network of mapped walks, picnic sites, information boards. Coach parking at main car park.

Public transport: Not to within a mile.

Habitat: Large area of standing water, shallow reedy bays, hedges, scrub, woodland, marsh, grassland.

Key birds: Wintering wildfowl and thrushes, breeding warblers/waterfowl. *Summer*: Lesser Whitethroat, Sedge and Grasshopper Warblers, Little and Great Crested Grebes, Tawny Owl, Barn Owl, Buzzard. *Winter*: Whooper Swan, Goldeneye, Hen Harrier, Short-eared Owl, Redwing, Fieldfare, Peregrine, Raven.

All year: Bullfinch, Siskin, Redpoll, Goldfinch, Stonechat. Passage waders: Ruff, Spotted Redshank, Curlew Sandpiper, Green Sandpiper.

Other notable flora and fauna: Bee and northern marsh orchid, royal fern, skullcap, needle spikerush. Migrant hawker, hairy, four-spotted chaser dragonflies, banded demoiselle, wall brown, gatekeeper, clouded yellow and orange tip butterflies. Hare, water vole.

Contact: The Warden, Llyn Alaw, Llantrisant, Holyhead LL65 4TW. 01407 730 762.

7. LLYN CEFNI

Welsh Water / Forestry Commission / United Utilities.

Location: Entrance at Bodffordd SH 433 775 and Rhosmeirch SH 451 783. A reservoir located two miles NW of Llangefni, in central Anglesey. Follow B5111 or B5109 from the village.

Access: Open at all times. Dogs allowed except in sanctuary area. Good footpath (wheelchair accessible) for most of the site, bridges over streams.

Facilities: Two picnic sites, good footpath, coach parking at Rhosmeirch car park SH451 783.

Public transport: Bus 32, 4 (44 Sun only, 52 Thu only). Tel 0871 200 2233 for information.

Habitat: Large area of open water, reedy bays, coniferous woodland, scrub, carr.

Key birds: *Summer*: Sedge, Whitethroat and Grasshopper Warblers, Buzzard, Tawny Owl, Little Grebe, Gadwall, Shoveler, Kingfisher.
Winter: Waterfowl (Whooper Swan, Goldeneye), Crossbill, Redpoll, Siskin, Redwing.
All year: Stonechat, Treecreeper, Song Thrush.

Other notable flora and fauna: Northern marsh orchid, rustyback fern, needle spikerush. Banded demoiselle, migrant hawker, golden-ringed dragonfly, emerald damselfly. Ringlet, gatekeeper, clouded yellow and wall butterflies. Bloody nose beetle.

Contact: The Warden, Llyn Alaw, Llantrisant, Holyhead LL65 4TW. 01407 730 762.

8. MAWDDACH VALLEY

RSPB (North Wales Office).

Location: Coed Garth Gell (SH 688 192) is adjacent to the main Dolgellau to Barmouth road (A496) near Taicynhaeaf. No reserve parking is available but lay-bys are found close to the reserve's entrances. Arthog Bog (SH630138) is off the main Dolgellau to Tywyn road (A493) west of Arthog. Parking is available near by at the Morfa Mawddach station.

Access: Nature trails are open at all times.

Facilities: Nature trails and information boards.

Public transport: Regular bus service between Dolgellau and Barmouth stops close to reserve entrance at Coed Garth Gell. The Arthog Bog part of

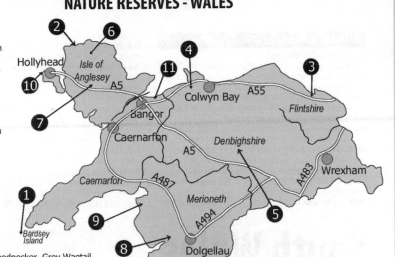

reserve served by Dolgallau to Tywyn bus, which stops close by at Arthog, and is a short distance from the Morfa Mawddach railway station.

Habitat: Oak woodland, bracken and heathland at Coed Garth Gell. Willow and alder scrub and raised bog at Arthog bog.

Key birds: At Coed Garth Gell: Buzzard, Sparrowhawk, Peregrine, Raven, Lesser Spotted Woodpecker, Grey Wagtail, Dipper and Hawfinch are joined in the summer by Pied Flycatcher, Spotted Flycatcher, Wood Warbler, Redstart, Tree Pipit and Cuckoo. At Arthog bog, Buzzard, Sparrowhawk, Peregrine and Raven are resident. Summer migrants include Tree Pipit, Grasshopper Warbler and Cuckoo. In winter flocks of Redpoll and Siskin are common and Red-breasted Merganser, Pintail and Little Egret are on the nearby estuary.

Other notable flora and fauna: Coed Garth Gell has Tunbridge filmy and beech ferns and a wide variety of butterflies. Golden-ringed dragonflies are regular at both reserves.

Contact: RSPB Ynys-Hir Reserve, Eglwys-fach, Machynlleth, Powys SY20 8TA. 01654 700 222. e-mail: ynyshir@rspb.org.uk

9. MORFA HARLECH NNR

CCW (North West Area).

Location: SH 574 317. On the A496 Harlech road.

Access: Open all year.

Facilities: Car park. Disabled parking bays and three coach parking spaces.

Public transport: The site is served by both bus and train. Train stations are at Harlech and Ty gwyn (Ty Gwyn is near the saltmarsh wintering birds.) Contact Arriva for details (0844 8004 411).

Habitat: Shingle (no shingle at Harlech), coast, marsh, dunes. Also forestry plantation, grassland, swamp.

Key birds: *Spring/summer:* Whitethroat, Spotted Flycatcher, Grasshopper Warbler, migrants. *Passage:* Waders, Manx Shearwater, ducks.
Winter: Divers, Whooper Swan, Wigeon, Teal, Pintail, Scaup, Common Scoter, Hen Harrier, Merlin, Peregrine, Short-eared Owl, Little Egret, Water Pipit, Snow Bunting, Twite.
All year/breeding: Redshank, Lapwing, Ringed Plover, Snipe, Curlew, Shelduck, Oystercatcher, Stonechat, Whinchat, Wheatear, Linnet, Reed Bunting, Sedge

Warbler. Also Red-breasted Merganser, Kestrel, gulls.

Other notable flora and fauna: Sand lizard, otter, water vole.

Contact: CCW, North West Wales, 0845 1306 229. e-mail: enquiries@ccw.gov.uk www.ccw.gov.uk

10. SOUTH STACK CLIFFS

RSPB (North Wales Office).

Location: RSPB Car Park SH 211 818, Ellins Tower information centre SH 206 820. Follow A55 to W end in Holyhead, proceed straight on at roundabout, continue straight on through traffic lights. After another half mile turn L and follow the Brown Tourist signs for RSPB Ynys Lawd/South Stack.

Access: RSPB car park with disabled parking, 'Access for all' track leading to a viewing area overlooking the lighthouse adjacent to Ellins Tower visitor centre. Access to Ellins Tower gained via staircase. Access to other areas of the reserve by an extensive network of paths, some of which are steep and uneven.
Coach parking by prior arrangement at The South Stack Kitchen Tel: 01407 762 181 (privately owned).

Facilities: Free access to Ellin's Tower which has windows overlooking main auk colony open daily (10am-5.30pm Easter-Sep).

Public transport: Mainline station Holyhead. Infrequent local bus service, Holyhead-South Stack. Tel. 0870 608 2608.

Habitat: Sea cliffs, maritime grassland, maritime heath, lowland heath.

Key birds: Peregrine, Chough, Fulmar, Puffin, Guillemot, Razorbill, Rock Pipit, Sky Lark, Stonechat, Linnet, Shag, migrant warblers and passage seabirds.

Contact: Dave Bateson, Plas Nico, South Stack, Holyhead, Anglesey LL65 1YH. 01407 764 973. www.rspb.org.uk

11. SPINNIES ABER OGWEN

North Wales Wildlife Trust.
Location: SH 613 721. From Bangor follow the Tal-y-Bont road from roundabout on A5122 near Penrhyn Castle entrance. Road to reserve is signposted on L after 1km. Reserve can also be approached from a road at J 12 off A55. Minor road leads to car park where reserve entrance is signposted.
Access: Open all year. Dogs on leads. Keep to the paths. Wheelchair accessible to the main hide.
Facilities: Two hides clearly signposted from the car park, main hide is wheelchair accessible and offers views of Traeth Lafan sands and the Spinnies lagoon. There is a drop-off point at the main entrance. Footpaths are good throughout.
Public transport: Take the 95 or 5X bus from Bangor or Llandudno.
Habitat: Woodland, scrub, grassland, shingle beach mudflats, reed swamp and open water.
Key birds: *Autumn/winter*: Large numbers of wintering wildfowl and waders such as Redshank, Greenshank, Wigeon and Teal. Kingfisher can be seen from Sep-Mar.
Spring/summer: Mergansers, feeding Sandwich Terns, large numbers of Mute Swans, Little Grebe, Blackcap and Sedge Warbler.
Other notable flora and fauna: Broad-leaved helleborine, snowdrops, dogs mercury, bulebells. Red admiral, Speckled wood, holly blue, orange-tip and small copper butterflies.
Contact: Jon Rowe, Assistant Reserves Officer, North Wales Wildlife Trust, 376 High Street, Bangor, Gwynedd LL57 1YE. 01248 351 541.

South Wales

1. CWM CLYDACH

RSPB Wales
Location: SN 584 026. Three miles N of J45 on M4, through the village of Clydach on B4291.
Access: Open at all times along public footpaths and waymarked trails. Coach parking not available.
Facilities: Nature trails, car park, information boards.
Public transport: Buses from Swansea stop at reserve entrance. Nearest railway station is eight miles away in Swansea.
Habitat: Oak woodland on steep slopes lining the banks of the fast-flowing Lower Clydach River.
Key birds: Red Kite, Sparrowhawk, Buzzard, Peregrine, Raven, Green Woodpecker, Dipper, Grey Wagtail and Marsh Tit are joined in the summer by Pied Flycatcher, Spotted Flycatcher, Wood Warbler, Redstart and Cuckoo. In winter Siskins and Redpolls are regular.
Contact: RSPB Ynys-Hir Reserve, Eglwys-fach, Machynlleth, Powys SY20 8TA. 01654 700 222.
e-mail: ynyshir@rspb.org.uk

2. CWM COL-HUW

The Wildlife Trust of South and West Wales.
Location: SS 957 674. Site includes Iron Age fort, overlooking Bristol Channel. From Bridgend take B4265 S to Llanwit Major. Follow beach road from village.
Access: Park in seafront car park. Climb steps. Open all year.
Facilities: All year toilets and café. Information boards.
Public transport: None.
Habitat: Unimproved grassland, woodland, scrub and Jurassic blue lias cliff.
Key birds: Cliff-nesting House Martin colony, breeding Fulmar, Grasshopper Warbler. Large autumn passerine passage. Peregrine. Seawatching vantage point. Occasional Chough.
Other notable flora and fauna: Common butterflies. Nationally scarce wild cabbage grows near the cliff edge.
Contact: Trust HQ, 01656 724 100.
e-mail: information@wtsww.cix.co.uk

3. KENFIG NNR

Bridgend County Borough Council.
Location: SS 802 811. Seven miles W of Bridgend. From J37 on M4, drive towards Porthcawl, then North Cornelly, then follow signs.
Access: Open at all times. Unsurfaced sandy paths, not suitable for wheelchairs. Flooding possible in winter and spring. Coach parking available.
Facilities: Toilets, hides, free car parking and signposted paths. Visitor centre open weekends and holidays (10am-4.30pm), weekdays (2pm-4.30pm).
Public transport: Local bus service – contact reserve for details.
Habitat: 1,300 acre sand dune system, freshwater lake with reeds, numerous wet dune slacks, sandy coastline with some rocky outcrops.
Key birds: *Summer*: Warblers including Cetti's, Grasshopper, Sedge, Reed and Willow Warbler, Blackcap and Whitethroat. One of the UK's best sites for orchids. *Winter*: Wildfowl, Water Rail, Bittern, grebes.
Other notable flora and fauna: 16 species of orchid, hairy dragonfly, red-veined and ruddy darters, small blue, dark green fritillary, grayling, brown argus butterflies.
Contact: David Carrington, Ton Kenfig, Bridgend, CF33 4PT 01656 743 386.
e-mail: david.carrington@bridgend.gov.uk

4. LAVERNOCK POINT

The Wildlife Trust of South and West Wales.
Location: ST 182 680. Public footpaths S of B4267 between Barry & Penarth.
Access: No restrictions.
Facilities: None.
Public transport: Call Trust for advice.
Habitat: Cliff top, unimproved grassland, dense scrub.
Key birds: Seawatching in late summer; Glamorgan's best migration hotspot in autumn.
Other notable flora and fauna: Various common butterflies, such as speckled wood, ringlet, gatekeeper, comma, red admiral and painted lady. Approx. 170 plant species have been listed, including the scarce adder's tongue fern.
Contact: Trust HQ, 01656 724 100.
e-mail: information@wtsww.cix.co.uk

4. MAGOR MARSH

Gwent Wildlife Trust.
Location: ST 427 867. S of Magor. Leave M4 at exit 23, turning R onto B4245. Follow signs for Redwick in Magor village. Take first L after railway bridge – reserve entrance is half mile further on R.
Access: Open all year. Keep to path. Wheelchair access to bird hide..
Facilities: Hide. Car park, footpaths and boardwalks.
Public transport: Bus service to Magor village. Reserve is approx 10 mins walk along Redwick road.
Habitat: Sedge fen, reedswamp, willow carr, damp hay meadows and open water.
Key birds: Important for wetland birds. *Spring*: Reed, Sedge and Grasshopper Warbler, occasional Garganey and Green Sandpiper on passage, Hobby. *Winter*: Teal, Peregrine, Jack Snipe, Snipe, occasional Shoveler and Gadwall, Bittern records in two recent years.
All year: Little Egret, Little Grebe, Reed Bunting, Cetti's Warbler and Water Rail.
Contact: Gwent Wildlife Trust, Seddon House, Dingestow, Monmouth NP25 4DY. 01600 740 358; Fax 01600 740 299. e-mail: info@gwentwildlife.co.uk www.gwentwildlife.org

6. OXWICH

CCW (Swansea Office).
Location: SS 872 773. 12 miles from Swansea, off A4118.
Access: NNR open at all times. No permit required for access to foreshore. Dunes, woodlands and facilities.
Facilities: Private car park, summer only. Toilets summer only. Marsh boardwalk and marsh lookout. No visitor centre, no facilities

for disabled visitors.
Public transport: Bus service Swansea/Oxwich. First Cymru, tel 01792 580 580.
Habitat: Freshwater marsh, saltmarsh, foreshore, dunes, woodlands.
Key birds: *Summer*: Breeding Reed, Sedge and Cetti's Warblers, Treecreeper, Nuthatch, woodpeckers. *Winter*: Wildfowl.
Contact: Countryside Council for Wales, RVB House, Llys Tawe, King's Road, Swansea SA1 8PG. 01792 634 960. e-mail: enquiries@ccw.gov.uk www.ccw.gov.uk

7. PARC SLIP NATURE PARK

The Wildlife Trust of South and West Wales.
Location: SS 880 840. Tondu, half mile W of Aberkenfig. From Bridgend take A4063 N, turning L onto B4281 after passing M4. Reserve is signposted from this road.
Access: Open dawn to dusk. Space for coach parking.
Facilities: Three hides, nature trail, interpretation centre.
Public transport: None.
Habitat: Restored opencast mining site, wader scrape, lagoons.
Key birds: *Summer*: Breeding Tufted Duck, Lapwing, Sky Lark. Migrant waders (inc. Little Ringed Plover, Green Sandpiper), Little Gull. Kingfisher, Green Woodpecker.
Other notable flora and fauna: 27 species of dragonfly have been recorded, including emperor, four spot chaser and scarce blue-tailed damselfy. 7 species of orchid, including bee, common spotted, southern marsh, twayblade and broad-leaved helleborine.
Contact: Trust HQ, 01656 724 100.
e-mail: information@wtsww.cix.co.uk

8. PETERSTONE WENTLOOGE

Gwent Wildlife Trust.
Location: ST 269 800. Reserve overlooks Severn Estuary, between Newport and

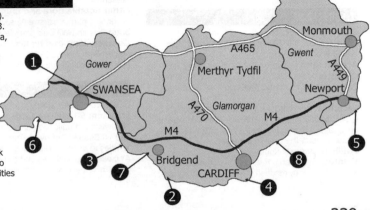

Cardiff. Take B4293 to Peterstone Wentlooge village.
Access: Park in large lay-by opposite the church and take path to the sea wall.
Facilities: None.
Public transport: None.

Habitat: Foreshore, inter-tidal mudflats, grazing.
Key birds: Passage waders and winter wildfowl.
Contact: Trust HQ, 01600 740 358; Fax 01600 740 299. e-mail: info@gwentwildlife.co.uk
www.gwentwildlife.org

West Wales

1. CASTLE WOODS

The Wildlife Trust of South and West Wales.
Location: SN 615 217. About 60 acres of woodland overlooking River Tywi, W of Llandeilo town centre.
Access: Open all year by footpath from Tywi Bridge, Llandeilo (SN 627 221).
Facilities: Call for advice.
Public transport: Train station at Llandeilo (2km), on Swansea to Shrewsbury route. Bus numbers X13 from Swansea and 280 from Carmarthen to Llandovery.
Habitat: Old mixed deciduous woodlands.
Key birds: All three woodpeckers, Buzzard, Raven, Sparrowhawk. *Summer*: Pied and Spotted Flycatchers, Redstart, Wood Warbler. *Winter*: On water meadows below, look for Teal, Wigeon, Goosander, Shoveler, Tufted Duck and Pochard.
Other notable flora and fauna: Butterflies including comma, silver-washed fritillary and speckled wood. Fallow deer, badger. Bluebell, dog's mercury, primrose and wood anemone, toothwort on roots of wych elm. The woodland is rich in mosses and lichens, including large lungwort.
Contact: Area Officer, 35 Maesquarre Road, Betws, Ammanford, Carmarthenshire SA18 2LF. 01269 594 293. e-mail: information@wtsww.cix.co.uk
www.wildlifetrust.org.uk/wtsww

2. CORS CARON

CCW (West Wales Area).
Location: SN 692 625 (car park). Reached from B4343 N of Tregaron.
Access: Open access to S of car park along the railway to boardwalk, out to SE bog. Access to rest of the reserve by permit. Dogs on lead. Access for coaches.
Facilities: New car park with toilets and picnic space. Bird hide along boardwalk. Riverside walk is open access. For access to the rest of the reserve please contact the reserve manager.
Public transport: None.
Habitat: Raised bog, river, fen, wet grassland, willow woodland, reedbed.

Key birds: *Summer*: Lapwing, Redshank, Curlew, Red Kite, Grasshopper Warbler, Whinchat. *Winter*: Teal, Wigeon, Whooper Swan, Hen Harrier, Red Kite.
Contact: CCW, Neuaddlas, Tregaron, Ceredigion. 01974 298 480. e-mail: p.culyer@ccw.gov.uk
www.ccw.gov.uk

3. GWENFFRWD & DINAS

RSPB Wales
Location: SN 788 471. North of Llandovery. From A483 take B road signposted to Llyn Brianne Reservoir.
Access: Public nature trail at Dinas open at all times.
Facilities: Nature trail including a board walk. Other parts of the trail are rugged. Car park and information board at start of trail. Coach parking can be arranged.
Public transport: Nearest station at Llandovery, 10 miles away.
Habitat: Hillside oak woods, streams and bracken slopes. Spectacular upland scenery.
Key birds: Upland species such as Red Kite, Buzzard, Peregrine, Raven, Goosander, Dipper And Grey Wagtail are joined in the summer by Pied Flycatcher, Spotted Flycatcher, Wood Warbler, Redstart, Tree Pipit, Common Sandpiper and Cuckoo. Marsh Tit and all three woodpecker species are present.
Other notable flora and fauna: Golden-ringed dragonfly, purple hairstreak, silver-washed fritillary butterflies and Wilson's filmy fern.
Contact: RSPB Ynys-Hir Reserve, Eglwys-fach, Machynlleth, Powys SY20 8TA. 01654 700 222. e-mail: ynyshir@rspb.org.uk

4. DYFI

CCW (West Wales Area).
Location: SN 610 942. Large estuary area W of Machyalleth. Public footpaths off A493 E of Aberdyfi, and off B4353 (S of river); minor road from B4353 at Ynyslas to dunes and parking area.
Access: Ynyslas dunes and the estuary have unrestricted access. No access to Cors Fochno

(raised bog) for casual birdwatching; permit required for study and research purposes. Good views over the bog and Aberleri marshes from W bank of Afon Leri.
Facilities: Public hide overlooking marshes beside footpath at SN 611 911.
Public transport: None.
Habitat: Sandflats, mudflats, saltmarsh, creeks, dunes, raised bog, grazing marsh.
Key birds: *Winter*: Greenland White-fronted Goose, wildfowl, waders and raptors. *Summer*: Breeding wildfowl and waders (inc. Teal, Shoveler, Merganser, Lapwing, Curlew, Redshank).
Contact: CCW Warden, Plas Gogerddan, Aberystwyth, Ceredigion SY23 3EE. 01970 821 100.

5. NATIONAL WETLANDS CENTRE WALES

The Wildfowl & Wetlands Trust.
Location: SS 533 984. Leave M4 at junction 48. Signposted from A484, E of Llanelli.
Access: Open daily 9.30am-5pm, except Christmas Eve and Christmas Day. Grounds are open until 6pm in summer. The centre is fully accessible. Mobility scooters and wheelchairs are free to hire.
Facilities: Visitor centre with disabled toilets, hides, restaurant, shop, education facilities, free car and coach parking. The centre has level access and hard-surfaced paths. Overlooks the Burry Inlet.
Public transport: Bus from Llanelli to Llwydhendy, approx 1 mile from the centre. Telephone Traveline Cymru 0871 200 2233 (7am-10pm daily).
Habitat: Inter-tidal mudflats, reedbeds, pools, marsh, waterfowl collection.
Key birds: Large flocks of Curlew, Oystercatcher, Redshank on saltmarsh. *Winter*: Pintail, Wigeon, Teal. Also Little Egret, Short-eared Owl, Peregrine.
Other notable flora and fauna: Bee and southern marsh orchids, yellow bartisa. Damselflies and dragonflies, water voles and otters.
Contact: WWT National Wetlands Centre Wales, Llwynhendy, Llanelli SA14 9SH. 01554 741 087; Fax 01554 744 101. e-mail: info.llanelli@wwt.org.uk www.wwt.org.uk

6. RAMSEY ISLAND

RSPB (CYMRU).
Location: SM 706 237. One mile offshore from St Justinians slipway, two miles W of St Davids.
Access: Open every day, Easter-Oct 31. No wheelchair access. Coach parking available at St Justinians. For boat bookings contact: Thousand Island expeditions: 01437 721 686.
Facilities: Toilets, small RSPB shop, tuck shop, hot drinks and snacks, self-guiding trail.
Public transport: Trains to Haverfordwest Station. Hourly buses to St Davids, bus to St Justinians.
Habitat: Acid grassland, maritime heath, seacliffs.
Key birds: *Spring/summer*: Cliff-nesting auks (Guillemot, Razorbill). Kittiwake, Lesser, Great Black-backed, Herring Gulls, Shag, Wheatear, Stonechat. *All year*: Peregrine, Raven, Chough, Lapwing.
Other notable flora and fauna: Grey seal, red deer, porpoise seen most days.
Contact: Warden: 07836 535 733. www.rspb.org.uk/reserves

7. SKOKHOLM ISLAND

The Wildlife Trust of South and West Wales.
Location: SM 735 050. Island lying S of Skomer.
Access: Occasional day visits, also 3 or 4 night stays available. Weekly accomm. Apr-Sep, tel 01239 621 212 for details and booking.
Facilities: Call for details.
Public transport: None.
Habitat: Cliffs, bays and inlets.
Key birds: *Summer*: Large colonies of Razorbill, Puffin, Guillemot, Manx Shearwater, Storm Petrel, Lesser Black-backed Gull. Migrants inc. rare species.
Contact: 01239 621 212.

8. SKOMER ISLAND

The Wildlife Trust of South and West Wales.
Location: SM 725 095. Fifteen miles from Haverfordwest. Take B4327 turn-off for Marloes, embarkation point at Martin's Haven, two miles past village.

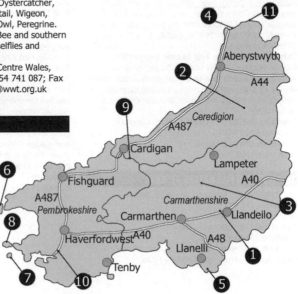

Access: Apr 1-Oct 31. Boats sail at 10am, 11am and noon every day except Mon (Bank Holidays excluded). Closed four days beginning of Jun for seabird counts. Not suitable for infirm (steep landing steps and rough ground).
Facilities: Information centre, toilets, two hides, wardens, booklets, guides, nature trails.
Public transport: None.
Habitat: Maritime cliff, bracken, bluebells and red campion, heathland, freshwater ponds.
Key birds: Largest colony of Manx Shearwater in the world (overnight). Puffin, Guillemot, Razorbill (Apr-end Jul). Kittiwake (until end Aug), Fulmar (absent Oct), Short-eared Owl (during day Jun and Jul), Chough, Peregrine, Buzzard (all year), migrants.
Contact: Skomer Island, Marloes, Pembs SA62 2BJ. 07971 114 302. e-mail: skomer@wtww.co.uk

9. WELSH WILDLIFE CENTRE

The Wildlife Trust of South and West Wales.
Location: SN 188 451. Two miles SE of Cardigan. River Teifi is N boundary. Sign posted from Cardigan to Fishguard Road.
Access: Open 10.30am-5pm all year. Free parking for WTSWW members, £3 non-members. Dogs on leads welcome. Disabled access to visitor centre, paths, four hides.
Facilities: Visitor centre, restaurant, network of paths and seven hides.
Public transport: Train station, Haverfordwest (23 miles). Bus station in Cardigan. Access on foot from Cardigan centre, ten mins.
Habitat: Wetlands, marsh, swamp, reedbed, open water, creek (tidal), river, saltmarsh, woodland.
Key birds: Cetti's Warbler, Kingfisher, Water Rail, Greater Spotted Woodpecker, Dipper, gulls, Marsh Harrier, Sand Martin, Hobby, Redstart, occasional Bittern and Red Kite.
Other notable flora and fauna: Dragonflies include emperor, broad-bodied Chaser, southern hawker and scarce blue-tailed damselfly. Otter, water shrew, sika and red deer. Fish including lamprey, stickleback, mullets, eel, sewin and salmon. Grass snake, adder.
Contact: The Welsh Wildlife Centre, Cilgerran, Cardigan SA43 2TB. 01239 621 212.
e-mail: wwc@welshwildlife.org
www.welshwildlife.org

10. WESTFIELD PILL NATURE RESERVE

The Wildlife Trust of South and West Wales.
Location: SM 958 073.
Access: Open all year.
Facilities: Car park, cycle track.
Public transport: None.
Habitat: Freshwater lagoons, disused railway embankment, scrub, woodland margins.

Key birds: *Spring/summer:* Hirundines, Whitethroat, Blackcap, Spotted Flycatcher.
Passage: waders.
Winter: Little Grebe, Peregrine, Water Rail, Woodcock, Fieldfare, Redwing, Siskin, Redpoll.
All year: Sparrowhawk, Kingfisher, Tawny Owl, Grey Wagtail, Dunnock, Raven, Bullfinch.
Other notable flora and fauna: Butterflies including holly blue and purple hairstreak. Numerous dragonflies and the tentacled lagoon worm (one of its few European sites). Adder, grass snake and slow worm. Otter and four species of bat, including Daubenton's.
Contact: The Wildlife Trust of South and West Wales, Nature Centre, Fountain Road, Tondu, Mid Glamorgan, CF32 0EH, 01239 621 212.

11. YNYS-HIR

RSPB (CYMRU).
Location: SN 68 29 63. Off A487 Aberystwyth - Machynlleth road in Eglwys-fach village. Six miles SW of Machynlleth.
Access: Open every day except Christmas Day (9am-9pm or dusk if earlier). Visitor centre open daily Apr-Oct (10am-5pm), Wed-Sun Nov-Mar (10am-4pm). Coaches welcome but please call for parking information. Sorry, no dogs allowed.
Facilities: Visitor centre and toilets. Numerous trails, six hides, drinks machine.
Public transport: Bus service to Eglwys-fach from either Machynlleth or Aberystwyth, tel. 01970 617 951. Rail service to Machynlleth.
Habitat: Estuary, freshwater pools, woodland and wet grassland.
Key birds: Large numbers of wintering waders, wildfowl and birds of prey on the estuary are replaced with breeding woodland birds in spring and summer.
All year: Red Kite, Buzzard, Little Egret, Lapwing, Teal.
Spring: Wood Warbler, Redstart, Pied Flycatcher, nine species of warbler.
Winter: Greenland white-fronted Goose, Barnacle Goose, Wigeon, Hen Harrier.
Other notable flora and fauna: Sixteen species of dragonfly and damselfly include small red damselfly and golden-ringed dragonfly. Butterflies include dark green fritillary, brimstone and speckled wood. Otters and brown hares are resident, though the former are rarely seen.
Contact: RSPB Ynys-Hir Reserve, Eglwys-fach, Machynlleth, Powys SY20 8TA. 01654 700 222.
e-mail: ynyshir@rspb.org.uk

NORTHERN IRELAND

Antrim

BOG MEADOWS

Ulster Wildlife Trust.
Location: J 315 726. Signposted from the Falls Road, West Belfast. (OS map 15).
Access: Open at all times. Coach parties welcome. Suitable for wheelchair users.
Facilities: Car park, network of paths – contact warden for toilets and bird hide access arrangements.
Public transport: Bus service from Belfast city along Falls Road. For more details contact Translink on 028 9066 6630.
Habitat: Unimproved grassland, scrub, ponds, reedbeds.
Key birds: *Summer*: Passage waders, Grey Wagtail, Stonechat, Sedge and Grasshopper Warblers, Reed Bunting. *Winter*: Water Rail, Snipe, Teal.
Contact: Tyrone Nelson, Bog Meadows reserve warden, Belfast UWT office, 163 Stewartstown Road, Dunmurry, Belfast BT19 9EP. 028 9062 8647.
e-mail: info@ulsterwildlifetrust.org
www.ulsterwildlifetrust.org

ECOS NATURE RESERVE

Ulster Wildlife Trust.
Location: D 118 036. 0.5 miles NE of Ballymena town centre.Signposted off M2 (OS map 9).
Access: Open at all times. Coaches welcome. Suitable for wheelchair users.
Facilities: Environmental centre (028 2566 4400), car park, toilets, bird hide, network of paths.
Public transport: Bus from Ballymena town centre or within easy walking distance. For more details contact Translink on 028 9066 6630.
Habitat: Lake, wet meadows, willow coppice, scrub.
Key birds: *Summer*: Breeding Snipe, Sedge Warbler, Grasshopper Warbler, Reed Bunting. *Winter*: Teal, Goldeneye, Lapwing, Curlew. Rarities have included, White-winged Black Tern and Hoopoe in recent years.
Contact: ECOS Warden, Ulster Wildlife Trust, 028 4483 0282. e-mail: info@ulsterwildlifetrust.org
www.ulsterwildlifetrust.org

GLENARM

Ulster Wildlife Trust.
Location: D 301 132. Gate by B97 0.5 mile SW Glenarm, 15 miles from Ballymena. OS 1:50 000 sheet 9.
Access: Wildlife Trust members. Not suitable for coaches. Parts of reserve accessible for wheelchair users.
Facilities: Forest tracks.

Public transport: Ulsterbus – from Ballymena. For more details contact Translink on 028 9066 6630.
Habitat: Species-rich grassland, oak woodland.
Key birds: *Summer*: Breeding Blackcap, Garden Warbler, Wood Warbler, Redpoll, Buzzard, Dippers, Common Crossbill, Grey Wagtail, Raven.
Contact: Ulster Wildlife Trust, 028 4483 0282.
e-mail: info@ulsterwildlifetrust.org
www.ulsterwildlifetrust.org

ISLE OF MUCK

Ulster Wildlife Trust.
Location: D 464 024. Situated off NE tip of Island Magee, Co Antrim (OS Map 9).
Access: Wildlife trust members only. Permit required to land on island from UWT.
Island only accessible by boat. Not suitable for coaches or disabled.
Facilities: None.
Public transport: None.
Habitat: Offshore island with cliffs and stack
Key birds: *Summer*: Fulmar, Manx Shearwater, Peregrine, Kittiwake, terns, Guillemot, Razorbill, Black Guillemot, Puffin. *Winter*: Red-throated Diver.
Contact: Ulster Wildlife Trust, 028 4483 0282.
e-mail: info@ulsterwildlifetrust.org
www.ulsterwildlifetrust.org

KEBBLE

Department of the Environment NI.
Location: D 095 515. W end of Rathlin Island, off coast from Ballycastle.
Access: Scheduled ferry service from Ballycastle.
Facilities: None.
Public transport: None.
Habitat: Sea cliffs, grass, heath, lake, marsh.
Key birds: Major cliff nesting colonies of auks (Inc. Puffin), Fulmar and Kittiwake; also Buzzard and Peregrine. Manx Shearwater and other seabirds on passage.
Contact: Dept of the Environment NI, Portrush Countryside Centre, 8 Bath Road, Portrush, Co Antrim BT56 8AP. 028 7082 3600.

LAGAN MEADOWS

Ulster Wildlife Trust.
Location: J 335 703. Signposted off Malone Road, South Belfast (OS map 15).
Access: Open at all times. Suitable for coach parties. Suitable for wheelchair users along Lagan towpath.
Facilities: Network of paths.
Public transport: Bus service from Belfast city centre along Malone/Stranmillis Roads. For more details contact Translink on 028 9066 6630.

Habitat: Species-rich meadows, marsh, pond and scrub.
Key birds: *Summer*: Sedge and Grasshopper Warblers, Blackcap and Reed Bunting. *Winter*: Water Rail, Snipe, Redpoll and Siskin.
Contact: Ulster Wildlife Trust, 028 4483 0282.
e-mail: info@ulsterwildlifetrust.org
www.ulsterwildlifetrust.org

RATHLIN ISLAND SEABIRD CENTRE

RSPB (Northern Ireland Office).
Location: NR 282 092. Nearest town is Ballycastle where ferry to Rathlin departs. From Rathlin Harbour it is a further four miles to the Seabird Centre. Private minibus service and bicycle hire available on the island.
Access: 11am-3pm daily (Apr -mid Sep). Viewing platform accessed by 89 steps down cliffside so access around the site not for all visitors. If you have any concerns, please contact the reserve or regional office.
Facilities: Car park with limited parking and limited vehicle access via ferry, cycle racks available. Binocular hire, group bookings accepted, remote location that is good for walking.
Public transport: None. **Habitat:** Coastal.
Key birds: *Spring/summer*: Breeding Puffin, Guillemot, Razorbill, Fulmar, Kittiwake.
Other notable flora and fauna: Ochids and hares possible close to reserve.
Contact: Seabird Centre (028 20 760 062), RSPB Norther Ireland HQ (028 9049 1547).

STRAIDKILLY

Ulster Wildlife Trust.
Location: D 302 165. Situated midway between Glenarm and Carnlough in the Glens of Antrim (OS map 9).
Access: Open at all times. Not suitable for coach parties or wheelchair users.
Facilities: Waymarked trail, picnic area and interpretation viewpoint.
Public transport: 128 Ballymena-Carnlough or 162 Larne-Cushendun. For more details contact Translink on 028 9066 6630.
Habitat: Semi-natural woodland.
Key birds: *Summer*: Buzzard, Raven, Blackcap and Bullfinch. *Winter*: Woodcock.
Contact: Ulster Wildlife Trust, 028 4483 0282.
www.ulsterwildlifetrust.org

Armagh

OXFORD ISLAND

Craigavon Borough Council.
Location: J 061 608. On shores of Lough Neagh, 2.5 miles from Lurgan, Co Armagh. Signposted from J10 of M1.
Access: Site open at all times. Car parks locked at varying times (see signs). Coach parking available.

Lough Neagh Discovery Centre open every day Apr-Sept (10am-5pm Mon-Sat, 10am-7pm Sun), Oct-Mar (10am-5pm every day) Closed Christmas Day. Dogs on leads please. Most of site and all of Centre accessible for wheelchairs. Wheelchairs and mobility scooters available for visitors.
Facilities: Public toilets, Lough Neagh Discovery Centre with loop system for hard-of-hearing, shop, Café and conference facilities. Four miles of footpaths, five birdwatching hides, children's play areas, trails, picnic tables, public jetties, museum. Guided walks and boat trips available (pre-booking essential). Varied programme of events.
Public transport: Ulsterbus Park'n Ride at Lough Road, Lurgan is 0.5 miles from reserve entrance. Tel 02890 333 000. Lurgan Railway Station, 3 miles from reserve entrance.
Habitat: Freshwater lake, ponds, wet grassland, reedbed, woodland.
Key birds: *Winter*: Large flocks of wildfowl, especially Pochard, Tufted Duck, Goldeneye and Scaup (mainly Dec/Jan). Whooper and Bewick's Swans and Greylag Geese (Oct-Apr). Tree Sparrows. *Summer*: Sedge Warbler, Grasshopper Warbler and Great Crested Grebe.
Other notable flora and fauna: Discovery Centre pond has interesting variety of pondweeds. Real's white butterfly (May-Jun). Rare Irish moiled cattle and Dexter cattle are used for conservation grazing.
Contact: Marcus Malley, Conservation Officer, Lough Neagh Discovery Centre, Oxford Island NNR, Lurgan, Co Armagh, N Ireland BT66 6NJ. 02838 322 205.
e-mail: oxford.island@craigavon.gov.uk
www.oxfordisland.com

Co. Down

BELFAST LOUGH RESERVE

RSPB (Northern Ireland Office).
Location: Take A2 N from Belfast and follow signs to Belfast Harbour Estate. Both entrances to reserve have checkpoints. From Dee Street 2 miles to reserve, from Tillysburn entrance 1 mile.
Access: Dawn to dusk.
Facilities: Lagoon overlooked by observation room (check for opening hours), two view points.
Public transport: Translink's metro bus stops close to reserve, service 26A and 27 (Translink 028 9066 6630).
Habitat: Mudflats, wet grassland, freshwater lagoon.
Key birds: Noted for Black-tailed Godwit numbers and excellent variety of waterfowl in spring, autumn and winter, with close views. Rarities have included Buff-breasted, Pectoral, White-rumped and Semi-palmated Sandpipers, Spotted Crake, American Wigeon, Laughing Gull.
Contact: Anthony McGeehan, 02891 479 009.

CASTLE ESPIE

The Wildfowl & Wetlands Trust.

Location: J 474 672. On Strangford Lough 10 miles E of Belfast, signposted from A22 in the Comber area.
Access: Open daily except Christmas Day (10.30am Mon-Sat, 11.30am Sun).
Facilities: Visitor centre, educational facilities, views over lough, three hides, woodland walk.
Public transport: Call for advice.
Habitat: Reedbed filtration system with viewing facilities.
Key birds: *Winter:* Wildfowl esp. pale-bellied Brent Goose, Scaup. *Summer:* Warblers. Wader scrape has attracted Little Egret, Ruff, Long-billed Dowitcher, Killdeer.
Contact: James Orr, Centre Manager, The Wildfowl & Wetlands Trust, Castle Espie, Ballydrain Road, Comber, Co Down BT23 6EA. 02891 874 146.

COPELAND BIRD OBSERVATORY

Location: Situated on a 40-acre island on outer edge of Belfast Lough, four miles N of Donaghadee.
Access: Access is by chartered boat from Donaghadee.
Facilities: Observatory open Apr-Oct most weekends and some whole weeks. Hostel-type accommodation for up to 20. Daily ringing, bird census, sea passage recording. General bookings: Neville McKee, (see below).
Public transport: None.
Habitat: Grassy areas, rock foreshore.
Key birds: Large colony of Manx Shearwaters; Black Guillemot, Eider, Water Rail also nest. *Summer:* Visiting Storm Petrels. Moderate passage of passerine migrants.
Contact: Bookings Secretary: Neville McKee, 67 Temple Rise, Templepatrick, Co. Antrim BT39 0AG 028 9443 3068 e-mail: Neville.McKee@btinternet.com www.cbo.org.uk

LOUGH FOYLE

RSPB (Northern Ireland Office).
Location: C 545 237. Large sea lough NE of Londonderry. Take minor roads off Limavady-Londonderry road to view-points (choose high tide) at Longfield Point, Ballykelly, Faughanvale.
Access: Open all year. No permit, but keep to trails.
Facilities: None. **Public transport:** None.
Habitat: Beds of eel-grass, mudflats, surrounding agricultural land.
Key birds: Staging-post for migrating wildfowl (eg. 15,000 Wigeon, 4,000 Pale-bellied Brent Geese in Oct/Nov).
Winter: Slavonian Grebe, divers, Bewick's and Whooper Swans, Bar-tailed Godwit, Golden Plover, Snow Bunting. *Autumn:* Waders (inc. Ruff, Little Stint, Curlew Sandpiper, Spotted Redshank).
Contact: RSPB N Ireland HQ, 02890 491 547

MURLOUGH

National Trust.
Location: J 394 338. Ireland's first nature reserve,

between Dundrum and Newcastle, close to Mourne Mountains.
Access: Permit needed except on marked paths.
Facilities: Visitor centre.
Public transport: Local bus service from Belfast-Newcastle passes reserve entrances.
Habitat: Sand dunes, heathland.
Key birds: Waders and wildfowl occur in Inner Dundrum Bay adjacent to the reserve; divers and large numbers of Scoter (inc. regular Surf Scoter) and Merganser in Dundrum Bay.
Contact: Murlough NNR, The Stable Yard, Keel Point, Dundrum, Newcastle, Co Down BT33 0NQ. Tel/Fax 02843 751 467; e-mail umnnrw@smtp.ntrust.org.uk.

NORTH STRANGFORD LOUGH

National Trust.
Location: J 510 700. View from adjacent roads and car parks; also from hide at Castle Espie (J 492 675).
Access: Call for advice.
Facilities: Hide.
Public transport: Bus service from Newtownards to Portaferry.
Habitat: Extensive tidal mudflats, limited saltmarsh.
Key birds: Major winter feeding area for pale-bellied Brent Goose, also Pintail, Wigeon, Whooper Swan. Waders (inc. Dunlin, Knot, Oystercatcher, Bar-tailed Godwit). During the summer months, Strangford's many islands provide the perfect breeding sites for thousands of gulls, terns and other waterfowl.
Other notable flora and fauna: Strangford Lough is an important refuge for substantial common and grey seal populations. Otters and porpoises are also regularly seen.
Contact: National Trust, Strangford Lough Wildlife Centre, Castle Ward, Strangford, Co Down BT30 7LS. Tel/Fax 02844 881 411; e-mail: strangford@nationaltrust.org.uk

QUOILE PONDAGE

Department of the Environment NI.
Location: J 500 478. One mile N of Downpatrick on road to Strangford, at S end of Strangford Lough.
Access: Open all year. No permit, but keep to trails.
Facilities: Large modern hide, visitor centre. Nature trail.
Public transport: None.
Habitat: Freshwater pondage to control flooding, with many vegetation types on shores.
Key birds: Many wildfowl species, woodland birds; migrant and wintering waders including Spotted Redshank, Ruff and Black-tailed Godwit.
Contact: Warden, Quoile Countryside Centre, 5 Quay Road, Downpatrick, Co Down BT30 7JB. 02844 615 520.

SLIEVENACLOY

Ulster Wildlife Trust.
Location: J 255 712. Situated in the Belfast Hills, take Ballycolin Road off A501 (OS map 14,15).

Access: Contact Reserve Warden. Unsuitable for coach parties and wheelchair users.
Facilities: Car park, waymarked trails.
Public transport: Bus service from Belfast to Glenavy. Contact Translink on 028 9066 6630.
Habitat: Unimproved grassland, scrub.
Key birds: *Summer*: Snipe, Curlew, Sky Lark, Grey Wagtail, Stonechat, Wheatear, Grasshopper Warbler and Reed Bunting. *Winter*: Hen Harrier, Merlin, Fieldfare and Snow Bunting.
Contact: Ulster Wildlife Trust, 028 4483 0282. www.ulsterwildlifetrust.org

UMBRA

Ulster Wildlife Trust.
Location: C 725 355. Ten miles W of Coleraine on A2 – entrance beside automatic railway crossing about 1.5 miles W of Downhill. OS 1:50 000 sheet 4.
Access: Wildlife Trust members. Not suitable for coaches. Unsuitable for wheelchair users.
Facilities: Informal paths.
Public transport: Ulsterbus service to Downhill from Coleraine. For more details contact Translink on 028 9066 6630.

Habitat: Sand dunes.
Key birds: *Summer*: Breeding Sky Lark. *Winter*: Woodcock, Peregrine, plus Great Northern Diver offshore.
Contact: Ulster Wildlife Trust, 028 4483 0282. www.ulsterwildlifetrust.orgyn

Co Tyrone

BLESSINGBOURNE

Ulster Wildlife Trust.
Location: H448487. Situated immediately NE of Fivemiletown (OS Map 18)
Access: Open at all times. Not suitable for coach parties. Unsuitable for wheelchair users.
Facilities: Paths
Public transport: For more details contact Translink on 028 9066 6630
Habitat: lake, reedbeds, mixed woodland
Key birds: *Summer*: Water Rail, Kingfisher, Sedge Warbler, Grasshopper Warbler, Blackcap
Contact: Ulster Wildlife Trust, 028 4483 0282. www.ulsterwildlifetrust.org

ISLE OF MAN

CALF OF MAN BIRD OBSERVATORY

Manx National Heritage.
Location: SC 15 65. Small island off the SW of the Isle of Man.
Access: Landings by private craft all year. No dogs, fires, camping or climbing.
Facilities: Accommodation for 8 people plus 2 volunteers sharing from Apr-Sept. Bookings: at contact address. Bird ringers welcome to join in ringing activities with prior notice.
Public transport: Local boat from Port Erin (Apr-Sept) or Port St Mary all year.
Habitat: Heather/bracken moor and seabird cliffs.
Key birds: *All year*: Hen Harrier, Peregrine and Chough. Breeding seabirds including Shag, Razorbill, Manx Shearwater etc. Excellent spring and autumn migration, seabird passage best in autumn.
Contact: Ben Jones, (Warden), Manx National Heritage, Douglas, Isle of Man IM1 3LY.

CLOSE SARTFIELD

Manx Wildlife Trust.
Location: SC 361 956. From Ramsey drive W on A3. Turn on to B9, take third R and follow this road for nearly a mile. Reserve entrance is on R.
Access: Open all year round. No dogs. Path and boardwalk suitable for wheelchairs from car park through wildflower meadow and willow scrub to hide.

Facilities: Car park, hide, reserve leaflet (50p, available from office) outlines circular walk.
Public transport: None.
Habitat: Wildflower-rich hay meadow, marshy grassland, willow scrub/developing birch woodland, bog.
Key birds: *Winter*: Large roost of Hen Harrier. *Summer*: Corn Crake, Curlew, warblers.
Contact: Manx Wildlife Trust, 01624 801 985. e-mail: manxwt@cix.co.uk www.wildlifetrust.org.uk/manxwt

CRONK Y BING

Manx Wildlife Trust.
Location: NX 381 017. Take A10 coast road N from Jurby. Approx two miles along there is a sharp R hand turn over a bridge. Before the bridge there is a track to the L. A parking area is available at end oftrack.
Access: Open all year round. Dogs to be kept on a lead. Not suitable for the disabled.
Facilities: None.
Public transport: None.
Habitat: Open dune and dune grassland.
Key birds: *Summer*: Terns. *Winter*: Divers, grebes, skuas, gulls.
Contact: Manx Wildlife Trust, 01624 801 985. e-mail: manxwt@cix.co.uk www.wildlifetrust.org.uk/manxwt

COUNTY DIRECTORY

Tufted Duck by David Cromack

ENGLAND

THE INFORMATION in the directory has been obtained either from the persons listed or from the appropriate national or other bodies. In some cases, where it has not proved possible to verify the details directly, alternative responsible sources have been relied upon. When no satisfactory record was available, previously included entries have sometimes had to be deleted. Readers are requested to advise the editor of any errors or omissions.

AVON

See Somerset.

BEDFORDSHIRE

Bird Atlas/Avifauna
An Atlas of the Breeding Birds of Bedfordshire 1988-92 by R A Dazley and P Trodd (Bedfordshire Natural History Society, 1994).

Bird Recorders
Nigel Willits, Orchard Cottage, 68 High Street, Wilden, Beds MK44 2QD. 01234 771 948; e-mail: willits1960@hotmail.com

Bird Report
BEDFORDSHIRE BIRD REPORT (1946-), from Mary Sheridan, 28 Chestnut Hill, Linslade, Leighton Buzzard, Beds LU7 2TR. 01525 378 245.

BTO Regional Representative
RR. Nigel Willits, Orchard Cottage, 68 High Street, Wilden, Beds MK44 2QD. 01234 771 948; e-mail: willits1960@hotmail.com

Club
BEDFORDSHIRE BIRD CLUB. (1992; 290). Miss Sheila Alliez, Flat 61 Adamson Court, Adamson Walk, Kempston, Bedford MK42 8QZ. e-mail: alliezsec@peewit.freeserve.co.uk www.bedsbirdclub.org.uk
Meetings: 8.00pm, last Tuesday of the month (Sep-Mar), Maulden Village Hall, Maulden, Beds.

Ringing Groups
IVEL RG. Graham Buss, 11 Northall Close, Eaton Bray, Dunstable, LU6 2EB. 01525 221 023; e-mail: g1j2buss@yahoo.co.uk

RSPB. WB Kirby. e-mail: will.kirby@rspb.org.uk

RSPB Local Groups
BEDFORD. (1970; 80). Bob Montgomery, 36 Princes Road, Bromham, Beds MK43 8QD. 01234 822 035;www.rspb.org.uk/groups/bedford/
Meetings: 7.30pm, 3rd Thursday of the month, A.R.A. Manton Lane, Bedford.

LUTON AND SOUTH BEDFORDSHIRE. (1973; 120+). Mick Price, 120 Common Road, Kensworth, Beds, LU6 3RG. 01582 873 268.
Meetings: 7.45pm, 2nd Wednesday of the month, Houghton Regis Social Centre, Parkside Drive, Houghton Regis, LU5 5QN.

Wildlife Trust
See Cambridgeshire,

BERKSHIRE

BirdAtlas/Avifauna
The Birds of Berkshire by P E Standley et al (Berkshire Atlas Group/Reading Ornithological Club, 1996).

Bird Recorder
RECORDER (Records Committee and rarity records). Chris DR Heard, 3 Waterside Lodge, Ray Mead Road, Maidenhead, Berkshire SL6 8NP. 01628 633 828; e-mail: chris.heard@virgin.net

Bird Reports
BERKSHIRE BIRD BULLETIN (Monthly,1986-) from Brian Clews, 118 Broomhill, Cookham, Berks SL6 9LQ. 01628 525 314; e-mail: brian.clews@btconnect.com

BIRDS OF BERKSHIRE (1974-), from Secretary of the Berkshire Ornithological Club, e-mail: renton.righelato@berksoc.org.uk

BIRDS OF THE THEALE AREA (1988-), from Secretary, Theale Area Bird Conservation Group.

NEWBURY DISTRICT BIRD REPORT (1959-), from Secretary, Newbury District Ornithological Club.

BTO Regional Representative & Regional Development Officer
RR. Chris Robinson, 2 Beckfords, Upper Basildon, Reading, RG8 8PB. 01491 671 420; e-mail: berks_bto_rep@btinternet.com

Clubs
BERKSHIRE BIRD BULLETIN GROUP. (1986; 100). Berkshire Bird Bulletin Group, PO Box 680, Maidenhead, Berks, SL6 9ST. 01628 525 314; e-mail: brian.clews@btconnect.com

BERKSHIRE ORNITHOLOGICAL CLUB. (1947; 320). Renton Righelato, 63 Hamilton Road, Reading, RG1 5RA. 0787 981 2564;
e-mail: renton.righelato@berksoc.org.uk
www.berksoc.org.uk
Meetings: 8pm, alternate Wednesdays (Oct-Mar). University of Reading.

NEWBURY DISTRICT ORNITHOLOGICAL CLUB. (1959; 110). Membership Secretary.
e-mail: info1@ndoc.org.uk
www.ndoc.org.uk

THEALE AREA BIRD CONSERVATION GROUP. (1988; 75). Catherine McEwan. 0118 941 5792;
e-mail catherine_j_mcewan@fsmail.net
www.freewebs.com/tabcg/index.htm
Meetings: 8pm, 1st Tuesday of the month, Englefield Social Club.

Ringing Groups
NEWBURY RG. J Legg, 31 Haysoms Drive, Greenham, Nr Newbury, Berks RG19 8EY.
e-mail: janlegg@btinternet.com
www.newburyrg.co.uk

RUNNYMEDE RG. D G Harris, 22 Blossom Waye, Hounslow, TW5 9HD.
e-mail: daveharris@tinyonline.co.uk

RSPB Local Groups
EAST BERKSHIRE. (1974; 200). Gerry Studd, 5 Cherry Grove, Holmer Green, High Wycombe, Bucks HP15 6RG. 01494 715 609;
e-mail: gerrystudd@aol.com
www.eastberksrspb.org.uk
Meetings: 7.30pm, Thursdays (Sept-April), Methodist Church Hall, High Street, Maidenhead.

EAST BERKS. LOCAL GROUP

READING. (1986; 80). David Glover. 0118 983 3812;
e-mail: davidglover@hotmail.co.uk
www.reading-rspb.org.uk

WOKINGHAM & BRACKNELL. (1979; 200). Les Blundell, Folly Cottage, Buckle Lane, Warfield, RG42 5SB. 01344 861 964;
e-mail: les@folly-cottage.fsnet.co.uk
www.wbrspb.btinternet.co.uk
Meetings: 8.00pm, 2nd Tuesday of the month (Sep-Jun), Finchampstead Memorial Hall, Wokingham, RG40 4JU.

Wildlife Hospitals
LIFELINE. Wendy Hermon, Treatment Centre Co-ordinator, Swan Treatment Centre, Cuckoo Weir Island, South Meadow Lane, Eton, Windsor, Berks SL4 6SS. 01753 859 397; (fax) 01753 622 709;
e-mail: wendyhermon@aol.com
www.zen117019.zen.co.uk
Registered charity. Thames Valley 24-hour swan rescue and treatment service. Veterinary support and hospital unit. Operates membership scheme.

Wildlife Trust
Director, See Oxfordshire,

BUCKINGHAMSHIRE

BirdAtlas/Avifauna
The Birds of Buckinghamshire ed by P Lack and D Ferguson (Buckinghamshire Bird Club, 1993). Now out of print.

Bird Recorder
Andy Harding, 93 Deanshanger Lane, Old Stratford, MK19 6AX. e-mail: a.v.harding@open.ac.uk

Bird Reports
AMERSHAM BIRDWATCHING CLUB ANNUAL REPORT (1975-), from Secretary.

BUCKINGHAMSHIRE BIRD REPORT (1980-), from John Gearing, Valentines, Dinton, Aylesbury, Bucks, HP17 8UW. e-mail: john_gearing@hotmail.com

NORTH BUCKS BIRD REPORT (12 pa), from Recorder.

BTO Regional Representative & Regional Development Officer
RR. David Lee. 01844 347 576;
e-mail: oldfield51@btinternet.com

RDO. Peter Hearn, 160 High Street, Aylesbury, Bucks, HP20 1RE. 01296 424 145; (fax)01296 581 520.

Clubs
BUCKINGHAMSHIRE BIRD CLUB. (1981; 340). Roger S Warren. 01491 638 544;
e-mail: Secretary@bucksbirdclub.co.uk
www.bucksbirdclub.co.uk

NORTH BUCKS BIRDERS. (1977; 40). Andy Harding, 15 Jubilee Terrace, Stony Stratford, Milton Keynes, MK11 1DU. H:01908 565 896; W:01908 653 328;
e-mail: a.v.harding@open.ac.uk
Meetings: Last Tuesday of the month (Nov, Jan, Feb, Mar), The Cock, High Street, Stony Stratford.

RSPB Local Groups
See also Herts: Chorleywood,

AYLESBURY. (1981; 220). Ann Wallington. 01295 253 330, e-mail: Jenny.wallington@btinternet.com

NORTH BUCKINGHAMSHIRE. (1976; 440). Chris Ward, 41 William Smith Close, Woolstone, Milton Keynes, MK15 0AN. 01908 669 448;
e-mail: cwphotography@hotmail.com
www.rspb.org.uk/groups/northbucks
Meetings: 8.00pm, 2nd Thursday of the month, Cruck Barn, City Discovery Centre, Bradwell Abbey, MK13 9AP.

Wildlife Hospitals
WILDLIFE HOSPITAL TRUST. St Tiggywinkles, Aston Road, Haddenham, Aylesbury, Bucks, HP17 8AF. 01844 292 292 (24hr helpline);
e-mail: mail@sttiggywinkles.org.uk
www.sttiggywinkles.org.uk
Registered charity. All British species. Veterinary referrals and helpline for vets and others on wild bird treatments. Full veterinary unit and staff. Pub: *Bright Eyes* (free to members - sae).

Wildlife Trust
Director, See Oxfordshire.

CAMBRIDGESHIRE

BirdAtlas/Avifauna
An Atlas of the Breeding Birds of Cambridgeshire (VC 29) P M M Bircham et al (Cambridge Bird Club, 1994).

The Birds of Cambridgeshire: checklist 2000 (Cambridge Bird Club)

Bird Recorders
CAMBRIDGESHIRE. Mark Hawkes, 7 Cook Drive, Eynesbury, St Neots, Cambs PE19 2JU. 01480 215 305; e-mail: marklhawkes@yahoo.co.uk

Bird Reports
CAMBRIDGESHIRE BIRD REPORT (1925-), from Bruce Martin, 178 Nuns Way, Cambridge, CB4 2NS. 01223 700656; e-mail: bruce.s.martin@ntlworld.com

PAXTON PITS BIRD AND WILDLIFE REPORT (1994-) £3.50 inc postage, from Trevor Gunton, 15 St James Road, Little Paxton, Cambs PE19 6QW. (Tel/fax)01480 473562.

PETERBOROUGH BIRD CLUB REPORT (1999-), from Secretary, Peterborough Bird Club.

BTO Regional Representatives
CAMBRIDGESHIRE RR. Tony Fulford, 19 Mallow Close, Ely, Cambs, CB6 3WH. 01353 659 524; e-mail: tonyfulford@gmail.com

HUNTINGDON & PETERBOROUGH. Phillip Todd. 01733 810 832; e-mail: huntspbororr@yahoo.co.uk

Clubs
CAMBRIDGESHIRE BIRD CLUB. (1925; 310). Bruce Martin, 178 Nuns Way, Cambridge, CB4 2NS. 01223 700 656; e-mail: bruce.s.martin@ntlworld.com
www.cambridgebirdclub.org.uk
Meetings: 2nd Friday of the month, St John's Church Hall, Hills Road, Cambridge/Milton CP Visitors Centre, Milton, Cambridge.

PETERBOROUGH BIRD CLUB. (1999; 210). David Cromack, 55 Thorpe Park Road, Peterborough, PE3 6LJ. 01733 566 815; www.pbc.codehog.co.uk

e-mail: d.cromack@btinternet.com
Meetings: Indoor last Tuesday of each month from Sep-Apr inclusive at 7.30pm at the Post Office Sports and Social Club on Bourges Boulevard, Peterborough. Outdoor meetings monthly throughout most of year.

Ringing Group
WICKEN FEN RG. Dr C J R Thorne. 17 The Footpath, Coton, Cambs CB23 7PX. 01954 210 566; e-mail: cjrt@cam.ac.uk

RSPB Local Group
CAMBRIDGE. (1977; 150). Melvyn Smith. 01799 500 482; e-mail: mel_brensmith@hotmail.co.uk
www.RSPB.org.uk/groups/cambridge.
Meetings: 3rd Wednesday of every month Jan-May and Sept-Dec 8pm. Chemistry Labs, Lensfield Road, Cambridge.

Wetland Bird Survey Organisers
CAMBRIDGESHIRE (including Huntingdonshire). Bruce Martin, 178 Nuns Way, Cambridge, CB4 2NS. 01223 700 656; e-mail: bruce.s.martin@ntlworld.com

NENE WASHES. Charlie Kitchin, RSPB Nene Washes, 21a East Delph, Whittlesey, Cambs PE7 1RH. 01733 205 140.

OUSE WASHES. Paul Harrington, Ouse Washes Reserve, Welches Dam, Manea, March, Cambs PE15 0NF. e-mail: paul.harrington@rspb.org.uk

HUNTINGDONSHIRE. (1982; 180). Martyn Stanley-Williams, Babinda House, High Street, Bury, Huntingdon PE26 2NR. 01487 710 456; e-mail: edunit@edunit.plus.com
www.huntsrspb.co.uk
Meetings: 7.30pm, last Wednesday of the month (Sep-Apr), Free Church, St Ives.

Wildlife Trust
THE WILDLIFE TRUST FOR BEDFORDSHIRE, CAMBRIDGESHIRE, NORTHAMPTONSHIRE AND PETERBOROUGH. (1990; 33,000). The Manor House, Broad Street, Great Cambourne, Cambridgeshire CB23 6DH. 01954 713 500; fax 01954 710 051;
e-mail: cambridgeshire@wildlifebcnp.org
www.wildlifebcnp.org

CHESHIRE

BirdAtlas/Avifauna
Birds in Cheshire and Wirral - A Breeding and Wintering Atlas 2004-2007 by Professor David Norman, Liverpool University Press, Autumn 2008.

ENGLAND

The Birds of Sandbach Flashes 1935-1999 by Andrew Goodwin and Colin Lythgoe (The Printing House, Crewe, 2000).

Bird Recorder (inc Wirral)
CHESHIRE & WIRRAL. Hugh Pulsford, 6 Buttermere Drive, Great Warford, Alderley Edge, Cheshire SK9 7WA. 01565 880 171; e-mail: countyrec@cawos.org

Bird Report
CHESHIRE & WIRRAL BIRD REPORT (1969-), from Peter Mathews, Hordern Farm Pottery, Buxton New Road, Macclesfield SK11 0AN.

HILBRE BIRD OBSERVATORY REPORT, from Hilbre Bird Observatory, c/o 129, Ennisdale Drive, West Kirby, Wirral, CH48 9UG, £3.

SOUTH EAST CHESHIRE ORNITHOLOGICAL SOCIETY BIRD REPORT (1985-), from Secretary, South East Cheshire Ornithol Soc. 01270 582642.

BTO Regional Representatives & Regional Development Officer
MID RR. Paul Miller. 01928 787 535; e-mail: huntershlll@worldonline.co.uk

NORTH & EAST RR. Mark Eddowes, 59 Westfield Drive, Knutsford, Cheshire WA16 0BH. 01565 621 683; e-mail: mark.eddowes@esrtechnology.com

SOUTH RR & RDO. Charles Hull, Edleston Cottage, Edleston Hall Lane, Nantwich, Cheshire CW5 8PL. 01270 628 194; e-mail: edleston@yahoo.co.uk

Clubs
CHESHIRE & WIRRAL ORNITHOLOGICAL SOCIETY. (1988; 375). David Cogger, 113 Nantwich Road, Middlewich, Cheshire, CW10 9HD. 01606 832 517; e-mail: memsec@cawos.org
www.cawos.org
Meetings: 7.45pm, 1st Friday of the month, Knutsford Civic Centre.

CHESTER & DISTRICT ORNITHOLOGICAL SOCIETY. (1967; 50). David King, 13 Bennett Close, Willaston, South Wirral, CH64 2XF. 0151 327 7212; e-mail: djmpkings@ntlworld.com .
Meetings: 7.30pm, 1st Thursday of the month (Oct-Mar), Caldy Valley Community Centre.

KNUTSFORD ORNITHOLOGICAL SOCIETY. (1974; 45). Derek A Pike, 2 Lilac Avenue, Knutsford, Cheshire, WA16 0AZ. 01565 653 811; www.10x50.com
Meetings: 7.30pm, 4th Friday of the month (not Dec), Jubilee Hall, Stanley Road, Knutsford.

LANCASHIRE & CHESHIRE FAUNA SOCIETY. (1914; 140). Dave Bickerton, 64 Petre Crescent, Rishton, Blackburn, Lancs, BB1 4RB. 01254 886257; e-mail: bickertond@aol.com
www.lacfs.org.uk

LYMM ORNITHOLOGY GROUP. (1975; 60). Mrs Ann Ledden, 4 Hill View, Widnes, WA8 9AL. 0151 424 0441; e-mail: secretary-log@tiscali.co.uk
Meetings: 8.00pm, last Friday of the month (Aug-May), Lymm Village Hall.

MID-CHESHIRE ORNITHOLOGICAL SOCIETY. (1963; 80). Paul Kenyon, 196 Chester Road, Hartford, Northwich, Cheshire CW8 1LG. 01606 779 60; e-mail: contact@midcheshireos.co.uk www.midcheshireos.co.uk
Meetings: 7.30pm, 2nd Friday of the month (Oct-Mar), Hartford Village Hall.

SOUTH EAST CHESHIRE ORNITHOLOGICAL SOCIETY. (1964; 150). Colin Lythgoe, 11 Waterloo Road, Haslington, Crewe, CW1 5TF. 01270 582 642. www.secos.org.uk
Meetings: 2nd Friday (Sept-Apr), 7.30pm, St Mathews Church Hall, Elworth.

WILMSLOW GUILD BIRDWATCHING GROUP. (1965; 67). Tom Gibbons, Chestnut Cottage, 37 Strawberry Lane, Wilmslow, Cheshire SK9 6AQ. 01625 520317.
Meetings: 7.30pm last Friday of the month, Wilmslow Guild, Bourne St, Wilmslow.

Ringing Groups
MERSEYSIDE RG. Bob Harris, 2 Dulas Road, Wavertree Green, Liverpool, L15 6UA. Work 0151 706 4311; e-mail: harris@liv.ac.uk

SOUTH MANCHESTER RG. Mr N.B. Powell, email: neville.powell@tiscali.co.uk

RSPB Local Groups
CHESTER. (1988; 220). Roger Nutter, Group Leader, 2 Lower Farm Court, Duckington, Malpas, Cheshire SY14 8LQ. 01829 782237; e-mail: roger@lexeme.co.uk www.rspb.org.uk/groups/chester7.30pm, 3rd Wednesday of the month (Sep-Apr), St Mary's Centre, Chester.

MACCLESFIELD. (1979; 394). Ray Evans. 01625 432 635; e-mail: ray@macclesfieldrspb.org.uk www.macclesfieldrspb.org.uk

NORTH CHESHIRE. (1976; 100). Paul Grimmet. 01925 268 770; e-mail: paulwtwitcher@hotmail.com www.rspb.org.uk/groups/north_cheshire
Meetings: 7.45pm, 3rd Friday (Jan-April and Sept-Nov), Appleton Parish Hall, Dudlow's Green Road, Appleton, Warrington.

Wildlife Hospitals
RSPCA STAPELEY GRANGE WILDLIFE CENTRE. London Road, Stapeley, Nantwich, Cheshire, CW5

7JW. 0870 442 7102. All wild birds. Oiled bird wash facilities and pools. Veterinary support.

Wildlife Trust
CHESHIRE WILDLIFE TRUST. (1962; 13,100). Bickley Hall Farm, Bickley, Malpas, Cheshire SY14 8EF. 01948 820 728; (fax) 0709 2888 469
e-mail: cheshirewt@cix.co.uk
www.cheshirewildlifetrust.co.uk

CLEVELAND

Bird Atlas/Avifauna
The Breeding Birds of Cleveland. Due for publication 2007/2008.

Bird Recorder
CLEVELAND. Tom Francis.
E-mail: mot.francis@ntlworld.com

Bird Report
CLEVELAND BIRD REPORT (1974-), from Mr J Fletcher, 43 Glaisdale Avenue, Middlesbrough TS5 7PF. 01642 818 825.

BTO Regional Representative
CLEVELAND RR. Vic Fairbrother, 8, Whitby Avenue, Guisborough, Cleveland, TS14 7AP. 01287 633 744; e-mail: vic.fairbrother@ntlworld.com

Club
TEESMOUTH BIRD CLUB. (1960; 340). Chris Sharp (Hon Sec.), 20 Auckland Way, Hartlepool, TS26 0AN. 01429 865 163. www.teesmouthbc.com
Meetings: 7.30pm, 1st Monday of the month (Sep-Apr), Stockton Library, Church Road, Stockton.

Ringing Groups
TEES RG. E Wood, Southfields, 16 Marton Moor Road, Nunthorpe, Middlesbrough, Cleveland TS7 0BH. 01642 323 563.

SOUTH CLEVELAND RG. W Norman, 2 Station Cottages, Grosmont, Whitby, N Yorks YO22 5PB. 01947 895 226; e-mail: wilfgros@lineone.net

RSPB Local Group
CLEVELAND. (1974; 200). Terry Reeve.
e-mail: ClevelandRSPB@googlemail.com
www.rspb.org.uk/groups/cleveland
Meetings: 7.30pm, 2nd Monday of the month (Sep-Apr), Lingfield Farm Countryside Centre, Mount Pleasant Way, Coulby Newham, MIddlesbrough (£1.50 members, £2.50 non-members).

Wetland Bird Survey Organiser
TEES ESTUARY. Mike Leakey, c/o Natural England, British Energy, Tees Road, Hartlepool TS25 2BZ. 01429 853 325;
e-mail: mike.leakey@naturalengland.org.uk

Wildlife Trust
TEES VALLEY WILDLIFE TRUST. (1979; 5,000). Margrove Heritage Centre, Margrove Park, Boosbeck, Saltburn-by-the-Sea, TS12 3BZ. 01287 636 382; fax 01287 636 383;
e-mail: info@teeswildlife.org www.teeswildlife.org

CORNWALL AND THE ISLES OF SCILLY

Bird Atlas/Avifauna
The Birds of the Isles of Scilly by P Robinson. Published by Christopher Helm 2003.

The Essential Guide to Birds of The Isles of Scilly 2007 by RL Flood, N Hudson and B Thomas, published by authors.

Bird Recorders
CORNWALL. Darrell Clegg, 55 Lower Fore Street, Saltash, Cornwall PL12 6JQ.
E-mail: recorder@cbwps.org.uk

ISLES OF SCILLY. Nigel Hudson, Post Office Flat, Hugh Street, St Mary's, Isles of Scilly TR21 0JE. 01720 422 267; e-mail: nigel-hudson1@tiscali.co.uk

Bird Reports
BIRDS IN CORNWALL (1931-), from Cornwall Birdwatching and Preservation Society.

ISLES OF SCILLY BIRD REPORT and NATURAL HISTORY REVIEW 2000 (1969-), from The Secretary, Lyonnesse Guest House, The Strand, St Mary's, Isles of Scilly TR21 0PS.
e-mail: scillybirding@scillybirding.co.uk
www.scillybirding.co.uk

BTO Regional Representative
CORNWALL. Stephen Jackson, 2, Trelawney Cottages, Falmouth, Cornwall TR11 3NY. 01326 313 533; e-mail: stephen.f.jackson@btinternet.com

ISLES OF SCILLY RR & RDO. Will Wagstaff, 42 Sally Port, St Mary's, Isles of Scilly, TR21 0JE. 01720 422212; e-mail: william.wagstaff@virgin.net

Clubs
CORNWALL BIRDWATCHING & PRESERVATION SOCIETY. (1931; 990). Darrell Clegg, 55 Lower Fore Street, Saltash, Cornwall PL12 6JQ.
E-mail: secretary@cbwps.org.uk www.cbwps.org.uk

CORNWALL WILDLIFE TRUST PHOTOGRAPHIC GROUP. (40). David Chapman, 41 Bosence Road, Townshend, Nr Hayle, Cornwall TR27 6AL. 01736 850287; e-mail: david@ruralimages.freeserve.co.uk www.ruralimages.freeserve.co.uk
Meetings: Mixture of indoor and outdoor meetings, please phone for details.

ISLES OF SCILLY BIRD GROUP. (2000; 510). The Secretary, Lyonnesse Guest House, The Strand, St Mary's, Isles of Scilly TR21 0PS.
www.scillybirding.co.uk

Ringing Group
SCILLONIA SEABIRD GROUP. Peter Robinson, Secretary, 19 Pine Park Road, Honiton, Devon EX14 2HR. (Tel/fax) 01404 549 873; (M)07768 538 132; e-mail: pjrobinson2@aol.com

RSPB Local Group
CORNWALL. (1972; 600). Gordon Mills, 11 Commercial Square, Camborne, Cornwall TR14 8JZ. 01209 718144; e-mail: GRSDMILLSFLORISTS@ camborne.fsbusiness.co.uk
www.RSPBcornwall.org.uk.
Meetings: Indoor meetings (Oct-Apr), outdoor throughout the year.

Wetland Bird Survey Organisers
CORNWALL (excl. Tamar complex). Graham Hobin, Lower Drift Farmhouse, Drift, Buryas Bridge, Penzance TR19 6AA.
e-mail: graham.hobin@sky.com

TAMAR COMPLEX. Gladys Grant, 18 Orchard Crescent, Oreston, Plymouth, PL9 7NF. 01752 406 287; e-mail: gladysgrant@talktalk.net

Wildlife Hospital
MOUSEHOLE WILD BIRD HOSPITAL & SANCTUARY ASSOCIATION LTD. Raginnis Hill, Mousehole, Penzance, Cornwall, TR19 6SR. 01736 731 386. All species. No ringing.

Wildlife Trust
CORNWALL WILDLIFE TRUST. (1962; 13,600). Five Acres, Allet, Truro, Cornwall, TR4 9DJ. 01872 273939; fax 01872 225476;
e-mail: info@cornwt.demon.co.uk
www.cornwallwildlifetrust.org.uk

THE ISLES OF SCILLY WILDLIFE TRUST. (462). Carn Thomas, Hugh Town, St Marys, Isles of Scilly TR21 0PT.01720 422 153; fax 01720 422 153; e-mail: enquiries@ios-wildlifetrust.org.uk
www.www.ios-wildlifetrust.org.uk

CUMBRIA

BirdAtlas/Avifauna
The Breeding Birds of Cumbria by Stott, Callion, Kinley, Raven and Roberts (Cumbria Bird Club, 2002).

Bird Recorders
CUMBRIA. Colin Raven, 18 Seathwaite Road, Barrow-in-Furness, Cumbria, LA14 4LX.
e-mail: colin@walneyobs.fsnet.co.uk

NORTH WEST (Allerdale & Copeland). Derek McAlone, 88 Whinlatter Road, Mirehouse, Whitehaven, Cumbria CA28 8DQ. 01946 691 370; e-mail: derek@derekmcalone3.wanadoo.co.uk

SOUTH (South Lakeland & Furness). Ronnie Irving. e-mail:ronnie@wsi-sign.co.uk

Bird Reports
BIRDS AND WILDLIFE IN CUMBRIA (1970-), from Dave Shackleton, 8 Burnbanks, Penrith, Cumbria CA10 2RW.

WALNEY BIRD OBSERVATORY REPORT, from Warden, see Reserves.

BTO Regional Representatives
CUMBRIA. Clive Hartley, Undercragg, Charney Well La, Grange Over Sands, LA11 6DB. 01539 532 856; e-mail: clive.hartley@tiscali.co.uk

Clubs
ARNSIDE & DISTRICT NATURAL HISTORY SOCIETY. (1967; 221). Jane Phillips. 01524 782 582.
Meetings: 7.30pm, 2nd Tuesday of the month (Sept-Apr). WI Hall, Arnside. (Also summer walks).

CUMBRIA BIRD CLUB. (1989; 230). Clive Hartley, Undercragg, Charney Well La, Grange Over Sands, LA11 6DB. 01539 532 856;
e-mail: clive.hartley@tiscali.co.uk
www.cumbriabirdclub.freeserve.co.uk
Meetings: Various evenings and venues (Oct-Mar) check on website for further details. £2 for non-members.

CUMBRIA RAPTOR STUDY GROUP. (1992). P N Davies, Snowhill Cottage, Caldbeck, Wigton, Cumbria CA7 8HL. 01697 371 249;
e-mail: pete.caldbeck@virgin.net

Ringing Groups
EDEN RG. G Longrigg, Mere Bank, Bleatarn, Warcop, Appleby, Cumbria CA16 6PX.

WALNEY BIRD OBSERVATORY. K Parkes, 176 Harrogate Street, Barrow-in-Furness, Cumbria, LA14 5NA. 01229 824 219.

RSPB Local Groups
CARLISLE. (1974; 400). Bob Jones, 130 Greenacres, Wetheral, Carlisle, 01225 561 684;
e-mail: bob@onethirty.force9.co.uk
www.rspb.org.uk/groups/carlisle
Meetings: 7.30pm, Wednesday monthly, Tythe Barn, Carlisle.

SOUTH LAKELAND. (1973; 340). Mr Martin Baines, 101 Serpentine Road, Kendal, Cumbria, LA9 4PP. 01539 732 214.
Meetings: Contact above.

WEST CUMBRIA. (1986; 270). Neil Hutchin, 3 Camerton Road, Gt Broughton, Cockermouth, Cumbria CA13 0YR. 01900 825 231; e-mail: majoriehutchin@btinternet.com
Meetings: 7.30pm, 1st Tuesday (Sept-Apr), United Reformed Church, Main St, Cockermouth

Wetland Bird Survey Organiser
DUDDON ESTUARY. Rosalyn Gay, 8 Victoria Street, Millom, Cumbria LA18 5AS. 01229 773 820; colinathodbarrow@aol.com

Wildlife Trust
CUMBRIA WILDLIFE TRUST. (1962; 15,000). Plumgarths, Crook Road, Kendal, Cumbria LA8 8LX. 01539 816 300; fax 01539 816 301; e-mail: mail@cumbriawildlifetrust.org.uk www.cumbriawildlifetrust.org.uk

DERBYSHIRE

BirdAtlas/Avifauna
The Birds of Derbyshire, ed. RA Frost (in preparation)

Bird Recorders
1. JOINT RECORDER. Roy A Frost, 66 St Lawrence Road, North Wingfield, Chesterfield, Derbyshire S42 5LL. 01246 850 037; e-mail: frostra66@btinternet.com

2. Records Committee & rarity records. Rodney W Key, 3 Farningham Close, Spondon, Derby, DE21 7DZ. 01332 678 571; e-mail: r_key@sky.com

3. JOINT RECORDER. Richard M R James, 10 Eastbrae Road, Littleover, Derby, DE23 1WA. 01332 771 787; e-mail: rmrjames@yahoo.co.uk

Bird Reports
CARSINGTON BIRD CLUB ANNUAL REPORT, from the club secretary.

DERBYSHIRE BIRD REPORT (1954-), from Bryan Barnacle, Mays, Malthouse Lane, Froggatt, Hope Valley, Derbyshire S32 3ZA. 01433 630 726; e-mail: barney@mays1.demon.co.uk

OGSTON BIRD CLUB REPORT (1970-), see contact for Ogston Bird Club below.

BTO Regional Representatives
NORTH RR. Dave Budworth, 121 Wood Lane, Newhall, Swadlincote, Derbys DE11 0LX. 01283 215 188; e-mail: dbud01@aol.com

SOUTH RR. Dave Budworth, 121 Wood Lane, Newhall, Swadlincote, Derbys DE11 0LX. 01283 215 188; e-mail: dbud01@aol.com

Clubs
BAKEWELL & DISTRICT BIRD STUDY GROUP.

(1987; 80).Bill Millward, Dale House, The Dale, Hope Valley, Derbys S32 1AQ.
Meetings: 7.30pm, 2nd Monday of the month, Friends Meeting House, Bakewell.

BUXTON FIELD CLUB. (1946; 68). B Aries, 1 Horsefair Avenue, Chapel-en-le-Frith, High Peak, Derbys SK23 9SQ. 01298 815 291; e-mail: brian.aries@btinternet.com
Meetings: 7.30pm, Saturdays fortnightly (Oct-Mar), Methodist Church Hall, Buxton.

CARSINGTON BIRD CLUB. (1992; 257). Maria Harwood/ Pat Wain, Joint Membership Secretary, 2 Yokecliffe Avenue, Wirksworth, Derbyshire DE4 4DJ. 01629 823 693; e-mail: membership@carsingtonbirdclub.co.uk www.carsingtonbirdclub.co.uk
Meetings: 3rd Tuesday of the month (Sep-Mar), Hognaston Village Hall, (Apr-Aug), outdoors.

DERBYSHIRE ORNITHOLOGICAL SOCIETY. (1954; 550). Steve Shaw, 84 Moorland View Road, Walton, Chesterfield, Derbys S40 3DF. 01246 236 090; e-mail: steveshaw84mrr@btinternet.com www.derbyshireOS.org.uk
Meetings: 7.30pm, last Friday of the winter months, various venues.

OGSTON BIRD CLUB. (1969; 1,126). Malcolm Hill, 2 Sycamore Avenue, Glapwell, Chesterfield, S44 5LH. 01623 812 159. www.ogstonbirdclub.co.uk

SOUTH PEAK RAPTOR STUDY GROUP. (1998; 12). M E Taylor, 76 Hawksley Avenue, Newbold, Chesterfield, Derbys S40 4TL. 01246 277 749.

Ringing Groups
DARK PEAK RG. W M Underwood, Ivy Cottage, 15 Broadbottom Road, Mottram-in-Longdendale, Hyde, Cheshire SK14 6JB.
e-mail: w.m.underwood@talk21.com

SORBY-BRECK RG. Dr Geoff P Mawson, Moonpenny Farm, Farwater Lane, Dronfield, Sheffield S18 1RA.
e-mail: moonpenny@talktalk.net www.sorbybreckringinggroup.co.uk

SOUDER RG. Dave Budworth, 121 Wood Lane, Newhall, Swadlincote, Derbys DE11 0LX.
e-mail: dbud01@aol.com

RSPB Local Groups
CHESTERFIELD. (1987; 274). Barry Whittleston. 01246 819 667; e-mail: barrymavis@whittleston. fsnet.co.uk
www.rspb.org.uk/groups/chesterfield
Meetings: 7.15pm, usually 3rd Monday of the month, Winding Wheel, New Exhibition Centre, 13 Holywell Street, Chesterfield.

DERBY LOCAL GROUP. (1973; 400). Chris Hunt, 38 Spenbeck Drive, Allestree, Derby, DE22 2UH. 01332 551 701; e-mail: chris.hunt42@ntlworld.com www.rspb.org.uk/groups/derby.
Meetings: 7.30pm, 2nd Wednesday of the month (Sep-Apr), Broughton Suite, Grange Banqueting Suite, 457 Burton Road, Littleover, Derby DE23 6FL.

HIGH PEAK. (1974; 175). Jim Jeffery.
E-mail: jim_jeffery1943@yahoo.co.uk
www.rspb.org.uk/groups/highpeak
Meetings: 7.30pm, 3rd Monday of the month (Sep-May), Marple Senior Citizens Hall.

Wildlife Trust
DERBYSHIRE WILDLIFE TRUST. (1962; 12,300). East Mill, Bridge Foot, Belper, Derbyshire DE56 1XH. 01773 881 188; fax 01773 821 826;
e-mail: enquiries@derbyshirewt.co.uk
www.derbyshirewildlifetrust.org.uk

DEVON

BirdAtlas/Avifauna
Tetrad Atlas of Breeding Birds of Devon by H P Sitters (Devon Birdwatching & Preservation Society, 1988).

The Birds of Darmoor by R Smaldon, published by Isabelline Books, 2005. (£18.95 from the publishers at 6 Bellevue, Enys, Penryn, Cornwall TR10 9LB).

The Birds of Lundy by Tim Davis and Tim Jones (Harpers Mill Publishing for Devon Bird Watching & Preservation Society and Lundy Field Society 2007), see www.birdsoflunday.org.uk for purchasing details.

Bird Recorder
Mr MW Tyler (until 31/12/08 - see entry under Ringing Groups). From 1st Jan 2009 - Mike Langman, 38 Brantwood Drive, Paignton, Devon TQ4 5HZ. 01803 528 008;
e-mail: devon-birdrecorder@lycos.com

Bird Reports
DEVON BIRD REPORT (1971) Previous annual reports since 1929, from DBWPS, PO Box 71, Okehampton, Devon EX20 1WF.

LUNDY FIELD SOCIETY ANNUAL REPORT (1946-). £3 each inc postage, check website for availability, from Frances Stuart, 3 Lower Linden Road, Clevedon, North Somerset BS21 7SU.
e-mail: lfssec@hotmail.co.uk

BTO Regional Representative
RR. John Woodland, Glebe Cottage, Dunsford, Exeter, EX6 7AA. 01647 252 494;
e-mail: jwoodland@btodv.fsnet.co.uk

BTO DEVON NATIONAL ATLAS ORGANISER. John Woodland, Glebe Cottage, Dunsford, Exeter, EX6 7AA. 01647 252 494;
e-mail: jwoodland@btodv.fsnet.co.uk

Clubs
DEVON BIRDWATCHING & PRESERVATION SOCIETY. (1928; 1200). Mrs Joy Vaughan, 28 Fern Meadow, Okehampton, Devon, EX20 1PB. 01837 53360; e-mail: joy@vaughan411.freeserve.co.uk

KINGSBRIDGE & DISTRICT NATURAL HISTORY SOCIETY. (1989; 130). Martin Catt, Migrants Rest, East Prawle, Kingsbridge, Devon TQ7 2DB. 01548 511 443; e-mail: martin.catt@btinternet.com
Meeting: 4th Monday of Sept-Apr, 7.30pm phone for venue.

LUNDY FIELD SOCIETY. (1946; 450). Frances Stuart, 3 Lower Linden Road, Clevedon, North Somerset, BS21 7SU. 01275 871 434; e-mail: lfssec@hotmail.co.uk www.lundy.org.uk
Meeting: AGM 1st Saturday in March, 1.45pm, Exeter University.

TOPSHAM BIRDWATCHING & NATURALISTS' SOCIETY. (1969; 140). Mrs Janice Vining, 2 The Maltings, Fore Street, Topsham, Exeter, EX3 0HF. 01392 873514; e-mail: tbnsociety@hotmail.com www.members.tripod.co.uk/tbns
Meetings: 7.30pm, 2nd Friday of the month (Sep-May), Matthews Hall, Topsham.

Ringing Groups
AXE ESTUARY RINGING GROUP. Mike Tyler, The Acorn, Shute Road, Kilmington, Axminster EX13 7ST. 01297 34958;
e-mail: mwtyler2@googlemail.com

DEVON & CORNWALL WADER RG. R C Swinfen, 72 Dunraven Drive, Derriford, Plymouth, PL6 6AT. 01752 704 184.

LUNDY FIELD SOCIETY. A M Taylor, 26 High Street, Spetisbury, Blandford, Dorset DT11 9DJ. 01258 857 336; e-mail: ammataylor@yahoo.co.uk

SLAPTON BIRD OBSERVATORY. R C Swinfen, 72 Dunraven Drive, Derriford, Plymouth, PL6 6AT. 01752 704 184.

RSPB Local Groups
EXETER & DISTRICT. (1974; 466). John Allan, Coxland-by-Sigford, Sigford, Near Newton Abbot, TQ12 6LE, 01626 821 344;
e-mail: johnallan@coxland.e7even.com
www.exeter-RSPB.org.uk
Meetings: 7.30p, various evenings, Southernhay United Reformed Church Rooms, Dix's Field, EXETER.

PLYMOUTH. (1974; 600). Mrs Eileen Willey, 11 Beverstone Way, Roborough, Plymouth, PL6 7DY. 01752 208 996.

Wetland Bird Survey Organiser
DEVON. Peter Reay, 10 Devon House, Bovey Tracey, Devon TQ13 9HB. 01626 834 486; e-mail: peter.p.j.reay@btinternet.com

TAMAR COMPLEX. Gladys Grant, 18 Orchard Crescent, Oreston, Plymouth, PL9 7NF. 01752 406 287; e-mail: gladysgrant@talktalk.net

Wildlife Hospitals
BIRD OF PREY CASUALTY CENTRE. Mrs J E L Vinson, Crooked Meadow, Stidston Lane, South Brent, Devon, TQ10 9JS. 01364 72174.
Birds of prey, with emergency advice on other species. Aviaries, rehabilitation facilities. Veterinary support.

Wildlife Trust
DEVON WILDLIFE TRUST. (1962; 33,000). Cricklepit, Commercial Road, Exeter, EX2 4AB. 01392 279244; fax 01392 433221; e-mail: contactus@devonwildlifewt.org www.devonwildlifetrust.org

DORSET

BirdAtlas/Avifauna
Dorset Breeding Bird Atlas (working title). In preparation.

The Birds of Dorset by Dr George Green (Christopher Helm 2004)

Bird Recorder
Kevin Lane, e-mail: kevin@broadstone heath.co.uk

Bird Reports
DORSET BIRDS (1977-), from Miss J W Adams, 16 Sherford Drive, Wareham, Dorset, BH20 4EN. 01929 552 299.

THE BIRDS OF CHRISTCHURCH HARBOUR (1956-), from Ian Southworth, 1 Bodowen Road, Burton, Christchurch, Dorset BH23 7JL. e-mail: ianbirder@aol.com

PORTLAND BIRD OBSERVATORY REPORT, from Warden, see Reserves,

BTO Regional Representatives
Mike Pleasants, 10 Green Lane, Bournemouth, BH10 5LB. 07751 555 033 or 01202 593 500; e-mail: mike@btorepdorset.org www.btorepdorset.org

Clubs
CHRISTCHURCH HARBOUR ORNITHOLOGICAL GROUP. (1956; 225). Mr. I.H. Southworth,

Membership Secretary, 1 Bodowen Road, Burton, Christchurch, Dorset BH23 7JL. 01202 478 093. www.chog.org.uk.

DORSET BIRD CLUB. (1987; 525). Mr Chris Chapleo, 15 Stour Way, Christchurch, Dorset BH23 2PF. 01202 419 867. www.dorsetbirdclub.org.uk
Meetings: Usually 7.30pm, no set day or venue.

DORSET NATURAL HISTORY & ARCHAEOLOGICAL SOCIETY. (1845; 2188). Dorset County Museum. High West Street, Dorchester, Dorset DT1 1XA. 01305 262 735; e-mail: secretary@dorsetcountymuseum.org www.dorsetcountymuseum.org

Ringing Groups
CHRISTCHURCH HARBOUR RS. E C Brett, 3 Whitfield Park, St Ives, Ringwood, Hants, BH24 2DX. e-mail: ed_brett@lineone.net

PORTLAND BIRD OBSERVATORY. Martin Cade, Old Lower Light, Portland Bill, Dorset, DT5 2JT. 01305 820553; e-mail: obs@btinternet.com www.portlandbirdobs.org.uk

STOUR RG. R Gifford, 62 Beacon Park Road, Upton, Poole, Dorset BH16 5PE.

RSPB Local Groups
BLACKMOOR VALE. (1981; 106). Mrs Margaret Marris, 15 Burges Close, Marnhull, Sturminster Newton, Dorset DT10 1QQ. 01258 820 091.
Meetings: 7.30pm, 3rd Friday in the month, Gillingham Primary School.

EAST DORSET. (1974; 435). Kenneth Baxter. 01202 474 204; e-mail: kenangela@ntlworld.com http://homepage.ntlworld.com/kenangela
Meetings: 7.30pm, 2nd Wednesday of the month, St Mark's Church Hall, Talbot Village, Wallisdown, Bournemouth.

POOLE. (1982; 305). John Derricott, 49 Medbourne Close, Blandford, Dorset DT11 7UA. 01258 450 927; e-mail: johnmal@derricott.fslife.co.uk www.RSPB.org.uk/groups/poole
Meetings: 7.30pm, Upton Community Centre, Poole Road, Upton.

SOUTH DORSET. (1976; 422). Andrew Parsons. 01305 772 678; e-mail: andrew_parsons_141@yahoo.co.uk www.rspb.org.uk/groups/southdorset
Meetings: 3rd Thursday of each month (Sep-Apr), Dorchester Town Hall.

Wildlife Hospital
SWAN RESCUE SANCTUARY. Ken and Judy Merriman, The Wigeon, Crooked Withies, Holt,

Wimborne, Dorset BH21 7LB. 01202 828 166; www.swan.jowebdesign.co.uk
24 hr rescue service for swans. Large sanctuary of 40 ponds and lakes. Hospital and intensive care. Veterinary support. Free advice and help line. Three fully equipped rescue ambulances. Rescue water craft for all emergencies. Viewing by appointment only.

Wetland Bird Survey Organisers
THE FLEET & PORTLAND HARBOUR. Steve Groves, Abbotsbury Swannery, New Barn Road, Abbotsbury, Dorset DT3 4JG. (W)01305 871 684; e-mail: swannery@gotadsl.co.uk

POOLE HARBOUR. Harold Lilley. 01202 889 633; e-mail: halilley@tiscali.co.uk

RADIPOLE & LODMOOR. Nick Tomlinson, RSPB Visitor Centre, Swannery Carpark, Weymouth, Dorset DT4 7TZ. 01305 778 313.

Wildlife Trust
DORSET WILDLIFE TRUST. (1961; 24,500). Brooklands Farm, Forston, Dorchester, Dorset, DT2 7AA. 01305 264 620; fax 01305 251 120; e-mail: enquiries@dorsetwildlife.co.uk
www.dorsetwildlife.co.uk

DURHAM

BirdAtlas/Avifauna
A Summer Atlas of Breeding Birds of County Durham by Stephen Westerberg/Kieth Bowey. (Durham Bird Club, 2000)

Bird Recorders
Mark Newsome, 69 Cedar Drive, Jarrow, NE32 4BF. e-mail: mvnewsome@hotmail.com

Bird Reports
BIRDS IN DURHAM (1971-), from D Sowerbutts, 9 Prebends Fields, Gilesgate, Durham, DH1 1HH. H:0191 386 7201; e-mail: d16lst@tiscali.co.uk

BTO Regional Representatives
David L Sowerbutts, 9 Prebends Field, Gilesgate Moor, Durham, DH1 1HH. H:0191 386 7201; e-mail: david.sowerbutts@dunelm.org.uk

Clubs
DURHAM BIRD CLUB. (1975; 280). Paula Charlton, Secretary, 14 Bywell Road, Cleadon SR6 7QT.. 0191 537 3178; e-mail: barryandpaula@tiscali.co.uk
www.durhambirdclub.org
Meetings: Monthly indoor meetings (Sept-Apr), in Durham and Sunderland.

SUMMERHILL (HARTLEPOOL) BIRD CLUB. (2000; 75). Paul Grinter, 11 Hawkridge Close, Hartlepool, TS26 8SA. 01429 422 313.
www.summerhillbirdclub.co.uk

Meetings: 7pm, 2nd Tuesday of the month (Sept-May), Summerhill Visitors Centre, Catcote Road, Hartlepool.

Ringing Groups
DURHAM DALES RG. J R Hawes, Fairways, 5 Raby Terrace, Willington, Crook, Durham DL15 0HR.

RSPB Local Group
DURHAM. (1974; 125). David Gibson. 0191 386 9793; e-mail: David@dgibson6.wanadoo.co.uk
www.durham-rspb.org.uk
Meetings: 7.30pm, 2nd Tuesday of the month (Oct-Mar), Room CG83, adjacent to Scarborough Lecture Theatre, University Science Site, Stockton Road entrance.

Wildlife Trust
DURHAM WILDLIFE TRUST. (1971; 4,000). Rainton Meadows, Chilton Moor, Houghton-le-Spring, Tyne & Wear, DH4 6PU. 0191 584 3112; fax 0191 584 3934; e-mail: info@durhamwt.co.uk
www.durhamwildlifetrust.org.uk

ESSEX

Bird Atlas/Avifauna
The Birds of Essex by Simon Wood (A&C Black, 2007).

The Breeding Birds of Essex by M K Dennis (Essex Birdwatching Society, 1996).

Bird Recorder
JOINT RECORDER. Roy Ledgerton, 25 Bunyan Road, Braintree, Essex CM7 2PL. 01376 326 103; e-mail: r.ledgerton@virgin.net

JOINT RECORDER. Les Steward, 6 Creek View, Basildon, Essex SS16 4RU. 01268 551 464 , e-mail: les.steward@btinternet.com

Bird Report
ESSEX BIRD REPORT (inc Bradwell Bird Obs records) (1950-), from Peter Dwyer, Sales Officer, 48 Churchill Avenue, Halstead, Essex, CO9 2BE. Tel/fax 01787 476524; e-mail: petedwyer@petedwyer.plus.com

BTO Regional Representatives
NORTH-EAST RR. Position vacant.

NORTH-WEST RR. Graham Smith. 01277 354 034; e-mail: silaum.silaus@tiscali.co.uk

SOUTH RR. Lynn Parr. e-mail: lynnparr99@hotmail.co.uk

Club
ESSEX BIRDWATCHING SOCIETY. (1949; 700). Carol O'Leary, 24 Horeshoe Crescent, The Garrison, Shoeburyness, Essex SS3 9WL. e-mail: carol@carololeary.wanadoo.co.uk

www.essexbirdwatchsoc.co.uk
Meetings: 1st Friday of the month (Oct-Mar), Friends' Meeting House, Rainsford Road, Chelmsford.

Ringing Groups
ABBERTON RG. C P Harris, Wylandotte, Seamer Road, Southminster, Essex, CM0 7BX.

BRADWELL BIRD OBSERVATORY. C P Harris, Wyandotte, Seamer Road, Southminster, Essex, CM0 7BX.

RSPB Local Groups
CHELMSFORD AND CENTRAL ESSEX. (1976; 5500). Mike Logan Wood, Highwood, Ishams Chase, Wickham Bishops, Essex, CM8 3LG. 01621 892045; e-mail: mike.lw@tiscali.co.uk
www.rspb.org.uk/groups/chelmsford
Meetings: 8pm, Thursdays, eight times a year. The Cramphorn Theatre, Chelmsford.

COLCHESTER. (1981; 250). Mr R Leavett, 10 Grove Road, Brantham, CO11 1TX.
Meetings: 7.45pm, 2nd Thursday of the month (Sep-Apr), Shrub End Community Hall, Shrub End Road, Colchester.

SOUTH EAST ESSEX. (1983; 200). Graham Mee, 108 Southsea Avenue, Leigh on Sea, Essex SS9 2BJ. 01702 478 876;
e-mail: grahamm@southendrspb.co.uk
www.southendrspb.co.uk
Meetings: 7.30pm, usually 1st Tuesday of the month (Sep-May), Belfairs School Hall, School Way, Leigh-on-Sea SS9 4HX.

Wetland Bird Survey Organisers
ESSEX (Other Sites). Gerry Johnson, 4 Bunting Close, Chelmsford, CM2 8XR. 01245 356 633.

LEE VALLEY. Cath Patrick, Myddelton House, Bulls Cross, Enfield, Herts EN2 9HG; 01992 717 711; e-mail: cpatrick@leevalleypark.org.uk

STOUR ESTUARY. Rick Vonk, RSPB, Unit 13 Court Farm, 3 Stutton Road, Brantham Suffolk CO11 1PW. (D)01473 328 006; e-mail:rick.vonk@rspb.org.uk

Wildlife Trust
ESSEX WILDLIFE TRUST. (1959; 36,000). The Joan Elliot Visitor Centre, Abbots Hall Farm, Great Wigborough, Colchester, CO5 7RZ. 01621 862 960; fax 01621 862 990; e-mail: admin@essexwt.org.uk
www.essexwt.org.uk

GLOUCESTERSHIRE

Bird Atlas/Avifauna
Atlas of Breeding Birds of the North Cotswolds. (North Cotswold Ornithological Society, 1990).

Birds of Gloucestershire CM Swaine (Alan Sutton 1982 - now out of print).

Birds of The Cotswolds Liverpool University Press (in preparation, due for publication in 2009)

Bird Recorder
GLOUCESTERSHIRE EXCLUDING S.GLOS (AVON). Richard Baatsen. E-mail: baatsen@surfbirder.com

Bird Reports
CHELTENHAM BIRD CLUB BIRD REPORT (1998-2001) - no longer published.

GLOUCESTERSHIRE BIRD REPORT (1953-). £7.50 including postage, from David Cramp, 2 Ellenor Drive, Alderton, Tewkesbury, GL20 8NZ. e-mail: djcramp@btinternet.com

NORTH COTSWOLD ORNITHOLOGICAL SOCIETY ANNUAL REPORT (1983-), from T Hutton, 15 Green Close, Childswickham, Broadway, Worcs, WR12 7JJ. 01386 858 511.

BTO Regional Representative
Mike Smart, 143 Cheltenham Road, Gloucester, GL2 0JH. Home/work 01452 421 131; e-mail: smartmike@btinternet.com

Clubs
CHELTENHAM BIRD CLUB. (1976; 94). Mrs Frances Meredith, 14 Greatfield Drive, Charlton Kings, Cheltenham, GL53 9BU. 01242 516 393; e-mail: chelt.birds@virgin.net
www.beehive.thisisgloucestershire.co.uk/cheltbirdclub
Meetings: 7.15pm, Mondays (Oct-Mar), Bournside School, Warden Hill Road, Cheltenham.

DURSLEY BIRDWATCHING & PRESERVATION SOCIETY. (1953; 350).
Jennifer Rogers, 15 Shadwell, Uley, Dursley, Glos GL11 5BW. 01453 860 128. email: j.rogers@btinternet.com
Meetings: 7.45pm, 2nd and 4th Monday (Sept-Mar), Dursley Community Centre.

GLOUCESTERSHIRE NATURALISTS' SOCIETY. (1948; 500). Mike Smart, 143 Cheltenham Road, Gloucester, GL2 0JH. 01452 421 131; e-mail: smartmike@btinternet.com
www.glosnats.org.uk

NORTH COTSWOLD ORNITHOLOGICAL SOCIETY. (1982; 70). T Hutton, 15 Green Close, Childswickham, Broadway, Worcs WR12 7JJ. 01386 858 511.
Meetings: Monthly field meetings, usually Sunday 9.30pm.

ENGLAND

Ringing Groups

COTSWOLD WATER PARK RG. John Wells, 25 Pipers Grove, Highnam, Glos, GL2 8NJ.
e-mail: john.wells2@btinternet.com

SEVERN ESTUARY GULL GROUP. M E Durham, 6 Glebe Close, Frampton-on-Severn, Glos, GL2 7EL. 01452 741 312.

SEVERN VALE RG. John Wells, 25 Pipers Grove, Highnam, Glos, GL2 8NJ. e-mail: john.wells2@btinternet.com

WILDFOWL & WETLANDS TRUST. Richard Hearn, Wildfowl & Wetlands Trust, Slimbridge, Glos, GL2 7BT. e-mail: richard.hearn@wwt.org.uk

RSPB Local Group

GLOUCESTERSHIRE. (1972; 600). David Cramp, 2 Ellenor Drive, Alderton, Tewkesbury, GL20 8NZ. 01242 620 281; www.rspbgloucestershire.co.uk
Meetings: 7.30pm, 3rd Tuesday of the month, Sir Thomas Rich's School, Gloucester.

Wildlife Hospital

VALE WILDLIFE RESCUE - WILDLIFE HOSPITAL + REHABILITATION CENTRE. Any staff member, Station Road, Beckford, Tewkesbury, GL20 7AN. 01386 882 288; (Fax)01386 882 299; e-mail: info@vwr.org.uk www.vwr.org.uk
All wild birds. Intensive care. Registered charity. Veterinary support.

Wetland Bird Survey Organisers

GLOUCESTERSHIRE (Inland). Jenny Worden, Wildfowl and Wetlands Trust, Slimbridge, Glos GL2 7BT. 01453 890 333; e-mail: jenny.worden@wwt.org.uk

COTSWOLD WATER PARK. Gareth Harris, Cotswold Water Park Society, Cotswold House, Down Ampney Estate, Cirencester, Glos GL7 5QF. 01793 752 413; e-mail: gareth.harris@waterpark.org www.waterpark.org

Wildlife Trust

GLOUCESTERSHIRE WILDLIFE TRUST. (1961; 20,000). Conservation Centre, Robinswood Hill Country Park, Reservoir Road, Gloucester, GL4 6SX. 01452 383 333; fax 01452 383334; e-mail: info@gloucestershirewildlifetrust.co.uk www.gloucestershirewildlifetrust.co.uk

HAMPSHIRE

Bird Atlas/Avifauna

Birds of Hampshire by J M Clark and J A Eyre (Hampshire Ornithological Society, 1993).

Bird Recorder

RECORDER. John Clark, 4 Cygnet Court, Old Cove Road, Fleet, Hants, GU51 2RL. Tel/fax 01252 623 397; e-mail: johnclark@cygnetcourt.demon.co.uk

ASSISTANT RECORDER.
Keith Betton. e-mail: keith_betton@hotmail.com

ASSISTANT RECORDER.
John Eyre, e-mail: john.eyre@ntlworld.com

Bird Reports

HAMPSHIRE BIRD REPORT (1955-). 2006 edition £11.90 inc postage, from Mrs Margaret Boswell, 5 Clarence Road, Lyndhurst, Hants, SO43 7AL. 023 8028 2105; e-mail: mag_bos@btinternet.com

BTO Regional Representative

RR. Glynne C Evans, Waverley, Station Road, Chilbolton, Stockbridge, Hants SO20 6AL. H:01264 860 697; e-mail: hantsbto@hotmail.com

Clubs

HAMPSHIRE ORNITHOLOGICAL SOCIETY. (1979; 1,200). Barrie Roberts, Honarary Secretary, 149 Rownhams Lane, North Baddesley, Southampton, SO52 9LU. 023 8073 7023; www.hos.org.uk/ e-mail: robertsbarrie@hotmail.com

SOUTHAMPTON & DISTRICT BIRD GROUP. (1994; 52). Dave Holloway, 73 Ampthill Road, Freemantle, Southampton, SO15 8LN. e-mail: david.holloway@solent.ac.uk
Meetings: Programme available.

Ringing Groups

FARLINGTON RG. D A Bell, 38 Holly Grove, Fareham, Hants, PO16 7UP.

ITCHEN RG. W F Simcox, 10 Holdaway Close, Kingsworthy, Winchester, SO23 7QH. e-mail: wsimcox@sparsholt.ac.uk

RSPB Local Groups

BASINGSTOKE. (1979; 90). Peter Hutchins, 35 Woodlands, Overton, Whitchurch, RG25 3HN. 01256 770 831; e-mail: fieldfare@jaybry.gotadsl.co.uk
Meetings: 7.30pm 3rd Wednesday of the month (Sept-May), The Barn, Church Cottage, St Michael's Church, Church Square, Basingstoke.

NORTH EAST HAMPSHIRE. (1976; 215). The Group leader, 4 Buttermer Close, Farnham, Surrey, GU10 4PN. 01252 724 093.
www.northeasthantsrspb.org.uk
Meetings: See website.

PORTSMOUTH. (1974; 210). Gordon Humby, 19 Charlesworth Gardens, Waterlooville, Hants, PO7 6AU. 02392 353 949.
Meetings: 7.30pm, 4th Saturday of every month. Colmans' Church Hall, Colman's Ave, Cosham. Programme and news letter issued to paid up members of the group who must be RSPB members.

WINCHESTER & DISTRICT LOCAL GROUP. (1974; 175). Maurice Walker, Jesmond, 1 Compton Way, Olivers Battery, Winchester, SO22 4EY. 01962 854

033. www.rspb.org.uk/groups/winchester
Meetings: 7.30pm, 1st Wednesday of the month (not Jul or Aug), Shawford Parish Hall, Pearson Lane, Shawford.

Wetland Bird Survey Organisers
AVON VALLEY. John Clark, 4 Cygnet Court, Old Cove Road, Fleet, Hants GU51 2RL. 01252 623 397; e-mail johnclark@cygnetcourt.demon.co.uk

HAMPSHIRE (Inland - excluding Avon Valley). Keith Wills, 51 Peabody Road, Farnborough, GU14 6EB. (H)01252 548408; e-mail: keithb.wills@ukgateway.net

HAMPSHIRE (estuaries/coastal). John Shillitoe e-mail: john@shillitoe.freeserve.co.uk

Wildlife Trust
HAMPSHIRE & ISLE OF WIGHT WILDLIFE TRUST. (1960; 27,000). Beechcroft House, Vicarage Lane, Curdridge, Hampshire SO32 2DP. 01489 774 400; fax 01489 774 401; e-mail: feedback@hwt.org.uk www.hwt.org.uk

HEREFORDSHIRE

Bird Atlas/Avifauna
The Birds of Herefordshire 2004, published by the Herefordshire Ornithological Club.

Bird Recorder
Steve Coney, 5 Springfield Road, Withington, Hereford, HR1 3RU. 01432 850 068; e-mail: coney@bluecarrots.com

Bird Report
THE YELLOWHAMMER - *Herefordshire Ornithological Club annual report, (1951-)*, from Mr I Evans, 12 Brockington Drive, Tupsley, Hereford , HR1 1TA. 01432 265 509; e-mail: iforelaine@btinternet.com

BTO Regional Representative
Steve Coney, 5 Springfield Road, Withington, Hereford, HR1 3RU. 01432 850 068; e-mail: coney@bluecarrots.com

Club
HEREFORDSHIRE ORNITHOLOGICAL CLUB. (1950; 360). TM Weale, Foxholes, Bringsty Common, Worcester, WR6 5UN. 01886 821 368; e-mail: weale@tinyworld.co.uk www.herefordshirebirds.org
Meetings: 7.30pm, 2nd Thursday of the month (Autumn/winter), Holmer Parish Centre, Holmer, Hereford.

Ringing Group
LLANCILLO RG. Dr G R Geen, 6 The Copse, Bannister Green, Felsted, Dunmow, Essex CM6

3NP. 01371 820 189; e-mail: graham.geen@gsk.com

Wildlife Trust
HEREFORDSHIRE NATURE TRUST. (1962; 2,535). Lower House Farm, Ledbury Road, Tupsley, Hereford, HR1 1UT. 01432 356 872; fax 01432 275 489; e-mail: enquiries@herefordshirewt.co.uk www .wildlifetrust.org.uk/hereford

HERTFORDSHIRE

Bird Atlas/Avifauna
Birds at Tring Reservoirs by R Young et al (Hertfordshire Natural History Society, 1996).

Mammals, Amphibians and Reptiles of Hertfordshire by Hertfordshire NHS in association with Training Publications Ltd, 3 Finway Court, Whippendell Road, Watford WD18 7EN, (2001).

The Breeding Birds of Hertfordshire by K W Smith et al (Herts NHS, 1993). Purchase from HNHS at £5 plus postage.
E-mail: herts.naturalhistorysociety@aol.com

Bird Recorder
Tony Blake, 9 Old Forge Close, Stanmore, Middx HA7 3EB. E-mail: recorder@hertsbirdclub.org.uk

Bird Report
HERTFORDSHIRE BIRD REPORT (1908-2006), from Linda Smith, 24 Mandeville Road, Welwyn Garden City, Herts AL8 7JU.
e-mail: herts.naturalhistorysociety@ntlworld.com
www.hnhs.org and www.hertsbirdclub.org.uk

BTO Regional Representative & Regional Development Officer
RR & RDO. Chris Dee, 26 Broadleaf Avenue, Thorley Park, Bishop's Stortford, Herts, CM23 4JY. H:01279 755 637; e-mail: hertsbto@hotmail.com

Clubs
FRIENDS OF TRING RESERVOIRS. (1993; 350). Rose Barr, Secretary, PO Box 1083, Tring HP23 5WU. 01296 424 145; (fax)01296 581 520. www.fotr.org.uk
Meetings: See website.

HERTFORDSHIRE BIRD CLUB. (1971; 330) Part of Hertfordshire NHS. Ted Fletcher, Beech House, Aspenden, Buntingford, Herts SG9 9PG. 01763 272 979. www.hertsbirdclub.org.uk

HERTFORDSHIRE NATURAL HISTORY SOCIETY AND HERTS BIRD CLUB. (1875; 320). Linda Smith, 24 Mandeville Rise, Welwyn Garden City, Herts, AL8 7JU. e-mail: herts.naturalhistorysociety@ntlworld.com

www.hnhs.org and www.hertsbirdclub.org.uk
Meetings: Saturday afternoon, Nov and Mar (date and venue varies).

Ringing Groups
MAPLE CROSS RG. P Delaloye.
e-mail: pdelaloye@tiscali.co.uk

RYE MEADS RG. Chris Dee, 26 Broadleaf Avenue, Thorley Park, Bishop's Stortford, Herts CM23 4JY. H:01279 755 637;
e-mail: ringingsecretary@rmrg.org.uk

TRING RG. Mick A'Court, 6 Chalkshire Cottages, Chalkshire road, Butlers Cross, Bucks HP17 0TW. H:01296 623 610; W:01494 462 246;
e-mail: mick@focusrite.com or a.arundinaceous@virgin.net

RSPB Local Groups
CHORLEYWOOD & DISTRICT. (1977; 142). Carol Smith, 24 Beacon Way, Rickmansworth, Herts WD3 7PE. 01923 897 885.
Meetings: 8pm, last Thursday of the month (Sept-May).

HARPENDEN. (1974; 1000). Geoff Horn, 41 Ridgewood Drive, Harpenden, Herts AL5 3LJ. 01582 765 443; e-mail: geoffrhorn@yahoo.co.uk
Meetings: Check with group contact for details.

HEMEL HEMPSTEAD. (1972; 150). Paul Green, 207 Northridge Way, Hemel Hempstead, Herts, HP1 2AU. 01442 266 637;
e-mail: paul@310nrwhh.freeserve.co.uk
www.hemelrspb.org.uk
Meetings: 8pm, 1st Monday of the month (Sep-Jun),The Cavendish School.

HITCHIN & LETCHWORTH. (1973; 110). Dr Martin Johnson, 1 Cartwright Road, Royston, Herts SG8 9ET. 01763 249 459;
e-mail: martinrjspc@hotmail.com
Meetings: 7.30pm, 1st Friday of the month, The Settlement, Nevells Road, Letchworth.

POTTERS BAR & BARNET. (1977; 1800). Stan Bailey, 23 Bowmans Close, Potters Bar, Herts, EN6 5NN. 01707 646 073.
Meetings: Afternoons — 2.00pm, 2nd Wednesday of the month, St Johns URC Hall, Mowbray Road, Barnet. Evening meetings — please check with contact as venue is likely to change.

ST ALBANS. (1979; 1550 in catchment area). Peter Antram, 6 Yule Close, Bricket Wood, St Albans, Herts AL2 3XZ. 01923 678 534;
www.rspb.org.uk/groups/stalbans
Meetings: 8.00pm, 2nd Tuesday of the month (Sep-May), St Saviours Church Hall, Sandpit Lane, St Albans.

SOUTH EAST HERTS. (1971; 2,400 in catchment area). Terry Smith, 31 Marle Gardens, Waltham Abbey, Essex, EN9 2DZ. 01992 715634;
e-mail: se_herts_rspb@yahoo.co.uk
www.rspb.org.uk/groups/southeasthertfordshire
Meetings: 7.30pm, usually last Tuesday of the month (Sept-June), URC Church Hall, Mill Lane, Broxbourne EN10 7BQ.

STEVENAGE. (1982; 1300 in the catchment area). Mrs Ann Collis, 16 Stevenage Road, Walkern, Herts, 01483 861 547.
Meetings: 7.30pm, 3rd Tuesday of the month, Friends Meeting House, Cuttys Lane, Stevenage.

WATFORD. (1974; 590). Janet Reynolds. 01923 249 647; e-mail: janet.reynolds@whht.nhs.uk
www.rspb.org.uk/groups/watford
Meetings: 7.30pm, 2nd Wednesday of the month (Sep-Jun), St Thomas' Church Hall, Langley Road, Watford.

Wetland Bird Survey Organiser
LEE VALLEY. Cath Patrick, Myddelton House, Bulls Cross, Enfield, Herts EN2 9HG; 01992 717 711;
e-mail: cpatrick@leevalleypark.org.uk

Wildlife Trust
HERTS & MIDDLESEX WILDLIFE TRUST. (1964; 18,500). Grebe House, St Michael's Street, St Albans, Herts, AL3 4SN. 01727 858 901; fax 01727 854 542; e-mail: info@hmwt.org
www.wildlifetrust.org.uk/herts/

ISLE OF WIGHT

Bird Recorder
G Sparshott, Leopards Farm, Main Road, Havenstreet, Isle of Wight, PO33 4DR. 01983 882 549; e-mail: grahamspa@aol.com

Bird Reports
ISLE OF WIGHT BIRD REPORT (1986-) (Pre-1986 not available), from Mr DJ Hunnybun, 40 Churchill Road, Cowes, Isle of Wight, PO31 8HH. 01983 292 880; email: davehunnybun@hotmail.com

BTO Regional Representative
James C Gloyn, 3 School Close, Newchurch, Isle of Wight, PO36 0NL. 01983 865 567; e-mail: gloynjc@yahoo.com

Clubs
ISLE OF WIGHT NATURAL HISTORY & ARCHAEOLOGICAL SOCIETY. (1919; 500). The Secretary, Salisbury Gardens, Dudley Road, Ventnor, Isle of Wight PO38 1EJ. 01983 855 385. www.iwnhas.org.

ISLE OF WIGHT ORNITHOLOGICAL GROUP. (1986; 155). Mr DJ Hunnybun, 40 Churchill Road, Cowes, Isle of Wight, PO31 8HH. 01983 292 880; email: davehunnybun@hotmail.com

Wetland Bird Survey Organiser
ISLE OF WIGHT. James Gloyn;
e-mail: gloynjc@yahoo.com

Wildlife Trust
Director, See Hampshire,

KENT

Bird Atlas/Avifauna
Birding in Kent by D W Taylor et al 1996. Pica Press

Bird Recorder
Don Taylor (retiring), 1 Rose Cottages, Old Loose Hill, Loose, Maidstone, Kent, ME15 0BN. 01622 745641; e-mail: don.taylor02@talktalk.net

Bird Reports
DUNGENESS BIRD OBSERVATORY REPORT (1989-), from Warden, see Reserves.

KENT BIRD REPORT (1952-), from Dave Sutton, 61 Alpha Road, Birchington, Kent, CT7 9ED. 01843 842541; e-mail: dave@suttond8.freeserve.co.uk

SANDWICH BAY BIRD OBSERVATORY REPORT, from Warden, see Reserves,

BTO Regional Representative & Regional Development Officer
RR. Sally Hunter. 01304 612 425;
e-mail: sally.hunter@tesco.net

Club
KENT ORNITHOLOGICAL SOCIETY. (1952; 720). Mrs Ann Abrams, 4 Laxton Way, Faversham, Kent, ME13 8LJ. 01795 533 453; e-mail: annie@chrisabrams.plus.com www.kentos.org.uk
Meetings: Indoor: October-April at various venues; the AGM in April is at Grove Green Community Hall, Grovewood Drive, Maidstone ME14 5TQ. See website for details: www.kentos.org.uk

Ringing Groups
DARTFORD RG. PE Jones.
e-mail: philjones@beamingbroadband.com

DUNGENESS BIRD OBSERVATORY. David Walker, Dungeness Bird Observatory, Dungeness, Romney Marsh, Kent TN29 9NA. 01797 321 309; e-mail: dungeness.obs@tinyonline.co.uk www.dungenessbirdobs.org.uk

RECULVER RG. Chris Hindle, 42 Glenbervie Drive, Herne Bay, Kent, CT6 6QL. 01227 373 070; e-mail: christopherhindle@hotmail.com

SANDWICH BAY BIRD OBSERVATORY. Mr KB Ellis, 6 Alderney Gardens, St Peters, Broadstairs, Kent CT10 2TN. 01304 617 341; e-mail: keithjulie@talktalk.net

SWALE WADER GROUP. Rod Smith, 67 York Avenue, Chatham, Kent, ME5 9ES. 01634 865 863; www.swalewaders.co.uk

RSPB Local Groups
CANTERBURY. (1973; 216). Chris Sproul. 01227 450 655; e-mail: cyasproul@yahoo.co.uk www.rspb.org.uk/groups/canterbury
Meetings: 8.00pm, 2nd Wednesday of the month (Sept-Apr), St Stephen's Hall, Hales Drive, Canterbury, CT2 7AB.

GRAVESEND & DISTRICT. (1977; 278). Malcolm Jennings, 206 Lower Higham Road, Gravesend, Kent, DA12 2NN. 01474 322 171; e-mail: malcolm.chalkland@btinternet.com www.rspbgravesend.org.uk
Meetings: 7.45pm, 2nd Wednesday of the month (Sep-May), St Botolph's Hall, North Fleet, Gravesend.

MAIDSTONE. (1973; 250). Dick Marchese, 11 Bathurst Road, Staplehurst, Tonbridge, Kent TN12 0LG. 01580 892 458; e-mail: marchese8@aol.com http://maidstone.localrspb.org.uk/
Meetings: 7.30pm, 3rd Thursday of the month, Grove Green Community Hall, Penhurst Close, Grove Green, opposite Tesco's.

MEDWAY. (1974; 230). Mrs Marie Tilley, 62 Eastcourt Lane, Gillingham, Kent ME8 6EY. 01634 387 431. www.medway-rspb.pwp.blueyonder.co.uk
Meetings: 7.45pm 3rd Tuesday of the month (except Aug), Strood Library, Bryant Road, Strood.

SEVENOAKS. (1974; 265). Bernard Morris, New House, Kilkhampton, Bude, Cornwall EX23 9RZ. 01288 321 727; or 07967 564 699; (Fax)01288 321 838; e-mail: bernard.morris5@btinternet.com www.rspb.org.uk/groups/sevenoaks
Meetings: 7.45pm 1st Thursday of the month, Otford Memorial Hall.

SOUTH EAST KENT. (1981; 165). Pauline McKenzie-Lloyd, Hillside, Old Park Avenue, Dover, Kent CT16 2DY. 01304 826 529; email: pauline.mcklloyd@tiscali.co.uk www.rspb.org.uk/groups/southeastkent
Meetings: 7.30pm, 3rd Wednesday of the month (Sep-May), United Reform Church, Folkestone. See details of field trips on website.

THANET. (1975; 119). Peter Radcliffe, Cottage of St John, Caterbury Road, Sarre, Kent CT7 0JY. 01843 847 345.

Meetings: 7.30pm last Tuesday of the month (Jan-Nov), Portland Centre.

TONBRIDGE. (1975; 150 reg attendees/1700 in catchment). Ms Gabrielle Sutcliffe, 1 Postern Heath Cottages, Postern Lane, Tonbridge, Kent TN11 0QU. 01732 365 583.
Meetings: 7.45pm 3rd Wednesday of the month (Sept-Apr), St Phillips Church, Salisbury Road.

Wetland Bird Survey Organisers
EAST KENT. Ken Lodge, 14 Gallwey Avenue, Birchington, Kent CT7 9PA. 01843 843 105; e-mail: kenlodge@minnisbay15.freeserve.co.uk

MEDWAY ESTUARY & NORTH KENT MARSHES. Sally Jennings, RSPB, Bromhey Farm, Cooling, Rochester, Kent ME3 8DS. 01634 222 480 .

SWALE ESTUARY. Sally Jennings, RSPB, Bromhey Farm, Cooling, Rochester, Kent ME3 8DS. 01634 222 480.

Wildlife Hospital
RAPTOR CENTRE. Eddie Hare, Ivy Cottage, Groombridge Place, Groombridge, Tunbridge Wells, Kent TN3 9QG. 01892 861 175;
www.raptorcentre.co.uk
Birds of prey. Veterinary support. 24hr rescue service for sick and injured birds of prey that covers the South-East.

Wildlife Trust
KENT WILDLIFE TRUST. (1958; 10500). Tyland Barn, Sandling, Maidstone, Kent, ME14 3BD. 01622 662 012; fax 01622 671 390;
e-mail: info@kentwildlife.org.uk
www.kentwildlifetrust.org.uk

LANCASHIRE

Bird Atlas/Avifauna
An Atlas of Breeding Birds of Lancaster and District by Ken Harrison (Lancaster & District Birdwatching Society, 1995).

Birds of Lancashire and North Merseyside by White, McCarthy and Jones (Hobby Publications 2008).

Bird Recorder (See also Manchester).
LANCASHIRE (Inc North Merseyside). Steve White, 102 Minster Court, Crown Street, Liverpool, L7 3QD. 0151 707 2744; e-mail: stephen.white2@tesco.net

Bird Reports
BIRDS OF LANCASTER & DISTRICT (1959-), from Secretary, Lancaster & District BWS, 01524 734 462.

BLACKBURN & DISTRICT BIRD CLUB ANNUAL REPORT (1992-), from Doreen Bonner, 6 Winston Road, Blackburn, BB1 8BJ. 01254 261 480;
e-mail: webmaster@blackburnbirdclub.co.uk
www.blackburnbirdclub.co.uk

CHORLEY AND DISTRICT NATURAL HISTORY SOCIETY ANNUAL REPORT (1979 -), published on website www.chorleynats.org.uk

EAST LANCASHIRE ORNITHOLOGISTS' CLUB BIRD REPORT (1982-), from Secretary, 01282 612 870;
e-mail: john.plackett@eastlancsornithologists.org.uk
www.eastlancashireornithologists.org.uk

FYLDE BIRD REPORT (1983-), from Secretary, Fylde Bird Club.

LANCASHIRE BIRD REPORT (1914-), from Secretary, Lancs & Cheshire Fauna Soc.

ROSSENDALE ORNITHOLOGISTS' CLUB BIRD REPORT (1977-) from Secretary, Rossendale Ornithologists Club.

BTO Regional Representatives & Regional Development Officer
EAST RR. Tony Cooper, 28 Peel Park Avenue, Clitheroe, Lancs, BB7 1ET. 01200 424 577;
e-mail: tony.cooper@eastlancsornithologists.org.uk

NORTH & WEST RR. Jean Roberts. 01524 770 295; e-mail: JeanRbrts6@aol.com

SOUTH RR. Position Vacant.

Clubs
BLACKBURN & DISTRICT BIRD CLUB. (1991; 134). Jim Bonner, 6 Winston Road, Blackburn, BB1 8BJ. 01254 261 480;
e-mail: webmaster@blackburnbirdclub.co.uk
www.blackburnbirdclub.co.uk
Meetings: Normally 7.30pm, 1st Monday of the month, (Sept-Apr), Church Hall, Preston New Road. Check website for all indoor and outdoor meetings.

CHORLEY & DISTRICT NATURAL HISTORY SOCIETY. (1979; 170). Phil Kirk, Millend, Dawbers Lane, Euxton, Chorley, Lancs PR7 6EB. 01257 266783; e-mail: secretary@chorleynats.org.uk
www.chorleynats.org.uk
Meetings: 7.30pm, 3rd Thursday of the month (Sept-Apr), St Mary's Parish Centre, Chorley

EAST LANCASHIRE ORNITHOLOGISTS' CLUB. (1955; 45). Dr JCW Plackett, 71 Walton Lane, Nelson, Lancs BB9 8BG. 01282 612 870; e-mail: john.plackett@eastlancsornithologists.org.uk
www.eastlancsornithologists.org.uk
Meetings: 7.30pm, 1st Monday of the month, St Anne's Church Hall, Feuce, Nr Burnley.

FYLDE BIRD CLUB. (1982; 110). Paul Ellis, 18 Staining Rise, Blackpool, FY3 0BU. 01253 891281; e-mail: paul.ellis24@btopenworld. com or kinta.beaver@man.ac.uk
www.fyldebirdclub.org

Meetings: 7.45pm, 4th Tuesday of the month, River Wyre Hotel, Breck Road, Poulton le Fylde.

FYLDE NATURALISTS' SOCIETY. (1946; 140). Julie Clarke, 7 Cedar Avenue, Poulton-le-Fylde, Blackpool, FY6 8DQ. 01253 883 785;
e-mail: secretary@fyldenaturalists.co.uk
www.fyldenaturalists.co.uk
Meetings: 7.30pm, fortnightly (Sep-Mar), Fylde Coast Alive, Church Hall, Raikes Parade, Blackpool unless otherwise stated in the Programme.

LANCASHIRE & CHESHIRE FAUNA SOCIETY. (1914; 150). Dave Bickerton, 64 Petre Crescent, Rishton, Lancs, BB1 4RB. 01254 886257;
e-mail: bickertond@aol.com www.lacfs.org.uk

LANCASHIRE BIRD CLUB. (1996). Dave Bickerton, 64 Petre Crescent, Rishton, Lancs, BB1 4RB. 01254 886257; e-mail: bickertond@aol.com
www.lacfs.org.uk

LANCASTER & DISTRICT BIRD WATCHING SOCIETY. (1959; 200). Andrew Cadman, 57 Greenways, Over Kellet, Carnforth, Lancs LA6 1DE. 01524 734462; e mail: andrewokuk@yahoo.co.uk
www.lancasterbirdwatching.org.uk
Meetings: 7.30pm, last Monday of the month (Sep-Nov, Feb-Mar), Bare Methodist Church Hall, St Margarets Road, Morecambe; (Jan and Apr) the Hornby Institute, Hornby.

ROSSENDALE ORNITHOLOGISTS' CLUB. (1976; 35). Ian Brady, 25 Church St, Newchurch, Rossendale, Lancs BB4 9EX. 01706 222120.
Meetings: 7.30pm, 3rd Monday of the month, Weavers Cottage, Bacup Road, Rawtenstall.

Ringing Groups
FYLDE RG. G Barnes, 17 Lomond Avenue, Marton, Blackpool, FY3 9QL.

NORTH LANCS RG. John Wilson BEM, 40 Church Hill Avenue, Warton, Carnforth, Lancs LA5 9NU.
E-mail: johnwilson711@btinternet.com

SOUTH WEST LANCASHIRE RG. I H Wolfenden, 35 Hartdale Road, Thornton, Liverpool, Merseyside L23 1TA. 01519 311 232.

RSPB Local Groups
BLACKPOOL. (1983; 170). Alan Stamford, 6 Kensington Road, Cleveleys, FY5 1ER. 01253 859 662.
Meetings: 7.30pm, 2nd Friday of the month (Sep-Jun), Frank Townsend Centre, Beach Road, Cleveleys.

LANCASTER. (1972; 176). Jill Blackburn, 13 Coach Road, Warton, Carnforth, Lancs LA5 9PR.
e-mail: jill.blackburn@dsl.pipex.com
www.rspb.org.uk/localgroups/lancaster

Wetland Bird Survey Organisers
NORTH LANCASHIRE (Inland). Mr Pete Marsh, Leck View Cottage, Ashley's farm, High Tatham, Lancaster LA2 8PH. 01524 264 944;
e-mail: pbmarsh@btopenworld.com

Wildlife Trust
THE WILDLIFE TRUST FOR LANCASHIRE, MANCHESTER AND NORTH MERSEYSIDE. (1962; 18,000). Mr Peter Mallon, Communications Officer, The Barn, Berkeley Drive, Bamber Bridge, Preston PR5 6BY. 01772 324 129; fax: 01772 628 849;
e-mail: pmallon@lancswt.org.uk
www.lancswt.org.uk

LEICESTERSHIRE & RUTLAND

The Birds of Leicestershire and Rutland by Rob Fray, Roger Davies, Dave Gamble, Andrew Harrop and Steve Lister (Christopher Helm due Dec 2008).

Bird Recorder
Steve Lister, 6 Albert Promenade, Loughborough, Leicestershire LE11 1RE. 01509 829 495;
e-mail: stevelister@surfbirder.com

Bird Reports
LEICESTERSHIRE & RUTLAND BIRD REPORT (1941-), from Mrs S Graham, 5 Lychgate Close, Cropston, Leicestershire LE7 7HU. 0116 236 6474.

RUTLAND NAT HIST SOC ANNUAL REPORT (1965-), from the Secretary, 01572 747 302.

BTO Regional Representative
LEICESTER & RUTLAND RR. Tim Grove, 35 Clumber Street, Melton Mowbray, Leicestershire, LE13 0ND. 01664 850766; e-mail: k.grove1@ntlworld.com

Clubs
BIRSTALL BIRDWATCHING CLUB. (1976; 50). Mr KJ Goodrich, 6 Riversdale Close, Birstall, Leicester, LE4 4EH. 0116 267 4813.
Meetings: 7.30pm, 2nd Tuesday of the month (Oct-Apr), The Rothley Centre, Mountsorrel Lane, Rothley, Leics LE7 7PR.

BURBAGE BIRDERS. info@burbagebirders.co.uk
www.burbagebirders.co.uk
Meetings: 7.30pm, 2nd Monday of the month, Burbage Common visitor centre.

LEICESTERSHIRE & RUTLAND ORNITHOLOGICAL SOCIETY. (1941; 580). Mrs Marion Vincent, 48 Templar Way, Rothley, Leicester, LE7 7RB. 0116 230 3405. www .lros.org.uk
Meetings: 7.30pm, 1st Friday of the month (Oct-May), Oadby Methodist Church, off Central Car Park, alternating with The Rothley Centre, Mountsorrel Lane, Rothley. Additional meeting at Rutland Water Birdwatching Cntr.

SOUTH LEICESTER BIRDWATCHERS. (2006;). Paul Seaton, 76 Roehampton Drive, Wigston, Leics, LE18 1HU. 07973 156 060;
e-mail: paul.lseaton@ntlworld.com
Meetings: 7.30 pm, 2nd Wednesday of the month (Sep-Jun), County Scout Centre, Winchester Road, Blaby, Leicester LE8 4HN.

Ringing Groups
RUTLAND WATER RG. Tim Appleton, Fishponds Cottage, Stamford Road, Oakham, LE15 8AB. (Day) 01572 770 651;
e-mail: awbc@rutland water.org.uk

STANFORD RG. John Cranfield, 41 Main Street, Fleckney, Leicester, LE8 8AP. 0116 240 4385;
e-mail: JacanaJohn@talktalk.net

RSPB Local Groups
LEICESTER. (1969; 1600 in catchement area). Chris Woolass, 136 Braunstone Lane, Leicester, LE3 2RW. 0116 299 0078;
e-mail: chris@jclwoolass.freeserve.co.uk
Meetings: 7.30pm, 3rd Friday of the month (Sep-May), Adult Education Centre, Wellington Street, Leicester.

LOUGHBOROUGH. (1970; 300). Robert Orton, 12 Avon Road, Barrow-on-Soar, Leics, LE12 8LE. 077 4887 6798.
www.rspb.org.uk/loughborough
Meetings: Monthly Friday nights, Loughborough University.

Wetland Bird Survey Organisers
LEICESTERSHIRE & RUTLAND (excl Rutland Water. Tim Grove, 35 Clumber Street, Melton Mowbray, Leics LE13 0ND. 01664 850 766;
e-mail: k.grove1@ntlworld.com

RUTLAND WATER. Tim Appleton, Fishponds Cottage, Stamford Road, Oakham, LE15 8AB. (Day) 01572 770 651.
e-mail: awbc@rutland water.org.uk

Wildlife Trust
LEICESTERSHIRE & RUTLAND WILDLIFE TRUST. (1956; 13,500). Brocks Hill Environment Centre, Washbrook Lane, Oadby, Leicestershire LE2 5JJ. 0116 272 0444; fax 0116 272 0404;
e-mail: info@lrwt.org.uk
www.lrwt.org.uk

LINCOLNSHIRE

Bird Atlas/Avifauna
The Status of Birds in Lincolnshire 1991-1995 (covers a five-year period) from Mr W Sterling, LBC Sales, Newlyn, Carlton Avenue, Healing, Grimsby DN37 7PN.

Bird Recorders
Steve Keightley, Redclyffe, Swineshead Road, Frampton Fen, Boston PE20 1SG. 01205 290 233;
e-mail: steve.keightley@btinternet.com

Bird Reports
LINCOLNSHIRE BIRD REPORT (1979-1996), 1990 is now sold out, from Bill Sterling, Newlyn, 5 Carlton Avenue, Healing, NE Lincs DN41 7PW.
e-mail: wbsterling@hotmail.com.

LINCOLNSHIRE RARE AND SCARCE BIRD REPORT (1997-1999) first edition, from Mr W Sterling, LBC Sales, Newlyn, Carlton Avenue, Healing, Grimsby DN37 7PN.

SCUNTHORPE & NORTH WEST LINCOLNSHIRE BIRD REPORT (1973-), from Secretary, Scunthorpe Museum Society, Ornithological Section, (Day)01724 402 871; (Eve)01724 734 261.

BTO Regional Representatives & Regional Development Officer
EAST RR. Position vacant.

NORTH RR. Position vacant.

SOUTH RR. Richard & Kay Heath, 56 Pennytoft Lane, Pinchbeck, Spalding, Lincs PE11 3PQ. 01775 767 055; e-mail: heathsrk@ukonline.co.uk

WEST RR. Peter Overton, Hilltop Farm, Welbourn, Lincoln, LN5 0QH. Work 01400 273 323;
e-mail: expeditions@biosearch.org.uk

RDO. Nicholas Watts, Vine House Farm, Deeping St Nicholas, Spalding, Lincs PE11 3DG. 01775 630 208.

Club
LINCOLNSHIRE BIRD CLUB. (1979; 220). Janet Eastmead, 3 Oxeney Drive, Langworth, Lincoln, LN3 5DD. 01522 754 522;
e-mail: janet.eastmead@talktalk.net
www.lincsbirdclub.co.uk
Meetings: Local groups hold winter evening meetings (contact Secretary for details).

SCUNTHORPE MUSEUM SOCIETY (Ornithological Section). (1973; 50). Keith Parker, 7 Ryedale Avenue, Winterton, Scunthorpe, Lincs DN15 9BJ.
Meetings: 7.15pm, 3rd Monday of the month (Sep-Apr), Scunthorpe Museum, Oswald Road.

Ringing Groups
GIBRALTAR POINT BIRD OBSERVATORY. Mr C.E. Perez. e-mail: cperez@gonhs.org

MID LINCOLNSHIRE RG. J Mawer, 2 The Chestnuts, Owmby Road, Searby, Lincolnshire DN38 6EH. 01652 628 583.

WASH WADER RG. P L Ireland, 27 Hainfield Drive, Solihull, W Midlands, B91 2PL. 0121 704 1168;
e-mail: enquiries@wwrg.org.uk

RSPB Local Groups
GRIMSBY AND CLEETHORPES. (1986; 2200 in catchment area). Barbara Stephenson. 01472 814 303; e-mail: terence@terencewhalin.wannado.co.uk www.rspb.org.uk/groups/grimsby
Meetings: 7.30pm, 1st Monday of the month (Sept-May), Corpus Christi Church Hall, Grimsby Road, Cleethorpes, DN35 7LJ.

LINCOLN. (1974; 250). Peter Skelson, 26 Parksgate Avenue, Lincoln, LN6 7HP. 01522 695 747; e-mail: peter.skelson@lincolnrspb.org.uk www.lincolnrspb.org.uk
Meetings: 7.30pm, 2nd Thursday of the month (not Jun, Jul, Aug, Dec), The Lawn, Union Road, Lincoln.

SOUTH LINCOLNSHIRE. (1987; 350). Barry Hancock, The Limes, Meer Booth Road, Antons Gowt, Boston, Lincs PE22 7BG. 01205 280 057; e-mail: info@southlincsrspb.org.uk www.southlincsrspb.org.uk
Meetings: 7.30pm, Thursdays,monthly, Sam Newson Music Centre, South Street, Boston.

Wetland Bird Survey Organisers
HUMBER ESTUARY - OUTER SOUTH. Rick Vonk; 01507 338 611; e-mail; dunewalker@btinternet.com

NORTH LINCOLNSHIRE (inland). Marcus Craythorne, Hartsholme Country Park, Skellingthorpe Road, Lincoln, LN6 0EY.
e-mail: marcus.craythorne@lincoln.gov.uk

THE WASH. Jim Scott, RSPB, Barn A, Home Farm Barns, Common Road, Snettisham, King's Lynn, Norfolk PE31 7PD.

Wildlife Trust
LINCOLNSHIRE WILDLIFE TRUST. (1948; 26,000). Banovallum House, Manor House Street, Horncastle, LIncs, LN9 5HF. 01507 526 667; fax 01507 525 732; e-mail: info@lincstrust.co.uk www.lincstrust.org.uk

LONDON, GREATER

Bird Atlas/Avifauna
The Breeding Birds Illustrated magazine of the London Area, 2002. ISBN 0901009 121 ed Jan Hewlett (London Natural History Society).

Two Centuries of Croydon's Birds by John Birkett (RSPB Croydon Local Group 2007).

Bird Recorder (see also Surrey)
Andrew Self, 16 Harp Island Close, Neasden, London, NW10 0DF. e-mail: andrewself@lineone.net www.londonbirders.com

Bird Report
CROYDON BIRD SURVEY (1995), from Secretary,

Croydon RSPB Group, 020 8640 4578; e-mail: johndavis.wine@care4free.net www.croydon-rspb.org.uk.

LONDON BIRD REPORT (20-mile radius of St Paul's Cath) (1936-), from Catherine Schmitt, Publications Sales, London Natural History Society, 4 Falkland Avenue, London N3 1QR.

BTO Regional Representatives
LONDON, NORTH. Ian Woodward, 245 Larkshall Road, Chingford, London, E4 9HY. 07947 321 889; e-mail: ianw_bto_nlon@hotmail.co.uk

LONDON, SOUTH. Richard Arnold. 020 8224 1135; e-mail: bto@thomsonecology.com

Clubs
LONDON NATURAL HISTORY SOCIETY (Ornithology Section). (1858; 1000). Mrs Angela Linnell, 20 Eleven Acre Rise, Loughton, Essex, IG10 1AN. 020 8508 2932; e-mail: Angela.Linnell@care4free.net. www.lnhs.org.uk
Meetings: Contact club secretary.

MARYLEBONE BIRDWATCHING SOCIETY. (1981; 110). Judy Powell, 7 Rochester Terrace, London, NW1 9JN. 020 7485 0863; e-mail: birdsmbs@yahoo.com www.geocities.com/birdsmbs
Meeting: 7.15pm, 2nd Friday of month (Sept-May), Gospel Oak Methodist Chapel, Lisburne Road, London NW3 2NR.

Ringing Groups
LONDON GULL STUDY GROUP - (SE including Hampshire, Surrey, Susex, Berkshire and Oxfordshire). This group is no longer active but still receiving sightings/recoveries of ringed birds. No longer In operation but able to give Information on gulls. Mark Fletcher, 24 The Gowans, Sutton-on-the-Forest, York, YO61 1DJ.
e-mail: m.fletcher@csl.gov.uk

RUNNYMEDE RG. D G Harris, 22 Blossom Waye, Hounslow, TW5 9HD.
e-mail: daveharris@tinyonline.co.uk

RSPB Local Groups
BEXLEY. (1979; 180). Tony Banks, 15 Boundary Road, Sidcup, Kent DA15 8SS. 020 8859 3518; email: tonybanks@fsmail.net www.bexleyrspb.org.uk
Meetings: 7.30pm, 3rd Friday of the month, Hurstmere School Hall, Hurst Road, Sidcup.

BROMLEY. (1972; 285). Val Bryant, 11 Hastings Road, Bromley, Kent BR2 8NZ.
e-mail: valbryant5@gmail.comt www.bromleyrspb.org.uk
Meetings: 2nd Wednesday of the month (Sep-

Jun), Large Hall, Bromley Central Library Building, Bromley High Street.

CROYDON. (1973; 4000 in catchment area). John Davis, 9 Cricket Green, Mitcham, CR4 4LB. 020 8640 4578; e-mail: johndavis.wine@care4free.net
www.croydon-rspb.org.uk
Meetings: 2nd Monday of each month at 2pm-4pm and again at 8pm-10pm at Old Whitgiftian Clubhouse, Croham Manor Road, South Croydon.

ENFIELD. (1971; 2700). Norman G Hudson, 125 Morley Hill, Enfield, Middx, EN2 0BQ. 020 8363 1431.
Meetings: 8pm, 1st Thursday of the month, St Andrews Hall, Enfield Town.

HAVERING. (1972; 270). David Coe, 8 The Fairway, Upminster, Essex, RM14 1BS. 01708 220710.
Meetings: 8pm, 2nd Friday of the month, Hornchurch Library, North Street, Hornchurch.

NORTH WEST LONDON RSPB GROUP. (1983; 2000 in catchment area). Bob Husband, The Firs, 49 Carson Road, Cockfosters, Barnet, Herts EN4 9EN. 020 8441 8742; e-mail: bobhusband@hotmail.co.uk
www.rspb.org.uk/groups/nwlondon
Meetings: 8pm, last Tuesday of the month (Sept-Apr), Union Church Hall, Eversfield Gardens, Mill Hill, NW7 (new for 2005).

PINNER & DISTRICT. (1972; 300). Dennis Bristow, 118 Crofts Road, Harrow, Middx, HA1 2PJ. 020 8863 5026.
Meetings: 8pm, 2nd Thursday of the month (Sept-May), Church Hall, St John The Baptist Parish church, Pinner.

RICHMOND & TWICKENHAM. (1979; 285). Keith Birch, 32 Broom Lock, Teddington, TW11 9QP. 020 8977 6496; e-mail: keithgbirch@aol.com.
Meetings: 8.00pm, 1st Wednesday of the month, York House, Twickenham.

Wetland Bird Survey Organiser
LEE VALLEY. Cath Patrick, Myddelton House, Bulls Cross, Enfield, Herts EN2 9HG; 01992 717 711; e-mail: cpatrick@leevalleypark.org.uk

Wildlife Trust
LONDON WILDLIFE TRUST. (1981; 7500). Skyline House, 200 Union Street, London, SE1 0LX. 0207 261 0447; fax 0207 633 0811; e-mail: enquiries@wildlondon.org.uk
www.wildlondon.org.uk

MANCHESTER, GREATER

Bird Atlas/Avifauna
Breeding Birds in Greater Manchester by Philip Holland et al (1984).

Bird Recorder
RECORDER AND REPORT EDITOR. Mrs A Judith Smith, 12 Edge Green Street, Ashton-in-Makerfield, Wigan, WN4 8SL. 01942 712 615; e-mail: judith@gmbirds.freeserve.co.uk
www.manchesterbirding.com

ASSISTANT RECORDER (Rarities). Ian McKerchar, 42 Green Ave, Astley, Manchester, M29 7EH . 01942 701 758; e-mail: ian@mckerchar1.freeserve.co.uk

Bird Reports
BIRDS IN GREATER MANCHESTER (1976-). Year 2001 onwards from County Recorder).

LEIGH ORNITHOLOGICAL SOCIETY BIRD REPORT (1971-), from Mr D Shallcross, 28 Surrey Avenue, Leigh, Lancs, WN7 2NN.
E-mail: chairman@leighos.org.uk
www.leighos.org.uk.

BTO Regional Representative & Regional Development Officer
RR. Steve Suttill, 94 Manchester Road, Mossley, Ashton-under-Lyne, Lancashire OL5 9AY. 01457 836 360; e-mail: suttill.parkinson@virgin.net

ASSISTANT RR. Steve Atkins, 33 Kings Grove, Wardle, Rochdale, Lancashire OL12 9HR. 01706 645 097; e-mail: steveatkins@tiscali.co.uk

Clubs
MANCHESTER ORNITHOLOGICAL SOCIETY. (1954; 70). Dr R Sandling, School of Mathematics, Manchester University, Manchester M13 9PL. e-mail: rsandling@manchester.ac.uk
Meetings: 7.30pm, 1st Tuesday (Oct-Apr), St James Church Hall, off Church Street, Gatley

GREATER MANCHESTER BIRD RECORDING GROUP. (2002: 40) Restricted to contributors of the county bird report. Mrs A Judith Smith. 01942 712 615; e-mail: judith@gmbirds.freeserve.co.uk
www.manchesterbirding.com

HALE ORNITHOLOGISTS. (1968; 77). Mrs E Hall, Flat 22, Shirley Court, Wardle Road, Sale M33 3DQ.
Meetings: 7.30pm, 2nd Wednesday of the month (Sept-July), St Peters Assembly Rooms, Hale.

LEIGH ORNITHOLOGICAL SOCIETY. (1971; 118). Mr D Shallcross, 28 Surrey Avenue, Leigh, Lancs, WN7 2NN. E-mail: chairman@leighos.org.uk
www.leighos.org.uk
Meetings: 7.15pm, Fridays, Leigh Library (check website for details).

ROCHDALE FIELD NATURALISTS' SOCIETY. (1970; 90). Mrs J P Wood, 196 Castleton Road, Thornham, Royton, Oldham OL2 6UP. 0161 345 2012;

www.rochdalefieldnaturalist-society.co.uk
Meetings: 7.30pm at Cutgate Baptist Church, Edenfield Rd, Rochdale. Yearly syllabus (out after AGM in Sept) states dates of lectures and outings.

STOCKPORT BIRDWATCHING SOCIETY. (1972; 80). Dave Evans, 36 Tatton Road South, Stockport, Cheshire, SK4 4LU. 0161 432 9513;
e-mail: windhover@ntlworld.com
Meetings: 7.30pm, last Wednesday of the month, Tiviot Dale Church.

Ringing Groups
LEIGH RG. A J Gramauskas, 21 Elliot Avenue, Golborne, Warrington, WA3 3DU. 0151 929 215.

SOUTH MANCHESTER RG. Mr N.B. Powell.
e-mail: neville.powell@tiscali.co.uk

RSPB Local Groups
BOLTON. (1978; 320). Mrs Alma Schofield, 29 Redcar Road, Little Lever, Bolton, BL3 1EW. 01204 791745.
Meetings: 7.30pm, Thursdays (dates vary), Main Hall, Smithills School, Smithills Dean Road, Bolton.

MANCHESTER. (1972; 3600 in catchment area). Peter Wolstenholme, 31 South Park Road, Gatley, Cheshire, SK8 4AL. 0161 428 2175.
Meetings: 7.30 pm, St James Parish Hall, Gatley Green, Church Road, Gatley, Cheadle.

STOCKPORT LOCAL GROUP. (1979; 200). Gay Crossley, 5 Broadhill Close, Bramhall, Stockport, Cheshire SK7 3BY. 0161 439 3210.
http://beatrice.mcc.ac.uk/stockport-rspb
Meetings: 7.30pm, 2nd Monday of the month (Sep-Apr), Stockport College of Technology, Lecture Theatre B.

WIGAN. (1973; 80). Graham Tonge. 01695 624 860; e-mail: neimaz07@yahoo.co.uk
www.rspb.uk/groups/wigan
Meetings: 7.45pm. St Anne's Parish Hall, Church Lane, Shevington, Wigan, Lancashire, WN6 8BD.

Wildlife Hospital
THREE OWLS BIRD SANCTUARY AND RESERVE. Trustee, Nigel Fowler, Wolstenholme Fold, Norden, Rochdale, OL11 5UD. 01706 642162; Emergency helpline 07973 819 389;
e-mail: info@threeowls.co.uk
www.threeowls.co.uk
Registered charity. All species of wild bird. Rehabilitation and release on Sanctuary Reserve. Open every Sunday (12pm-4pm), otherwise visitors welcome by appointment. Quarterly newsletter. Veterinary support.

Wildlife Trust
Director, See Lancashire,

MERSEYSIDE & WIRRAL

Bird Atlas see Cheshire

Bird Recorders see Cheshire; Lancashire

Bird Reports see also Cheshire
HILBRE BIRD OBSERVATORY REPORT, from Warden, see Reserves,

BTO Regional Representatives
MERSEYSIDE RR and RDO. Bob Harris, 2 Dulas Road, Wavertree Green, Liverpool, L15 6UA. Work 0151 706 4311; e-mail: harris@liv.ac.uk

WIRRAL RR. Paul Miller. 01928 787 535;
e-mail: huntershill@worldonline.co.uk

Clubs
MERSEYSIDE NATURALISTS' ASSOCIATION. (1938; 150). John Clegg, MNA Membership Secretary, 29 Barlow Lane, Liverpool, L4 3QP. www.geocities.com/mnahome.
Meetings: 3rd Saturday afternoon (winter only), Bootle Cricket Club. Coach outings throughout the year. New publication due 2008: *In the Footsteps of Eric Hardy* by David Bryant (John Bannon Press).

WIRRAL BIRD CLUB. (1977; 150). The Secretary. E-mail: info@wirralbirdclub.com
www.wirralbirdclub.com

Ringing Groups
MERSEYSIDE RG. Bob Harris, 2 Dulas Road, Wavertree Green, Liverpool, L15 6UA. Work 0151 706 4311; e-mail: harris@liv.ac.uk

SOUTH WEST LANCASHIRE RG. I H Wolfenden, 35 Hartdale Road, Thornton, Liverpool, Merseyside L23 1TA. 01519 311 232.

RSPB Local Groups
LIVERPOOL. (1966; 162). Chris Tynan, 10 Barker Close, Huyton, Liverpool, L36 0XU. 0151 480 7938; e-mail: christtynan@aol.com
www.rspbliverpool.org.uk
Meetings: 7 for 7.30pm, 3rd Monday of the month (Sep-Apr), Mossley Hill Parish Church, Junc. Rose Lane and Elmswood Rd.

SEFTON COAST. (1980; 62). Peter Taylor, 26 Tilston Road, Walton, Liverpool, L9 6AJ. 0151 524 1905;
e-mail: ptaylor@liv.ac.uk
www.scmg-rspb.org.uk
Meetings: 7.30pm, 2nd Tuesday of the month, St Lukes Church Hall, Liverpool Road, Crosby.

RSPB
SEFTON COAST
LOCAL GROUP

SOUTHPORT. (1974; 300). Roy Ekins. 01704 875 898; e-mail: royekins@yahoo.co.uk
Meetings: 7.45pm, Lord Street West Church Hall, Duke Street, SOUTHPORT.

WIRRAL. (1982; 120). Jeremy Bradshaw. 0151 632 2364; email: Info@wirralRSPB.org.uk www.rspb.org.uk/groups/wirral
Meetings: 7.30pm, 1st Thursday of the month, Bromborough Civic Centre, 2 Bromborough Village Road, WIRRAL.

Wetland Bird Survey Organiser
DEE ESTUARY. Colin Wells, Burton Farm Point, Station Road, Nr Neston, South Wirra CH64 5SB. 01513 367 681; e-mail: colinwells@rspb.org.uk

Wildlife Trust
Director, See Lancashire,

NORFOLK

Bird Atlas/Avifauna
The Birds of Norfolk by Moss Taylor, Michael Seago, Peter Allard & Don Dorling (Pica Press, 1999).

Bird Recorder
JOINT COUNTY RECORDERS. Dave and Jacquie Bridges, 27 Swan Close, Hempstead Road, Holt, Norfolk NR25 6DP. 01263 713 249; e-mail: dnjnorfolkrec@aol.com

Bird Reports
CLEY BIRD CLUB 10-KM SQUARE BIRD REPORT (1987-), from Peter Gooden, 45 Charles Road, Holt, Norfolk, NR25 6DA. 01263 712368

NAR VALLEY ORNITHOLOGICAL SOCIETY ANNUAL REPORT (1976-), from The Secretary, Ian Black.

NORFOLK BIRD & MAMMAL REPORT (1953-), from DL Paull, 8 Lindford Drive, Eaton, Norwich NR4 6LT

NORFOLK ORNITHOLOGISTS' ASSOCN ANNUAL REPORT (1961-), from Secretary.

WENSUM VALLEY BIRDWATCHING SOCIETY (2003-) from e-mail: admin@wvbs.co.uk www.wvbs.co.uk

BTO Regional Representatives
NORTH-EAST RR. Chris Hudson, Cornerstones, 5 Ringland Road, Taverham, Norwich, NR8 6TG. 01603 868 805;(M)07771 635 844; e-mail: Chris697@btinternet.com

NORTH-WEST RR. Allan Hale. 01366 328 421; e-mail: allan.heidi@eidosnet.co.uk

SOUTH-EAST RR. Rachel Warren. 01603 593 912; e-mail: campephilus@btinternet.com

SOUTH-WEST RR. Vince Matthews, Rose's Cottage, The Green, Merton, Thetford, Norfolk IP25 6QU.

Clubs
CLEY BIRD CLUB. (1986; 500). Peter Gooden, 45 Charles Road, Holt, Norfolk, NR25 6DA. 01263 712 368.
Meetings: 8.00pm, Wednesdays, monthly (Dec-Feb), White Horse Hotel, Blakeney.

GREAT YARMOUTH BIRD CLUB. (1989; 30). Keith R Dye, 104 Wolseley Road, Great Yarmouth, Norfolk, NR31 0EJ. 01493 600705; www.gybc.org.uk
Meetings: 7.45pm, 4th Monday of the month, Rumbold Arms, Southtown Road.

NAR VALLEY ORNITHOLOGICAL SOCIETY. (1976; 125). Ian Black, Three Chimneys, Tumbler Hill, Swaffham, Norfolk, PE37 7JG. 01760 724 092; e-mail: ian_a_black@hotmail.com www.accessbs.com/narvos
Meetings: 7.30pm, last Tuesday of the month (Jul-Nov and Jan-May), Barn Theatre, Convent of The Sacred Heart, Mangate Street, Swaffham, PE37 7QW.

NORFOLK & NORWICH NATURALISTS' SOCIETY. (1869; 630). DL Paull. 8 Lindford Drive, Eaton, Norwich NR4 6LT. 01603 457 270; www.NNNS.org.uk
Meetings: 7.30pm, 3rd Tuesday of the month (Sep-Apr), Easton College, Norwich.

NORFOLK ORNITHOLOGISTS' ASSOCIATION. (1962; 1100). Jed Andrews, Broadwater Road, Holme-next-Sea, Hunstanton, Norfolk PE36 6LQ. 01485 525 406; e-mail: info@noa.org.uk www.noa.org.uk

WENSUM VALLEY BIRDWATCHING SOCIETY. (2003; 110). Colin Wright, 7 Hinshalwood Way, Old Costessey, Norwich, Norfolk NR8 5BN. 01603 740548; e-mail: admin@wvbs.co.uk www.wvbs.co.uk
Meetings: 7.30pm, 3rd Thursday of the month, Weston Longville village hall.

Ringing Groups
BTO NUNNERY RG. Kate Risely, c/o BTO, The Nunnery, Thetford, Norfolk IP24 2PU. e-mail: kate.risely@bto.org

HOLME BIRD OBSERVATORY. Miss SA Barker. e-mail: info@noa.org.uk.

NORTH NORFOLK FARMLAND STUDY & RINGING GROUP. Keith Herber, laleham, 60 Dale End, Brancaster Staithe, Kings Lynn PE31 8DA. 01328 711 635; e-mail: keith.herber@btopenworld.com

ENGLAND

NORTH WEST NORFOLK RG. Mr J L Middleton, 18 Back Lane, Burnham Market, Norfolk PE31 8EY. E-mail: middleton@bmarket.freeserve.co.uk

SHERINGHAM RG. D Sadler, 26 Abbey Road, Sheringham, Norfolk, NR26 8NN. 01263 821 904.

WASH WADER RG. P L Ireland, 27 Hainfield Drive, Solihull, W Midlands, B91 2PL. 0121 704 1168; e-mail: enquiries@wwrg.org.uk

RSPB Local Groups
NORWICH. (1971; 360). Robert Pindar. 01692 582 689; e-mail: rpindar@yahoo.co.uk
www.rspb.org.uk/groups/norwich
Meetings: 7.30pm, 2nd Monday of the month (except Aug), Hellesdon Community Centre, Middletons Lane, Hellesdon, Norwich (entrance of Woodview Road).

WEST NORFOLK. (1977; 247). Ken Bayliss, 23 Church Lane, Roydon, King's Lynn, Norfolk PE32 1AR. 01485 600 446; e-mail: ken.bayliss3@btopenworld.com
rspb-westnorfolk.org
Meetings: 7.30pm, 3rd Wednesday of the month (Sep-Apr), South Wootton Village Hall, Church Lane, South Wootton, King's Lynn.

Wetland Bird Survey Organisers
NORTH NORFOLK COAST. Michael Rooney, English Nature, Hill Farm Offices, Main Road, Well-next-the-Sea Norfolk NR23 1AB. 01328 711 635; e-mail: michael.rooney@naturalengland.org.uk

INLAND. Tim Strudwick, RSPB Strumpshaw Fen, Staithe Cottage, Low Road, Strumpshaw Norfolk NR13 4HS. 01603 715 191

THE WASH. Jim Scott, RSPB, Barn A, Home Farm Barns, Common Road, Snettisham, King's Lynn, Norfolk PE31 7PD.

Wildlife Trust
NORFOLK WILDLIFE TRUST. (1926; 34,000). Bewick House, 22 Thorpe Road, Norwich, Norfolk NR1 1RY. 01603 625 540; fax 01603 598 300; e-mail: info@norfolkwildlifetrust.org.uk
www.norfolkwildlifetrust.org.uk

NORTHAMPTONSHIRE

Bird Recorder
POSITION VACANT: Enquiries to Mike Alibone, 25 Harrier Park, East Hunsbury, Northants NN4 0QG. E-mail: northantsbirds@ntlworld.com

Bird Report
NORTHAMPTONSHIRE BIRD REPORT (1969-), from Mr John Coleman, 2 Marsons Drive, Crick, Northants NN6 7TD.

BTO Regional Representative
RR. Barrie Galpin. 01780 444 351; e-mail: barrie.galpin@zen.co.uk

Clubs
NORTHAMPTONSHIRE BIRD CLUB. (1973; 100). Mrs Eleanor McMahon, Oriole House, 5 The Croft, Hanging Houghton, Northants, NN6 9HW. 01604 880 009; e-mail:eleanor1960@btinternet.com
www.northamptonshirebirdclub.org.uk
Meetings: 7.30pm, 1st Wednesday of the month. Village Hall, Pound Lane, Moulton, Northants.

Ringing Group
NORTHANTS RG. D M Francis, 2 Brittons Drive, Billing Lane, Northampton, NN3 5DP.

RSPB Local Groups
MID NENE. (1975; 350). Hilary Guy. 01536 516 422; e-mail: hilary@snowdrop.demon.co.uk
Meetings: 7.30pm, 2nd or 3rd Thursday of the month (Sep-Apr), The Saxon Hall, Thorpe Street/Brook Street, Raunds.

NORTHAMPTON. (1978; 3000). Liz Wicks, 6 Waypost Court, Lings, Northampton, NN3 8LN. 01604 513 991; e-mail: lizydrip@ntlworld.com
Meetings: 7.30pm, 2nd Thursday of the month, Northampton Academy, Drama Suite, Wellingborough Road, Northampton NN3 8NH.

Wetland Bird Survey Organiser
Jim Williams, Langsend, Newnham, Nr Daventry, Northants NN11 3HQ. 01230 402 121; e-mail: jim.williams4@btinternet.com.

Wildlife Trust
Director, See Cambridgeshire,

NORTHUMBERLAND

Bird Atlas/Avifauna
The Atlas of Breeding Birds in Northumbria edited by J C Day et al (Northumberland and Tyneside Bird Club, 1995).

The Atlas of Wintering Birds in Northumbria (Northumberland and Tyneside Bird Club).

Bird Recorder
Tim Dean, 2 Knocklaw Park, Rothbury, Northumberland NE65 7PW. 01669 621 460; (M)07766 263 167; e-mail: t.r.dean@btopenworld.com

Bird Reports
BIRDS IN NORTHUMBRIA (1970-), from Trevor Blake, 6 Glenside, Ellington, Morpeth, Northumberland NE61 5LS. 01670 862 635; e-mail: trevor.blake@castlemorpeth.gov.uk

BIRDS ON THE FARNE ISLANDS (1971-), from Secretary, Natural History Society of Northumbria, 0191 2326 386; e-mail: NHSN@ncl.ac.uk

BTO Regional Representative & Regional Development Officer
RR. Tom Cadwallender, 22 South View, Lesbury, Alnwick, Northumberland NE66 3PZ. H:01665 830 884; W:01670 533 039;
e-mail: tomandmurielcadwallender@hotmail.com

RDO. Muriel Cadwallender, 22 South View, Lesbury, Alnwick, Northumberland NE66 3PZ. 01665 830 884; e-mail: tomandmurielcadwallender@hotmail.com

Clubs
NATURAL HISTORY SOCIETY OF NORTHUMBRIA. (1829; 850). The Natural History Society of Northumbria, Hancock Museum, Barras Bridge, Newcastle upon Tyne, NE2 4PT. 0191 232 6386; e-mail: nhsn@ncl.ac.uk www.NHSN.ncl.ac.uk
Meetings: 7.00pm, every Friday (Oct-Mar), Percy Building, Newcastle University.

NORTH NORTHUMBERLAND BIRD CLUB. (1984; 210). Richard Narraway, Workshop Cottage, The Friary, Bamburgh, NE69 7AE. 01668 214 759 www.northnorthumberlandbirdclub.co.uk
Meetings: 7.30pm, 2nd Friday of the month (Sep-Jun), Bamburgh Pavilion (below castle).

NORTHUMBERLAND & TYNESIDE BIRD CLUB. (1958; 270). Alan Watson, Secretary, 3 Green Close, Whitley Bay, Northumberland NE25 9SH. 0191 252 2744; e-mail: apusx@blueyonder.co.uk www.ntbc.org.uk

Ringing Groups
NATURAL HISTORY SOCIETY OF NORTHUMBRIA. Dr C P F Redfern, Westfield House, Acomb, Hexham, Northumberland NE46 4RJ.

NORTHUMBRIA RG. Secretary. B Galloway, 34 West Meadows, Stamfordham Road, Westerhope, Newcastle upon Tyne NE5 1LS. 0191 286 4850.

Wetland Bird Survey Organisers
NORTHUMBERLAND COAST. J Roper, 1 Long Row, Howick, Alnwick, Northumberland NE66 3LQ. e-mail: roperjuliea@hotmail.com

NORTHUMBERLAND (Inland). Steve Holliday, 2 Larriston Place, Cramlington, Northumberland NE23 8ER. 01670 731 963;
e-mail: steveholliday@hotmail.co.uk

Wildlife Hospitals
BERWICK SWAN & WILDLIFE TRUST. The Honorary Secretary, North Road Industrial Estate, Berwick upon Tweed, TD15 1UN. 01289 302882;
e-mail: swan-trust@hotmail.co.uk
www.swan-trust.org
Registered charity. All categories of wildlife. Pools for swans and other waterfowl. Veterinary support.

Wildlife Trust
NORTHUMBERLAND WILDLIFE TRUST. (1962; 13,000). The Garden House, St Nicholas Park, Jubilee Road, Gosforth, Newcastle upon Tyne, NE3 3XT. 0191 284 6884; fax 0191 284 6794;
e-mail: mail@northwt.org.uk
www.nwt.org.uk

NOTTINGHAMSHIRE

Bird Recorders
Andy Hall, E-mail: andy.h11@ntlworld.com

Bird Reports
LOUND BIRD REPORT (1990-), from Gary Hobson, 18 Barnes Avenue, Wrenthorpe, Wakefield, WF1 2BH. 01924 384 419;
e-mail: gary.lbc1@tiscali.co.uk.

BIRDS OF NOTTINGHAMSHIRE (1943-). £8 for current report, £4 for previous issues, plus p&p, from Ms Jenny Swindells, 21 Chaworth Road, West Bridgford, Nottingham NG2 7AE. 0115 9812 432;
e-mail: j.swindells@btinternet.com
www.nottsbirders.net

NETHERFIELD WILDLIFE GROUP ANNUAL REPORT (1999-). £5 inc postage, from Mr Niel Matthews, 4 Shellbourne Close, Heronridge, Nottingham, NG5 9LL.

BTO Regional Representative
RR. Mrs Lynda Milner, 6 Kirton Park, Kirton, Newark, Notts NG22 9LR. 01623 862 025;
e-mail: lyndamilner@hotmail.com

Clubs
ATTENBOROUGH BIRD CLUB. (1996; 45). John Ellis, 67 Springfield Avenue, Sandiacre, Nottingham, NG10 5NA. E-mail: jellis@trent.83.freeserve.co.uk

LOUND BIRD CLUB. (1991; 50). Gary Hobson, 18 Barnes Avenue, Wrenthorpe, Wakefield, WF1 2BH. 01924 384 419; e-mail: gary.lbc1@tiscali.co.uk www.loundbirdclub.piczo.com

NETHERFIELD WILDLIFE GROUP. (1999; 130). Philip Burnham, 57 Tilford Road, Newstead Village, Nottingham, NG15 0BU. 01623 401 980; e-mail: philip.burnham1@ntlworld.com.

NOTTINGHAMSHIRE BIRDWATCHERS. (1935; 370). Ms Jenny Swindells, 21 Chaworth Road, West Bridgford, Nottingham, NG2 7AE. 0115 9812 432;

e-mail: j.swindells@btinternet.com
www.nottsbirders.net
Meetings and events: Please see website for details.

WOLLATON NATURAL HISTORY SOCIETY. (1976; 86). Mrs P Price, 33 Coatsby Road, Hollycroft, Kimberley, Nottingham NG16 2TH. 0115 938 4965.
Meetings: 7.30pm, 3rd Wednesday of the month, St Leonards Community Centre, Wollaton Village, HG8 2ND.

Integrated Population Monitoring Group
TRESWELL WOOD INTEGRATED POPULATION MONITORING GROUP. Chris du Feu, 66 High Street, Beckingham, Notts, DN10 4PF.
e-mail: chris@chrisdufeu.force9.co.uk

Ringing Groups
BIRKLANDS RG. A D Lowe, 159 Sherwood Street, Market Warsop, Mansfield, Notts NG20 0JX.
e-mail: alowe@nottswt.co.uk

NORTH NOTTS RG. Adrian Blackburn, Willows End, 27 Palmer Road, Retford, Notts DN22 6SS. 01777 706 516; (M)07718 766 873:
e-mail: adrian.blackburn@sky.com

SOUTH NOTTINGHAMSHIRE RG. K J Hemsley, 8 Grange Farm Close, Toton, Beeston, Notts NG9 6EB.
e-mail: k.hemsley@ntlworld.com

RSPB Local Groups
MANSFIELD AND DISTRICT. (1986; 200). John Barlow, 240 Southwell Road West, Mansfield, Notts NG18 4LB. 01623 626647.
Meetings: 7pm, 1st Wednesday of the month (Sep-Jun), Bridge St Methodist Church, Rock Valley, Mansfield.

NOTTINGHAM. (1974; 514). Andrew Griffin, Lindholme, New Hill, Walesby, Newark, Notts NG22 9PB. 01623 860 529;
e-mail: amg1963@btinternet.com
www.notts-rspb.org.uk
Meetings: 7.30pm, 1st Wednesday of the month, Nottingham Mechanics, North Sherwood Street, Nottingham.

Wetland Bird Survey Organiser
Gary Hobson, 18 Barnes Avenue, Wrenthorpe, Wakefield, WF1 2BH. 01924 384 419;
e-mail: gary.lbc1@tiscali.co.uk.

Wildlife Trust
NOTTINGHAMSHIRE WILDLIFE TRUST. (1963; 4,300). The Old Ragged School, Brook Street, Nottingham, NG1 1EA. 0115 958 8242; fax 0115 924 3175; e-mail: info@nottswt.co.uk
www.wildlifetrust.org.uk/nottinghamshire

OXFORDSHIRE

Bird Atlas/Avifauna
Birds of Oxfordshire by J W Brucker et al (Oxford, Pisces, 1992).

The New Birds of the Banbury Area by T G Easterbrook (Banbury Ornithological Society, 1995).

Bird Recorder
Ian Lewington, 119 Brasenose Road, Didcot, Oxon, OX11 7BP. 01235 819 792; e-mail: ian@recorder.fsnet.co.uk

Bird Reports
BIRDS OF OXFORDSHIRE (1921-), from Barry Hudson, Pinfold, 4 Bushy Row, Bampton, Oxon OX18 2JU. 01865 775 632.

BANBURY ORNITHOLOGICAL SOCIETY ANNUAL REPORT (1952-). £5 each including postage, from MJ Lewis, Old Mill Cottage, Avon Dassett, Southam, Warwickshire, CV47 2AE. 01295 690 643; e-mail: mikelewisad@hotmail.com.

BTO Regional Representatives & Regional Development Officer
NORTH. Frances Buckel, Witts End, Radbones Hill, Over Norton, Chipping Norton, Oxon OX7 5RA. 01608 644 425; e-mail: fran.buckel@binternet.com

SOUTH RR & RDO. Mr John Melling, 17 Lime Grove, Southmoor, Nr Abingdon, Oxon OX13 5DN.
e-mail: bto-rep@oos.org.uk

Clubs
BANBURY ORNITHOLOGICAL SOCIETY. (1952; 100). Frances Buckel, Witts End, Radbones Hill, Over Norton, Chipping Norton, Oxon OX7 5RA. 01608 644 425; e-mail: fran.buckel@binternet.com
www.banburyornithologicalsociety.org.uk
Meetings: 7.30pm, 2nd Monday of the month, Freemason's Hall, Marlborough Road, Banbury.

OXFORD ORNITHOLOGICAL SOCIETY. (1921; 330). Barry Hudson, Pinfold, 4 Bushy Row, Bampton, Oxon OX18 2JU. 01993 852 028;
e-mail: secretary@oos.org.uk
www.oos.org.uk
Meetings: Various dates, Stratfield Brake, Kidlington.

Ringing Group
EDWARD GREY INSTITUTE. Dr A G Gosler, c/o Edward Grey Institute, Department of Zoology, South Parks Road, Oxford OX1 3PS. 01865 271 158; e-mail: andrew.gosler@zoo.ox.ac.uk

RSPB Local Groups
OXFORD. (1977; 100). Ian Kilshaw, 6 Queens Court, Bicester, Oxon, OX26 6JX. Tel 01869 601 901;

e-mail: ian.kilshaw@ntlworld.com
www.rspb-oxford.org.uk
Meetings: 7.45pm, normally 1st Thursday of the
month, Sandhills Primary School, Terret Avenue,
Headington, Oxford (opposite Thornhill park and
ride).

VALE OF WHITE HORSE. (1977; 330). Philip Morris .
01367 710 285; e-mail: Philip.P.Morris@tsco.net
www.rspb-vwh.org.uk
Meetings: 7.30pm, 3rd Monday of the month (Sep-
May). Didcot Civic Hall.

Wetland Bird Survey Organiser
OXFORDSHIRE (NORTH). Sandra Bletchly,
e-mail: sandra@banornsoc.fsnet.co.uk

Wildlife Trust
BBOWT. (1959; 24,000). The Lodge, 1 Armstrong
Road, Littlemore, Oxford, OX4 4XT. 01865 775 476;
fax 01865 711 301; e-mail: info@bbowt.org.uk
www.bbowt.org.uk

SHROPSHIRE

Bird Atlas/Avifauna
Atlas of the Breeding Birds of Shropshire
(Shropshire Ornithological Society, 1995).

Bird Recorder
Geoff Holmes, 22 Tenbury Drive, Telford Estate,
Shrewsbury, SY2 5YF. 01743 364 621;
e-mail: geoff.holmes4@tiscali.co.uk

Bird Report
SHROPSHIRE BIRD REPORT (1956-) Annual, from
Helen Griffiths (Hon Secretary), 104 Noel Hill Road,
Cross Houses, Shrewsbury SY5 6LD. 01743 761507;
e-mail: helen.griffiths@english-nature.org.uk
www.shropshirebirds.com

BTO Regional Representative
RR. Allan Dawes, Rosedale, Chapel Lane, Trefonen,
Oswestry, Shrops SY10 9DX. 01691 654245;
e-mail: allandawes@btinternet.com

Club
SHROPSHIRE ORNITHOLOGICAL SOCIETY. (1955;
800). Helen Griffiths, 104 Noel Hill Road, Cross
Houses, Shrewsbury, SY5 6LD. 01743 761 507;
e-mail: helen.griffiths@english-nature.org.uk
www.shropshirebirds.com
Meetings: 7.15pm, 1st Thursday of month (Oct-
Apr), Shirehall, Shrewsbury.

RSPB Local Group
SHROPSHIRE. (1992; 320). Roger M Evans, 31 The
Wheatlands, Bridgnorth, WV16 5BD. 01746 766
042; e-mail: revans4@toucansurf.com
www.rspb.org.uk/groups/shropshire
Meetings: 3rd Thursday of the month (Sep-Apr),

Council Chamber, Shirehall, Shrewsbury. Also field
trip year round. 3rd Wednesday in the month (Oct-
March) Secret Hills Centre Craven Arms.

SOUTH SHROPSHIRE. Alan Botting (Group Leader).
01547 540 176 or Christine Bateman (Secretary),
01584 878 362;
e-mail: Christinelbateman@yahoo.com
www.rspbsouthshropshire.org.uk
Meetings: 7.30pm (Sep-Apr), Shropshire Hills
Discovery Centre (Secret Hills), Craven Arms.

Wetland Bird Survey Organiser
Michael Wallace, 01743 25 234;
e-mail: michael@wallace7536.freeserve.co.uk

Wildlife Trust
SHROPSHIRE WILDLIFE TRUST. (1962; 10,000).
193 Abbey Foregate, Shrewsbury, Shropshire SY2
6AH. 01743 284 280; fax 01743 284281;
e-mail: shropshirewt@cix.co.uk
www.shropshirewildlifetrust.org.uk

SOMERSET & BRISTOL

Bird Atlas/Avifauna
A History of the Birds of Somerset by DK Ballance.
(Isabelline Books, 6 Bellevue, Enys, Penryn,
Cornwall TR10 9LB. 2006).

The Birds of Exmoor and the Quantocks by DK
Ballance and BD Gibbs. (Isabelline Books, 6
Bellevue, Enys, Penryn, Cornwall TR10 9LB. 2003).

Bird Recorders
AVON. Martin John,
e-mail: avonbirdrecorder@googlemail.com

SOMERSET. Brian D Gibbs, 23 Lyngford Road,
Taunton, Somerset, TA2 7EE. 01823 274 887;
e-mail: brian.gibbs@virgin.net
www.somersetbirds.net

Bird Reports
AVON BIRD REPORT (1977-), from Harvey Rose,
12 Birbeck Road, Bristol, BS9 1BD. 0117 968 1638;
e-mail: h.e.rose@bris.ac.uk

EXMOOR NATURALIST (1974-), from Secretary,
Exmoor Natural History Society.

SOMERSET BIRDS (1913-),
www.somersetbirds.net

BTO Regional Representatives
AVON RR. Richard L Bland, 11 Percival Road, Bristol,
BS8 3LN. Home/W:01179 734 828;
e-mail: richardbland@blueyonder.co.uk

AVON ASSISTANT RR. John Tully, 6 Falcondale
Walk, Westbury-on-Trym, Bristol, BS9 3JG. 0117
950 0992; e-mail: johntully4@aol.com

SOMERSET RR. Eve Tigwell, Hawthorne Cottage, 3 Friggle Street, Frome, Somerset BA11 5LP. 01373 451630; e-mail: eve.tigwell@zen.co.uk

Clubs

BRISTOL NATURALISTS' SOCIETY (Ornithological Section). (1862; 550). Dr Mary Hill, 15 Montrose Avenue, Redland, Bristol, BS6 6EH. 0117 942 2193; e-mail: mary@jhill15.fsnet.co.uk www.bristolnats.org.uk

Meetings: 7.30pm, monthly Wednesday (check for dates, Oct-Mar), Westmorland Hall, Westmorland Road, Bristol

BRISTOL ORNITHOLOGICAL CLUB. (1966; 670). Mrs Judy Copeland, 19 St George's Hill, Easton-in-Gordano, North Somerset, BS20 0PS. Tel/fax 01275 373554; judy.copeland@ukgateway.net www.boc-bristol.org.uk
Meetings: 7.30pm, 3rd Thursday of the month, Newman Hall, Grange Court Road, Westbury-on-Trym.

CAM VALLEY WILDLIFE GROUP. (1994; 356). André Fournier, 1 Boomfield Lane, Paulton, Bristol BS39 7QU. 01761 148 153.
e-mail: andre.fournier@btinternet.com www.somersetmade.co.uk/cvwg/

EXMOOR NATURAL HISTORY SOCIETY. (1974; 480). Miss Caroline Giddens, 12 King George Road, Minehead, Somerset, TA24 5JD. 01643 707 624; e-mail: carol.enhs@virgin.net www.enhs.org.uk
Meetings: 7.30pm, 1st Wednesday of the month (Oct-Mar), Methodist Church Hall, The Avenue, Minehead.

SOMERSET ORNITHOLOGICAL SOCIETY. (1923; 350). e-mail: brian.hill@somersetbirds.net www.somersetbirds.net
Meetings: 7.30pm, various Thursdays (Oct-Apr), Ruishton Village Hall, Taunton.

Ringing Groups

CHEW VALLEY RS. Mr A Ashman.
e-mail: alan.ashman@talktalk.net

GORDANO VALLEY RG. Lyndon Roberts, 20 Glebe Road, Long Ashton, Bristol, BS41 9LH. 01275 392 722; e-mail: mail@lyndonroberts.com

RSPCA. Mr K Leighton.
e-mail: kev.leighton@O2.co.uk

STEEP HOLM RS. A J Parsons, Barnfield, Tower Hill Road, Crewkerne, Somerset, TA18 8BJ. 01460 73640.

RSPB Local Groups

BATH AND DISTRICT. (1989; 220). Alan Barrett. 01225 310 905; www.rspb.org.uk/groups/bath e-mail: alan_w_h_barrett@yahoo.co.uk
Meetings: 7.30pm, 3rd Wednesday of the month (Sep-Mar), Bath Society Meeting Room, Green Park Station, Bath

CREWKERNE & DISTRICT. (1979; 340). Denise Chamings, Daniels Farm, Lower Stratton, South Petherton, Somerset TA13 5LP. 01460 240 740; e-mail: denise.chamings@virgin.net WWW.rspb.org.uk/groups/crewkerne
Meetings: 7.30pm, 3rd Thursday of the month (Sep-Apr), The Henhayes Centre, Crewkerne.

TAUNTON. (1975; 148). Frances Freeman. 01823 674 182; e-mail: francesfreeman@yahoo.com www.rspb.org.uk/groups/taunton

WESTON-SUPER-MARE (N SOMERSET). (1976; 215). Don Hurrell, Freeways, Star, Winscombe, BS25 1PS. 01934 842 717;
e-mail: hurrell@cpsmail.co.uk www.rspb.org.uk/groups/westonsupermare
Meetings: 7.30pm, 1st Thursday of the month (Sep-Apr), St Pauls Church Hall, Walscote Road.

Wetland Bird Survey Organisers

SOMERSET LEVELS. Steve Meen, RSPB West Sedgemoor, Dewlands Farm, Redhill, Curry Rivel, Langport Somerset TA10 0PH. 01458 252805; e-mail: steve.meen@rspb.org.uk

SEVERN ESTUARY - SOUTHERN COAST. Harvey Rose, 12 Birbek Road, Stoke Bishop, Bristol, BS9 1BD. 0117 968 1638; e-mail: h.e.rose@bris.ac.uk

Wildlife Trusts

AVON WILDLIFE TRUST. (1980; 7,000). The Old Police Station , 32 Jacobs Wells Road, Bristol, BS8 1DR. 0117 917 7270; fax 0117 929 7273; e-mail: mail@avonwildlifetrust.org.uk www.avonwlldlIfetrust.org.uk

SOMERSET WILDLIFE TRUST. (1964; 19,500). Tonedale Mill,Tonedale,Wellington,Somerset TA21 0AW. 01823 652 400; fax 01823 652 411; e-mail: enquiries@somersetwildlife.org www.somersetwildlife.org www.enhs.org.uk

STAFFORDSHIRE

Bird Recorder

Nick Pomiankowski,22 The Villas, West End, Stoke ST4 5AQ; 01782 849 682; e-mail: staffs-recorder@westmidlandbirdclub.com

Bird Report See West Midlands

BTO Regional Representatives

NORTH EAST. Gilly Jones, 4 The Poplars, Lichfield

Road, Abbots Bromley, Rugeley Staffs WS15 3AA.
01283 840 555; e-mail: g.n.jones@wlv.ac.uk

SOUTH & CENTRAL. Gilly Jones, 4 The Poplars,
Lichfield Road, Abbots Bromley, Rugeley Staffs
WS15 3AA. 01283 840 555; e-mail: g.n.jones@wlv.
ac.uk

WEST. Gilly Jones, 4 The Poplars, Lichfield Road,
Abbots Bromley, Rugeley Staffs WS15 3AA. 01283
840 555; e-mail: g.n.jones@wlv.ac.uk

Clubs
SOUTH PEAK RAPTOR STUDY GROUP. (1998;
12). M E Taylor, 76 Hawksley Avenue, Newbold,
Chesterfield, Derbys S40 4TL. 01246 277 749.

WEST MIDLAND BIRD CLUB (STAFFORD BRANCH).
Gerald Ford. 01630 673 409;
e-mail: gerald.ford@westmidlandbirdclub.com
www.westmidlandbirdclub.com/stafford
Meetings: 7.30pm, 2nd Friday of the month
(Oct-Mar), The Centre for The Blind, North Walls,
Stafford.

WEST MIDLAND BIRD CLUB (TAMWORTH BRANCH).
(1992). Barbara Stubbs, 19 Alfred Street, Tamworth,
Staffs, B79 7RL. 01827 57865;
e-mail: tamworth@westmidlandbirdclub
www.westmidlandbirdclub.com/tamworth
Meetings: 7.30pm, 3rd Friday of the month (Sep-
Apr), Phil Dix Centre, Corporation Street, Tamworth.

RSPB Local Groups
BURTON-ON-TRENT AND SOUTH DERBYSHIRE.
(1973; 50). Dave Lummis, 121 Wilmot Road,
Swadlincote, Derbys, DE11 9BN. 01283 219 902.
www.basd-rspb.co.uk
Meetings: 7.30pm 1st Wednesday of the month,
All Saint's Church, Branston Road, Burton.

LICHFIELD & DISTRICT. (1977; 1150). Ray Jennett,
12 St Margarets Road, Lichfield, Staffs, WS13 7RA.
01543 255 195.
Meetings: 7.30pm, 2nd Tuesday of the month
(Jan-May, Sept-Dec), St Mary's Centre.

NORTH STAFFS. (1982; 187). John Booth, 32 St
Margaret Drive, Sneyd Green, Stoke-on-Trent, ST1
6EW. 01782 262 082; www.rspb.org.uk/groups/
northstaffordshire
Meetings: 7.30pm, normally 3rd Wednesday of
the month, North Staffs Conference Centre (Medical
Institute).

SOUTH WEST STAFFORDSHIRE. (1972; 185).
Mrs Theresa Dorrance, 39 Wilkes Road, Codsall,
Wolverhampton, WV8 1RZ. 01902 847 041;
e-mail: dorrancesteve@fsmail.net
Meetings: 8.00pm, 2nd Tuesday of the month
(Sep-May), Codsall Village Hall.

Wildlife Hospitals
BRITISH WILDLIFE RESCUE CENTRE. Alfred
Hardy, Amerton Working Farm, Stowe-by-Chartley,
Stafford, ST18 0LA. 01889 271308.
On A518 Stafford/Uttoxeter road. All species,
including imprints and permanently injured.
Hospital, large aviaries and caging. Open to the
public every day. Veterinary support.

GENTLESHAW BIRD OF PREY HOSPITAL. Jenny
Smith, Gentleshaw Wildlife Centre, Stone Road,
Eccleshall, Staffs ST21 6JY. 01785 850 379; e-mail:
gentleshaw1@btconnect.com
www.gentleshawwildlife.co.uk Registered charity.
All birds of prey (inc. owls). Hospital cages and
aviaries; release sites. Veterinary support. Also
GENTLESHAW BIRD OF PREY AND WILDLIFE
CENTRE, Fletchers Country Garden Centre, Stone
Road, Eccleshall, Stafford. 01785 850379 (1000-
1700).

Wildlife Trust
STAFFORDSHIRE WILDLIFE TRUST. (1969; 14,000).
The Wolseley Centre, Wolseley Bridge, Stafford,
ST17 0WT. 01889 880 100; fax 01889 880 101;
e-mail: staffs-wildlife.org.uk
www.staffs-wildlife.org.uk

SUFFOLK

Bird Atlas/Avifauna
Birds of Suffolk by S H Piotrowski (February 2003)
Quatermelon.

Bird Recorders
NORTH EAST. David Fairhurst.
e-mail: davidfairhurst@lycos.com

SOUTH EAST (inc. coastal region from Slaughden
Quay southwards). Eddie Marsh.
e-mail: marshharrier@btinternet.com

WEST (whole of Suffolk W of Stowmarket, inc.
Breckland). Colin Jakes, 7 Maltward Avenue, Bury St
Edmunds, Suffolk IP33 3XN. 01284 702 215;
e-mail: colin.jakes@stedsbc.gov.uk

Bird Report
*SUFFOLK BIRDS (inc Landguard Bird Observatory
Report) (1950-)*, from Ipswich Museum, High Street,
Ipswich, Suffolk.

BTO Regional Representative
Mick T Wright, 15 Avondale Road,
Ipswich, IP3 9JT. 01473 710 032;
e-mail: micktwright@btinternet.com

Clubs
LAVENHAM BIRD CLUB. (1972; 54).
Mr G Pattrick, Brights Farmhouse,
Brights Lane, Lavenham, Suffolk
CO10 9PH. 01787 248 128.

Meetings: 7.30pm, normally 3rd Saturday (Sep-Mar, except Dec), Lavenham Guildlhall.

SUFFOLK ORNITHOLOGISTS' GROUP. (1973; 650). Andrew M Gregory, 1 Holly Road, Ipswich, IP1 3QN. 01473 253 816.
Meetings: Last Thursday of the month (Jan-Mar, Oct-Nov), Holiday Inn, Ipswich.

Ringing Groups
DINGLE BIRD CLUB. Dr D Pearson, 4 Lupin Close, Reydon, Southwold, Suffolk IP18 6NW. 01502 722348.

LACKFORD RG. Dr Peter Lack, 11 Holden Road, Lackford, Bury St Edmunds, Suffolk IP28 6HZ. e-mail: peter.diane@tinyworld.co.uk

LANDGUARD RG. Landguard Ringing Group, Landguard Bird Observatory, View Point Road, Felixstowe, Suffolk, IP11 3TW. 01394 673782; e-mail: landguardbo@yahoo.co.uk www.lbo.co.uk

MARKET WESTON RG. Dr R H W Langston, Walnut Tree Farm, Thorpe Street, Hinderclay, Diss, Norfolk IP22 1HT. e-mail: rlangston@wntfarm.demon.co.uk

RSPB Local Groups
BURY ST EDMUNDS. (1982; 150). John Sharpe . 01359 230 045; e-mail: sharpix@tiscali.co.uk www.rspb.org.uk/groups/burystedmunds
Meetings: 7.30pm, 3rd Tuesday of the month (Sep-May), County Upper School, Beetons Way, Bury St Edmunds.

IPSWICH. (1975; 275). Mr Chris Courtney, St Elmo, 19 Marlborough Road, Ipswich, Suffolk IP4 5AT. 01473 423 213; www.ipswichrspb.org.uk. e-mail: chrisc.courtney@yahoo.co.uk
Meetings: 7.30pm, 2nd Thursday of the month (Sep-Apr), Sidegate Lane Primary School, Sidegate Lane, Ipswich.

LOWESTOFT & DISTRICT. (1976; 130). Mrs E Beaumont, 52 Squires Walk, Lowestoft, Suffolk, NR32 4LA. 01502 560 126; e-mail: embeaumont@supanet.com www.rspb.org.uk/groups/lowestoft
Meetings: Friday 7.15pm 1st Monday in the month, St Marks Church Hall, Oulton Broad.

WOODBRIDGE. (1987; 450). Malcolm Key, Riverside, Parham, Suffolk, IP13 9LZ. 01728 723 155; e-mail: malcolm.key@btopenworld.com
Meetings: 7.30pm, 1st Thursday of the month (Oct-May), Woodbridge Community Hall.

Wetland Bird Survey Organisers
DEBEN ESTUARY. Nick Mason, The Decoy, 8 Mallard Way, Hollesley, Nr Woodbridge, Suffolk IP12 3QJ. (H)01359 411 150; e-mail: nick.mason4@btinternet.com

STOUR ESTUARY. Rick Vonk, RSPB, Unit 13 Court Farm, 3 Stutton Road, Brantham Suffolk CO11 1PW. (D)01473 328 006; e-mail:rick.vonk@rspb.org.uk

SUFFOLK (other sites). Alan Miller, Suffolk Wildlife Trust, Moonrakers, Back Lane, Wenhaston, Halesworth, Suffolk, IP19 9DY. e-mail: alan.miller@suffolkwildlifetrust.org

Wildlife Trust
SUFFOLK WILDLIFE TRUST. (1961; 25,000). Brooke House, The Green, Ashbocking, Ipswich, IP6 9JY. 01473 890 089; fax 01473 890 165; e-mail: info@suffolkwildlifetrust.org www.suffolkwildlifetrust.org

SURREY

Bird Atlas/Avifauna
Birds of Surrey by Jeffery Wheatley (Surrey Bird Club 2007).

Bird Recorder (inc London S of Thames & E to Surrey Docks)
SURREY (includes Greater London south of the Thames and east to the Surrey Docks, excludes Spellthorne). Jeffery Wheatley, 9 Copse Edge, Elstead, Godalming, Surrey, GU8 6DJ. 01252 702 450; e-mail: j.j.wheatley@btinternet.com.

Bird Report
SURBITON AND DISTRICT BIRD WATCHING SOCIETY (1972-), from Thelma Caine, 21 More Lane, Esher, Surrey KT10 8AJ.

SURREY BIRD REPORT (1952-), from J Gates, 5 Hillside Road, Weybourne, Farnham, Surrey GU9 9DW. 01252 315 047; e-mail: jeremygates@hotmail.co.uk

BTO Regional Representative
RR. Hugh Evans. 01932 227 781; e-mail: hugh.evans31@tiscali.co.uk

Clubs
SURBITON & DISTRICT BIRDWATCHING SOCIETY. (1954; 165). Gary Caine, 21 More Lane, Esher, Surrey, KT10 8AJ. 01372 468 432; e-mail: hockley@sdbws.ndo.co.uk www.sdbws.ndo.co.uk
Meetings: 7.30pm, 3rd Tuesday of the month, Surbiton Library Annex.

SURREY BIRD CLUB. (1957; 350). Charlotte Gray, 24 Nursery Hill, Shamley Green, Surrey GU5 0UN. 01483 894 144; e-mail: webmaster@surreybirdclub.org.uk www.surreybirdclub.org.uk
Meetings: See website for details.

ENGLAND

Ringing Groups
HERSHAM RG. A J Beasley, 29 Selbourne Avenue, New Haw, Weybridge, Surrey KT15 3RB.
e-mail: abeasley00@hotmail.com

RUNNYMEDE RG. D G Harris, 22 Blossom Waye, Hounslow, TW5 9HD.
e-mail: daveharris@tinyonline.co.uk

RSPB Local Groups
DORKING & DISTRICT. (1982; 280). John Burge, Broughton Norrels Drive, East Horsley, Leatherhead, KT24 5DR. 01483 283 803;
e-mail: burgejs@googlemail.com
Meetings: 8.00pm, Fridays once a month (Sep-Apr), Christian Centre, next to St Martin's Church, Dorking.

EAST SURREY. (1984; 150-200). Brian Hobley, 26 Alexandra Road, Warlingham, Surrey, CR6 9DU. 01883 625 404; e-mail: brianhobley@btinternet.com
www.eastsurreyrspb.co.uk
Meetings: 8.00pm, 2nd Wednesday of the month (Sep-Jul), Whitehart Barn, Godstone.

EPSOM & EWELL. (1974; 168). Janet Gilbert, 78 Fairfax Avenue, Ewell, Epsom, Surrey KT17 2QQ. 0208 394 0405;
e-mail: janetegilbert@btinternet.com
www.rspb.org.uk/groups/epsom
Meetings: 7.45pm, 2nd Friday of the month, All Saints Church Hall, Fulford Road, West Ewell.

GUILDFORD AND DISTRICT. (1974; 600). Roger Beck, 14 Overbrook, West Horsley, KT24 6BH. 01483 282 417;
e-mail: rogerbeck@beck40.fsnet.co.uk
www.rspb.org.uk/groups/guildford
Meetings: 2.15pm 2nd Tuesday and 7.45pm 4th Wednesday of the month, Onslow Village Hall, Guildford.

NORTH WEST SURREY. (1973; 140). Ms Mary Braddock, 20 Meadway Drive, New Haw, Surrey, KT15 2DT. 01932 858692;
e-mail: mary@braddock3.wanadoo.co.uk
www.nwsurreyrspb.org.uk
Meetings: 7.45pm, 4th Wednesday of the month (not Dec, Jul, Aug), Sir William Perkins School, Chertsey.

Wetland Bird Survey Organiser
SURREY (includes Greater London south of the Thames and east to the Surrey Docks, excludes Spellthorne). Jeffery Wheatley, 9 Copse Edge, Elstead, Godalming, Surrey GU8 6DJ. 01252 702 450; e-mail: j.j.wheatley@btinternet.com

Wildlife Hospitals
THE SWAN SANCTUARY. See National Directory

WILDLIFE AID. Randalls Farm House, Randalls Road, Leatherhead, Surrey, KT22 0AL. 01372 377 332; 24-hr emergline 09061 800 132 (50p/min); fax 01372 375183; e-mail: wildlife@pncl.co.uk
www.wildlifeaid.com
Registered charity. Wildlife hospital and rehabilitation centre helping all native British species. Special housing for birds of prey. Membership scheme and fund raising activities. Veterinary support.

Wildlife Trust
SURREY WILDLIFE TRUST. (1959; 25,700). School Lane, Pirbright, Woking, Surrey, GU24 0JN. 01483 795 440; fax 01483 486 505;
e-mail: info@surreywt.org.uk
www.surreywildlifetrust.org

SUSSEX

Bird Atlas/Avifauna
The Birds of Selsey Bill and the Selsey Peninsular (a checklist to year 2000) From: Mr O Mitchell, 21 Trundle View Close, Barnham, Bognor Regis, PO22 0JZ.

Birds of Sussex ed by Paul James (Sussex Ornithological Society, 1996).

Fifty Years of Birdwatching, a celebration of the acheivements of the Shoreham District OS from 1953 onwards. from Shoreham District Ornithological Society, 7 Berberis Court, Shoreham by Sea, West Sussex BN43 6JA. £15 plus £2.50 p&p.

Bird Recorder
Mr CW Melgar, 36 Victoria Road, Worthing, W Sussex, BN11 1XB. 01903 200 064;
e-mail: cwmelgar@yahoo.com

Bird Reports
BIRDS OF RYE HARBOUR NR ANNUAL REPORT (1977- published every 5 years), from Dr Barry Yates, see Clubs.

HENFIELD BIRDWATCHER Reports 2000 and 2005 ed Mike Russell et al, Henfield Birdwatch

PAGHAM HARBOUR LOCAL NATURE RESERVE ANNUAL REPORT, from Warden, see Reserves,

SHOREHAM DISTRICT ORNITHOLOGICAL SOCIETY ANNUAL REPORT (1952-) - back issues available, from Mrs. Shena Maskell, SDOS Membership Administrator, 41 St. Lawrence Avenue, Worthing, West Sussex BN14 7JJ.
www.sdos.org

SUSSEX BIRD REPORT (1963-), from J E Trowell, Lorrimer, Main Road, Icklesham, Winchelsea, E

Sussex, TN36 4BS. e-mail: membership@sos.org.uk
www.sos.org.uk

BTO Regional Representative
Dr Helen Crabtree, 01444 441 687;
e-mail: hcrabtree@gmail.com.

Clubs
FRIENDS OF RYE HARBOUR NATURE RESERVE.
(1973; 1800). Dr Barry Yates, 2 Watch Cottages,
Nook Beach, Winchelsea, E Sussex TN36 4LU.
01797 223862; e-mail: yates@clara.net
www.wildrye.info
Meetings: Monthly talks in winter, monthly walks
all year.

HENFIELD BIRDWATCH. (1999; 135). Mike Russell,
31 Downsview, Small Dole, Henfield, West Sussex
BN5 9YB. 01273 494311;
e-mail: mikerussell@sussexwt.org.uk

SHOREHAM DISTRICT ORNITHOLOGICAL SOCIETY.
(1953; 150). Mrs. Shena Maskell, SDOS Membership
Administrator, 41 St. Lawrence Avenue, Worthing,
West Sussex BN14 7JJ.
www.sdos.org.
Meetings: 7.30pm, 1st Tuesday of the month (Oct-
Apr), St Peter's Church Hall, Shoreham-by-Sea. (7
indoor meetings, 16 field outings)

SUSSEX ORNITHOLOGICAL SOCIETY. (1962; 1502).
Nigel Bowie, 55 Rochester Street, Brighton, BN2
0EJ. 01273 571 266; e-mail:secretary@sos.org.uk
www.sos.org.uk

Ringing Groups
BEACHY HEAD RS. R D M Edgar, 32 Hartfield Road,
Seaford, E Sussex BN25 4PW.

CUCKMERE RG. Tim Parmenter, 18 Chapel Road,
Plumpton Green, East Sussex, BN7 3DD. 01273 891
881.

RYE BAY RG. P Jones, Elms Farm, Pett Lane,
Icklesham, Winchelsea, E Sussex TN36 4AH. 01797
226374; e-mail: philjones@beamingbroadband.com

STEYNING RINGING GROUP. B R Clay, Meghana,
Honeysuckle Lane, High Salvington, Worthing, West
Sussex BN13 3BT. e-mail: brian.clay@ntlworld.com

RSPB Local Groups
BATTLE. (1973; 80). Miss Lynn Jenkins, 61 Austen
Way, Guestling, Hastings, E Sussex TN35 4JH.
01424 432 076;
e-mail: Lynn.jenkins@battlerspb.org.uk
www.battlerspb.org.uk
Meetings: 7.30pm, 4th Tuesday of the month,
Battle and Langton Primary School, Battle.

BRIGHTON & DISTRICT. (1974; 350). Ian Booth.
01273 588 288; e-mail: Ian@batatzes.fsnet.co.uk
www.rspb.org.uk/groups/brighton

Meetings: 7.30pm, 4th Thursday of the month, All
Saints Church Hall, Eaton Road, Hove.

CHICHESTER & SW SUSSEX. (1979; 245). David
Hart, Heys Bridle Rd, Slindon Common, Arundel,
BN18 0NA. 01243 814 497; e-mail: heather.
dave1@tiscali.co.uk
www.rspb.org.uk/groups/chichester
Meetings: 7.30 pm 2nd Thursday of each month,
Newell Centre, Newell Centre, Tozer Way, St
Pancras, Chichester.

CRAWLEY & HORSHAM. (1978; 148). Andrea
Saxton, 104 Heath Way, Horsham, W Sussex, RH12
5XS. 01403 242 218;
e-mail: Andrea.saxton@sky.com
www.rspb.org.uk/groups/crawley
Meetings: 8.00pm, 3rd Wednesday of the month
(Sept-Apr), The Friary Hall, Crawley.

EAST GRINSTEAD. (1998; 185). Nick Walker, 14
York Avenue, East Grinstead, W Sussex RH19 4TL.
01342 315 825; e-mail: gnwalker@tiscali.co.uk
www.rspb.org.uk/groups/egrinstead
Meetings: 8.00pm, last Wednesday of the month,
Large Parish Hall, De La Warr Road, East Grinstead.

EASTBOURNE & DISTRICT. (1993; 520).
Ian Muldoon. 01273 476852; e-mail:
ian1muldoon@yahoo.co.uk
www.rspb.org.uk/groups/eastbourne
Meetings: 2.15 pm and 7.30 pm ,1st Wednesday
of the month (Sep-Jun), St. Wilfreds Church Hall,
Eastbourne Road, Pevensey Bay.

HASTINGS & ST LEONARDS. (1983; 110). Susan
Neighbour, 9 Gainsborough Road, Bexhill on
Sea, E Sussex TN40 2UL. 01424 211 140; e-mail:
s92neighbour@tesco.net
Meetings: 7.30pm, 3rd Friday of the month, Taplin
Centre, Upper Maze Hill.

Wildlife Hospital
BRENT LODGE BIRD &
WILDLIFE TRUST. Penny
Cooper, Brent Lodge,
Cow Lane, Sidlesham,
Chichester, West Sussex,
PO20 7LN. 01243 641 672
(emergency number);
www.brentlodge.org.
All species of wild birds
and small mammals. Full
surgical and medical facilities (inc. X-ray). Purpose-
built oiled bird washing unit. Veterinary support.

Wildlife Trust
SUSSEX WILDLIFE TRUST. (1961; 24,000). Woods
Mill, Shoreham Road, Henfield, W Sussex, BN5 9SD.
01273 492630; fax 01273 494500;
e-mail: enquiries@sussexwt.org.uk
www.sussexwt.org.uk

ENGLAND

TYNE & WEAR

Bird Recorders
See Durham; Northumberland.

Bird Report See Durham; Northumberland.

Clubs
NATURAL HISTORY SOCIETY OF NORTHUMBRIA.
(1829; 900). The Natural History Society of
Northumbria, Hancock Museum, Barras Bridge,
Newcastle upon Tyne, NE2 4PT. 0191 232 6386;
e-mail: nhsn@ncl.ac.uk
www.NHSN.ncl.ac.uk
Meetings: 7.00pm, every Friday (Oct-Mar), Percy
Building, Newcastle University.

NORTHUMBERLAND & TYNESIDE BIRD CLUB.
(1958; 270). Alan Watson, Secretary, 3 Green Close,
Whitley Bay, Northumberland NE25 9SH. 0191 252
2744; e-mail: apusx@blueyonder.co.uk
www.ntbc.org.uk

RSPB Local Groups
NEWCASTLE UPON TYNE. (1969; 250). Brian
Moorhead. 07903 387 429;
e-mail: ncastlerspbgroup@btinternet.com
www.rspb.org.uk/groups/newcastle
Meetings: 7pm, (Mar, Jun, Sep, Nov), Northumbria
University, Ellison Place, Newcastle upon Tyne.

WARWICKSHIRE

Bird Recorder
Jonathan Bowley, 17 Meadow Way, Fenny Compton,
Southam, Warks, CV47 2WD. 01295 770069; e-mail:
warks-recorder@westmidlandbirdclub.com

Bird Report See West Midlands.

BTO Regional Representatives
WARWICKSHIRE. Mark Smith. 01926 735 398;
e-mail: mark.smith36@ntlworld.com

RUGBY. Position vacant.

Clubs
NUNEATON & DISTRICT BIRDWATCHERS' CLUB.
(1950; 78). Alvin K Burton, 23 Redruth Close,
Horeston Grange, Nuneaton, Warwicks CV11 6FG.
024 7664 1591.
Meetings: 7.30pm, 3rd Thursday of the month
(Sep-Jun), Hatters Space Community Centre, Upper
Abbey Street, Nuneaton.

Ringing Groups
ARDEN RG. Roger J Juckes, 24 Croft Lane, Temple
Grafton, Alcester, Warks B49 6PA. 01789 778748.

BRANDON RG. David Stone, Overbury, Wolverton,
Stratford-on-Avon, Warks CV37 0HG. 01789 731488.

RSPB Local Group
See West Midlands.

Wildlife Trust
WARWICKSHIRE WILDLIFE TRUST. (1970; 13,000).
Brandon Marsh Nature Centre, Brandon Lane,
Coventry, CV3 3GW. 024 7630 2912; fax 024 7663
9556; e-mail: enquiries@wkwt.org.uk
www.warwickshire-wildlife-trust.org.uk

WEST MIDLANDS

Bird Atlas/Avifauna
The Birds of the West Midlands edited by Graham
Harrison et al (West Midland Bird Club, 1982). Rev
ed due 2000/2001.

Bird Recorder
Kevin Clements, 26 Hambrook Close, Dunstall Park,
Wolverhampton, West Midlands WV6 0XA. email:
west-mids-recorder@westmidlandbirdclub.com

Bird Reports
*THE BIRDS OF SMESTOW VALLEY AND
DUNSTALL PARK (1988-)*, from Secretary,
Smestow Valley Bird Group.

*THE BIRDS OF STAFFORDSHIRE, WARWICKSHIRE,
WORCESTERSIRE AND THE WEST MIDLANDS
(1934-)*, £9 inc p&p, from John Hoyle, 22 Montford
Road, Coleshill B46 3LT,
e-mail: membership@westmidlandbirdclub.com

BTO Regional Representative
BIRMINGHAM & WEST MIDLANDS. Steve Davies.
07882 891 726;
e-mail:stevendavies907@btinternet.com

Clubs
SMESTOW VALLEY BIRD GROUP. (1988; 56). Frank
Dickson, 11 Bow Street, Bilston, Wolverhampton,
WV14 7NB. 01902 493 733.

WEST MIDLAND BIRD CLUB.
(1929; 2000). Barbara Oakley,
147 Worlds End, Quinton,
Birmingham B32 1JX.
e-mail: secretary@
westmidlandbirdclub.com
www. westmidlandbirdclub.com
Meetings: Check website for
details of the different branches
and their events.

WEST MIDLAND BIRD CLUB (BIRMINGHAM
BRANCH). (1995; 800). Martin Kenrick.
e-mail: birmingham@westmidlandbirdclub.com
www.westmidlandbirdclub.com/birmingham
Meetings: 7.30pm, usually last Tuesday (Oct-Apr),
Birmingham Medical Institute, in Harborne Road,
Edgbaston, near Five Ways.

WEST MIDLAND BIRD CLUB (SOLIHULL BRANCH).
Raymond Brown, The Spinney, 63 Grange Road,
Dorridge, Solihull B93 8QS. 01564 772 550;
e-mail: solihull@westmidlandbirdclub
www.westmidlandbirdclub.com/solihull
Meetings: 7.30 pm, Fridays, Solihull College's,
New Lecture Rooms, Blossomfield Road, Solihull.

Ringing Groups
MERCIAN RG (Sutton Coldfield). Mr DJ Clifton.
e-mail: djc.dab@talk21.com

RSPB Local Groups
BIRMINGHAM. (1975; 100). John Bailey, 52
Gresham Road, Hall Green, Birmingham, B28 0HY.
0121 777 4389; e-mail: jvbailey@btinternet.com
www.rspb-birmingham.org.uk
Meetings: 7.30pm, 3rd Thursday of the month
(Sep-Jun), Salvation Army Citadel, St Chads,
Queensway, Birmingham.

COVENTRY & WARWICKSHIRE. (1969; 130). Alan
King, 69 Westmorland Road, Coventry, CV2 5BP.
01926 428 365;
e-mail: Ron@speddings.spacomputers.com
www.rspb.org.uk/groups/coventryandwarwickshire.

SOLIHULL. (1983; 2600). John Roberts, 115
Dovehouse Lane, Solihull, West Midlands, B91 2EQ.
0121 707 3101; e-mail: johnbirder@care4free.net
www.rspb.org.uk/groups/solihull
Meetings: 7.30pm, usually 2nd Tuesday of the
month (Sep-Apr), Oliver Bird Hall, Church Hill Road,
Solihull.

STOURBRIDGE. (1978; 150). Pat Ackland. 01384
293 090; www.rspb.org.uk/groups/stourbridge
Meetings: 2nd Wednesday of the month (Sep-
May), Woollaston Suite, Stourbridge Town Hall,
Crown Centre, STOURBRIDGE, West Midlands, DY8
1YE

SUTTON COLDFIELD. (1986; 250). Martin Fisher.
0121 308 4400; e-mail: martinjfisher@care4free.net
Meetings: 7.30pm, 1st Monday of the month,
Bishop Vesey's Grammer School.

WALSALL. (1970). Mike Pittawa y, 2 Kedleston
Close, Bloxwich, Walsall, WS3 3TW. 01922 710568;
e-mail: chair@rspb-walsall.org.uk
www.rspb-walsall.org.uk
Meetings: 7.30pm, 3rd Wednesday of the month,
St Marys School, Jesson Road, Walsall.

WOLVERHAMPTON. (1974; 110). Barry Proffitt.
07900 431 820;
e-mail: RSPBwolverhampton@hotmail.co.uk
www.rspb.org.uk/groups/wolverhampton
Meetings: 7.30pm, 2nd Wednesday of the month
(Sept-Apr), The Newman Centre, Haywood Drive,
Tettenhall, Wolverhampton.

Wildlife Trust
THE WILDLIFE TRUST FOR BIRMINGHAM AND
BLACK COUNTRY. (1980; 2,000). 28 Harborne Road,
Edgbaston, Birmingham, B15 3AA. 0121 454 1199;
fax 0121 454 6556; e-mail: info@bbcwildlife.org.uk
www.bbcwildlife.org.uk

WILTSHIRE

Bird Atlas/Avifauna
Birds of Wiltshire by James Ferguson-Lees 2007,
Wiltshire Ornithological Society

Bird Recorder
Rob Turner, 14 Ethendun, Bratton, Westbury, Wilts,
BA13 4RX. 01380 830862;
e-mail: robt14@btopenworld.com

Bird Report
*Published in Hobby (journal of the Wiltshire OS)
(1975-),* from John Osborne, 4 Fairdown Avenue,
Westbury, Wiltshire BA13 3HS. 01373 864 598

BTO Regional Representatives
NORTH. Bill Quantrill. 01225 866 245;
e-mail: william.quantrill@btinternet.com

SOUTH. Bill Quantrill. 01225 866 245;
e-mail: william.quantrill@btinternet.com

Clubs
SALISBURY & DISTRICT NATURAL HISTORY
SOCIETY. (1952; 151). J Pitman, 10 The Hardings,
Devizes Road, Salisbury, SP2 9LZ. 01722 327395.
Meetings: 7.30pm, 3rd Thursday of the month
(Sept-Apr), Lecture Hall, Salisbury Museum, King
House, The Close, Salisbury.

WILTSHIRE ORNITHOLOGICAL
SOCIETY. (1974; 450). Phil
Deacon, 12 Rawston Close,
Nythe, Swindon, Wilts SN3
3PW. 01793 528 930;
e-mail:
phil.deacon@ntlworld.com
www.wiltshirebirds.co.uk
Meetings: See website for details.

Ringing Group
COTSWOLD WATER PARK RG. John Wells, 25 Pipers
Grove, Highnam, Glos, GL2 8NJ.
e-mail: john.wells2@btinternet.com

WEST WILTSHIRE RG. Mr M.J. Hamzij, 13 Halfway
Close, Trowbridge, Wilts BA14 7HQ.
e-mail: m.hamzij@btinternet.com

RSPB Local Groups
NORTH WILTSHIRE. (1973; 115). Derek Lyford, 9
Devon Road, Swindon, SN2 1PQ. 01793 520 997;
e-mail: derek.lyford@virgin.net
www.rspb.org.uk/groups/northwiltshire

Meetings: 7.30pm, 1st Tuesday of the month (Sep-Jun), Even Swindon Community Centre, Jennings St, Swindon SU 137 849.

SOUTH WILTSHIRE. (1986; 820). Tony Goddard, Clovelly, Lower Road, Charlton All Saints, Salisbury, SP5 4HQ. 01725 510 309.
Meetings: 7.30pm, Tuesday evenings (monthly), Salisbury Arts Centre, Salisbury.

Wetland Bird Survey Organiser
COTSWOLD WATER PARK. Gareth Harris, Keynes Country Park, Spratsgate Lane, Shorncote, Glos GL7 6DF. e-mail: gareth.harris@waterpark.org

Wildlife Trust
WILTSHIRE WILDLIFE TRUST. (1962; 18,000). Elm Tree Court, Long Street, Devizes, Wilts, SN10 1NJ. 01380 725 670; fax 01380 729 017;
e-mail: info@wiltshirewildlife.org
www.wiltshirewildlife.org

WORCESTERSHIRE

Bird Recorder
Brian Stretch, 13 Pitmaston Road, Worcester WR2 4HY. 01905 423 417;
e-mail: worcs-recorder@westmidlandbirdclub.com
www.westmidlandbirdclub.com

Bird Report See West Midlands.

BTO Regional Representative
G Harry Green MBE, Windy Ridge, Pershore Road, Little Comberton, Pershore, Worcs, WR10 3EW. 01386 710 377;
e-mail: harrygreen_worcs@yahoo.co.uk

VALE WILDLIFE RESCUE - WILDLIFE HOSPITAL + REHABILITATION CENTRE. Any staff member, Station Road, Beckford, Tewkesbury, Glos GL20 7AN. 01386 882 288; (Fax)01386 882 299;
e-mail: info@vwr.org.uk
website: www.vwr.org.uk
All wild birds. Intensive care. Registered charity. Veterinary support.

Ringing Group
WYCHAVON RG. J R Hodson, 15 High Green, Severn Stoke, Worcester, WR8 9JS. 01905 754 919(day), 01905 371 333(eve);
e-mail: hodson77@btinternet.com

Club
WEST MIDLAND BIRD CLUB (KIDDERMINSTER BRANCH). Celia Barton, 28A Albert Street, Wall Heath, Kingswinford, DY6 0NA. 01384 839 838;
e-mail: kidderminster@westmidlandbirdclub.com
Meetings: 7.30pm, 4th Wednesday of the month (Sep-Apr), St Oswalds Church Centre, Broadwaters, Kidderminster.

RSPB Local Group
WORCESTER & MALVERN. (1980; 300). Garth Lowe, Sunnymead, Old Storridge, Alfrick, Worcester WR6 5HT. 01886 833 362.
Meetings: 7.30pm, 2nd Wednesday in month (Sept-May), Powick Village Hall.

Wildlife Trust
WORCESTERSHIRE WILDLIFE TRUST. (1968; 9,000). Lower Smite Farm, Smite Hill, Hindlip, Worcester, WR3 8SZ. 01905 754 919; fax 01905 755 868;
e-mail: enquiries@worcestershirewildlifetrust.co.uk
www.worcswildlifetrust.co.uk

YORKSHIRE

Bird Atlas/Avifauna
*An Atlas of the Breeding Birds of the Huddersfield Area, 1987-1992.*by Brian Armitage et al (2000) - very few copies left.

Atlas of Breeding Birds in the Leeds Area 1987-1991 by Richard Fuller et al (Leeds Birdwatchers' Club, 1994).

Birds of Barnsley by Nick Addey (Pub by author, 114 Everill Gate Lane, Broomhill, Barnsley S73 0YJ, 1998).

Birds of The Lower Derwent Valley by CS Ralston. English Nature (E and N Yorks) 2005.

The Birds of Halifax by Nick Dawtrey (only 20 left), 14 Moorend Gardens, Pellon, Halifax, W Yorks, HX2 0SD.

The Birds of Wintersett by S Denny. Wintersett Wildlife Group 2003, available from the author.

The Birds of Yorkshire by John Mather (Croom Helm, 1986).

Vice County Bird Recorders
VC61 (East Yorkshire) and Editor of *Yorkshire Bird Report*. Geoff Dobbs, 1 Priory Road, Beverley, East Yorkshire HU17 0EG. 07778 559 763;
e-mail: geoffdobbs@aol.com

VC62 (North Yorkshire East). Alistair Forsyth.
e-mail: birdsvc62@gmail.com

VC63 (South & West Yorkshire). Covering the following groups - Barnsley Bird Study, Blacktoft Sands RSPB, Doncaster and District OS, Rotherham and District OS, Sheffield Bird Study and SK58 Birders. John Wint, 9 Yew Tree Park, Whitley, Goole, DN14 0NZ. 01977 662 826;
e-mail: john.wint@tiscali.co.uk

VC64 (West Yorkshire)/HARROGATE & CRAVEN. Phil Bone, 11 Dorrington Close, Pocklington, York, YO42 2GS. 01904 655 770; e-mail: p.bone@csl.gov.uk

VC65 (North Yorkshire West). Steve Worwood, 18 Coltsgate Hill, Ripon, HG4 2AB. 01765 602 518; e-mail: steve@worwood.entadsl.com

Bird Reports

BARNSLEY & DISTRICT BIRD STUDY GROUP REPORT (1971-), from Secretary.

BRADFORD NATURALISTS' SOCIETY ANNUAL REPORT, from Mr I Hogg, 23 St Matthews Road, Bankfoot, Bradford, BD5 9AB. 01274 727902.

BRADFORD ORNITHOLOGICAL GROUP REPORT (1987-), from Jenny Barker, 3 Chapel Fold, Slack Lane, Oakworth, Keighley, BD22 0RQ.

DONCASTER BIRD REPORT (1955-), from Mr M Roberts, 8 Sandbeck court, Rossington, Doncaster, DN11 0FN. 01302 326 265.

FILEY BRIGG BIRD REPORT (1976-), from Mr C Court, 12 Pinewood Avenue, Filey, YO14 9NS.

FIVE TOWNS BIRD REPORT (1995-), from Secretary, Five Towns Bird Group.

HARROGATE & DISTRICT NATURALISTS' ORNITHOLOGY REPORT (1996-), from Secretary.

HULL VALLEY WILDLIFE GROUP REPORT (2000-) covering Hull Valley. from Roy Lyon, 670 Hotham Road South, Hull, HU5 5LE. 07754 439 496.

BIRDS IN HUDDERSFIELD (1966-), from Mr Brian Armitage, 106 Forest Road, Dalton, Huddersfield HD5 8ET.01484 305054; e-mail: brian.armitage@ntlworld.com

LEEDS BIRDWATCHERS' CLUB ANNUAL REPORT (1949-), from Peter Murphy, 12 West End Lane, Horsforth, Leeds LS18 5JP.

BIRDS OF ROTHERHAM (1975-), from Secretary, Rotherham Orn Soc, www.rotherhambirds.co.uk (check website for current publication details).

BIRDS IN THE SHEFFIELD AREA (1973-), from Margaret Miller, e-mail: margmiller@talktalk.net www.sbsg.org

THE BIRDS OF SK58 (1993-), from Secretary, SK58 Birders. e-mail: recorder@skbirders.com www.sk58birders.com

SPURN BIRD OBSERVATORY ANNUAL REPORT, from Warden, see Reserves.

WINTERSETT AREA ANNUAL REPORT (1988-), from Steve Denny, 13 Rutland Drive, Crofton, Wakefield, WF4 1SA.01924 864487.

YORK ORNITHOLOGICAL CLUB ANNUAL REPORT (1970-), from Peter Watson, 1 Oak Villa, Hodgson Lane, Upper Poppleton, York YO26 6EA. 01904 795063; e-mail: peterewwatson@aol.com.

YORKSHIRE NATURALISTS' UNION: BIRD REPORT (1940-). £10 including postage, from Craig Thomas, 16 Scarborough Road, Filey, North Yorkshire YO14 9EF. 01723 513 055; e-mail: craigthomas@yahoo.co.uk

BTO Regional Representatives & Regional Development Officers

NORTH-EAST RR. Michael Carroll. 01751 476 550.

NORTH-WEST RR. Gerald Light. 01756 753 720; e-mail: gerald@uwlig.plus.com

SOUTH-EAST AND SOUTH-WEST RR. David Gains. E-mail: bto-rep@fireflyuk.net

EAST RR. Position vacant.

BRADFORD RR & RDO. Mike L Denton, 77 Hawthorne Terrace, Crosland Moor, Huddersfield, HD4 5RP. 01484 646 990; e-mail: Dentonatheta@aol.com

LEEDS & WAKEFIELD RR. Position vacant.

RICHMOND RR. John Edwards, 7 Church Garth, Great Smeaton, Northallerton, N Yorks DL6 2HW. H:01609 881 476; e-mail: john@jhedwards.plus.com

YORK RR. Rob Chapman, 12 Moorland Road, York, YO10 4HF. 01904 633 558; e-mail: robert.chapman@tinyworld.co.uk

YORKSHIRE (HARROGATE) RR. Mike Brown, 48 Pannal Ash Drive, Harrogate, N Yorks, HG2 0HU. 01423 567 382; e-mail: mike@thebrownsathome.plus.com

Clubs

BARNSLEY BIRD STUDY GROUP. (1970; 35). Graham Speight, 58 Locke Avenue, Barnsley, South Yorkshire S70 1QH. 01226 321 300. **Meetings:** 7.15pm, 1st Thursday in the month (Nov-Mar), RSPB Old Moor, Barnsley.

BRADFORD ORNITHOLOGICAL GROUP. (1987; 180). Shaun Radcliffe, 8 Longwood Avenue, Bingley, W Yorks, BD16 2RX. 01274 770 960; www.bradfordbirding.org **Meetings:** 1st Tuesday of the month - see website for details.

CASTLEFORD & DISTRICT NATURALISTS' SOCIETY. (1956; 15). Michael J Warrington, 31 Mount Avenue, Hemsworth, Pontefract, W Yorks WF9 4QE. 01977 614 954; e-mail: michaelwarrington@talktalk.net **Meetings:** 7.30pm, Tuesdays monthly (Sep-Mar), Whitwood College, Castleford (check with above for dates).

ENGLAND

DONCASTER & DISTRICT ORNITHOLOGICAL SOCIETY. (1955; 30). Dave Ward, Membership Secretary, 11 Newstead Road, Scawthorpe, Doncaster DN5 9JS.
www.birdingdoncaster.org.uk
Meetings: 7.15pm, last Thursday of the month (Jan-May and Sep-Nov), Parklands Sports and social club, Wheatley Hall Road.

FILEY BRIGG ORNITHOLOGICAL GROUP. (1977; 100). Sue Hull. 01723 515 042;
e-mail:secretary-at-fbog.co.uk
www.fbog.co.uk

HARROGATE & DISTRICT NATURALISTS' SOCIETY. (1947; 350). Mrs Pat Cook, General Secretary, 1 Millbank Terrace, Shaw Mills, Harrogate. 01423 772 953; e-mail: gensec.hdns@talktalk.net www.knaresborough.co.uk/hdns/index.html
Meetings: 7.45pm, St. Roberts Centre, 2/3 Robert Street, Harrogate. The programme of meetings is sent out to members in September.

HORNSEA BIRD CLUB. (1967; 42). John Eldret, 44 Rolston Road, Hornsea, HU18 1UH. 01964 532 854.
Meetings: 7.30pm, 3rd Friday of the month (Sep-Mar), Hornsea Library.

HUDDERSFIELD BIRDWATCHERS' CLUB. (1966; 80). Chris Abell, 57 Butterley Lane, New Mill, Holmfirth, HD9 7EZ. 01484 681 499;
e-mail: cdabell@gmail.com
www.huddersfieldbirdwatchersclub.org.uk
Meetings: 7.30pm, Tuesday's fortnightly (Sep-May), Children's Library (section), Huddersfield Library and Art Gallery, Princess Alexandra Walk, Huddersfield.

HULL VALLEY WILDLIFE GROUP. (1997; 175). The Secretary, 29 Beech View, Cranswick, East Yorkshire YO25 9QQ. 01377 270 957.
www.hullvalleywildlifegroup.org.uk

LEEDS BIRDWATCHERS' CLUB. (1949; 60). Peter Murphy, 12 West End lane, Horsforth, Leeds, LS18 5JP. 0113 293 0188;
e-mail: pandbmurphy@ntlworld.com
Meetings: 7.15pm Monday fortnightly, Quaker Meeting House, Woodhouse Lane, Leeds.

PUDSEY ORNITHOLOGY CLUB. (1989; 26). Alan Patchett, 102 Half Mile Lane, Leeds, LS13 1DB. 0113 229 9038.
Meetings: Contact for details.

ROTHERHAM & DISTRICT ORNITHOLOGICAL SOCIETY. (1974; 80). Malcolm Taylor, 18 Maple Place, Chapeltown, Sheffield, S30 4QW. 0114 246 1848; e-mail: rdos@hotmail.co.uk
www.rotherhambirds.co.uk
Meetings: 7.30pm, 2nd Friday of the month, United Reform church hall, Herringthorpe.

SCARBOROUGH BIRDERS. (1993; 20). R.N.Hopper (Membership Secretary), 10A Ramshill Road, Scarborough, N Yorkshire YO11 2QE. 01723 369 537. www.scarborough-birding.org.uk

SHEFFIELD BIRD STUDY GROUP. (1972; 160). Richard Dale, 109 Main Road, Wharncliffe Side, Sheffield, S35 0DP. 0114 286 2513;
e-mail: richarddale9@hotmail.com
www.sbsg.org
Meetings: 7.15pm, 2nd Wednesday of the month (Sep-Jun), Lecture Theatre 5, Sheffield University Arts Tower.

SK58 BIRDERS. (1993; 66). Andy Hirst, 15 Hunters Drive, Dinnington, Sheffield, S25 2TG. 07947 068 125; e-mail: contact@skbirders.com www.sk58birders.com Chair: Mick Clay, 2 High St, S.Anston, Sheffield. 01909 566 000.
Meetings: 7.30pm, last Wednesday of the month (except July and Aug), Upstairs Room, Loyal Trooper pub, South Anston.

SK58 BIRDERS

SORBY NHS (ORNITHOLOGICAL SECTION). (1918; 400). The Secretary, C/O 159 Bell Hagg Road, Sheffield, S6 5DA, e-mail: secretary@sorby.org.uk www.sorby.org.uk

SWILLINGTON INGS BIRD GROUP. (1989; 83). Chris Robinson, 20 Luke Williams House, Horsefair, Pontefract, WF8 1PP. 01977 798 040 or 07534 271 254; e-mail: GBFShrike@hotmail.com
Blog: http://se3828.wordpress.com
Meetings: 7.30pm, 1st Thursday of even months with informal social evenings 1st Thursday of odd months (please phone for details of venue).

WAKEFIELD NATURALISTS' SOCIETY. (1851; 35). Michael Warrington, 31 Mount Avenue, Hemsworth, Pontefract, W Yorks WF9 4QE. 01977 614 954; michaelwarrington@talktalk.net
Meetings: 7.30pm, 2nd Tuesday of the month (Sep-Apr), Friends Meeting House, Thornhill Street, Wakefield.

YORK ORNITHOLOGICAL CLUB. (1967; 80). Linda Newton, 5 Fairfields Drive, Skelton, York YO30 1YP, 01904 471 446;
e-mail: secretary@yorkbirding.org.uk
www.yorkbirding.org.uk
Meetings: 7.30pm, 1st Tuesday of the month, Friends' Meeting House, Friargate, York (see website).

YORKSHIRE NATURALISTS' UNION (Ornithological Section). (1875; 500). Jim Pewtress, 31 Piercy End,

Kirbymoorside, York, YO62 6DQ. 01751 431 001;
e-mail: trivialis@operamail.com

Ringing Groups

BARNSLEY RG. M C Wells, 715 Manchester Road,
Stocksbridge, Sheffield, S36 1DQ. 0114 288 4211;
e-mail: barnsleybsg-plus.com

DONCASTER RG. D Hazard, 41 Jossey Lane,
Scawthorpe, Doncaster, S Yorks DN5 9DB. 01302
788 044; e-mail: dave.hazard@tiscali.co.uk

EAST DALES RG. Mr P. Bone, 11 Dorrington Close,
Pocklington, York, YO42 2GS.
E-mail: p.bone@csl.gov.uk

EAST YORKS RG. Peter J Dunn, 43 West Garth
Gardens, Cayton, Scarborough, N Yorks YO11 3SF.
01723 583149; e-mail: pjd@fbog.co.uk

SORBY-BRECK RG. Geoff P Mawson, Moonpenny
Farm, Farwater Lane, Dronfield, Sheffield S18 1RA.
e-mail: moonpenny@talktalk.net

SPURN BIRD OBSERVATORY. Paul Collins, Kew Villa,
Seaside Road, Kilnsea, Hull HU12 0UB. 01964 650
479; e-mail: pcnfa@hotmail.com

WINTERSETT RG. P Smith, 16 Templar Street,
Wakefield, W Yorks, WF1 5HB. 01924 375 082.

RSPB Local Groups

AIREDALE AND BRADFORD. (1972; 3500 in
catchment area). Ruth Porter . 01524 703 019;
e-mail: Carol.bamber@RSPB.org.uk
www.rspb.org.uk/groups/airedaleandbradford
Meetings: 7.30pm, monthly on Fridays, Room 3,
Shipley Library.

CRAVEN & PENDLE. (1986; 300). Colin Straker.
01756 751 888;
e-mail: colin.straker@btinternet.com
www.cravenandpendlerspb.org
Meetings: 7.30pm 2nd Wednesday of the month
(Sep-May), St Andrews Church Hall, Newmarket
Street, Skipton.

DONCASTER. (1984; 100). Sue Clifton, West Lodge,
Wadworth Hall Lane, Wadworth, Doncaster, DN11
9BH. Tel/fax 01302 854 956;
e-mail: sue.cl.@waitrose.com
www.rspb.org.uk/groups/doncaster
Meetings: 7.30pm 2nd Wednesday of the month
(Sept-May), Salvation Army Community Church,
Lakeside.

EAST YORKSHIRE. (1986;110). Trevor Malkin, 49
Taylors Field, Driffield, E Yorks, YO25 6FQ. 01377
257 325; e-mail: EastyorksRSPB@yahoo.co.uk
www.rspb.org.uk/groups/eastyorkshire
Meetings: 7.30pm, North Bridlington Library,
Martongate, BRIDLINGTON (check website for
details).

HUDDERSFIELD & HALIFAX. (1981; 140). David
Hemingway, 267 Long Lane, Dalton, Huddersfield,
HD5 9SH. 01484 301 920;
e-mail: d.hemingway@ntlworld.com
www.rspb.org.uk/groups/huddersfieldandhalifax

HULL & DISTRICT. (1983; 334). Betty Hilton. 01482
849 503; e-mail: betty_hilton@hotmail.com
Meetings: 7.30pm, Tuesdays (Sept-May), United
Reformed Church, Southella Way, Kirkella, HULL.
(£1.50 for Local Group Members and £2.00 for Non
Members).

LEEDS. (1974; 450). Linda Jenkinson, 112 Eden
Crescent, Burley, Leeds, LS4 2TR. 0113 230 4595;
E-mail: linda.jenkinson@leeds.gov.uk
www.RSPB.org.uk/groups/leeds
Meetings: 7.30pm, 3rd Wednesday of the month
(Sep-Apr), Lecture Theatre B, School of Mechanical
Engineering, University of Leeds.

SHEFFIELD. (1981; 500). Malcolm Dyke, Flat 5, 648
Abbeydale Road, Sheffield, S7 2BB. 07947 605 959;
www.rspb-sheffield.org.uk
Meetings: 7.30pm 1st Thursday of the month
(Sept-May), Central United Reformed Church,
Norfolk St, Sheffield.

WAKEFIELD. (1987; 150). Duncan Stokoe, 12 New
Road, Horbury, Wakefield, West Yorkshire WF4 5LR.
e-mail: duncanstokoe@talktalk.net
www.rspb.org.uk/groups/wakefield
Meetings: 7.30pm, 4th Thursday of the month
(Sep-Apr), Ossett War Memorial Community Centre,
Prospect Road, Ossett, WF5 8AN.

WHITBY. (1977; 120). John Woolley, 2 Upgang
Lane, Whitby, N Yorks YO21 3EA. 01947 604505.
Meetings: 7.15pm, 2nd Wednesday of the month,
St John Ambulance Hall, back St Hilda's Terrace,
Whitby.

YORK. (1973; 600). Chris Lloyd, 7 School Lane,
Upper Poppleton, York, YO26 6JS. 01904 794865;
e-mail: chris.a.lloyd@care4free.net
www.yorkrspb.org.uk
Meetings: 7.30pm, Tues, Wed or Thurs, Temple
Hall, York St John College, Lord Mayors Walk, York.

Wildlife Hospital

ANIMAL HOUSE WILDLIFE WELFARE. Mrs C
Buckroyd, 14 Victoria Street, Scarborough, YO12
7SS. 01723 371 256 (please leave a message on
the answer machine and callers will be contacted as
soon as possible); e-mail: cynthiabuckroyd@talktalk.
net or cindybuckroyd@hotmail.com.
All species of wild birds. Oiled birds given treatment
before forwarding to cleaning stations. Incubators,
hospital cages, heat pads, release sites. Birds ringed
before release. Prior telephone call requested.
Collection if required. Veterinary support. Charity
shop at 127 Victoria Road.

Wildlife Trusts

SHEFFIELD WILDLIFE TRUST. (1985; 4,200). 37 Stafford Road, Sheffield, S2 2SF. 0114 263 4335; fax 0114 263 4345; e-mail: mail@wildsheffield.com www.wildsheffield.com

YORKSHIRE WILDLIFE TRUST. (1946; 21,500). 1 St George's Place,Tadcaster Road,YorkYO24 1GN. 01904 659 570; fax 01904 613 467; e-mail: info@ywt.org.uk www.ywt.org.uk

SCOTLAND

Bird Report
SCOTTISH BIRD REPORT From, The SOC, The Scottish Birdwatching Resource Centre, Waterston House, Aberlady, East Lothian, EH32 0PY.

Club
See Scottish Ornithologists' Club in National Directory.

ANGUS & DUNDEE

Bird Recorder
ANGUS & DUNDEE. John Ogilvie, 23 Church Street, Brechin, Angus, DD9 6HB. 01356 662 672; e-mail: johncogilvie@aol.com

Bird Report
ANGUS & DUNDEE BIRD REPORT (1974-), from The Secretary, Angus & Dundee Bird Club.

BTO Regional Representatives & Regional Development Officer
ANGUS RR & RDO. Ken Slater, Braedownie Farmhouse, Glen Clova, Kirriemuir, Angus, DD8 4RD. 01575 550 233; e-mail: rec_glendoll@angus.sol.co.uk

Clubs
ANGUS & DUNDEE BIRD CLUB. (1997; 211). Bob McCurley, 22 Kinnordy Terrace, Dundee,DD4 7NW. 01382 462 944; e-mail: lunanbay1@btinternet.com www.angusbirding.com
Meetings: 7.30pm, Tuesdays, Montrose Basin Wildlife Centre.

SOC TAYSIDE BRANCH. (145). Brian Boag, Birch Brae, Knapp, Inchture, Perthshire PH14 9RN. 01828 686 669.

Ringing Group
TAY RG. Ms S Millar, Edenvale Cottage, 1 Lydox Cottages, Dairsie, Fife, KY15 4RN. e-mail: shirley@edenecology.co.uk

RSPB Members' Groups
DUNDEE. (1972;110). Graham Smith, 01382 532 461; e-mail: grahamnjen@hotmail.com www.RSPB.org.uk/groups/dundee
Meetings: 7.30 pm, monthly Wednesdays (Sep-Mar), Methodist Church, 20, West Marketgait, DUNDEE. Admission £1.00 for all, including refreshments.

Wetland Bird Survey Organisers
MONTROSE BASIN. Neil Mitchell. 01674 676 336; e-mail: nmitchell@swt.org.uk

ARGYLL

Birds of Argyll (Argyll Bird Club 2007, £45 inc postage), available from Bob Furness, The Cnoc, Tarbert, Arrochar, Dunbartonshire G83 7DG. 01301 702 603.

Bird Recorder
ARGYLL. Paul Daw, Tigh-na-Tulloch, Tullochgorm, Minard, Argyll, PA32 8YQ. 01546 886 260; e-mail: monedula@globalnet.co.uk

Bird Reports
ARGYLL BIRD REPORT (1984-), From Dr Bob Furness, The Cnoc, Tarbert, Dunbartonshire G83 7DG. 01301 702 603; e-mail: r.furness@bio.gla.ac.uk

ISLE OF MULL BIRD REPORT (2004-), From Mr Alan Spellman, Maridon, Lochdon, Isle of Mull, Argyll. PA73 7AP.

MACHRIHANISH SEABIRD OBSERVATORY REPORT (1992-), from the Observatory, see Reserves & Observatories.

BTO Regional Representatives
ARGYLL (MULL, COLL, TIREE AND MORVERN). Sue Dewar, 01680 812 594; e-mail: sue.dewar@btconnect.com

ARGYLL SOUTH, BUTE, GIGHA AND ARRAN. Richard Allen, e-mail: richardallan@compuserve.com

ISLAY, JURA, COLONSAY RR. John S Armitage, Airigh Sgallaidh, Portnahaven, Isle of Islay, PA47 7SZ. 01496 860 396; e-mail: jsa@ornquest.plus.com www.islaybirder.blogspot.com

Club
ARGYLL BIRD CLUB. (1983;270). Sue Furness, The Cnoc, Tarbet, Argyll, G83 7DG.01301 702 603; e-mail: r.furness@bio.gla.ac.uk www.argyllbirdclub.org

ISLE OF MULL BIRD CLUB. (2001;150), Mrs Janet T Hall, Membership Secretary, Druim Mhor, Craignure, Isle of Mull, Argyll PA65 6AY.01680 812 441; e-mail: oystercatcher@dee-emm.co.uk www.mullbirdclub.org.uk
Meetings: 7 for 7.30pm start, 3rd Friday of the month (Oct-Apr), Craignure Village Hall.

Ringing Group
TRESHNISH AUK RG. Robin Ward, e-mail: robin. ward807@ntlworld.com

RSPB Members' Group
HELENSBURGH. (1975; 62). Steve Chadwin, 01436 670 158.
Meetings: The Guide Halls, The Guide Halls, Lower John Street, HELENSBURGH.

Wildlife Hospital
WINGS OVER MULL. Richard and Sue Dewar, Auchnacroish House, Torosay, Craignure, Isle of Mull PA65 6AY. Tel/fax: 01680 812 594; email: dewars@wingsovermull.com www.wingsovermull.com

AYRSHIRE

Bird Recorder
AYRSHIRE. Fraser Simpson, 4 Inchmurrin Drive, Kilmarnock, Ayrshire KA3 2JD. e-mail: recorder@ayrshire-birding.org.uk

Bird Reports
AYRSHIRE BIRD REPORT (1976-), From The Recorder or Dr RG Vernon, 29 Knoll Park, Ayr KA7 4RH.

BTO Regional Representatives
AYRSHIRE RR. Brian Broadley, 01290 424 241; e-mail: brianbroadley@onegreendoor.com

Club
SOC AYRSHIRE. (1962; 154). Duncan Watt, Wildings Studio, 28 Greenbank, Dalry, Ayrshire, KA24 5AY. 01294 832 361; www.ayrshire-birding.org.uk
Meetings: 7.30pm, Tuesdays monthly, Monkton Community Church, Monkton by Prestwick.

RSPB Members' Groups
CENTRAL AYRSHIRE LOCAL GROUP. (1978; 85). Tony Scott (Group Leader), 4 Hilltop Place, Ayr,KA7 3PB. 01292 281 045; e-mail: da.scott@tiscali.co.uk
Meetings: 7.40pm, 3rd Monday of the month (Sep-Apr), Carnegie Library, Main Street, Ayr.

NORTH AYRSHIRE. (1976; 180). Duncan Watt, 28 Greenbank, Dalry, Ayrshire, KA24 5AY.01294 832 361; e-mail: duncan@spectrus.co.uk www.narspb.org.uk
Meetings: 7.30pm, various Fridays (Aug-Apr), Ardrossan Civic Centre, open to all. Full list available.

Wetland Bird Survey Organiser
AYRSHIRE. Mr David Grant, e-mail: d.grant@au.sac.as.uk

Wildlife Hospital
HESSILHEAD WILDLIFE RESCUE CENTRE. Gay & Andy Christie, Gateside, Beith, Ayrshire, KA15 1HT. 01505 502 415; e-mail: info@hessilhead.org.uk www.hessilhead.org.uk
All species. Releasing aviaries. Veterinary support. Visits only on open days please.

BORDERS

Bird Atlas/Avifauna
The Breeding Birds of South-east Scotland, a tetrad atlas 1988-1994 by R D Murray et al. (Scottish Ornithologists' Club, 1998).

Bird Recorder
Ray Murray, 4 Bellfield Crescent, Eddleston, Peebles, EH45 8RQ. 01721 730677; e-mail: ray.d.murray@ukgateway.net

Bird Report
BORDERS BIRD REPORT (1979-), From Malcolm Ross, Westfield Cottage, Smailholm, Kelso TD5 7PN.01573 460 699; e-mail: eliseandmalcolm@btinternet.com

BTO Regional Representative
RR. Graham Pyatt. 01721 740 319; e-mail: d.g.pyatt@btinternet.com

Club
SOC BORDERS BRANCH. (100). Graham Pyatt, The Schoolhouse, Manor, Peebles EH45 9JN. 01721 740 319.
Meetings: 7.30pm, 2nd Monday of the month, George & Abbotsford Hotel, Melrose.

Ringing Group
BORDERS RG. (1991; 10). Dr T W Dougall, 38 Leamington Terrace, Edinburgh, EH10 4JL. (Office) 0131 344 2600.

RSPB Members' Group
BORDERS. (1995; 94). John Marshall, 01896 850 564; e-mail: n-jmarshall@tiscali.co.uk
Meetings: 7.30pm, 3rd Wednesday of the month, The Corn Exchange, Market Square, MELROSE.

SCOTLAND

CAITHNESS

Bird Recorders
CAITHNESS. Stan Laybourne, Old Schoolhouse, Harpsdale, Halkirk, Caithness, KW12 6UN. 01847 841244; e-mail:stanlaybourne@talk21.com

Bird Reports
CAITHNESS BIRD REPORT (1983-97). Now incorporated into *The Highland Bird Report*, from Julian Smith, St John's, Brough, Dunnet, Caithness; KW14 8YD; e-mail: designsmith@madasafish.com

BTO Regional Representative
CAITHNESS. D Omand, 9 Skiall, Shebster, Thurso, Caithness KW14 7YD. 01847 811 403; e-mail: achreamie@yahoo.co.uk

Clubs
SOC CAITHNESS BRANCH. (51). Stan Laybourne, Old Schoolhouse, Harpsdale, Halkirk, Caithness, KW12 6UN. 01847 841 244; e-mail:stanlaybourne@talk21.com

CLYDE

Bird Atlas/Avifauna
*A Guide to Birdwatching in the Clyde Area (2001)*by Cliff Baister and Marin Osler (Scottish Ornithologists' Club, Clyde branch).

Clyde Breeding Bird Atlas (working title). In preparation.

Bird Recorder
CLYDE ISLANDS. Bernard Zonfrillo, 28 Brodie Road, Glasgow,G21 3SB. e-mail:b.zonfrillo@bio.gla.ac.uk

CLYDE. Iain P Gibson, 8 Kenmure View, Howwood, Johnstone, Renfrewshire, PA9 1DR. 01505 705 874; e-mail: iain.gibson@land.glasgow.gov.uk

Bird Reports
CLYDE BIRDS (1973-), From Jim & Valerie Wilson, 76 Laigh Road, Newton Mearns, Glasgow, G77 5EQ. e-mail: jim.val@btinternet.com

BTO Regional Representatives
LANARK, RENFREW, DUMBARTON. John Knowler, 0141 584 9117; e-mail: john.knowler@ntlworld.ocm

Club
SOC CLYDE BRANCH. (300). Sandra Hutchinson, 52 Station Road, Bearsden, Glasgow, G61 4AL.0141 943 1816; e-mail: hutchinson_80hotmail.com

Ringing Groups
CLYDE RG. (1979; 18)I Livingstone, 57 Strathview Road, Bellshill, Lanarkshire, ML4 2UY.01698 749 844; e-mail: iainlivcrg@googlemail.com

RSPB Members' Groups
GLASGOW. (1972;141). Roger Adams. 0141 942 6920; e-mail: rogerlpadams7@aol.com
www.rspb.org.uk/groups/glasgow
Meetings: 7.30pm, generally 1st Wednesday of the month (Sep-Apr), Woodside Halls or Fotheringay Centre.

HAMILTON. (1976;90). Jim Lynch, 0141 583 1044; e-mail: birder45a@yahoo.co.uk
www.baronshaugh.co.uk
Meetings: 7.30pm, 3rd Thursday of the month (Sept-May), Watersports Centre, Motherwell (next to Strathclyde Loch).

RENFREWSHIRE. (1986; 200). George Bissett. 01236 732 796;
e-mail: georgenmoira@googlemail.com
Meetings: 1st Friday of the month (Sep-Apr), The McMaster Centre, 2a Donaldson Drive, RENFREW

Wetland Bird Survey Organisers
CLYDE ESTUARY. Jim & Valerie Wilson, 76 Laigh Road, Newton Mearns, Glasgow G77 5EQ. (H)0141 639 2516; e-mail: Jim.Val@btinternet.com

GLASGOW/RENFREWSHIRE/LANARKSHIRE/DUNBARTONSHIRE. Jim & Valerie Wilson, 76 Laigh Road, Newton Mearns, Glasgow G77 5EQ. (H)0141 639 2516; e-mail: Jim.Val@btinternet.com

DUMFRIES & GALLOWAY

Bird Recorders
Paul Collin, Gairland, Old Edinburgh Road, Minnigaff, Newton Stewart, DG8 6PL. 01671 402 861; e-mail: pncollin@live.co.uk

Bird Report
DUMFRIES & GALLOWAY REGION BIRD REPORT (1985-), from Duncan Irving, 12 Great Eastern Drive, Glancaple, Dumfries, DG1 4QZ. e-mail: duncanirving@btinternet.com

BTO Regional Representatives
DUMFRIES RR. Edmund Fellowes, 01387 262 094; e-mail: edmundfellowes@aol.com

KIRKCUDBRIGHT RR and Atlas Co-ordinator. Andrew Bielinski, 41 Main Street, St Johns Town of Dalry, Castle Douglas, Kirkcudbright, DG7 3UP. 01644 430 418 (evening); e-mail: andrewb@bielinski.fsnet.co.uk

WIGTOWN RR. Geoff Sheppard, The Roddens, Leswalt, Stranraer, Wigtownshire, DG9 0QR. 01776 870 685;
e-mail: geoff.sheppard@tesco.net

Clubs
SOC DUMFRIES BRANCH. (1961; 105). Mrs Pat Abery, East Daylesford, Colvend, Dalbeattie,

Dumfries, DG5 4QA. 01556 630 483.
Meetings: 7.30pm, 2nd Wednesday of the month (Sept-Apr), Cumberland St Day Centre.

SOC STEWARTRY BRANCH. (1976; 80). Miss Joan Howie, 60 Main Street, St Johns Town of Dalry, Castle Douglas, Kirkcudbrightshire, DG7 3UW. 01644 430226
Meetings: 7.30pm, usually 2nd Thursday of the month (Sep-Apr), Kells School, New Galloway.

SOC WEST GALLOWAY BRANCH. (1975; 50). Geoff Sheppard, The Roddens, Leswalt, Stranraer, Wigtownshire, DG9 0QR. 01776 870 685; e-mail: geoff.sheppard@tesco.net
Meetings: 7.30pm, 2nd Tuesday of the month (Oct-Mar), Stranraer Library.

Ringing Group
NORTH SOLWAY RG. Geoff Sheppard, The Roddens, Leswalt, Stranraer, Wigtownshire, DG9 0QR. 01776 870 685; e-mail: geoff.sheppard@tesco.net

RSPB Members' Group
GALLOWAY. (1985;150). Cynthia Douglas, Midpark, Balmaclellan, Castle Douglas, DG7 3PX. 01644 420 605; www.gallowayrspb-localgroup.org.uk
Meetings: 7.30pm 3rd Tuesday in the month, Castle Douglas High School.

Wetland Bird Survey Organisers
AUCHENCAIRN. Euan MacAlpine, Auchenshore, Auchencairn, Castle Douglas, Galloway DG7 1QZ . 01556 640 244;
e-mail: js.eamm@sky.com

FLEET BAY. David Hawker. 01556 610 086;
e-mail: dheco@dsl.pipex.com

LOCH RYAN. Geoff Shepherd, The Roddens, Leswalt, Stranraer, Wigtonshire DG9 0QR. 01776 870 685; e-mail: geoff.sheppard@tesco.net

ROUGH FIRTH. Judy Baxter, Saltflats Cottage, Rockcliffe, Dalbeattie, DG5 4QQ. 01556 630 262; e-mail: Jbaxter@nts.org.uk

WIGTOWN. Paul Collin, Gairland, Old Edinburgh Road, Minnigaff, Newton Stewart, DG8 6PL. 01671 402 861; e-mail: pncollin@live.co.uk

FIFE

Bird Atlas/Avifauna
The Fife Bird Atlas 2003 by Norman Elkins, Jim Reid, Allan Brown, Derek Robertson & Anne-Marie Smout. Available from Allan W. Brown (FOAG), 61 Watts Gardens, Cupar, Fife KY15 4UG, Tel. 01334 656804, email: swans@allanwbrown.co.uk

Bird Recorders
FIFE REGION INC OFFSHORE ISLANDS (NORTH FORTH). Rab Shand.
e-mail: rabshand@blueyonder.co.uk

ISLE OF MAY BIRD OBSERVATORY. Iain English, 19 Nethan Gate, Hamilton, S Lanarks, ML3 8NH.
e-mail: i.english@talk21.com

Bird Reports
FIFE BIRD REPORT (1988-) (FIFE & KINROSS BR 1980-87), From Willie McBay, 41 Shamrock Street, Dunfermline, Fife, KY12 0JQ.01383 723464;
e-mail: wmcbay@aol.com

ISLE OF MAY BIRD OBSERVATORY REPORT (1985-), From Jonathan Osborne, The Shieling, Halcombe Crescent, Earlston, Berwickshire TD4 6DA.

BTO Regional Representative
FIFE & KINROSS RR. Norman Elkins, 18 Scotstarvit View, Cupar, Fife, KY15 5DX. 01334 654 348;
e-mail: jandnelkins@btinternet.com

Clubs
FIFE BIRD CLUB. (1985; 250). Willie McBay, 41 Shamrock Street, Dunfermline, Fife, KY12 0JQ. 01383 723 464;
www.fifebirdclub.org
Meetings: 7.30pm, (various evenings), Dean Park Hotel, Chapel Level, Kirkcaldy.

LOTHIANS AND FIFE SWAN & GOOSE STUDY GROUP.
(1978). Allan & Lyndesay Brown, 61 Watts Gardens, Cupar, Fife, KY15 4UG.
e-mail: swans@allanwbrown.co.uk
www.swanscot.org.uk

SOC FIFE BRANCH. (1956;170). Robert Armstrong, Straun House, Old St Andrews Road, Guardbridge, Fife KY16 0UD. 01334 828 279.
Meetings: 7.30pm, 2nd Wednesday of the month (Sep-Apr), St Andrews Town Hall.

Ringing Groups
ISLE OF MAY BIRD OBSERVATORY. David Grieve, 50 Main Street, Symington, Biggar, South Lanarkshire ML12 6LJ. 01899 309 176.

TAY RG. Ms S Millar, Edenvale Cottage, 1 Lydox Cottages, Dairsie, Fife, KY15 4RN.e-mail: shirley@edenecology.co.uk

Wetland Bird Survey Organisers
FIFE (excluding estuaries). Grey Goose count organiser for Fife, Lothians and Borders. Allan Brown, 61 Watts Gardens, Cupar, Fife KY15 4UG;
e-mail: swans@allanwbrown.co.uk

EDEN ESTUARY. Norman Elkins, 18 Scotstarvit View, Cupar, Fife KY15 5DX. 01334 654 348;
e-mail: jandnelkins@btinternet.com

SCOTLAND

TAY ESTUARY. Norman Elkins, 18 Scotstarvit View, Cupar, Fife KY15 5DX. 01334 654 348; e-mail: jandnelkins@btinternet.com

Wildlife Hospital
SCOTTISH SPCA WILD LIFE REHABILITATION CENTRE. Middlebank Farm, Masterton Road, Dunfermline, Fife, KY11 8QN. 01383 412 520
All species. Open to visitors, groups and school parties. Illustrated talk on oiled bird cleaning and other aspects of wildlife rehabilitation available. Veterinary support.

FORTH

Bird Recorder
UPPER FORTH (Does not include parts of Stirling in Loch Lomondside/Clyde Basin). Dr C J Henty, Edgehill East, 7b Coneyhill Road, Bridge of Allan, Stirling, FK9 4EL. 01786 832 166; e-mail: cjh@cliffhenty.plus.com

Bird Report
FORTH AREA BIRD REPORT (1975-) - enlarged report published annually in The Forth Naturalist and Historian, University of Stirling. From Dr Roy Sexton, 22 Alexander Drive, Bridge of Allan, Stirling FK9 4QB. 01786 833 409.

BTO Regional Representative
CENTRAL RR. Neil Bielby, 56 Ochiltree, Dunblane, Perthshire, FK15 0DF. 01786 823 830; e-mail: n.bielby@sky.com

Club
SOC CENTRAL SCOTLAND BRANCH. (1968; 101). Mr RL Gooch, The Red House, Dollarfield, Dollar, Clacks FK14 7LX. 01259 742 326.
Meetings: 7.30pm, 1st Thursday of the month (Sep-Apr), The Smith Art Gallery and Museum, Dumbarton Road, Stirling.

RSPB Members' Group
FORTH VALLEY. (1995; 150). David Redwood, 8 Strathmore Avenue, Dunblane, Perthshire FK15 9HX. 01786 825 493;
e-mail: david.redwood1@btinternet.com
http://forthrspb.p5.org.uk
Meetings: 7.30pm, 3rd Thursday of the month (Sept-Apr), Hill Park Centre, Stirling.

Wetland Bird Survey Organiser
CENTRAL (excl Forth Estuary. Neil Bielby, 56 Ochiltree, Dunblane, Perthshire FK15 0DF. 01786 823 830; e-mail: n.bielby@sky.com

HIGHLAND

Bird Atlas/Avifauna
The Birds of Sutherland by Alan Vittery (Colin Baxter Photography Ltd, 1997).

Birds of Skye by Andrew Currie. In preparation.

Bird Recorders
ROSS-SHIRE, INVERNESS-SHIRE, SUTHERLAND. Alastair McNee, Liathach, 4 Balnafettack Place, Inverness IV3 8TQ. 01463 220493; (M)07763 927814; e-mail: aj.mcnee@care4free.net

Bird Reports
HIGHLAND BIRD REPORT (1991-), From the Recorder. 2004 edition £7.50, 2005 £9.50 including p&p.

SUTHERLAND BIRD REVIEW (2002-) sold out.

BTO Regional Representatives & Regional Development Officer
INVERNESS & SPEYSIDE RR & RDO. Hugh Insley, 1 Drummond Place, Inverness,IV2 4JT. 01463 230 652; e-mail: hugh.insley@btinternet.com

RUM, EIGG, CANNA & MUCK RR & RDO. Bob Swann, 14 St Vincent Road, Tain, Ross-shire, IV19 1JR. 01862 894 329;
e-mail: robert.swann@homecall.co.uk

ROSS-SHIRE RR. Simon Cohen,
E-mail: saraandsimon@hotmail.com

SUTHERLAND. Position vacant.

SKYE. Bob McMillan, 01471 866 305;
e-mail: bob@skye-birds.com

Clubs
EAST SUTHERLAND BIRD GROUP. (1976; 100). Tony Mainwood, 13 Ben Bhraggie Drive, Golspie, Sutherland KW10 6SX. 01408 633 247; e-mail: tony.mainwood@btinternet.com
Meetings: 7.30pm, Last Monday of the month (Oct, Nov, Jan, Feb, Mar), Golspie Community Centre.

SOC HIGHLAND BRANCH. (1955; 151). Ann Sime, Drumrunie House, Myrtlefield Lane, Westhill, Inverness IV2 5UE. 01463 790 249.
Meetings: 7.45pm, 1st Tuesday of the month (Sep-Mar), Culloden Library.

Ringing Groups
HIGHLAND RG. Bob Swann, 14 St Vincent Road, Tain, Ross-shire, IV19 1JR. e-mail: robert. swann@homecall.co.uk

RSPB Members' Group
HIGHLAND. (1987; 214). Richard Prentice, Lingay, Lewiston, Drumnadrochit, Inverness, IV63 6UW. 01456 450 526;
e-mail: richard@rprentice.wanadoo.co.uk
www.rspb.org.uk/groups/highland
Meetings: 7.30pm, last Thursday of the month (Sep-Apr), Kingsmill Hotel, Culcabock Road, Inverness.

SCOTLAND

Wetland Bird Survey Organisers
MORAY & NAIRN (Inland). David Law, Hollybrae, South Darkland, Elgin, Moray IV30 8NT.

SKYE & LOCHALSH. Bob McMillan, 11 Elgol, Nr Broadford, Isle of Skye IV49 9BL. 01471 866 305; e-mail: bob@skye-birds.com

LOTHIAN

Bird Atlas/Avifauna
The Breeding Birds of South-east Scotland, a tetrad atlas 1988-1994 by R D Murray et al. (Scottish Ornithologists' Club, 1998).

Bird Recorder
David J Kelly, 01875 6140 72; e-mail: dj_kelly@btinternet.com

Bird Reports
LOTHIAN BIRD REPORT (1979-), from the Lothian SOC Branch Secretary.

BTO Regional Representative
RR. Alan Heavisides, 9 Addiston Crescent, Balerno, Edinburgh, EH14 7DB. 0131 449 3816; e-mail: a.heavisides@napier.ac.uk

Clubs
EDINBURGH NATURAL HISTORY SOCIETY. (1869; 200). Mrs Joan McNaughton, 14 Relugas Road, Edinburgh EH9 2ND. 0131 477 0270.
www.edinburghnaturalhistorysociety.org.uk

LOTHIANS AND FIFE MUTE SWAN STUDY GROUP. (1978; 12). Allan & Lyndesay Brown, 61 Watts Gardens, Cupar, Fife, KY15 4UG. e-mail: swans@allanwbrown.co.uk

LOTHIAN SOC. (1936; 450). Doreen and James Main, Seatoller, Broadgate, Gullane, East LothianEH31 2DH. 01620 844 532; e-mail: doreen.main@yahoo.com
Meetings: 7.30pm, 2nd Tuesday (Sep-Dec and Jan-Apr), Lounge 2, Meadowbank Sports Stadium.

Ringing Group
LOTHIAN RG. Mr M Cubitt, 12 Burgh Mills Lane, Linlithgow,West Lothian EH49 7TA.

RSPB Members' Group
EDINBURGH. (1974;480). Mark Stephen, 25 Newcroft Drive, Glasgow G44 5RT. 07796 538 837; e-mail: markws_2000@yahoo.co.uk
www.rspb.org.uk/groups/edinburgh/
Meetings: 7.30pm, 3rd Tuesday or Wednesday of the month (Sep-Apr), Napier University, Craiglockhart Campus, Edinburgh.

Wetland Bird Survey Organisers
FORTH ESTUARY (North). Alastair Inglis, 5 Crowhill Road, Dalgety Bay, Fife KY11 5LJ.e-mail: aandjinglis@hotmail.com

FORTH ESTUARY (Outer South). Duncan Priddle, 19c High Street, Haddington, East Lothian EH41 3ES. 01620 827 459; e-mail: dpriddle@eastlothian.gov.uk

LOTHIAN (excl estuaries). Joan Wilcox, 18 Howdenhall Gardens, Edinburgh, Midlothian EH16 6UN. (H)0131 6648 893; e-mail: webs@bto.org

TYNINGHAME ESTUARY. Mr R Anderson, John Muir Country Park, Town House, Dunbar, East Lothian EH42 1ER. (W)01368 863 886; e-mail: randerson@eastlothian.gov.uk

MORAY & NAIRN

Bird Atlas/Avifauna
The Birds of Moray and Nairn by Martin Cook (Mercat Press, 1992.

Bird Recorder
NAIRN. Martin J H Cook, Rowanbrae, Clochan, Buckie, Banffshire, AB56 5EQ. 01542 850 296; e-mail: martin.cook99@btinternet.com

MORAY. Martin J H Cook, Rowanbrae, Clochan, Buckie, Banffshire, AB56 5EQ. 01542 850 296; e-mail: martin.cook99@btinternet.com

Bird Reports
BIRDS IN MORAY AND NAIRN (1999-), from the Moray Recorder, 01542 850 296; e-mail: martin.cook99@btinternet.com

MORAY & NAIRN BIRD REPORT (1985-1998), from the Moray Recorder, 01542 850 296; e-mail: martin.cook99@btinternet.com

BTO Regional Representatives
NAIRN RR. Bob Proctor, 78 Marleon Field, Elgin, Moray, IV30 4GE.
e-mail: bobandlouise@proctor8246.fsnet.co.uk

MORAY RR. Bob Proctor, 78 Marleon Field, Elgin, Moray, IV30 4GE.
e-mail: bobandlouise@proctor8246.fsnet.co.uk

Wetland Bird Survey Organisers
LOSSIE ESTUARY. Bob Proctor, 78 Marleon Field, Silvercrest, Bishopmill, Elgin, IV30 4GE; e-mail: bobandlouise@proctor8246.fsnet.co.uk

MORAY & NAIRN (Inland). David Law, Hollybrae, South Darkland, Elgin, Moray IV30 8NT.

NORTH EAST SCOTLAND

Bird Atlas/Avifauna
The Birds of North East Scotland by S T Buckland,

M V Bell & N Picozzi (North East Scotland Bird Club, 1990).

Bird Recorder
NORTH-EAST SCOTLAND. Hywel Maggs, 4 Merlin Terrace, Newburgh, Ellon, Aberdeenshire AB41 6FA. 01358 788 106;
e-mail: hywelmaggs@hotmail.com

Bird Reports
NORTH-EAST SCOTLAND BIRD REPORT (1974-), From Dave Gill, Drakemyre Croft, Cairnorrie, Methlick, Aberdeenshire, AB41 7JN. 01651 806 252; e-mail: david@gilldavid1.orangehome.co.uk

NORTH SEA BIRD CLUB ANNUAL REPORT (1979-), From Andrew Thorpe, Ocean Laboratory and Centre for Ecology, Aberdeen University, Newburgh, Ellon, Aberdeenshire, AB41 6AA01224 274428; e-mail: nsbc@abdn.ac.uk

BTO Regional Representatives
ABERDEEN. Paul Doyle, 01358 751 365;
e-mail: paul@albaecology.co.uk

KINCARDINE & DEESIDE. Graham Cooper, Westbank, Beltie Road, Torphins, Banchory, Aberdeen, AB31 4JT. 01339 882 706;
e-mail: grm.cooper@btinternet.com

Clubs
SOC GRAMPIAN BRANCH. (1956; 110). John Wills, Bilbo, Monymusk, Inverurie, Aberdeenshire, AB51 7HA. 01467 651296;
e-mail: bilbo@monymusk.freeserve.co.uk
Meetings: 7.30pm, 1st Monday of the month (Sep-Apr), venue to be arranged.

Ringing Groups
ABERDEEN UNIVERSITY RG. Andrew Thorpe, e-mail: andrewthorpe4@aol.com

GRAMPIAN RG. R Duncan, 86 Broadfold Drive, Bridge of Don, Aberdeen, AB23 8PP.
e-mail: Raymond@waxwing.fsnet.co.uk

RSPB Local Group
ABERDEEN. (1975; 210). Rodney Payne, 2 Arbuthnott Court, Stonehaven,AB39 2GW. 01569 763742; www.rspb-abdn-mbrsgp.org.uk.
Meetings: 7.30pm, monthly in the winter, Lecture Theatre, Zoology Dept, Tillydrone Av, Aberdeen. Two birding trips monthly throughout the year.

Wildlife Hospital
GRAMPIAN WILDLIFE REHABILITATION TRUST. 40 High Street, New Deer, Turriff, Aberdeenshire, AB53 6SX. 01771 644 489; (M)07803 235 383;
e-mail: laurence.brain@btconnect.com
Veterinary surgeon. Access to full practice facilities. Will care for all species of birds.

ORKNEY

Bird Atlas/Avifauna
The Birds of Orkney by CJ Booth et al (The Orkney Press, 1984).

Bird Recorder
Mr EJ Williams, Fairholm, Finstown, Orkney, KW17 2EQ. e-mail: jim@geniefea.freeserve.co.uk

Bird Report
ORKNEY BIRD REPORT (inc North Ronaldsay Bird Report) (1974-), From Mr EJ Williams, Fairholm, Finstown, Orkney, KW17 2EQ.
e-mail: jim@geniefea.freeserve.co.uk

BTO Regional Representative
Colin Corse, Garrisdale, Lynn Park, Kirkwall, Orkney, KW15 1SL. 01856 874 484; e-mail: ccorse@aol.com

Club
SOC ORKNEY BRANCH. (1993; 15). Colin Corse, Garrisdale, Lynn Park, Kirkwall, Orkney, KW15 1SL. H:01856 874 484;
e-mail: ccorse@aol.com.

Ringing Groups
NORTH RONALDSAY BIRD OBSERVATORY. Ms A E Duncan, Twingness, North Ronaldsay, Orkney, KW17 2BE. e-mail: alison@nrbo.prestel.co.uk www.nrbo.f2s.co.uk

ORKNEY RG. Colin Corse, Garrisdale, Lynn Park, Kirkwall, Orkney, KW15 1SL. H:01856 874 484; e-mail: ccorse@aol.com

SULE SKERRY RG. Dave Budworth, 121 Wood Lane, Newhall, Swadlincote, Derbys, DE11 0LX. 01283 215 188.

RSPB Members' Group
ORKNEY. (1985;300 in catchment area). Mrs Pauline Wilson, Sunny Bank, Deerness, Orkney KW17 2QQ. 01856 741 382;
e-mail: p.wilson410@btinternet.com
Meetings: Meetings advertised in newsletter and local press, held at Kirkwall Community Centre.

Wetland Bird Survey Organiser
ORKNEY (other sites). Eric Meek, RSPB, 12/14 North End Road, Stromness, Orkney KW16 3AG. 01856 850 176.

OUTER HEBRIDES

Bird Recorder
OUTER HEBRIDES AND WESTERN ISLES. Brian Rabbitts, 01876 580 328;
e-mail: rabbitts@hebrides.net

Bird Report
OUTER HEBRIDES BIRD REPORT (1989-), from the Recorder.

BTO Regional Representatives & Regional Development Officer
BENBECULA & THE UISTS RR & RDO. 01876 580 328; e-mail: rabbitts@hebrides.net

LEWIS & HARRIS RR. Chris Reynolds, 11 Reef, Isle of Lewis, HS2 9HU. 01851 672 376; e-mail: cmreynolds@btinternet.com

Ringing Group
SHIANTS AUK RG. David Steventon, Welland House, 207 Hurdsfield Road, Macclesfield, Cheshire, SK10 2PX. 01625 421 936.

UISTS AND BENBECULA. Brian Rabbitts, 01876 580 328; e-mail: rabbitts@hebrides.net

PERTH & KINROSS

Bird Recorder
PERTH & KINROSS. Ron Youngman, Blairchroisk Cottage, Ballinluig, Pitlochry, Perthshire, PH9 0NE. 01796 482324; e-mail: blairchroisk@aol.com

Bird Report
PERTH & KINROSS BIRD REPORT (1974-), from the Recorder.

BTO Regional Representative
PERTHSHIRE RR. Richard Paul. 01882 632 212; e-mail: richard@rannoch.biz t www.perthshire-birds.org.uk

Clubs
PERTHSHIRE SOCIETY OF NATURAL SCIENCE (Ornithological Section). (1964; 37). Miss Esther Taylor, 23 Verena Terrace, Perth, PH2 0BZ. 01738 621 986; www.psns.org.uk
Meetings: 7.30pm, Wednesdays monthly (Oct-Mar), Perth Museum. Summer outings.

RSPB Members' Groups

Wetland Bird Survey Organiser
TAY ESTUARY. Norman Elkins, 18 Scotstarvit View, Cupar, Fife KY15 5DX. 01334 654 348; e-mail: jandnelkins@rapidial.co.uk

SHETLAND

Bird Recorders
FAIR ISLE. Deryk Shaw, Bird Observatory, Fair Isle, Shetland, ZE2 9JU.
e-mail: fairisle.birdobs@zetnet.co.uk

SHETLAND. Paul Harvey, SBRC, Shetland Amenity Trust, Garthspool, Lerwick, ShetlandZE1 0NY. 01595 694 688; e-mail: sbrc@shetlandamenity.org

Bird Reports
FAIR ISLE BIRD OBSERVATORY REPORT (1949-) from Scottish Ornithologists' Club, 21 Regent Terrace, Edinburgh, EH7 5BT. 0131 556 6042

SHETLAND BIRD REPORT (1969-) no pre 1973 available,
From Martin Heubeck, East House, Sumburgh Lighthouse, Virkie, Shetland, ZE3 9JN.e-mail: martinheubeck@btinternet.com

BTO Regional Representative
RR and RDO. Dave Okill, Heilinabretta, Cauldhame, Trondra, Shetland, ZE1 0XL. 01595 880 450.

Club
SHETLAND BIRD CLUB. (1973; 200). Russ Haywood, Lamnaberg, Wester Quarff, Shetland ZE2 9EZ. 01950 477 451; e-mail: haywood712ATbtinternet.com www.nature-shetland.co.uk

Ringing Groups
FAIR ISLE BIRD OBSERVATORY. Deryk Shaw, Bird Observatory, Fair Isle, Shetland, ZE2 9JU. e-mail: fairisle.birdobs@zetnet.co.uk

SHETLAND RG. Dave Okill, Heilinabretta, Cauldhame, Trondra, Shetland, ZE1 0XL. H:01595 880450; W:01595 696926.

Wetland Bird Survey Organiser
Paul Harvey, Shetland Biological Records Centre, Shetland Amenity Trust, 22-24 North Road, Lerwick, Shetland, ZE1 3NG. (Day)01595 694 688; e-mail: shetamenity.trust@zetnet.co.uk

WALES

BTO WALES OFFICER. John Lloyd, Cynghordy Hall, Cynghordy, Llandovery, Carms SA20 0LN. e-mail: the.lloyds@dsl.pipex.com

Club
See Welsh Ornithological Society in National Directory.

EAST WALES

Bird Atlas/Avifauna
The Birds of Montgomeryshire by Brayton Holt & Graham Williams (Powysland Club 2008). Contact Brayton Holt (see below) for availability and price.

The Gwent Atlas of Breeding Birds by Tyler, Lewis, Venables & Walton (Gwent Ornithological Society, 1987).

Bird Recorders
BRECONSHIRE. Andrew King, Heddfan, Pennorth, Brecon, Powys LD3 7EX. 01874 658 351; e-mail: andrew.king53@virgin.net

GWENT. Chris Jones. e-mail: countyrecorder@gwentbirds.org.uk

MONTGOMERYSHIRE. Brayton Holt, Scops Cottage, Pentrebeirdd, Welshpool, Powys SY21 9DL. 01938 500 266; e-mail: brayton.wanda@virgin.net

RADNORSHIRE, Pete Jennings, Penbont House, Elan Valley, Rhayader, Powys LD6 5HS. H:01597 811522; W:01597 810880; e-mail: petejelanvalley@hotmail.com

Bird Reports
BRECONSHIRE BIRDS (1962-), from Brecknock Wildlife Trust.

GWENT BIRD REPORT (1964-), from Jerry Lewis, Y Bwthyn Gwyn, Coldbrook, Abergavenny, Monmouthshire NP7 9TD. (H)01873 855 091; (W)01633 644 856

MONTGOMERYSHIRE BIRD REPORT (1981-82-), from Montgomeryshire Wildlife Trust.

RADNOR BIRDS (1987/92-), from Radnorshire Recorder.

BTO Regional Representatives
BRECKNOCK RR. John Lloyd, Cynghordy Hall, Cynghordy, Llandovery, Carms, SA20 0LN. e-mail: the.lloyds@dsl.pipex.com

GWENT RR. Jerry Lewis, Y Bwthyn Gwyn, Coldbrook, Abergavenny, Monmouthshire NP7 9TD. H:01873 855 091; W:01633 644 856

MONTGOMERY RR. Jane Kelsall, Holly Bank, Moel y Garth, Welshpool, Powys SY21 9JA. 01938 556 438; e-mail: janekelsall@phonecoop.coop

RADNORSHIRE RR. Brian Jones. e-mail: jones.brn10@virgin.net

Clubs
THE GWENT ORNITHOLOGICAL SOCIETY. (1964; 420). T J Russell. 01600 716 266; e-mail: secretary@GwentBirds.org.uk www.gwentbirds.org.uk
Meetings: 7.30pm, alternate Saturdays (Sept-Apr), Goytre Village Hall.

MONTGOMERYSHIRE FIELD SOCIETY. (1946; 190). Maureen Preen, Ivy House, Deep Cutting, Pool Quay, Welshpool, Powys SY21 9LJ. Tel: Mary Oliver, 01686 413 518.
Meetings: 2.30pm, 2nd Saturday of the month (Nov, Jan, Feb, Mar), Methodist Church Hall, Welshpool. Field trips (Apr-Oct) weekdays.

MONTGOMERYSHIRE WILDLIFE TRUST BIRD GROUP. (1997; 110). A M Puzey, Four Seasons, Arddleen, Llanymynech, Powys SY22 6RU. 01938 590 578.
Meetings: 7.30pm, Welshpool Methodist Hall.

Ringing Groups
GOLDCLIFF RG. Mr RM Clarke. e-mail: chykembro2@aol.com.

LLANGORSE RG. Group name: (1987; 15). Jerry Lewis, Y Bwthyn Gwyn, Coldbrook, Abergavenny, Monmouthshire NP7 9TD. H:01873 855 091; W:01633 644 856.

Wetland Bird Survey Organisers
RADNORSHIRE. Peter Jennings, Pentbont House, Elan Valley, Rhayader, Powys LD6 5HS. H:01597 811 522; W:01597 810 880; e-mail: petejelanvalley@hotmail.com

BRECONSHIRE. Andrew King, Heddfan, Pennorth, Brecon LD3 7EX. e-mail: heddfan25@hotmail.com

POWYS. Andrew King, Heddfan, Pennorth, Brecon, Powys LD3 7EX. 01874 658 351y

Wildlife Trusts
BRECKNOCK WILDLIFE TRUST. (1963; 650). Lion House, Bethel Square, Brecon, Powys LD3 7AY. 01874 625 708;

WALES

e-mail: enquiries@brecknockwildlifetrust.org.uk
www.brecknockwildlifetrust.org.uk

GWENT WILDLIFE TRUST. (1963; 5,000). Seddon House, Dingestow, Monmouth, NP25 4DY. 01600 740 358; fax 01600 740 299;
e-mail: info@gwentwildlife.org
www.gwentwildlife.org

MONTGOMERYSHIRE WILDLIFE TRUST. (1982; 1000). Collot House, 20 Severn Street, Welshpool, Powys, SY21 7AD. 01938 555 654; fax 01938 556 161; e-mail: info@montwt.co.uk
www.montwt.co.uk

RADNORSHIRE WILDLIFE TRUST. (1987; 878). Warwick House, High Street, Llandrindod Wells, Powys LD1 6AG. 01597 823 298; fax 01597 823 274; e-mail:info@radnorshirewildlifetrust.org.uk
www.radnorshirewildlifetrust.org.uk

NORTH WALES

Bird Atlas/Avifauna
Birds of Anglesey/Adar Môn by PH Jones and P Whalley. (Menter Mon, 2004).

The Birds of Caernarfonshire by John Barnes (1998, from Lionel Pilling, 51 Brighton Close, Rhyl LL18 3HL).

Bird Recorders
ANGLESEY. Stephen Culley, 22 Cae Derwydd, Cemaes Bay, Anglesey, LL67 0LP.
e-mail: SteCul10@aol.com

CAERNARFONSHIRE. John Barnes, Fach Goch, Waunfawr, Caernarfon, LL55 4YS. 01286 650 362.

DENBIGHSHIRE & FLINTSHIRE. Ian Spence, 43 Blackbrook, Sychdyn, Mold, Flintshire CH7 6LT. Tel/fax 01352 750 118;
e-mail: ianspence.cr@btinternet.com.
www.cbrg.org.uk

MEIRIONNYDD. Jim Dustow, Afallon, 7 Glan y Don, Rhiwbryfdir, Blaenau Ffestiniog, Gwynedd LL41 3LW. e-mail: Jim.Dustow@rspb.org.uk.

Bird Reports
BARDSEY BIRD OBSERVATORY ANNUAL REPORT, from the Warden, see Reserves.

CAMBRIAN BIRD REPORT (sometime Gwynedd Bird Report) (1953-), from Stephen Culley, 22 Cae Derwydd, Cemaes Bay, Anglesey, LL67 0LP.
e-mail: SteCul10@aol.com

CLWYD BIRD REPORT (2002-) - changing to NE Wales Bird Report, from Ian M Spence, Ty'r Fawnog, 43 Blackbrook, Sychdyn, Mold, Flints CH7 6LT. 01352 750 118;
e-mail: ianspence.cr@btinternet.com

MEIRIONNYDD BIRD REPORT Published in Cambrian Bird Report (above).

WREXHAM BIRDWATCHERS' SOCIETY ANNUAL REPORT (1982-), from The Secretary, Wrexham Birdwatchers' Society.

BTO Regional Representatives
ANGLESEY RR. Tony White. 01407 710 137;
e-mail: wylfor@treg5360.freeserve.co.uk

CAERNARFON RR. Geoff Gibbs. 01248 681 936;
e-mail: geoffkate.gibbs@care4free.net

CLWYD EAST RR. Dr Anne Brenchley, Ty'r Fawnog, 43 Black Brook, Sychdyn, Mold, Flints CH7 6LT. 01352 750 118;
e-mail: anne.brenchley@btinternet.com

CLWYD WEST RR. Mel ab Owain, 31 Coed Bedw, Abergele, Conwy, LL22 7EH. 01745 826528;
e-mail: melabowain@btinternet.com

MEIRIONNYDD RR. David Anning. 01654 761 481;
e-mail: davidanning@freeuk.com

Clubs
BANGOR BIRD GROUP. (1947; 100). Jane Prosser, 15 Victoria Street, Bangor, Gwynedd LL57 2HD. 01248 364 632.
Meetings: 7.30pm, Semester terms, Bramble Building, University of Bangor.

CLWYD BIRD RECORDING GROUP (committee that produces the Bird Report).
e-mail: julie.s.rogers@talktalk.net

CLWYD ORNITHOLOGICAL SOCIETY. (1956; 45). Jaquie Irving, 01745 854 132.
Meetings: 7.30pm (Sep-Apr), Farmers Arms, Waen, St. Asaph.

DEE ESTUARY CONSERVATION GROUP. (1973; 25 grps).
e-mail: decg@deeestuary.co.uk
www.deeestuary.co.uk/decg.htm

DEESIDE NATURALISTS' SOCIETY. (1973; 700). Mrs Janice Jones, Secretary, 21 Woodlands Court, Hawarden, Deeside, Flints CH5 3NB. 01244 537 440; e-mail: deenaturalists@btinternet.com
www.deesidenaturalists.org.uk

WREXHAM BIRDWATCHERS' SOCIETY. (1974; 90). Miss Marian Williams, 10 Lake View, Gresford, Wrexham, Clwyd LL12 8PU. 01978 854 633.
Meetings: 7.30pm, 1st Friday of the month (Sep-Apr), Gresford Memorial Hall, Gresford.

WALES

Ringing Groups
BARDSEY BIRD OBSERVATORY. Steven Stansfield, Bardsey Island, off Aberdaron, Pwllheli, Gwynedd LL53 8DE. 07855 264 151;
e-mail: warden@bbfo.org.uk

MERSEYSIDE RG. Bob Harris, 2 Dulas Road, Wavertree Green, Liverpool, L15 6UA. Work 0151 706 4311; e-mail: harris@liv.ac.uk

SCAN RG. Dr D. Moss.
e-mail: dorian@dorianmoss.com

RSPB Local Group
NORTH WALES. (1986; 80). Maureen Douglas, 57 Penrhyn Beach East, Penrhyn Bay, Llandudno, Conwy LL30 3RW. 01492 547 768.
Meetings: 7.30pm, 3rd Friday of the month (Sep-Apr), St Davids Church Hall, Penrhyn Bay, LLANDUDNO, Gwynedd, LL30 3EJ.

Wetland Bird Survey Organisers
ANGLESEY (other sites). Ian Sims, RSPB Malltraeth Marsh, Tai'r Gors, Pentre Berw, Gaerwen, Anglesey, LL60 6LB.e-mail: ian.sims@rspb.org.uk

CAERNARFONSHIRE (excl Traeth Lafan). Rhion Pritchard, Pant Afonig, Hafod Lane, Bangor, Gwynedd LL57 4BU. (H)01248 671 301;
e-mail: rhion678pritchard@btinternet.com

CLWYD (Coastal). Mr Peter Wellington, 4 Cheltenham Avenue, Rhyl, Clwyd LL18 4DN. (H)01745 3542 32; e-mail: webs@bto.org.

MEIRIONNYDD ESTUARIES (not Dyfi). Jim Dustow, Afallon, 7 Glan y Don, Rhiwbryfdir, Blaenau Ffestiniog, Gwynedd LL41 3LW.
e-mail: Jim.Dustow@rspb.org.uk.

MEIRIONNYDD (other sites). Mr Trefor Owen, Crochendy Twrog, Maentwrog, Blaenau Ffestiniog, LL41 3YU. (H)01766 590 302.

DEE ESTUARY. Colin Wells, Burton Point Farm, Station Road, Burton, Nr Neston, South Wirral CH64 5SB. 0151 336 7681.

FORYD BAY. Simon Hugheston-Roberts, Oakhurst, St David's Road, Caernarfon, LL55 1EL.
e-mail: sm.roberts@ccw.gov.uky

Wildlife Trust
NORTH WALES WILDLIFE TRUST. (1963; 4,609). 376 High Street, Bangor, Gwynedd, LL57 1YE. 01248 351 541; fax 01248 353 192;
e-mail: nwwt@wildlifetrustswales.org
www.wildlifetrust.org.uk/northwales

SOUTH WALES

Bird Atlas/Avifauna
An Atlas of Breeding Birds in West Glamorgan

by David M Hanford et al (Gower Ornithological Society, 1992).

Birds of Glamorgan by Clive Hurford and Peter Lansdown (Published by the authors, c/o National Museum of Wales, Cardiff, 1995)

Bird Recorders
GLAMORGAN (EAST). Geri Thomas, 9 Julian's Close, Gelligaer, Glamorgan CF82 8DT. (H)01443 836 949; (M)07984 591 983;
e-mail: merlinbiosurveys@btinternet.com

GOWER (WEST GLAMORGAN). Robert Taylor, 285 Llangyfelach Road, Brynhyfryd, Swansea, SA5 9LB. 01792 464 780; (M) 07970 567 007;
e-mail: rob@birding.freeserve.co.uk

Bird Reports
EAST GLAMORGAN BIRD REPORT (title varies 1963-95) 1996-2003, from Mr John D Wilson, 122 Westbourne Road, Penarth, Vale of Glamorgan, CF64 3HH. 029 2033 9424;
e-mail: john_wilson@glamorganbirds.org

GOWER BIRDS (1965-), from Heather Coats, 3 Brynawel Close, Crynant, Neath, SA10 8TG.
e-mail: gowerblrdsf@hotmail.com
www.glamorganbirds.org.uk

BTO Regional Representatives
EAST GLAMORGAN (former Mid & South Glam) RR. Rob Nottage, 32 Village Farm, Bonvilston, Cardiff, CF5 6TY. e-mail: nottage@dsl.pipex.com

WEST RR. Bob Howells, Ynys Enlli, 14 Dolgoy Close, West Cross, Swansea SA3 5LT.
e-mail: bobhowells31@hotmail.com

Clubs
CARDIFF NATURALISTS' SOCIETY. (1867; 225). Stephen R Howe, National Museum of Wales, Cardiff, CF10 3NP.
e-mail: steve.howe@museumwales.ac.uk
www.cardiffnaturalists.org.uk
Meetings: 7.30pm, various evenings, Llandaff Campus Uwic, Western Avenue, Cardiff.

GLAMORGAN BIRD CLUB. (1990; 300+).
Membership Secretary. 01443 841 555;
e-mail: rosney@nantgarw.freeserve.co.uk
www.glamorganbirds.org.uk
Meetings: 7.30pm, 2nd Tuesday of winter months, Kenfig Reserve Centre.

GOWER ORNITHOLOGICAL SOCIETY. (1956; 120). Peter Douglas-Jones, 28 Brynfield Road, Langland, Swansea, SA3 4SX. e-mail: gowerbirdsf@hotmail.com www.glamorganbirds.org.uk
Meetings: 7.15pm, last

WALES

Friday of the month (Sep-Mar), The Environment Centre, Pier Street, Swansea.

Ringing Groups
FLAT HOLM RG. Group name: Brian Bailey, Tamarisk House, Wards Court, Frampton-on-Severn, Glos, GL2 7DY.
e-mail: brian.bailey@sandbservices.eclipse.co.uk

KENFIG RG. Group name: Mr D.G. Carrington, 44 Ogmore Drive, Nottage, Porthcawl, Mid Glamorgan CF36 3HR.

RSPB Local Groups
CARDIFF & DISTRICT. 1973. Joy Lyman, 5 Dros-Y-Morfa, Rumney, Cardiff, CF3 3BL. 02920 770 031; e-mail: joy@lyman.plus.com
www.RSPB.org.uk/groups/cardiff.
Meetings: 7.30pm, various Fridays (Sept-May), Llandaff Parish Hall, Llandaff, Cardiff.

WEST GLAMORGAN. (1985; 346). Maggie Cornelius. 01792 229 244;
e-mail: maggie.cornelius@tiscali.co.uk
www.westglam-RSPB.org.uk

Wetland Bird Survey Organisers
EAST GLAMORGAN (former Mid & South Glam), Rob Nottage, 32 Village Farm, Bonvilston, Cardiff, CF5 6TY. e-mail: nottage@dsl.pipex.com

SEVERN ESTUARY, Niall Burton, c/o BTO, The Nunnery, Thetford, Norfolk, IP24 2PU.
e-mail: niall.burton@bto.org

WEST GLAMORGAN, Bob Howells, Ynys Enlli, 14 Dolgoy Close, West Cross, Swansea SA3 5LT. 01792 405 363; e-mail: bobhowells31@hotmail.com

Wildlife Hospital
GOWER BIRD HOSPITAL. Karen Kingsnorth and Simon Allen, Valetta, Sandy Lane, Pennard, Swansea, SA3 2EW. 01792 371 630;
e-mail: info@gowerbirdhospital.org.uk
www.gowerbirdhospital.org.uk
All species of wild birds, also hedgehogs and small mammals. Prior phone call essential. Gower Bird Hospital cares for sick, injured and orphaned wild birds and animals with the sole intention of returning them to the wild. Post release radio tracking projects, ringing scheme. Contact us for more information.

Wildlife Trust
WILDLIFE TRUST OF SOUTH AND WEST WALES. (2002; 6,000). Nature Centre, Parc Slip, Fountain Road, Tondu, Bridgend CF32 0EH. 01656 724 100; fax 01656 726 980; e-mail: info@welshwildlife.org
www.welshwildlife.org

Bird Atlas/Avifauna
Birds of Pembrokeshire by Jack Donovan and Graham Rees (Dyfed Wildlife Trust, 1994).

Bird Recorders
CARMARTHENSHIRE. Derek Moore, Rowan Howe, Gors Road, Salem, Llandeilo, Carmarthenshire SA19 7LY. 01558 823 708;
e-mail: DerekBirdBrain@aol.com

CEREDIGION. Russell Jones, Bron y Gan, Talybont, Ceredigion, SY24 5ER. 07753 774 891;
e-mail: russell.jones@rspb.org.uk

PEMBROKESHIRE 1. Stephen Berry, 1 Cunard House, Quay Road, Goodwick, SA64 0BS. 01348 872 233; e-mail: stephen.berry16@btinternet.com.

PEMBROKESHIRE 2. Jon Green, Crud Yr Awel, Bowls Road, Blaenporth, Ceredigion SA43 2AR. 01239 811 561; e-mail: jonrg@tiscali.co.uk.

Bird Reports
CARMARTHENSHIRE BIRD REPORT (1982-), from Mrs Angela Lovegrove, Newton Park Farm House, Cynwyl Elfed, Carmarthenshire SA33 6SP..

CEREDIGION BIRD REPORT (biennial 1982-87; annual 1988-), from Wildlife Trust West Wales.

PEMBROKESHIRE BIRD REPORT (1981-), from Ms Barbara Priest, The Pines, Templeton, Pembs, SA67 8RT. e-mail: barbara.priest@tiscali.co.uk

BTO Regional Representatives
CARDIGAN RR. Moira Convery, 41 Danycoed, Aberystwyth, SY23 2HD. 01970 612 998;
e-mail: moira.convery@dsl.pipex.com

CARMARTHEN RR. Colin Jones. 01554 821 632; e-mail: colinjones25@yahoo.co.uk

PEMBROKE RR. Annie and Bob Haycock, 1 Rushmoor, Martletwy, Pembrokeshire, SA67 8BB. 01834 891 667; e-mail: rushmoor1@tiscali.co.uk

Clubs
CARMARTHENSHIRE BIRD CLUB.(2008; 100). Owen Harris, 2 Marine Cottages, Water Street, Ferryside, SA17 5SB.
www.carmarthenshirebirds.co.uk
Meetings: Winter evenings at WWT Penclacwydd (check website for details).

WALES

LLANELLI NATURALISTS. (1971; 100). Richard Pryce, Trevethin, School Road, Pwll, Llanelli, Carmarthenshire SA15 4AL.
e-mail: Contact@llanellinaturalists.org.uk
www.llanellinaturalists.org.uk
Meetings: 1st Thursday of the month, YWCA Llanelli (see programme in local libraries).

PEMBROKESHIRE BIRD GROUP. (1993; 60). Ms Barbara Priest, The Pines, Templeton, Pembs, SA67 8RT. e-mail: barbara.priest@tiscali.co.uk.
Meetings: 7.30pm, 1st Tuesday of the month (Oct-Apr), The Patch, Furzy Park, Haverfordwest.

Ringing Group
PEMBROKESHIRE RG. Group name: J Hayes, 3 Wades Close, Holyland Road, Pembroke, SA71 4BN. 01646 687 036;
e-mail: hayesj@chevron.com.

Wetland Bird Survey Organisers
DYFI ESTUARY, Dick Squires, Cae'r Berllan, Eglwysfach, Machynlleth, Powys SY20 8TA.
e-mail: dick.squires@rspb.org.uk

DYSINNI ESTUARY. Jim Dustow, Afallon, 7 Glan y Don, Rhiwbryfdir, Blaenau Ffestiniog, Gwynedd LL41 3LW. e-mail: Jim.Dustow@rspb.org.uk.

CARDIGAN, Dick Squires, Cae'r Berllan, Eglwysfach, Machynlleth, Powys SY20 8TA.
e-mail: dick.squires@rspb.org.uk

CARMARTHEN, BAY AND INLAND. Ian Hainsworth, 23 Rhyd y Defaid Drive, Swansea, SA2 8AJ. 01792 205 693; e-mail: ian.hains@ntlworld.com

Wildlife Hospitals
NEW QUAY BIRD HOSPITAL. Jean Bryant, Penfoel, Cross Inn, Llandysul, Ceredigion, SA44 6NR. 01545 560 462. All species of birds. Fully equipped for cleansing oiled seabirds. Veterinary support.

WEST WILLIAMSTON OILED BIRD CENTRE. Mrs J Hains, Lower House Farm, West Williamston, Kilgetty, Pembs, SA68 0TL. 01646 651236. Facilities for holding up to 200 Guillemots, etc. for short periods. Initial treatment is given prior to despatch to other washing centres during very large oil spills; otherwise birds are washed at the Centre with intensive care and rehabilitation facilities. Also other species. Veterinary support.

Wildlife Trust
See South Wales.

ISLE OF MAN

Bird Atlas/Avifauna
Manx Bird Atlas. 5-yr BBS and Winter Atlas research completed. (Liverpool University 2007). Contact: Chris Sharpe (see below, BTO Representative).

Bird Recorder
Dr Pat Cullen, Troutbeck, Cronkbourne, Braddan, Isle of Man, IM4 4QA. Home: 01624 623308; Work 01624 676774; e-mail: bridgeen@mcb.net

Bird Reports
MANX BIRD REPORT (1947-), published in *Peregrine*. Mrs A C Kaye, Cronk Ny Ollee, Glen Chass, Port St Mary, Isle of Man, IM9 5PL.

CALF OF MAN BIRD OBSERVATORY ANNUAL REPORT, from The Secretary, Manx National Heritage, Manx Museum, Douglas, Isle of Man, IM1 3LY.

BTO Regional Representative & Regional Development Officer
RR. Dr Pat Cullen, as above, 01624 623 308.

RDO. Chris Sharpe, 33 Mines Road, Laxey, Isle of Man, IM4 7NH. 01624 861 130;
e-mail: chris@manxbirdatlas.org.uk

Club
MANX ORNITHOLOGICAL SOCIETY. (1967; 150). Mrs A C Kaye, Cronk Ny Ollee, Glen Chass, Port St Mary, Isle of Man, IM9 5PL. 01624 834 015
Meetings: 1st Tues in month, 7.30pm, Union Mills Hall.

Ringing Group
MANX RINGING GROUP. Mr K. N. Scott.
e-mail: kev@manxbroadband.com

Wetland Bird Survey Organiser
Pat Cullen, Troutbeck, Cronkbourne, Braddan, Isle of Man, IM4 4QA. (H)01624 623 308; (W)01624 676 774;
e-mail: bridgeen@mcb.net

Wildlife Trust
MANX WILDLIFE TRUST. (1973; 900). The Courtyard, Tynwald Mills, St Johns, Isle of Man IM4 3AE. 01624 801 985; (Fax) 01624 801 022; e-mail: manxwt@cix.co.uk
www.wildlifetrust.org.uk/manxwt/

CHANNEL ISLANDS

ALDERNEY

Bird Recorder
Mark Atkinson. E-mail: atkinson@cwgsy.net.

Bird Report
*ALDERNEY SOCIETY ORNITHOLOGY REPORT
(1992-)*, from the Recorder.

BTO Regional Representative
Philip Alexander. 01481 726 173;
e-mail: alybru@cwgsy.net

Wildlife Trust
ALDERNEY WILDLIFE TRUST (2002; 460). Alderney
Information Centre, 34 Victoria Street, St Anne
Alderney GY9 3AA. 01481 822 935; (Fax) 01481 822
935; e-mail: info@alderneywildlife.org
www.alderneywildlife.org

GUERNSEY

Bird Atlas/Avifauna
Birds of the Bailiwick of Guernsey (working title). In
preparation.

Bird Recorder
Mark Lawlor; e-mail: mplawlor@cwgsy.net

Bird Report
*REPORT & TRANSACTIONS OF LA SOCIETE
GUERNESIAISE (1882-)*, from the Recorder.

BTO Regional Representative
Philip Alexander. 01481 726 173;
e-mail: alybru@cwgsy.net

Clubs
LA SOCIÉTIÉ GUERNESIAISE (Ornithological
Section). (1882; 30). The Secretary,
e-mail: societe@cwgsy.net
www.societe.org.gg
Meetings: First Thurs of month, 8pm, Candie
Gardens lecture theatre.

RSPB Local Group
GUERNSEY. (1975; 350+). Michael Bairds, Les
Quatre Vents, La Passee, St Sampsons, Guernsey,
GY2 4TS. 01481 255 524;
e-mail: mikebairds@cwgsy.nett
www.rspbguernsey.co.uk

Wetland Bird Survey Organiser
GUERNSEY COAST. Mary Simmons, Les Maeures,
Mont d'Aval, Castel, Guernsey, GY5 7UQ. 01481 256
016; e-mail: msim@cwgsy.net

Wildlife Hospital
GUERNSEY. GSPCA ANIMAL SHELTER. Mrs Jayne
Le Cras, Rue des Truchots, Les Fiers Moutons, St
Andrews, Guernsey, Channel Islands, GY6 8UD.
01481 257 261; e-mail: jaynelecras@gspca.org.gg.
All species. Modern cleansing unit for oiled seabirds.
24-hour emergency service. Veterinary support.

JERSEY

Bird Recorder
Tony Paintin, 16 Quennevais Gardens, St Brelade,
Jersey, Channel Islands, JE3 8FQ. 01534 741 928;
e-mail: cavokjersey@hotmail.com

Bird Report
JERSEY BIRD REPORT, from La Société Jersiaise, 7
Pier Road, St Helier, Jersey JE2 4XW.
e-mail: societe@societe-jersiaise.org

BTO Regional Representative
Tony Paintin, 16 Quennevais Gardens, St Brelade,
Jersey, Channel Islands, JE3 8FQ. 01534 741 928;
e-mail: cavokjersey@hotmail.com

Club
SOCIÉTIÉ JERSIAISE (Ornithological Section).
(1948; 40). C/O La Société Jersiaise, 7 Pier Road, St
Helier, Jersey JE2 4XW. 01534 758 314;
e-mail: societe@societe-jersiaise.org
www.societe-jersiaise.org
Meetings: 8.00pm, alternate Thursdays throughout
the year, Museum in St.Helier.

Wildlife Hospital
JERSEY. JSPCA ANIMALS' SHELTER. The Secretary,
89 St Saviour's Road, St Helier, Jersey, JE2 4GJ.
01534 724 331; (Fax) 01534 871797;
e-mail: info@jspca.org.je
www.jspca.org.je All species. Expert outside support
for owls and raptors. Oiled seabird unit. Veterinary
surgeon on site. Educational Centre.

NORTHERN IRELAND

Bird Recorder
George Gordon, 2 Brooklyn Avenue, Bangor, Co Down, BT20 5RB. 028 9145 5763;
e-mail: gordon@ballyholme2.freeserve.co.uk

Bird Reports
NORTHERN IRELAND BIRD REPORT, from Secretary, Northern Ireland, Birdwatchers' Association (see National Directory).

IRISH BIRD REPORT, Included in Irish Birds,, BirdWatch Ireland in National Directory.

COPELAND BIRD OBSERVATORY REPORT, see Reserves.

BTO Regional Representatives
BTO IRELAND OFFICER. Shane Wolsey. 028 9146 7947; e-mail: shane@swolsey.biz

ANTRIM & BELFAST. Position vacant.

ARMAGH. David W A Knight, 20 Mandeville Drive, Tandragee, Craigavon, Co Armagh BT62 2DQ. 028 38 840 658; e-mail: david.knight@niwater.com

DOWN. Position vacant.

FERMANAGH. Position vacant.
LONDONDERRY. Charles Stewart, Bravallen, 18 Duncrun Road, Bellarena, Limavady, Co Londonderry BT49 0JD. 028 7775 0468;
e-mail: charles.stewart2@btinternet.com

TYRONE. Position vacant.

Clubs
NORTHERN IRELAND BIRDWATCHERS' ASSOCIATION See National Directory.

NORTHERN IRELAND ORNITHOLOGISTS' CLUB. See National Directory.

CASTLE ESPIE BIRDWATCHING CLUB (COMBER). (1995; 60). Dot Blakely, 8 Rosemary Park, Bangor, Co Down, BT20 3EX. 028 9145 0784

Ringing Groups
COPELAND BIRD OBSERVATORY. C W Acheson, 28 Church Avenue, Dunmurry, Belfast, BT17 9RS.

NORTH DOWN RINGING GROUP. Mr D C Clarke. e-mail: declan.clarke@homecall.co.uk

RSPB Local Groups
ANTRIM. (1977; 23). Brenda Campbell . 02893 323 657; e-mail: brendacampbell@supanet.com
Meetings: 8pm, 2nd Monday of the month, College of Agriculture Food & Rural Enterprise, 22 Greenmount Road, ANTRIM.

BANGOR. (1973; 25). Fulton Somerville. E-mail: fulton.somerville@newryandmourne.gov.uk
Meetings: Trinity Presbyterian Church Hall, Main Street, BANGOR, County Down.

BELFAST. (1970; 130). Ron Houston. 028 9079 6188.
Meetings: Cooke Centenary Church Hall, Cooke Centenary Church Hall, Ormeau Rd, BELFAST

COLERAINE. (1978; 45). Peter Robinson, 34 Blackthorn Court, Coleraine, Co Londonderry, BT52 2EX. 028 7034 4361;
e-mail: robinson493@btinternet.com
Meetings: 7.30pm, third Monday of the month (Sept-Apr), St Patricks Church, Minor Church Hall, Corner of Brook St and Circular Road, Coleraine

FERMANAGH. (1977; 28). Barbara Johnston. 028 6634 1708; e-mail: johnston.cb@googlemail.com
Meetings: 7.30pm, 4th Tuesday of the month, St Macartans Church Hall.

LARNE. (1974; 35). Jimmy Christie, 314 Coast Road, Ballygally, Co Antrim, BT40 2QZ. 028 2858 3223;
e-mail: candjchristie@btinternet.com
Meetings: 7.30pm, 1st Wednesday of the month, Larne Grammar School.

LISBURN. (1978; 30). Peter Galloway. 028 9266 1982; e-mail: peter.dolly@virgin.net
www.rspblisburn.com
Meetings: 7.30pm, 4th Monday of the month, Friends Meeting House, 4 Magheralave Road, LISBURN

Wetland Bird Survey Organisers
LARNE LOUGH. Doreen Hilditch.
e-mail:18brae@btinternet.com

BELFAST LOUGH. Shane Wolsey, 25 Ballyholme Esplanade, Bangor, County Down, BT20 5LZ. 02891 467947; e-mail: shane@swolsey.biz

CARLINGFORD LOUGH. Frank Carroll, 292 Barcroft Park, Newry, County Down, Northern Ireland, BT35 8ET. 02830 268 015;
E-mail: francis.carroll292@btinternet.com

DUNDRUM BAY. Malachy Martin, Murlough NNR, Keel Point, Dundrum, Co. Down, BT33 0NQ. 028 4375 1467;
E-mail: Malachy.Martin@nationaltrust.org.uk

BANN ESTUARY. Hill Dick, 3 Willowfield Mews, Coleraine, County Londonderry, BT52 2BH. 02870 329 720; e-mail: webs@bto.org

LOUGH FOYLE. Matthew Tickner, RSPB, Belvoir Park

Forest, Belfast, Co Antrim, BT8 7QT. 028 491547(c/o Belfast RSPB);
e-mail: matthew.tickner@rspb.org.uk

CO. LONDONDERRY (OTHER SITES). Alan Hetherington, 1 Sperrin Park, Caw, Waterside, Londonderry, Northern Ireland, BT47 6NG. 028 7128 1367; e-mail: whitesiskin@ntlworld.com

Wildlife Hospital
TACT WILDLIFE CENTRE. Mrs Patricia Nevines, 2 Crumlin Road, Crumlin, Co Antrim, BT29 4AD. Tel/fax 028 9442 2900;

e-mail: tactwildlife@btinternet.com
www.tactwildlifecentre.org.u All categories of birds treated and rehabilitated; released where practicable, otherwise given a home. Visitors (inc. school groups and organisations) welcome by prior arrangement. Veterinary support.

Wildlife Trust
ULSTER WILDLIFE TRUST. (1978; 6,000). 3 New Line, Crossgar, Co Down, BT30 9EP. 028 4483 0282; fax 028 4483 0888;
e-mail: info@ulsterwildlifetrust.org
www.ulsterwildlifetrust.org

REPUBLIC OF IRELAND

Bird Recorders
BirdWatch Ireland, P.O. Box 12, Greystones, Co. Wicklow, Ireland. 353 (0)1 2819 878 (Fax) 353 (0)1 2810 997; e-mail: info@birdwatchireland.ie
www.birdwatchireland.ie

Rarities. Paul Milne, 100 Dublin Road, Sutton, Dublin 13, +353 (0)1 832 5653;
e-mail: paul.milne@oceanfree.net

CLARE. John Murphy;
e-mail: jemurphy@esatclearie

CORK. Mark Shorten; e-mail: mshorten@indigo.ie

DONEGAL. Ralph Sheppard;
e-mail: rsheppard@eircom.net

DUBLIN, LOUTH, MEATH AND WICKLOW. Declan Murphy; e-mail: dmurphy@birdwatchireland.ie

Dick Coombes;
e-mail: rcoombes@birdwatchireland.ie

GALWAY. Tim Griffin; 74 Monalee Heights, Knocknacarra.

KERRY. Edward Carty; 3 The Orchard, Ballyrickard, Tralee.

LIMERICK. Tony Mee; Ballyorgan, Kilfinane, Co. Limerick.

MAYO. Tony Murray; National Parks and Wildlife, Lagduff More, Ballycroy, Westport

MID-SHANNON. Stephen Heery;
e-mail: sheery@eircom.net

MONAGHAN. Joe Shannon;
e-mail: joeshan@eircom.net

WATERFORD. Paul Walsh;
e-mail: pmwalsh@waterfordbirds.com

WEXFORD. Wexford Wildfowl Reserve, North Slob

Bird Reports
IRISH BIRD REPORT, contact BirdWatch Ireland in National, Directory).

CAPE CLEAR BIRD OBSERVATORY ANNUAL REPORT, from the observatory.

CORK BIRD REPORT (1963-71; 1976-), Cork Bird Report Editorial Team, Long Strand, Castlefreke, Clonakilty, Co. Cork; e-mail: cbr@corkecology.net

EAST COAST BIRD REPORT (1980-), Contact BirdWatch Ireland.

BirdWatch Ireland Branches
Branches may be contacted in writing via BirdWatch Ireland HQ (see entry in National Directory).

Ringing Groups
CAPE CLEAR B.O, Mr M.E. O'Donnell, Barnlands, Killinieran, Gorey, Co Wexford,
e-mail: micealodonnell@eircom.net

GREAT SALTEE RINGING STATION, Mr O J Merne, 20 Cuala Road, Bray, Co Wicklow, Ireland,
e-mail: omerne@eircom.net

MUNSTER RG, Mr K.P.C. Collins, Ballygambon, Lisronagh, Clonmel, County Tipperary,
e-mail: kcsk@eircom.net

ARTICLES IN
BIRD REPORTS

Angus and Dundee Bird Report 2005
- Laughing Gull, Carnoustie Bay by Richard Bramhall
- Yellowhammers in a Monifieth garden by Arthur c Bastable
- The first Rustic Bunting for Angus by Richard Bramhall
- Breeding terns at GlaxoSmithKline, Montrose by Les Hatton
- First Isabelline Shrike for Angus by Richard Bramhall
- NB: The articles by Richard Bramhall have previously been published in *Birding Scotland*

Avon Bird Report 2005
- Unusual ornithological events in the Avon area 1945-1980 by AH Davis
- Historical perspective of Feral Pigeon populations by J Tully
- Identification of Marsh and Willow Tits by JP Martin
- Upland Sandpiper at Channel View Farm by R Hunt
- The Waxwing invasion by RL Bland
- BBS for Avon 2005 by J Tully
- Avon Ringing report by LF Roberts

Ayrshire Bird Report 2006
- The birds of the Hunterston area 1968-1999 by Marco McGinty and James Towill
- Skuas at Saltcoats in 2006 by Jason McManus
- Analysis of Barn Owl pellets in East Ayrshire by Allstair Murdoch
- Kestrel in Ayrshire 2006 by Gordon Riddle
- Sparrow breeding details 2006 by Ian Todd

Birds of Berkshire 2000-7
- Cormorant breeding survey 2000 by Pat Martin
- House Sparrows in College Town by Des Sussex
- Honey Buzzard influx in 2000 by Chris Heard
- Autumn passage of Yellow Wagtails by Pete Standley and Richard Crawford
- A Black Kite in West Berkshire by Chris Heard

Borders Bird Report No. 23 2005
- Ringing in Borders 2005
- Tree Sparrow Survey 1998-9
- Bird crime report for Borders 2005

Cambridgeshire Bird Report 2005
- Great Fen Project by Chris Gerrard
- Numbers of water birds at Grafham Water reservoir 1964-2002 by Daniel Piec
- An exceptional influx of Tundra Bean Geese in winter 2004/5 by Mark Ward
- The breeding birds of Monks Wood by Richard Broughton, Shelley Hinsley, Paul Bellamy

Carmarthenshire Birds 2004-5
- The BTO in Carmarthenshire by Colin Jones
- National Wetland Centre - ringing report 2005 by Heather Coats
- Ceredigion Bird Report 2004-2005
- Bonaparte's Gull - first county record by Mark Hughes
- Nightjar Survey by Ray Bamford
- Ringing Report by Dave Reed

Cheshire and Wirral Bird Report 2005
- Report on bird ringing in Cheshire and Wirral by Prof D Norman
- Chimney Swift at Wooston Eyes by D Riley
- Black Kite at Moore by A Wraithnel et al
- Pallas's Warbler wintering in Cheshire by RM Blindell et al
- Whiskered Terns at Ashtons Flash by M Fearn
- Long-billed Dowitcher at IMF RSPB reserve by S Hinde
- Cetti's Warblers at Neston reedbed by S Williams
- Breeding Little Egrets on the Dee Estuary 2005 by C Wells
- Waxwing influx 2004/5 by P Oddy
- 'Channel' Wagtail by AM Pulsford

Birds and Wildlife in Cumbria 2005
- Birds wintering in the Kendal/Killington area 2005/6 by Clive Hartley

Derbyshire Bird Report 2005
- Surf Scoter (at Foremark Reservoir - a new species for Derbyshire by RW Key
- White-tailed Eagle at Bueley Moor and Harland Edge - a new species for Derbyshire by ME Taylor
- Dartford Warbler at The Sanctuary, Derby - a new species for the society by RW Key
- Cormorants apparently rearing two broods by T Cockburn
- Pale female Yellowhammer at Barlow Edge during spring/summer 2005 by RW Key

Birds in Dumfries and Galloway 2005
- Donald Watson 1918-2005 an appreciation
- Systematic species accounts 2002-5
- Table summarising Galloway Mute Swan survey 2002
- North Solway Ringing Group constant effort site 2005, Lochfoot summary table

Birds in Greater Manchester; County Report 2006
- The breeding Peregrines in the City Centre by Judith Smith
- Greater Manchester County Year List 2006 (Birding on the edge!) by Robert Adderley
- Wintering birds in SD91 East Rochdale and Littleborough area (The Atlas 2007-11 winter pilot) by Steve Adkins and Steve Suttill.
- The BTO/RSPB/JNCC Breeding Bird Survey in the Manchester Region, 2006 by Judith Smith

Hampshire Bird Report 2005
- Tawny Owl Survey 2005 by BS Sharkey
- The Hobby in The Twilight Zone by I Pibworth
- Corn Bunting survey 2005 by KF Betton
- Birding by Bike by JM Clark
- Desert Wheatear by AC Johnson and SK Woolley
- First for Hampshire - Laughing Gull by JA Norton and PN Raby
- First for Hampshire - Radde's Warbler by NJ Montefriffo and A Pink

ARTICLES IN BIRD REPORTS

The Hertfordshire Bird Report 2004
- Review of the year by Ted Fletcher
- Bird Ringing report 2004 by Chris Dee
- BTO Breeding Bird Survey results for 2004 by Chris Dee
- Winter Gull Roost Survey January 2004 by Joan Thompson

Highland Bird Report 2005
- Highland Ringing Group report 2005 by Bob Swan et al
- The dynamics of a Highland Swallow Roost by Hugh Insley et al
- *Birds of the Cromarty Firth 1867* by W Vincent Legge (reprint of historical article)

Kent Bird Report 2005
- Marsh Harriers in Kent and the 2005 Breeding Survey by Peter Oliver
- Changes in Bird Populations at Bough Beech 1969-71 to 2005-7 by Chas Langton

The Leicestershire and Rutland Bird Report 2005
- Review of the year by Rob Fray
- Leicestershire and Rutland Wetland Bird Survey counts Rob Fray
- The arrival and departure of summer migants by Rob Fray
- Long-billed Dowitcher - new to county list by Steve Lister
- Visible migration at Deans Lane in autumn 2005 by Steve Lister
- Waxwings in Leicestershire and Rutland in 2005 by Rob Fray

Lincolnshire Rare and Scarce Bird report 1997-1999
- Summary of rare and scarce birds in Lincolnshire, reviews for 1997, 1998, 1999 by Steve Keightley
- Selected systematic list 1997-1999 by J Eastmead et al
- Accounts of Lincolnshire rarities 1997-1999
- Whistling Swan by Kevin Durose
- Franklin's Gull by Kevin Durose
- River Warbler by Kevin Durose
- Little Swift by Graham Catley
- Red flanked Bluetail by Kevin Durose

London Bird Report 2004
- Ringing report by Roger Taylor
- Breeding bird survey by Ian Woodward
- House Sparrow monitoring 1995-2003 by Helen Baker
- Meadow Pipits at Walton Heath by Alan Prowse

The Manx bird Report for 2005 by Pat Cullen
- Red Grouse in the Isle of Man 2005 by Bruce Walker
- Early and late dates of migrants in 2005 by Allen S. Moore
- Choughs in the Isle of Man 2005 by Allen S. Moore
- 2004 - a very good year for Choughs in the Isle of Man by Allen S. Moore
- Welsh Choughs in the Isle of Man by Allen S. Moore
- Report of the Manx Ringing Group 1997-2005 by Kevin Scott

Norfolk Bird Report 2006
- The Rook/Jackdaw roost at Buckenham Carrs by Mark Cocker

- Population explosion of nesting gulls in Great Yarmouth by Peter Allan
- First recorded roof-nesting of Common Terns in Norfolk by C Dye
- An interesting Pied Flycatcher on Blakeney Point by Mick Fiszer and Keith Dye
- Rose-breasted Grosbeak at Holme - addition to the Norfolk list by Jed Andrews

North East Scotland Bird Report 2005
- Black Grouse in NE Scotland in 2005 by I Francis and A Pout
- Barrow's Goldeneye at Meikle Loch - the first record for NE Scotland by P Shepard
- Bonaparte's Gull at Peterhead - a first for NE Scotland by A Thiel
- Belted Kingfisher in Aberdeen - the first Scottish record by K Landsman

Northern Ireland Bird Report 2003-4
- Little Shearwater at Ramore Head by Anthony McGeehan
- Polygamy - A new phase in Hen Harrier ecology by Don Scott

Birds in Northumbria 2005
- Franklin's Gull at Woodhorn by Jimmy Steele
- Chimney Swift at Holt Island by Michael Frankis
- Wetland bird survey 2005 by Steve Holliday et al
- Breeding bird survey report 2003-5 by Tom and Muriel Cadwallender
- Historical bird notes from Seaton sluice to Tynemouth by Peter Tapsell
- Rare birds in Northumberland by Andy Mould

Orkney Bird Report 2006
- Ringing report 2006 by Jim Williams
- North Ronaldsay Bird Observatory report 2006 by Alison Duncan
- Breeding Red-breasted Mergansers by Chris Booth
- Red-throated Diver survey 2006 by Stuart J Williams
- Hen Harriers in Orkney 2002-6 by Jim Williams
- The North Ronaldsay seawatch on Aug 31 by Bob Simpson

The Sussex Bird Report no.58 - 2005
- The Sussex Ringing Report for 2005 by RDM Edgar and S McKenaie
- Ivory Gulls in Sussex by RJ Fairbank
- Diseases of Garden Birds by RT Pepper
- The 2004/5 Waxwing invasion by A.Thomas
- Expansion of the Breeding Bird Survey in Sussex by Dr H. Crabtree
- Gull-billed Tern Lingering on the Sussex Coast, Summer 2005 by CW Melgar
- A Review of the Results of the WeBs in Sussex by Dr JA Newnham et al.

Hobby 2005 (Wiltshire OS)
- Species new to Wiltshire - Red-rumped Swallow at Corsham Lake
- Porton Down breeding bird survey 2005
- Salisbury Plain breeding bird survey 2005
- Stonehenge World Heritage Site breeding bird survey 2005
- Wiltshire Yellow Wagtail survey 2004

NATIONAL DIRECTORY

White-tailed Eagle by David Cromack

ARMY ORNITHOLOGICAL SOCIETY (1960; 200).

Open to serving and retired MOD employees who have an interest in their local MOD estate. Activities include field meetings, expeditions, the preparation of checklists of birds on Ministry of Defence property, conservation advice and an annual bird count. Annual journal *Adjutant.*

Contact: The Secretary, Army Ornithological Society, JAMES Project Team, Battlesbury Brks, Warminster BA12 9DT. 01985 223 682; e-mail: secretary@aos-uk.com www.aos-uk.com

ASSOCIATION FOR THE PROTECTION OF RURAL SCOTLAND (1926).

Works to protect Scotland's countryside from unnecessary or inappropriate development, recognising the needs of those who live and work there and the necessity of reconciling these with the sometimes competing requirements of recreational use.

Contact: Association for the Protection Rural Scotland, Gladstone's Land, 3rd Floor, 483 Lawnmarket, Edinburgh EH1 2NT. 0131 225 7012; e-mail: info@ruralscotland.org www.ruralscotland.org

ASSOCIATION OF COUNTY RECORDERS AND EDITORS (1993; 120).

The basic aim of ACRE is to promote best practice in the business of producing county bird reports, in the work of Recorders and in problems arising in managing record systems and archives. Organises periodic conferences and publishes newsACRE.

Contact: The Secretary, Association of County Recorders & Editors, e-mail: judith@gmbirds.freeserve.co.uk

BARN OWL TRUST (1988)

Registered charity. Aims to conserve the Barn Owl and its environment through conservation, education, research and information. Free leaflets on all aspects of Barn Owl conservation. Educational material inc. video and resource pack. Book `Barn Owls on Site', a guide for planners and developers. Works with and advises landowners, farmers, planners, countryside bodies and others to promote a brighter future for Britain's Barn Owls. Currently providing training for ecological consultants via a one-day training course, `Barn Owl Ecology, Surveys and Signs'. Open to phone calls Mon-Fri (9.00-5.00). Send SAE for information.

Contact: Barn Owl Trust, Waterleat, Ashburton, Devon TQ13 7HU. 01364 653 026; e-mail: info@barnowltrust.org.uk www.barnowltrust.org.uk

BIRD OBSERVATORIES COUNCIL (1970).

Objectives are to provide a forum for establishing closer links and co-operation between individual autonomous observatories and to help co-ordinate the work carried out by them. All accredited bird observatories affiliated to the Council undertake a ringing programme and provide ringing experience to those interested, most also provide accommodation for visiting birdwatchers.

Contact: Peter Howlett, Bird Observatories Council, c/o Dept of Biodiversity, National Museum Wales, Cardiff CF10 3NP. 0292 057 3233; (Fax)0292 023 9009; e-mail: info@birdobscouncil.org.uk www.birdobscouncil.org.uk

BIRD STAMP SOCIETY (1986; 220).

Quarterly journal Flight contains philatelic and ornithological articles. Lists all new issues and identifies species. Runs a quarterly Postal Auction; number of lots range from 400 to 800 per auction. UK subs £14 per annum from 1st August.

Contact: Mrs R Bradley, Bird Stamp Society, 31 Park View, Crossway Green, Chepstow NP16 5NA. 01291 625 412; e-mail: bradley666@lycos.co.uk www.bird-stamps.org

BIRDWATCH IRELAND (1968; 10,000).

The trading name of the Irish Wildbird Conservancy, a voluntary body founded in 1968 by the amalgamation of the Irish Society for the Protection of Birds, the Irish Wildfowl Conservancy and the Irish Ornithologists' Club. Now the BirdLife International partner in Ireland with 21 voluntary branches. Conservation policy is based on formal research and surveys of birds and their habitats. Owns or manages an increasing number of reserves to protect threatened species and habitats. Publishes Wings quarterly and Irish Birds annually, in addition to annual project reports and survey results.

Contact: BirdWatch Ireland, PO Box 12, Greystones, Co. Wicklow, Ireland. +353 (0)1 2819 878; (Fax)+353 (0)1 2819 763; e-mail: info@birdwatchireland.org www.birdwatchireland.ie

BRITISH BIRDS RARITIES COMMITTEE (1959).

The Committee adjudicates records of species of rare occurrence in Britain (marked `R' in the Log

Charts). Its annual report, which is published in British Birds. The BBRC also assesses records from the Channel Islands. In the case of rarities trapped for ringing, records should be sent to the Ringing Office of the British Trust for Ornithology, who will in turn forward them to the BBRC.
Contact: Mr N Hudson, Hon Secretary, British Birds Rarities Committee, Post Office Flat, Hugh Street, St Mary's, Isles of Scilly TR21 0JE TR21 0JE. e-mail: secretary@bbrc.org.uk
www.bbrc.org.uk

BRITISH DRAGONFLY SOCIETY 1983; 1604.
The BDS aims to promote the conservation and study of dragonflies. Members receive two issues of Dragonfly News and BDS Journal each year in spring and autumn. There are countrywide field trips, an annual members day and training is available on aspects of dragonfly ecology.
Contact: Mr H Curry, Hon Secretary, British Dragonfly Society, 23 Bowker Way, Whittlesey, Cambs PE7 1PY.
e-mail: bdssecretary@dragonflysoc.org.uk
www.dragonflysoc.org.uk

BRITISH FALCONERS' CLUB (1927; 1200).
Largest falconry club in Europe, with regional branches. Its aim is to encourage responsible falconers and conserve birds of prey by breeding, holding educational meetings and providing facilities, guidance and advice to those wishing to take up the sport. Publishes The Falconer annually and newsletter twice yearly.
Contact: British Falconers' Club, Westfield, Meeting Hill, Worstead, North Walsham, Norfolk NR28 9LS. 01692 404 057;
e-mail: admin@britishfalconersclub.co.uk
www.britishfalconersclub.co.uk

BRITISH MUSEUM (NAT HIST) see Walter Rothschild Zoological Museum

BRITISH ORNITHOLOGISTS' CLUB (1892; 450).
A registered charity, the Club's objects are `the promotion of scientific discussion between members of the BOU, and others interested in ornithology, and to facilitate the publication of scientific information in connection with ornithology'. The Club maintains a special interest in avian systematics, taxonomy and distribution. About eight dinner meetings are held each year. Publishes the Bulletin of the British Ornithologists' Club quarterly, also (since 1992) a continuing series of occasional publications.
Contact: BOC Office, British Ornithologists' Club, PO Box 417, Peterborough, PE7 3FX. (Tel/Fax) 01733 844 820; e-mail: boc.admin@bou.org.uk
www.boc-online.org

BRITISH ORNITHOLOGISTS' UNION (1858; 1,250).
Founded by Professor Alfred Newton FRS, the BOU is one of the world's oldest and most respected ornithological societies and it celebrates its 150th anniversary during 2008. It aims to promote ornithology within the scientific and birdwatching communities, both in Britain and around the world. This is largely achieved by the publication of its quarterly international journal, Ibis (1859-), featuring  work at the cutting edge of our understanding of the world's birdlife. It also publishes an ongoing series of country/island group 'checklists' (22 titles to date – see BOU website for details). It operates an active programme of meetings, seminars and conferences to inform birdwatchers and ornithologists about ornithological work being undertaken around the world. This can include research projects that have received financial assistance from the BOU's ongoing programme of Ornithological Research Grants. Copies of journals and offprints received and books reviewed in Ibis are held as part of the Alexander Library in the Zoology Department of the University of Oxford (see Edward Grey Institute). The BOU Records Committee maintains the official British List (see below).
Contact: Steve Dudley, British Ornithologists' Union, PO Box 417, Peterborough, PE7 3FX. (Tel/Fax) 01733 844 820; e-mail: bou@bou.org.uk
www.ibis.ac.uk and www.bouproc.net

BRITISH ORNITHOLOGISTS' UNION RECORDS COMMITTEE .
The BOURC is a standing committee of the British Ornithologists' Union. Its function is to maintain the British List, the official list of birds recorded in Great Britain. The up-to-date list can be viewed on the BOU website. Where vagrants are involved it is concerned only with those which relate to potential additions to the British List (ie first records). In this it differs from the British Birds Rarities Committee (qv). In maintaining the British List, it also differs from the BBRC in that it examines, where necessary, important pre-1950 records, monitors introduced species for possible admission to or deletion from the List, and reviews taxonomy and nomenclature relating to the List. BOURC reports are published in Ibis and are also available via the BOU website. Decisions contained in these reports which affect the List are also announced direct to the birdwatching public via egroups, web forums and the popular birdwatching press.
Contact: Steve Dudley, BOURC, PO Box 417, Peterborough, PE7 3FX. (Tel/Fax) 01733 844 820; e-mail: bourc@bou.org www.bou.org.uk

BRITISH TRUST FOR ORNITHOLOGY (1933; 13,200).
A registered charity governed by an elected
Council, it has a rapidly growing membership and
enjoys the support of a large number of county
and local birdwatching
clubs and societies
through the BTO/Bird
Clubs Partnership.

Its aims are: `To
promote and
encourage the wider
understanding,
appreciation and
conservation of birds through scientific studies
using the combined skills and enthusiasm of its
members, other birdwatchers and staff.'

Through the fieldwork of its members and
other birdwatchers, the BTO is responsible for
the majority of the monitoring of British birds,
British bird population and their habitats. BTO
surveys include the National Ringing Scheme,
the Nest Record Scheme, the Breeding Bird
Survey (in collaboration with JNCC and RSPB),
and the Waterways Breeding Bird Survey --- all
contributing to an integrated programme of
population monitoring.

The BTO also runs projects on the birds of
farmland and woodland, also (in collaboration with
WWT, RSPB and JNCC) the Wetland Bird Survey,
in particular Low Tide Counts. Garden BirdWatch,
which started in 1995, now has more than 14,000
participants. The Trust has 140 voluntary regional
representatives (see County Directory) who
organise fieldworkers for the BTO's programme of
national surveys in which members participate.

The results of these co-operative efforts are
communicated to government departments, local
authorities, industry and conservation bodies for
effective action. For details of current activities see
National Projects.

Members receive *BTO News* six times a year and
have the option of subscribing to the thrice-yearly
journal, *Bird Study* and twice yearly *Ringing &
Migration*. Local meetings are held in conjunction
with bird clubs and societies; there are regional
and national birdwatchers' conferences, and
specialist courses in bird identification and
modern censusing techniques. Grants are made
for research, and members have the use of a
lending and reference library at Thetford and the
Alexander Library at the Edward Grey Institute of
Field Ornithology (qv).
Contact: British Trust for OrnithologyThe
Nunnery, Thetford, Norfolk IP24 2PU. 01842 750
050; (Fax)01842 750 030; e-mail: info@bto.org
www.bto.org

BTO SCOTLAND (2000; 989).
BTO Scotland is now in its eighth year of
operation. Its main functions are to promote the
work of the BTO in Scotland, to develop wider
coverage for surveys in Scotland, by encouraging
greater participation in BTO survey work by
Scottish birdwatchers, and to develop contract
research income within Scotland. BTO Scotland
ensures that the work the Trust does is not just
related to the priorities of the UK as a whole but
is also focused on the priorities of Scotland, with
a landscape and wildlife so different from the rest
of the UK.
Contact: BTO Scotland, British Trust
for Ornithology, School of Biological and
Environmental Sciences, Cottrell Building,
University of Stirling, Stirling FK9 4LA. 01786 466
560 (Fax)01786 466 561;
e-mail: scot.info@bto.org www.bto.org

BRITISH WATERFOWL ASSOCIATION
The BWA is an association of enthusiasts
interested in keeping, breeding and conserving
all types of waterfowl, including wildfowl and
domestic ducks and geese. It is a registered
charity, without trade
affiliations, dedicated
to educating the public
about waterfowl and the
need for conservation
as well as to raising the
standards of keeping and
breeding ducks, geese
and swans in captivity.
Contact: Mrs Sue
Schubert, British
Waterfowl Association,
PO Box 163, Oxted, RH8 0WP. 01892 740212;
e-mail: Info@waterfowl.org.uk
www.waterfowl.org.uk

BRITISH WILDLIFE REHABILITATION COUNCIL (1987).
Its aim is to promote the care and rehabilitation
of wildlife casualties through the exchange of
information between people such as rehabilitators,
zoologists and veterinary surgeons who are active
in this field. Organises an annual symposium
or workshop. Publishes a regular newsletter.
Supported by many national bodies including the
Zoological Society of London, the British Veterinary
Zoological Society, the RSPCA, the SSPCA, and the
Vincent Wildlife Trust.
Contact: To make a contribution - Janet Peto,
BWRC, PO Box 8686, Grantham, Lincolnshire NG31
0AG. www.bwrc.org.uk

BTCV (formerly British Trust for Conservation Volunteers)
(1959).
It's mission is to create a more sustainable future

NATIONAL ORGANISATIONS

by inspiring people and improving places. Between 2004 and 2008 it aims to enrich the lives of one million people, through involvement with BTCV, through volunteering opportunities, employment, improved health, and life skills development; to Improve the biodiversity and local environment of 20,000 places and to support active citizenship in 5,000 community based groups. BTCV is governed by a board of 6 volunteer trustees elected by the charity membership and currently supports 140,000 volunteers to take practical action to improve their urban and rural environments. Publishes a quarterly magazine, *Roots*, a series of practical handbooks and a wide range of other publications. Further information and a list of local offices is available from the above address.
Contact: BTCV, Sedum House, Mallard Way, Potteric Carr, Doncaster DN4 8DB. 01302 388 883; e-mail: Information@btcv.org.uk
www.btcv.org.uk

BTCV CYMRU
The Conservation Centre, BTCV Cymru, Forest Farm Road, Whitchurch, Cardiff, CF14 7JJ. 029 2052 0990; Fax: 029 2052 2181;
e-mail: wales@btcv.org.ukwww.btcvcymru.org

BTCV SCOTLAND
Runs 7-14 day `Action Breaks' in Scotland during which participants undertake conservation projects; weekend training courses in environmental skills; midweek projects in Edinburgh, Glasgow, Aberdeen, Stirling and Inverness.
Contact: BTCV Scotland, Balallan House, 24 Allan Park, Stirling FK8 2QG. 01786 479697; (Fax)01786 465359; e-mail: scotland@btcv.org.uk
www2.btcv.org.uk/display/btcv_scotland

BTCV CONSERVATION VOLUNTEERS NORTHERN IRELAND
(1983).
Conservation Volunteers Northern Ireland, Beech House, 159 Ravenhill Road, , BELFAST BT6 0BP. 028 9064 5169; (Fax)028 9064 4409;
e-mail: CVNI@btcv.org.uk
www.cvni.org

CAMPAIGN FOR THE PROTECTION OF RURAL WALES (1928; 2,800)
Its aims are to help the conservation and enhancement of the landscape, environment and amenities of the countryside, towns and villages of rural Wales and to form and educate opinion to ensure the promotion of its objectives. It recognises the importance of the indigenous cultures of rural Wales and gives advice and information upon matters affecting protection, conservation and improvement of the visual environment.

Contact: Peter Ogden, Director, CPRW, Tŷ Gwyn, 31 High Street, Welshpool, Powys SY21 7YD. 01938 552 525/556 212; (Fax)552 741; www.cprw.org.uk

CENTRE FOR ECOLOGY & HYDROLOGY (CEH)
The work of the CEH, a component body of the Natural Environment Research Council, includes a range of ornithological research, covering population studies, habitat management and work on the effects of pollution. The CEH has a long-term programme to monitor pesticide and pollutant residues in the corpses of predatory birds sent in by birdwatchers, and carries out detailed studies on affected species. The Biological Records Centre (BRC), which Is part of the CEH, Is responsible for the national biological data bank on plant and animal distributions (except birds).
Contact: Centre for Ecology & Hydrology, Maclean Building, Crowmarsh Gifford, Wallingford, Oxfordshire OX10 8BB. 01491 692 560.
www.ceh.ac.uk

COUNTRY LAND AND BUSINESS ASSOCIATION (1907; 36,000).
The CLA is at the heart of rural life and is the voice of the countryside for England and Wales, campaigning on issues which directly affect those who live and work in rural communities. Its members together manage 50% of the countryside. CLA members range from some of the largest landowners, with interests in forest, moorland, water and agriculture, to some of the smallest with little more than a paddock or garden.
Contact: Country Land and Business Association, 16 Belgrave Square, London, SW1X 8PQ. 020 7235 0511;(Fax) 020 7235 4696;
e-mail: mail@cla.org.uk www.cla.org.uk

COUNTRYSIDE AGENCY
This is now part of Natural England, please see entry later in this section.

COUNTRYSIDE COUNCIL FOR WALES
The Government's statutory adviser on wildlife, countryside and maritime conservation matters in Wales. It is the executive authority for the conservation of habitats and wildlife. Through partners, CCW promotes protection of landscape, opportunities for enjoyment, and support of those who live, work in, and manage the countryside. It enables thesepartners, including local authorities, voluntary organisations and interested individuals, to pursue countryside management projects through grant aid. CCW is accountable to the National Assembly for Wales which appoints its

NATIONAL ORGANISATIONS

Council members and provides its annual grant-in-aid.

Contact: Countryside Council for Wales, Maes-y-Ffynnon, Penrhosgarnedd, Bangor, Gwynedd LL57 2DL. 01248 385 500; (Fax)01248 355 782; (Enquiry unit) 0845 1306229; e-mail: enquiries@ccw.gov.uk www.ccw.gov.uk

CPRE (formerly Council for the Protection of Rural England) (1926; 60,000).

Patron HM The Queen. CPRE now has 43 county branches and 200 local groups. We are people who care passionately about our countryside and campaign for it to be protected and enhanced for the benefit of everyone. Membership open to all.

Contact: CPRE, CPRE National Office, 128 Southwark Street, London SE1 0SW. 020 7981 2800; (fax)020 7981 2899; e-mail: info@cpre.org.uk www.cpre.org.uk

DEPARTMENT OF THE ENVIRONMENT FOR NORTHERN IRELAND

Responsible for the declaration and management of National Nature Reserves, the declaration of Areas of Special Scientific Interest, the administration of Wildlife Refuges, the classification of Special Protection Areas under the EC Birds Directive, the designation of Special Areas of Conservation under the EC Habitats Directive and the designation of Ramsar sites under the Ramsar Convention. It administers the Nature Conservation and Amenity Lands (Northern Ireland) Order 1985, the Wildlife (Northern Ireland) Order 1985, the Game Acts and the Conservation (Natural Habitats, etc) Regulations (NI) 1995 and the Environment (Northern Ireland) Order 2002.

Contact: Environment and Heritage Service, Klondyke Building, Cromac Avenue, Gasworks Business Park, Lower Ormeau Road, Belfast BT7 2JA., Department of the Environment (NI), (028) 9056 9515; (polution hotline; 0800 807 060); www.ehsni.gov.uk

DISABLED BIRDER'S ASSOCIATION (2000;700).

The DBA is a registered charity and international movement, which aims to promote access to reserves and other birding places and to a range of services, so that people with different needs can follow the birding obsession as freely as able-bodied people. Membership is currently free and open to all, either disabled or able-bodied. We are keen for new members to help give a strong voice to get our message across to those who own and manage nature reserves to ensure that they think access when they are planning and improving their facilities. We are also seeking to influence those

who provide birdwatching services and equipment. The DBA also runs overseas trips. Chairman, Bo Beolens.

Contact: The Membership Secretary, Margaret Read MBE, Disabled Birder's Association, 121 Lavernock Road, Pengarth, Vale of Glamorgan CF64 3QG. e-mail: bo@fatbirder.com www.disabledbirdersassociation.co.uk

EDWARD GREY INSTITUTE OF FIELD ORNITHOLOGY (1938).

The EGI takes its name from Edward Grey, first Viscount Grey of Fallodon, a life-long lover of birds and former Chancellor of the University of Oxford, who gave his support to an appeal for its foundation capital.

The Institute now has a permanent research staff; it usually houses some 12-15 research students, two or three senior visitors and post-doctoral research workers. The EGI also houses Prof Sir John Krebs's Ecology & Behaviour Group, which studies the ecology, demography and conservation of declining farmland birds. Field research is carried out mainly in Wytham Woods near Oxford and on the island of Skomer in West Wales.

In addition there are laboratory facilities and aviary space for experimental work. The Institute houses the Alexander Library, one of the largest collections of 20th century material on birds in the world. The library is supported by the British Ornithologists Union who provides much of the material. Included in its manuscript collections are diaries, notebooks and papers of ornithologists. It also houses the British Falconers Club library.

The Library is open to members of the BOU and the Oxford Ornithological Society; other bona fide ornithologists may use the library by prior arrangement.

Contact: Clare Harvey, PA to Prof. Sheldon, Edward Grey Institute, Department of Zoology, South Parks Road, Oxford OX1 3PS. 01865 271274, Alexander Library 01865 271143; e-mail: lynne.bradley@zoology.oxford.ac.uk; e-mail:clare.rowsell@zoo.ox.ac.ukweb-site, EGI: http://egizoosrv.zoo.ox.ac.uk/EGI/EGIhome. htm web-site library http://users.ox.ac.uk/~zoolib/

ENVIRONMENT AGENCY (THE)

A non-departmental body that aims to protect and improve the environment and to contribute towards the delivery of sustainable developmentthrough the integrated management

NATIONAL ORGANISATIONS

of air, land and water. Functions include pollution prevention and control, waste minimisation,management of water resources, flood defence, improvement of salmon and freshwater fisheries, conservation of aquatic species,navigation and use of inland and coastal waters for recreation. Sponsored by the Department of the Environment, Transport and the Regions, MAFF and the Welsh Office.
Contact: Environment Agency, Rio House, Waterside Drive, Aztec West, Almondsbury, Bristol BS32 4UD. 01454 624 400; (Fax)01454 624 409; www.environment-agency.gov.uk

Regional Offices
Anglian. Kingfisher House, Goldhay Way, Orton Goldhay, Peterborough PE2 5ZR. 01733 371 811; fax 01733 231 840.

North East. Rivers House, 21 Park Square South, Leeds LS1 2QG. 0113 244 0191; fax 0113 246 1889.

North West. Richard Fairclough House, Knutsford Road, Warrington WA4 1HG. 01925 653 999; fax 01925 415 961.

Midlands. Sapphire East, 550 Streetsbrook Road, Solihull B91 1QT. 0121 711 2324; fax 0121 711 5824.

Southern. Guildbourne House, Chatsworth Road, Worthing, W Sussex BN11 1LD. 01903 832 000; fax 01903 821 832.

South West. Manley House, Kestrel Way, Exeter EX2 7LQ. 01392 444 000; fax 01392 444 238.

Thames. Kings Meadow House, Kings Meadow Road, Reading RG1 8DQ. 0118 953 5000; fax 0118 950 0388.

Wales. Rivers House, St Mellons Business Park, St Mellons, Cardiff CF3 0EY. 029 2077 0088; fax 029 2079 8555.

FARMING AND WILDLIFE ADVISORY GROUP (FWAG)
(1969).
An independent UK registered charity led by farmers and supported by government and leading countryside organisations. Its aim is to unite farming and forestry with wildlife and landscape conservation. Active in most UK counties.

There are 120 Farm Conservation Advisers who give practical advice to farmers and landowners to help them integrate environmental objectives with commercial farming practices.

Contact:
English Head Office, FWAG, National Agricultural Centre, Stoneleigh, Kenilworth, Warwickshire CV8 2RX. 02476 696 699;(Fax) 02476 696 699; e-mail: info@fwag.org.uk   www.fwag.org.uk

Northern Ireland, FWAG, National Agricultural Centre, 46b Rainey Street, Magherafelt, Co. Derry BT45 5AH. 028 7930 0606; (fax)028 7930 0599; e-mail: n.ireland@fwag.org.uk

Scottish Head Office, FWAG Scotland, Algo Business Centre, Glenearn Road, Perth PH2 ONJ. 01738 450 500; (Fax) 01738 450 495; e-mail: steven.hunt@fwag.org.uk

Wales Head Office. FWAG Cymru, Ffordd Arran, Dolgellau, Gwynedd LL40 1LW. 01341 421 456; (Fax) 01341 422 757; e-mail: cymru@fwag.org.

FIELD STUDIES COUNCIL (1943).
Manages Centres where students from schools, universities and colleges of education, as well as individuals of all ages, could stay and study various aspects of the environment under expert guidance. The courses include many for birdwatchers, providing opportunities to study birdlife on coasts, estuaries, mountains and islands. There are some courses demonstrating bird ringing and others for members of the BTO. The length of the courses varies: from a weekend up to seven days' duration. Research workers and naturalists wishing to use the records and resources are welcome.

Contact: Field Studies Council, Preston Montford, Montford Bridge, Shrewsbury SY4 1HW. 01743 852 100; (Fax)01743 852 101; e-mail: fsc.headoffice@field-studies-council.org www.field-studies-council.org

Centres:
Blencathra Field Centre, Threlkeld, Keswick, Cumbria CA12 4SG, 01768 77 9601; e-mail: enquiries.bl@field-studies-council.org

Castle Head Field Centre, Grange-over-Sands, Cumbria LA11 6QT, 0845 330 7364;

e-mail: enquiries.ch@field-studies-council.org

Dale Fort Field Centre, Haverfordwest, Pembs SA62 3RD, 0845 330 7365; e-mail: enquiries.df@field-studies-council.org

Epping Forest Field Centre, High Beach, Loughton, Essex, IG10 4AF, 020 8502 8500; e-mail: enquiries.ef@field-studies-council.org

Flatford Mill Field Centre, East Bergholt, Suffolk, CO7 6UL, 0845 330 7368;
e-mail: enquiries.fm@field-studies-council.org

Derrygonnelly Field Centre, Tir Navar, Creamery St, Derrygonnelly, Co Fermanagh, BT93 6HW. 028 686 41673;
e-mail: enquiries.dg.@field-studies-council.org

Juniper Hall Field Centre, Dorking, Surrey, RH5 6DA, 0845 458 3507;
e-mail: enquiries.jh@field-studies-council.org

Kindrogan Field Centre, Enochdhu, Blairgowrie, Perthshire PH10 7PG. 01250 870 150;
e-mail: admin.kd@field-studies-council.org

Margam Park Field Centre, Port Talbot SA13 2TJ. 01639 8956 36;
e-mail: margam_sustainable_centre@hotmail.com

Malham Tarn Field Centre, Settle, N Yorks, BD24 9PU, 01729 830 331;
e-mail: fsc.malham@ukonline.co.uk

Nettlecombe Court, The Leonard Wills Field Centre, Williton, Taunton, Somerset, TA4 4HT, 01984 640 320; e-mail: enquiries.nc@field-studies-council.org

Orielton Field Centre, Pembroke, Pembs,SA71 5EZ, 0845 330 7372;
e-mail: enquiries.or@field-studies-council.org

Preston Montford Field Centre, Montford Bridge, Shrewsbury, SY4 1DX, 0845 330 7378;
e-mail: enquiries.pm@field-studies-council.org

Rhyd-y-creuau, the Drapers' Field Centre Betws-y-coed, Conwy, LL24 0HB, 01690 710 494;
e-mail: enquiries.rc@field-studies-council.org

Slapton Ley Field Centre, Slapton, Kingsbridge, Devon, TQ7 2QP, 01548 580 466;
e-mail: enquiries.sl@field-studies-council.org

FLIGHTLINE
Northern Ireland's daily bird news service. Run under the auspices of the Northern Ireland Birdwatchers' Association (qv).
Contact: George Gordon, Flightline, 2 Brooklyn Avenue, Bangor, Co Down BT20 5RB. 028 9146 7408; e-mail: gordon@ballyholme2.freeserve.co.uk

FORESTRY COMMISSION
The Forestry Commission of Great Britain is the government department responsible for the protection and expansion of Britain's forests and woodlands. The organisation is run from national offices in England, Wales and Scotland, working to targets set by Commissioners and Ministers in each of the three countries. Its objectives are to protect Britain's forests and resources, conserve and improve the biodiversity, landscape and cultural heritage of forests and woodlands, develop opportunities for woodland recreation and increase public understanding and community participation in forestry.
Contact: Forestry Commission, 231 Corstorphine Road, Edinburgh, EH12 7AT. 0131 334 0303; (Fax)0131 334 4473; www.forestry.gov.uk

FRIENDS OF THE EARTH (1971; 100,000).
The largest international network of environmental groups in the world, represented in 68 countries. It is one of the leading environmental pressure groups in the UK. It has a unique network of campaigning local groups, working in 200 communities in England, Wales and Northern Ireland. It is largely funded by supporters with more than 90% of income coming from individual donations, the rest from special fundraising events, grants and trading.
Contact: Friends of the Earth, 26-28 Underwood Street, London, N1 7JQ. 020 7490 1555; (Fax)020 7490 0881; www.foe.co.uk
e-mail: info@foe.co.uk

GAME CONSERVANCY TRUST (1933; 22,000).
A registered charity which researches the conservation of game and other wildlife in the British countryside. More than 60 scientists are engaged in detailed work on insects, pesticides, birds (30 species inc. raptors) mammals (inc. foxes), and habitats. The results are used to advise government, landowners, farmers and conservationists on practical management techniques which will benefit game species, their habitats, and wildlife. Each June an Annual Review of 100 pages lists about 50 papers published in the peer-reviewed scientific press.
Contact: Game Conservancy Trust, Fordingbridge, Hampshire, SP6 1EF. 01425 652 381; (Fax)01425 655 848; e-mail: info@gct.org.uk www.gct.org.uk

GAY BIRDERS CLUB (1995; 300+).
A voluntary society for lesbian, gay and bisexual birdwatchers, their friends and supporters, over the age of consent, in the UK and worldwide. The club has 3-400 members and a network of regional contacts. It organises day trips, weekends and longer events at notable birding locations in the UK and abroad; about 200+ events in a year. Members receive a quarterly newletter with details of all events. There is a Grand Get-Together every 18 months. Membership £12 waged and £5 unwaged.

NATIONAL ORGANISATIONS

Contact: Gay Birders Club, GeeBeeCee, BCM-Mono, London WC1N 3XX.
e-mail: contact@gbc-online.org.uk
www.gbc-online.org.uk

GOLDEN ORIOLE GROUP (1987; 15). .
Organises censuses of breeding Golden Orioles in parts of Cambridgeshire, Norfolk and Suffolk. Maintains contact with a network of individuals in other parts of the country where Orioles may or do breed. Studies breeding biology, habitat and food requirements of the species.
Contact: Jake Allsop, Golden Oriole Group, 5 Bury Lane, Haddenham, Ely, Cambs CB6 3PR. 01353 740 540; www.goldenoriolegroup.org.uk

HAWK AND OWL TRUST (1969).
Registered charity dedicated to the conservation and appreciation of wild birds of prey and their habitats. Publishes a newsletter *Peregrine* and educational materials for all ages.The Trust achieves its major aim of creating and enhancing nesting, roosting and feeding habitats for birds of prey through projects which involve practical research, creative conservation and education, both on its own reserves and in partnership with landowners, farmers and others. Members are invited to take part in fieldwork, population studies, surveys, etc. Studies of Kestrel and Little, Long-eared and Tawny Owls are in progress, as well as annual monitoring of Hen Harrier winter roosts.
The Trust manages three main reserves: Sculthorpe Moor Community Nature Reserve, Norfolk; Shapwick Moor on the Somerset Levels; and Fylingdales Moor conservation area on the North York Moors. Its Sculthorpe reserve near Fakenham, Norfolk and National Conservation and Education Centre at Chiltern Open Air Museum near Chalfont St Giles, Buckinghamshire, offer

 schools and other groups cross-curricular environmental activities
Contact: Hawk and Owl Trust, PO Box 100, Taunton TA4 2WX. Tel: 0870 990 3889. e-mail: enquiries@hawkandowl.org Website: www.hawkandowl.org

JOINT NATURE CONSERVATION COMMITTEE (1990).
A committee of the three country agencies (English Nature, Scottish Natural Heritage, and the Countryside Council for Wales), together with independent members and representatives from Northern Ireland and the Countryside Agency. It is supported by specialist staff. Its statutory responsibilities include the establishment of common standards for monitoring, the analysis of information and research; advising Ministers on the development and implementation of policies for or affecting nature conservation; the provision of advice and the dissemination of knowledge to any persons about nature conservation; and the undertaking and commissioning of research relevant to these functions. JNCC additionally has the UK responsibility for relevant European and wider international matters. The Species Team, located at the HQ address above, is responsible for terrestrial bird conservation.
Contact: Joint Nature Conservation Committee, Monkstone House, City Road, Peterborough PE1 1JY. 01733 562 626; (Fax)01733 555 948; e-mail: comment@jncc.gov.uk
www.jncc.gov.uk

LINNEAN SOCIETY OF LONDON (1788, 2,000).
Named after Carl Linnaeus, the 18th century Swedish biologist, who created the modern system of scientific biological nomenclature, the Society promotes all aspects of pure and applied biology. It houses Linnaeus's collection of plants, insects and fishes, library and correspondence. The Society has a major reference library of some 100,000 volumes. Publishes the Biological, Botanical and Zoological Journals, and the Synopses of the British Fauna.
Contact: Linnean Society of London, Burlington House, Piccadilly, London W1J 0BF. 020 7434 4479; (Fax)020 7287 9364; e-mail: info@linnean.org
www.linnean.org

MANX ORNITHOLOGICAL SOCIETY see County Directory

MANX WILDLIFE TRUST see County Directory

NATIONAL BIRDS OF PREY CENTRE (1967).
Seeks to deliver conservation of birds of prey through captive breeding, rescue and rehabilitation, and research. The Centre is home to some 170 birds of prey and has an active captive breeding programme of many of its residents and also contributes to conservation, rescue, and rehabilitation of the many species brought into the Centre each year. Open all year 1030am-5.30pm (or dusk if earlier). Closed Christmas and Boxing Day.
Contact: National Birds of Prey Centre, Newent, Glos, GL18 1JJ. 0870 990 1992; e-mail: kb@nbpc.org www.nbpc.co.uk

NATIONAL TRUST (1895; 3.1million).
Charity that works for the preservation of places of historic interest or natural beauty in England, Wales and Northern Ireland for ever, for everyone.

They rely on their 3.5 million members, 49,000 volunteers, 500,000 school children and millions of visitors, donors and supporters. The Trust protects and opens to the public more than 300 historic houses and gardens, 49 industrial monuments and mills, plus more than 617,500 acres of land and 700 miles of coast. About 10% of SSSIs and ASSIs in England, Wales and Northern Ireland are wholly or partially owned by the Trust, as are 63 NNRs (e.g. Blakeney Point, Wicken Fen, Murlough and Dinefwr Estate). 33% of Ramsar sites include Trust land as do 45% of SPAs.

Central Office: Heelis, Kemble Drive, Swindon, Wiltshire SN2 2NA. Tel: 01793 817 400; (fax) 01793 817 401.

Enquiries: PO Box 39, Warrington, WA5 7WD. Tel: 0870 458 4000; (fax) 0870 609 0345. e-mail: enquiries@thenationaltrust.org.uk www.nationaltrust.org.uk

Contact: National Trust, PO Box 39, Warrington, WA5 7WD. 0870 458 4000; (Fax)020 8466 6824; e-mail: enquiries@thenationaltrust.org.uk www.nationaltrust.org.uk

NATIONAL TRUST FOR SCOTLAND (1931; 297,000).

An independent charity, its 128 properties open to the public are described in its annual guide.

Contact: National Trust for Scotland, Wemyss House, 28 Charlotte Square, Edinburgh, EH2 4ET. 0844 493 2100; (Fax)0131 243 9301; e-mail: information@nts.org.uk www.nts.org.uk

NATURAL ENGLAND

Natural England has been formed by bringing together English Nature, the landscape, access and recreation elements of the Countryside Agency and the environmental land management functions of the Rural Development Service.

Natural England works for people, places and nature, to enhance biodiversity, landscapes and wildlife in rural, urban, coastal and marine areas; promoting access, recreation and public well-being; and contributing to the way natural resources are managed so that they can be enjoyed now and in the future.

Natural England is working towards the delivery of four strategic outcomes:

- A healthy natural environment: England's natural environment will be conserved and enhanced.

- Enjoyment of the natural environment: more people enjoying, understanding and

acting to improve, the natural environment, more often.

- Sustainable use of the natural environment: the use and management of the natural environment is more sustainable.

A secure environmental future: decisions which collectively secure the future of the natural environment.

Contact: Natural England, Northminster House, Peterborough, PE1 1UA. 0845 600 3078; (Fax)01733 455 103; e-mail: enquiries@naturalengland.org.uk www.naturalengland.org.uk

NATURE PHOTOGRAPHERS' PORTFOLIO (1944).

A society for photographers of wildlife, especially birds. Circulates postal portfolios of prints and transparencies and an on-line folio.

Contact: A Winspear-Cundall, Hon Secretary, Nature Photographers' Portfolio, 8 Gig Bridge Lane, Pershore, Worcs WR10 1NH. 01386 552 103; www.nature-photographers-portfolio.co.uk

NORTHERN IRELAND BIRDWATCHERS' ASSOCIATION (1991; 120).

The NIBA Records Committee, established in 1997, has full responsibility for the assessment of records in N Ireland. NIBA also publishes the Northern Ireland Bird Report.

Contact: Wilton Farrelly, Hon Secretary, Northern Ireland Birdwatchers' Assoc, 24 Cabin Hill Gardens, Knock, Belfast BT5 7AP. 028 9022 5818; e-mail: wilton.farrelly@ntlworld.com

NORTHERN IRELAND ORNITHOLOGISTS' CLUB (1965; 150).

Operates a Tree Sparrow and Barn Owl nestbox scheme and a winter feeding programme for Yellowhammers. Has a regular programme of lectures and field trips for members. Publishes The Harrier quarterly.

Contact: C Gillespie, Northern Ireland Ornithologists Club, 4 Demesne Gate, Saintfield, Co. Down, BT24 7BE. www.nioc.co.uk

NORTH SEA BIRD CLUB (1979; 200).

The stated aims of the Club are to: provide a recreational pursuit for people employed offshore; obtain, collate and analyse observations of all birds seen offshore; produce reports of observations, including an annual report; promote the collection of data on other wildlife offshore. Currently we hold in excess of 100,000 records of birds, cetaceans and insects reported since 1979.

Contact: Andrew Thorpe, The North Sea Bird Club, Ocean Laboratory and Culterty Field Station, University of Aberdeen, Newburgh, Aberdeenshire

AB41 6AA. 01224 274 428. fax: 01224 274 402;
e-mail: nsbc@abdn.ac.uk
www.abdn.ac.uk/nsbc

PEOPLE'S DISPENSARY FOR SICK ANIMALS (1917).
Registered charity. Provides free veterinary
treatment for sick and injured animals whose
owners qualify for this charitable service.
Contact: PDSA, Whitechapel Way, Priorslee,
Telford, Shrops TF2 9PQ. 01952 290 999;
(Fax)01952 291 035; e-mail: pr@pdsa.org.uk
www.pdsa.org.uk

RAPTOR RESCUE, BIRD OF PREY REHABILITATION.
Birds of prey only. Heated hospital units.
Indoor flights, secluded aviaries, hacking
sites, rehabilitation aviaries/flights. Falconry
rehabilitation techniques, foster birds for rearing
young to avoid imprinting. Veterinary support. Reg
charity no. 283733
Contact: Raptor Rescue, Bird of Prey
Rehabilitation, 28 Victoria Road, Great Sankey,
Warrington, WA5 2ST. (National advice line) 0870
241 0609; e-mail: info@raptorrescue.org.uk
www.raptorrescue.org.uk

RARE BIRDS COMMITTEE (1985).
Assesses records of species of rare occurrence
in the Republic of Ireland. Details of records
accepted and rejected are incorporated in the Irish
Bird Report, published annually in Irish Birds. In
the case of rarities trapped for ringing, ringers
in the Republic of Ireland are required to send
their schedules initially to the National Parks and
Wildlife Service, 51 St Stephen's Green, Dublin 2. A
copy is taken before the schedules are sent to the
British Trust for Ornithology.
Contact: Paul Milne, Hon Secretary, Irish Rare
Birds Committee, 100 Dublin Road, Sutton, Dublin
13. +353 (0)1 8325 653;
e-mail: pjmilne@hotmail.com

RARE BREEDING BIRDS PANEL (1973; 7).
An independent body funded by the JNCC and
RSPB. Both bodies are represented on the panel
as are BTO and ACRE. It collects all information
on rare breeding birds in the United Kingdom, so
that changes in status can be monitored as an
aid to present-day conservation and stored for
posterity. Special forms are used (obtainable free
from the secretary and the website) and records

Rare Breeding Birds Panel

should if possible be
submitted via the
county and regional
recorders. Since 1996
the Panel also monitors
breeding by scarcer
non-native species and
seeks records of these in the same way. Annual
report is published in British Birds. For details of
species covered by the Panel see Log Charts and
the websites.
Contact: Mark Holling, Secretary, Rare Breeding
Birds Panel, The Old Orchard, Grange Road, North
Berwick, East Lothian EH39 4QT. 01620 894 037;
e-mail: secretary@rbbp.org.uk
www.rbbp.org.uk

ROYAL AIR FORCE ORNITHOLOGICAL SOCIETY (1965; 295).
RAFOS organises regular field meetings for
members, carries out ornithological census work
on MOD properties and mounts major expeditions
annually to various UK and overseas locations.
Publishes a Newsletter twice a year, a Journal
annually, and reports on its expeditions and
surveys.
Contact: General Secretary, RAFOS, R
e-mail: rafos_secretary@hotmail.com
www.rafos.org.uk

ROYAL NAVAL BIRDWATCHING SOCIETY (1946; 167 full and 93 associate members and library).
Covers all main ocean routes, the Society has a
system for reporting the positions and identity
of seabirds and landbirds at sea by means of
standard sea report forms. Maintains an extensive
world wide sea bird database. Members are
encouraged to photograph birds while at sea and
a library of photographs and
slides is maintained. Publishes
a Bulletin and an annual report
entitled The Sea Swallow.
The Simpson Scholarship
provides assistance to embryonic
ornithologists for studies
regarding seabirds and landbirds
at sea.
Contact: Cdr FS Ward RN,
Gen Secretary, Royal Naval
Birdwatching Society, 16 Cutlers
Lane, Stubbington, Fareham,
Hants PO14 2JN. +44 1329 665931;
e-mail: francisward@btopenworld.com
www.rnbws.org.uk

ROYAL PIGEON RACING ASSOCIATION (1897; 39,000).
Exists to promote the sport of pigeon racing and
controls pigeon racing within the Association.
Organises liberation sites, issues rings, calculates
distances between liberation sites and home lofts,
and assists in the return of strays. May be able to
assist in identifying owners of ringed birds caught
or found.
Contact: General Manager, RPRA, Royal Pigeon
Racing Association, The Reddings, Cheltenham,

313

GL51 6RN. 01452 713529;
e-mail: gm@rpra.org or strays@rpra.org
www.rpra.org

ROYAL SOCIETY FOR THE PREVENTION OF CRUELTY TO ANIMALS (1824; 43,690).

In addition to its animal centres, the Society also runs a woodland study centre and nature reserve at Mallydams Wood in East Sussex and specialist wildlife rehabilitation centres at West Hatch, Taunton, Somerset TA3 5RT (0870 0101847), at Station Road, East Winch, King's Lynn, Norfolk PE32 1NR (0870 9061420), and London Road, Stapeley, Nantwich, Cheshire CW5 7JW (not open to the public). Inspectors are contacted through their National Communication Centre, which can be reached via the Society's 24-hour national cruelty and advice line: 08705 555 999.
Contact: RSPCA Headquarters, RSPCA, Willberforce Way, Horsham, West Sussex RH13 9RS. 0300 1234 999; (fax)0303 123 0284. www.rspca.org.uk

ROYAL SOCIETY FOR THE PROTECTION OF BIRDS

UK Partner of BirdLife International, and Europe's largest voluntary wildlife conservation body. The RSPB, a registered charity, is governed by an elected body (see also RSPB Phoenix and RSPB Wildlife Explorers). Its work in the conservation of wild birds and habitats covers the acquisition and management of nature reserves; research and surveys; monitoring and responding to development proposals, land use practices and pollution which threaten wild birds and biodiversity; and the provision of an advisory service on wildlife law enforcement.

Work in the education and information field includes formal education in schools and colleges, and informal activities for children through Wildlife Explorers; publications (including *Birds*, a quarterly magazine for members, *Bird Life*, a bi-monthly magazine for RSPB Wildlife Explorers, *Wild Times* for under-8s); displays and exhibitions; the distribution of moving images about birds; and the development of membership activities through Members' Groups.

The RSPB currently manages 182 nature reserves in the UK, covering more than 313,000 acres; more than 50% of this area is owned. Sites are carefully selected, mostly as being of national or international importance to wildlife conservation. The aim is to conserve a countrywide network of reserves with all examples of the main bird communities and with due regard to the conservation of plants and other animals. Visitors are generally welcome to most reserves, subject to any restrictions necessary to protect the wildlife or habitats.

Current national projects include extensive work on agriculture, and conservation and campaigning for the conservation of the marine environment and to halt the illegal persecution of birds of prey. Increasingly, there is involvement with broader environmental concerns such as climate change and transport.

The RSPB's International Dept works closely with Birdlife International and its partners in other countries and is involved with numerous projects overseas, especially in Europe and Asia.

Contact: RSPB, The Lodge, Sandy, Beds SG19 2DL. 01767 680 551; (Fax)01767 692 365; e-mail: (firstname.name)@rspb.org.uk www.rspb.org.uk

Regional Offices:

ENGLAND

RSPB North England, 1 Sirius House, Amethyst Road, Newcastle Business Park, Newcastle upon Tyne NE4 7YL. 0191 256 8200.

RSPB North West, Westleigh Mews, Wakefield Road, Denby Dale, Huddersfield HD8 8QD. 01484 861 148.

RSPB Central England, 46 The Green, South Bar, Banbury, Oxon OX16 9AB. 01295 253 330.

RSPB East Anglia, Stalham House, 65 Thorpe Road, Norwich NR1 1UD. 01603 661 662.

RSPB South East, 2nd Floor, Frederick House, 42 Frederick Place, Brighton BN1 4EA. 01273 775 333.

RSPB London, 2nd Floor, 65 Petty France, London, SW1H 9EU, 0207 808 1240;

e-mail: london@rspb.org.uk

RSPB South West, Keble House, Southernhay Gardens, Exeter EX1 1NT. 01392 432 691.

SCOTLAND

RSPB Scotland HQ, Dunedin House, 25 Ravelston Terrace, Edinburgh EH4 3TP. 0131 311 6500; e-mail: rspb.scotland@rspb.org.uk

RSPB North Scotland, Etive House, Beechwood Park, Inverness IV2 3BW. 01463 715 000.

RSPB East Scotland, 10 Albyn Terrace, Aberdeen AB1 1YP. 01224 624 824.

RSPB South & West Scotland, 10 Park Quadrant, Glasgow G3 6BS. 0141 331 0993.

NATIONAL ORGANISATIONS

WALES

RSPB North Wales, Maes y Ffynnon, Penrhosgarnedd, Bangor, Gwynedd LL57 2DW. 01248 363 800.

RSPB South Wales, Sutherland House, Castlebridge, Cowbridge Road East, Cardiff CF11 9AB. 029 2035 3000.

RSPB WILDLIFE EXPLORERS and RSPB PHOENIX (formerly YOC) (1965; 168,000).

Junior section of the RSPB. There are more than 100 groups run by 300 volunteers. Activities include projects, holidays, roadshows, competitions, and local events for children, families and teenagers. Publishes 2 bi-monthly magazines, Bird Life (aimed at 8-12 year olds) and Wild Times (aimed at under 8s) and 1 quarterly magazine Wingbeat (aimed at teenagers).
Contact: Mark Boyd, Youth Manager, RSPB, RSPB Youth and Education Dept, The Lodge, Sandy, Beds SG19 2DL. 01767 680 551; e-mail: explorers@rspb.org.uk and phoenix@rspb.org.uk www.rspb.org.uk/youth

SCOTTISH BIRDS RECORDS COMMITTEE (1984; 7 members + secretary).

Set up by the Scottish Ornithologists' Club to ensure that records of species not deemed rare enough to be considered by the British Birds Rarities Committee, but which are rare in Scotland, are fully assessed; also maintains the official list of Scottish birds.
Contact: Angus Hogg, Secretary, Scottish Birds Records Committee, 11 Kirkmichael Road, Crosshill, Maybole, Ayrshire KA19 7RJ. e-mail: dcgos@globalnet.co.uk www.the-soc.org.uk

SCOTTISH ORNITHOLOGISTS' CLUB (1936; 2250).

The Club has 14 branches (see County Directory). Each with a programme of winter meetings and field trips throughout the year. The SOC organises an annual weekend conference in the autumn anda joint SOC/BTO one-day birdwatchers' conference in spring. Publishes quarterly newsletter Scottish Bird News, the bi-annual Scottish Birds, the annual Scottish Bird Report and the Scottish Raptor. The SOC has opened a new resource centre in Scotland, at Aberlady, details of which can be found on the website.

Contact: The Scottish Birdwatching Resource Centre, The SOC, Waterston House, Aberlady, East Lothian EH32 0PY. 01875 871 330; (Fax)01875 871 035; e-mail: mail@the-soc.org.uk www.the-soc.org.uk

SCOTTISH NATURAL HERITAGE (1991).

Is the Scottish Executive's statutory advisor in respect to the conservation, enhancement, enjoyment, understanding and sustainable use of the natural heritage.
Contact: Scottish Natural Heritage, Great Glen House, Inverness IV3 8NW. 01463 725 000; e-mail: fergus.macneill@snh.gov.uk www.snh.org.uk

SCOTTISH SOCIETY FOR THE PREVENTION OF CRUELTY TO ANIMALS (1839; 45,000 supporters).

Represents animal welfare interests to Government, local authorities and others. Educates young people to realise their responsibilities. Maintains an inspectorate to patrol and investigate and to advise owners about the welfare of animals and birds in their care. Maintains welfare centres, two of which include oiled bird cleaning centres. Bird species, including birds of prey, are rehabilitated and where possible released back into the wild.
Contact: Scottish SPCA, Braehead Mains, 603 Queensferry Road, Edinburgh EH4 6EA. 03000 999 999; (Fax)0131 339 4777; e-mail: enquiries@scottishspca.org www.scottishspca.org

SCOTTISH WILDLIFE TRUST (1964; 30,000).

Has members' centres throughout Scotland. Aims to conserve all forms of wildlife and has over 120 reserves, many of great birdwatching interest, covering some 20,000 hectares. Member of The Wildlife Trusts partnership and organises Scottish Wildlife Week. Publishes Scottish Wildlife three times a year.
Contact: Scottish Wildlife Trust, Cramond House, Cramond Glebe Road, Edinburgh EH4 6NS. 0131 312 7765; (Fax)0131 312 8705; e-mail: enquiries@swt.org.uk www.swt.org.uk

SEABIRD GROUP (1966; 350).

Concerned with conservation issues affecting seabirds. Co-ordinates census and monitoring work on breeding seabirds; has established and maintains the Seabird Colony Register in collaboration with the JNCC; organises triennial conferences on seabird biology and conservation topics. Small grants available to assist with research and survey work on seabirds.

Publishes the Seabird Group Newsletter every four months and the journal, Atlantic Seabirds, quarterly in association with the Dutch Seabird Group.
Contact: Alan Leitch, Seabird Group, 2 Burgess Terrace, Edinburgh, EH9 2BD. 0131 667 1169; e-mail: alan.leitch1@virgin.net
www.seabirdgroup.org.uk

SOCIETY OF WILDLIFE ARTISTS (1964; 70 Members, 68 Associates).
Registered charity. Annual exhibition held in Sept/Oct at the Mall Galleries, London.
Contact: The Secretary, Society of Wildlife Artists, Federation of British Artists, 17 Carlton House Terrace, London SW1Y 5BD. 020 7930 6844; e-mail: info@mallgalleries.com
www.swla.co.uk

SWAN SANCTUARY (THE)
Founded by Dorothy Beeson BEM. A registered charity which operates nationally. Has a fully equipped swan hospital with an operating theatre, x-ray facilities and a veterinary surgeon. New site has several nursing ponds and a four acre rehabilitatin lake where around 4,000 swans and the same number of other forms of wildlife are treated. 24-hour service operated, with volunteer rescuers on hand to recover victims of oil spills, vandalism etc. Reg. charity number 1002582.
Contact: The Swan Sanctuary, Felix Lane, Shepperton, Middlesex TW17 8NN. 01932 240 790; e-mail: swans@swanuk.org.uk
www.swanuk.org.uk

SWAN STUDY GROUP (80).
An association of both amateur and professionals, from around the UK. Most are concerned with Mute Swans, but Bewick's and Whooper Swan biologists are also active members. The aim of the Group is to provide a forum for communication and discussion, and to help co-ordinate co-operative studies. Annual meetings are held at various locations in the UK at which speakers give presentations on their own fieldwork.
Contact: Dr Helen Chisholm, Swan Study Group, 14 Buckstone Howe, Edinburgh, EH10 6XF. 0131 445 2351; e-mail: h.chisholm@blueyonder.co.uk

THE BRITISH LIBRARY SOUND ARCHIVE WILDLIFE SECTION (1969).
(Formerly BLOWS - British Library of Wildlife Sounds). The most comprehensive collection of bird sound recordings in existence: over 150,000 recordings of more than 8000 species of birds worldwide, available for free listening. Copies or sonograms of most recordings can be supplied for private study or research and, subject to copyright clearance, for commercial uses. Contribution of new material and enquiries on all aspects of wildlife sounds and recording techniques are welcome. Publishes Bioacoustics journal, CD guides to bird songs and other wildlife, including ambience titles. Comprehensive catalogue available on-line at http:\\cadensa.bl.uk
Contact: Cheryl Tipp, British Library Sound Archive Wildlife Sctn, British Library, National Sound Archive, 96 Euston Road, London NW1 2DB. 020 7412 7403; e-mail: cheryl.tipp@bl.uk
www.bl.uk/collections/sound-archive/wild.html

THE MAMMAL SOCIETY (1954; 2,500).
The Mammal Society is the voice for British mammals and the only organisation solely dedicated to the study and conservation of all British mammals. They seek to raise awareness of mammals, their ecology and their conservation needs, to survey British mammals and their habitats to identify the threats they face, to promote mammal studies in the UK and overseas, to advocate conservation plans based on sound science, to provide current information on mammals through their publications, to involve people of all ages in their efforts to protect mammals, to educate people about British mammals and to monitor mammal population changes.

Contact: The Mammal Society, 2B Inworth StreetLondon, SW11 3EP. 020 7350 2200; (Fax)020 7350 2211; e-mail: enquiries@mammal.org.uk
www.mammal.org.uk

THE NATURAL HISTORY MUSEUM AT TRING
Founded by Lionel Walter (later Lord) Rothschild, the Museum displays British and exotic birds (1500 species) including many rarities and extinct species. Galleries open all year except 24-26 Dec. Adjacent to the Bird Group of the Natural History Museum - with over a million specimens and an extensive ornithological library, an internationally important centre for bird research.
Contact: The Natural History Museum at Tring, Akeman Street, Tring, Herts HP23 6AP. 020 7942 6171; (Fax)020 7942 6150; e-mail: tring-enquiries@nhm.ac.uk
www.nhm.ac.uk/tring

UK400 CLUB (1981).
Serves to monitor the nation's leading twitchers and their life lists, and to keep under review contentious species occurrences. Publishes a bi-monthly magazine Rare Birds and operates a website; www.uk400clubonline.co.uk. Membership open to all.
Contact: L G R Evans, UK400 Club, 8 Sandycroft Road, Little Chalfont, Amersham, Bucks HP6 6QL. 01494 763 010; e-mail: LGREUK400@aol.com www.uk400clubonline.co.uk

ULSTER WILDLIFE TRUST see County Directory
Ulster Wildlife Trust,

WADER STUDY GROUP (1970; 600).
An association of wader enthusiasts, both amateur and professional, from all parts of the world. The Group aims to maintain contact between them, to help in the organisation of co-operative studies, and to provide a vehicle for the exchange of information. Publishes the Wader Study Group Bulletin three times a year and holds annual meetings throughout Europe.
Contact: , The General Secretary, Wader Study Group, The National Centre for Ornithology, The Nunnery, Thetford, Norfolk IP24 2PU. www.waderstudygroup.org

WELSH KITE TRUST (1996; 1200).
A registered charity that undertakes the conservation and annual monitoring of Red Kites in Wales. It attempts to locate all the breeding birds, to compile data on population growth, productivity, range expansion etc. The Trust liaises with landowners, acts as consultant on planning issues and with regard to filming and photography, and represents Welsh interests on the UK Kite Steering Group. Provides a limited rescue service for injured kites and eggs or chicks at risk of desertion or starvation. Publishes a newsletter Boda Wennol twice a year, sent free to subscribing Friends of the Welsh Kite and to all landowners with nesting Kites.
Contact: Tony Cross, Project Officer, Welsh Kite Trust, Samaria, Nantmel, Llandrindod Wells, Powys LD1 6EN. 01597 825 981; e-mail: tony.cross@welshkitetrust.org www.welshkitetrust.org

WELSH ORNITHOLOGICAL SOCIETY (1988; 250).
Promotes the study, conservation and enjoyment of birds throughout Wales. Runs the Welsh Records Panel which adjudicates records of scarce species in Wales. Publishes the journal Welsh Birds twice a year, along with newsletters, and organises an annual conference.
Contact: Membership details from - Welsh Ornithological Society, Alan Williams, Treasurer WOS, 30 Fairfield, Penperlleni, PONTYPOOL, NP4 0AQ. e-mail: alan.williams6@virgin.net Welshos.org.uk

WETLAND TRUST
Set up to encourage conservation of wetlands and develop study of migratory birds, and to foster international relations in these fields. Destinations for recent expeditions inc. Brazil, Senegal, The Gambia, Guinea-Bissau, Nigeria, Kuwait, Thailand, Greece and Jordan. Large numbers of birds are ringed each year in Sussex and applications are invited from individuals to train in bird ringing or extend their experience.
Contact: Phil Jones, Wetland Trust, Elms Farm, Pett Lane, Icklesham, Winchelsea, E Sussex TN36 4AH. 01797 226374; e-mail: phil@wetlandtrust.org

WILDFOWL & WETLANDS TRUST (THE) (1946; 130,000 members and 4,700 bird adopters).
Registered charity founded by the late Sir Peter Scott, its mission - to conserve wetlands and their biodiversity. WWT has nine centres with reserves (see Arundel, Caerlaverock, Castle Espie, Llanelli, Martin Mere, Slimbridge, Washington, Welney, and The London Wetland Centre in Reserves and Observatories section). The centres are nationally or internationally important for wintering wildfowl; they also aim to raise awareness of and appreciation for wetland species, the problems they face and the conservation action needed to help them. Programmes of walks and talks are available for visitors with varied interests - resources and programmes are provided for school groups. Centres, except Caerlaverock and Welney, have wildfowl from around the world, inc. endangered species. Research Department works on population dynamics, species management plans and wetland ecology. The Wetland Advisory Service (WAS) undertakes contracts, and Wetland Link International promotes the role of wetland centres for education and public awareness.
Contact: Wildfowl and Wetlands Trust, Slimbridge, Glos, GL2 7BT. 01453 891900; (Fax)01453 890827; e-mail: info.slimbridge@wwt.org.uk www.wwt.org.uk

WILDLIFE SOUND RECORDING SOCIETY (1968; 327).
Works closely with the Wildlife Section of the National Sound Archive. Members carry out recording work for scientific purposes as well as for pleasure. A field weekend is held each spring,

317

and members organise meetings locally. Four CD sound magazines of members' recordings are produced for members each year, and a journal, Wildlife Sound, is published twice a year.
Contact: Hon Membership Secretary, WSRS, Wildlife Sound Recording Society, e-mail: enquiries@wildlife-sound.org
www.wildlife-sound.org/

WILDLIFE TRUSTS (THE) (765,000)
We're the largest UK charity exclusively dedicated to conserving all our habitats and species, with a membership of more than 660,000 people including 108,000 junior members. We campaign for the protection of wildlife and invest in the future by helping people of all ages to gain a greater appreciation and understanding of wildlife. Collectively, we also manage more than 2,200 nature reserves spanning over 80,000 hectares. The Wildlife Trusts also lobby for better protection of the UK's natural heritage and are dedicated to protecting wildlife for the future. Publ Natural World. See also Wildlife Watch.

Contact: The Wildlife Trusts, The Kiln, Waterside, Mather Road, Newark NG24 1WT. 0870 036 7711; (Fax)0870 036 0101;
e-mail: enquiry@wildlifetrusts.org
www.wildlifetrusts.org

WILDLIFE WATCH (1971; 24,000+).
The junior branch of The Wildlife Trusts (see previous entry). It supports 1500 registered volunteer leaders running Watch groups across the UK. Publishes Watchword and Wildlife Extra for children and activity books for adults working with young people.
Contact: Wildlife Watch, The Wildlife Trusts, The Kiln, Waterside, Mather Road, Newark NG24 1WT.

0870 036 7711; (Fax)00870 0360101;
e-mail: watch@wildlife-trusts.cix.co.uk
www.wildlifewatch.org.uk

WWF-UK (1961).
WWF is the world's largest independent conservation organisation, comprising 27 national organisations. It works to conserve endangered species, protect endangered spaces, and address global threats to nature by seeking long-term solutions with people in government and industry, education and civil society. Publishes WWF News (quarterly magazine).

Contact: WWF-UK (World Wide Fund for Nature), Panda House, Weyside Park, Catteshall Lane, Godalming, Surrey GU7 1XR. 01483 426 444; (Fax)01483 426 409;
www.wwf-uk.org

ZOOLOGICAL PHOTOGRAPHIC CLUB (1899).
Circulates black and white and colour prints of zoological interest via a series of postal portfolios.
Contact: Martin B Withers, Hon Secretary, Zoological Photographic Club, 93 Cross Lane, Mountsorrel, Loughborough, Leics LE12 7BX. 0116 229 6080.

ZOOLOGICAL SOCIETY OF LONDON (1826).
Carries out research, organises symposia and holds scientific meetings. Manages the Zoological Gardens in Regent's Park (first opened in 1828) and Whipsnade Wild Animal Park near Dunstable, Beds, each with extensive collections of birds. The Society's library has a large collection of ornithological books and journals. Publications include the Journal of Zoology, Animal Conservation, Conservation Biology book series, The Symposia and The International Zoo Yearbook.
Contact: Zoological Society of London, Regent's Park, London, NW1 4RY. 020 7722 3333; www.zsl.org

NATIONAL PROJECTS

National ornithological projects depend for their success on the active participation of amateur birdwatchers. In return they provide birdwatchers with an excellent opportunity to contribute in a positive and worthwhile way to the scientific study of birds and their habitats, which is the vital basis of all conservation programmes. The following entries provide a description of each particular project and a note of whom to contact for further information (full address details are in the previous section).

ATLAS 2007-11
(BTO, run in partnership with BirdWatch Ireland and the Scottish Ornithologists' Club)
Atlases have provided a periodic stock-take of the birds of Britain and Ireland, and this latest Atlas will do just that, only this time in both the breeding season and in winter. It will generate range and abundance maps for all species while giving the opportunity to contrast past and present distributions and assess changes, for better or worse. Fieldwork will start in earnest in November 2007 and run for 4 winters and 4 summers. Observers will be able to submit their records and see periodic sneak previews of the results online. Mapping Britain and Ireland's birds is a major undertaking and the BTO will need your support.
Contact: birdatlas@bto.org
www.birdatlas.net

BARN OWL MONITORING PROGRAMME
A BTO project
Volunteers monitor nest sites to record site occupancy, clutch size, brood size and breeding success. Qualified ringers may catch and ring adults and chicks and record measurements. Volunteers must be qualified bird ringers or nest recorders with a Schedule 1 licence for Barn Owl.
Contact: Carl Barimore,
e-mail: barnowls@bto.org

BirdTrack
Organised by BTO on behalf of BTO, RSPB and BirdWatch Ireland.
BirdTrack is a year-round bird recording scheme, designed to collect large numbers of lists of birds. The idea is simple – you make a note of the birds seen at each site you visit and enter your daily observations on a simple-to-use web page. Birdwatchers can also send in other types of records, including counts and casual observations. The focus of the website (www.birdtrack.net) will be spring and autumn migration, seasonal movements and the distribution of scarce species. BirdTrack is also an ideal electronic notebook to store your own bird records, allowing queries and reports by sites and species.
Contact: Mark Grantham, BTO

BREEDING BIRD SURVEY
Supported by the BTO, JNCC and the RSPB.
Begun in 1994, the BBS is designed to keep track of the changes in populations of our common breeding birds. It is dependent on volunteer birdwatchers throughout the country who can spare about five hours a year to cover a 1x1km survey square. There are just two morning visits to survey the breeding birds each year. Survey squares are picked at random by computer to ensure that all habitats and regions are covered. Since its inception it has been a tremendous success, with more than 3,000 squares covered and more than 200 species recorded each year.
Contact: Census Unit, e-mail: bbs@bto.org, or your local BTO Regional Representative (see County Directory).

CORE MONITORING CENSUS (formerly COMMON BIRDS CENSUS)
This survey has officially finished. This was the main source of population monitoring in the wider countryside from 1962-2000, but has now been superceded by the Breeding Bird Survey. Nevertheless, CBC is still the best method to use at a local scale, producing maps showing the locations of bird's territories for a defined area. This is especially useful to study the relationship of breeding birds with their habitats. Although new participants are not needed currently, the method is still valuable and will be available on the BTO website.

CONSTANT EFFORT SITES SCHEME
A BTO project for bird ringers, funded by a partnership of the BTO, the JNCC, The

Environment and Heritage Service in Northern Ireland - National Parks & Wildlife Service (Ireland) and the ringers themselves.

Participants in the scheme monitor common songbird populations by standardized mist-netting and ringing of birds throughout the summer at more than 130 sites across Britain and Ireland. Changes in numbers of adults captured provide an index of population changes between years, while the ratio of juveniles to adults gives a measure of productivity. Between-year recaptures of birds are used to study variations in adult survival rates. Information from CES complements that from other long-term BTO surveys.

Contact: Mark Grantham, BTO.

GARDEN BIRD FEEDING SURVEY

A BTO project.

The 2006/07 season completed 37 years of the GBFS. Each year 250 observers record the numbers and variety of garden birds fed by man in the 26 weeks between October and March. It is the longest running survey of its type in the world. Gardens are selected by region and type, from city flats, suburban semis and rural houses to outlying farms.

Contact: David Glue, BTO.

BTO/CJ GARDEN BIRDWATCH

A BTO project, supported by C J WildBird Foods.

Started in January 1995, this project is a year-round survey that monitors the use that birds make of gardens. Approximately 17,000 participants from all over the UK and Ireland keep a weekly log of species using their gardens. The data collected are used to monitor regional, seasonal and year-to-year changes in the garden populations of our commoner birds. To cover costs there is an annual fee of £12. There is a quarterly colour magazine and all new joiners receive a full-colour, garden bird handbook. Results and more information are available online: www.bto.org/gbw. E-mail: gbw@bto.org

Contact: Garden BirdWatch Team, BTO.

GOOSE CENSUSES

A WWT project

Britain and Ireland support internationally important goose populations. During the day, many of these feed away from wetlands and are therefore not adequately censused by the Wetland Bird Survey. Additional surveys are therefore undertaken to provide estimates of population size. These primarily involve roost counts, supplemented by further counts of feeding birds.

Most populations are censused up to three times a year, typically during the autumn, midwinter, and spring. In addition, counts of the proportion of juveniles in goose flocks are undertaken to provide estimates of annual productivity. Further volunteers are always needed. In particular, counters in Scotland, Lancashire and Norfolk are sought. For more information

Contact: Richard Hearn, Programme Manager, E-mail: richard.hearn@wwt.org.uk
T: +44 (0)1453 891 185;
e-mail: monitoring@wwt.org.uk

HERONRIES CENSUS

A BTO project.

This survey started in 1928 and has been carried out under the auspices of the BTO since 1934. It represents the longest continuous series of population data for any European breeding bird. Counts are made at as many heronries as possible each year, throughout the UK to provide an index of the current population level; data from Scotland and Northern Ireland are scant and more contributions from these countries would be especially welcomed.

Herons may be hit hard during periods of severe weather but benefit by increased survival over mild winters. Their position at the top of a food chain makes them particularly vulnerable to pesticides and pollution.

Contact: John Marchant, BTO.

IRISH WETLAND BIRD SURVEY (I-WeBS)

A joint project of BirdWatch Ireland, the National Parks & Wildlife Service of the Dept of Arts, Culture & the Gaeltacht, and WWT, and supported by the Heritage Council and WWF-UK.

Established in 1994, I-WeBS aims to monitor the numbers and distribution of waterfowl populations wintering in Ireland in the long term, enabling the population size and spatial and temporal trends in numbers to be identified and described for each species. Methods are compatible with existing schemes in the UK and Europe, and I-WeBS collaborates closely with the Wetland Bird Survey (WeBS) in the UK. Synchronised monthly counts are undertaken at wetland sites of all habitats during the winter.

Counts are straightforward and counters receive a newsletter and full report annually. Additional help is always welcome, especially during these

initial years as the scheme continues to grow.
Contact: BirdWatch Ireland;
www.birdwatchireland.ie

NEST RECORD SCHEME

*A BTO Project forming part of the BTO's Integrated
Population Monitoring programme carried out
under contract with the JNCC.*

All birdwatchers can contribute to this scheme
by sending information about nesting attempts
they observe into the BTO on standard Nest
Record Cards or electronically via the IPMR
computer package. The NRS monitors changes
in the nesting success and the timing of breeding
of Britain's bird species. Guidance on on how to
record and visit nests safely, without disturbing
breeding birds, is available in a free starter pack
from the Nest Records Unit.
Contact: Carl Barimore;
e-mail: nest.records@bto.org

RAPTOR AND OWL RESEARCH REGISTER

A BTO project

The Register has helped considerably over
the past 30 years in encouraging and guiding
research, and in the co-ordination of projects.
There are currently almost 500 projects in
the card index file through which the Register
operates.

The owl species currently receiving most
attention are Barn and Tawny. As to raptors,
the most popular subjects are Kestrel, Buzzard,
Sparrowhawk, Hobby and Peregrine, with
researchers showing increasing interest in
Red Kite, and fewer large in-depth studies of
Goshawk, Osprey and harriers.

Contributing is a simple process and involves
all raptor enthusiasts, whether it is to describe
an amateur activity or professional study. The
nature of research on record varies widely
– from local pellet analyses to captive breeding
and rehabilitation programmes to national
surveys of Peregrine, Buzzard and Golden Eagle.
Birdwatchers in both Britain and abroad are
encouraged to write for photocopies of cards
relevant to the species or nature of their work.
The effectiveness of the Register depends upon
those running projects (however big or small)
ensuring that their work is included.
Contact: David Glue, BTO.

RED KITE RE-INTRODUCTION PROJECT

*An English Nature/SNH/RSPB project supported
by Forest Enterprise, Yorkshire Water and
authorities in Germany and Spain*

The project involves the translocation of birds
from Spain, Germany and the expanding

Chilterns population for release at sites in
England and Scotland.

Records of any wing-tagged Red Kites in
England should be reported to Natural Engand,
Northminster House, Peterborough, PEI IUA (tel
01733 455 281). Scottish records should be sent
to the RSPB's North Scotland Regional Office,
Etive House, Beechwood Park, Inverness, IV2
3BW (tel 01463 715 000).

Sightings are of particular value if the letter/
number code (or colour) of wing tags can be
seen or if the bird is seen flying low over (or
into) woodland. Records should include an
exact location, preferably with a six figure grid
reference.

RETRAPPING ADULTS FOR SURVIVAL PROJECT

*A BTO project for bird ringers, funded by
a partnership of the BTO, the JNCC, The
Environment and Heritage Service in Northern
Ireland - National Parks & Wildlife Service (Ireland)
and the ringers themselves.*

This project started in 1998 and is an initiative
of the BTO Ringing Scheme. It aims to gather
re-trap information for a wide range of species,
especially those of conservation concern, in
a variety of breeding habitats, allowing the
monitoring of survival rates.

Detailed information about survival rates from
the RAS Project will help in the understanding
of changing population trends. Ringers choose
a target species, decide on a study area and
develop suitable catching techniques. The aim
then is to catch all the breeding adults of the
chosen species within the study area. This is
repeated each breeding season for a minimum
of five years. The results will be relayed to
conservation organisations who can use the
information to design effective conservation
action plans.
Contact: John Marchant, BTO.

RINGING SCHEME

*A BTO project for bird ringers, funded by a
partnership of the BTO, the JNCC, The National
Parks & Wildlife Service (Ireland) and the ringers
themselves.*

The purpose of the Ringing Scheme is to study
survival, productivity and movements by marking
birds with individually numbered metal rings
which carry a return address. About 2,000 trained
and licensed ringers operate in Britain and
Ireland, and together they mark around 800,000
birds each year.

All birdwatchers can contribute to the scheme
by reporting any ringed or colour-ringed birds

they find either. Reports can be submitted online at www.ring.ac or direct to the BTO in writing. Anyone finding a ringed bird should note the ring number, species (if known), when and where the bird was found, and what happened to it. If the bird is dead, please remove and keep the ring, or if writing, flatten it out and tape it to your letter and send it to us. If details are reported via the website, or phoned in, please keep the ring in case there is a query. Finders who send their name and address will be given details of where and when the bird was ringed. About 12,000 ringed birds are reported each year and an annual report is published.
Contact: Jacquie Clark, BTO.

SWIFT CONSERVATION

A Concern for Swifts Group project.
Endorsed by the BTO and the RSPB, the Group monitors Swift breeding colonies, especially where building restoration and maintenance are likely to cause disturbance. Practical information can be provided to owners, architects, builders and others. The help of interested birdwatchers is always welcome.
Contact: Jake Allsop, 01353 740 540; www.swift-conservation.org

TOOTH & CLAW

An independent project aimed at improving knowledge about Britain's predators and

promoting discussion on the issues that surround them.

Tooth & Claw explores some of the complex issues surrounding our relationship with wild predators and questions how we really feel and why?

Through the web site, Tooth & Claw provides a meeting place between anecdotal input and scientific research and encourages constructive and imaginative dialogue on predator issues.

A series of case studies led by powerful imagery will provide insightful interviews and personal accounts of our lives alongside the likes of eagles and foxes with a glimpse into the future and

the return of creatures we have not known for centuries.
Contact: Peter Cairns, Northshots, Ballintean, Glenfeshie, Kingussie, Scotland, PH21 1NX. (44) (0)1540 651 352;
e-mail: peter@toothandclaw.org.uk
www.toothandclaw.org.uk

WATERWAYS BREEDING BIRD SURVEY

A BTO project, supported by the Environment Agency
WBBS uses transect methods like those of the Breeding Bird Survey to record bird populations along randomly chosen stretches of river and canal throughout the UK. Just two survey visits are needed during April-June. WBBS began in 1998 and has now taken over from the Waterways Bird Survey as the main monitoring scheme for birds in this habitat.
Contact: BTO Regional Representative (see County Directory) to enquire if any local stretches require coverage, otherwise John Marchant at BTO HQ.

WETLAND BIRD SURVEY

A joint scheme of BTO, WWT, RSPB & JNCC.
The Wetland Bird Survey (WeBS) is the monitoring scheme for non-breeding waterbirds in the UK.

The principal aims are:
1. to determine the population sizes of waterbirds
2. to determine trends in numbers and distribution
3. to identify important sites for waterbirds

WeBS data are used to designate important waterbird sites and protect them against adverse development, for research into the causes of declines, for establishing conservation priorities and strategies and to formulate management plans for wetland sites and waterbirds.

Monthly, synchronised Core Counts are made at as many wetland sites as possible. Low Tide Counts are made on about 20 estuaries each winter to identify important feeding areas. Counts take just a few hours and are relatively straightforward. The 3,000 participants receive regular newsletters and a comprehensive annual report. New counters are always welcome.
Contacts: WeBS Office, BTO (Core Counts - Mark Collier, Low Tide Counts - Alex Banks and general enquiries - Andy Musgrove, at BTO HQ, E-mail WeBS@bto.org www.bto.org/webs

INTERNATIONAL DIRECTORY

Red-necked Phalarope by David Cromack

The BirdLife Partnership

BirdLife is a Partnership of non-governmental organisations (NGOs) with a special focus on conservation and birds. Each NGO Partner represents a unique geographic territory/country.

The BirdLife Network explained

Partners: Membership-based NGOs who represent BirdLife in their own territory. Vote holders and key implementing bodies for BirdLife's Strategy and Regional Programmes in their own territories.

Partners Designate: Membership-based NGOs who represent BirdLife in their own territory, in a transition stage to becoming full Partners. Non-vote holders.

Affiliates: Usually NGOs, but also individuals, foundations or governmental institutions when appropriate. Act as a BirdLife contact with the aim of developing into, or recruiting, a BirdLife Partner in their territory.

Secretariat: The co-ordinating and servicing body of BirdLife International.

Secretariat Addresses

BirdLife Global Office

BirdLife International
Wellbrook Court
Girton Road
Cambridge CB3 0NA
UNITED KINGDOM
Tel. +44 1 223 277 318
Fax +44 1 223 277 200
E-mail: birdlife@birdlife.org.uk
www.birdlife.org

Birdlife Africa Regional Office

c/o ICIPE Campus
Kasarani Road, off Thika Road
Nairobi KENYA

Postal Address

PO Box 3502
00100 GPO
Nairobi KENYA
+254 20 862246
+254 20 862246
E-mail: birdlife@birdlife.or.ke
www.birdlife.org/regional/africa/
partnership

BirdLife Americas Regional Office

Birdlife International
Vicente Cárdenas 120 y Japon,
3rd Floor
Quito ECUADOR

Postal address

BirdLife International
Casilla 17-17-717
Quito ECUADOR
Tel. +593 2 453 645
Fax +593 2 459 627
E-mail: birdlife@birdlife.org.ec
www.birdlife.org/regional/
americas/partnership

BirdLife Asia Regional Office

Toyo-Shinjuku Building
2nd Floor, Shinjuku 1-12-15
Shinkuju-ku
Tokyo 160-0022, JAPAN
Tel.+3 3351 9981
Fax.+3 3351 9980
E-mail: info@birdlife-asia.org
www.birdlife.org/regional/asia/
partnership

BirdLife European Regional Office

Droevendaalsesteeg 3a PO Box
127, NL- 6700 AC, Wageningen
THE NETHERLANDS
Tel. +31 317 478831
Fax +31 317 478844
E-mail: birdlife@birdlife.agro.nl

European Community Office (ECO)

BirdLife International
Avenue de la Toison d'Or 67
(2nd floor), B-1060 Brussels
BELGIUM
Tel. +32 2280 08 30
Fax +32 2230 38 02
E-mail: bleco@birdlifeeco.net
www.birdlife.org/regional/europe/
partnership

BirdLife Middle East Regional Office

BirdLife International - Amman
P. O. Box 2295
Amman 11953
JORDAN
Tel: +962 (6) 566-2945
Fax: +962 (6) 569-1838
E-mail: birdlife@nol.com.jo
www.birdlife.org/regional/middle_
east/partnership

INTERNATIONAL ORGANISATIONS

AFRICA

PARTNERS

Burkina Faso
Fondation des Amis de la Nature (NATURAMA), 01 B.P. 6133, Ouagadougou 01.
e-mail: naturama@fasonet.bf

Ethiopia
Ethiopian Wildlife and Natural History Society, PO Box 13303, Addis Ababa, Pub: *Agazen; Ethiopian Wildl. and Nat. Hist. News. (& Annual Report); Ethiopian Wildl. and Nat. Hist. Soc. Quarterly News (WATCH); Walia (WATCH) (Ethiopia).*
e-mail: ewnhs@telecom.net.et
http://ewnhs.ble@telecom.net.et

Ghana
Ghana Wildlife Society, PO Box 13252, Accra, Pub: *Bongo News; NKO (The Parrots).*
e-mail: wildsoc@ighmail.com

Kenya
Nature Kenya, PO Box 44486, 00100 GPO. Nairobi. Pub: *Bulletin of the EANHS; Journal of East African Natural; Kenya Birds.*
e-mail: office@naturekenya.org
www.naturekenya.org

Nigeria
Nigerian Conservation Foundation, PO Box 74638, Victoria Island, Lagos. Pub: *NCF Matters/News/ Newsletter; Nigerian Conservation Foundation Annual Report.*
e-mail: enquiries@ncf-nigeria.org
www.africanconservation.org/ncftemp/

Seychelles
Nature Seychelles, Roche Caiman, Box 1310, Victoria, Mahe, Seychelles. Pub: *Zwazo - a BirdLife Seychelles Newsletter.*
e-mail: nature@seychelles.net
www.nature.org.sc

Sierra Leone
Conservation Society of Sierra Leone, PO BOX 1292, Freetown. Pub: *Rockfowl Link, The.*
e-mail: cssl@sierratel.sl

South Africa
BirdLife South Africa, PO Box 515, Randburg, Johannesburg 2125, South Africa, Pub: *Newsletter of BirdLife South Africa; Ostrich.*
e-mail: info@birdlife.org.za
www.birdlife.org.za

Tanzania
Wildlife Conservation Society of Tanzania, PO Box 70919, Dar es Salaam, Pub: *Miombo.*
e-mail: wcst@africaonline.co.tz

Uganda
Nature Uganda, PO Box 27034, Kampala. Pub: *Naturalist - A Newsletter of the East Africa Nat. His. Soc.*
e-mail: nature@natureuganda.org
www.natureuganda.org/

PARTNERS DESIGNATE

Tunisia
Association "Les Amis des Oiseaux", Avenue 18 Janvier 1952, Ariana Centre, App. C209, 2080 Ariana, Tunis. Pub: *Feuille de Liaison de l'AAO; Houbara, l'.* e-mail: aao.bird@planet.tn

Zimbabwe
BirdLife Zimbabwe, P O Box RV 100, Runiville, Harare, Zimbabwe. Pub: *Babbler (WATCH) (Zimbabwe); Honeyguide.*
e-mail: birds@zol.co.zw

AFFILIATES

Botswana
Birdlife Botswana, Private Bag 003 # Suite 348, Mogoditshane, Gaborone, Botswana
e-mail: blb@birdlifebotswana.org.bw
www.birdlifebotswana.org.bw

Burundi
Association Burundaise pour la Protection des Oiseaux, P O Box 7069, Bujumbura, Burundi
e-mail: aboburundi@yahoo.fr

Cameroon
Cameroon Biodiversity Conservation Society (CBCS), PO Box 3055, Messa, Yaoundé.
e-mail: gdzikouk@yahoo.fr

Egypt
Sherif Baha El Din, 3 Abdala El Katib St, Dokki, Cairo. e-mail: baha2@internetegypt.com

Rwanda
Association pour la Conservation de la Nature au Rwanda, P O Box 4290, Kigali,
e-mail: acnrwanda@yahoo.fr

Zambia
Zambian Ornithological Society, Box 33944, Lusaka 10101, Pub: *Zambian Ornithological Society Newsletter.* e-mail: zos@zamnet.zm
www.wattledcrane.com

INTERNATIONAL ORGANISATIONS

AMERICAS

PARTNERS

Argentina
Aves Argentina / AOP, 25 de Mayo 749, 2 piso, oficina 6, 1002 Buenos Aires. Pub: *Hornero; Naturaleza & Conservacion; Nuestras Aves; Vuelo de Pajaro.*
e-mail: info@avesargentinas.org.ar
www.avesargentinas.org.ar

Belize
The Belize Audubon Society, 12 Fort Street, PO Box 1001, Belize City. Pub: *Belize Audubon Society Newsletter.*
e-mail: base@btl.net
www.belizeaudubon.org

Bolivia
Asociacion Armonia, 400 Avenidad Lomas de Arena, Casilla 3566, Santa Cruz, Bolivia. Pub: *Aves en Bolivia.*
e-mail: armonia@scbbs-bo.com

Canada
Bird Studies Canada, PO Box/160, Port Rowan, Ontario N0E 1M0. Pub: *Bird Studies Canada - Annual Report; Birdwatch Canada.*
e-mail: generalinfo@bsc-eoc.org
www.bsc-eoc.org

Canada
Nature Canada, 1 Nicholas Street, Suite 606, Ottawa, Ontario, K1N 7B7. Pub: *Grass 'n Roots; IBA News Canada; Nature Canada; Nature Matters; Nature Watch News (CNF).*
e-mail: info@naturecanada.ca
www.naturecanada.ca

Ecuador
Fundación Ornithológica del Ecuador, La Tierra 203 y Av. de los Shyris, Casilla 17-17-906, Quito.
e-mail: cecia@uio.satnet.net
www.cecia.org/

Jamaica
BirdLife Jamaica, 2 Starlight Avenue, Kingston 6, Pub: *Broadsheet: BirdLife Jamaica; Important Bird Areas Programme Newsletter.*
e-mail: birdlifeja@yahoo.com
www.birdelifejamaica.com

Panama
Panama Audubon Society, Apartado 2026, Ancón, Balboa. Pub: *Toucan.*
e-mail: info@panamaaudubon.org
www.panamaaudubon.org

Venezuela
Sociedad Conservacionista Audubon de, Apartado 80.450, Caracas 1080-A, Venezuela. Pub: *Audubon (Venezuela) (formerly Boletin Audubon).*
e-mail: audubon@cantv.net

PARTNERS DESIGNATE

Mexico
CIPAMEX, Apartado Postal 22-012, D.F. 14091, Mexico. Pub: *AICA's; Cuauhtli Boletin de Cipa Mex.*
e-mail: cipamex@campus.iztacala.unam.mx
http://coro@servidor.unam.mx

Paraguay
Guyra Paraguay,, Coronel Rafael Franco 381 c/ Leandro Prieto, Casilla de Correo 1132, Asunción. Pub: *Boletin Jara Kuera.*
e-mail: guyra@guyra.org.py
or guyra@highway.com.py
www.guyra.org.py/

United States
National Audubon Society, 700 Broadway, New York, NY, 10003 -9562. Pub: *American Birds; Audubon (USA); Audubon Field Notes; Audubon Bird Conservation Newsletter.*
e-mail: audubonaction@audubon.org
www.audubon.org

Chile
Union de Ornitologis de Chile (UNORCH), Casilla 13.183, Santiago 21. Pub: *Boletin Chileno de Ornitologia; Boletin Informativo (WATCH) (Chile).*
e-mail: unorch@entelchile.net
www.geocities.com/RainForest/4372

AFFILIATES

Bahamas
Bahamas National Trust, PO Box N-4105, Nassau. Pub: *Bahamas Naturalist; Currents; Grand Bahama Update.*
e-mail: bnt@batelnet.bs
www.thebahamasnationaltrust.org/

Cuba
Centro Nacional de Áreas Protegidas (CNAP). Calle 18 a, No 1441, e/ 41 y 47, Playa, Ciudad Habana, Cuba. e-mail: cnap@snap.cu
www.snap.co.cu/

El Salvador
SalvaNATURA, 33 Avenida Sur #640, Colonia Flor Blanca, San Salvador.
e-mail: salvanatura@saltel.net
www.salvanatura.org

Falkland Islands
Falklands Conservation, PO Box 26, Stanley,. or Falklands Conservation, 1 Princes Avenue, Finchley, London N3 2DA, UK. Pub: *Falklands Conservation*.
e-mail: conservation@horizon.co.fk
www.falklandsconservatlon.com

Honduras
Sherry Thorne, c/o Cooperación Técnica, Apdo 30289 Toncontín, Tegucigalpa.
e-mail: pilar_birds@yahoo.com

Suriname
Foundation for Nature Preservation in Suriname, Cornelis Jongbawstraat 14, PO BOX 12252, Paramaribo
e-mall: research@stinasu.sr
www.stinasu.sr

Uruguay
GUPECA, Casilla de Correo 6955, Correo Central, Montevideo. Pub: *Achara*.
e-mail: info@avesuruguay.org.uy
www.avesuruguay.org.uy/

ASIA

PARTNERS

Japan
Wild Bird Society of Japan (WBSJ), 1/F Odakyu Nishi Shinjuku Building, 1-47-1 Hatsudai Shibuya-ku, Tokyo 151-061, Japan. Pub: *Strix; Wild Birds; Wing*.
e-mail: int.center@wing-wbsj.or.jp
www.wing-wbsj.or.jp

Malaysia
Malaysian Nature Society, PO Box 10750, 50724 Kuala Lumpur. Pub: *Enggang; Suara Enggang; Malayan Nature Journal; Malaysian Naturalist*.
www.mns.org.my
e-mail: natsoc@po.jaring.my

Philippines
Haribon Foundation, Suites 401-404 Fil-Garcia Bldg, 140 Kalayaan Avenue cor. Mayaman St, Diliman, Quezon CIty 1101. Pub: *Haribon Foundation Annual Report; Haring Ibon; Philippine Biodiversity*.
e-mail: birdlife@haribon.org.ph
www.haribon.org.ph

Singapore
Nature Society (Singapore), 510 Geylang Road, #02-05, The Sunflower, 398466. Pub: *Nature News; Nature Watch (Singapore)*.
e-mail: nss@nss.org.sg
www.nss.org.sg

Taiwan
Wild Bird Federation Taiwan (WBFT), 1F, No. 3, Lane 36 Jing-Long St., 116 Taipei, Taiwan, R.O.C. Pub: *Yuhina Post*.
e-mail: wbft@bird.org.tw
www.bird.org.tw

Thailand
Bird Conservation Society of Thailand, 43 Soi Chok Chai Ruam Mit 29, Vipahvadee-Rabgsit Road, Sansaen-nok, Dindaeng, Bangkok 10320 Thailand. Pub: *Bird Conservation Society of Thailand*.
e-mail: bcst@bcst.or.th
www.bcst.or.th

PARTNER DESIGNATE

India
Bombay Natural History Society, Hornbill House, Shaheed Bhagat Singh Road, Mumbai-400 023. Pub: *Buceros; Hornbill; Journal of the Bombay Natural History Society*.
e-mail: bnhs@bom4.vsnl.net.in
www.bnhs.org

AFFILIATES

Hong Kong
The Hong Kong Birdwatching Society, Room 1612 Beverley Commercial Building, 87-105 Chatham Road South, Tsim Sha Tsui, Kowloon, Hong Kong. Pub: *Hong Kong Bird Report*.
e-mail: hkbws@hkbws.org.uk
www.hkbws.org.hk

Indonesia
BirdLife Indonesia (Perhimpunan Pelestari Burung dan Habitatnya), Jl. Dadali 32, Bogor 16161, PO. Box 310/Boo, Bogor 16003, Indonesia.
e-mail: birdlife@burung.org
www.burung.org

INTERNATIONAL DIRECTORY

INTERNATIONAL ORGANISATIONS

Nepal
Bird Conservation Nepal, P.O.Box 12465, Lazimpat, Kathmandu, Nepal. Pub: *Bird Conservation Nepal (Danphe); Ibisbill.*
e-mail: bcn@mail.com.np
www.birdlifenepal.org

Pakistan
Ornithological Society of Pakistan, PO Box 73, 109D Dera Ghazi Khan, 32200. Pub: *Pakistan Journal of Ornithology.*
e-mail: osp@mul.paknet.com.pk

Sri Lanka
Field Ornithology Group of Sri Lanka, Dept of Zoology, University of Colombo, Colombo 03. Pub: *Malkoha - Newsletter of the Field Ornithology Group of Sri Lanka.*
e-mail: fogsl@slt.lk

EUROPE

PARTNERS

Austria
BirdLife Austria, Museumplatz 1/10/8, AT-1070 Wien. Pub: *Egretta; Vogelschutz in Osterreich.*
e-mail: office@birdlife.at
www.birdlife.at/

Belgium
BirdLife Belgium (BNVR-RNOB-BNVS), Natuurpunt, Kardinaal, Mercierplein 1, 2800 Mechelen, Belgium.
e-mail: wim.vandenbossche@natuurpunt.be
www.natuurreservaten.be

Bulgaria
Bulgarian Society for the Protection of Birds (BSPB), PO Box 50, Musagenitza Complex, Block 104, Entrance A, Floor 6, BG-1111, Sofia, Bulgaria. Pub: *Neophron (& UK).*
e-mail: bspb_hq@bspb.org
www.bspb.org

Czech Republic
Czech Society for Ornithology (CSO), Hornomecholupska 34, CZ-102 00 Praha 10. Pub: *Ptaci Svet; Sylvia; Zpravy Ceske Spolecnosti Ornitologicke.* e-mail: cso@birdlife.cz
www.birdlife.cz

Denmark
Dansk Ornitologisk Forening (DOF), Vesterbrogade 138-140, DK-1620, Copenhagen V, Denmark. Pub:

DAFIF - Dafifs Nyhedsbrev; Dansk Ornitologisk Forenings Tidsskrift; Fugle og Natur.
e-mail: dof@dof.dk
www.dof.dk

Estonia
Estonian Ornithological Society (EOU), PO Box 227, Vesti Str. 4, EE-50002 Tartu, Estonia. Pub: *Hirundo Eesti Ornitoogiauhing.*
e-mail: eoy@eoy.ee
www.eoy.ee

Finland
BirdLife SUOMI Finland, Annankatu 29 A, PO Box 1285, FI 00101, Helsinki. Pub: *Linnuston-Suojelu; Linnut; Tiira.*
e-mail: office@birdlife.fi
www.birdlife.fi

France
Ligue pour la Protection des Oiseaux (LPO), La Corderie Royale, B.P. 90263, 17305 ROCHEFORT CEDEX, France. Pub: *Lettre Internationale; Ligue Francaise Pour La Protection des Oiseaux; Oiseau, L' (LPO); Outarde infos.*
e-mail: lpo@lpo.fr
www.lpo.fr/

Germany
Naturschutzbund Deutschland, Herbert-Rabius-Str. 26, D-53225 Bonn, Germany. Pub: *Naturschutz Heute (NABU) Naturschutzbund Deutschland.*
e-mail: nabu@nabu.de
www.nabu.de

Gibraltar
Gibraltar Ornithological and Nat. History Society, Jew's Gate, Upper Rock Nature Reserve, PO Box 843, GI. Pub: *Alectoris; Gibraltar Nature News.*
e-mail: gohns@gibnet.gi
www.gibraltar.gi/gonhs

Greece
Hellenic Ornithological Society (HOS), Vas. Irakleiou 24, GR-10682 Athens, Greece. Pub: *HOS Newsletter.*
e-mail: birdlife-gr@ath.forthnet.gr
www.ornithologiki.gr

Hungary
Hungarian Orn. and Nature Cons. Society (MME), Kolto u. 21, Pf. 391, HU-1536, Budapest. Pub: *Madartani Tajekoztato; Madartavlat; Ornis Hungarica; Tuzok.*
e-mail: mme@mme.hu
www.mme.hu

INTERNATIONAL ORGANISATIONS

Iceland
Icelandic Society for the Protection of Birds, Fuglaverndarfélag Islands, PO Box 5069, IS-125 Reykjavik, Iceland.
e-mail: fuglavernd@fuglavernd.is
www.fuglavernd.is

Ireland
BirdWatch Ireland, Rockingham House, Newcastle, Co. Wicklow, Eire. Pub: *Irish Birds; Wings (IWC Birdwatch Ireland)*.
e-mail: info@birdwatchireland.org
www.birdwatchireland.ie

Israel
Society for the Protection of Nature in Israel, Hashsela 4, Tel-Aviv 66103. Pub: *SPNI News*.
e-mail: ioc@netvision.net.il
www.birds.org.il

Italy
Lega Italiana Protezione Uccelli (LIPU), Via Trento 49, IT-43100, Parma. Pub: *Ali Giovani; Ali Notizie*.
e-mail: lipusede@box1.tin.it
www.lipu.it

Latvia
Latvijas Ornitologijas Biedriba (LOB), Ak 1010, LV-1050 Riga, Latvia. Pub: *Putni Daba*.
e-mail: putni@lob.lv
www.lob.lv

Luxembourg
Letzebuerger Natur-a Vulleschutzliga (LNVL), Kraizhaff, rue de Luxembourg.L-1899 Kockelscheuer. Pub: *Regulus (WATCH); Regulus Info (& Annual Report) (WATCH); Regulus Wissenschaftliche Berichte (WATCH)*.
e-mail: secretary@luxnatur.lu
www.luxnatur.lu

Malta
BirdLife Malta, 57 Marina Court, Flat 28, Triq Abate Rigord, MT-Ta' Xbiex, MSD 12, MALTA. Pub: *Bird Talk (WATCH) (Malta); Bird's Eye View (WATCH) (Malta); Il-Merill*.
e-mail: info@birdlifemalta.org
www.birdlifemalta.org

Netherlands
Vogelbescherming Nederland, PO Box 925, NL-3700 AX Zeist. Pub: *Vogelniews; Vogels*.
e-mail: info@vogelbescherming.nl
www.vogelbescherming.nl/

Norway
Norsk Ornitologisk Forening, Sandgata 30 B,

N-7012 Trondheim, Norway. Pub: *Fuglearet; Fuglefauna; Var; Ringmerkaren*.
e-mail: nof@birdlife.no
www.birdlife.no

Poland
Ogólnopolskie Towarzystwo Ochrony Ptaków (OTOP), Ul. Hallera 4/2, PL-80-401 Gdansk, Poland. Pub: *Ptaki; Ptasie Ostoje*.
e-mail: office@otop.most.org.pl
www.otop.org.pl/

Portugal
Sociedade Portuguesa para o Estuda das, Aves (SPEA), Rua da Vitoria, 53-3° Esq, 1100-618, Lisboa. Pub: *Pardela*.
e-mail: spea@spea.pt
www.spea.pt

Romania
Romanian Ornithological Society (SOR), Str. Gheorghe Dima 49/2, RO-3400 Cluj. Pub: *Alcedo; Buletin AIA; Buletin de Informare Societatea Ornitologica Romana; Milvus (Romania)*.
e-mail: office@sor.ro
www.sor.ro/

Slovakia
Soc. for the Prot. of Birds in Slovakia (SOVS), PO Box 71, 093 01 Vranov nad Topl'ou. Pub: *Spravodaj SOVS; Vtacie Spravy*.
e-mail: sovs@changenet.sk
www.sovs.miesto.sk

Slovenia
BirdLife Slovenia (DOPPS), Trzaska 2, PO Box 2990, SI-1000 Ljubljana, Slovenia. Pub: *Acrocephalus; Svet Ptic*.
e-mail: dopps@dopps-drustvo.si
www.ptice.org

Spain
Sociedad Espanola de Ornitologia (SEO), C/ Melquiades Biencinto 34, E-28053, Madrid. Pub: *Ardeola; Areas Importantes para las Aves*.
e-mail: seo@seo.org
www.seo.org

Sweden
Sveriges Ornitologiska Forening (SOF), Ekhagsvagen 3, SE 104-05, Stockholm. Pub: *Fagelvarld; var; Ornis Svecica*.
e-mail: birdlife@sofnet.org
www.sofnet.org

Switzerland
SVS/BirdLife Switzerland, Wiedingstrasse 78, PO

Box, CH-8036, Zurich, Switzerland. Pub: *Oiwvos Ornis; Ornis Junior; Ornithologische Beobachter; Der Ornithos; Steinadler.*
e-mail: svs@birdlife.ch
www.birdlife.ch

Turkey
Doga Dernegi, PK: 640 06445, Yenişehir, Ankarae, Turkey. Pub: *Kelaynak; Kuscu Bulteni.*
e-mail: doga@dogadernegi.org
www.dogadernegi.org/

United Kingdom
Royal Society for the Protection of Birds, The Lodge, Sandy, Bedfordshire, SG19 2DL.
e-mail: info@RSPB.org.uk
www.rspb.org.uk

PARTNERS DESIGNATE

Belarus
BirdLife Belarus (APB), PO Box 306, Minsk, 220050 Belarus. Pub: *Subbuteo - The Belarusian Ornithological Bulletin.*
e-mail: apb@tut.by
http://apb.iatp.by/

Lithuania
Lietuvos Ornitologu Draugija (LOD), Naugarduko St. 47-3, LT-2006, Vilnius, Lithuania. Pub: *Baltasis Gandras.*
e-mail: lod@birdlife.lt
www.birdlife.lt

Russia
Russian Bird Conservation Union (RBCU), Building 1, Shosse Entuziastov 60, 111123, RU-Moscow. Pub: *Newsletter of the Russian Bird Conservation Union.*
e-mail: mail@rbcu.ru
www.rbcu.ru/en/

Ukraine
Ukrainian Union for Bird Conservation (UTOP), PO Box 33, Kiev, 1103, UA. Pub: *Life of Birds.*
e-mail: utop@iptelecom.net.ua
www.utop.org.ua/

AFFILIATES

Liechtenstein
Botanish-Zoologische Gesellschaft, Im Bretscha 22, FL-9494 Schaan, Liechtenstein.
e-mail: broggi@pingnet.li or renat@pingnet.li

Andorra
Associacio per a la Defensa de la Natura, Apartado de Correus Espanyols No 96, Andora La Vella, Principat d'Andorra. Pub: *Aiguerola.*
e-mail: and@andorra.ad
www.adn-andorra.org/

Croatia
Croatian Society for Bird and Nature Protection, Gunduliceva 24, HR-10000 Zagreb, Croatia. Pub: *Troglodytes.*
e-mail: jasmina@hazu.hr

Cyprus
BirdLife Cyprus, PO Box 28076, 2090 Lefkosia, Cyprus.
e-mail: melis@cytanet.com.cy
www.birdlifecyprus.org

Faroe Islands (to Denmark)
Føroya Fuglafrødifelag (Faroese Orginithological Society) (FOS), Postssmoga 1230, FR-110 Torshavn, Faroe Islands.
e-mail: doreteb@ngs.fo

Georgia
Georgian Centre for the Conservation of Wildlife, PO Box 56, GE-Tbilisi 0160, Georgia.
e-mail: office@gccw.org
www.gccw.org/

MIDDLE EAST

PARTNERS

Jordan
Royal Society of the Conservation of Nature, PO Box 6354, Jubeiha-Abu-Nusseir Circle, Amman 11183. Pub: *Al Reem.*
e-mail: adminrscn@rscn.org.jo
www.rscn.org.jo

Lebanon
Society for the Protection of Nature in Lebanon, Awad Bldg, 6th Floor, Abdel Aziz Street, P.O.Box: 11-5665, Beirut, Lebanon.
e-mail: spnlorg@cyberia.net.lb
www.spnlb.org

PARTNER DESIGNATE

Palestine
Palestine Wildlife Society (PWLS), Beit Sahour, PO

Box 89. Pub: *Palestine Wildlife Society - Annual Report*. www.wildlife-pal.org
e-mail: wildlife@palnet.com

AFFILIATES

Bahrain
Dr Saeed A. Mohamed, PO Box 40266, Bahrain.
e-mail: sam53@batelco.com.bh

Iran, Islamic Republic of
Dr Jamshid Mansoori, Assistant Professor, College of Natural Resources, Tehran University, Mojtame Sabz, Golestan Shamali, Mahestan Ave, Shahrake Qarb, Phase 1, P.O.Box 14657, Tehran, I.R. of Iran.
e-mail: birdlifeiran@yahoo.com

Kuwait
Kuwait Environment Protection Society, PO Box 1896, Safat 13019, Kuwait.
e-mail: rasamhory@hotmail.com
www.keps74.com

Saudi Arabia
National Commission for Wildlife Cons & Dev, NCWDC, PO Box 61681, Riyadh 11575. Pub: *Phoenix; The*. e-mail: ncwcd@zajil.net
www.ncwcd.gov.sa/

Yemen
Yemen Society for the Protection of Wildlife (YSPW), 29 Alger Street, PO Box 19759, Sana'a, Yemen.
e-mail: wildlife.yemen@y.net.ye

PACIFIC

PARTNER

Australia
Birds Australia, 415 Riversdale Road, Hawthorn East, VIC 3123, Australia. Pub: *Australia Garcilla; Birds Australia Annual Report; Eclectus;*

Emu; Wingspan (WATCH) (Australia); from wingspan@birdsaustralia.com.au.
e-mail: mail@birdsaustralia.com.au
www.birdsaustralia.com.au

AFFILIATES

Cook Islands
Taporoporo'anga Ipukarea Society (TIS), PO Box 649, Rarotonga, Cook Islands.
e-mail: 2tis@oyster.net.ck

Fiji
Dr Dick Watling, c/o Environment Consultants Fiji, P O Box 2041, Government Buildings, Suva, Fiji.
e-mail: watling@is.com.fj
www.environmentfiji.com

French Polynesia
Société d'Ornithologie de Polynésie "Manu", B.P. 21 098, Papeete, Tahiti.
e-mail: sop@manu.pf
www.manu.pf

Palau
Palau Conservation Society, PO BOX 1811, Koror, PW96940. Pub: *Ngerel a Biib.*
e-mail: pcs@palaunet.com
www.palau-pcs.org/

Samoa
O le Si'osi'omaga Society Incorporated, O le Si'osi'omaga Society Inc., P O Box 2282, Apia, Western Samoa.
e-mail: ngo_siosiomaga@samoa.ws

New Zealand
Royal Forest & Bird Protection Society of, PO Box 631, Wellington. Pub: *Forest & Bird; Forest & Bird Annual Report; Forest & Bird Conservation News.*
e-mail: office@forestandbird.org.nz
www.forestandbird.org.nz/

SPECIAL INTEREST ORGANISATIONS

AFRICAN BIRD CLUB.
c/o Birdlife International as below.
e-mail (general): contact@africanbirdclub.org
e-mail (membership and sales):
membership@africanbirdclub.org
www.africanbirdclub.org
Pub: *Bulletin of the African Bird Club*.

BIRDLIFE INTERNATIONAL.
Wellbrook Court, Girton Road, Cambridge, CB3
ONA, +44 (0)1223 277 318; (Fax) +44 (0)1223
277 200,
Pub:*World Birdwatch*. www.birdlife.net

**EAST AFRICA NATURAL HISTORY SOCIETY
see Kenya in preceding list.**

EURING (European Union for Bird Ringing).
Euring Data Bank, c/o BTO, The Nunnery,
Thetford, Norfolk IP24 2PU. 01842 750 050.
www.euring.org

FAUNA AND FLORA INTERNATIONAL.
Jupiter House, 4th Floor, Station Road, Cambridge,
CB1 2JD. Call on +44 (0)1223 571 000; (Fax) +44
(0)1223 461 481. www.fauna-flora.org
e-mail: info@fauna-flora.org
Pub:*Fauna & Flora News; Oryx*.

LIPU-UK

**(the Italian League
for the Protection of
Birds).**
David Lingard, Fernwood,
Doddington Road,
Whisby, Lincs, LN6 9BX,
+44 (0)1522 689 030,
e-mail: david@lipu-
uk.org   www.lipu-uk.org
Pub:*The Hoopoe*, annually, *Ali Notizie*, quarterley.

NEOTROPICAL BIRD CLUB.
c/o The Lodge, Sandy,
Bedfordshire, SG19 2DL.
Pub:*Cotinga*.
email: secretary@neotropicalbirdclub.org
www.neotropicalbirdclub.org

ORIENTAL BIRD CLUB.
P.O.Box 324, Bedford,
MK42 0WG
Pub:*The Forktail; OBC Bulletin*.

email: mail@orientalbirdclub.org
www.orientalbirdclub.org

**ORNITHOLOGICAL SOCIETY OF THE MIDDLE
EAST (OSME).**
c/o The Lodge, Sandy, Beds, SG19 2DL.
Pub:*Sandgrouse*.
www.osme.org

**TRAFFIC International (formerly Wildlife
Trade Monitoring Unit).**
219a Huntingdon Road, Cambridge, CB3 ODL,
+44 (0)1223 277 427; (Fax) +44 (0)1223 277 237.
Pub:*TRAFFIC Bulletin*.
e-mail: traffic@traffic.org
www.traffic.org

WEST AFRICAN ORNITHOLOGICAL SOCIETY.
R E Sharland, 1 Fisher's Heron, East Mills, Hants,
SP6 2JR. Pub: *Malimbus*.
e-mail bob@sharland2002.fsnet.co.uk
http://malimbus.free.fr

WETLANDS INTERNATIONAL.
PO Box 471, 6700 AL Wageningen, Netherlands,
+31 317 485 774; (Fax) +31 317 486 770,
Pub:*Wetlands*.
e-mail: post@wetlands.org
www.wetlands.org

WORLD OWL TRUST.
The World Owl Centre, Muncaster Castle,
Ravenglass, Cumbria, CA18 1RQ, +44 (0)1229
717393; (Fax) +44 (0)1229 717107,
www.owls.org

WORLD PHEASANT ASSOCIATION.
7-9 Shaftesbury St, Fordingbridge, Hants SP6 1JF.
01425 657 129; (Fax) 01425 658 053.
Pub:*WPA News*. www.pheasant.org.uk

WORLD WIDE FUND FOR NATURE.

Panda House, Weyside
Park, Godalming
United Kingdom. +44
1483 426 444;
(Fax) +44 1483 426 409,
e-mail: supporterrelations
@wwf.org.uk
www.panda.org

QUICK REFERENCE SECTION

Nesting Kittiwakes by David Cromack

BRITISH SUMMER TIME

In 2009 BST applies from 01:00 on March 29 to 01:00 on October 25.
Note that all the times in the following tables are GMT.

| Shetland 42, 43 |
| Orkney 44, 45 |

During British Summer Time one hour should be added.

Predictions are given for the times of high water at
Dover throughout the year.

The times of tides at the locations shown here may
be obtained by adding or subtracting their 'tidal
difference' as shown opposite (subtractions
are indicated by a minus sign).

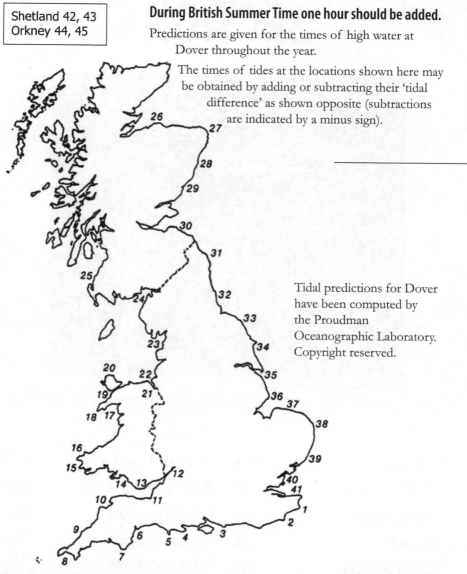

Tidal predictions for Dover
have been computed by
the Proudman
Oceanographic Laboratory.
Copyright reserved.

Map showing locations for which tidal differences are given on facing page.

TIDE TABLES 2009

Example 1
To calculate the time of first high water at Girvan on February 21
1. Look up the time at Dover (09 02)*
   = 9:02 am
2. Add the tidal difference for Girvan
   = 0.54
3. Therefore the time of high water at Girvan = 9:56 am

Example 2
To calculate the time of second high water at Blakeney on June 28
1. Look up the time at Dover (15 15)
   = 3:15 pm
2. Add 1 hour for British Summer Time (16 15) = 4:15 pm
3. Subtract the tidal difference for Blakeney = - 4.07
4. Therefore the time of high water at Blakeney = 12:08 pm

*All Dover times are shown on the 24-hour clock. Thus, 08 14 = 08.14 am; 14 58 = 2.58pm Following the time of each high water the height of the tide is given, in metres.

(Tables beyond April 2010 are not available at the time of going to press.)

TIDAL DIFFERENCES

1	Dover	See pp 338-341		23	Morecambe	0	20
2	Dungeness	-0	12	24	Silloth	0	51
3	Selsey Bill	0	09	25	Girvan	0	54
4	Swanage (lst H.W.Springs)	-2	36	26	Lossiemouth	0	48
5	Portland	-4	23	27	Fraserburgh	1	20
6	Exmouth (Approaches)	-4	48	28	Aberdeen	2	30
7	Salcombe	-5	23	29	Montrose	3	30
8	Newlyn (Penzance)	5	59	30	Dunbar	3	42
9	Padstow	-5	47	31	Holy Island	3	58
10	Bideford	-5	17	32	Sunderland	4	38
11	Bridgwater	-4	23	33	Whitby	5	12
12	Sharpness Dock	-3	19	34	Bridlington	5	53
13	Cardiff (Penarth)	-4	16	35	Grimsby	-5	20
14	Swansea	-4	52	36	Skegness	-5	00
15	Skomer Island	-5	00	37	Blakeney	-4	07
16	Fishguard	-3	48	38	Gorleston	-2	08
17	Barmouth	-2	45	39	Aldeburgh	-0	13
18	Bardsey Island	-3	07	40	Bradwell Waterside	1	11
19	Caernarvon	-1	07	41	Herne Bay	1	28
20	Amlwch	-0	22	42	Sullom Voe	-1	34
21	Connahs Quay	0	20	43	Lerwick	0	01
22	Hilbre Island (Hoylake/West Kirby)	-0	05	44	Kirkwall	-0	26
				45	Widewall Bay	-1	30

NB. Care should be taken when making calculations at the beginning and end of British Summer Time. See worked examples above.

Time Zone **GMT** Units **METRES**

Tidal Predictions : **HIGH WATERS 2009**

Datum of Predictions = **Chart Datum : 3.67 metres below Ordnance Datum (Newlyn)**

British Summer Time : **29th March to 25th October**

Moon phases: ◐ = First Quarter ○ = Full Moon ◑ = Last Quarter ● = New Moon

DOVER — January

Day	Morning hr min	m	Afternoon hr min	m
1 Th	01 31	6.3	13 43	6.1
2 F	02 04	6.3	14 19	6.0
3 Sa	02 41	6.2	15 01	5.8
4 Su ◐	03 25	6.1	15 53	5.7
5 M	04 19	5.9	16 55	5.6
6 Tu	05 24	5.8	18 04	5.6
7 W	06 34	5.8	19 17	5.7
8 Th	07 45	5.9	20 30	5.9
9 F	08 52	6.2	21 34	6.2
10 Sa	09 54	6.4	22 32	6.5
11 Su ○	10 50	6.6	23 23	6.7
12 M	11 44	6.7	** **	*
13 Tu	00 11	6.8	12 33	6.7
14 W	00 56	6.9	13 18	6.6
15 Th	01 38	6.8	14 02	6.5
16 F	02 19	6.7	14 42	6.2
17 Sa	03 01	6.5	15 27	6.0
18 Su ◑	03 47	6.2	16 19	5.7
19 M	04 43	5.8	17 23	5.4
20 Tu	05 52	5.5	18 39	5.2
21 W	07 11	5.3	19 55	5.3
22 Th	08 23	5.4	20 56	5.5
23 F	09 20	5.6	21 46	5.8
24 Sa	10 07	5.8	22 25	6.0
25 Su	10 45	6.0	23 00	6.2
26 M ●	11 17	6.1	23 33	6.4
27 Tu	11 47	6.3	** **	*
28 W	00 05	6.5	12 18	6.3
29 Th	00 36	6.5	12 49	6.3
30 F	01 07	6.6	13 18	6.3
31 Sa	01 36	6.5	13 50	6.2

DOVER — February

Day	Morning hr min	m	Afternoon hr min	m
1 Su	02 09	6.5	14 27	6.1
2 M ◐	02 47	6.3	15 12	6.0
3 Tu	03 39	6.1	16 12	5.7
4 W	04 43	5.8	17 28	5.5
5 Th	06 05	5.6	18 58	5.4
6 F	07 35	5.6	20 28	5.7
7 Sa	08 55	5.9	21 36	6.1
8 Su	09 57	6.3	22 28	6.5
9 M ○	10 49	6.5	23 13	6.7
10 Tu	11 34	6.7	23 55	6.9
11 W	** **	7.0	12 18	6.7
12 Th	00 34	6.9	12 56	6.7
13 F	01 12	6.8	13 32	6.7
14 Sa	01 48	6.8	14 07	6.3
15 Su	02 26	6.6	14 47	6.1
16 M ◑	03 06	6.2	15 30	5.7
17 Tu	03 54	5.7	16 26	5.3
18 W	05 02	5.3	17 47	5.0
19 Th	06 35	5.1	19 18	5.0
20 F	07 57	5.1	20 31	5.3
21 Sa	09 02	5.4	21 23	5.6
22 Su	09 49	5.7	22 03	5.9
23 M	10 24	5.9	22 36	6.2
24 Tu	10 52	6.1	23 07	6.4
25 W ●	11 20	6.3	23 37	6.5
26 Th	11 49	6.4	** **	*
27 F	00 08	6.6	12 20	6.5
28 Sa	00 37	6.7	12 51	6.5

DOVER — March

Day	Morning hr min	m	Afternoon hr min	m
1 Su	01 07	6.7	13 24	6.4
2 M	01 41	6.6	14 02	6.3
3 Tu	02 20	6.4	14 47	6.0
4 W ◐	03 12	6.1	15 49	5.7
5 Th	04 22	5.7	17 10	5.3
6 F	05 58	5.4	18 58	5.3
7 Sa	07 45	5.5	20 27	5.7
8 Su	08 59	5.9	21 27	6.1
9 M	09 54	6.2	22 14	6.5
10 Tu	10 38	6.5	22 53	6.7
11 W ○	11 17	6.6	23 33	6.9
12 Th	11 54	6.7	** **	*
13 F	00 34	6.9	12 29	6.7
14 Sa	00 44	6.9	13 03	6.5
15 Su	01 18	6.7	13 35	6.4
16 M	01 52	6.4	14 10	6.1
17 Tu	02 27	6.1	14 49	5.8
18 W ◑	03 11	5.6	15 40	5.4
19 Th	04 05	5.1	16 53	5.0
20 F	05 51	4.8	18 32	4.9
21 Sa	07 25	4.9	20 12	5.2
22 Su	08 31	5.2	20 56	5.5
23 M	09 18	5.6	21 29	5.8
24 Tu	09 50	5.9	22 03	6.1
25 W	10 18	6.3	22 34	6.4
26 Th ●	10 46	6.5	23 03	6.6
27 F	11 15	6.6	23 34	6.7
28 Sa	11 51	6.8	** **	*
29 Su	00 08	6.8	12 27	6.6
30 M	00 43	6.7	13 04	6.5
31 Tu	01 21	6.6	13 48	6.3

DOVER — April

Day	Morning hr min	m	Afternoon hr min	m
1 W	02 06	6.3	14 40	6.0
2 Th ◐	03 06	5.9	15 47	5.7
3 F	04 26	5.5	17 13	5.4
4 Sa	06 09	5.4	18 54	5.4
5 Su	07 43	5.6	20 11	5.8
6 M	08 47	5.9	21 06	6.1
7 Tu	09 36	6.2	21 50	6.4
8 W	10 17	6.4	22 28	6.6
9 Th ○	10 52	6.6	23 06	6.7
10 F	11 27	6.6	23 42	6.8
11 Sa	** **	6.7	12 02	6.5
12 Su	00 18	6.7	12 36	6.5
13 M	00 51	6.5	13 10	6.3
14 Tu	01 25	6.2	13 43	6.1
15 W	01 59	5.9	14 21	5.8
16 Th	02 40	5.6	15 08	5.5
17 F ◑	03 39	5.2	16 11	5.0
18 Sa	05 01	4.9	17 31	4.9
19 Su	06 30	4.9	18 54	5.1
20 M	07 39	5.2	19 56	5.4
21 Tu	08 27	5.5	20 41	5.8
22 W	09 04	5.8	21 18	6.1
23 Th	09 37	6.1	21 53	6.3
24 F	10 11	6.3	22 26	6.5
25 Sa ●	10 48	6.5	23 03	6.7
26 Su	11 27	6.6	23 44	6.7
27 M	** **	*	12 11	6.6
28 Tu	00 27	6.7	12 57	6.5
29 W	01 15	6.5	13 50	6.3
30 Th	02 11	6.2	14 48	6.1

Time Zone **GMT**

Tidal Predictions : **HIGH WATERS 2009**

Units **METRES**

Datum of Predictions = Chart Datum : 3.67 metres below Ordnance Datum (Newlyn)

British Summer Time : 29th March to 25th October

DOVER — May

Date	Day	Morning hr min	m	Afternoon hr min	m
1	F ◗	03 18	5.9	15 51	5.8
2	Sa	04 34	5.6	17 06	5.7
3	Su	06 02	5.5	18 30	5.7
4	M	07 19	5.7	19 39	5.9
5	Tu	08 19	5.9	20 34	6.0
6	W	09 06	6.0	21 19	6.3
7	Th	09 47	6.2	22 00	6.4
8	F	10 25	6.3	22 41	6.5
9	Sa ○	11 03	6.4	23 20	6.5
10	Su	11 41	6.4	23 58	6.4
11	M	* *		12 18	6.4
12	Tu	00 33	6.3	12 53	6.3
13	W	01 08	6.1	13 28	6.1
14	Th	01 43	5.9	14 04	5.9
15	F	02 23	5.6	14 47	5.7
16	Sa	03 11	5.4	15 37	5.5
17	Su ◖	04 12	5.2	16 38	5.3
18	M	05 21	5.1	17 45	5.3
19	Tu	06 27	5.2	18 50	5.5
20	W	07 25	5.5	19 43	5.7
21	Th	08 13	5.7	20 30	6.0
22	F	08 56	6.0	21 13	6.3
23	Sa	09 39	6.3	21 56	6.5
24	Su ●	10 24	6.5	22 41	6.6
25	M	11 11	6.6	23 30	6.7
26	Tu	* *		12 04	6.6
27	W	00 23	6.6	12 58	6.5
28	Th	01 19	6.5	13 52	6.3
29	F	02 19	6.3	14 45	6.2
30	Sa	03 18	6.1	15 40	6.2
31	Su ◗	04 21	5.9	16 41	6.0

DOVER — June

Date	Day	Morning hr min	m	Afternoon hr min	m
1	M	05 30	5.7	17 48	5.9
2	Tu	06 37	5.7	18 56	5.9
3	W	07 38	5.7	19 55	6.0
4	Th	08 31	5.8	20 47	6.0
5	F	09 19	5.9	21 34	6.1
6	Sa	10 03	6.1	22 19	6.2
7	Su ○	10 43	6.2	23 02	6.2
8	M	11 23	6.3	23 41	6.2
9	Tu	* *		12 01	6.3
10	W	00 19	6.1	12 36	6.3
11	Th	00 54	5.9	13 11	6.1
12	F	01 28	5.8	13 46	6.0
13	Sa	02 03	5.7	14 23	5.8
14	Su	02 41	5.7	15 04	5.9
15	M ◖	03 23	5.5	15 50	5.7
16	Tu	04 21	5.4	16 43	5.6
17	W	05 20	5.5	17 45	5.7
18	Th	06 23	5.7	18 47	5.9
19	F	07 24	5.9	19 46	6.2
20	Sa	08 21	6.1	20 42	6.4
21	Su	09 16	6.3	21 36	6.4
22	M ●	10 11	6.4	22 29	6.5
23	Tu	11 06	6.5	23 24	6.6
24	W	11 59	6.7	* *	
25	Th	00 17	6.6	12 51	6.8
26	F	01 17	6.6	13 41	6.7
27	Sa	02 09	6.5	14 28	6.6
28	Su	02 59	6.3	15 15	6.5
29	M ◗	03 49	6.1	16 05	6.3
30	Tu	04 43	5.8	17 03	6.0

DOVER — July

Date	Day	Morning hr min	m	Afternoon hr min	m
1	W	05 45	5.6	18 08	5.8
2	Th	06 53	5.5	19 15	5.7
3	F	07 57	5.7	20 20	5.8
4	Sa	08 55	5.7	21 16	5.8
5	Su	09 44	5.9	22 04	5.9
6	M	10 26	6.1	22 46	6.0
7	Tu ○	11 06	6.2	23 24	6.1
8	W	11 42	6.3	23 59	6.1
9	Th	* *		12 16	6.4
10	F	00 33	6.1	12 50	6.4
11	Sa	01 05	6.1	13 22	6.4
12	Su	01 36	6.1	13 55	6.3
13	M	02 09	6.0	14 27	6.2
14	Tu	02 44	5.9	15 04	6.1
15	W ◖	03 24	5.7	15 50	5.9
16	Th	04 24	5.6	16 41	5.8
17	F	05 30	5.5	17 59	5.7
18	Sa	06 44	5.5	19 20	5.8
19	Su	08 00	5.7	20 26	6.0
20	M	09 09	6.0	21 29	6.2
21	Tu	10 08	6.4	22 26	6.5
22	W ●	11 00	6.7	23 20	6.7
23	Th	11 48	6.8	* *	
24	F	00 11	6.8	12 36	7.0
25	Sa	01 00	6.6	13 19	6.9
26	Su	01 46	6.4	14 02	6.7
27	M	02 27	6.4	14 42	6.7
28	Tu ◗	03 09	6.2	15 27	6.4
29	W	03 55	6.0	16 19	6.2
30	Th	04 55	5.6	17 24	6.0
31	F	06 08	5.3	18 41	5.4

DOVER — August

Date	Day	Morning hr min	m	Afternoon hr min	m
1	Sa	07 26	5.3	19 59	5.4
2	Su	08 34	5.5	21 02	5.6
3	M	09 27	5.8	21 51	5.8
4	Tu	10 10	6.0	22 31	6.0
5	W	10 46	6.2	23 06	6.1
6	Th ○	11 20	6.4	23 37	6.2
7	F	11 52	6.5	* *	
8	Sa	00 06	6.5	12 23	6.5
9	Su	00 36	6.3	12 53	6.5
10	M	01 04	6.3	13 21	6.5
11	Tu	01 31	6.4	13 48	6.4
12	W	02 04	6.1	14 23	6.3
13	Th ◖	02 35	6.1	15 06	6.1
14	F	03 39	5.8	16 08	5.8
15	Sa	04 52	5.5	17 28	5.6
16	Su	06 20	5.4	19 01	5.6
17	M	07 57	5.6	20 26	5.9
18	Tu	09 08	6.0	21 30	6.2
19	W	10 01	6.5	22 23	6.6
20	Th ●	10 46	6.8	23 07	6.8
21	F	11 30	7.0	23 52	7.0
22	Sa	* *		12 12	7.1
23	Su	00 34	6.8	12 51	7.1
24	M	01 14	6.7	13 29	6.9
25	Tu	01 50	6.5	14 07	6.7
26	W	02 30	6.2	14 48	6.3
27	Th ◗	03 13	5.9	15 37	5.9
28	F	04 08	5.5	16 42	5.5
29	Sa	05 08	5.2	18 11	5.2
30	Su	06 56	5.1	19 39	5.1
31	M	08 11	5.3	20 47	5.4

Time Zone **GMT**

Units **METRES**

Tidal Predictions : **HIGH WATERS 2009**

Datum of Predictions = **Chart Datum : 3.67 metres below Ordnance Datum (Newlyn)**

British Summer Time : **29th March to 25th October**

DOVER — September

Date	Day	Morning hr min	m	Afternoon hr min	m
1	Tu	09 06	5.7	21 34	5.8
2	W	09 49	6.0	22 14	6.0
3	Th	10 22	6.3	22 41	6.2
4	F	10 53	6.5	23 07	6.2
5	Sa	11 21	6.6	23 35	6.4
6	Su	11 51	6.7	** **	* *
7	M	00 04	6.5	12 18	6.7
8	Tu	00 32	6.5	12 46	6.6
9	W	01 03	6.4	13 15	6.6
10	Th	01 36	6.3	13 52	6.4
11	F	02 17	6.1	14 38	6.1
12	Sa	03 13	5.8	15 44	5.7
13	Su	04 34	5.5	17 19	5.4
14	M	06 19	5.4	19 08	5.5
15	Tu	07 55	5.7	20 28	5.9
16	W	08 49	6.1	21 25	6.3
17	Th	09 46	6.6	22 10	6.6
18	F	10 26	6.9	22 49	6.8
19	Sa	11 06	7.0	23 28	6.8
20	Su	11 44	7.1	** **	* *
21	M	00 00	6.8	12 22	7.0
22	Tu	00 41	6.7	12 57	6.8
23	W	01 17	6.5	13 34	6.6
24	Th	01 53	6.3	14 11	6.2
25	F	02 35	5.9	14 58	5.8
26	Sa	03 26	5.6	16 01	5.3
27	Su	04 36	5.2	17 33	4.9
28	M	06 11	5.0	19 10	5.0
29	Tu	07 35	5.2	20 19	5.3
30	W	08 33	5.6	21 06	5.7

DOVER — October

Date	Day	Morning hr min	m	Afternoon hr min	m
1	Th	09 16	6.0	21 40	6.0
2	F	09 49	6.5	22 08	6.2
3	Sa	10 18	6.4	22 34	6.4
4	Su	10 46	6.6	23 00	6.5
5	M	11 16	6.7	23 31	6.6
6	Tu	11 45	6.7	** **	* *
7	W	00 05	6.6	12 18	6.7
8	Th	00 40	6.6	12 54	6.6
9	F	01 19	6.4	13 35	6.4
10	Sa	02 07	6.1	14 28	6.0
11	Su	03 11	5.8	15 46	5.6
12	M	04 34	5.5	17 26	5.4
13	Tu	06 12	5.5	19 05	5.6
14	W	07 36	5.8	20 16	5.9
15	Th	08 35	6.2	21 06	6.3
16	F	09 22	6.5	21 49	6.5
17	Sa	10 01	6.8	22 25	6.6
18	Su	10 39	6.9	23 02	6.7
19	M	11 17	6.9	23 40	6.7
20	Tu	11 55	6.8	** **	* *
21	W	00 16	6.6	12 32	6.6
22	Th	00 51	6.5	13 08	6.4
23	F	01 28	6.3	13 45	6.1
24	Sa	02 07	6.0	14 28	5.7
25	Su	02 55	5.7	15 25	5.3
26	M	03 53	5.4	16 41	5.0
27	Tu	05 06	5.2	18 13	5.0
28	W	06 34	5.2	19 28	5.2
29	Th	07 41	5.5	20 19	5.5
30	F	08 28	5.8	20 56	5.8
31	Sa	09 05	6.1	21 26	6.1

DOVER — November

Date	Day	Morning hr min	m	Afternoon hr min	m
1	Su	09 37	6.3	21 57	6.3
2	M	10 10	6.5	22 29	6.5
3	Tu	10 43	6.7	23 06	6.6
4	W	11 20	6.8	23 47	6.7
5	Th	** **	* *	12 05	6.6
6	F	00 30	6.6	12 46	6.5
7	Sa	01 19	6.5	13 36	6.3
8	Su	02 14	6.2	14 38	6.0
9	M	03 16	6.0	15 51	5.8
10	Tu	04 25	5.8	17 16	5.6
11	W	05 44	5.9	18 39	5.9
12	Th	07 01	6.1	19 45	6.1
13	F	08 02	6.4	20 38	6.3
14	Sa	08 55	6.5	21 22	6.4
15	Su	09 34	6.5	22 03	6.4
16	M	10 17	6.6	22 42	6.5
17	Tu	10 57	6.6	23 28	6.5
18	W	11 37	6.4	23 58	6.3
19	Th	** **	* *	12 15	6.3
20	F	00 34	6.4	12 51	6.1
21	Sa	01 11	6.4	13 28	5.8
22	Su	01 49	6.2	14 07	5.5
23	M	02 30	5.9	14 52	5.3
24	Tu	03 16	5.7	15 47	5.1
25	W	04 11	5.5	16 55	5.1
26	Th	05 15	5.4	18 06	5.3
27	F	06 25	5.4	19 08	5.6
28	Sa	07 24	5.6	19 57	5.6
29	Su	08 13	5.9	20 41	5.9
30	M	08 55	6.1	21 23	6.2

DOVER — December

Date	Day	Morning hr min	m	Afternoon hr min	m
1	Tu	09 37	6.4	22 05	6.4
2	W	10 21	6.6	22 50	6.6
3	Th	11 06	6.7	23 38	6.7
4	F	11 54	6.7	** **	* *
5	Sa	00 29	6.7	12 46	6.6
6	Su	01 21	6.7	13 42	6.5
7	M	02 11	6.5	14 38	6.3
8	Tu	03 05	6.3	15 39	6.0
9	W	04 01	6.2	16 42	5.8
10	Th	05 02	6.0	17 51	5.7
11	F	06 12	5.9	19 00	5.7
12	Sa	07 19	5.9	20 02	5.8
13	Su	08 19	6.0	20 55	5.9
14	M	09 12	6.1	21 43	6.1
15	Tu	10 00	6.2	22 26	6.2
16	W	10 43	6.3	23 06	6.4
17	Th	11 24	6.3	23 44	6.3
18	F	** **	* *	12 37	6.2
19	Sa	00 20	6.4	13 11	6.1
20	Su	00 56	6.4	13 45	6.0
21	M	01 29	6.3	14 20	5.8
22	Tu	02 04	6.0	14 59	5.6
23	W	02 41	5.8	15 45	5.5
24	Th	03 22	5.7	16 45	5.5
25	F	04 11	5.6	17 49	5.3
26	Sa	05 10	5.6	18 56	5.3
27	Su	06 15	5.6	19 59	5.4
28	M	07 19	5.7	20 58	5.6
29	Tu	08 20	5.9	21 51	5.9
30	W	09 15	6.2	22 42	6.3
31	Th	10 07	6.5	23 13	6.5

TIDE TABLES 2010

Time Zone **GMT**

Units **METRES**

Tidal Predictions : **HIGH WATERS 2010**

Datum of Predictions = **Chart Datum : 3.67 metres below Ordnance Datum (Newlyn)**

British Summer Time : **28th March to 31st October**

DOVER — January

Date	Day	Morning hr min	m	Afternoon hr min	m
1	F	10 59	6.7	23 33	6.8
2	Sa	11 49	6.8	** **	* *
3	Su	00 22	6.9	12 41	6.8
4	M	01 11	6.9	13 34	6.7
5	Tu	01 57	6.8	14 23	6.5
6	W	02 42	6.7	15 11	6.3
7	Th	03 30	6.5	16 01	6.0
8	F	04 24	6.2	17 00	5.7
9	Sa	05 26	5.9	18 08	5.5
10	Su	06 37	5.7	19 22	5.5
11	M	07 52	5.6	20 31	5.6
12	Tu	08 56	5.9	21 27	5.8
13	W	09 49	6.1	22 12	6.0
14	Th	10 32	6.2	22 52	6.2
15	F	11 10	6.3	23 27	6.4
16	Sa	11 45	6.5	** **	* *
17	Su	00 02	6.5	12 19	6.3
18	M	00 34	6.5	12 50	6.2
19	Tu	01 07	6.4	13 19	6.1
20	W	01 35	6.3	13 48	5.9
21	Th	02 03	6.2	14 17	5.8
22	F	02 34	6.0	14 54	5.6
23	Sa	03 15	5.8	15 41	5.4
24	Su	04 10	5.8	16 46	5.4
25	M	05 19	5.6	18 04	5.3
26	Tu	06 39	5.5	19 28	5.5
27	W	07 57	5.7	20 42	5.8
28	Th	09 05	6.0	21 43	6.2
29	F	10 01	6.4	22 34	6.6
30	Sa	10 52	6.7	23 21	6.8
31	Su	11 40	6.8	** **	* *

DOVER — February

Date	Day	Morning hr min	m	Afternoon hr min	m
1	M	00 08	7.0	12 29	6.9
2	Tu	00 51	7.1	13 14	6.8
3	W	01 34	7.0	13 57	6.7
4	Th	02 16	6.9	14 38	6.4
5	F	02 58	6.6	15 23	6.1
6	Sa	03 46	6.2	16 17	5.7
7	Su	04 45	5.8	17 24	5.4
8	M	06 02	5.4	18 49	5.2
9	Tu	07 29	5.3	20 10	5.3
10	W	08 42	5.5	21 11	5.6
11	Th	09 37	5.7	21 56	5.9
12	F	10 19	5.9	22 34	6.2
13	Sa	10 55	6.1	23 07	6.4
14	Su	11 26	6.2	23 40	6.5
15	M	11 56	6.3	** **	* *
16	Tu	00 11	6.5	12 23	6.3
17	W	00 41	6.6	12 50	6.3
18	Th	01 03	6.5	13 14	6.3
19	F	01 56	6.4	13 42	6.1
20	Sa	01 56	6.3	14 16	6.1
21	Su	02 34	6.2	15 01	5.9
22	M	03 27	5.9	16 04	5.5
23	Tu	04 41	5.5	17 30	5.3
24	W	06 15	5.4	19 12	5.3
25	Th	07 49	5.6	20 34	5.6
26	F	08 58	6.0	21 32	6.2
27	Sa	09 53	6.4	22 19	6.6
28	Su	10 39	6.7	23 03	6.9

DOVER — March

Date	Day	Morning hr min	m	Afternoon hr min	m
1	M	11 24	6.8	23 47	7.1
2	Tu	** **	* *	12 08	6.9
3	W	00 27	7.1	12 50	6.8
4	Th	01 08	7.1	13 28	6.7
5	F	01 46	6.8	14 07	6.4
6	Sa	02 27	6.5	14 49	6.1
7	Su	03 12	6.1	15 40	5.7
8	M	04 11	5.6	16 45	5.3
9	Tu	05 30	5.3	18 13	5.0
10	W	07 07	5.3	19 42	5.2
11	Th	08 24	5.6	20 45	5.5
12	F	09 19	5.9	21 30	5.8
13	Sa	10 00	5.9	22 10	6.1
14	Su	10 32	6.1	22 42	6.3
15	M	11 00	6.2	23 11	6.4
16	Tu	11 27	6.3	23 40	6.5
17	W	11 52	6.4	** **	* *
18	Th	00 06	6.5	12 19	6.4
19	F	00 30	6.5	12 46	6.3
20	Sa	00 57	6.4	13 15	6.3
21	Su	01 29	6.4	13 53	6.2
22	M	02 10	6.2	14 40	5.9
23	Tu	03 05	5.9	15 47	5.6
24	W	04 26	5.5	17 20	5.3
25	Th	06 11	5.3	19 01	5.4
26	F	07 42	5.6	20 17	5.8
27	Sa	08 47	6.0	21 12	6.3
28	Su	09 36	6.4	21 58	6.6
29	M	10 21	6.6	22 41	6.9
30	Tu	11 02	6.8	23 21	7.0
31	W	11 44	6.8	** **	* *

DOVER — April

Date	Day	Morning hr min	m	Afternoon hr min	m
1	Th	00 02	7.0	12 23	6.7
2	F	00 41	6.9	13 03	6.6
3	Sa	01 21	6.7	13 41	6.4
4	Su	02 00	6.3	14 23	6.1
5	M	02 45	5.9	15 11	5.7
6	Tu	03 43	5.5	16 11	5.4
7	W	04 57	5.1	17 31	5.1
8	Th	06 32	5.0	18 58	5.1
9	F	08 04	5.2	20 06	5.4
10	Sa	08 44	5.5	20 55	5.7
11	Su	09 25	5.8	21 34	6.0
12	M	09 57	6.0	22 22	6.2
13	Tu	10 25	6.1	22 36	6.3
14	W	10 52	6.3	23 10	6.4
15	Th	11 21	6.4	23 33	6.5
16	F	11 52	6.5	** **	* *
17	Sa	00 00	6.5	12 26	6.5
18	Su	00 37	6.5	13 03	6.3
19	M	01 17	6.3	13 46	6.2
20	Tu	02 04	6.1	14 42	5.7
21	W	03 09	5.8	15 53	5.5
22	Th	04 32	5.5	17 14	5.5
23	F	06 04	5.5	18 40	5.7
24	Sa	07 24	5.7	19 50	6.0
25	Su	08 23	6.0	20 44	6.3
26	M	09 13	6.3	21 30	6.5
27	Tu	09 57	6.5	22 14	6.7
28	W	10 39	6.6	22 57	6.8
29	Th	11 21	6.6	23 40	6.8
30	F	** **	* *	12 04	6.6

SUNRISE AND SUNSET TIMES

Predictions are given for the times of sunrise and sunset on every Saturday throughout the year. For places on the same latitude as the following, add 4 minutes for each degree of longitude west (subtract if east).

These times are in GMT, except between 01:00 on Mar 29 and 01:00 on Oct 25, when the times are in BST (1 hour in advance of GMT).

		London		Manchester		Edinburgh	
		Rise	Set	Rise	Set	Rise	Set
Jan	4	08 06	16 06	08 24	16 04	08 43	15 53
	11	08 03	16 15	08 20	16 14	08 38	16 04
	18	07 57	16 26	08 14	16 26	08 30	16 17
	25	07 49	16 38	08 05	16 38	08 20	16 31
Feb	1	07 39	16 50	07 54	16 52	08 07	16 46
	8	07 27	17 03	07 41	17 06	07 53	17 02
	15	07 14	17 16	07 27	17 20	07 38	17 17
	22	07 00	17 29	07 12	17 33	07 21	17 32
Mar	1	06 46	17 41	06 57	17 47	07 04	17 47
	8	06 30	17 53	06 40	18 00	06 46	18 02
	15	06 15	18 05	06 24	18 13	06 28	18 17
	22	05 59	18 17	06 07	18 26	06 10	18 31
	29	06 43	19 29	06 50	19 39	06 51	19 45
Apr	5	06 27	19 41	06 33	19 52	06 33	19 59
	12	06 11	19 53	06 16	20 05	06 15	20 14
	19	05 56	20 04	06 00	20 17	05 57	20 28
	26	05 42	20 16	05 45	20 30	05 41	20 42
May	3	05 29	20 27	05 30	20 43	05 25	20 56
	10	05 17	20 39	05 17	20 55	05 10	21 10
	17	05 06	20 49	05 05	21 07	04 57	21 23
	24	04 57	20 59	04 55	21 17	04 45	21 35
	31	04 50	21 07	04 48	21 27	04 36	21 46
Jun	7	04 45	21 14	04 42	21 34	04 30	21 54
	14	04 43	21 19	04 40	21 39	04 27	22 00
	21	04 43	21 22	04 40	21 42	04 26	22 03
	28	04 46	21 22	04 42	21 42	04 29	22 03

SUNRISE AND SUNSET TIMES

		London		Manchester		Edinburgh	
		Rise	Set	Rise	Set	Rise	Set
Jul	5	04 51	21 19	04 48	21 39	04 35	21 59
	12	04 58	21 14	04 55	21 33	04 44	21 52
	19	05 06	21 07	05 05	21 25	04 54	21 43
	26	05 16	20 58	05 15	21 15	05 06	21 31
Aug	2	05 26	20 47	05 26	21 03	05 19	21 18
	9	05 37	20 35	05 38	20 50	05 32	21 03
	16	05 48	20 21	05 50	20 35	05 46	20 47
	23	05 59	20 06	06 02	20 20	06 00	20 30
	30	06 10	19 51	06 15	20 03	06 13	20 12
Sep	6	06 21	19 36	06 27	19 47	06 27	19 54
	13	06 32	19 20	06 39	19 30	06 41	19 36
	20	06 44	19 04	06 51	19 12	06 54	19 17
	27	06 55	18 47	07 04	18 55	07 08	18 58
Oct	4	07 06	18 31	07 16	18 38	07 22	18 40
	11	07 18	18 16	07 29	18 22	07 36	18 22
	18	07 30	18 01	07 42	18 06	07 50	18 05
	25	06 42	16 47	06 55	16 50	07 05	16 48
Nov	1	06 54	16 34	07 08	16 36	07 20	16 32
	8	07 07	16 22	07 22	16 23	07 35	16 18
	15	07 19	16 11	07 35	16 12	07 49	16 05
	22	07 30	16 03	07 47	16 02	08 03	15 54
	29	07 41	15 56	07 59	15 55	08 16	15 46
Dec	6	07 51	15 53	08 09	15 51	08 27	15 40
	13	07 58	15 52	08 17	15 49	08 36	15 38
	20	08 03	15 53	08 23	15 51	08 42	15 39
	27	08 06	15 58	08 25	15 55	08 44	15 44

GRID REFERENCES

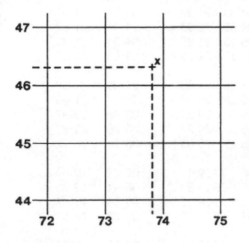

A grid reference is made up of letters and numbers. Two-letter codes are used for 100km squares on the National Grid (opposite) and single-letter codes on the Irish Grid (below).

The squares may be further subdivided into squares of 10km, 1km or 100m, allowing for increasingly specific references. On a given map the lines forming the squares are numbered in the margins, those along the top and bottom being known as 'eastings' and those along the sides as 'northings'. A reference number is made up of the relevant letter code plus two sets of figures, those representing the easting followed by the northing. According to the scale of the map they can either be read off directly or calculated by visually dividing the intervals into tenths. For most purposes three-figure eastings plus three-figure northings are adequate.

The example above, from an Ordnance Survey 'Landranger' map, illustrates how to specify a location on a map divided into lkm squares: the reference for point X is 738463. If that location lies in square SP (see map opposite), the full reference is SP738463.

Letter codes for Irish grid 10km squares

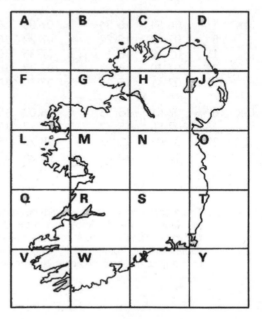

GRID REFERENCES

Letter codes for national
grid 10km squares

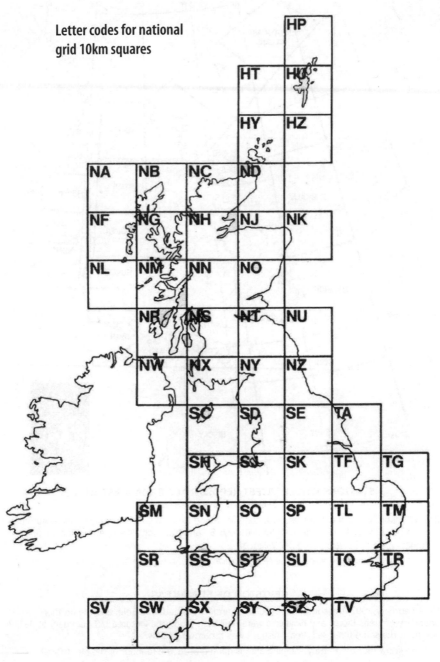

SEA AREAS

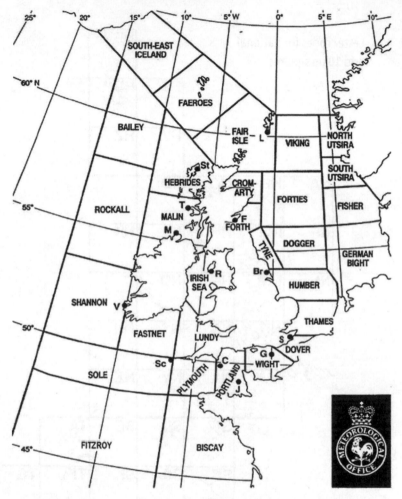

STATIONS WHOSE LATEST REPORTS ARE BROADCAST IN THE 5-MINUTE FORECASTS

Br Bridlington; C Channel Light-Vessel Automatic; F Fife Ness; G Greenwich Light-Vessel Automatic; J Jersey; L Lerwick; M Malin Head; R Ronaldsway; S Sandettie Light-Vessel Automatic; Sc Scilly Automatic; St Stornoway; T Tiree; V Valentia.

From information kindly supplied by the Meteorological Office

REVISION OF SEA AREAS

On 4 February 2002, the southern boundary of areas Plymouth and Sole, and the northern boundary of areas Biscay and Finisterre were realigned along the Metarea I/II boundary at 48°27' North. At the same time, sea area Finisterre was renamed FitzRoy.

Did you know that the FitzRoy shipping area is named after the founder of the Met Office?

THE BIRDWATCHER'S CODE OF CONDUCT

Around three million adults go birdwatching every year in the UK. Following The birdwatchers' code is good practice, common sense and will help everybody to enjoy seeing birds.

This code puts the interests of birds first, and respects other people, whether or not they are interested in birds. It applies whenever you are watching birds in the UK or abroad. Please help everybody to enjoy birdwatching by following the code, leading by example and sensitively challenging the minority of birdwatchers who behave inappropriately.

1. The interests of the birds come first

Birds respond to people in many ways, depending on the species, location and time of year.

If birds are disturbed they may keep away from their nests, leaving chicks hungry or enabling predators to take their eggs or young. During cold weather, or when migrants have just made a long flight, repeatedly disturbing birds can mean they use up vital energy that they need for feeding.

Intentionally or recklessly disturbing some birds at or near their nest is illegal in Britain.

Whether you are particularly interested in photography, bird ringing, sound-recording or birdwatching, remember to always put the interests of the birds first.

- Avoid going too close to birds or disturbing their habitats – if a bird flies away or makes repeated alarm calls, you're too close. If it leaves, you won't get a good view of it anyway.
- Stay on roads and paths where they exist and avoid disturbing habitat used by birds.
- Think about your fieldcraft. You might disturb a bird even if you are not very close, eg a flock of wading birds on the foreshore can be disturbed from a mile away if you stand on the seawall.
- Repeatedly playing a recording of bird song or calls to encourage a bird to respond can divert a territorial bird from other important duties, such as feeding its young. Never use playback to attract a species during its breeding season.

2. Be an ambassador for birdwatching

Respond positively to questions from interested passers-by. They may not be birdwatchers yet, but good views of a bird or a helpful answer may ignite a spark of interest. Your enthusiasm could start lifetime's interest in birds and a greater appreciation of wildlife and its conservation.

Consider using local services, such as pubs, restaurants, petrol stations, and public transport. Raising awareness of the benefits to local communities of trade from visiting birdwatchers may, ultimately, help the birds themselves.

3. Know the Countryside Code, and follow it

Respect the wishes of local residents and landowners and don't enter private land without permission, unless it is open for public access on foot.

Follow the codes on access and the countryside for the place you're walking in. Irresponsible behaviour may cause a land manager to deny access to others (eg for important bird survey work). It may also disturb the bird or give birdwatching bad coverage in the media.

Access to the countryside

Legislation provides access for walkers to open country in Britain, and includes measures to protect wildlife. Note that the rules and codes are different in each part of Britain, so plan ahead and make sure you know what you can do legally.

4. The law

Laws protecting birds and their habitats are the result of hard campaigning by generations of birdwatchers. We must make sure that we don't allow them to fall into disrepute. In England, Scotland and Wales, it is a criminal offence to disturb, intentionally or recklessly, at or near the nest, a species listed on Schedule 1 of the Wildlife & Countryside Act 1981 (see www.rspb.org.uk/policy/wildbirdslaw for a full list). Disturbance could include playback of songs and calls. In Scotland, disturbing Capercaillie and Ruffs at leks is also an offence. It is a criminal offence to intentionally disturb a bird at or near the nest under the Wildlife (Northern Ireland) Order 1985.

The Government can, for particular reasons such as scientific study, issue licences to individuals that permit limited disturbance, including monitoring of nests and ringing. It is a criminal offence to destroy or damage, intentionally or recklessly, a special interest feature of a Site of Special Scientific Interest (SSSI) or to disturb the wildlife for which the site was notified.

If you witness anyone who you suspect may be illegally disturbing or destroying wildlife or habitat, phone the police immediately (ideally, with a six-figure map reference) and report it to the RSPB.

5. Rare birds

Mobile phones, telephone and pager services and the internet mean you can now share your sightings instantly. If you discover a rare bird, please bear the following in mind

- Consider the potential impact of spreading the news and make an effort to inform the landowner (or, on a nature reserve, the warden) first. Think about whether the site can cope with a large number of visitors and whether sensitive species might be at risk, such as breeding terns, flocks of wading birds or rare plants. The county bird recorder or another experienced birdwatcher can often give good advice.
- On private land, always talk to the landowner first. With a little planning, access can often be arranged.
- People coming to see a rare bird can raise money for a local reserve, other wildlife project or charity. Consider organising a voluntary collection at access points to the site.
- Rare breeding birds are at risk from egg-collectors and some birds of prey from persecution. If you discover a rare breeding species that you think is vulnerable, contact the RSPB; it has considerable experience in protecting rare breeding birds. Please also report your sighting to the county bird recorder or the Rare Breeding Birds Panel. (www.rbbp.org.uk). Also, consider telling the landowner – in most cases, this will ensure that the nest is not disturbed accidentally. If you have the opportunity to see a rare bird, enjoy it, but don't let your enthusiasm override common sense.

THE BIRDWATCHER'S CODE OF CONDUCT

In addition to the guidelines above:
- park sensibly, follow instructions and consider making a donation if requested
- don't get too close so that you can take a photograph – you'll incur the wrath of everyone else watching if you scare the bird away
- be patient if the viewing is limited, talk quietly and give others a chance to see the bird too
- do not enter private areas without permission
- not everyone likes to see an 'organised flush' and it should never be done in important wildlife habitats or where there are other nesting or roosting birds nearby. A flush should not be organised more frequently than every two hours and not within two hours of sunrise or sunset, so the bird has chance to feed and rest.

6. Make your sightings count
Add to tomorrow's knowledge of birds by sending your sightings to www.birdtrack.net This online recording scheme from the BTO, the RSPB and BirdWatch Ireland

allows you to input and store all of your birdwatching records, which in turn helps to support species and site conservation. With one click, you can also have your records forwarded automatically to the relevant county recorder.

County recorders and local bird clubs are the mainstay of bird recording in the UK. Your records are important for local conservation and help to build the county's ornithological history. For a list of county bird recorders, look in the County Directory of *The Yearbook,* ask at your local library, or visit www.britishbirds.co.uk/countyrecorders

You can also get involved in a UK-wide bird monitoring scheme, such as the Breeding Bird Survey and the Wetland Bird Survey (see www.bto.org for details). If you've been birdwatching abroad, you can give your sightings to the BirdLife International Partner in that country by visiting www.worldbirds.org Your data could be vital in helping to protect sites and species in the country you've visited.

SCHEDULE 1 SPECIES

Under the provisions of the Wildlife and Countryside Act 1981 the following bird species (listed in Schedule 1 - Part I of the Act) are protected by special penalties at all times.

Avocet	Falcon, Gyr	Owl, Barn	Lark, Shore
Bee-eater	Fieldfare	Owl, Snowy	Shrike, Red-backed
Bittem	Firecrest	Peregrine	Spoonbill
Bittern, Little	Garganey	Petrel, Leach's	Stilt, Black-winged
Bluethroat	Godwit, Black-tailed	Pintail	Stint, Temminck's
Brambling	Goshawk	Phalarope, Red-necked	Swan, Bewick's
Bunting, Cirl	Grebe, Black-necked	Plover, Kentish	Swan, Whooper
Bunting, Lapland	Grebe, Slavonian	Plover, Little Ringed	Tern, Black
Bunting, Snow	Greenshank	Quail, Common	Tern, Little
Buzzard, Honey	Gull, Little	Redstart, Black	Tern, Roseate
Chough	Gull, Mediterranean	Redwing	Tit, Bearded
Crake, Corn	Harriers (all species)	Rosefinch, Scarlet	Tit, Crested
Crake, Spotted	Heron, Purple	Ruff	Treecreeper, Short-toed
Crossbills (all species)	Hobby	Sandpiper, Green	Warbler, Cetti's
Stone-curlew	Hoopoe	Sandpiper, Purple	Warbler, Dartford
Divers (all species)	Kingfisher	Sandpiper, Wood	Warbler, Marsh
Dotterel	Kite, Red	Scaup	Warbler, Savi's
Duck, Long-tailed	Merlin	Scoter, Common	Whimbrel
Eagle, Golden	Oriole, Golden	Scoter, Velvet	Lark, Wood
Eagle, White-tailed	Osprey	Serin	Wryneck

The following birds and their eggs (listed in Schedule 1 - Part II of the Act) are protected by special penalties during the close season, which is Feb 1 to Aug 31 (Feb 21 to Aug 31 below high water mark), but may be killed outside this period - Goldeneye, Greylag Goose (in Outer Hebrides, Caithness, Sutherland, and Wester Ross only), Pintail.

THE COUNTRYSIDE CODE

Launched on 12 July 2004, this Code for England has been produced through a partnership between the Countryside Agency and Countryside Council for Wales.

The Countryside Code has been revised and re-launched to reflect the introduction of new open access rights (Countryside & Rights of Way Act 2000) and changes in society over the last 20 years.

• Be safe – plan ahead
Follow any signs, even when going out locally, it's best to get the latest information about where and when you can go; for example, your rights to go onto some areas of open land may be restricted while work is carried out, for safety reasons or during breeding seasons. Follow advice and local signs, and be prepared for the unexpected.

• Leave gates and property as you find them
Please respect the working life of the countryside, as our actions can affect people's livelihoods, our heritage, and the safety and welfare of animals and ourselves.

• Protect plants and animals, and take your litter home
We have a responsibility to protect our countryside now and for future generations, so make sure you don't harm animals, birds, plants, or trees.

• Keep dogs under close control
The countryside is a great place to exercise dogs, but it's every owner's duty to make sure their dog is not a danger or nuisance to farm animals, wildlife or other people.

• Consider other people
Showing consideration and respect for other people makes the countryside a pleasant Environment for everyone – at home, at work and at leisure.

BIRDLINE NUMBERS - National and Regional

Birdline name	To obtain information	To report sightings (hotlines)
National		
Bird Information Service www.birdingworld.co.uk	09068 700 222	
Flightline (Northern Ireland)	028 9146 7408	
Regional		
Northern Ireland	028 9146 7408	
Scotland	09068 700 234	01292 611 994
Wales	09068 700 248	01492 544 588
East Anglia	09068 700 245	01603 763 388
Midlands	09068 700 247	01905 754 154
North East	09068 700 246	07974 358 988
North West	09068 700 249	01492 544 588
South East www.southeastbirdnews.co.uk	09068 700 240	01845 570 444 or 08000 377 240
South West	09068 700 241	0845 4567 938

Charges
At the time of compilation, calls to premium line numbers cost 60p per minute.

Key contributors in this Edition

ANDREW BECKETT

A part-time lecturer in natural history illustration at Blackpool College of Art & Design, Andrew has been firmly established as a freelance artist for more than 16 years with patronage from companies such as Marks & Spencer, Dorling Kindersley and TimeLife. In 2007 Andrew won the *Birds Illustrated* Award at the National Exhibition of Wildlife Art and this led to him being commissioned to produce the cover image for the *2009 Birdwatcher's Yearbook*. More of his work can be seen at: www.illustrationweb.com

STEVE CALE

A wellknown figure on the British birding scene, Steve was born in the West Midlands but now lives in Norfolk, where there is constant inspiration for his acrylic and watercolour painting of birds and wildlife. Steve has travelled widely in search of subject matter and to further his interest in conservation. In recent times he has become an enthusiastic tour leader to Gambia, Northern Cyprus, Turkey and Tobago and has just published the first birding guide for North Cyprus. His work has been widely published in books, magazines and on greetings cards. Steve also conducts painting workshops – for more details, visit his website at: www.steve-cale-artist.co.uk

JACQUIE CLARK

As Head of Ringing at the British Trust for Ornithology, Jacquie is responsible for all aspects of running and developing the scheme in Britain. This includes being the Managing Editor of Ringing & Migration. She is a qualified ringer herself, with a licence to use cannon nets for catching waders. She has written or contributed to many papers in scientific journals on all aspects of ringing, migration and conservation. Jacquie can be contacted at: jacquie.clarke@bto.org

RICHARD FACEY

As well working as Conservation Officer for the Countryside Council for Wales (CCW), Richard is a regular contributor to Birds Illustrated magazine. After graduating in zoology, he worked on contract for the RSPB in Wales. An eager birder with a keen interest in bird behaviour and ecology, Richard is also an active bird-ringer.

GORDON HAMLETT

Gordon's annual survey of the most pertinent websites for birdwatchers was initiated in 2003 and has been a valuable and popular feature in *The Birdwatcher's Yearbook* ever since. A freelance writer and reviewer, Gordon has for many years edited the *UK Bird Sightings* section of *Bird Watching* magazine and has also contributed reviews of bird books, DVDs and other media to that magazine and *Birds Illustrated*. In 2005 his much-acclaimed *Best Birdwatching Sites in the Scottish Highlands* was published by Buckingham Press. He now lives in Norfolk and can be contacted at: gordon.hamlett@btinternet.com

HEARTFELT THANKS

The publishers would like to thank the scores of club secretaries, reserve wardens, national and international conservation groups for their continuing support of *The Birdwatcher's Yearbook*. Their willingness to take the time to update information on an annual basis ensures that the *Yearbook* remains both a pertinent and accurate resource for the greater birdwatching community.

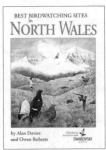

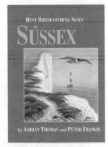

INDEX TO RESERVES